KARL MARX
FREDERICK ENGELS
COLLECTED WORKS
VOLUME
43

KARL MARX
FREDERICK ENGELS

COLLECTED
WORKS

INTERNATIONAL PUBLISHERS

NEW YORK

KARL MARX
FREDERICK ENGELS

Volume
43

MARX AND ENGELS: 1868-70

INTERNATIONAL PUBLISHERS
NEW YORK

This volume has been prepared jointly by Lawrence & Wishart Ltd., London, International Publishers Co. Inc., New York, and Progress Publishers, Moscow, in collaboration with the Institute of Marxism-Leninism, Moscow.

Editorial commissions:

GREAT BRITAIN: Eric Hobsbawm, John Hoffman, Nicholas Jacobs, Monty Johnstone, Martin Milligan, Jeff Skelley, Ernst Wangermann.
USA: Louis Diskin, Philip S. Foner, James E. Jackson, Leonard B. Levenson, Victor Perlo, Betty Smith, Dirk J. Struik.
USSR: for Progress Publishers—A. K. Avelichev, N. P. Karmanova, M. K. Shcheglova; for the Institute of Marxism-Leninism—P. N. Fedoseyev, L. I. Golman, A. I. Malysh, M. P. Mchedlov, V. N. Pospelova, G. L. Smirnov.

Library of Congress Cataloging in Publication Data

Marx, Karl, 1818-1883.
  Karl Marx, Frederick Engels: collected works.

  1. Socialism—Collected works. 2. Economics—Collected works. I. Engels, Friedrich, 1820-1895. Works. English. 1975. II. Title.
HX 39. 5. A 16 1975   335.4   73-84671
ISBN 0-7178-0543-3 (v. 43)

Printed in the Union of Soviet Socialist Republics

Contents

KARL MARX AND FREDERICK ENGELS
LETTERS
April 1868-July 1870

1868

1869

1870

Contents

XIII

APPENDICES

NOTES AND INDEXES

ILLUSTRATIONS

TRANSLATORS:

JOHN PEET: Letters 1-100, 102-17, 119-215, 217, 219-20, 222-42, 244-79, 281-307, 309-43, 345-46; Appendices: Letters 1-7, 9-11

MICHAEL SLATTERY: Letters 118, 216, 243; Appendices: Letter 8

SERGEI SYROVATKIN: Letters 101, 218, 221, 280, 308, 344, 347

Preface

Volume 43 of the *Collected Works* of Karl Marx and Frederick Engels contains their correspondence from April 1868 to July 1870. Chronologically it completes the period from 1864 to 1870, an important one in the history of Marxism and the international working-class movement, which laid the basis for Marxism's great influence on the mass working-class movement. The years 1868-1870 witnessed the formation of the first workers' parties in a number of countries and the establishment of socialist principles in the programme documents of the International Working Men's Association (the First International). The Association's activity during these years took place against the background of the growing class struggle, the aggravation of economic and social contradictions in Europe, the upsurge in the national liberation struggle of the Irish people, the crisis of the Second Empire and the imminent military conflict between Bonapartist France and Bismarck's Prussia. The international situation was also made more tense as a result of the bourgeois revolution which began in Spain in 1868.

The material in this volume, like that of the preceding one, reflects the remarkably varied activity of Marx and the General Council of the International led by him, activity aimed at strengthening the unity of the working class and educating it in the spirit of proletarian internationalism. The letters illustrate Marx's active participation in all the theoretical discussions which took place in the Council, in drafting the resolutions of the General Council and in preparing the congresses of the International Working Men's Association. They also throw light on Marx's and Engels's work on the drafting and writing of documents for the International in 1868-1870 (published in vols 20 and 21 of the present edition). The correspondence makes clear the great extent to which Engels assisted Marx in leading the International. Marx systematically discussed all important questions with him, kept him informed of the course of discussions in the Council, and of its draft resolutions, and made use of his recommendations. Engels took an active part in working out the International's tactics, explaining it in letters to eminent members of the working-class movement, in particular the Germans (Wilhelm Liebknecht and Wilhelm Bracke) and frequently defended the position of the International Working Men's Association on various questions in the press.

In the history of the International, the 1868-1870 period was a time of ideological and organisational strengthening. The Association's federations and sections were active in many European countries and the USA. In Britain it was the trade unions which provided its mass base. Trade unions as class organisations of the workers also began to take shape in other countries. 'The International Association..., as a result of conditions on the continent, ... is beginning to become a serious power,' Marx wrote in a letter to Engels of 7 July 1868 (see this volume, p. 63). After the adoption, in November 1864, of the 'Inaugural Address of the Working Men's International Association' and the 'Provisional Rules of the Association', Marx was faced with the task of drawing up a united theoretical programme for the international working-class movement and substantiating and openly proclaiming the principles of scientific socialism in the International's programme. At the same time he saw clearly that before these principles could be assimilated by the various working-class national organisations a great deal of preparatory work in the press, at congresses and in the local sections would have to be done. 'As the stage of development reached by different sections of the workers in the same country and by the working class in different countries necessarily varies considerably, the actual movement also necessarily expresses itself in very diverse theoretical forms,' Marx wrote to Engels on 5 March 1869. 'The community of action the International Working Men's Association is calling into being, the exchange of ideas by means of the different organs of the sections in all countries and, finally, the direct discussions at the general congresses would also gradually create a common theoretical programme for the general workers' movement' (pp. 235-36). Marx was guided by the fact that the ideological and organisational unity of action of the working class should be formed on the basis of the real class struggle. He saw this as the way to overcome reformism and sectarianism in the working-class movement.

The correspondence shows that the Association's success in this direction was due largely to Marx's organisational talent, his ability in the course of everyday struggle to stimulate the class consciousness of the workers and lead them to an understanding of common theoretical and practical tasks. These tactics of Marx's were a sure pledge of the victory of scientific communism over the sectarian trends in the working-class movement.

As the correspondence in this volume shows, in 1868-1870 the General Council of the Association continued as before to give material assistance and moral support to those taking part in the strike movement, which embraced broad sections of the working class in Britain, France, Germany, Belgium and Switzerland (pp. 82, 203-04, and 209-10). During these years international solidarity became a most important factor in the economic struggle of the working class. The organisation of help to strikers promoted the growth of the authority and popularity of the International Working Men's Association among the masses (pp. 8, 350).

As before, Marx participated directly in the preparation of the congresses of the International and had a decisive influence on their work. He wrote the reports of the General Council to the Brussels (September 1868) and Basle (September 1869) congresses. Particularly noteworthy is Marx's letter of 10 September 1868 to Johann Georg Eccarius and Friedrich Lessner, in which he outlined the tactics to be adopted by the General Council's delegates to the Brussels Congress. Here Marx also explains the position of the working class on the question of war in the concrete historical situation at the end of the 1860s in connection with the imminent war between France and Prussia. Noting the insufficient organisation of the workers, Marx nevertheless considered it necessary to state clearly in the resolution to be adopted that 'the congress protests in the name of the working class, and denounces those who instigate war' (p. 94). The campaign for peace was becoming one of the programme aims of the international working-class movement, and its success depended largely on the international unity of the workers.

As the letters show, Marx and Engels expressed their complete satisfaction with the success of the struggle against Proudhonism at the Brussels Congress (p. 102). The adoption by the Congress of resolutions on the need to turn the land, mines, etc., into common property was a convincing victory for socialist principles over the petty-bourgeois views of the Proudhonists. Thus, the inclusion of the demand for the socialist reorganisation of society in the programme of the International became possible only as a result of progressive workers overcoming the petty-bourgeois world outlook. It is no accident that the bourgeois press began panic-stricken talk about the communist nature of the Congress's decisions on property (pp. 101, 107).

As can be seen from the correspondence, Marx and Engels linked the demand to abolish private ownership of land very closely with the question of the workers' ally in the countryside, the question of the attitude to small peasant property. It was precisely from this angle that the question was considered at the Basle Congress. On 30 October 1869 Marx wrote to Engels about the need for a differentiated approach by the working class to big and small land ownership (p. 364). In his reply to Marx of 1 November 1869 Engels agreed with his point of view and paid special attention to the heterogeneity of the peasantry, the existence, alongside the big peasant proprietors who exploit day labourers and peasant tenants, of middle and small peasant proprietors. Engels pointed out that the working class should adopt a flexible policy in relation to the poor sections of the peasantry, taking their interests into account (p. 365). These ideas of Engels' were elaborated by him in greater detail in his preface to the second edition of *The Peasant War in Germany* at the beginning of February 1870 (see present edition, Vol. 21).

A number of letters published in this volume reflect the struggle waged by Marx, Engels and the General Council of the International against the disorganising activity of Bakunin and his supporters in the International, against Bakunin's anarchist views on major questions of the theory and tactics of the workers' movement. Bakuninism, a form of anarchism, expressed the protest of the petty bourgeoisie against capitalist exploitation and ruin. It reflected the mood of petty proprietors unable to find a real way of freeing themselves from capitalist oppression. In their works and letters Marx and Engels roundly criticised the theory and practice of Bakuninism, pointing out the harm which sectarianism caused to the working-class movement.

The International Alliance of Socialist Democracy set up in the autumn of 1868 in Geneva by Bakunin claimed ideological leadership of the International and at the same time an autonomous existence within it. The leaders of the Alliance hoped to use the International to propagate anarchist ideas and establish their influence throughout the working-class movement.

Bakunin's plans encountered strong opposition from the General Council. After receiving the documents of the Alliance and its request for membership of the International Working Men's Association, Marx deemed it necessary to refuse this request. In a letter to Marx of 18 December 1868 Engels also expressed his strong opposition to allowing the Alliance to join the Association. 'This would be a state within the state,' he wrote to Marx (p. 192). Engels' proposals contained in this letter were included by Marx in the reply compiled by him on behalf of the General Council and entitled *The International Working Men's Association and the Alliance of Socialist Democracy* in which he defended the principles of setting up workers' organisations which ensured their unity and solidarity. In this 'elaborate document the General Council declared the 'Alliance' to be an instrument of disorganisation, and rejected every connexion with it' (p. 491).

In reply to the Alliance's repeated request, Marx drew up a circular letter, *The General Council of the International Working Men's Association to the Central Bureau of the International Alliance of Socialist Democracy.* This document was actually based on Marx's letter to Engels of 5 March 1869. It contains criticism of the basic precept of the Bakuninist programme—the demand for 'the political, economic and social equalisation of *the classes*'. Marx showed convincingly that the demand for the 'equalisation of the classes' was equivalent to the bourgeois socialists' slogan about 'harmony of capital and labour' and fundamentally opposed to 'the general tendency of the International Working Men's Association—the complete emancipation of the working classes' (p. 236).

The history of the General Council's struggle against subsequent attempts by Bakunin and his supporters to disorganise the International Working Men's Association and also lengthy criticism of the main points of Bakunin's programme are to be found in Marx's letter to Lafargue of 19 April 1870. Describing Bakuninism as a sectarian tendency alien to the working-class movement, Marx focuses his criticism mainly on two of Bakunin's demands: the demand to abolish the right of inheritance, which was declared to be the point of departure of social revolution and the only way to abolish private property, and the renunciation of the political activity of the working class.

The theoretical weakness of Bakunin's recipe, Marx pointed out, lay in the fact that he did not understand the objective link between the basis and the superstructure of capitalist society. 'The whole thing rests on a superannuated idealism, which considers the actual jurisprudence as the basis of our economical state, instead of seeing that our economical state is the basis and source of our jurisprudence!' (p. 490). Marx also stressed the political and tactical harm of Bakunin's thesis. Proclaiming the abolition of the right of inheritance, Marx believed, would inevitably alienate the working class from its ally, the peasantry. This demand would be 'not a serious act, but a foolish menace, rallying the whole peasantry and the whole small middle-class round the reaction' (ibid.).

Marx also showed how mistaken was Bakunin's demand that the working class should be restrained from taking any part in the political struggle. It misled the workers and prevented the adoption of an independent working-class policy, the growth of class consciousness and the formation of political parties of the working class (pp. 490-91).

As their correspondence shows, Marx and Engels focused their attention on the destiny of the international working-class movement.

With the creation of the North German Confederation in 1867 the German working class was faced with the task of closing its ranks and setting up an independent proletarian party. Its ties with the International were of great importance for the ideological and organisational development of the German working-class movement in the latter half of the 1860s. Marx, who performed the duties of the Corresponding Secretary for Germany from the moment of the founding of the International Working Men's Association, was very closely linked with the German workers. Certain aspects of the activity of one of the German sections, that of Solingen, are revealed by Engels' letter of 8 February 1870 to Karl Klein and Friedrich Moll.

A serious obstacle to educating the German workers in the spirit of scientific communism and proletarian internationalism was Lassalleanism. The correspondence published in this volume enables us to trace the way in which Marx, Engels and their supporters Wilhelm Liebknecht and August Bebel, who led the revolutionary wing of the German working-class movement, opposed the Lassallean programme and tactics. In his letter of 13 October 1868 to the President of the General Association of German Workers, J. B. Schweitzer, Marx gave an objective appraisal of Lassalle's role in the German working-class movement. It was to Lassalle's credit, Marx wrote, that he had revived 'after fifteen years of slumber' an independent working-class movement in Germany free from the influence of the liberal bourgeoisie

(p. 132). But Lassalle's essentially reformist programme was an eclectic one. His overestimation of setting up workers' co-operatives with state assistance as a means to the social transformation of society (he viewed universal suffrage as the chief way of attaining this aim), his political orientation towards an alliance with Bismarck's government in the matter of German unification, and the sectarian nature of the organisation created by him, were at variance with the aims of the German working-class movement and laid the foundations for the opportunist trend within it (pp. 132-34).

Marx noted that the leaders of the General Association of German Workers, afraid of losing their influence with the masses, had been forced to make important additions to Lassalle's agitational demands. In particular, the programme adopted at the Hamburg Congress (August 1868) included the following points: 'agitation for complete political freedom, regulation of the working day and international co-operation of the working class', i.e. 'the starting points of any "serious" workers' movement' (see Marx's letter to Engels of 26 August 1868). The questions concerning the economic struggle, which Lassalle ignored (the staging of strikes, organisation of trade unions), were considered at the general German workers' congress in Berlin, called by the leaders of the General Association of German Workers in September 1868. However, only representatives of the Lassallean trade unions were admitted to the Berlin Congress, which testified to a continuation of the former sectarian course. In the above-mentioned letter to Schweitzer of 13 October 1868, and many other letters, Marx criticised him strongly for these tactics which led to a split in the trade-union movement and for anti-democratic methods of leadership, as well as criticising the anti-democratic way he set up trade associations. Marx told Schweitzer that the organisation created by him, 'suitable as it is for secret societies and sect movements, contradicts the nature of the trade unions' (p. 134).

From the letters it is clear how carefully Marx and Engels followed the activity of Bebel and Liebknecht at this time, giving them constant advice and supporting their struggle against the Lassalleans to unite the proletarian masses. While he fully understood the need for co-operation with the petty-bourgeois German People's Party against Prussian reaction, Liebknecht on a number of occasions conceded too much to this party; it was precisely this that provoked the strong criticism of Liebknecht's actions by Marx and Engels (pp. 15-16, 38, 141).

Thanks to tireless agitation by Liebknecht and Bebel there was a shift to the left in the Union of German Workers' Associations, which gradually freed itself from bourgeois influence and drew increasingly close to the International. In a letter to Engels of 29 July 1868 Marx noted with satisfaction that at the forthcoming Congress of the Union of German Workers' Associations in Nuremberg in September 1868 it was certain to join the International Working Men's Association and adopt its programme (p. 75). Marx and Engels believed that this success should be consolidated and the prerequisites created for the formation of a proletarian party in Germany by a further break with Lassalleanism and the complete overcoming by the German workers of their ideological dependence on non-proletarian elements alien to them. 'The dissolution of the Lassallean sect and, on the other hand, the severence of the Saxon and South German workers from the leading-strings of the 'People's Party' are the two fundamental conditions for the new formation of a genuine German workers' party,' Marx wrote to Ludwig Kugelmann on 10 July 1869 (p. 313).

In their correspondence Marx and Engels recorded the rapid 'process of the disintegration of specific Lassalleanism', which speeded up the withdrawal of progressive workers from the General Association of German Workers (pp. 255, 304). A number of former Lassalle's supporters (Wilhelm Bracke, Theodor York and others) agreed to the proposal made by Bebel and Liebknecht to call a general congress of German Social-Democrats. At this Congress, which took place in Eisenach from 7 to 9 August 1869, the Social-Democratic Workers' Party was founded. The creation of an independent workers' party in Germany was a great victory for Marxism and for the ideas of the International in the German working-class movement (see Engels' letter to Wilhelm Bracke of 28 April 1870, pp. 498-99). As Lenin pointed out later, in Eisenach a firm foundation was laid for 'a genuinely Social-Democratic workers' party. And in those days the essential thing was the *basis* of the party'. (V. I. Lenin, *Collected Works*, Vol. 19, p. 298.)

A number of letters published in this volume reflect the desire of Marx and Engels to raise the level of the theoretical awareness of members of the German working-class movement by means of propagating in the press the ideas of scientific communism and their criticism of Lassalleanism.

This volume also contains material concerning the preparation for publication of a short biography of Marx written by Engels (p. 76) and a new edition of *The Eighteenth Brumaire of Louis Bonaparte* and *The Peasant War in Germany*, which Marx and Engels supplied with new prefaces. Marx had a very high opinion of Engels' Preface to *The Peasant War in Germany*, which was published in *Der Volksstaat*:

'Your introduction is very good. I know of nothing that should be altered or added...' (p. 428).

The letters in this volume show how closely Marx and Engels followed the development of the working-class movement in France on the eve of the Franco-Prussian war and the Paris Commune. The deepening crisis of the Second Empire and the growth of revolutionary activity among the masses helped to extend the influence of the International in France. Within the French working class the characteristic Proudhonist renunciation of active forms of organising workers (economic and political) was gradually being overcome. There was a growing trend towards the emergence of a workers' party. Alarmed by the growing influence of the International in the country, the French government tried to check the revolutionary movement with mass reprisals, and also to provoke premature action by the masses in order to strike a blow at the working class. Marx wrote to Engels on 18 November 1868: 'In France things look very serious... The government wants to force the lads on to the streets so that *chassepot* and rifled cannon may then *laisser "faire merveille"'* (p. 162).

In March and May of 1868 and June-July of 1870 the Bonapartist government organised three trials against the French sections of the International Working Men's Association. Leaders of sections of the Association were arrested and accused of plotting against the Emperor. Noting the provocative character of the victimisation of French members of the International, Marx wrote to his daughter Jenny on 31 May 1870 in connection with the third trial, that the Bonapartist officials were busying themselves in Paris 'to hatch a new complot, in which the "Intern. W. Ass." is to play the principal part and where I, as ... *"wirklicher geheimer Oberhauptchef"* must of course put in my appearance' (p. 525). He stressed that all the repressive acts of the Bonapartist government were merely leading to a growth in the International's influence in France. 'Our French members are demonstrating *ad oculos* the French Government the difference between a political secret society and a genuine workers' association. No sooner had the government jailed all the members of the Paris, Lyons, Rouen, Marseilles etc., committees ... than committees *twice as numerous* announced themselves in the newspapers as their successors with the most daring and defiant declarations (and, as an added touch, with their *private addresses* as well). The French Government has finally done what we so long wanted it to do: transform the political question — Empire or Republic — into a question *de vie ou de mort* for the working class!' (pp. 522-23).

As leader of the International Marx attached great importance to the consolidation of the truly proletarian elements in France, to their ideological and organisational strengthening. With his direct help and support the official founding of the Paris Federation of the International took place in Paris on 18 April 1870. In his letters to Paul Lafargue of 18 and 19 April 1870 Marx advised the leaders of the Federation to adopt firm class positions, not to allow sectarian tendencies and not to give way to the influence of the various petty-bourgeois Proudhonist and Bakuninist doctrines. '*Il faut éviter les "étiquettes" sectaires dans l'Association Internationale*, he wrote. 'Those who interpret best the hidden sense of the class struggle going on before our eyes—the Communists are the last to commit the blunder of affecting or fostering sectarianism' (p. 485).

Marx's and Engels' letters about France included in this volume are full of hopes for a new outburst of the emancipation struggle of the working class, full of revolutionary optimism based on their belief in the inevitability of a crisis of the Bonapartist regime and major social changes, and full of the awareness that 'the whole historic witches' brew is simmering' (p. 233).

The correspondence shows the deep and constant interest which Marx and Engels took in the problems of the British working-class movement. In this period, as before, Marx made use of the experience of the mass organisations of the British working class— the trade unions. Under his leadership the General Council of the International maintained constant connections with a number of the largest trade unions in Manchester, Birmingham and Salford, particularly during their struggle for the full legalisation of trade unions and their national unification. Marx linked the successful solution of these questions first and foremost with active struggle by rank-and-file trade-union members. 'The squabble among the authorities of the trades unions,' which in fact paralysed them for years, has at last been settled...,' Marx wrote to Engels on 26 September 1868 in connection with the formation of the British Trades Union Congress, when the trade unions 'have finally agreed on *joint action*' (p. 114).

Some of the letters also contain criticism of the reformist leaders of the British trade unions who sought to solve social problems by means of reforms and compromises with the ruling classes (pp. 3-4, 253 and 394-95). However, the very course of the class struggle (strikes and the mass movement for electoral reform, etc.), and also the influence of the International, sometimes encouraged British trade unionists in practice to go beyond their socially pacifist and reformist ideas. This gave Marx a basis for collaborating with the trade-union leaders in the International Working Men's Association up to the time of the Paris Commune. Simultaneously Marx fought uncompromisingly against their reformist views, urging them to rely on the masses.

However, the revolutionary tendencies which continued to exist in the British mass working-class movement were challenged as before by the strong reformist influence of the trade-union leaders. Explaining the failure of the first working-class candidates at the parliamentary elections in 1868, Marx and Engels pointed above all to the ideological and political dependence of the working class on liberal bourgeois leaders, to the fact that the working class did not have its own political party and its own programme. 'Everywhere the proletariat are the rag, tag and bobtail of the official parties...,' Engels wrote on 18 November 1868 (p. 163). Marx's letters clearly show that the electoral defeat forced some of the London trade-union leaders who were members of the General Council to admit the soundness of his criticism and, to a certain extent, to agree with his view of the need for workers to act independently, to fight against them being turned into an appendage of the liberal bourgeoisie. '...the English too late but unanimously acknowledged that I had forecast *literally* for them, the ... highly amusing upshot of the elections,' he wrote to Engels on 18 November 1868 (p. 161).

The letters tell the story of the International Working Men's Association's break with the trade-unionist newspaper *The Bee-Hive,* which had been the official organ of the General Council since 22 November 1864. Under the leadership of bourgeois liberals the newspaper adopted a conciliatory position, ignoring and distorting the documents of the International. On Marx's initiative the General Council discussed the situation with *The Bee-Hive* in April 1870 and the newspaper ceased to be the International's organ. 'I denounced the paper as being sold to the bourgeois (S. Morley, etc.), mentioned particularly its treatment of our Irish resolutions and debates, etc.,' Marx wrote to Engels on 28 April 1870 (pp. 497-98).

After the Basle Congress of the International the question of the abolition of large-scale land-ownership as an effective means of fighting poverty, a very topical question for Britain, was actively discussed in democratic circles and among the workers. Marx saw this as an opportunity to create in Britain an independent political workers' organisation of a non-trade-union nature, an organisation whose programme would be originally based on the resolutions of the International's congresses. Thus, the *Land and Labour*

League was founded on 27 October 1869. Marx became an active member. Concerning the actual fact of the founding of the League Marx wrote to Engels on 30 October 1869: 'The creation of the *Land and Labour League* (incidentally, directly inspired by the General Council) should be regarded as an outcome of the Basle Congress; here, the workers' party makes a clean break with the bourgeoisie, nationalisation of land [being] the starting point' (p. 364).

In the second half of the 1860s the growing national liberation movement in Ireland began to have a great influence on British social and political life.

Some of the letters in this volume give a detailed account of the course of the discussion on the Irish question which took place in autumn 1869 in the General Council on Marx's initiative (pp. 371-72, 375-76, 386-87, 392-93) and was connected with the widespread campaign launched at that time in Britain for an amnesty for imprisoned Fenians. Marx was hoping in the course of this discussion to state in a resolution of the General Council the British working class's internationalist attitude to its ally, the fighters for the national liberation of Ireland. Illness prevented him from realising this intention, however. Nevertheless, his point of view was reflected in other General Council documents, in particular, the 'Confidential Communication' (see present edition, Vol. 21) and in letters to active members of the working-class movement in Germany, France and the USA (see this volume, pp. 390-91, 449, 472-76). In these letters Marx elaborated the thesis that the abolition of the Irish people's colonial enslavement and the granting to the Irish themselves of the right to decide their own fate was the most important condition for the emancipation of the working class in Britain. Thus he used the example of Anglo-Irish relations to illustrate a most important thesis in the national colonial question, namely, the community of interests between the participants in the national liberation struggle in the colonies and the workers' movement in the metropolis, and their interaction as a major prerequisite for the emancipation of the working people both in the metropolis and in the colonies.

Ireland, a British colony, Marx explained in his correspondence, was the citadel of British landlordism. The landed aristocracy mercilessly exploited the Irish peasants. The colonial enslavement of Ireland was also an important source of the strength of the British bourgeoisie. Irish workers in Britain were forced to agree to any wage, thereby lowering the standard of living of British workers. This brought about a split in the working class of Great

Britain and strengthened the position of the capitalists (pp. 473-75). To destroy the foundations of the rule of the British landed magnates and the financial and industrial bourgeoisie in Ireland would be to weaken the power of these classes in England itself. Consequently the liberation of Ireland would help the English working class considerably to attain its class aims (pp. 473-75). In this connection Marx wrote: 'For a long time I believed it would be possible to overthrow the Irish regime by English working class ascendancy... Deeper study has now convinced me of the opposite. The English working class will *never accomplish anything* before it has got rid of Ireland. The lever must be applied in Ireland. This is why the Irish question is so important for the social movement in general' (p. 398).

Marx emphasised that the English working class 'will never be able to do anything decisive here in England before they separate their attitude towards Ireland quite definitely from that of the ruling classes, and not only make common cause with the Irish, but even take the initiative in dissolving the Union established in 1801, and substituting a free federal relationship for it' (p. 390). 'Only by putting forward this demand was Marx really educating the English workers in the spirit of internationalism,' stressed Lenin (V. I. Lenin, *Collected Works*, Vol. 22, pp. 149-50).

The internationalist ideas of Marx and Engels on the Irish question were the result of their deep study of the historical past and present condition of this country and the long history of Anglo-Irish relations. Engels wrote: 'Irish history shows what a misfortune it is for one nation to subjugate another' (p. 363).

The correspondence throws light on Engels' work on his book on Irish history. The Franco-Prussian war which began in the summer of 1870 and the revolution which followed in Paris did not, however, allow him to complete this work.

A number of letters in this volume show Marx's constant and profound interest in the development of the American working-class movement. As the General Council's Corresponding Secretary for the German language sections in the USA, Marx corresponded with representatives of the German workers in America. He urged them to struggle to overcome sectarianism and strive for the international unity of the American working-class movement and to draw it into the sphere of activity of the International. '*A coalition of the German workers with the Irish workers* (naturally, also, with the English and American workers who wish to join in) is the greatest thing you could undertake now. This must be done in the name of the "International"', he wrote to Sigfrid

Meyer and August Vogt on 9 April 1870 (p. 476). Marx wrote with
profound regret of the sudden death of William Sylvis, the
President of the National Labor Union of the USA, of whose
achievements he thought highly, particularly of his struggle to
overcome national and local separatism in the American working-
class movement (p. 351).

Some of the letters in this volume also indicate the constant
interest with which Marx and Engels followed the growth of the
revolutionary movement in Russia. Marx's letter to N. F. Danielson of 7 October, 1868 marked the beginning of regular
correspondence between the founders of Marxism and the leaders
of the Russian revolutionary democratic movement. During this
period Marx was strongly aware of the need for more detailed
knowledge of life inside Russia after the abolition of serfdom in
1861. A study of the socio-economic relations of this huge peasant
country which had embarked on the path of capitalist development led Marx to feel 'deeply convinced that a ... social revolution ...
is irrepressible in Russia and near at hand' (see Marx's letter to Laura and Paul Lafargue of 5 March 1870). Marx was convinced that the victory of a popular revolution and the overthrow
of tsarism in Russia would provide a powerful impetus for the
development of the revolutionary movement throughout the
world. In the concrete historical conditions of the late 1860s Marx
regarded the victory of the revolutionary forces in Britain and
Russia as one of the main and decisive conditions for the
overthrow of capitalist society and the social reorganisation of
Europe.

During this period Marx and Engels also established contact
with the Russian revolutionary youth educated on the ideals of the
great Russian revolutionary democrats N. G. Chernyshevsky and
N. A. Dobrolyubov. Early in 1870 a Russian section of the
International was set up in Geneva. Concerning this Marx
informed Engels on 12 February 1870: 'In Geneva, by the by, a
new colony of exiled Russian students has grown up with a
programme proclaiming opposition to pan-Slavism, which should be
replaced by the "International"' (p. 430). On 12 March 1870 the
members of the Russian section, one of the organisers of which was
N. Utin, sent a letter to London announcing its constitution. Inviting
Marx to represent their section on the General Council, they
declared themselves to be in full agreement with the principles of the International (pp. 480, 493). He readily agreed to
their request. 'Enclosed, a letter from the *Russian colony* in Geneva,' he wrote to Engels on 24 March 1870. 'We have admitted

them; I have *accepted* their commission to be their representative on the General Council, and have also sent them a short reply...' (p. 462).

The propagation and dissemination of Marxism and the overcoming of petty-bourgeois utopias in the working class were greatly assisted by the publication in September 1867 of Volume I of Marx's *Capital*. After it came out Marx continued to work on its second and third books, which he intended should form Volume II. In spite of his bad health and constant financial difficulties, Marx nevertheless believed that for him 'there could never, from the outset, have been any question of ... taking over a business before ...' the 'book was finished' (p. 185).

In the summer of 1868 Marx embarked upon further intensive study in the British Museum library. Resuming his work on Volume II of *Capital*, he decided first and foremost to rewrite and expand the preliminary draft of the second book (Manuscript I). From the end of 1868 to the middle of 1870 he wrote a new version of the whole of second book of *Capital*, which he later called Manuscript II. In the Preface to Volume II Engels subsequently evaluated it as 'the only somewhat complete elaboration of Book II...' (see present edition, Vol. 36). It was at this time that Marx made use of *The Position of the Working Class in Russia* by V. V. Bervi (Flerovsky), published in 1869, for his work on Volume II of *Capital*. Marx considered Flerovsky's work to be the most important socio-economic study of the condition of the workers after Engels' book *The Condition of the Working-Class in England* (pp. 423-24). In this connection Marx began 'to study Russian hammer and tongs' (p. 551) and by the beginning of February 1870 had made considerable progress in the language.

Alongside his work on Book II of *Capital*, Marx paid considerable attention during this period to the study of problems relating to Book III. In his letter to Engels of 30 April 1868 Marx outlined his plan for the structure and main contents of the whole of Book III (pp. 21-25).

To be well-equipped with facts Marx continued to study world economic literature. Thus, in his letter of 7 October 1868 to N. F. Danielson he wrote that he could not prepare Volume II of *Capital* for the press 'until certain official *enquêtes*, instituted during last year (and 1866) in France, the United States and England, have been completed or published' (p. 123).

Marx made an intensive study of new material on agricultural development and agrarian relations in a number of countries. He sent various requests for the necessary literature to his comrades and his daughter Laura, who had moved to Paris after her marriage (pp. 9 and 97). Thus, Marx requested De Paepe to let him have the titles of the main works on the structure of land holding in Belgium and Belgian agriculture (p. 412). He wrote to Sigfrid Meyer, one of the leaders of the German and American working-class movement, on 4 July 1868 asking him to send him American newspapers from time to time. 'In particular, it would be of great value to me,' Marx wrote, 'if you could dig up some anti-bourgeois material about land-ownership and agrarian relations in the United States.' Marx needed this material, inter alia, for his polemic with the American economist H. Ch. Carey on the question of land rent. Engels' letters of 9 and 19 November to Marx and Marx's letter to Engels of 26 November 1869 contain a critical examination of Carey's mistaken ideas, and also point out errors in Ricardo's theory of land rent. Marx and Engels substantiate their views on the emergence of land rent, quoting convincing examples and facts in support of their theory.

As can be seen from Marx's letters, the agrarian system in Russia was of considerable interest to him in his treatment of the genesis of capitalist land rent in Book III of *Capital.* In the middle of 1868 Marx embarked upon a careful study of Russian sources, in the belief that in 'dealing with the land question, it has become essential to study Russian land-owning relationships from primary sources' (Marx to Kugelmann, 27 June 1870).

Describing Marx's studies of a large number of Russian sources in the 1870s, Engels noted later in the Preface to Volume III of *Capital* that according to Marx's plan Russia 'was to play the same role in the part dealing with rent in land that England played in Book I in connection with industrial wage-labour' (see present edition, Vol. 37).

As well as continuing to elaborate economic theory Marx and Engels devoted considerable attention in this period to circulating Volume I of *Capital* and propagating its ideas. Some of the letters in this volume refer to the steps taken by Marx and Engels to popularise the work. Engels rendered great service in this respect. Thus, besides some reviews of the volume for German newspapers, in 1868 Engels also wrote a review for the English bourgeois journal *The Fortnightly Review* (see present edition, Vol. 20).

In a number of letters Marx and Engels touch upon reviews and comments by bourgeois economists on Volume I of *Capital.* Here, alongside a critical appraisal of the views expressed by the authors of these reviews ('specialist mandarins', as Marx so aptly puts it) (p. 213), they set out in clear and concise form the most important theses of Marx's economic theory (see, for example, Marx's letter to Ludwig Kugelmann of 11 July 1868).

The main aim behind the efforts by Marx and Engels to disseminate the ideas of *Capital* was to equip the working class with a scientific revolutionary economic theory in its struggle to free itself from capitalist exploitation. Linking the elaboration of an economic theory very closely with practical aims, Marx attached great importance to the propagation of his views to a working-class audience. He delivered a lecture on wages for German workers in London, about which he wrote to Engels on 23 May 1868 (see p. 40). Engels constantly showed genuine concern for the fate of the working-class movement and the practical application of the conclusions of Marx's political economy. He intended to write a popular brochure on the contents of Volume I of *Capital* for the workers (see Engels' letter to Marx of 16 September 1868, this volume, p. 100).

The correspondence of Marx and Engels in this period also illustrates the great importance they attached to the publication of *Capital* in different languages (French, Russian and English). In October 1869 Charles Keller, a member of the Paris section of the First International, began work on a translation of *Capital* (pp. 399, 546), greatly assisted by Marx (p. 359). The work was not completed, however. One of the leaders of revolutionary Chartism, George Harney, a companion-in-arms and friend of Marx and Engels, offered his services for the publication of Volume I of *Capital* in English in New York (p. 276).

Marx was delighted to hear that his book was being translated into Russian (p. 130), and wrote on 7 October 1868 to one of the translators, N. F. Danielson. It was the first translation of *Capital*, and appeared in 1872.

The letters indicate the truly encyclopaedic knowledge possessed by Marx and Engels, the breadth and variety of their scholarly interests. During this period they devoted considerable attention to philosophical problems. In a number of letters Marx criticises Eugen Dühring and F. A. Lange for their deprecatory attitude to Hegelian dialectics.

In October-November 1868 Marx and Engels read and discussed in detail the manuscript of the book entitled *Das Wesen der menschlichen Kopfarbeit* by the German leather-worker Joseph Dietzgen. They stressed Dietzgen's considerable learning and his independent discovery of the laws of the materialist theory of knowledge. On 28 October 1868, in direct response to the impression which the manuscript had made upon him, Marx wrote:

'He is one of the most gifted workers I know' (p. 149).

The correspondence also bears witness to the constant interest which Marx and Engels took in the development of the natural sciences, physics, chemistry and biology, and their study of the most important discoveries in these areas (pp. 33 and 246). As can be seen from Marx's letter to Engels of 18 November 1868, Marx was interested in the problem of the origin of life on earth in connection with research by the Viennese Professor Gustav Jäger and the German scientist Ernst Haeckel, followers of Darwin's theory of evolution (p. 162).

In his letter to Kugelmann of 27 June 1870, Marx sharply criticised the book *On the Workers' Question* by one of the so-called social Darwinists, F. A. Lange, who automatically transferred the law of the struggle for existence discovered by Darwin in the animal and plant world to the history of mankind. There is also sharp criticism of 'social Darwinism' in Marx's letter to Paul and Laura Lafargue of 15 February 1869.

As before, linguistics remained the special sphere of Engels' scientific interests. In spring 1869 he resumed his studies of the Friesian and Old Irish languages (pp. 247, 257, 410, 501, 514, 517-18).

The correspondence published in this volume contains extensive biographical material on Marx and Engels and gives a clear picture of their everyday life and struggle, their process of creation and their practical activity during this period, when they were in effect leading the mass international working-class movement. The letters fully reflect the growing friendship between the two men over the years, their constant collaboration both in the elaboration of theory and in leading the workers' revolutionary struggle, and their touching affection for each other. For Marx Engels was the person with whom he shared his most intimate thoughts and new scientific ideas. Engels' attachment to Marx extended to the members of his family, especially his daughters for whom he showed a truly paternal concern.

As the correspondence shows, Marx and Engels devoted considerable attention to the training and ideological education of progressive fighters from the working class. In the General Council and the administrative bodies of the International in the various countries Marx sought to create a firm backbone of proletarian revolutionaries. Under the direct influence of Marx, with the assistance of veterans of the working-class movement who had been members of the Communist League and taken part in the Revolution of 1848-49, such as Johann Becker, Johann Georg

Eccarius, Friedrich Lessner, Karl Pfänder, Wilhelm Liebknecht and Victor Schily, young members of the working-class movement, such as César de Paepe, Sigfrid Meyer and August Vogt, were introduced to scientific socialism. The letters published show how patiently and determinedly Marx and Engels sought to educate their comrades-in-arms, helping them with advice, responding to their requests and criticising their errors and shortcomings.

An example of the considerate and comradely attitude of Marx and Engels to their friends and comrades-in-arms is the help which they gave to Eugene Dupont, a General Council member, when he was in great need after his wife died and he lost his job (p. 481). Marx also gave financial assistance to the German worker Eccarius (pp. 284-85).

The correspondence presents us with vivid portraits of Marx's and Engels' comrades-in-arms and friends, active members of the working-class movement, such as Friedrich Lessner, Wilhelm Liebknecht and Ernest Jones.

It also shows us the new generation of revolutionaries—Paul Lafargue; the French ethnographer Gustave Flourens, a man of unusual bravery and courage; the Russian naturalist and revolutionary Hermann Lopatin, whom Marx considered as 'a very wide-awake *critical* brain' (p. 530), and the young August Bebel. Marx and Engels spoke with affection and respect of the German chemist and Social-Democrat Carl Schorlemmer; of the English lawyer, member of the International and future translator of Volume I of *Capital*, Samuel Moore; the English geologist Dakyns, who joined the socialist movement under the influence of Marx and Engels; the German doctor Ludwig Kugelmann and others.

In addition to the correspondence there is Engels' 'Confession' (answers to questions on a semi-humorous questionnaire) which reveals his personal merits, his warm sense of humour and his well-balanced personality.

* * *

Volume 43 contains 347 letters by Marx and Engels. The majority were written in German, 21 in English, 6 in French and several in a combination of two or three languages. Most of the letters are published in English for the first time; 125 letters have been published in English before, 87 of these in part only. All previous publications are indicated in the notes. Engels' letter of 26 November 1868 to W. Holzenhauer is published here for the first time. The Appendices contain 11 letters and documents, which are published in English for the first time.

During work on the text and other sections of this volume the dating of certain letters was established more accurately as a result of additional research.

The text of earlier English publications has been checked and verified against the originals. Obvious errors have been silently corrected. Abbreviated proper names, geographical names and individual words are given in full, except when these abbreviations were made for conspiratorial reasons or cannot be deciphered. Defects in the manuscript are indicated in the footnotes, and passages where the text is lost or illegible are indicated by dots. If the context makes it possible to provide a hypothetical reconstruction of the lost or illegible passages, this is given in square brackets. Passages deleted by the authors are reproduced at the bottom of the page in cases where there is a significant discrepancy. The special nature of certain letters which were drafts or fragments reproduced in other documents is indicated either in the text itself or in the notes.

Foreign words and expressions in the text of the letters are retained in the form in which they were used by the authors, with a translation where necessary in the footnotes and italicised (if they were underlined by the authors they are italicised and spaced out).

English words and expressions used by Marx and Engels in texts originally written in German, French or other languages are printed in small caps. Whole passages originally written in English are marked by asterisks. Some of the words are now somewhat archaic or have undergone changes in usage. For example, the term 'nigger', which has acquired generally—but especially in the USA—a more profane and unacceptable status than it had in Europe during the 19th century.

The numbering of the notes relating to one and the same fact or event in the texts of different letters is duplicated.

The volume was compiled, the texts of the letters and notes prepared by Irina Shikanyan (letters from April 1868 to April 1869 inclusive) and Alexander Vatutin (letters from May 1869 to July 1870). The Preface was written by Irina Shikanyan and Alexander Vatutin. The volume was edited by Velta Pospelova. The name index and the index of periodicals were prepared by Alexander Vatutin, the index of quoted and mentioned literature jointly by Irina Shikanyan and Alexander Vatutin (Institute of Marxism-Leninism of the CC CPSU).

The translations were done by John Peet (Lawrence & Wishart),

Michael Slattery and Sergei Syrovatkin (Progress Publishers) and edited by Eric Hobsbawm, Nicholas Jacobs (Lawrence & Wishart) and Glenys Ann Kozlov, Jane Sayer, Svetlana Gerasimenko, Yelena Kalinina, Natalia Karmanova, Mzia Pitskhelauri, Viktor Schnittke (Progress Publishers), and Norire Ter-Akopyan, scientific editor (USSR Academy of Sciences).

The volume was prepared for the press by Yelena Vorotnikova and Nadezhda Rudenko (Progress Publishers).

KARL MARX
and
FREDERICK ENGELS

LETTERS

April 1868-July 1870

1868

1

MARX TO LUDWIG KUGELMANN[1]

IN HANOVER

London, 6 April 1868

Dear Kugelmann,

The young pair[a] were registered at a civil ceremony last Thursday[b] (since a *church* wedding is not legally necessary here), and have left for France to celebrate their HONEYMOON. They send their best greetings to you and Mrs Gertrud.

Coppel paid a call on me here. Unfortunately, I could not receive him, since I was wrapped in cataplasms. Engels was here during the wedding, and left again yesterday.[2] In response to his urgings, I have decided to take the arsenic cure, since an end must at last be put to this state of affairs. One of his friends in Manchester[c] was completely cured by this method in a relatively short time. I had certain prejudices against arsenic after reading in the *Gazette médicale* about a discussion among French doctors.[d]

The Irish question predominates here just now. It has naturally only been exploited by Gladstone and consorts to take over the helm again, and particularly to have an ELECTORAL CRY[e] at the next elections, which will be based on HOUSEHOLD SUFFRAGE.[3] *At the moment,* this turn of affairs is detrimental to the workers' party, because the intriguers among the workers, such as Odger, Potter, etc., who want to get into the next Parliament, have now found a new *excuse* for attaching themselves to the bourgeois liberals.[4]

This is, however, only a *penalty* that England—and thus, also, the English working class—is paying for the great centuries-old

---

[a] Paul and Laura Lafargue - [b] 2 April - [c] Presumably Schorlemmer (see this volume, p. 12). - [d] 'Traitement arsénial de la phthisie pulmonaire', *Gazette médicale de Paris*, 11 January 1868. - [e] This English phrase is given in brackets after its German equivalent.

crime against Ireland. IN THE LONG RUN it will benefit the English working class itself. You see, the ENGLISH ESTABLISHED CHURCH IN IRELAND—OR WHAT THEY USE TO CALL HERE THE IRISH CHURCH—is the religious bulwark of English LANDLORDISM IN IRELAND and, at the same time, the outpost of the Established Church in England itself (I am speaking here of the Established Church as a *landowner*). The overthrow of the Established Church in Ireland would mean its fall in England, and the two will be followed (in their downfall) by LANDLORDISM, first in Ireland and then in England. And I have always been convinced that the social revolution must begin *seriously* from the ground, i.e. from landed property.

In addition, the whole thing will have the very useful result that, once the IRISH CHURCH is dead, the *PROTESTANT* IRISH TENANTS in the province of Ulster will make common cause with the Catholic TENANTS and their movement in the 3 other provinces of Ireland, whereas so far LANDLORDISM has been able to exploit this *religious* antagonism.

The day before yesterday I received a letter from Freiligrath (wedding cards were, of course, sent to him), containing the following curious sentence.[5]—It will perhaps amuse you more, however, if *I enclose the letter itself,* which I now do. But you must *return* it to me. So that you understand the letter properly, the following: In Berlin, shortly before my book[a] came out, there appeared *Zwölf Streiter der Revolution von G. Struve und Gustav Rasch.* In this publication, Freiligrath is acclaimed as 'one' of the 12 apostles and, at the same time, it is proved in great detail that he *never* was a communist, in fact that it was only through TOO GREAT A CONDESCENSION that he became associated with such monsters as Marx, Engels, Wolff, etc.[b] Since Wolff was slandered here too, I wrote to Freiligrath for an explanation, particularly since I knew that G. Rasch (a scoundrel) headed his begging committee in Berlin.[6] He replied very dryly, and with evasive philistine cunning. Later I sent him my book without, however, as was formerly our mutual custom, signing it. He appears to have taken the HINT.

My best regards to your dear wife and Fränzchen. If at all feasible, I shall come UNDER ALL CIRCUMSTANCES and pay you a visit.

Yours

K. Marx

---

[a] the first volume of *Capital* - [b] G. Struve and G. Rasch, *Zwölf Streiter der Revolution,* Berlin, 1867, pp. 59-61.

Apropos. Borkheim will visit you IN A FEW DAYS. Don't forget that, despite all comradeship with him, I always *observe reserve!*

Liebknecht's paper[a] is much too narrow-mindedly 'southern'.[b] (He has not enough dialectic to strike out on two sides at once.)

First published abridged in *Die Neue Zeit,* Bd. 2, Nr. 6, Stuttgart, 1901-1902 and in full in: Marx and Engels, *Works,* Second Russian Edition, Vol. 32, Moscow, 1964

Printed according to the original

Published in English in full for the first time

2

ENGELS TO MARX

IN LONDON

Manchester, 10 April 1868

Dear Moor,

Enclosed letters from Wilhelmchen[7] and Siebel, please return the former to me. Poor Siebel seems to be having a bad time indeed. I shall see him in about 10 days.

Further, the draft of an advertisement for Meissner[8]; what do you think of it? So far it has not been pressing, since he could not advertise because of the Easter Fair anyway.

Yesterday I sent you Nos. 4 to 14 of Wilhelmchen's rag.[c] It is dreadfully stupid. One who was in England for such a long time and who has your book and mine[d] should really know how to put the material supplied to him by the workers to other use than simply reproducing it at full length. Some anti-federalist passages with us in mind are rather comical in connection with the whole federalist-Struveist nature of the sheet.[e][9]

When I got back here[2] I found such a pile of work waiting that I could only see Gumpert yesterday. Enclosed the prescription: on the

---

[a] *Demokratisches Wochenblatt* - [b] See next letter and Engels' letter to Marx of 2 February 1868 (present edition, Vol. 42). - [c] *Demokratisches Wochenblatt* - [d] Presumably the first volume of *Capital* and *The Condition of the Working-Class in England.* - [e] See previous letter.

first 4-5 days you should take it only twice daily, then 3 times, always 1 $1/_2$-2 hours after a meal. And also live well and get plenty of exercise. Gumpert laughs at your assertion that arsenic makes you stupid.

The vote on parliamentary freedom of speech is explained by the fact that Bismarck had stated previously that for Prussia, for the sake of peace, he would concede this point. So it was not even, as we thought, proof of the courage of the philistines.

What Wilhelm says about the American treaty is of course nonsense from beginning to end.[10]

Unfortunately, I have a death to announce to Tussy. The poor hedgehog ate a round hole in his blanket, put his head through it, and got so stuck in it that he was found strangled yesterday morning. Peace to his ashes, and BETTER LUCK TO THE NEXT ONE.

During the 3 days of my absence, the fellows in Liverpool swindled cotton up by no less than 3d., from 10d. to 13d. Hence so much work. Luckily the holidays intervene, which I am using to complete the extracts for the Beesly article.[11] I am starting right away, and thus close for today. Best greetings to your wife and the girls.

Your
F. E.

The wedding was celebrated here with great festivity: the dogs had green collars, a TEA PARTY for 6 children, Lafargue's glass basin served as a punch-bowl, and the poor hedgehog was made drunk for the last time.

First published abridged in *Der Briefwechsel zwischen F. Engels und K. Marx*, Bd. 4, Stuttgart, 1913 and in full in *MEGA*, Abt. III, Bd. 4, Berlin, 1931

Printed according to the original

Published in English for the first time

3

MARX TO ENGELS

IN MANCHESTER

London, 11 April 1868

DEAR FRED,

D'abord[a] the GENERAL CONDOLATIONS, and especially from Tussychen, about the departed RIGHT HONOURABLE HEDGEHOG.

It is a good thing that the opium prescription arrived today.[b] The affairs under my arm have become very vexatious since your departure.[2]

From the young couple,[c] who are now in Paris, the most satisfying news.[12] They are obviously very happy. Lafargue has sent me Horn's pamphlet[d] and another one on French finance. The second is twaddle, the first I shall send you soon. I wrote to Lafargue[e] that the fact that he finds time 'AT SUCH A CRITICAL JUNCTURE' to think of me and send me printed matter goes a long way to prove 'THAT HE MUST BELONG TO A BETTER THAN THE EUROPEAN RACE'.[f] WE ARE ALWAYS 'CHAFFING' AT EACH OTHER.

I have read the *Histoire du Crédit mobilier.*[g] As far as the real essence of the matter is concerned, I really wrote better stuff on it years ago in the *Tribune.*[13] The author knows the business. He is himself a Paris banker. But he has in fact nothing to draw on except the *official* material, provided by the Crédit itself in its reports, and the facts noted in the stock market quotations. The secret material could only be obtained *by legal steps.* What astonishes me particularly is this: the actual TRICKS all reduce themselves to stock-jobbing on the exchange,[h] and in this department *au fond*[i] there has been *nothing new since Law,*[14] whatever the disguise. Neither on this side of the Channel, nor on the other. The interesting aspect of these things is the practice, not the theory.

I enclose a letter from Kugelmann (*à renvoyer*[j]). After you had left, I wrote to him.[k] But since writing is a nuisance for me at the moment because of my left arm, I enclosed Freiligrath's letter to

---

[a] First of all - [b] See previous letter. - [c] Paul and Laura Lafargue - [d] I. E. Horn, *Frankreichs Finanzlage.* - [e] See this volume, p. 9. - [f] An allusion to J. G. Seume's poem 'Der Wilde'. - [g] M. Aycard, *Histoire du Crédit Mobilier. 1852-1867.* - [h] See this volume, p. 11. - [i] basically - [j] to be returned - [k] See this volume, pp. 3-5.

me,[5] so that Kugelmann should receive the SUFFICIENT quantum of written matter. I told him also, in reply to a previous enquiry, that I would visit him in any case for A FEW DAYS. However, he 'erred' about the date. It is not so close.

Do not forget to send me the *Schweitzer*[15] BY NEXT POST.

From *The Times* of today (telegraphic dispatch)[a] you will see that we have won a complete victory in Geneva, working day reduced from 12 to 11 hours, wages increased by 10%.[16] The matter went like this. Scarcely had you left when a deputy arrived from Geneva.[17] This FACT, that the workers sent an *envoy* to London, to the fearsome secret tribunal, *was decisive*, as earlier in the STRIKE of the bronze workers of Paris.[18] The MASTERS believe in the power and the fighting fund in London. This should show the workers in England and on the continent the power they would possess in us if they really put at our disposal the appropriate means, etc.

Enclosed returned Wilhelm,[7] Siebel. Your draft[b] is not written in your EASYGOING style. Today I have particular pain in my left arm. As soon as this has passed, I shall return your draft with my probable emendations.

The children send their best greetings. In fact, if only for their sake, I wish you lived in London instead of Manchester.

MY COMPLIMENTS TO MRS BURNS.

Your

K. M.

First published in *Der Briefwechsel zwischen F. Engels und K. Marx*, Bd. 4, Stuttgart, 1913

Printed according to the original

Published in English for the first time

---

[a] 'Switzerland, Geneva, April 10', *The Times*, No. 26096, 11 April 1868.- [b] See this volume, p. 5, and Note 8.

4

MARX TO LAURA AND PAUL LAFARGUE [19]

IN PARIS

London, 11 April 1868

My dear Cacadou,

You know I am a slow hand at writing, but this time the shortcomings of my left arm are responsible for the sins of my right hand. Under those circumstances I missed the more my secretary who might have addressed to himself, on my behalf, the most charming letters.[20]

I am happy to see from your scribblings (you excuse the 'term', Borkheim with his 'scribaille' is still dinning my ears[21]) and those of your helpmate[12] that you are thoroughly enjoying your *Brautfahrt*,[a] and that all the outer circumstances, spring and sun and air and Paris jollities, conjure in your favour. As to that said helpmate, his sending books to me, at such a critical juncture, speaks volumes for the innate kindness of the 'young man'. This simple fact would go far to prove that he must belong to a better than the European race.[b] By the by, as we have just touched the chapter of books, you might pay a visit to Guillaumin (14, rue Richelieu)[22] and get his (economical) *bulletins de librairie* for 1866-1868. You might also wend your steps to the *Librairie Internationale* (15, Boulevard Montmartre) and ask for their catalogues (1865-68). Of course, if you get these *desiderata*, you will not *send* them, but bring them on your return to this dreary place.

I am expecting, from Meissner, 3 copies of my book.[c] On their arrival, I shall send two to Caesar de Paepe, one for himself, the other for Altmayer.[d] Meanwhile, if you should find the time to see Schily (that is to say if you write to him 4, rue St. Quentin to come and see you) be so kind to ask him what has become of the 3 copies, 1 I sent for Jacquelard,[e] 1 for Taine, 1 for Réclus. If Jacquelard was not to be found, you might give his copy to Altmayer, since Meissner *is very slow* in forwarding the copies. In that case, however, I ought to be informed. You'll certainly fancy, my dear child, that I am very fond of books, because I trouble you with them at so unseasonable a time. But you would

---

[a] honeymoon trip - [b] An allusion to J. G. Seume's poem 'Der Wilde'. - [c] the first volume of *Capital* - [d] Altmeyer - [e] Jaclard

be quite mistaken. I am a machine, condemned to devour them and, then, throw them, in a changed form, on the dunghill of history. A rather dreary task, too, but still better than that of Gladstone's, who is obliged, at a day's notice, to work himself into 'states of mind', yclept 'earnestness'.

We feel here rather somewhat lonely. First you disappeared together with the meridional 'silent man', and then Engels left us.[2] In lieu of an 'excitement' we had the Lormiers yesterday evening. I played with Louis two parties of chess and allowed him to win one. What do you think the strange Caliban boy told me, in the most solemn manner of the world, on taking leave? '*Sans rancune, j'espère!*'[a]

And now, my dear Cacadou, *Adio*.

Old Nick

Dear Lafargue,[23]

Do you not find that staying in Paris WITH A YOUNG LOVABLE WIFE is much pleasanter than with politics? When your father[b] arrives in Paris, give him my best regards, and, in particular, you and Laura should not forget to make his stay SO PLEASANT as possible. Given the state of his eyes, he needs diversion, and nothing will divert him more than that the young pair should devote to him completely the short time they have with the old gentleman. I am writing to you in German so that you may, or may not, as you wish, inform the private secretary[c] of the contents of these lines. And now, with heartiest greetings.

Yours faithfully,
K. M.

First published in *Annali dell'Istituto Giangiacomo Feltrinelli*, an. 1, Milano, 1958

Printed according to the original

Published in English in full for the first time

---

[a] '*No offence taken*, I hope!' - [b] François Lafargue - [c] Laura

5

ENGELS TO MARX

IN LONDON

Manchester, 17 April 1868

Dear Moor,

Horn[a] 'awaits receipt', as commercial style puts it.

It is certain that there is theoretically nothing of interest and nothing new to be said about agiotage. It all comes down to fraud under false pretences and nothing can change here except the manner. The secret material about the history of the Crédit mobilier[13] can, by the way, and probably will, reach the light of day by itself on the fall of the Empire, even if there is no intervention by the courts.

I had already seen about the glorious victory in Geneva[16] in the newspapers on Saturday[b] morning. The business is all the better since the stupid philistines had made out the International Association to be the real motive force of the affair, and it now receives all the glory. You will have seen that the intermediaries in the business were Police Prefect Camperio and the noble and serrrious *Amand Goegg*. This will have instilled new respect for our power in Mr Amand. Incidentally, I should like to know how long—following this business—they will leave the International Association unmolested in *Germany*.

BY THE BY, the workers' affairs are proceeding famously. First Belgium, then Geneva, now Bologna[24]—I am only surprised that the International has not yet been blamed for this—it keeps going everywhere.

You will have received the Schweitzer.[15]

Tomorrow I shall send you—I have forgotten it at the office—1. a new copy of Wilhelmchen's rag,[c] 2. Eichhoff's further jeremiad,[25] 3. a section of an editorial declaration from the *Zukunft* about the curious article *ad vocem*[d] Vogt, from which you will see what shits they are.

Making extracts from your book is, with my limited time, giving me more work than I expected, *car enfin*[e] if this job is to be done, it must be done properly and not just for this special purpose.[26]

---

[a] I. E. Horn, *Frankreichs Finanzlage*. See this volume, p. 7. - [b] 11 April - [c] *Demokratisches Wochenblatt* - [d] concerning - [e] because after all

Next week I expect to have more time, there is a pause in business, and if I can get away between 4 and 5 in the evening, this gives the whole evening a different character for working.

Kugelmann returned enclosed.[27] I was very interested in his uterine polyp removed by splitting and compressed sponge; he will have to tell me about it personally in more detail in good time. But the attempt to turn Virchow into a communist with the aid of this polyp looks very much like an extra-uterine pregnancy. Even if Virchow had knowledge and theoretical interest in politics or political economy, this upright citizen is after all much too deeply engaged.[28]

Incidentally, you will come here before you leave for the continent, *cela est entendu*,[a] and bring Tussy with you as promised.

Your arm must surely have settled down by now? The fact that Kugelmann recommends arsenic will certainly have allayed some of your anxieties. Schorlemmer took a lot of it in his time, and never noted the slightest ill effects.

Heartiest greetings to the ladies.

Your
F. E.

First published abridged in *Der Briefwechsel zwischen F. Engels und K. Marx*, Bd. 4, Stuttgart, 1913 and in full in *MEGA*, Abt. III, Bd. 4, Berlin, 1931

Printed according to the original

Published in English for the first time

6

MARX TO LUDWIG KUGELMANN [29]

IN HANOVER

London, 17 April 1868

Dear Kugelmann,

You must regard me as a great criminal for taking so long to reply to the friendly letter from your dear wife[b] and yourself.[27] The situation is simply this. The old sanguinary herpes (to express myself poetically) attacked me with such tactical dexterity that I

---

[a] that is understood - [b] Gertrud Kugelmann

could not adopt the posture necessary for writing. I could, of course, have dictated, but you know that in such cases one always hopes to be ALL RIGHT next morning. Thus the delay, and thus, also, the brevity of these lines.

It is still *quite uncertain* when I shall be travelling to Germany for a few days; in any case, it won't be soon. At all events, I shall come at a time when I know that you will not be away.

You have done me a great service with your lines to Virchow, though I doubt whether he will have the patience and the time to immerse himself in a subject out of his line.[a] I know it cost me a great effort to read his *Cellularpathologie* in Manchester, particularly because of the way it was written.

The issues of *Social-Demokrat* hitherto concerned with my book are: No. 10 (22 Jan. 1868), No. 11 (24 Jan.), No. 12 (26 Jan.), No. 14 (31 Jan.), No. 15 (2 Feb.), No. 24 (23 Feb.), No. 25 (26 Feb.), No. 30 (8 March),[15] and another number, which I don't have at the moment, but which contains only extracts.[b]

With heartiest greetings to your dear wife and Fränzchen

Yours

K. Marx

Meyer[c] paid me a visit here.

First published abridged in *Die Neue Zeit,* Bd. 2, Nr. 7, Stuttgart, 1901-1902 and in full in *Pisma Marksa k Kugelmanu* (Letters of Marx to Kugelmann), Moscow-Leningrad, 1928

Printed according to the original

7

MARX TO ENGELS

IN MANCHESTER

[London,] 18 April 1868

DEAR FRED,

I have been lying fallow until today and could not leave the house. My arm was so inflamed, and there was so much suppuration, that I could wear nothing on that arm and

---

[a] See this volume, p. 12. - [b] *Der Social-Demokrat*, No. 39, 29 March 1868. - [c] Gustav Meyer

movement was upsetting, too. The suppuration has stopped completely this morning. The wounds themselves heal rapidly. I shall go out again today. With the help of arsenic I now hope that this disgusting muck is finished.

The Viennese affairs enclosed were sent by Fox, who is also responsible for the pencil marks.

On *Tuesday*[a] I have to pay £5 for school and £1 5s. for gymnastic classes for Tussy. If it is possible for you to send this *by return*, I would appreciate it very much, for the sake of the child.

The departure is still a good way off. Kugelmann jumps to conclusions too rapidly. I only wrote to him that I would be coming SOME TIME OR OTHER.[b]

Becker's appeal,[30] which is enclosed, demonstrates again the great lack of discipline. We stopped the collections in the London UNIONS, and the Parisians did the same, because it is *only now* that we are informed that further money is needed. If they had telegraphed from Geneva on the same day, it would have been ALL RIGHT.

Salut.

Your
K. M.

First published in *Der Briefwechsel zwischen F. Engels und K. Marx*, Bd. 4, Stuttgart, 1913

Printed according to the original

Published in English for the first time

8

ENGELS TO MARX

IN LONDON

Manchester, 20 April 1868

Dear Moor,

Enclosed two fivers to satisfy the schoolmasters.

Just like the Geneva people to dawdle. It is a naïve presumption too that, now that the STRIKE[16] is over, the world should help the Genevans to pay the debts contracted during the STRIKE. I have never seen anything like that in this country. Here they only ask

---

[a] 21 April - [b] See this volume, p. 13.

for support as long as the STRIKE lasts.

The Vienna paper[a] appears to contribute to a deliberate confusion created by the industrial interests, which is obviously grafted on to the spontaneous naive-helpless confusion. In the end, you always encounter a distinctly bourgeois tendency— accordingly, the paper no longer *reports* the workers' meetings, but *instructs* them.

With best greetings.

Your
F. E.

First published in *Der Briefwechsel zwischen F. Engels und K. Marx*, Bd. 4, Stuttgart, 1913

Printed according to the original

Published in English for the first time

9

MARX TO ENGELS

IN MANCHESTER

[London,] 21 April 1868

DEAR FRED,

BEST THANKS FOR THE £10.

Yesterday I went out for a walk again, and now here comes Jennychen to drive me out again on the pretext that you entrusted her with supervision over me.

My arm is in order again, there is just the healing itch. For some years now I have made the curious observation that my urine, which in my normal state deposits chalk or whatever it is, becomes quite clear when I have carbuncles. And in fact the mineral deposit is now appearing again. Perhaps Gumpert knows something about it.

Apropos. Wilhelm is now sending me his rag, too.[b] How loyal it is of the man to call my *Herr Vogt* a '*deserving* book' instead of saying that there are many bad jokes in it.[31] And then: the Prussians persecute Hanoverians who were 'loyal to their king'! Then: regarding Edgar Bauer on the paying of the South German

---

[a] Presumably *Neues Wiener Tagblatt* - [b] *Demokratisches Wochenblatt*

press, that, if things go on like that, '*all*' men of honour (country squires, priests, democrats, the Elector of Hesse,[a] etc.) will combine against Prussia.[32] Poor Wilhelm!

Blind has again made one of his great coups. With the aid of a servile message he has squeezed a reply from Juárez, which is in the *Courrier français* today.[b] It is time this clown got a bang on the head for his buffoonery.

Salut.

Your
K. M.

First published in *Der Briefwechsel zwischen F. Engels und K. Marx*, Bd. 4, Stuttgart, 1913   Printed according to the original

Published in English for the first time

10

MARX TO ENGELS[33]

IN MANCHESTER

London, 22 April 1868

Dear Fred,

I have resumed work, and it's going well. Only I have to limit the working *time*, for after ABOUT 3 hours my head starts to buzz and prickle. I shall now tell you briefly a 'morsel' which *occurred* to me when I was just glancing at the part of my manuscript about the rate of profit.[c] It provides a simple solution to one of the most difficult questions. The question is how it can happen that as the value of money, or gold, falls, *the rate of profit* rises; and that it falls with the rise in the value of money.

Let us assume the value of money falls by $\frac{1}{10}$. Then, other things remaining equal, the price of commodities rises by $\frac{1}{10}$.

If, on the other hand, the value of money rises by $\frac{1}{10}$, then the price of commodities falls by $\frac{1}{10}$, other things remaining equal.

Given a fall in the value of money, the price of labour, unless it rises in the same proportion, *falls*, the rate of surplus value rises,

---

[a] Ludwig III - [b] B. P. Juárez, 'Mexico, 9 mars 1868", *Le Courrier français,* 21 April 1868. - [c] Marx has in mind the beginning of the manuscript of Book III of *Capital,* written in 1864-65 (for a discussion of this see Engels' Preface to Volume III of *Capital,* present edition, Vol. 37).

and therefore, ALL OTHER THINGS REMAINING THE SAME, the rate of profit rises too. This rise of the latter—as long as the DESCENDANT OSCILLATION in the value of money continues—is due solely to the fall in wages, and this fall is due to the fact that the change in wages is slow to match the change in the value of money. (As was the case at the end of the 16th and in the 17th century.) Conversely, if, with the value of money rising, wages do not fall in the same proportion, the rate of surplus value falls, and therefore, *caeteris paribus*,[a] the rate of profit.

These two movements, the rise in the rate of profit when money falls in value, and its fall when the value of money rises, are, *under these circumstances*, both due solely to the FACT that the price of labour has not yet been adjusted to the new value of money. These phenomena (and how they are explained has long been known) cease after the adjustment of the price of labour to the value of money.

This is where the difficulty begins. The so-called theorists say: As soon as the price of labour corresponds to the new value of money, e.g. has risen with the falling value of money, both profit and wages are expressed in so much more money. Their *relation thus remains the same*. Therefore there can be no change in the rate of profit. The specialists who concern themselves with the history of prices reply to this with FACTS. Their explanations are mere phrases.

The whole difficulty arises from confusing the *rate of surplus value* with the *rate of profit*. Let us assume that the rate of surplus value remains *the same*, e.g. 100%. Then, if the value of money falls by $^1/_{10}$, wages of £100 (say for 100 men) rise to 110 and surplus value likewise to 110. The same total quantity of labour, formerly expressed in 200, is now expressed in £220. If the price of labour is adjusted to the value of money, the *rate of surplus value* can neither rise nor fall as the result of any change in the value of money. Assume, however, that the elements, or some elements, of the *constant* part of capital were to fall in value owing to the growing productivity of labour, whose products they are. If the fall in their value is greater than the fall in the value of money, their price will fall, despite the drop in the value of money. If the fall in their value only corresponded to the fall in the value of money, then their price would remain unchanged. Let us assume the latter case.

For instance, in a certain branch of industry the capital of 500 is composed of $400c + 100v$, so *with a rate of surplus value of 100%* we

---

[a] other things remaining equal

have: $400c + 100v \mid + 100m = \dfrac{100}{500} = 20\%$ *rate of profit*[a] (in Volume II I intend to use $400c$, etc., instead of $\dfrac{c}{400}$, etc., as it is less complicated. *Qu'en penses tu?*[b]). If the value of money falls by $^1/_{10}$, then wages rise to 110 and ditto surplus value. If the money price of the *constant* capital remains the same because the value of its component parts has fallen by $^1/_{10}$ as a result of the increased productivity of labour, then now: $400c + 100v \mid + 110m$ or $\dfrac{110}{510} = 21\,^{29}/_{50}\%$ rate of profit, which would therefore have risen by ABOUT $1\,^1/_2\%$, while the rate of surplus value, $\dfrac{110m}{110v}$, remains as before 100%.

The *rise in the rate of profit* would be greater if the value of the constant capital sank faster than the value of money, and less if it sank more slowly. It will continue as long as any fall in the value of the constant capital is taking place, i.e. as long as the same quantity of means of production does not cost £440 where it formerly cost £400.

And it is an historical fact, and can be specially demonstrated from the years 1850-1860, that the productivity of labour, especially in industry proper, receives an impetus from the falling value of money, the mere inflation of money prices, and the general international rush for the increased quantity of money.

The opposite case can be developed in an analogous manner.

The extent to which, in one case, the rise of the rate of profit with the sinking value of money, and, in the other, the sinking of the rate of profit with the rising value of money, affect the *general rate of profit* will depend partly upon the *relative size* of the particular branch of production in which the change takes place, and partly upon the *length* of the change, for the rise and fall of the rate of profit in particular branches of industry takes time to infect the other branches. If the oscillation lasts a relatively short time, it remains local.

I am sending you the *Courrier*[c] and *Nain jaune* which Lafargue sent me.

Salut.

Your

K. M.

First published in *Der Briefwechsel zwischen F. Engels und K. Marx*, Bd. 4, Stuttgart, 1913

Printed according to the original

Published in English in full for the first time

---

[a] c stands for constant capital, v for variable capital, m for surplus value. - [b] What do you think about this? - [c] Probably *Le Courrier français* of 21 April 1868 (see this volume, p. 16).

11

ENGELS TO MARX[34]

IN LONDON

Manchester, 26 April 1868

Dear Moor,

The business with the rate of profit and the value of money is very neat and very clear. The only thing that is unclear to me is how you can assume $\frac{m}{c+v}$ as *rate of profit*, for m does not flow solely into the pockets of the industrialist who produces it, but has to be shared with the merchant, etc.; unless you are taking the whole branch of business together here, therefore disregarding how m is divided up between manufacturer, wholesaler, retailer, etc. In general, I am very keen to see your exposition of this point.

Wilhelmchen, as you will have seen, is now also singing the praises of the *honourable Jakobus Venedey*! And they resemble one another just like one jackass resembles another. I have had enough of it now, I shall not write to him any more. Let him make a fool of himself on his own account.

To write $400c + 100v + 100m$ is quite acceptable, just as is £400 3s. 4d.

You have seen that the comfortable relationship between the honest Bismarck and his Reichstagers is beginning to come to an end; the latter want to make the officials of the debt administration legally answerable, and Otto the Great[a] cannot stand that, naturally. He'll not build them no fleet for that.[35]

To give full expression to the hangover affecting handsome William[b] because he confiscated the lands and property of his cousin Georg,[c][36] the Prussian commission to administer King Georg's property is composed of General von *Kotze* and Regierungsrat *Sauerhering* (literally).[d]

It is very nice of Jenny that she dutifully drags you out to go for walks. I hope that she does not allow herself to be scared off by your physical indolence disguised as your need to work; in the present fine weather it would be shameful if you stayed at home. I hope that no traces of new carbuncles have shown themselves.

---

[a] Otto von Bismarck - [b] William I - [c] Georg V - [d] *Kotze* means 'vomit', *Sauerhering* means 'pickled herring'.

In the Customs Parliament[37] old Rothschild sits right near to Wilhelmchen, and behind them the bunch of jackasses called the 'People's Party'.[38]

Could you not collect some of the mineral stuff and send it here for analysis?[a] I have not yet seen Gumpert.

The recent WOMEN'S SUFFRAGE MEETING here[39] was of course attended by the whole Borchardt family, male and female (only Mama Borchardt absent). Gumpert has a nice row with Borchardt. Borchardt had accused him of an infringement NOT ONLY OF MEDICAL PROFESSIONAL ETIQUETTE, BUT OF *ALL ETHICS* (because in the house of friends, where Borchardt is the doctor and a child had died of scarlet fever, Gumpert had expressed his surprise and astonishment that Borchardt should have allowed the other children and their friends to view the body—Borchardt has 'grounds' for declaring scarlet fever non-contagious)—and Gumpert has brought the case before the medical society here, whereby he has little to gain, however, since the committee consists of nothing but jackasses, a fact which he should, of course, have considered earlier.

When will the young married couple[b] return, and have you found an apartment?[40]

Best greetings to all.

Your

F. E.

First published abridged in *Der Briefwechsel zwischen F. Engels und K. Marx*, Bd. 4, Stuttgart, 1913 and in full in *MEGA*, Abt. III, Bd. 4, Berlin, 1931

Printed according to the original

Published in English in full for the first time

12

MARX TO ENGELS[33]

IN MANCHESTER

London, 30 April 1868

DEAR FRED,

For the CASE under discussion it is immaterial whether m (the surplus value) is *quantitatively* $>$ or $<$ than the surplus value created in the given branch of production itself. E.g., if

---

[a] See this volume, p. 15. - [b] Paul and Laura Lafargue

$\dfrac{100m}{400c+100v}$ =20%, and this becomes, owing to a fall in the value of money by $^1/_{10}$, = $\dfrac{110m}{400c+110v}$ (assuming that the value of the constant capital sinks), it is immaterial if the capitalist producer pockets only half of the surplus value which he himself produces. For the rate of profit for him then = $\dfrac{55m}{400c+110v}$ > than the former $\dfrac{50m}{400c+100v}$. I retain m here in order to show *qualitatively* in the expression itself where the profit comes from.

But it is proper that you should know the method by which the rate of profit is developed. I shall therefore give you the process in the *most general* outline. In *Book II*,[41] as you know, the *process of circulation* of capital is presented on the basis of the premisses developed in Book I. I.e. the new determinations of form which arise from the process of circulation, such as fixed and circulating capital, turnover of capital, etc. Finally, in Book I we content ourselves with the assumption that when, in the valorisation process,[a] £100 becomes £110, it *finds* the elements into which it is converted anew *already in existence* in the market. But now we investigate the conditions under which these elements are to be found in existence, that is to say, the social intertwining of the different capitals, of parts of capital and of REVENUE (=m).

In Book III[41] we then come to the conversion of surplus value into its different forms and separate component parts.

I. *Profit* is for us, for the time being, only *another name* for or another category of *surplus value*. As, owing to the form of wages, the whole of labour appears to be paid for, the unpaid part of it seems necessarily to come not from labour but from capital, and not from the variable part of capital but from the total capital. As a result, *surplus value* assumes the form of *profit*, without there being any *quantitative* difference between the one and the other. It is only an illusory manifestation of surplus value.

Further, the part of capital consumed in the production of a commodity (the capital, constant and variable, advanced for its production, *minus* the utilised but not consumed part of *fixed* capital) now appears as the *cost price* of the commodity, since for the capitalist that part of the value of the commodity that it costs *him* is *its* cost price, while the unpaid labour contained in the commodity does not enter into *its* cost price, from his point of view. The surplus value=profit now appears as the *excess of the*

---

[a] In the original: Verwertungsprozeß. See also this volume, p. 360.

selling price of the commodity over its cost price. Let us call the value of the commodity W and its cost price K; then $W = K + m$, therefore $W - m = K$, therefore $W > K$. This new category, cost price, is very necessary for the details of the later analysis. It is evident from the outset that the capitalist can sell a commodity at a profit *below its value* (as long as he sells it *above* its cost price), and this is the *fundamental law* for comprehending the equalisations effected by competition.

Therefore, while profit is at first *only formally* different from surplus value, the *rate of profit* is, by contrast, at once really different from the *rate of surplus value*, for in one case we have $\dfrac{m}{v}$ and in the other $\dfrac{m}{c+v}$, from which it follows from the outset, since $\dfrac{m}{v} > \dfrac{m}{c+v}$, that the rate of profit < than the rate of surplus value, unless $c = 0$.

In view of what has been developed in Book II, it follows, however, that we cannot compute the rate of profit on the commodity product of any period we select, e.g. that of a week, but that $\dfrac{m}{c+v}$ denotes here the surplus value produced *during the year* in relation to the capital *advanced* during the year (as distinct from the capital *turned over*). Therefore, $\dfrac{m}{c+v}$ stands here for the *annual rate of profit.*

Then we shall first examine how variations in the *turnover* of capital (partly depending on the relation of the circulating to the fixed portions of capital, partly on the number of times the circulating capital turns over in a year, etc., etc.) modify the *rate of profit* while the *rate of surplus value remains the same.*

Now, taking the turnover as given, and $\dfrac{m}{c+v}$ as the annual rate of profit, we examine how the latter can change, independently of changes in the rate of surplus value, and even of its total amount. Since m, the total amount of surplus value, = *the rate of surplus value multiplied by the variable capital,* then, if we call the rate of surplus value r[a] and the rate of profit p', $p' = \dfrac{r \cdot v}{c+v}$. Here we have the 4 quantities p', r, v, c, with any 3 of which we can work, always seeking the 4th as unknown. This covers all possible cases of movements in the rate of profit, in so far as they are distinct from

---

[a] Otherwise Marx designates the rate of surplus value as r only in his economic manuscript of 1861-63. In Volume I of *Capital* he designates it as the ratio $\dfrac{m}{v}$, and in Volumes II and III as m'.

the movements in the rate of surplus value and, TO A CERTAIN EXTENT, even in its total amount. This has, of course, hitherto been *inexplicable* to everybody.

The laws thus found—very important, e.g., for understanding how the price of the raw material influences the rate of profit—hold good *no matter how* the surplus value is later divided among the producer, etc. This can only change the *form of appearance*. Moreover, they remain *directly* applicable if $\frac{m}{c+v}$ is treated as the relation of the socially produced surplus value to the social capital.

II. What were treated in I as *movements*, whether of capital in a particular branch of production or of social capital—movements changing its composition, etc.—are now conceived as *differences* of the *various masses of capital invested in the different branches of production*.

Then it turns out that, assuming *the rate of surplus value*, i.e. the exploitation of labour, as *equal*, the production of value and therefore the production of surplus value and therefore the *rate of profit* are *different* in different branches of production. But from these varying rates of profit a mean or general rate of profit is formed by competition. This rate of profit, expressed absolutely, can be nothing but the *surplus value* produced (annually) by the *capitalist class* in relation to the total of *social* capital advanced. E.g., if the social capital$=400c+100v$, and the surplus value annually produced by it$=100m$, the composition of the social capital$=80c+20v$, and that of the product (in percentages)$=80c+20v \mid +20m=20\%$ rate of profit. This is the *general rate of profit*.

What the competition among the various masses of capital—invested in different spheres of production and differently composed—is striving for is *capitalist communism*, namely that the *mass of capital employed in each sphere of production* should get a fractional part of the total surplus value proportionate to the part of the total social capital that it forms.

This can only be achieved if in each sphere of production (assuming as above that the total capital$=80c+20v$ and the social rate of profit$=\dfrac{20m}{80c+20v}$) the annual commodity product is sold at *cost price + 20% profit on the value of the capital advanced* (it is immaterial how much of the advanced fixed capital enters into the annual cost price or not). But this means that the *price determination* of the commodities must *deviate* from their *values*.

Only in those branches of production where the percentual composition of capital is $80c+20v$ will the price K (*cost price*) + *20% on the capital advanced* coincide with the *value* of the commodities. Where the composition is higher (e.g. $90c+10v$), the price is *above* their value; where the composition is lower (e.g. $70c+30v$), the price is *below* their value.

The price thus equalised, which divides up the social surplus value equally among the various masses of capital in proportion to their sizes, is the *price of production* of commodities, the centre around which the oscillation of the market prices moves.

Those branches of production which constitute a natural *monopoly* are exempted from this *equalisation process*, even if their rate of profit is higher than the social rate. This is important later for the development of *rent*.[a]

In this chapter,[42] there must be further developed the various *causes of equalisation* of the various capital investments, which appear to the vulgar conception as so many *sources* of profit.

Also to be developed: the *changed form of manifestation* that the previously developed and still valid laws of value and surplus value assume now, *after the transformation of values into prices of production.*

III. *The tendency of the rate of profit to fall as society progresses.* This already follows from what was developed in Book I on the *change in the composition of capital with the development of the social productive power.*[43] This is one of the greatest triumphs over the *pons asini*[b] of all previous political economy.

IV. Until now we have only dealt with *productive capital.*[44] Now there enters modification through *merchant capital.*

According to our previous assumption the *productive capital* of society = 500 (millions or billions, *n'importe*[c]). And the formula was $400c+100v \mid +100m$. The general rate of profit, p', = 20%. Now let the merchant capital=100.

So, the $100m$ has now to be calculated on 600 instead of 500. The general rate of profit is thus reduced from 20% to $16\,{}^2/_3\%$. The *price of production* (for the sake of simplicity we will assume here that all of the $400c$, i.e. the whole fixed capital, enters into the *cost price* of the annual output of commodities) now=$583\,{}^1/_3$. The merchant sells at 600 and therefore realises, if we ignore the fixed portion of his capital, $16\,{}^2/_3\%$ on his 100, as much as the productive capitalists; or, in other words, he appropriates $\,{}^1/_6$ of the social surplus value. The commodities—*en masse* and on a social

---

[a] Marx means the theory of absolute rent (see present edition, Vol. 37). - [b] asses' bridge - [c] it doesn't matter

scale—are sold at *their value*. His £100 (apart from the fixed portion) only serve him as circulating money capital. Whatever the merchant swallows over and above that, he gets either simply by trickery, or by speculation on the oscillation of commodity prices, or, in the case of the actual retailer, as wages for labour— wretched unproductive labour that it is—in the form of profit.

V. We have now reduced profit to the form in which it appears in practice, according to our assumptions $16\,^2/_3\%$. *Next comes the division of this profit into entrepreneur's gain and interest. Interest-bearing capital. The credit system.*

VI. *Transformation of surplus profit into rent.*

VII. At last we have arrived at the *forms of manifestation* which serve as the *starting point* in the vulgar conception: rent, coming from the land; profit (interest), from capital; wages, from labour. But from our standpoint things now look different. The apparent movement is explained. Furthermore, A. Smith's nonsense, which has become the *main pillar* of all political economy hitherto, the contention that the price of the commodity consists of those three revenues, i.e. only of variable capital (wages) and surplus value (rent, profit (interest)), is overthrown.[45] The entire movement in this apparent form. Finally, since those 3 items (wages, rent, profit (interest)) constitute the sources of income of the 3 classes of landowners, capitalists and wage labourers, we have the *class struggle*, as the conclusion in which the movement and disintegration of the whole shit resolves itself.

Our young couple[a] back again since last week, very love-SICK. Apartment for them near Primrose Hill, where they moved in this evening.

Enclosed letters from Kugelmann, etc. I have sent Schily what he wanted,[46] but not in the childish way he requested. In a few days I shall be 50. As that Prussian lieutenant said to you: '20 years of service and still lieutenant', I can say: half a century on my shoulders, and still a pauper. How right my mother was: 'If only Karell had made capital instead of etc.'

Salut.

Your

K. Marx

Of carbuncles only a very small trace on the right thigh, but will probably vanish without trace.

----

[a] Paul and Laura Lafargue

Ernest Jones has made a fool of himself by his lukewarm and *nisi prius*[a] way of defending Burke.[47] Burke has at least won a victory in forcing the old jackass Bramwell to abandon the hypocrisy of TEMPER, and allowing his mean dog's soul to rampage free of *carrière*.[b]

First published in *Der Briefwechsel zwischen F. Engels und K. Marx*, Bd. 4, Stuttgart, 1913

Printed according to the original

Published in English in full for the first time

13

MARX TO ENGELS[48]

IN MANCHESTER

London, 4 May 1868

DEAR FRED,

This morning I received enclosed letter and cutting from Schweitzer. Since he addresses himself to me as workers' representative of one of the most industrial districts, I must naturally reply.[49]

My view is that the Germans can stand a reduction of the protective tariff on pig iron and that the manufacturers of other articles are also exaggerating their howls. This view is based upon a comparison of the English and German exports to neutral markets. Enclosed, by way of example, a note on exports to Belgium.[c]

At the same time, in my opinion, the point is to exploit this question in the interests of the party, without, however, procuring any new reliefs to the English.

My proposal would therefore be:

1. *No reduction of tariffs* before a parliamentary *enquête*[d] into the state of the German iron-mining production and iron manufacture. This *enquête* should not, however, be confined, as the bourgeois gentlemen desire, simply to chambers of commerce and 'experts' but should, at the same time, include the *workers'*

---

[a] half-hearted - [b] reins - [c] See the table on p. 27. - [d] enquiry

Imports into Belgium for the years 1865, 1866, 1867 (year ended 31 December)ᵃ

Kilogs	Kilogs	1865	1866	1867				
Iron, ore and filings	From Customs Union	161,496,808	155,584,195	213,049,319				
	France	138,370,214	130,382,679	96,761,074				
Pig and old iron	Total	24,864,110	32,508,242	56,233,219	+	−		
	From United Kingdom	23,421,806	28,450,976	50,722,330				
Iron rails, sheet, etc.	Total	1,555,576	1,579,999	2,136,652				
	United Kingdom	668,140	698,984	1,008,674				
	Holland	312,984	237,241	403,468			−	+
Iron wire	Total	501,380	710,335	1,108,038				
	From Customs Union	32,631	226,993	1,472,714				
	United Kingdom	442,107	445,265	350,064				
	France	26,979	36,075	284,348				
Steel, Bars, Sheets, Wire	Total		4,320,429	2,484,240				
	From United Kingdom		3,468,280	1,453,007	−	+		
	Customs Union		697,295	905,108				
Steel wrought	Total		1,257,973	914,633				
	From United Kingdom		761,234	548,396				
Metal wares of wrought iron	Total	940,763	993,581	1,307,407				
	Customs Union	256,138	305,909	385,148				
	United Kingdom	283,164	285,001	331,732			+	−
Metal wares of cast iron	Total	290,715	274,784	385,325				
	Customs Union	18,931	13,901	26,145				
	*United Kingdom	37,853	45,239	59,946				
Machines and machinery	Total	4,908,078	5,437,599	5,114,905				
	United Kingdom	3,081,942	3,888,891	2,859,729				
	France	1,322,155	1,052,857	1,699,102				

* To the heading *Metal wares of cast iron* should be added *France:* 1865—238,905; 1866—205,264; 1867—247,527.

ᵃ Marx gives the table in English.

conditions in these branches; all the more so since Messrs manufacturers are 'demanding' the protective tariffs solely 'for the protection' of the workers, and have in addition discovered that *'the value of iron'* consists only 'of *wages* and freight'.

2. *No reduction of tariffs* before an *enquête* into how the *railways* misuse their monopoly, and before their freight (and passenger) tariffs are controlled by legal regulations.

I would like your view *immediately*, and also immediate return of the enclosures.

Very nice that your home-town chamber of commerce should bemoan the growing power and menace of the International Working Men's Association.

Salut.

Your
K. M.

First published abridged in *Der Briefwechsel zwischen F. Engels und K. Marx*, Bd. 4, Stuttgart, 1913 and in full in *MEGA*, Abt. III, Bd. 4, Berlin, 1931. Marx's note appended to the letter was first published in: Marx and Engels, *Works*, Second Russian Edition, Vol. 32, Moscow, 1964

Printed according to the original

Published in English in full for the first time

14

ENGELS TO MARX [48]

IN LONDON

Manchester, 6 May 1868

Dear Moor,

I congratulate ANYHOW on the half *saeculum*,[a] from which, incidentally, I am also only a short span away. Indeed, what juvenile enthusiasts we were 25 years ago when we boasted that by this time we would long have been beheaded.

Enclosed returning Kugelmann, Büchner, Schily, Reclus,[46] Schweitzer[49] and the *Elberfelder Zeitung*, and additionally something on your book which Siebel's wife sent me[50]; he appears to be

---

[a] century

no longer capable of writing, is in Barmen and going to Godesberg.

The profit story is very nice,[a] but I shall have to think it over further in order to grasp the *portée*[b] in all its aspects.

Ad vocem[c] Schweitzer. The rascal is utilising this business simply as an inducement to make us take the bait again. Of course, it does not matter that you give him information this time, but *principiis obsta*[d]! Don't let the fellow catch your little finger lest he make an attempt on your whole hand. On the subject itself, I have no doubt at all that the German iron industry could dispense with the protective tariff, *a majore*,[e] therefore, could also stand the reduction of the tariff on pig iron from $7\frac{1}{2}$ groschen to 5 groschen per hundredweight (from 15s. to 10s. per ton), and the other reductions likewise. The export of iron is increasing every year, and not only to Belgium. This would bring ruin to a few ironworks established during the wave of speculation in the 50s, situated a long way from the coal and otherwise based on insufficient, poor pits. But these are for the most part already *kaputt*, and the vicinity of a railway would be more use to them than any protective tariff if they should ever become viable again. (There is one like this in Engelskirchen, 500 paces from my brothers' factory—the coal has to be brought from Siegburg, $2\frac{1}{2}$ German miles,[f] by wagon—no wonder it lies idle. *This* sort of works cries out for protective tariff, and is cited as proof that it is necessary.)

The Elberfeld-Barmen Chamber of Commerce is the nastiest protective tariff institution there is, and *notorious* for it. Even though the main industry of the district is aimed at *export*. However, there are always a lot of trades in decline there, hence the lamentations.

For the rest, your plan about the *enquête*[g] is rather good, and I like it very much. As far as railways go, the freight charges in Germany are *lower* than elsewhere, and, since goods traffic is the *main thing* in Germany, this could not be otherwise. They could be pushed still lower, and the governments have the power to do it, but what is most necessary is greater centralisation and equalisation in administration and freight charges, and constitutionally this is a matter for the Reichstag. By and large, the iron-chaps have no cause to yell about high freights.

---

[a] See this volume, pp. 21-25. - [b] meaning - [c] As regards - [d] guard against the first step (Ovid, *Remedia amoris*) - [e] even more - [f] The German mile (*Meile*) was a linear measure of different length in different German states, but it can be regarded as roughly $4\frac{1}{2}$ miles. - [g] enquiry

Liebknecht has sent me the trades regulations, on which I have promised him some critical comments.[51] Progress compared to the regression under Frederick William IV, but what bureaucratic confusion. I am sending you the stuff for the fun of it.

Yesterday the inevitable Leibel Choras arrived and prevented me writing. I asked him about the persecution of Jews in Moldavia; he wailed a bit, but it does not appear to be all that bad: we have to bear it, we Jews do not have the power; he would like to be Russian or Austrian, but it does not occur to him to leave. The Hohenzollern is a stupid boy, and the government in the hands of the 'clerks' (boyars in reduced circumstances playing at bureaucracy) and they squeeze the Jews so.

Many greetings to your wife, the girls and Monsieur and Madame Lafargue.

Your
F. E.

First published in *Der Briefwechsel zwischen F. Engels und K. Marx*, Bd. 4, Stuttgart, 1913

Printed according to the original

Published in English in full for the first time

15

MARX TO ENGELS[48]

IN MANCHESTER

[London,] 7 May 1868

DEAR FRED,

BEST THANKS for your marginal notes. I have included them in the letter to Schweitzer as far as necessary. My letter is so coolly phrased that it will not be 'shown around'.[49]

Now I would like to ask you for information on another subject. However, you can postpone this if it should interrupt the work for the *Fortnightly*, which is urgent.[11]

The point is that I would like to link up with Volume I in the examples given in Volume II.[41]

In order to use the data on your factory given on p. 186[52]— completely sufficient to illustrate the rate of surplus value—for the *rate of profit*, the following would be necessary:

1. The missing data on the capital advanced for the *factory building* and the percentage of the SINKING FUND for this. Ditto WAREHOUSE. In both cases, the RENT should be given, if paid. Also the office costs and costs of staff for the WAREHOUSE.

With regard to the *steam engine*, no data is given on the *percentage* at which the weekly wear and tear is calculated, and therefore the capital advanced for the steam engine is not visible either.

2. *Now the real question.* How do you calculate the *turnover* of the *circulating part of capital* (i.e. raw material, auxiliary materials, wages)? How great then is the *circulating* capital *advanced*? I would like to receive this answered *in detail,* even illustrated, particularly the turnover calculation of the circulating capital advanced.

Tomorrow I shall send you the crazy Urquhart for your amusement.

Salut.

Your
K. M.

First published in *Der Briefwechsel zwischen F. Engels und K. Marx,* Bd. 4, Stuttgart, 1913

Printed according to the original

Published in English in full for the first time

16

MARX TO JOSEPH DIETZGEN [53]

IN PETERSBURG

[London, 9 May 1868]

...When I have cast off the burden of political economy, I shall write a 'Dialectic'. The true laws of dialectics are already contained in Hegel, though in a mystical form. What is needed is to strip away this form...

First published in *Der Volksstaat,* Nr. 3, 9 January 1876

Printed according to the newspaper

Published in English for the first time

17

ENGELS TO MARX [48]

IN LONDON

Manchester, 10 May 1868

Dear Moor,

You received the information about the factory at that time direct from Henry Ermen—it is G. Ermen's spinning mill, with which I have nothing to do, and about which the young Ermens have been specifically forbidden to tell me anything. If you write to Henry Ermen, Bridgewater Mill, Pendlebury (*private*), he will probably tell you what you want to know. But you will have to tell him that he should give you the data as they were in *1860*, since much has been built since then. I would say, approximately, that a factory building for 10,000 spindles, including cost of land, will come to £4,000 à £5,000 (in the given case a bit less is probably to be assumed, since it was only a one-storey SHED, and land up there, unless containing coal, costs almost nothing). Rate of wear and tear on the building (£500-600 to be subtracted as ground price) $7\,^1/_2\%$ *including interest*. At £3,600 therefore £18 ground rent (à 3%) + ($7\,^1/_2\%$ on 3,000=) 225=£243 rent for the building.

WAREHOUSE does not exist for this factory, since G. Ermen only sells through or to us or through an agent to other people, and pays 2% commission on the turnover for this. Assuming the turnover à £13,000, we get £260 as substitute for WAREHOUSE costs.

As far as calculating the turnover of the circulating capital is concerned, I do not really know what you mean by this. We calculate only the *total turnover*, that is the total of annual sales. If I understand rightly, you want to know how many times a year the circulating part of capital is turned over, or, in other words, how much circulating capital is *in business*. This, however, differs in almost all cases. A prosperous owner of a spinning mill has almost always (that is except when he is expanding, or immediately afterwards) some spare capital that he invests in some other way, but uses, when the chance offers itself, to buy cotton cheaply, etc. Or he uses credit, if he can and it is worthwhile. It may be assumed that a mill-owner who invests £10,000 in machines (apart from the *building*, which he can and mostly will rent) can get along with $^1/_5$ à $^1/_4$ of the fixed capital in circulating capital; that is for

£10,000 fixed capital put into machines, £2,000 à £2,500 circulating capital will do. This is the *average* assumption here.

Here I leave out of account the steam engines. On this score H. Ermen has obviously provided you, from memory, a completely absurd story. Weekly wear and tear of the steam engine £20, that is £1,040 a year! At a $12\,^1/_2\%$ rate the steam engine will cost £8,320, *ce qui est absurde.*[a] The entire machine cannot have cost more than £1,500 à £2,000, and that G. Ermen wanted to write off his whole machine in 2 years is just like him, but not businesslike. You can ask him about this, too. But I fear that Monsieur Gottfried[b] has long taken these old account books into his own custody, and then Henry Ermen will not be able to help you either.

Schorlemmer will probably visit you on Wednesday or Thursday.[c] The Royal Society[54] has invited him to read his PAPER on the boiling points of C_nH_{2n+2} on Thursday and to take part in the debate.[d] Since the main chemist there is Frankland, whom Schorlemmer has attacked in all his works, this is a great triumph, and a few more invitations like this WILL BE THE MAKING OF HIM. I am very happy for the fellow, who has only stayed at his rather pitiful position here because it places at his disposal the laboratory and thus the means of doing theoretical work. He is really one of the best fellows I have got to know for a long time; he is so totally free of prejudices this freedom appears to be almost spontaneous, but must in fact be based upon much thought. At the same time, the notable modesty. Incidentally, he has again made a handsome discovery. On pages 264 and 297 of his book you will find that propyl alcohol and *iso*propyl alcohol are two isomeric combinations.[e] It had hitherto been impossible to obtain pure propyl alcohol, so the Russians had already claimed that it did not exist, there was only *iso*propyl alcohol. Last autumn at the meeting of natural scientists Schorlemmer replied to them: by next autumn he would have obtained it, and he has really done it.

This week I do at last have no more meetings and similar calls upon my time, and will be able to get down to the *Fortnightly.*[11] But I still do not know *how* to start. It is clear to me that I will

---

a which is absurd - b Ermen - c 13 or 14 May - d C. Schorlemmer, 'Researches on the Hydrocarbons of the Series C_nH_{2n+2}', *Proceedings of the Royal Society,* No. 94, 1867 and No. 102, 1868. - e This refers to H. E. Roscoe's chemistry textbook, the German edition of which, *Kurzes Lehrbuch der Chemie nach den neuesten Ansichten der Wissenschaft* (Brunswick, 1867), was prepared by Carl Schorlemmer in conjunction with the author. The isomerism of the alcohols named is stated on pp. 296-98.

begin with the conversion of money into capital, but *how* is still quite unclear. What do you think about this?

With best greetings,

Your
F. E.

First published in *Der Briefwechsel zwischen F. Engels und K. Marx*, Bd. 4, Stuttgart, 1913

Printed according to the original
Published in English in full for the first time

18

ENGELS TO MARX

IN LONDON

Manchester, 15 May 1868

Dear Moor,

You will probably have heard that Siebel died on the 9th inst. My mother wrote me that shortly before he had told his wife she should go to bed, which she did; suddenly she could no longer hear his breath, jumped up and found him dead. I am sending you 2 notices from his wife, one of which I ask you to send to Freiligrath.

Enclosed 6 prints of Lupus'[a] photograph.

Further something about Kobes'[b] present activities.

Have you read about the Ebergenyi trial?[55] Chorinsky's letters are in fact unparalleled. One can see that the Austrians are still awaiting their 1789. I shall send you the relevant *Zukunft* this evening. The Ebergenyi woman is said to receive masses of visitors in her 'convict prison' with a cigarette in her mouth and as merry as a cricket.

Best greetings.

Your
F. E.

Apropos. The articles in the *Fortnightly* are *all signed*. If this is the *rule*, it would be most unfortunate, since then it would be easy to see through the business. In any case, I would have to know if

---

[a] Wilhelm Wolff's - [b] Jakob Venedey's

the article *must* be signed, for this would change the formulation a lot, and know right away for I have reached the stage where I can start.^a What is your answer to these questions?

First published abridged in *Der Briefwechsel zwischen F. Engels und K. Marx*, Bd. 4, Stuttgart, 1913 and in full in *MEGA*, Abt. III, Bd. 4, Berlin, 1931

Printed according to the original

Published in English for the first time

19

MARX TO ENGELS[56]

IN MANCHESTER

[London,] 16 May 1868

DEAR FRED,

My silence for a week has perhaps already been explained to you by Schorlemmer.^b Two carbuncles on the scrotum would perhaps have made even Sulla peevish. How greatly that man, despite his more-than-Palmerstonian TEMPER, was affected by his mythical but anyway lousy sickness, is shown by the fact that just 10 days before his death he had the decurion seized in a neighbouring city, and 1 day before he himself croaked had him strangled in his own house.[57]

In addition, I have all sorts of trouble. For example, on the 28th of this month a bill for £15 due at the butcher's, etc. To my urgent petitions to Holland no answer.[58]

Finally I had cajoled myself with the illusion that by this time I would have a 2nd edition,^c and thus see money for the first. But I had added up the bill without the host—I do not mean the Volkswirt,^d but the Germans in general.

POOR Siebel! In a way he had himself prepared his premature death. But WITH ALL THAT he was a good fellow. We are unlucky—Daniels, Wolff, Schramm, Weydemeyer, Siebel, Weerth! Not to speak of the living dead.

As regards *The Fortnightly Review*,[11] I had long considered this point, and had long arranged with Lafargue (the actual negotiator with Beesly) that you should appear under any old *nom de guerre*,

---

^a See this volume, pp. 35-36 and 37, and Note 11. - ^b See this volume, p. 33. - ^c of the first volume of *Capital* - ^d Marx plays on the words *Wirt* (host) and *Volkswirt* (political economist).

which you must let us know. Beesly himself will not be informed who the man is. And it is all the same to him. Apart from other considerations, the impact in Germany would be greatly lessened if the stuff appeared under your name.

In your last letter[a] you made a mistake on one point. The notes used on p. 186[52] you yourself wrote late one evening in my notebook, which still exists.[59] The notes of the Russian Ermen,[b] on the other hand, referred mainly to technical things.

Incidentally, the main thing for me was to ascertain the magnitude of the *advanced* circulating capital, i.e. advanced in raw material, etc., and wages, as against the circulating capital *turned over*. I have enough STATEMENTS, part of them from manufacturers, handed in either to the COMMISSIONERS[c] or to private economists. But everywhere only the annual accounts. The devil of the thing is that there is a wide divergence in political economy between what is of practical interest and what is theoretically necessary, so that one cannot even find the necessary material, as in other sciences.

I have received cuttings from Berlin newspapers from Eichhoff and sent him cuttings from here in RETURN. We have also exchanged two letters.[60] But now the enclosed shows, what Borkheim half guessed on his last visit to Berlin, that Eichhoff has let himself into concessions *quoad*[d] Stieber. Probably from sheer stupidity. For this reason he has taken up political economy as a neutral field.[61] For the rest, it appears that he feels uneasy, and he told Borkheim that, after swotting up properly on economy, he will exchange Berlin for Vienna, IN ABOUT 6 MONTHS.

In the *Essener Zeitung* a pompous denunciation of the International Working Men's Association.

Did you read the warlike SPEECH by Failly when taking over the command of Châlons? I have once again worked through the finances of the Empire. And only one thing appears clear to me, that Badinguet[e] *must* make war.

Salut.

Your

K. M.

First published in *Der Briefwechsel zwischen F. Engels und K. Marx*, Bd. 4, Stuttgart, 1913

Printed according to the original

Published in English in full for the first time

20

ENGELS TO MARX

IN LONDON

Manchester, 22 May 1868

Dear Moor,

Schorlemmer had told me about *one* carbuncle, but two *a tempo*,[a] and in addition in that place where, it is true, everything exists in pairs, *c'est vraiment trop*.[b] I hope they have gone, and that the arsenic will hold back further ones.

I shall send you the money for the bill.

Have you heard anything from Meissner? If not, the time would have come to ask how sales have been going; on this point he owes you an accounting after the Easter Fair as *associé* in the business. Then you could also refer to the *advertisement* asked for by Meissner,[8] the man is still waiting for a reply from me.

The *Fortnightly* article[11] will thus be written as though by an *Englishman*—that is how I understand you. Incidentally, I still cannot get past the beginning. It is damned difficult to make clear the dialectical method to the English who read the reviews, and I surely cannot approach the crowd with the equations $C-M-C$, etc.

Did my last letter give you the data you need?[c] If not, formulate your questions and I shall see what can be done.

Schorlemmer says that you spoke of coming here soon, which would be very desirable. The change of air will do you more good than anything else. This week and the beginning of next our house is in a revolution because of CLEANING AND WHITEWASHING, but if you can come at the end of next week, that would be very nice; you know that in the Whit week I always have plenty of time to spare. Don't forget that you promised to bring Tussy with you.

Eichhoff has finally terminated his lectures on crises.[25] As was to be expected, the mortgage crisis in Berlin was the core and finale of the whole thing. But the poor devil appears finally to have bored even the reporter of the *Zukunft* so much that he only reported on it quite briefly and incomprehensibly.[d]

---

[a] at a time - [b] that is really too much - [c] See this volume, pp. 32-34. - [d] *Die Zukunft*, No. 174, 15 May 1868 (morning edition). Engels refers to the report on the last of Eichhoff's series of lectures, 'Die Ursachen der Handelsstockungen der Gegenwart', delivered in Alt-Kölln, Berlin.

Liebknecht has this time committed great folly. First he has completely identified himself with the South German federalists, ultramontanes, etc., by signing their protest,[62] and always votes with them, and in addition has so lost all fruitfulness in his speechifying that the impertinent Lasker could tell him—and rightly so—that he was making the same speech once again which he had delivered for weeks past in all popular meetings.[63] The cunning Schweitzer, who confines himself simply to workers' representation, has quite overshadowed him.

The rag,[a] too, as you will have seen, is achieving the impossible: it is getting even more stupid.

Enclosed Borkheim returned.

Your

F. E.

First published abridged in *Der Briefwechsel zwischen F. Engels und K. Marx*, Bd. 4, Stuttgart, 1913 and in full in *MEGA*, Abt. III, Bd. 4, Berlin, 1931

Printed according to the original

Published in English for the first time

21

MARX TO ENGELS [48]

IN MANCHESTER

London, 23 May 1868

DEAR FRED,

It appears to me that you are on the wrong track with your fear of presenting such simple formulas as $M—C—M$, etc.[11] to the English review philistines. On the contrary. If you were forced, as I am, to read the economic articles of Messrs Lalor, Herbert Spencer, Macleod, etc., in *The Westminster Review*, etc., you would see that all of them are fed up with the economic trivialities—and know their readers are fed up, too—so they try to give their scribblings some flavour through PSEUDOPHILOSOPHICAL or PSEUDOSCIENTIFIC SLANG. The pseudocharacter in no way makes the writing (content=0) easy to understand. On the contrary. The trick lies in so mystifying the reader and causing him to rack his brain, that he may finally be relieved to discover that these HARD WORDS are only

---

^a *Demokratisches Wochenblatt*

fancy dress for *loci communes*.[a] Add to this that the readers of the *Fortnightly* and *The Westminster Review* flatter themselves that they are the LONGEST HEADS OF ENGLAND (let alone the rest of the world, naturally). Even apart from that, if you had seen what Mʀ *James Hutchinson Stirling* dares to present to the public as *The Secret of Hegel*,[b] not only in books but also in REVIEWS,—Hegel himself would not understand it—you would realise—Mr J. H. Stirling is regarded as a great thinker—that you are really being too timid. People demand something *new*, new in form and content.

Since you want to start with Chapter II[64] (you must not, however, forget to draw the reader's attention somewhere to the fact that in Chapter I he will find a *new* treatment of that value and money stuff[65]) the following should, in my opinion, be used for the beginning, naturally in the form agreeable to you.

In his investigations into CURRENCY *Th. Tooke*[c] underlines that money in its function as capital flows back to its starting point (REFLUX OF MONEY TO ITS POINT OF ISSUE), but in its function simply as CURRENCY does not flow back. This distinction, noted by Sir James Steuart,[d] among others, long before Tooke, serves the latter simply for a polemic against what the preachers of the CURRENCY PRINCIPLE[66] claim to be the influence the issue of credit money (BANKNOTES, etc.) exercises upon commodity prices. Our author, however, makes this peculiar form of circulation of money which functions as capital ('SERVE IN THE *FUNCTION OF CAPITAL*', *A. Smith*[e]) the starting point for his investigation into the nature of capital itself, and in the first place for an answer to the question: How is money, this independent form of value, converted into capital? ('CONVERSION INTO CAPITAL' the official expression.)

All sorts of businessmen, says Turgot, '*ont cela de commun qu'ils achètent pour vendre... leurs achats sont une avance qui leur rentre*'.[f] *Buying to sell*, this is in fact the transaction in which money functions as capital, and which conditions its reflux to ɪᴛs ᴘᴏɪɴᴛ ᴏғ ɪssuᴇ, in distinction to *selling to buy*, where it *need* only function as CURRENCY. The differing sequence of the acts of SELLING and BUYING imposes upon money two different circulation movements. What is hidden behind this is the different behaviour of

---

a platitudes - b An allusion to J. H. Stirling's work *The Secret of Hegel: Being the Hegelian System in Origin, Principle, Form, and Matter*. - c Th. Tooke, *An Inquiry into the Currency Principle...* - d J. Steuart, *An Inquiry into the Principles of Political Oeconomy*. - e A. Smith, *An Inquiry into the Nature and Causes of the Wealth of Nations*, Vol. 1, Edinburgh, 1814, p. 441. - f 'have in common that they *buy to sell*... their *purchases* are an *advance* which *returns* to them' (Turgot, *Réflexions sur la formation et la distribution des richesses*. In: *Oeuvres de Turgot*, Vol. 1, Paris, 1844, p. 43).

the *value* itself expressed in money form. To illustrate this, the author gives the following formulas, etc., etc., for the two different circulation movements.

I believe that you will make the matter easier for yourself and the reader by quoting the formulas.

I shall reply later to the other points of your letter. Of the carbuncles there remains only one, also soon finished. Last Wednesday I gave a lecture (ABOUT $^5/_4$ of an hour) on wages (especially the *form* of the same) to about 100 German PICKED workers.[67] I was very unwell that day, and I was advised to telegraph that I could not come. However, this was impossible, since some of the people had come from very distant parts of London. So I went there. The business went off very well, and after the lecture I felt better than before.

I have made concessions to my family doctor Lafargue in that I have *not yet* visited the Museum[a] again. But I have perhaps, during the past weeks, meditated too much AT HOME.

I shall, IF POSSIBLE, come to Manchester with Tussychen at the end of *next* week (SAY SATURDAY[b]). But you will have to send me the money for the fares and SOME SHILLINGS which I shall leave for my wife.

Tussychen, OF COURSE, has reminded me of the trip ABOUT every day.

Enclosed new Liebknecht stuff.

Salut.

Your
K. M.

First published in *Der Briefwechsel zwischen F. Engels und K. Marx*, Bd. 4, Stuttgart, 1913

Printed according to the original

Published in English in full for the first time

---

[a] Marx means the British Museum Library. - [b] 30 May

Frederick Engels. 1860s

22

ENGELS TO MARX

IN LONDON

Manchester, 25 May 1868

Dear Moor,

You must come on *Friday*,[a] because I have the afternoon free on Saturday and by then we shall be finished with everything in the house.

Enclosed $^1/_2$ £20 and $^1/_2$ £5 notes, the two other halves follow in another envelope. Till Friday then, let me know which train you are taking. You can travel from King's Cross by the new (Midland) line, which passes through the most beautiful part of Derbyshire.

9.10 from London 2.15 in Manchester
11.30   ”   ”   5.45 ”   ”
3.   ”   ”   8.5 ”   ”

Your
F. E.

First published in *Der Briefwechsel zwischen F. Engels und K. Marx*, Bd. 4, Stuttgart, 1913

Printed according to the original

Published in English for the first time

---

[a] 29 May

4—983

23

MARX TO ENGELS

IN MANCHESTER

London, 27 May 1868

DEAR FRED,

THANKS FOR £25.
Departure: Friday[a] from King's Cross 11.30.
Salut.

Your
K. M.

First published in *Der Briefwechsel zwischen F. Engels und K. Marx*, Bd. 4, Stuttgart, 1913

Printed according to the original

Published in English for the first time

24

MARX TO ENGELS

IN MANCHESTER

[London,] 20 JUNE 1868

DEAR FRED,

Immediately after my return to London[68]—our trip was marvelous—I found whole bundles of dunning and threatening letters. The people had been turned away with the excuse that I was 'travelling'. But one might think the electric telegraph had announced my return to these fellows. *Si licet parva componere magnis*,[b] OLD Niebuhr (the father of the HISTORIAN) relates with what speed the FACTS of the SILESIAN WAR [69] travelled from Europe to Asia IN NO TIME simply through the telegraphy of people's tongues. And among creditors this form of natural telegraphy appears to work even more efficiently. Among the bills there are various ones that can *scarcely* be delayed for one week; the worst, however, is the

---

a 29 May - b If one may compare the small with the great

enclosed scrawl payable *on Tuesday*,[a] for, if the GAS SUPPLY is publicly cut off, things will get quite out of control.

Last Tuesday[b] there was a meeting of the International. In the meantime, papers have come into my hands which have made unavoidable a RESCINDING of the RESOLUTIONS AS TO THE CONGRESS.[70] *D'abord*,[c] the declaration by Minister of Justice Bara that the Congress *is not permitted* to take place *in Brussels*.[d] Secondly, a printed manifesto of the COMMITTEES of Brussels and Verviers in which they throw down the gauntlet to the Minister.[e] *Thirdly*, letters from De Paepe and Vandenhouten that we would ruin the Association in Belgium by transferring the Congress. This would be interpreted as a concession to the government, etc.

I do not even mention the lousy intrigues of Vésinier, who is now here, and also Pyat, etc. Naturally they have been spreading the rumour that we are working at the dictation of Bonaparte.

They believed that a big scandal was to be expected at this last meeting and therefore sent guests to us. They were very *désappointés* when I withdrew my RESOLUTIONS after reading and referring to the documents, etc. I put the matter thus: The law against the FOREIGNERS was in no way a special threat against the International. It was *general*. The International would, however, have made a *concession* to the Belgian government if, under such legislation, it had selected Brussels as its MEETING PLACE. Now the matter was the other way round. Now that the Belgian government had directly threatened and provoked us we would be making a concession to it if we moved the Congress away from Brussels, etc. At the same time, I made a few very contemptuous jokes about the heroic tone adopted by those who attacked my RESOLUTIONS (Odger, etc.) before they knew the CHANGED STATE OF CIRCUMSTANCES. THE ONLY DANGER THAT COULD HAVE BEEN INCURRED, WAS THAT OF CHEAP MARTYRDOM AND RIDICULE. Mrs Law shouted 'HEAR, HEAR' for me several times, and showed her support by drumming on the table. Anyhow I managed things so that the laughter turned against Odger, etc., and that the RESCINDING of the RESOLUTIONS did not appear as a victory on their part.

The heat is very nasty for me. I shall have Gumpert's medicine made up for me, since I have 'puked' (as Mrs Blind would say) for

---

a 23 June - b 9 June - c First of all - d J. Bara's speech in the Chamber of Deputies of 16 May 1868, reported in *La Voix de l'avenir*, No. 23, 7 June 1868 and *La Liberté*, No. 47, 17 May 1868. - e 'À Monsieur Bara, ministre de la justice', *La Tribune du peuple*, No. 5, 24 May 1868.

several consecutive days, despite exemplary abstention from food and drink.

Salut.

Your

K. M.

Apropos. Tussychen generated something approaching bad blood here in the house with her dithyrambic praise of the Manchester HOME and her openly declared wish to return there as soon as possible.

First published in *Der Briefwechsel zwischen F. Engels und K. Marx*, Bd. 4, Stuttgart, 1913

Printed according to the original

Published in English for the first time

25

ENGELS TO MARX

IN LONDON

Manchester, 22 June 1868

Dear Moor,

In great haste enclosed £10 in one note. Tomorrow I shall send you a further £10, which should help to meet the most urgent and most pressing needs.

The article[11] is coming along well and will certainly be finished this week; I am, however, much more satisfied with the quantitative aspect than the qualitative.[a] A 2nd article[71] will then, I think, complete the whole thing. What do you think of the idea that Lafargue should put his name to it?

More tomorrow.

Your

F. E.

First published in *Der Briefwechsel zwischen F. Engels und K. Marx*, Bd. 4, Stuttgart, 1913

Printed according to the original

Published in English for the first time

---

[a] In the original: quantitative.

26

MARX TO ENGELS[48]

IN MANCHESTER

London, 23 JUNE 1868

DEAR FRED,

BEST THANKS FOR THE £10.

Tussychen and Jennychen are both unfortunately very unwell—sore throats and vomiting. If things do not get better TODAY, I shall have to call a doctor. Our Allen suddenly became paralysed a week ago, so he cannot leave his house.

Vésinier is wrangling here in the FRENCH BRANCH[72] against Dupont and Jung, both of whom he brands 'as Bonapartists'. During my absence[68] he attended a meeting of the CENTRAL COUNCIL[73] (which he has no right to do) and has written a fantastic report in the *Cigale* (Brussels paper).[74] The venue of the Congress was just being discussed.[70]

Lafargue cannot possibly sign,[a] since he is a FRENCHMAN, and in addition, my SON-IN-LAW. Sign it A. Williams or SOMETHING OF THE SORT. It would be best if Sam Moore signed.

Salut.

Your

K. M.

Yesterday BY ACCIDENT I came across a fine passage in A. Smith. After he had explained that LABOUR the PRIME COST, etc., and *nearly* said the right things though with constant contradictions; after he had ditto declared:

'THE PROFITS OF STOCK, IT MAY PERHAPS BE THOUGHT, ARE ONLY A DIFFERENT NAME FOR THE WAGES OF A PARTICULAR SORT OF LABOUR, THE LABOUR OF INSPECTION AND DIRECTION. THEY ARE, HOWEVER, ALTOGETHER DIFFERENT, ARE REGULATED BY QUITE DIFFERENT PRINCIPLES, AND BEAR NO PROPORTION TO THE QUANTITY, THE HARDSHIP, OR THE INGENUITY OF THIS SUPPOSED LABOUR OF INSPECTION AND DIRECTION',[b]

after that he suddenly does an about turn and wants to develop WAGES, PROFIT, RENT, as the 'COMPONENT PARTS OF NATURAL PRICE' (with him = VALUE). Among other things, there is the following fine passage:

---

[a] See this volume, p. 44. - [b] A. Smith, *An Inquiry into the Nature and Causes of the Wealth of Nations*, Vol. 1, Edinburgh, 1814, p. 78.

'WHEN THE PRICE OF ANY COMMODITY IS NEITHER MORE NOR LESS THAN WHAT IS SUFFICIENT TO PAY THE RENT OF THE LAND, THE WAGES OF THE LABOUR, AND THE PROFITS OF THE STOCK EMPLOYED IN RAISING, PREPARING AND BRINGING IT TO MARKET, ACCORDING TO THEIR NATURAL RATES, THE COMMODITY IS THEN SOLD FOR WHAT MAY BE CALLED ITS NATURAL PRICE. THE COMMODITY IS THEN SOLD *PRECISELY FOR WHAT IT IS WORTH*, OR *FOR WHAT IT REALLY COSTS THE PERSON* WHO BRINGS IT TO MARKET; *FOR* THOUGH IN COMMON LANGUAGE *THE PRIME COST* OF *ANY COMMODITY* DOES *NOT COMPREHEND THE PROFIT* OF THE PERSON WHO IS TO SELL IT AGAIN, YET, IF HE SELLS IT AT A PRICE WHICH DOES NOT ALLOW HIM THE *ORDINARY RATE OF PROFIT IN HIS NEIGHBOURHOOD*, HE IS EVIDENTLY A *LOSER* BY THE TRADE; SINCE, BY EMPLOYING HIS STOCK IN SOME OTHER WAY, HE MIGHT HAVE MADE THAT PROFIT.' (The existence of profit in the 'neighbourhood' as an explanation for the same!) 'HIS PROFIT, *BESIDES, IS HIS REVENUE*, THE PROPER FUND OF HIS SUBSISTENCE. AS, WHILE HE IS PREPARING AND BRINGING THE GOODS TO MARKET, HE ADVANCES TO HIS WORKMEN THEIR WAGES, OR THEIR SUBSISTENCE; SO *HE ADVANCES TO HIMSELF*, IN THE SAME MANNER, HIS OWN SUBSISTENCE; WHICH IS GENERALLY SUITABLE TO THE *PROFIT* WHICH HE MAY REASONABLY EXPECT FROM THE SALE OF HIS GOODS. UNLESS THEY YIELD HIM THIS PROFIT, THEREFORE, *THEY DO NOT REPAY HIM WHAT THEY MAY VERY PROPERLY BE SAID TO HAVE COST HIM*.'[a]

This second manner of pressing the profit into the PRIME COST—because already consumed—is really fine.

The same man, in whom the organs of pissing and generation also coincide mentally,[75] stated previously:

'AS SOON AS STOCK HAS ACCUMULATED IN THE HANDS OF PARTICULAR PERSONS ... *THE VALUE* WHICH THE *WORKMEN ADD* TO THE MATERIALS ... *RESOLVES ITSELF INTO TWO PARTS*, OF WHICH THE ONE PAYS THEIR WAGES, THE OTHER THE *PROFITS OF THEIR EMPLOYER* UPON THE WHOLE STOCK OF MATERIALS AND WAGES WHICH HE ADVANCED.'[b]

First published abridged in *Der Briefwechsel zwischen F. Engels und K. Marx*, Bd. 4, Stuttgart, 1913 and in full in *MEGA*, Abt. III, Bd. 4, Berlin, 1931

Printed according to the original

Published in English in full for the first time

27

ENGELS TO MARX

IN LONDON

Manchester, 24 June 1868

Dear Moor,

Enclosed S/K 60 115 and 60 116—two fivers. Yesterday I had such a fuss because of the building work in the Schiller Institute[76]

---

[a] Ibid., pp. 88-89. - [b] Ibid., pp. 77-78.

that I left the WAREHOUSE without sending them to you and had not a moment until it was too late. Today again all sorts of things are preventing me from writing to you more fully, if I am not to sacrifice the time which should be devoted to the article[11] this evening; in any case yesterday nothing was done on it.

Regarding the sore throats, be careful.[a] Of course, they are now epidemic and mostly innocent, but since the time when diphtheria became epidemic here it has always been better to consult a doctor quickly so that you know where you are.

Your
F. E.

First published in *Der Briefwechsel zwischen F. Engels und K. Marx*, Bd. 4, Stuttgart, 1913

Printed according to the original

Published in English for the first time

28

MARX TO ENGELS

IN MANCHESTER

London, 24 JUNE 1868

Dear FRED,

Unfortunately, the sickness of both girls turns out to be SCARLATINA and Tussychen has it in a very malignant form.
Salut.

Your
K. M.

First published in *Der Briefwechsel zwischen F. Engels und K. Marx*, Bd. 4, Stuttgart, 1913

Printed according to the original

Published in English for the first time

---

[a] See this volume, p. 45.

29

MARX TO LUDWIG KUGELMANN [29]

IN HANOVER

London, 24 June 1868

Dear Friend,

All sorts of incidents have prevented me from writing to you. Now, too, only a few lines.

My eldest and youngest daughters[a] both have SCARLATINA. I now recall that you spoke to me in Hanover [77] about a method of treatment as soon as the crisis has passed and the scaling process commences. Please be so kind as to explain this to me by return.

With best greetings to your dear wife and Fränzchen,

Yours

K. Marx

Liebknecht is growing increasingly dull under the impact of the South German stupidity. He is not enough of a dialectician to criticise both sides at once.[b]

First published in *Pisma Marksa k Kugel-manu* (Letters of Marx to Kugelmann), Moscow-Leningrad, 1928

Printed according to the original

30

ENGELS TO MARX

IN LONDON

Manchester, 25 June 1868

Dear Moor,

We were never so shocked here as this morning when your news arrived that your girls have scarlet fever. The thing has been on my mind all day; I hope everything goes well, and *here*, as I see from a medical report, all cases of that sort this year have passed

---

[a] Jenny and Eleanor Marx - [b] See this volume, p. 5.

off remarkably benignly. What sort of a doctor have you got, for you cannot take risks in such cases; *my means are at your disposal,* write or telegraph if you need anything, and you will have it immediately if it is at all possible.

Yesterday I sent you two five-pound notes S/K 60 115 and 60 116 *unregistered.*

Let me know very frequently how things are going. Lizzie was terribly upset when I read this out to her; she has a tremendous affection for Tussy and talks about her all day long.[68] And now good little Jenny has to get the sickness, too. You have really been terribly unlucky.

Under these circumstances, I do not wish to write about other things, and they would not interest you as long as the present state of affairs continues. I enclose a few lines to Tussy to entertain her, and on the orders of Lizzie.[78] On no account leave us without news.

Your
F. E.

First published in *Der Briefwechsel zwischen F. Engels und K. Marx*, Bd. 4, Stuttgart, 1913

Printed according to the original

Published in English for the first time

31

MARX TO ENGELS

IN MANCHESTER

London, 26 June 1868 [a]

DEAR FRED,

BEST THANKS FOR £10.

The business with the children is going relatively *well.* (Tussychen was very pleased with your letter.[78]) Our doctor is our neighbour, the Irishman Dr Korklow, who is known in the neighbourhood particularly as a scarlet-fever doctor (also in the school which my children attended). In case of need, i.e. as soon as there is the slightest disquieting change, Lafargue will bring a doctor from his hospital. So far this has not been necessary.

---

[a] 1868 is not in Marx's handwriting.

I would appreciate it if you could send me a bit more money, since the major part of the £20 had to be spent to partly pay off the most urgent small debts.

Lafargue has told Beesly that 1 article is pending.[11] Beesly says it must come in good time to find a place in the *August* number.[a]

My head is naturally IN TURMOIL. Since I can do nothing serious, I am writing up the stuff for Eichhoff.[79] It will go off tomorrow. *Salut.*

Your
Moor (*verte*[b])

Jennychen told Tussy that she had turned from her former higher Chinese character into a LOCALISED (IRISH) BEING and was therefore no longer showing due respect to the EMPEROR.[c] Tussy replied: FORMERLY I CLUNG TO A MAN, NOW I CLING TO A NATION.

First published abridged in *Der Briefwechsel zwischen F. Engels und K. Marx*, Bd. 4, Stuttgart, 1913 and in full in *MEGA*, Abt. III, Bd. 4, Berlin, 1931

Printed according to the original

Published in English for the first time

32

ENGELS TO MARX

IN LONDON

Manchester, 26 June 1868

Dear Moor,

Yesterday evening, after I had written to you, I went to Gumpert to ask him about SCARLATINA, but found his house so full of patients and Solomonic persons that I couldn't really approach him. I therefore saw him again today and asked him whether he could recommend a doctor, since Allen was sick. He said the main thing was to have a man who, even if not excessively CLEVER, should really live nearby, should come 3-4 times a day at critical times, and always be on call. In his opinion, Lafargue is quite capable of handling this case properly, and if you want further assistance,

---

[a] of *The Fortnightly Review* - [b] turn (the postscript is on the back of the sheet) - [c] pet name for Marx's daughter Jenny

Allen would be the best man to recommend one of the doctors in the vicinity. Apart from this, *fresh air* and PLENTY OF IT is the main thing; he himself usually prescribes washing with vinegar and water and disinfection of the house with chloride of lime; all this cannot, however, be decreed from a distance. In such acute sicknesses medicines are not really much use.

You will have received the second ten pounds in 2 fivers which I sent you the day before yesterday. Enclosed a further five pounds S/K 46 795, and next week I shall send you some more.

Incidentally, Gumpert did comfort me greatly and he confirmed that this year this sickness occurs in an exceptionally mild form.

Lizzie is afraid that you might think that Tussy could have caught the germ of the sickness here and she has urged me to write that everybody here is healthy.

Sincere greetings to your wife, the two patients,[a] Laura and Lafargue.

Your

F. E.

First published abridged in *Der Briefwechsel zwischen F. Engels und K. Marx*, Bd. 4, Stuttgart, 1913 and in full in *MEGA*, Abt. III, Bd. 4, Berlin, 1931

Printed according to the original

Published in English for the first time

33

MARX TO ENGELS[80]

IN MANCHESTER

London, 27 June 1868

DEAR FRED,

£5 received with THANKS.

The children are getting along *very well*. The suppuration and swelling of the throat has improved so much that today the doctor prescribed a hearty DINNER for them (hitherto they had only port and Liebig[b]). They consumed the DINNER with ZEST. From the beginning Korklow prescribed *air*. Instead of the CHLORIDE OF LIME

---

[a] Jenny and Eleanor Marx - [b] beef tea

another (newer) disinfectant, since he regards the former as injurious to the lungs. Luckily our house is built in such a way, and in particular the children's rooms are so situated, that they are plentifully provided with ventilation coming from every side.

Tell Mrs Lizzy (TO WHOM Tussy SENDS HER LOVE) that Manchester was not for a moment held responsible here. SCARLATINA and MEASLES are now epidemic in London. Tussy probably CAUGHT THE INFECTION FROM THE DAUGHTER OF PROFESSOR FRANKLAND.

Best greetings to Lizzy from me.

Your
Moor

Today I received a curious document. I have been summoned to appear next Wednesday[a] before the VESTRY of St. Pancras TO SHOW CAUSE WHY MY GOODS AND CHATTELS SHOULD NOT BE DISTRAINED. For the accursed VESTRY elected me *bon gré mal gré*[b] as 'CONSTABLE OF THE VESTRY OF ST. PANCRAS', and I went to Manchester[68] instead of taking over the office and swearing the appropriate oath of office. Dr Korklow, to whom I showed the SUMMONS today, said that it WAS AN HONOUR MUCH VALUED BY THE PHILISTINES OF ST. PANCRAS. I SHOULD TELL THEM THAT I WAS A FOREIGNER AND THAT THEY SHOULD KISS ME ON THE ARSE.

First published abridged in *Der Briefwechsel zwischen F. Engels und K. Marx*, Bd. 4, Stuttgart, 1913 and in full in *MEGA*, Abt. III, Bd. 4, Berlin, 1931   Printed according to the original

34

ENGELS TO MARX[56]

IN LONDON

Manchester, 28 June 1868

Dear Moor,

You lifted a heavy stone from all our hearts with your letter of yesterday. The day before yesterday and even yesterday everybody here in the house was very depressed, but today everybody is merry as a cricket again, and I myself feel quite different.

The article is finished.[11] You are quite right, Sam[c] is the man to

---

[a] 1 July - [b] whether I would or not - [c] Samuel Moore

sign it. I shall tell him today and at the same time give him the article to look through and to note possible Germanisms. But let me know by return whether I can keep it for a few days more, say, till Wednesday[a] evening; if not, I can send it off on Monday. The second and final article[71] (the first goes up to the conclusion of *absolute* surplus value) can then be finished by the end of this inst., since I am unlikely to leave here before then, so the two articles can directly follow one another. First I shall send the *Zukunft* the article about Prussian military nomenclature.[81]

Salut, ô connétable de Saint Pancrace![b] Now you should get yourself a worthy outfit: a red nightshirt, white nightcap, down-at-the-heel slippers, white pants, a long clay pipe and a POT OF PORTER. Lafargue, as your squire, can invent his uniform himself. As you see, the Pancratian philistines insist that you should sacrifice yourself for the common good. And this year-long, touching attachment which nothing could shake—this you intend to reciprocate with the cold negation of KISS MY—? But 'that's just like the communists'.

Give Jennychen my heartiest greetings and tell her that since she has now finally had a fever, I would like to have heard her speaking in delirium; there would have been more sense and poetry in it than fat Freiligrath will ever develop. Ditto best greetings to your wife and the two Lafargues.

Your

F. E.

First published abridged in *Der Briefwechsel zwischen F. Engels und K. Marx*, Bd. 4, Stuttgart, 1913 and in full in *MEGA*, Abt. III, Bd. 4, Berlin, 1931

Printed according to the original

Published in English in full for the first time

35

MARX TO ENGELS

IN MANCHESTER

London, 29 JUNE 1868

DEAR FRED,

BEST COMPLIMENTS FROM Tussy and Jennychen. The doctor[c] is very satisfied although POOR Jenny is suffering from SLEEPLESSNESS and also

---

[a] 1 July - [b] Greetings, constable of St. Pancras! (See previous letter.) - [c] Korklow

from coughing. He said today: as soon as the children are over their illness, they should leave London immediately and be sent to the seaside. (Perhaps they could go together with Lizzie?)

Enclosed copies of *Elberfelder Zeitung* which reached me today from Germany. *Dr. Fr. Schnacke* is named on the ENVELOPE as the author[a] and sender; I remember his name from 1848, but do not know him personally. THERE IS MUCH MUDDLING IN HIS ARTICLES.

There is time enough if you send me the ARTICLE by the end of this week.[11]

I am very TIRED as the anxiety of the recent period completely prevented me from sleeping.

Salut.

Your
K. M.

Today a letter from Kugelmann. 4 pages about the treatment of SCARLATINA.[b] Dietzgen from Petersburg visited him at Whitsun on his way to the Rhine.

First published in *MEGA*, Abt. III, Bd. 4, Berlin, 1931

Printed according to the original

Published in English for the first time

36

MARX TO ENGELS

IN MANCHESTER

London, 2 July 1868

DEAR FRED,

D'abord[c] best thanks for the article.[11]

And secondly for the 2 5-pound halves. At the same time, I received a dunning letter from the LANDLORD, whom tomorrow (on arrival of the second halves) I shall first pay the remainder for the quarter which ended on March 25th.

---

[a] This refers to Schnacke's review, signed E. F. S., of Volume I of *Capital* by Karl Marx in *Elberfelder Zeitung* of 17, 20, 23, 25 and 27 June 1868. The concluding part of the review appeared on 2 and 3 July. - [b] See this volume, p. 48. - [c] First of all

Enclosed a letter from Eichhoff.[82] Meissner should have sent me the scrawl from Faucher.[83] It is a good thing that the fellows are beginning to give vent to their annoyance.

The children are progressing well. Naturally very weak. Tussychen also still has a little suppuration in the throat. The doctor is on the whole very satisfied. He will only know in a few days when they will be well enough to go out.

Yesterday, when buying a pencil, I found upon it Russian letters in golden script. Русскій Графитъ.[a] But behind the Russian there appears to be a German named Theodor Stal (Schtal), namely Теодоръ Шталъ. This is the first time that I found something like that in a small local shop here. Borkheim would smell treason behind this.

Best greetings to Lizzy and the little one.[b]

Your
K.M.

First published in *Der Briefwechsel zwischen F. Engels und K. Marx*, Bd. 4, Stuttgart, 1913

Printed according to the original

Published in English for the first time

37

ENGELS TO MARX [48]

IN LONDON

[Manchester,] 2 July 1868

Dear Moor,

Enclosed the two second halves of the two fivers, S/K 11 185 Manchester, 14 January 1867, S/K 79 542 Manchester, 12 January 1867.

I have written to Borkheim[84] to get himself a new Russian book: *Zemlya i volya*, Land and Freedom, in which a German Russian, a landowner,[c] shows that since the emancipation of the peasants[85]

---

[a] Russian graphite. Marx gives these words and, further on, the name Theodor Schtal in Russian letters. - [b] Mary Ellen Burns - [c] [Lilienfeld, Pawel] Л. П., *Земля и воля*, St. Petersburg, 1868.

the Russian peasant is being *ruined through communal property*, and ditto Russian agriculture—small and large. The book is said to contain much statistical proof. Exchange value has already penetrated too deeply into these primitive communities, so that after the abolition of serfdom the situation no longer appears to be viable.

Tomorrow I hope to receive good news from you again. In the meantime, best greetings for the patients,[a] your wife and the Lafargues.

Your
F. E.

First published in *Der Briefwechsel zwischen F. Engels und K. Marx*, Bd. 4, Stuttgart, 1913

Printed according to the original

Published in English in full for the first time

38

MARX TO LUDWIG KUGELMANN[29]

IN HANOVER

London, 2 July 1868

Dear Kugelmann,

Many thanks for your letter.[b] The children are getting along well, though (today is the 9th day) they are not yet fit to go out.

With regard to my book,[c] the day before yesterday I received 5 issues of the *Elberfelder Zeitung* containing a very well-disposed review by Dr Schnacke.[d] (I recall the name from 1848, but do not know him personally.) There is a lot of confusion in his presentation of the matter. On the other hand, I have received information from Berlin that that clown Faucher made fun of my book in the June issue of his magazine.[83] It's a good thing these gentry are at last blurting out their annoyance.

---

[a] Jenny and Eleanor Marx - [b] See this volume, p. 54. - [c] the first volume of *Capital* - [d] *Elberfelder Zeitung* of 17, 20, 23, 25 and 27 June 1868. The review was signed E. F. S. The concluding part appeared on 2 and 3 July.

When and if I shall come to Germany, I do not yet know. I am finally rid of my carbuncles.

Engels will certainly come here in August or September.

Salut! and MY COMPLIMENTS TO MRS KUGELMANN AND THE LITTLE ONE.[a]

Yours

K. M.

First published abridged in *Die Neue Zeit*, Bd. 2, Nr. 7, Stuttgart, 1901-1902 and in full in *Pisma Marksa k Kugelmanu* (Letters of Marx to Kugelmann), Moscow-Leningrad, 1928

Printed according to the original

39

MARX TO ENGELS

IN MANCHESTER

[London,] 4 July 1868

DEAR FRED,

I am acknowledging the receipt (yesterday) of both second halves.

THANKS, ditto, FOR THE TWO little books of Schorlemmer.[b]

The children are getting along well. Yesterday they were up for part of the day, and Jennychen was even downstairs in the PARLOUR. The doctor[c] is now coming only every second day. Therefore he was not here yesterday, and I still await him today.

In today's *Hermann* the reception for Freiligrath in Cologne. Cups, etc. Nothing better than the *quid pro quo* to the effect that Freiligrath changed his seat 9 times, with the hint that this change was politically motivated!

Orsini's brother[d] is here again. He is accused of having betrayed the Fenians,[86] whose agent he was. His accuser is COLONEL Nagle and the French landlady in whose house he lived here at that time (at the time of the Fenian unrest and before he left for the UNITED

---

[a] Franziska Kugelmann - [b] C. Schorlemmer, 'Researches on the Hydrocarbons of the Series C_nH_{2n+2}', *Proceedings of the Royal Society*, No. 94, 1867 and No. 102, 1868. - [c] Korklow - [d] Cesare Orsini

STATES). His methods of exonerating himself are reminiscent of Bangya and he will clear out of London as soon as possible. Beust's action with the Czechs does not appear clear.[a]
Salut.

Your
Moor

First published abridged in *Der Briefwechsel zwischen F. Engels und K. Marx*, Bd. 4, Stuttgart, 1913 and in full in *MEGA,* Abt. III, Bd. 4, Berlin, 1931

Printed according to the original

Published in English for the first time

40

MARX TO SIGFRID MEYER [87]

IN NEW YORK

London, 4 July 1868
1 Modena Villas, Maitland Park,
Haverstock Hill

Dear Friend,

Your letter of 20 May arrived while I was away from London, a fairly long absence.[68] Hence the delay in replying.

Concerning Liebknecht's connections with New York, I know nothing, but will write to him on the subject.

For Sorge I enclose the following credentials.[b] Our direct connection is with Whaley, Sylvis AND Jessup.

The Commonwealth has long ceased to exist. The weekly reports on the proceedings of the CENTRAL COUNCIL appear in *The Bee-Hive*. This far from means, however, that this paper, a narrow-minded TRADES-UNION-ORGAN, represents our views.

In the German press, my book[c] has hitherto been reviewed—and mostly very favourably—in the *Zukunft*, the Stuttgart *Beobachter*,[d] the Württemberg *Staatszeitung*,[e] the Frankfurt *Börsenzeitung*,[f] ditto the *Hamburger Börsenzeitung*,[g] the Hamburg *Anzeiger*, etc., in various papers in Hanover and Rhine Province-Westphalia, particularly extensively in a series of articles in Schweitzer's

---

[a] See this volume, p. 64. - [b] See this volume, p. 59. - [c] the first volume of *Capital* - [d] The reviews for the *Zukunft* and the *Beobachter* were written by Engels. - [e] Marx means Engels' review for the *Staats-Anzeiger für Württemberg*. - [f] Marx evidently means the *Frankfurter Zeitung und Handelsblatt*. The review has not been found. - [g] *Die Börsen-Halle. Hamburgische Abendzeitung*, 14 February 1868.

London, 4th 1868.

We recommend Mr. Sorge to all the friends of the International Workingmen's Association and, at the same time, empower him to act in the name and on behalf of that Association.

By order of the General Council of the Intern. W. Assoc.

Karl Marx,
Secretary for Germany.

Credentials of the General Council of the International written in Friedrich Sorge's name (in Marx' hand)

Social-Demokrat (Berlin)[15] and the *Elberfelder Zeitung.*[a] The last two papers, although the latter is liberal bourgeois, are openly partisan.

The big bourgeois and reactionary papers like the *Kölnische*, the *Augsburger*, the *Neue Preussische*, the *Vossische*, etc., are carefully keeping their mouths shut.

From the ranks of the official economists, to date only in the Hildburghausen *Ergänzungsblätter* at the beginning of this year the review by *Dr Dühring*[b] (privatdozent at the University of Berlin, *supporter of Carey*) (this review was timid but, on the whole, appreciative)—and in the June issue of the economic magazine published by Faucher and Michaelis.[c] Mr Faucher naturally provides nothing except such remarks as one might expect from the comedian and hired jester of the German Bastiatites.

I would be grateful if you would send me a few newspapers from time to time. In particular, it would be of great value to me if you could dig up some anti-bourgeois material about land-ownership and agrarian relations in the United States. Since I shall be dealing with *rent* in my 2nd volume,[41] material against *H. Carey's* 'harmonies'[d] would be especially welcome.

Salut.

Yours

K. Marx

[Appendix]

London, 4 July 1868

We recommend Mr Sorge to all the friends of the International Work-ingmen's Association, and, at the same time, empower him to act in the name, and on behalf, of that Association.

By order of the General Council of the Intern. W. Assoc.

Karl Marx,
Secretary for Germany

First published in: Marx and Engels, *Works*, First Russian Edition, Vol. XXV, Moscow, 1934

Printed according to the original

Published in English in full for the first time

---

[a] The review by F. Schnacke (signed: E. F. S.) in the issues of 17, 20, 23, 25 and 27 June and 2 and 3 July 1868. - [b] E. Dühring, 'Marx. *Das Kapital. Kritik der politischen Oekonomie*, I. Band, Hamburg, 1867', *Ergänzungsblätter zur Kenntniss der Gegenwart*, Bd. 3, Heft 3, Hildburghausen, 1867, pp. 182-86. - [c] '*Das Kapital. Kritik der politischen Oekonomie* von Karl Marx. Erster Band. Buch I. Der Produktionsprozess des Kapitals. Hamburg. Otto Meissner, 1867', *Vierteljahrschrift für Volkswirthschaft und Kulturgeschichte*, Bd. XX, 5. Jg., Berlin, 1868, pp. 206-19. - [d] H. Ch. Carey, *The Harmony of Interests, Agricultural, Manufacturing, and Commercial.*

41

MARX TO ENGELS

IN MANCHESTER

London, 7 July 1868

DEAR FRED,

The children are progressing well. Yesterday for the first time they were outside for half an hour. The peeling is still very pronounced. Only when this is finished will they be MOVABLE.

During the past few days I have been pressed very hard by the baker, CHEESEMONGER, ASSESSED TAXES, God and the Devil.

You will recall that the German Workers' Educational Society here has celebrated the June Insurrection[88] for ABOUT 18 years now. Only in the last few years have the French (their society here now exists as the FRENCH BRANCH of the International[72]) taken part. And the old *meneurs*[a] always stayed away. I mean the *petits grands hommes*.[b]

But this year, IN PUBLIC MEETING, along came Mr Pyat and read out an alleged address of the Paris Commune (this is a *euphemism* for the IDENTICAL Pyat, who is in no way inferior to Blind in this LINE) in which the *assassinat* of Bonaparte was preached, as it was years ago in his *Lettre aux étudians*.[c] The FRENCH BRANCH, reinforced by other bawlers, acclaimed this. Vésinier had it printed in *Cigale*[d] and *Espiègle*,[e] Belgian PAPERS, and presents Pyat as giving his direction to the 'International'.[89]

As a result, we get a letter from the Brussels committee,[90] which just at the moment is making great propaganda, under difficult circumstances (Charleroi affair[24]). Contents: This demonstration threatens to wreck the entire Association on the continent. Will the FRENCH BRANCH never move forward from the old demagogic phrases, etc.? etc., etc. It should be remembered that, at this very time, our people are behind bars in Paris.[91] *We* yesterday issued a declaration (to be printed in Brussels), disavowing any connection between the above-mentioned Pyat and the International.[f]

Indeed I regard the whole affair (naturally based upon the

---

[a] leaders - [b] little great men - [c] F. Pyat, *Lettre aux étudians*, London, 1866. - [d] F. Pyat's speech at a meeting in Cleveland Hall on 29 June 1868. In: *La Cigale*, No. 29, 19 July 1868. - [e] Address to the Parisians by the Paris Central Committee of Action, 24 June 1868. In: *L'Espiègle*, No. 27, 5 July 1868. - [f] K. Marx, 'Resolution of the General Council on Félix Pyat's Provocative Behaviour'.

background of the enormous stupidity of the FRENCH BRANCH) as an intrigue of the old parties, the republican jackasses of 1848, especially the *petits grands hommes* who represent them in London. Our Association is a thorn in their flesh. After trying in vain to work against the Association, THE NEXT BEST THING, of course, is to compromise it. Pyat is just the man to do this *de bonne foi.*[a] The cleverer ones therefore push him forward.

What could be funnier than this squint-eyed melodrama-writer and *Charivari* man before 1848, this TOASTMASTER of 1848 who now plays Brutus, but from a safe distance!

The FRENCH BRANCH here will have to be thrown out of the International if it does not put a stop to its asininity. One cannot allow 50 unprincipled louts, round whom loudmouths of all nationalities gather at such public opportunities, to endanger the International Association at a moment when, as a result of conditions on the continent, it is beginning to become a serious power.

Salut.   Your

                                                        K. M.

First published in *Der Briefwechsel zwischen F. Engels und K. Marx*, Bd. 4, Stuttgart, 1913

Printed according to the original

Published in English for the first time

42

ENGELS TO MARX

IN LONDON

                                    Manchester, 10 July 1868

Dear Moor,

Enclosed 2 fivers, S/K 93 518 and 19, Manchester, 14 January 1867, to pacify the CHEESEMONGER and other Manicheans.

Everybody here was overjoyed by your good news about the patients.[b]

Hopefully you will really be able to calm down the FRENCH BRANCH.[72] Once again there appears to be sufficient confusion in that nation to guarantee the mess-up of any revolution that may break out. Wherever you look among these fellows, nothing but stupidity.

---

[a] in good faith - [b] Marx's daughters Eleanor and Jenny

Ad vocem[a] Pyat, Blind must not be forgotten. I believe I told you that the Bradford Schiller Society (*id est* Dr Bronner) approached the Schiller Institute[76] here, in order to organise there, here, and in Liverpool 'Readings by famous Germans living in England'. I told the people right away that the whole thing revolved round Karl Blind; all the same they should, as far as I was concerned, agree to the plan *sous réserve*[b] in order to see for themselves. So, last week a letter arrived from Bradford with further information. It said approaches had been made to Prof. Goldstücker, Max Müller, *K. Blind* and *A. Ruge*! The *first* two had accepted, yet only *sous réserve* with regard to their time and health, but the latter two had accepted immediately and unconditionally, and Ruge had immediately asked whether an historical or philosophical theme would be preferred. In short, the bomb had burst, and the gentlemen received the reply that Goldstücker and Max Müller would be quite acceptable here, but there could be no question of Blind and Ruge. And this puts paid to the attempt.

Beust[c] has once again made himself suspicious in my eyes. The serious attempt of the Russians to have the Eastern business explode this spring, in spite of the fact that their railway was not yet finished, only appears explicable in that they wished to exploit the presence of a Palmerston as Austrian Prime Minister as long as it lasted. According to one version, he told the Czechs, incidentally, that he was in possession of plans which had been agreed between Prussia and Russia for the eventuality of the dissolution of Austria, and that under these plans Bohemia would not become Russian, but would be sacrificed by the Russians.

I have read the conclusion of the Prussian war of 1866 (Main campaign).[d] According to it, the South Germans were even more stupid than one had thought and known; the blame is, incidentally, distributed more evenly, so that Charlemagne of Bavaria[e] appears as at least as great an ass as Alexander the Great of Hesse.[f]

Best greetings to your wife, the girls and the Lafargues.

Your
F. E.

First published abridged in *Der Briefwechsel zwischen F. Engels und K. Marx*, Bd. 4, Stuttgart, 1913 and in full in *MEGA*, Abt. III, Bd. 4, Berlin, 1931

Printed according to the original

Published in English for the first time

---

[a] Regarding - [b] with reservations - [c] Friedrich Ferdinand Count von Beust, then Chancellor of Austria - [d] *Der Feldzug der preussischen Main-Armee im Sommer 1866*. - [e] Karl Theodor Maximilian August - [f] Alexander Ludwig Georg, Prince of Hesse

43

MARX TO ENGELS[92]

IN MANCHESTER

London, 11 July 1868

DEAR FRED,

The £10 received with BEST THANKS. I immediately paid £3 5s. for taxes, £3 to the CHEESEMONGER (whom, by the way, I have been paying cash for weeks, since he, just like the TEA-GROCER, no longer puts it on the slate), £1 10s. to the chemist. I owe the baker about £17 and the man, who was always very friendly with us, is in great difficulties. It is awful for me that I have to press you like this. If I only knew how to find any *direct* way out!

The children[a] are doing fairly well, though Jennychen is still very weak. The ruling TEMPER here in the house is not exactly made for convalescents. My wife is not in the best of shape either, and therefore unnecessarily IRRITABLE.

Enclosed:

1. *Kugelmann*: I answered him right away[b] saying he should *be sure not* to loose the intended letter upon Faucher, the Mannequin Pisse.[93]

2. The review by the worthy Faucher[83]; another in the *Literarisches Zentralblatt*.[c] Both to be returned to me.

3. Letter from Dietzgen, who has also written an article on my book for me.[94]

You cannot fully appreciate the farce Mannequin Pisse Faucher is putting on in making me a pupil of Bastiat. Bastiat states in his *Harmonies*[d]:

'If anybody were to explain to him, on the basis of the determination of value by labour time, why air has *no* value and a *diamond* a *high* value, he would throw his book into the fire.'

Since I have now accomplished this terrible trick, Faucher must prove that I, in fact, accept Bastiat, who declares that there exists 'no measure' of value.

The manner in which Mr Bastiat derives the value of the

---

a Jenny and Eleanor Marx - b See this volume, pp. 67-70. - c *Literarisches Centralblatt für Deutschland*, No. 28, 4 July 1868, pp. 754-56: 'Marx, Karl. *Das Kapital. Kritik der politischen Oekonomie* (in 3 Bdn.). Erster Bd. Buch I. Der Produktionsprozess des Kapitals. Hamburg, 1867. O. Meissner' (signed 'h'). - d Marx quotes from F. Bastiat's *Harmonies économiques*, Paris, 1850, pp. 181-82.

diamond is given in the following truly commercial-traveller-type conversation:

'Monsieur, cédez-moi votre diamant.—Monsieur, je veux bien; cédez-moi en échange votre travail de toute une année.'[a]

Instead of the business friend answering: *'Mon cher, si j'étais condamné à travailler, vous comprenez bien que j'aurai autre chose à acheter que des diamants',*[b] he says:

'Mais, monsieur, vous n'avez pas sacrifié à votre acquisition une minute.—Eh bien, monsieur, tâchez de rencontrer une minute semblable.—Mais, en bonne justice, nous devrions échanger à *travail égal.*—Non, en bonne justice, vous appréciez vos services et moi les miens. Je ne vous force pas; pourquoi me forceriez-vous? Donnez-moi un an tout entier, ou cherchez vous même un diamant.—Mais cela m'en entraînerait à dix ans de pénibles recherches, sans compter une déception probable au bout. Je trouve plus sage, plus profitable d'employer ces dix ans d'une autre manière.—C'est justement pour cela que je crois vous rendre encore *service* en ne vous demandant qu'un an. Je vous en épargne neuf, et voilà pourquoi j'attache beaucoup de *valeur* à ce *service.'*[c]

Is it not a wine salesman to the very life?

Incidentally—and the German Bastiatites do not know this— that unhappy assertion that the value of commodities is deter- mined, not by the labour they cost, but by the labour which they *spare* the buyer (the babbling about the connection between exchange and the division of labour is childish talk) is just as little Bastiat's discovery as any of the other of his wine-salesman categories.

The old jackass Schmalz, the Prussian demagogue-catcher,[95] says (German edition 1818, *French* 1826):

'Le travail d'autrui en général ne produit jamais pour nous qu'une *économie de temps*, et cette économie de temps est tout ce qui constitue sa *valeur* et son *prix.* Le menuisier, par exemple, qui me fait une table, et le domestique qui porte mes lettres à la poste, qui bat mes habits, ou qui cherche pour moi les choses qui me sont nécessaires, me rendent l'un et l'autre *un service* absolument de même nature: l'un et l'autre *m'épargne* et le temps que je serais obligé d'employer moi-même à mes [ces] occupations, et celui qu'il m'aurait fallu consacrer à m'acquérir l'aptitude et les talents qu'elles exigent.'[d]

---

[a] 'Monsieur, give me your diamond.—Gladly, monsieur; give me in exchange your work for a whole year.' - [b] 'My dear Sir, if I were condemned to work, you will understand that I would have something other to buy than diamonds.' - [c] 'But monsieur, you did not sacrifice a minute for your acquisition.— All right, monsieur, try to find a similar minute.—But, in fairness, we should exchange *equal labour.*—No, in fairness, you should put a value on your services, and I on mine. I am not forcing you; why would you force me? Give me a whole year or look for a diamond yourself.—But that would involve me in ten years exhausting search, quite apart from the probable disappointment at the end. I find it wiser and more profitable to employ these ten years in a different manner.—That is exactly why I believe I am indeed doing you a *service* when I only demand one year from you. I save you nine, and that is why I attach a high *value* to this *service.'* - [d] 'In general, the work of others only

Old Schmalz was an epigone of the physiocrats.[96] He says this in a polemic directed against A. Smith's *travail productif* and *improductif*,[a] and proceeds from their thesis that only agriculture produces real value. He found that in *Garnier*.[b] Similar stuff, on the other hand, in *Ganilh*,[c] epigone of the mercantilists. Ditto in polemics against the same differentiation made by A. Smith. Thus, polemics by epigones representing two standpoints, with neither having the slightest conception of value,—and Bastiat copies them! And this is the latest discovery in Germany! A pity that no paper exists in which one can expose this plagiarism by Bastiat.[97]

Salut.

Your

K. M.

First published abridged in *Der Briefwechsel zwischen F. Engels und K. Marx*, Bd. 4, Stuttgart, 1913 and in full in *MEGA*, Abt. III, Bd. 4, Berlin, 1931

Printed according to the original

Published in English in full for the first time

44

MARX TO LUDWIG KUGELMANN[29]

IN HANOVER

London, 11 July 1868

Dear Friend,

The children are getting on well, though still weak.

Thank you very much for the things you sent. *Definitely do not* write to Faucher,[98] otherwise this *mannequin pisse* will feel too

---

produces a *saving of time* for us, and this saving of time is the only thing which constitutes its *value* and its *price.* For example, the carpenter who makes me a table, and the servant who takes my letters to the post, cleans my clothes, and procures for me the things I need—the one and the other render me *services* of absolutely the same nature. The one and the other *save* me both the time that I myself would be obliged to use for my [these] occupations, and the time that I would have had to devote to acquiring the skills they require' ([Th.] Schmalz, *Économie politique, ouvrage traduit de l'allemand...*, Vol. I, Paris, 1826, p. 304). - [a] productive and unproductive labour - [b] [G. Garnier,] *Abrégé élémentaire des principes de l'économie politique.* - [c] Ch. Ganilh, *Des systèmes d'économie politique, de la valeur comparative de leurs doctrines, et de celle qui parait la plus favorable aux progrès de la richesse.*

important.[93] All he has achieved is that, if a second edition appears, I shall aim a few necessary blows at Bastiat where I speak about the *magnitude of value*.[99] This wasn't done before, since the 3rd volume[41] will contain a separate and extensive chapter about the 'vulgar economy' gentry.[100] Incidentally, you will find it quite natural that Faucher and consorts derive the 'exchange value' of their own scribblings not from the *amount of labour power expended*, but from the *absence of such expenditure*, that is from *'saved labour'*. Moreover, the worthy Bastiat did not even himself make this 'discovery', so welcome to these gentry, but just 'cribbed' it, in his usual manner, from much earlier authors. His sources are of course unknown to Faucher and consorts.

As for the *Centralblatt*, the man is making the greatest concession possible by admitting that, if value means anything at all, then my conclusions must be conceded.[a] The unfortunate fellow does not see that, even if there were no chapter on 'value' at all in my book,[65] the analysis I give of the real relations would contain the proof and demonstration of the real value relation. The chatter about the need to prove the concept of value arises only from complete ignorance both of the subject under discussion and of the method of science. Every child knows that any nation that stopped working, not for a year, but let us say, just for a few weeks, would perish. And every child knows, too, that the amounts of products corresponding to the differing amounts of needs demand differing and quantitatively determined amounts of society's aggregate labour. It is SELF-EVIDENT that this *necessity* of the *distribution* of social labour in specific proportions is certainly not abolished by the *specific form* of social production; it can only change *its form of manifestation*. Natural laws cannot be abolished at all. The only thing that can change, under historically differing conditions, is the *form* in which those laws assert themselves. And the form in which this proportional distribution of labour asserts itself in a state of society in which the interconnection of social labour expresses itself as the *private exchange* of the individual products of labour, is precisely the *exchange value* of these products.

Where science comes in is to show *how* the law of value asserts itself. So, if one wanted to 'explain' from the outset all phenomena

---

[a] This refers to the review, in *Literarisches Centralblatt für Deutschland*, No. 28, 4 July 1868, 'Marx, Karl. *Das Kapital. Kritik der politischen Oekonomie* (in 3 Bdn.). Erster Bd. Buch I. Der Produktionsprozess des Kapitals. Hamburg, 1867. O. Meissner' (signed 'h').

that apparently contradict the law, one would have to provide the science *before* the science. It is precisely Ricardo's mistake that in his first chapter, on value,[a] all sorts of categories that still have to be arrived at are assumed *as given*, in order to prove their harmony with the law of value.

On the other hand, as you correctly believe, *the history of the theory* of course demonstrates that the understanding of the value relation has *always been the same*, clearer or less clear, hedged with illusions or scientifically more precise. Since the reasoning process itself arises from the existing conditions and is itself a *natural process*, really comprehending thinking can always only be the same, and can vary only gradually, in accordance with the maturity of development, hence also the maturity of the organ that does the thinking. Anything else is drivel.

The vulgar economist has not the slightest idea that the actual, everyday exchange relations and the value magnitudes *cannot be directly identical*. The point of bourgeois society is precisely that, *a priori*, no conscious social regulation of production takes place. What is reasonable and necessary by nature asserts itself only as a blindly operating average. The vulgar economist thinks he has made a great discovery when, faced with the disclosure of the intrinsic interconnection, he insists that things look different in appearance. In fact, he prides himself in his clinging to appearances and believing them to be the ultimate. Why then have science at all?

But there is also something else behind it. Once interconnection has been revealed, all theoretical belief in the perpetual necessity of the existing conditions collapses, even before the collapse takes place in practice. Here, therefore, it is completely in the interests of the ruling classes to perpetuate the unthinking confusion. And for what other reason are the sycophantic babblers paid who have no other scientific trump to play except that, in political economy, one may not think at all!

But *satis superque*.[b] In any case, it shows the depth of degradation reached by these priests of the bourgeoisie: while workers and even manufacturers and merchants have understood my book and made sense of it, these 'learned scribes' (!) complain that I make excessive demands on their comprehension.

I would *not* advise reprinting Schweitzer's articles, though Schweitzer has made a good job of them for his paper.[101]

---

[a] D. Ricardo, *On the Principles of Political Economy, and Taxation*, Ch. I: On Value. - [b] enough and more than enough

You would oblige me if you sent me a few issues of the *Staats-Anzeiger*.

You should be able to get Schnacke's address by enquiring at the *Elberfelder*.

Best greetings to your wife and Fränzchen.

Yours

K. M.

Apropos. I have received an article by Dietzgen about my book[94]; I am sending it to Liebknecht.

First published abridged in *Die Neue Zeit*, Bd. 2, Nr. 7, Stuttgart, 1901-1902 and in full in *Pisma Marksa k Kugelmanu* (Letters of Marx to Kugelmann), Moscow-Leningrad, 1928

Printed according to the original

45

ENGELS TO MARX

IN LONDON

Manchester, 14 July[a] 1868

Dear Moor,

Enclosed another two fivers, S/K 92 566 and 93 517. Manchester, 14 January [18]67.

I do not know whether I shall manage to finish the article. On Sunday during a meal a small blood-vessel burst in the conjunctiva of my left eye and since then this eye has been very sensitive, so that it is at present quite impossible for me to write with a light; I think, however, it will soon pass.

Do not forget to order 40-50 *separate reprints* of the article in the *Fortnightly*[11] so that we can distribute them.

Best greetings.

Your

F. E.

First published in *Der Briefwechsel zwischen F. Engels und K. Marx*, Bd. 4, Stuttgart, 1913

Printed according to the original

Published in English for the first time

---

[a] In the original: 14 January.

46

ENGELS TO MARX

IN LONDON

Manchester, 21 July 1868

Dear Moor,

I concluded from Tussy's letter the receipt of the £10, and also that both patients[a] must have reached the point at which they should be sent to the SEASIDE, the sooner the better. So that there shall be no delay I enclose £25 (1 of 20 and 1 of 5). It is still uncertain when I shall get away from here, and it will therefore be better for the time being to drop the attempt at a combined SEASIDE operation, so that the girls' health may not suffer.

I believe you said recently that Borkheim himself would be inclined to advance the £150 if he was not at the moment short of money. Is he now perhaps in a position to provide the sum, or at least £100? It would be absolute folly to toss into the maw of this miserable society 20% interest per annum against the finest security. Even if Borkheim can get us only £100, of which £50 might be repaid in case of need in January or February and the rest on 10/20 July 1869 (though it would be best if *the whole sum* need not be repaid until next July), everything could be fixed up easily. He really only needs to commit himself to pay £100 on the loan in September, so that I would then only need to send him the *remainder*. This would free £100 for me, which I could send you right now. If nothing of this sort happens, you will understand that I am very tied, as long as the heavy load of £175 is hanging over my head, and especially as long as I do not know how the balance has come out, and I probably won't know for another 3-4 weeks.

Think over the business with Borkheim. Maybe something can be done; if so we would be, at least for the time being, out of all our troubles, and would once again have gained time.

The pamphlets and journals I sent back to you yesterday. Who is this sultry Dr Boruttau, who displays such a sensitive organ for sexual love?[b]

Jones is hard put to it whether to stand for Manchester or for Dewsbury.[102] The Dewsburyans have sent him a requisition signed

---

[a] Marx's daughters Eleanor and Jenny - [b] This refers to C. Boruttau's book *Gedanken über Gewissens-Freiheit*. See also this volume, p. 72.

by 2,000 voters; he wants 1,000 more since there will be 6,000 voters. Now they are pressing *here* in Manchester whether he will accept or not.

Best greetings.

Your

F. E.

First published in *Der Briefwechsel zwischen F. Engels und K. Marx*, Bd. 4, Stuttgart, 1913

Printed according to the original

Published in English for the first time

47

MARX TO ENGELS

IN MANCHESTER

London, 23 July 1868

DEAR FRED,

BEST THANKS for the £25. The children will probably go to the sea next week together with MR and MRS Lafargue. Since yesterday Lafargue has been ' MEMBER OF THE ROYAL COLLEGE OF SURGEONS' and has received his patent for the KILLING OF MEN AND BEASTS. Then, in 4-5 weeks, he will go to Paris. As a result, we are in a very embarrassing position, since my wife still has to buy linen for Laura for at least £20.

I do not think we can do any business with Borkheim. Yesterday he told me that 'money was very tight' in his case, etc. The Dutchmen, of whom I can, in fact, only use August Philips, are travelling. But I shall use my head to see how and where to get a loan, since it is *absolutely necessary*. The practice of borrowing at 20% can in fact only happen with institutions like those utilised by Borkheim, where people lose the capital advanced if one kicks the bucket before the date of maturity.

About Dr Boruttau, the man with the sultry prick, I know nothing except that he also ' runs with' the Lassalleans (Schweitzer FRACTION). The funniest thing is the 'French' of his dedication to a sympathetic soul in Moscow.[103]

You will have seen that my book[a] forms a point of discussion in

---

[a] the first volume of *Capital*

the programme of the General Association of German Workers.[a][104]

I have sent you a scrawl by Dühring which despite the heat you might read. You could also tell me your impressions of it, since it is certainly not overtaxing. But all the more boring, to be sure.

I saw Prof. Beesly last week at Lafargue's. Beesly was absent when your article[11] arrived. Immediately after his return he received it and sent it to Henry Morley[b] (CHIEF EDITOR of *The Fortnightly Review*) in Scotland, from whence we have received no further NEWS as yet.

How do you live in this heat? I lose all capacity for thought, and without Gumpert's medicine I COULD NOT STAND IT AT ALL.

Salut.

Your
K. M.

First published abridged in *Der Briefwechsel zwischen F. Engels und K. Marx*, Bd. 4, Stuttgart, 1913 and in full in *MEGA*, Abt. III, Bd. 4, Berlin, 1931

Printed according to the original

Published in English for the first time

48

ENGELS TO MARX

IN LONDON

Manchester, 29 July 1868

Dear Moor,

Enclosed Liebknecht returned.[105] What a feeble business with Schweitzer. He should *recognise* 1. you and 2. the International Working Men's Association! Wilhelmchen appears to me to have once again failed to control his tendency to stupidities. Incidentally, you see that Schweitzer did, after all, show off with your letters.[c]

As regards Liebknecht's promises about Nuremberg and the Swiss workers, I SHALL WAIT FOR PERFORMANCE BEFORE GIVING AN OPINION.

Now enclosed a letter from Kugelmann.[106] The business with Keil is splendid—if Kertbény is not in fact inventing a bit. Just in

---

[a] This refers to the programme of the Hamburg Congress of the General Association of German Workers then forthcoming. See J. B. Schweitzer, 'An die Mitglieder des Allgemeinen deutsch. Arbeiter-Vereins', *Der Social-Demokrat*, No. 80, 10 July 1868. - [b] John Morley is meant. - [c] See this volume, pp. 26 and 28-30.

case, I sat down and scribbled in great haste the enclosed scrawl, trying to make it as Beta-like as possible[107]—as is suitable for that miserable rag[a]; kindly let me have your comments on it by return so that we may send the stuff off without delay and strike while the iron is hot. We may not despise this bit of humbug, any more than we despise the stratagems through Siebel's mediation.[50] And the Kinkels, Freiligraths and Blinds, etc., will be badly annoyed; the philistine, however, as you know, trusts his *Gartenlaube*, and it will greatly impress Meissner. Your wife will also enjoy it very much—I think it would be best if you keep it secret for the time being, because of possible disappointment, and then you will surprise her when the paper comes out.

It is a good thing that owing to the delay of the article[11] caused by Beesly's absence I get some time for the second one.[71] Working at night still affects my eye slightly, and it then hurts all the next day.

Best greetings to your wife, the girls and Lafargue and his spouse. In haste.

Your
F. E.

First published abridged in *Der Briefwechsel zwischen F. Engels und K. Marx*, Bd. 4, Stuttgart, 1913 and in full in *MEGA*, Abt. III, Bd. 4, Berlin, 1931

Printed according to the original

Published in English for the first time

49

MARX TO ENGELS

IN MANCHESTER

[London,] 29 July 1868

DEAR FRED,

I hope that the business with your eye is nothing serious. Small blood vessels will burst now and then, without any particular consequence. Have you consulted Gumpert about it?

Unfortunately, the household will only go to the sea next week. And that is because of the *Lafargue family*, who wanted to join in and rent a LODGING, etc., together. Because of Lafargue's ties with

---

[a] *Die Gartenlaube. Illustrirtes Familienblatt*

his hospital (where he has been operating for weeks as house SURGEON) the departure has been delayed from day to day, despite my curses, threats and shouts, so that now it is to take place at the beginning of next week, when my wife will go OFF with the rest, and Laura of course arguing that she will soon part completely from the FAMILY, etc. Tussy (highly delighted by your letter, I believe, she knows *par coeur*[a] your 6 letters to her [78]) is hale and hearty again. Not so Jennychen, who is also worrying about all sorts of things, etc. If I HAD MADE UP MY MIND where on the continent I could just now depend with certainty upon a LOAN (especially since I would, if necessary, have your guarantee), I would cross over and take Jennychen with me. But this is perhaps the best time of the year to find nobody at home.

There have been all sorts of scandals here RELATING TO Pyat, FRENCH BRANCH [72] and GENERAL COUNCIL. On this tomorrow.[b] Today only this. Schweitzer in his 2nd programme for the congress of the *General Association of German Workers* in Hamburg has an item about the *International Working Men's Association* and another about *my book*.[c] The programme was printed in the *Zukunft*[d] [104] and elsewhere. On the other hand, *A. Bebel*, as president of the Workers' Union meeting in Nuremberg, has sent an invitation to the General Council.[108] We should send a delegate (Eccarius will go). That they will join the International Working Men's Association and adopt our programme is already *certain*, he says. Finally, we have received an invitation from Vienna where the Austrian workers' fraternal festival will be held, also at the beginning of September.[109] We have sent to Fox, who is in Vienna, the authorisation to represent us there.

About the private negotiations between Wilhelmchen and Schweitzer[e] I know no more than the former writes. Yet I know from another source that the influence of that cunning fox Schweitzer has grown to the same extent as Wilhelmchen has discredited himself among the workers by his over-close alliance with the South German provincial pettifoggers. It was evidently *for this reason* that Wilhelm found it necessary to set up a sort of cartel with Schweitzer, who is at present inside and who, moreover, was clever enough to have his title of nobility revoked by the Prussian court 'for *lèse-majesté*'.[110] As far as I am concerned—I mean as MEMBER of the GENERAL COUNCIL—I must

---

[a] by heart - [b] See this volume, pp. 78-79. - [c] the first volume of *Capital* - [d] 'Programm der Generalsammlung des Allgemeinen deutschen Arbeiter-Vereins, stattfindend in Hamburg, vom 22. bis 25. August 1868', *Die Zukunft*, No. 266, 10 July 1868. - [e] See this volume, p. 73.

conduct myself impartially between the various *organised* groups of workers. It is their business and not mine whom they have as leader. As SECRETARY FOR GERMANY I must answer all those who apply to me in their official capacity as presidents, etc., of workers' groups. In this sense, I have also written to Schweitzer (always WITH AN EYE to the possible publication of the entire correspondence).[111] Faced with the intrigues of the old '48 democrats here, it was, however, high time to be able to display influence among the German workers in Germany.

That you, poor devil, with your sore eye, should also have to water the *Gartenlaube*—and in this weather, too—really cries to the heavens.[a]

My comments are confined to:

Page 2 where I have put 1 x).[112] The FACT was actually this! For us the government sent, instead of the city censor, a special fellow from Berlin (Mr von St. Paul, etc.). When even this did not help, yet another tier of censorship, that of the *Regierungspräsident* of Cologne,[b] was added. Finally, the Berlin cabinet, driven wild, issued a sort of manifesto against us, apprising the world of all our offences, and concluding with the announcement that at the end of the quarter they would shut up our shop. I resigned because the shareholders—even if in vain, as it later turned out—tried to negotiate with the Prussian government.

Page 3 (2x). It would perhaps be good to add here for the benefit of the philistines that the provisional government had invited me in writing to return to France.[c]

Ditto page 3 (x3). You might add for the benefit of the democratic philistines that the Prussians expelled me *par ordre du Muphti*,[d] after they had failed in the law courts.[113]

Finally, would it not be better, instead of the title: 'A German Political Economist', to have: 'A German Socialist'? Both are 'hideous', but the former probably more so.

More tomorrow about affairs here.

Salut.

Your
Moor

First published abridged in *Der Briefwech-sel zwischen F. Engels und K. Marx*, Bd. 4, Stuttgart, 1913 and in full in *MEGA*, Abt. III, Bd. 4, Berlin, 1931

Printed according to the original

Published in English for the first time

---

a Marx plays on the name of the magazine: 'Gartenlaube' means 'arbour'. See also this volume, p. 74. - b Karl Heinrich von Gerlach - c See 'Ferdinand Flocon to Marx in Brussels. March 1, 1848' (present edition, Vol. 6, p. 649). - d on orders from the mufti (i.e. by Royal order)

50

ENGELS TO LUDWIG KUGELMANN

IN HANOVER

York, 31 July 1868

Dear Kugelmann,

This scrawl must be excused by the fact that I am on my way for a few days to bring my dear spouse[a] to the seaside resort at Bridlington (I bet you couldn't guess how this name is pronounced), and by the haste in which I send you the enclosed composition.[106] The business is splendid, that is, if it can be done and Kertbény is not bragging.[b] The enclosed scribble has been composed, as far as possible, in the spirit of the rag,[c] but it should possibly be made milder here and there. Marx thinks the title 'A German *Socialist*'[d] would be better, which would be very nice, if Monsieur Kertbény did not object; but this must be prevented *above all*, so I find your suggestion, being the 'milder' one, is better.[114]

Marx has, for the time being, kept your letter with him, and since it is already late today anyway, and everybody in the hotel is hurrying to bed, I shall have to answer it next week. I put Lupus' photogram aside for you some time ago; luckily it is still one of the old good prints; recently I had another 24 prints made, but in the meantime the negative had faded so much that they turned out very badly. As for me, a blood vessel burst in the conjunctiva of my left eye a fortnight ago, and left behind a red patch on the apple (south-west side) which has not yet vanished, and with which I would not like to be eternised. So you will just have to wait for a while.

N.B. There are two corrections, marked A and B, written here later; please insert them in the right place.[e] It would be desirable for Kertbény neither to know the author of the article, nor see the original handwriting.

So until next week.

Yours

F. E.

First published in: Marx and Engels, *Works*, First Russian Edition, Vol. XXV, Moscow, 1934

Printed according to the original

Published in English for the first time

---

[a] Lydia Burns - [b] See this volume, p. 73. - [c] *Die Gartenlaube. Illustrirtes Familienblatt* - [d] See this volume, p. 76. - [e] Ibid.

51

MARX TO ENGELS

IN MANCHESTER

[London,] 4 August 1868

Dear Fred,

How is your eye?

You will probably have received the Eichhoff stuff.[a] In the *Zukunft* there are 'Economic Letters'[b] singing the praises of my book.[c] In fact these letters are largely cribbed from the book. In the *Social-Demokrat* the Executive of the General Association of German Workers is urged by the presidium to invite me as a guest of honour to the congress at Hamburg at the end of August.[d]

A few days ago I wrote to Meissner[84] to find out at last where and how.

Kugelmann has written me a few lines saying that the chamber of commerce and the polytechnical school in Hanover have ordered a number of copies of my book.

In the meantime, I am really more BOTHERED by PRIVATE ECONOMY or, as the English say, DOMESTIC ECONOMY, than by political economy. My LANDLORD has dunned me and, unfortunately for me, is staying FOR SOME TIME AT London. I have also been forced to sign diverse smaller bills of exchange, etc.

The filthy French branch[72] has created a fine scandal for us. The Pyatists have published a *blâme*[e] of the *conseil général* in the *Cigale*. Their channel was the infamous Vésinier. We ignored this VOTE OF CENSURE and simply passed *à l'ordre du jour*.[f] There followed a MEETING of the FRENCH BRANCH where there were fisticuffs. Dupont, Jung, Lafargue, Johannard, Lassassie and various others have quit this gang of scoundrels. This rabble now amounts to a total of perhaps 15 persons, although they confront us as the '*souveraineté du peuple*'.[g] We are '*des endormeurs*', '*des ambitieux*',[h] etc. Apart from

---

[a] W. Eichhoff, *Die Internationale Arbeiterassociation. Ihre Gründung, Organisation, politisch-sociale Thätigkeit und Ausbreitung*. See also Note 79. - [b] 'Oekonomische Briefe', *Die Zukunft*, Nos 292 and 298, 25 and 29 July 1868. - [c] the first volume of *Capital* - [d] 'An die Vorstands-Mitglieder des Allgemeinen deutschen Arbeiter-Vereins' (signed: W. Real), *Der Social-Demokrat*, No. 90, 2 August 1868. See also Note 130. - [e] censure - [f] to next business - [g] 'sovereignty of the people' - [h] 'humbugs', 'the ambitious'

the little bit of scandal which these Spiegelbergs are making in that obscure Belgian paper, they are naturally NOWHERE. Nothing is more grotesque than the way in which this mob play Jacobin Club.[115]

Apropos. Moses' article[116] has, after all, turned up. It is in the hands of Massol, who will print it shortly in his *Morale indépendante*, now that this has changed its skin to become a political journal. Reclus will ditto wade in with his *Coopération*, now that this ditto has be-butterflied itself into a political paper.

My wife went to Ramsgate in advance on Monday[a] to prepare the quarters. The gang will follow tomorrow.

Lafargue is only free from tomorrow. In the meantime, he has been operating like mad as assistant to the HOME SURGEON of St. Bartholomew's. Yesterday, e.g., from 9 in the morning until 11 in the evening. Woe to the *corpus vile*[b] of male or female kind on which he gets his practice.

Best greetings from Tussy to you and Lizzy. The child declares to all and sundry that she is READY to emigrate to Manchester. MEANWHILE she is teased here with the NICKNAME 'THE POOR NEGLECTED NATION'.[c]

Salut.

Your
K. M.

How do you translate GRAVEL as distinct from SAND and FLINT? And how PEAT as distinct from BOG? Incidentally, there are perhaps 6 further different names for what are, more or less, nuances of peat-ground in the 'POOR NEGLECTED COUNTRY'.

Finally, how do you manage to live in this heat? I would like best to hang on a tree in the air.

P. S. Now, when the Germans will join the 'INTERNATIONAL WORKINGMEN'S ASSOCIATION' *en masse*, with the Association, for the time being, filling out at least the boundaries of its main territory—though it is still thin on the ground—my plan is that the GENERAL COUNCIL should move to Geneva for the next year[117] and that we should function here only as the BRITANNIC COUNCIL. It appears a shrewd move to me if the proposal comes from us. At the same

---

[a] 3 August - [b] living body - [c] An allusion to Tussy's Irish sympathies.

time, it will show the jackasses in Paris, etc., that we are in no way anxious for this pleasant dictatorship. *Qu'en penses tu?*[a]

First published abridged in *Der Briefwechsel zwischen F. Engels und K. Marx*, Bd. 4, Stuttgart, 1913 and in full in *MEGA*, Abt. III, Bd. 4, Berlin, 1931

Printed according to the original

Published in English for the first time

52

ENGELS TO MARX

IN LONDON

[Manchester,] 6 August 1868

Dear Moor,

What do I do in this heat? Languish and drink. Today it is raining, the air is muggy and saturated with humidity, it is therefore doubly horrible, the sweat does not evaporate and you are damp all over.

Last Friday[b] I took Lizzie and M. Ellen[c] to Bridlington Quay and returned on Monday; tomorrow I shall return there with Moore, and I would take my HOLIDAY and stay the week, but Charles[d] has gout and is all in, so I must do his work as well as my own, and there can be no question of going away.

Eichhoff's pamphlet[e] proves something which I had scarcely credited him with—that he is capable of reporting facts objectively. Of course, you had also made it easy for him.[79] The thing will have a very good effect. Now as regards the transfer to Geneva, it reminds me of the Central Authority's move to Cologne.[118] I would think this coup over *very thoroughly*. First, are the few jackasses worth it that you should take this step for their sake and hand over responsibility for the whole thing to people who, for all their good will, and also probably instinct, just do not have the stuff to lead a movement like this? Second, once we start moving house, and the holy respect for London, which is still the Medina of the emigration, has been replaced by a very doubtful respect for Geneva—what is the guarantee that the Proudhonists will not succeed in one fine day having the Council transferred, if only as

---

[a] What do you think about this? - [b] 31 July - [c] Lydia (Lizzie) and Mary Ellen Burns - [d] Charles Roesgen - [e] W. Eichhoff, *Die Internationale Arbeiterassociation...*

a matter of international *courtoisie*,[a] to Brussels or Paris? Finally: such centres should never be put in places where *deportation* is possible, as long as we have a spot free from this risk.

The more splendidly things go, the more important it is that you should keep them in *your* hands, and now that the business is also beginning to get under way in Germany, I do not believe that Becker[b] has the stuff to manage it.

I sent Kugelmann the biographical stuff on Friday from York.[106] It is a very good thing that something about your book[c] should now simultaneously appear in French papers, too. Nota bene, have at least 20-30 reprints made of my article in the *Fortnightly*[11] (for which we will naturally pay, *s'il le faut*[d]), they can be used very well. ANYHOW, the conspiracy of silence is now over, and if the thing is only blazing a path slowly, it is now doing it surely.

GRAVEL is *Kies*. For the various stages of the Irish peat-ground I have no expressions, you will have to ask an East Frisian.

Borkheim has already reminded me of the 'date of maturity'. Best greetings to the entire sea-bathing company.

Your
F. E.

First published abridged in *Der Briefwechsel zwischen F. Engels und K. Marx*, Bd. 4, Stuttgart, 1913 and in full in *MEGA*, Abt. III, Bd. 4, Berlin, 1931

Printed according to the original

Published in English for the first time

53

MARX TO ENGELS

IN MANCHESTER

London, 10 August 1868

DEAR FRED,

Enclosed letter from J. Morley, the CHIEF EDITOR of the *Fortnightly*. Beesly did everything he could, but Mr Morley found the matter not to his taste.[119] NEVER MIND!

The family is fortunately at the SEASIDE, which they all needed very much.

---

[a] politeness - [b] Johann Philipp Becker - [c] the first volume of *Capital*; see also Note 116 - [d] if necessary

What you say about the transfer of the CENTRAL COUNCIL[73] to Geneva is very correct. It remains possible that in Brussels, *malgré nous et contre nous*,[a] they will propose a CHANGE in order to document their heroic resistance to the *principe autoritaire*.[b] At least in this case our delegates will have to vote for Geneva as *pis aller*.[c]

Salut.

Your

K. M.

First published in *Der Briefwechsel zwischen F. Engels und K. Marx*, Bd. 4, Stuttgart, 1913

Printed according to the original

Published in English for the first time

54

MARX TO LUDWIG KUGELMANN[29]

IN HANOVER

London, 10 August 1868

Dear Kugelmann,

On receipt of your letter, I asked around, but in vain. At the moment it is impossible to get money from the UNIONS here for foreign STRIKES.[120] The various data about the Linden factory contained in the latest Hanoverian papers sent me are of great interest to me.

My family is, at present, at the seaside, which was all the more necessary since both GIRLS[d] seemed very delicate after their illness. Lafargue, after passing his SURGEON examinations here in London, will operate as assistant at his hospital for a few weeks, and then move to Paris where, however, he will still have to pass the French medical examinations.[121]

At the moment I am more occupied with PRIVATE than with PUBLIC ECONOMY. Engels has offered to be my guarantor for a loan of £100-150 at 5% interest, the first half payable in January, the second in July. So far, however, I have not been able to find a creditor.

I hope 'verry' much that the *state of my work* will allow me to abandon London for good and all and move to the continent next year, at the end of September. I shall strike my tents as soon as I

---

a despite us and against us - b authoritarian principle - c the lesser evil - d Jenny and Eleanor Marx

can dispense with the Museum[a] here. The high cost of living here is becoming increasingly burdensome as time goes on. It is true that the pettiness of conditions over there is not much to my taste, but 'tranquillity is the first duty of citizens',[122] and this is the only way to achieve tranquillity. There have been all sorts of rows here, in and with the so-called FRENCH BRANCH[72] of the INTERNATIONAL WORKINGMEN'S ASSOCIATION, about which I shall report in my next letter.[b]

I am at present *solus*,[c] and I feel strange, missing all the children's noise.

Salut.

Yours

K. Marx

First published abridged in *Die Neue Zeit,* Bd. 2, Nr. 7, Stuttgart, 1901-1902 and in full in *Pisma Marksa k Kugelmanu* (Letters of Marx to Kugelmann), Moscow-Leningrad, 1928

Printed according to the original

55

MARX TO FRIEDRICH LESSNER[123]

IN LONDON

London, 11 August 1868

Dear Lessner,

Because of the orthographic mistakes, I have re-written the whole appeal, enclosed herewith. Now you should copy it in *your own handwriting*.

Salut.

Your

K. M.

First published in: Marx and Engels, *Works,* First Russian Edition, Vol. XXIX, Moscow, 1946

Printed according to the original

Published in English for the first time

---

[a] the British Museum Library - [b] See this volume, pp. 173-75. - [c] alone

56

ENGELS TO MARX [48]

IN LONDON

[Manchester,] 12 August 1868

Dear Moor,

It would be worth the trouble to find out more about Mr Morley's motives,[a] even if this only leads to the conclusion that the petty, lousy cliquishness, which we used to assume only existed in Germany, also flourishes here. If Morley refuses the piece [119] despite Beesly's influence, then he has his *reasons*. These men are, *au fond*,[b] bourgeois, and MR Morley has all the reasons in the world to prevent giving publicity to things like those you have presented in your analysis. These are no *isms*; THAT KNOCKS HIM ON THE HEAD, and hence the lack of space. Still, I have no fear that we shall therefore be unable to present the book [c] to the English public, but the easiest and simplest way is cut off, and we shall have to search until we find a new one. In the meantime, the French articles will produce their effect,[116] and it would be a good thing if they could be shown to the gentlemen of the *Fortnightly*; it would be very nice if Mr Morley could still be forced to accept the piece.

The day after tomorrow I shall probably go for 10 days to Bridlington Quay (address: Mr *Burns*, 3 Burlington Place, Bridlington Quay, Yorkshire), since Charles [d] is recovering; but, of course, something may still crop up, in which case I shall write to you. I was there with Moore from Friday till Monday [e]; we made quite interesting geological studies.

Best greetings from Lizzie.

Your

F. E.

First published in *Der Briefwechsel zwischen F. Engels und K. Marx*, Bd. 4, Stuttgart, 1913

Printed according to the original

Published in English in full for the first time

---

[a] See this volume, p. 81.- [b] basically - [c] the first volume of *Capital*- [d] Charles Roesgen; see this volume, p. 80.- [e] from 7 to 10 August

57

MARX TO ENGELS [124]

IN MANCHESTER

[London,] 13 August 1868

DEAR FRED,

I hope that these lines will reach you before your departure, for there is *periculum in mora*.[a]

Firstly, I must send money to Ramsgate, so they can stay there another week. As their departure was delayed for weeks after your last remittance, smaller domestic debts were paid; on the other hand, my wife had to retrieve watches and other things from the pawnshop so that they could appear RESPECTABLE at the watering place.

Secondly, one of the *épiciers*,[b] who is owed £6 and a few shillings, must be paid this week, since the man is shutting up shop.

Thirdly, I have already received 2 SUMMONS for QUEEN'S TAXES (about £8). The LOCAL TAXES are paid, as you know. I absolutely cannot put off these sums.

For two further pressing items—the LANDLORD, who is unfortunately in London now, and a bill of exchange for £12 payable on the 25th of this month—I shall still perhaps receive money in time from Germany.

I have written to my cousins August and Karl Philips in Amsterdam and Aachen in order to find out whether they are back.[125] It would be a sheer waste of money to go to the continent in order to borrow, before one is sure that the people are there.

For the past week I have not had a wink of sleep and *l'illustre* Gaudissart[c] Borkheim, who visited me the day before yesterday to take leave, said I really should get rid of my jaundice. He entertained me with the story of the £1,000 he is trying to blackmail out of Oppenheim.

In great haste.

Your

K. M.

First published in *Der Briefwechsel zwischen F. Engels und K. Marx*, Bd. 4, Stuttgart, 1913

Printed according to the original

Published in English in full for the first time

---

[a] danger in delay (Titus Livius, *Rerum Romanorum ab Urbe condita libri*, Book XXXVIII, Ch. 25) - [b] grocers - [c] *L'illustre Gaudissart* was Borkheim's nickname (after the title character of a novel by Balzac).

58

ENGELS TO MARX [124]

IN LONDON

[Manchester, about 14 August 1868]

Dear Moor,

I shall send you money tomorrow, our cashier had no more notes this afternoon. Do not feel awkward about 'pressing', I only wish there were more there to be pressed out; but bear in mind as well that in 6 weeks we shall have to pay the £150 with interest, and Borkheim says that the interest will bring the total up to 165! I think you will have to make up your mind to go to Holland; we cannot 'afford' to borrow at *such* interest.

Faucher made me laugh very much.[83] Absolutely the noble arrogance of this fellow. The patronising introduction and then criticism (and what criticism!) of a very elementary thing in which you present the views of the *economists*, thus only make a resumé; he wisely keeps his fingers off your own things. Also very good is his admission that the present generation, including Faucher, knows nothing of either Jacob or Joseph, thus confirming your opinion that they 'really have learned nothing'. Incidentally, the impudence of the fellow is comic. He really assumes that his public knows nothing, will learn nothing, and even wishes to read nothing except such Faucherist piss. And the man is right about it.

Best greetings.

Your
F. E.

First published in *Der Briefwechsel zwischen F. Engels und K. Marx*, Bd. 3, Stuttgart, 1913

Printed according to the original

Published in English in full for the first time

59

MARX TO ENGELS

IN BRIDLINGTON QUAY

London, 21 August 1868

Dear Fred,

My wife returned from Ramsgate yesterday, but the children are still there. Since I have been puking gall for about 1 week, and, in addition, cholera is developing here, my wife insists that I should also go to the sea at Ramsgate for at least 2-3 days. So I shall be leaving today.[126]

The £25 received with many thanks: the bill of exchange for £12, as I assured myself today, falls due on 28 August. So far I have not yet received anything from the continental side.

It would be best if you send the money for the LIFE INSURANCE to me myself, on the date due, when I can pay the people. For they must, after all, hand over to me the promissory note that I signed. Dealing with this via Schyler would in fact compromise me.

Salut.

Your
K. M.

First published in *Der Briefwechsel zwischen F. Engels und K. Marx*, Bd. 4, Stuttgart, 1913

Printed according to the original

Published in English for the first time

60

ENGELS TO MARX

IN LONDON

Bridlington Quay, 22 August 1868

Dear Moor,

Best thanks for the *Lanterne* and the B. Becker.[a] The closer one comes to see the details of the Lassalle tragicomedy, the more the

---

[a] B. Becker, *Enthüllungen über das tragische Lebensende Ferdinand Lassalle's.*

comical side emerges. This man was ruined by his IRREPRESSIBLE reflection upon himself, his permanent self-contemplation. 'How do I appear to myself?' was the eternal refrain. Poor Baron Izzy! Comic at that exalted moment when he commissioned his *alter ego*, Rüstow, to bed the beautiful Helen[a] *per procura*[b] if necessary—he well knew how little danger this involved—as at that other moment when the Wallachian[c] shot away his genitals. Poor Izzy! To be gelded by a shot from a Wallachian.[d] You always found it so comical that his *gob* had been stopped, but now *this* as well.

Seiler! That is the impression of the whole story. Sebastian Seiler, the only worthy historiographer of this tragicomedy—he will hang himself that he missed this putrid scene. *En attendant*[e] it is quite amusing that the 'testamentary successor of Lassalle'[127] declares him an aristocrat, traitor and cad, and is forced to appropriate all those things that we formerly had published *against him himself* and against Schweitzer.[128] Bastards!

On Wednesday or Thursday[f] I shall go back to Manchester from here and shall then visit my mother for a week—probably in Ostend. I am still waiting for a letter from her, and have no idea where I stand in the meantime.[129]

Naturally I would have sent the money for the loan from the insurance company *only to you*, if you had not from the start shoved the whole affair away from you and onto Borkheim, so that I had to turn to him simply to find out how much had to be paid. *That* I could, of course, only do with the simultaneous remark that I would send the sum to him, since he was indeed standing surety for the money. As I already wrote to you, it would never have occurred to me to send the money to that jackass Schyler.[g] But I expect to see you before then, in London at the end of next week.

Your
F. E.

First published in *MEGA*, Abt. III, Bd. 4, Berlin, 1931

Printed according to the original

Published in English for the first time

---

[a] Helene von Dönniges - [b] by proxy - [c] Janko von Racowiţa - [d] In the original, a play on the word *Wallach* (Wallachian), also German for a gelding. - [e] Meanwhile - [f] 26 or 27 August - [g] See this volume, p. 87.

61

MARX TO ENGELS[33]

IN MANCHESTER

London, 26 August 1868

DEAR FRED,

Still no 'SUPPLIES' from Germany. It is, of course, idiotic to depend completely upon half-promises. But if you are drowning you clutch at every straw. On Friday[a] the bill of exchange for £12, about which I wrote to you,[b] is due. Since nothing had arrived by today, and to have no protest in the house, I just visited my baker, who told me he could '*perhaps*' get the money by tomorrow evening, but only for a few days. At the same time, I have received the enclosed scrawl from my LANDLORD. That everything should happen to one just at this time. It is enough to drive one mad.

Bring me back or send me the screed by Becker.[c] His theoretical-political-economic criticisms of Lassalle have been copied from your pamphlet on the military question.[d]

This Becker has done us a great service with his Seileriana. He deserves to be Lassalle's 'testamentary successor'.[127]

The invitation which I received to the congress of the General Association of German Workers (Hamburg, 22-25 August)[130] is signed by Schweitzer as President and by more than 20 workers from different districts of Germany (members of the *Executive Committee*). I had to take the latter into consideration in my reply.[e] I explained that I could not come because of the work of the Central Council of the International Working Men's Association, and said I was glad to see that the starting points of any 'serious' workers' movement—agitation for complete political freedom, regulation of the working day and international co-operation of the working class—were emphasised in their *programme* for the congress.[f] That is to say, in other words, I congratulated them on

---

a 28 August - b See this volume, p. 87. - c B. Becker, *Enthüllungen über das tragische Lebensende Ferdinand Lassalle's.* - d F. Engels, *The Prussian Military Question and the German Workers' Party.* - e 'To the President and Executive Committee of the General Association of German Workers'. - f 'Programm der Generalversammlung des Allgemeinen deutschen Arbeiter-Vereins, stattfindend in Hamburg, vom 22. bis 25. August 1868', *Die Zukunft*, No. 266, 10 July 1868, and *Der Social-Demokrat*, No. 98, 21 August 1868.

having abandoned *Lassalle's programme*.[a] Whether they will notice the point remains to be seen. Schweitzer, the only man with brains in the whole Lassalle gang, will certainly detect it. But whether he will think it advisable to show this or to pretend to be dense, *nous verrons*.[b]

Your

K. M.

First published abridged in *Der Briefwechsel zwischen F. Engels und K. Marx*, Bd. 4, Stuttgart, 1913 and in full in *MEGA*, Abt. III, Bd. 4, Berlin, 1931

Printed according to the original

Published in English in full for the first time

62

ENGELS TO MARX

IN LONDON

Manchester, 28 August 1868

Dear Moor,

I found your letter of the 25th[c] waiting for me here, and as promised yesterday,[131] I enclose 2 fivers and 1 tenner, with which his lordship the LANDLORD will have to content himself for the time being.

I expect a letter from my mother any day that she has arrived in Ostend, and I will immediately dash there[129]; I shall see you in London in any case, but it is doubtful whether I shall be able to stay there for a day on my outward journey.

In haste.

Your

F. E.

First published in *MEGA*, Abt. III, Bd. 4, Berlin, 1931

Printed according to the original

Published in English for the first time

---

[a] F. Lassalle, 'Offenes Antwortschreiben an das Central-Comité zur Berufung eines Allgemeinen Deutschen Arbeitercongresses zu Leipzig vom 1. März'.- [b] we shall see - [c] Engels apparently means Marx's letter of 26 August 1868.

63

MARX TO ENGELS

IN MANCHESTER

London, 29 August 1868

DEAR FRED,

The £20 received with BEST THANKS.

Tussy had a great shock today. She found Dicky dead in his cage although he was still singing merrily yesterday. He has been buried with full honours.

Dupont has received the mandate from Naples to represent the Neapolitan branch.[132] Since the Mentana business, as we see from Italian reports, there has been a general reactionary trend in domestic affairs, and in particular the workers' right to meet and form societies has almost been done away with.[133]

In Paris, happily, we still have our old people, *behind bars.* The committee there will send a *délégué* to Brussels, but against that the various *corps de métier*[a] will send 8-9.[134] Our people have written to us from prison suggesting that these *corps de métier* MEN should be 'compromised politically' so that there should be no way back for them. Just to show the sort of methods to which the Paris police have recourse: A gentleman calling himself 'Eugène Dupont' from London visited the wives of several of the prisoners to pump them. He was a police agent, but his play-acting did not work anywhere.

Eccarius left for Nuremberg as our *délégué* today.[135] From there he will go to Brussels. He is correspondent of *The Times* in both cases.[136]

The so-called *branche française,*[72] under the leadership of Messrs Pyat and Vésinier, is sending a delegate to Brussels in order— *horribile dictu*[b]—to put us in the dock!

Apropos. If Moore is still there, tell him it would be good if he could pay to me his USUAL CONTRIBUTION to the INTERNATIONAL WORKINGMEN'S ASSOCIATION *by Tuesday.*[c] We are weakly represented in Brussels, and every shilling that we can raise now will be used to

_____
[a] trade societies - [b] horrible to say - [c] 1 September

send one MEMBER MORE there. TUESDAY NEXT IS OUR LAST SITTING this year before the congress.[137]

Salut.

Your

K. M.

First published abridged in *Der Briefwech-sel zwischen F. Engels und K. Marx*, Bd. 4, Stuttgart, 1913 and in full in *MEGA*, Abt. III, Bd. 4, Berlin, 1931

Printed according to the original

Published in English for the first time

64

ENGELS TO MARX

IN LONDON

Manchester, 1 September 1868

Dear Moor,

Enclosed the £5 for Moore's SUBSCRIPTION to the INTERNATIONAL. So get me the receipt for him.

I am waiting on tenterhooks for a letter from my mother informing me of her arrival in Ostend and of her address. I am to go there for a few days,[129] and hear and see nothing. If there is no news by the day after tomorrow, hardly anything will come of it, since good old Gottfried[a] wishes to go away next week. As soon as I have news, I shall notify you by telegraph of my forthcoming arrival[b] in London.

I shall bring the Lassalle swindle[c] with me, or Schorlemmer, who has it, will send it to you as soon as he's read it.

Jones is holding OPEN AIR MEETINGS here for the workers,[102] but acts so tamely that he is already being attacked for it by his rival Henry. On Saturday[d] evening he called Gladstone 'THAT GREAT LEADER OF THE *WORKING CLASSES*!' I heard this myself. He is being *too* clever once again.

Your

F. E.

First published abridged in *Der Briefwech-sel zwischen F. Engels und K. Marx*, Bd. 4, Stuttgart, 1913 and in full in *MEGA*, Abt. III, Bd. 4, Berlin, 1931

Printed according to the original

Published in English for the first time

---

[a] Gottfried Ermen - [b] In the original: reply. - [c] B. Becker, *Enthüllungen über das tragische Lebensende Ferdinand Lassalle's.* - [d] 29 August

65

MARX TO ENGELS

IN MANCHESTER

London, 9 September 1868

DEAR FRED,

The £167 paid on 8 September, RECEIPT received and BOND received back.

I am sending you enclosed *The Times* and 2 issues of *The Daily News* about the INTERNATIONAL WORKINGMEN'S CONGRESS.[a][138] You must send back the *2 'Daily News' by return.*

You see from the FIRST LEADER of *The Times*[b] what a good policy it was to send our report[c] to it alone, with a few words TO THAT EFFECT.

In great haste.
Salut.

Your
K. Marx

First published in *Der Briefwechsel zwischen F. Engels und K. Marx*, Bd. 4, Stuttgart, 1913

Printed according to the original

Published in English for the first time

66

MARX TO GEORG ECCARIUS AND FRIEDRICH LESSNER[139]

IN BRUSSELS

London, 10 September 1868

Dear Eccarius and Lessner,

FIRST MY THANKS TO LESSNER FOR HIS LONG AND INTERESTING LETTER.[140]

You must not allow the congress[138] to last beyond this week.

---

[a] 'The Congress of the International Association of Workmen. From Our Special Correspondent. Brussels, Sept. 6, 7', *The Daily News*, 8 and 9 September 1868. - [b] *The Times*, No. 26225, 9 September 1868. - [c] K. Marx, 'The Fourth Annual Report of the General Council of the International Working Men's Association', contained in Eccarius' first dispatch on the congress (see Note 136). 'International Working Men's Congress (From a Correspondent)', *The Times*, No. 26225, 9 September 1868.

Until now—AS FAR AS ENGLAND IS CONCERNED—there has been nothing to discredit it.

If the Belgians and French should once again place masses of new stuff on the agenda, let them know it will not do,[141] since

1. the Germans are very poorly represented, as their congresses are being held almost simultaneously in Germany[142];

2. England is almost not represented because of the suffrage movement;

3. the German Swiss are not yet represented at all, since they have only just affiliated, and those branches long in existence have exhausted their funds in the Geneva strike[16];

4. the discussions are being conducted one-sidedly, in French;

5. therefore, *decisions on general theoretical questions* must be avoided, since this can only lead to protests later from the non-Belgians and non-French.

The public is naturally interested mainly in the question of war. Pompous declamations and high-faluting phrases do no HARM here. The decision to be taken in this connection would seem to be simply that the working class is not yet sufficiently organised to throw any decisive weight onto the scales; that, however, the congress protests in the name of the working class, and denounces those who instigate war; that a war between France and Germany is a civil war, ruinous for both countries and for Europe as a whole. A statement that war could only benefit the Russian government can hardly be made acceptable to the French and Belgian gentlemen.[a]

Greetings to friend Becker.[b]

K. Marx

If the question of *crédit mutuel* is raised, Eccarius should simply declare that the workers in England, Germany and the United States have nothing to do with Proudhonist dogmas and consider the credit question to be of secondary importance.

The resolutions of the congress should be telegraphed to the London newspapers. So don't do anything discreditable.

K. M.

First published in *Deutsche Worte*, Nr. 5,   Printed according to the journal
Jg. XVIII, 1898

---

[a] See this volume, p. 101. - [b] Johann Philipp Becker

67

MARX TO ENGELS

IN MANCHESTER

London, 12 September 1868

DEAR FRED,

Luckily the congress [138] ends today and up to Thursday [a]—that is as far as the news goes—it had only compromised itself tolerably. But one must always fear some public disgrace, since the Belgians form the enormous majority. Mr Tolain and other Parisians want to have the GENERAL COUNCIL moved to Brussels. They are very JEALOUS OF London. It is a great step forward that the Proudhonist 'braves Belges' [b] and French, who dogmatically declaimed against TRADES UNIONS, etc., in Geneva (1866) and Lausanne (1867), [143] are now most fanatically in favour. In spite of all their boasting, the 'braves Belges' had made no preparations. For example, the correspondent of The Daily News hunted in vain for 3 days for the possible meeting place until he accidentally ran into Jung and Stepney. In fact, the premises had not been booked in advance, and the 'braves Belges' wanted to charge the expenses (among others, those for their 250 participants) to the London GENERAL COUNCIL, to which they and the French owe about 3,000 frs. The sum is now being raised by private collections among the delegates.

I am in a bad scrape. Laura has fallen sick since you were here, [129] and my wife was forced to borrow £10 from her simply to meet the extra expenses, as we are absolutely broke.

I have heard nothing at all from Holland [c] and must therefore regard the silence as intentional. I really do not know what to do.

Apropos. It was a good thing that we changed the word CONVICTS into VICTIMS. [d]

---

[a] 10 September - [b] plucky Belgians - [c] from the Philips family - [d] This evidently refers to changes in 'The Fourth Annual Report of the General Council of the International Working Men's Association' written by Marx (present edition, Vol. 21, p. 13).

On the return of Shaw—who was sent at Moore's expense[a]—the latter will receive his RECEIPT.

Salut.

Your

K. M.

First published abridged in *Der Briefwechsel zwischen F. Engels und K. Marx,* Bd. 4, Stuttgart, 1913 and in full in *MEGA,* Abt. III, Bd. 4, Berlin, 1931

Printed according to the original

Published in English for the first time

68

MARX TO SIGFRID MEYER

IN NEW YORK

London, 14 September 1868
1 Modena Villas, Maitland Park,
Haverstock Hill

Dear Meyer,

Enclosed the issue of *The Times* containing the 4th ANNUAL REPORT of the GENERAL COUNCIL (written by *me*), and the very interesting *Times* FIRST LEADER on this document.[b] This is the first time that it has abandoned its tone of *moquerie* about the working class, and taken it 'verry' *au sérieux.* Spread this around. Inform Jessup of this.

I must reply to both your letters, the first to me and the 2nd to Eccarius, which was handed me in his absence (he has not yet returned from Brussels).

As far as the first letter is concerned, it is your fault if *Sorge* (who is *completely unknown* to me) has received credentials.[144] If you wanted simply to give him a recommendation for a particular purpose, you should have written so clearly. The way you put it in your letter, I believed that Sorge was *your and A. Vogt's man.* So be more careful in future. Then you made the second mistake of *giving* the credentials to Sorge, instead of writing to me first about the misunderstanding!

The mistake has been made, but it is not irreparable.

The Brussels Congress[138] has once again allotted the General

---

[a] See this volume, pp. 91 and 92. - [b] *The Times,* No. 26225, 9 September 1868.

Council to London. But it is now to be regarded as a *new* COUNCIL, which *revises* all *old* credentials. So write to me whether you and A. Vogt want credentials. Write, too, *in which manner* we should withdraw Sorge's credentials or, alternatively, inform him that the new General Council has changed the credentials.[145]

Drury was here for a while. Recently, shortly before the Brussels Congress, he was *proposed* as authorised agent of the INTERNATIONAL WORKINGMEN'S ASSOCIATION to the AMERICAN LABOR UNION[146] and its congress. We *did not agree to this at the time*, since the source of the suggestion[a] appeared *suspicious* to us. Please observe the man more closely first, either yourself or through friends.

No COPIES remain of the *Commonwealth* PAPER. For the past few years there have *not* been any *agitational* writings in our sense in England. *My book[b] has not yet been translated into English.*[147] Eccarius, otherwise very capable, but at the same time very AMBITIOUS, has *intentionally not mentioned it* in *The Commonwealth* or at other opportunities. He likes to appropriate my propositions *for himself.* At the congress in Brussels, Lessner mentioned *my book* in his speech about machinery. The correspondent of *The Daily News* reported this.[c] Eccarius, who reported the congress sessions for *The Times, suppressed* it.[136] His conduct is all the more absurd since he owes me not only his knowledge, but also his post as general secretary on the GENERAL COUNCIL. I alone supported him (at *The Commonwealth* too) against attacks by the English and French.[148] He relies upon the experience he already has with me, that I am only concerned with the cause, and ignore personal stupidities!

I shall *not* give him your letter.

The more English excerpts from my book you can get into the American press the better.[149]

Send them to me!

I attach the enclosed card. It was sent to us, with a letter, to establish contact with us. Address: G. W. Randall, SECRETARY, WORKINGMEN'S INSTITUTE, 3 Tremont Row, ROOM 52, *Boston* N. E.

I lost contact years ago with all my acquaintances in America. I am still in touch only with Meyer[d] in St. Louis, the friend of our J. Weydemeyer (deceased last year).

Write me all you can find out about the relationship between the railways and real estate.

a W. R. Cremer and Huleck (see this volume, pp. 177-78). - b the first volume of *Capital* - c 'The International Working Men's Congress. From Our Special Correspondent. Brussels, Sept. 9', *The Daily News*, 11 September 1868. - d Hermann Meyer

You may have seen that, at its congress in Hamburg, the General Association of German Workers passed a special resolution giving recognition to my book.[104]

Write to Randall on my behalf as GERMAN SECRETARY of the GENERAL COUNCIL.

Best greetings to A. Vogt and yourself.

Yours
K. Marx

I am sending 2 copies of *The Times*, one for you, the other for Jessup.[a]

<table>
<tr>
<td>First published in: Marx and Engels, Works, First Russian Edition, Vol. XXV, Moscow, 1934</td>
<td>Printed according to the original

Published in English for the first time</td>
</tr>
</table>

69

MARX TO HERMANN JUNG

IN LONDON

London, 14 September 1868

Dear Jung,

The Times today carries Eccarius' reports of the 9th and 10th.[b]

In the debate on machinery, he makes Lessner's SPEECH *worse*; it was much better in *The Daily News*. Lessner quoted my book,[c] as you have seen in *The Daily News*.[d] Eccarius *suppresses* the quotation.

Yet even better. In *The Daily News* the resolution about machines, etc., was noted as a *proposal from the GENERAL COUNCIL*.[e] In *The Times*, Mr Eccarius converts this into his *personal proposal*.[f]

---

[a] This sentence was inserted by Marx immediately under the address. - [b] [J. G. Eccarius,] 'The International Working Men's Congress. (From a Correspondent)', *The Times*, No. 26229, 14 September 1868 (see also Note 136). - [c] the first volume of *Capital* - [d] 'The International Working Men's Congress. From Our Special Correspondent. Brussels, Sept. 9', *The Daily News*, 11 September 1868. - [e] K. Marx, 'Draft Resolution on the Consequences of Using Machinery under Capitalism Proposed by the General Council to the Brussels Congress'. - [f] See this volume, p. 101.

This is a point on which you must collar him. His egotism needs a cuff TO SET HIM RIGHT AGAIN.

Yours

K. M.

First published in: G. Jaeckh, *Die Internationale*, Leipzig, 1904

Printed according to the original

Published in English for the first time

70

ENGELS TO MARX [34]

IN LONDON

Manchester, 16 September 1868

Dear Moor,

I can only write briefly and badly, I have rheumatism in my right hand and have been writing all the afternoon.

Enclosed a ten-pound note. When Borkheim returns, you absolutely must force him to undertake some sort of coup, if nothing else can be done. You will understand that I myself find things rather tight at the moment. Did you ever write to *Meissner* asking for a settling of accounts? With the workers bombarding from all sides now, the burking will soon come to an end, and the second edition [a] will not have to be awaited for long. *Now is the time* to insert a new advertisement for the book. Think one out, I shall send it to Meissner, whom I owe an answer anyway. But don't put it off. Furthermore, Meissner should be sent *The Times* with the resolution of the Germans in Brussels, the *Demokratisches Wochenblatt* of yesterday,[150] etc., the man must be kept happy. If you have not done it, do it (I can no longer get that No. of *The Times* here). And then the exchange value, too, will gradually come into effect for you.

The things in *The Times* in Eccarius' report [b] will be a big help to you here, and Mr Morley will be amazed.[c] The papers here also carry fairly full extracts from the report (but most in *The Daily News*).

---

[a] the second German edition of Volume I of *Capital*- [b] [J. G. Eccarius,] 'The International Working Men's Congress. (From a Correspondent)', *The Times*, No. 26230, 15 September 1868. - [c] See this volume, p. 81.

The congress went well after all. The method of conducting the babble in public and the BUSINESS on the quiet has worked splendidly. So, the COUNCIL will remain in London, and once again the Proudhonists have only the satisfaction of having resolved that *they* are Proudhonists, and nobody else is.

One might also send Meissner the No. of the *Zukunft* about Lloyd, etc., in which you are mentioned twice. I can do all this, if you want.

Moses Hess amused me greatly.[151]

But the question now arises: Has not a popular short presentation of the content of your book *for workers* become an urgent necessity? If it is not written, some Moses or other will come along and do it and botch it up. What do you think of it?

Enclosed also Eichhoff back.[a]

It is impossible to leave without stupidities being committed. While I was away,[129] the fellows on the *comité* of the Schiller Institute,[76] acting on the suggestion of the Bradfordians, invited that swine Vogt to give a lecture here. I naturally announced my resignation at once, 'in order not to give an indirect vote of confidence to a man who, I considered it proved, was a paid Bonapartist agent in 1859'.[b] The swine is coming tomorrow.

Your
F. E.

First published abridged in *Der Briefwechsel zwischen F. Engels und K. Marx*, Bd. 4, Stuttgart, 1913 and in full in *MEGA*, Abt. III, Bd. 4, Berlin, 1931

Printed according to the original

Published in English in full for the first time

71

MARX TO ENGELS

IN MANCHESTER

London, 16 September 1868

Dear Engels,

THANKS FOR THE £10. At the end of the letter I shall say more about money matters. First about 'general items'.

---

[a] W. Eichhoff, *Die Internationale Arbeiterassociation. Ihre Gründung, Organisation, politisch-sociale Thätigkeit und Ausbreitung.* - [b] F. Engels, 'To the Directorate of the Schiller Institute'.

The policy of sending the report solely to *The Times* has proved itself.[136] It has forced all London newspapers to speak, with the exception of the deeply-indignant Levy.[a] *The Times* did not accept Eccarius' reports from Nuremberg. It only took the bait after it had received the report from me.[b] *The Morning Advertiser* of yesterday carried (upsetting Blind) A FIRST LEADER in favour of the *International* against *The Times*.[c] The *Star* declares the congress to have been a 'SUCCESS'.[d] *The Standard*, which first attacked us, SNEAKS before the WORKING CLASS in a leading article yesterday.[e] It knocks the capitalists and will now even pull grimaces about the LAND QUESTION. The *Journal des Débats* regrets that the English and the Germans and the Belgians, as shown by the resolution on the land,[152] belong to the *'secte communiste'* and that the French, on the other hand, keep on reproducing *'les déclamations ridicules de Proudhon'*.[f]

People are very dissatisfied with Eccarius and next Tuesday[g] a storm will break that will do him good.[153] The points of the indictment are as follows:

He took almost *no part at all* in the congress and afterwards posed in *The Times* as the LEADING MIND. Also in *The Times*, he took over the *proposals of the GENERAL COUNCIL* as his private property, and ditto the applause for them as due to him. He suppressed as far as possible the speeches *of the others* and, to flatter *The Times*, *falsified* Dupont's concluding speech. Apart from this, Lessner has the GRIEVANCE that when he (Lessner) read from my book, Eccarius suppressed this in *The Times*,[154] ditto that he only included the resolution on the book[150] in his correspondence under HIGH PRESSURE, and finally that he falsified the German resolution on war.[155] He said that a European war would be a civil war, instead of saying, as the German resolution stated, THAT 'A WAR BETWEEN FRANCE AND GERMANY WAS A CIVIL WAR *FOR THE PROFIT OF RUSSIA*'. He completely omits the latter point. On the other hand, he attributes to the Germans and the English the Belgian nonsense that it was necessary TO STRIKE AGAINST WAR.

On the other hand, as a reporter he has done us some service. The long and the short of it is that he will be told that he should figure only as *reporter* in future, with the COUNCIL paying his

---

[a] of *The Daily Telegraph* - [b] K. Marx, 'The Fourth Annual Report of the General Council of the International Working Men's Association'. See also this volume, p. 93. - [c]'London, Wednesday, September 16', *The Morning Advertiser,* 16 September 1868. - [d] 'The International Congress of Workmen', *The Evening Star,* 15 September 1868. - [e] *The Standard,* 16 September 1868. - [f] 'Proudhon's ridiculous declamations' - [g] 22 September

travelling expenses and *The Times* paying for the articles. But he will *never again* be named as DELEGATE. Thus preserved from the CONFLICT OF FRACTIONS.

Lessner says that we accomplished so much despite being so little represented at the congress, which was almost entirely Belgian (with the addition of FRENCHMEN), because on all decisive points the Belgian workers, notwithstanding their Brussels LEADERS, voted with London. Moses is said to have made the best SPEECH against the Proudhonists.[151] Tolain was so furious that he did not appear at the banquet. Not only has the Central Council[73] here been appointed once again, but the list of members, *purified* by us, was accepted. Within four weeks Vésinier is to submit to a commission in Brussels proof of his suspicions regarding Tolain.[156] In case these are *baseless* (and they are), the congress has already conditionally *expelled* him from the Association as a slanderer. The delegate of the FRENCH BRANCH tabled a bill of indictment against the GENERAL COUNCIL which, among other things, contained the *modeste* demand that the French member of the GENERAL COUNCIL should be named by the FRENCH BRANCH. In response, the congress simply proceeded with the agenda (exactly as we have treated the GRIEVANCES of these fellows in the GENERAL COUNCIL).

At Nuremberg,[135] *Liebknecht* committed a completely useless stupidity (even one *contrary to the Rules*) by forcing upon the people Becker's confused wishy-washy stuff as the *Programme of the International Working Men's Association*.[157] Sonnemann remarked correctly that this was a *quid pro quo*.[a] But Mr Wilhelm wanted to have *democratic babble* for the *'People's Party'*![38]

Meissner wrote a few lines some weeks ago. He would only be able to render an account in some weeks. It appeared to him that up to the present *no profit* had been made. I am sending him *The Times* and Liebknecht[b] and the *Zukunft*[c] today. The *advertisement* will have to be done by you. I cannot advertise my own book.[d] And it would be a very good thing if you yourself wrote a small popular explanatory pamphlet. Let us hope that things will now get going.

As regards money matters, I simply cannot go on in this way. It makes all work impossible. I believe it would be best if you would write to Borkheim and ask him whether it was not possible to raise money for me somehow since, *after paying off the LOAN SOCIETY* and other accumulated debts, I was now in great difficulties because of

---

[a] confusion - [b] Liebknecht's paper, the *Demokratisches Wochenblatt* - [c] See this volume, p. 100. - [d] the first volume of *Capital*

extra expenses, including trousseau for Laura, who was soon going to Paris. (And this is in fact an *aggravating* circumstance!) I have studied Borkheim enough to know that he must believe that I have, WITHIN CERTAIN LIMITS, A SETTLED INCOME, but that I am in particular difficulties because there is as yet no income from the book, etc. He should think that you are writing to him behind my back. Of course, you must give him your guarantee, or rather promise it.

It is a very good thing that *Vogt* is in England[a] just when the INTERNATIONAL is arousing such interest. *He* can put two and two together.
Salut.

Your
K. M.

First published abridged in *Der Briefwech-sel zwischen F. Engels und K. Marx*, Bd. 4, Stuttgart, 1913 and in full in *MEGA*, Abt. III, Bd. 4, Berlin, 1931

Printed according to the original

Published in English for the first time

72

ENGELS TO MARX

IN LONDON

Manchester, 18 September 1868

Dear Moor,

I think you will not be able to enforce the intended exclusion of Eccarius from the congress; he will be indispensable, as a delegate too. Apart from this, it is very good, however, that he does not get away with this, and that there are various people WHO WILL WASH HIS HEAD, as Lafargue says.

As regards the advertisement (*annonce*) about your book,[b] it is absurd to claim that you could not write it yourself. You even wanted to write it yourself when I sent you one that you did not like.[c] Be so kind as to return to this matter, and send me the advertisement you promised me then. I shall then pass it on to

---

[a] See this volume, p. 100. - [b] the first volume of *Capital* - [c] See this volume, p. 8.

Meissner. But we shall have to support him somewhat so that his good will does not weaken.

In puncto[a] money I shall write to Borkheim willingly as soon as you inform me that he is back. Apropos this matter, you must, however, let me know what happened when you drew the loan. For how much did you insure your life, at what premium, and is the policy still valid? Because it might still be possible to get a new loan or an advance on the policy itself from the same society. But how am I to raise money for you if you leave me quite in the dark about all these matters? If I can reach agreement with Gottfried Ermen, who will scarcely return before the end of October, I shall immediately be able to raise some funds once again, but everything depends on this. If I can *not* reach agreement with him, my own position will become very uncertain. It can, however, take until the end of this year before the matter is settled, and this means another $3^1/_2$ months.[158]

William the Handsome[b] is getting exuberant now that his Bismarck has left him.[159] The drive towards war is becoming ever clearer. For all that, I believe it is now too late for this year. Purchasing horses and the actual mobilisation still require more time in France than in Prussia, and despite all the preparations and bragging I do not believe that the French need less than 6 weeks for this. As the domestic supply of horses is insufficient, the beginning of the actual mobilisation, that is to say, now, the firm decision to strike, will inevitably be marked by large purchases of horses abroad, which immediately becomes public knowledge. Even now it will be a long time before they can have the *entire* number of horses necessary for war. Little Louis[c] will have to give 5-6 weeks NOTICE, and this brings us to the end of October; and especially with the enormous masses now involved, a winter campaign would certainly only be waged in an extreme emergency. If there are not quite special reasons, we are pretty safe until March-April, and all sorts of things can happen before then.

In addition, Louis still does not *have* anything like the number of men he needs. He will hardly be able to raise more than 650,000 troops of the line (*gendarmerie, garde municipale* and all sorts of other police troops figure in the army budget), and much of the *garde mobile* does not even exist on paper. It takes at least 6/7 years to fully implement a changed military system, and his is only one year old. I do not believe that Louis wants a war precisely at this moment, if he can avoid it, since every month of delay

---

a As regards - b William I - c Napoleon III

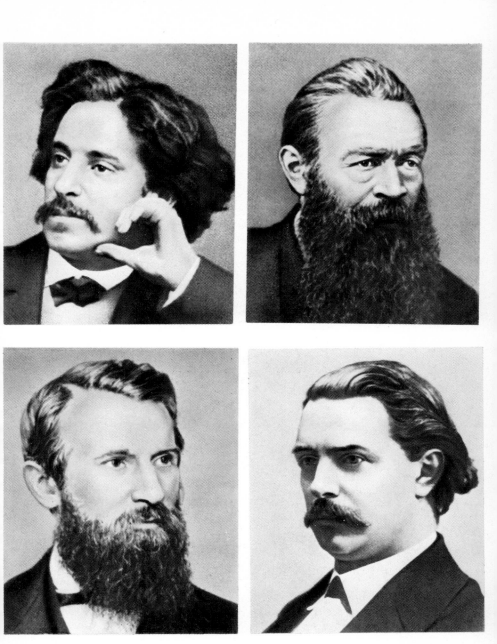

Marx's and Engels' correspondents:
Paul Lafargue, Johann Philipp Becker, Friedrich Lessner, Ludwig Kugelmann

Georg Eccarius, Robert Applegarth, Nikolai Danielson

brings stronger reinforcement to *his* forces than to those of Prussia.

I hope Laura is well again? Best greetings.

Your
F. E.

First published in *Der Briefwechsel zwischen F. Engels und K. Marx*, Bd. 4, Stuttgart, 1913

Printed according to the original

Published in English for the first time

73

MARX TO ENGELS

IN MANCHESTER

London, 19 September 1868

DEAR FRED,

Enclosed a letter from Schweitzer,[160] ditto one from Essen and also 6 numbers of the *Social-Demokrat*. I must have all this stuff back by *Tuesday*.[a] What answer should I give the cunning Schweitzer? You will see from the debates of the *General Association of German Workers congress*[104] (in the *Social-Demokrat*) that the 'true-blue' Lassalleans smelt that their president was leaving Lassalle's course in proposing a congress for the establishment of TRADES UNIONS and settlement of STRIKES.[161] He only received permission to launch this agitation independently of the Association of German Workers by threatening to resign. His purpose, of course, is to get in ahead of Liebknecht, etc. He was also aware that, with the development of a *real* workers' organisation in Germany based on TRADES UNIONS, his artificial sectarian Association WOULD SOON BE NOWHERE. What he now describes in a LEADER (No. 104)[b] as the summa of Lassalle's discoveries: 'state credit for the foundation of productive associations', is literally copied from the programme of French *Catholic* socialism, *duce*[c] Buchez, in the *Atelier* at the time of Louis Philippe.[162] I must answer diplomatically and would like to know your view.

---

[a] 22 September - [b] 'Der allgemeine deutsche Arbeiter-Congress. II', *Der Social-Demokrat*, No. 104, 6 September 1868. - [c] led by

Vogt is no longer available here.[a] But yesterday I wrote to Liebknecht and categorically requested information about the copies (perhaps 150) sent to him.[163]

Next Tuesday[b] at the first session of the GENERAL COUNCIL there will be stormy weather. Dupont is also furious about Eccarius because he took as good as no part in the congress.[153] I shall try to protect Eccarius against 'positive' measures,[c] but this time I shall not be able to take sides for him so strongly as I did last year against Fox, Carter, etc.[148]

A *Bordelais*,[d] merchant, friend of Lafargue, English-speaking, passed through here after a journey through Sweden and Denmark. He told Lafargue that in higher circles there they speak much about my book,[e] which does not sound very likely to me.

Laurachen is somewhat better. Her SUFFERINGS are connected with certain natural processes of development. They want to leave at the beginning of October, and this is awkward because the linen part of the trousseau is still incomplete.

L'illustre Gaudissart[f] returned today.

The loan was like this: You borrow money FOR A CERTAIN TERM. If you die before maturity, the sum need *not* be paid back. On the other hand, in the contrary case repayment must be made on the date of maturity with the STIPULATED interest. The transaction is then *at an end*. It is thus no life insurance. You do not receive a policy, but the money, for which you make out a BOND. This was naturally returned to me. It is the peculiar form that makes the whole business so expensive—certainly the worst and the dearest way to borrow money.

The sole circumstance which would, in my opinion, favour Bonaparte in a belated campaign is that Russia would then be more paralysed, at least for military action. One thing is certain. The whole of France believes that war is IMMINENT.

As for the advertisement, I shall *d'abord*[g] see what Meissner answers. I have asked him about it.[h]

How did things go with fat Vogt?[i]

Salut.

Your

K. M.

The report on the Brussels Congress in the *Opinion nationale* states, inter alia:

---

[a] Marx means his book *Herr Vogt.* - [b] 22 September - [c] See this volume, pp. 101-02. - [d] man from Bordeaux - [e] the first volume of *Capital* - [f] Sigismund Borkheim - [g] first - [h] See this volume, p. 102. - [i] Ibid., p. 100.

'Je dois mentionner ici le rapport général de l'Association, rédigé par le conseil de Londres. *Mentionner*, c'est bien le seul mot que je puisse employer, car, je ne suis point assez fort légiste pour trier et élaguer les phrases incriminables par les lois de France, et il s'en pourrait trouver quelques-unes de ce genre.'[a] Speaks then of the PASSAGES dealing with *'le gouvernement français'.* 'La critique y est verte parfois, et souvent ironique. Je le répète, je ne puis m'en faire juge; mais je dois avouer que le public a été moins timide que votre correspondant; il a couvert d'applaudissements frénétiques tous les passages que je m'abstiens de citer.'[b]

There were 12 REPORTERS from France there.

The *Émancipation*[c] and the *Journal de Bruxelles*[d] attacked the congress in exactly the same way as they attacked us 20 years ago.

One Russian was there as a journalist. He said he would send the General Council the Russian papers that wrote about the congress.

First published abridged in *Der Briefwechsel zwischen F. Engels und K. Marx*, Bd. 4, Stuttgart, 1913 and in full in *MEGA*, Abt. III, Bd. 4, Berlin, 1931

Printed according to the original

Published in English for the first time

74

ENGELS TO MARX

IN LONDON

Manchester, 21 September 1868

Dear Moor,

Enclosed returned the Schweitzer stuff.[160] The man is an idiot to believe that he can bribe you with such a letter. In making you chief of 'Europe' in general, he hints delicately that your kingdom

---

[a] 'I must mention here the general report of the Association, drafted by the Council in London. *Mention* is in fact the only word which I can use since I am not sufficiently qualified in law to identify and weed out the phrases punishable under French law, and there could well be some of this sort in it' (from J. I. Blanc's report on the Brussels Congress of the International Working Men's Association in *L'Opinion nationale*, 10 September 1868). - [b] 'The criticism here is sometimes sharp and often ironical. I repeat I cannot make a judgment; but I must admit that the audience was less timid than your correspondent; it received with frantic applause all those passages which I refrain from quoting' (ibid). - [c] *L'Émancipation belge*, No. 254, 10 September 1868, leading article. - [d] *Journal de Bruxelles*, Nos 252, 254-260; 8, 10-16 September 1868.

is, for this very reason, not in any country in particular, i.e., strictly speaking, not of this world. He appoints you Pope so that you may anoint him Kaiser of Germany, and thus give a kick to Wilhelm.[a] In any case, it is worth much that you have *this* letter in your hands.

I think you should, above all, point out to the philistine that his workers' congress[164] only makes sense if it is a *genuine* workers' congress, not merely a feeble imitation of his Hamburg congress; i.e. if Schweitzer sees to it that non-Lassallean elements are also represented. So far, there is no sign of this, and Schweitzer does not appear to have taken any steps in this direction. Whether he 'can make friends' with Wilhelm and others or not, is completely immaterial; in a matter like this he must go along with them. Then, regarding the statutes, you could write to him that what counts is less what is in them than how they are handled.

The fellow obviously wishes to push out Wilhelmchen, Bebel and consorts, and be able to appeal to something in writing from you for this purpose. That must be very important to him, otherwise he would never have written you this letter, which delivers him absolutely into your hands for ever. You are quite right that he sees that a few Lassallean phrases will no longer do and that he must expand.

If I am not mistaken you also gave Wilhelmchen copies of the *18th Brumaire.*[b] Some of them should be brought here, I no longer have a copy.

I shall write to Gaudissart.[c]

The Spanish business[165] could end all the war clamour. *La innocente Isabel*[d] was the only reliable ally that Louis[e] had, and if a revolution should be victorious in Spain, the whole constellation will assume a different character. The affair will probably be decided very quickly; I believe the Innocent Lady is *foutue.*[f]

Your
F. E.

First published in *Der Briefwechsel zwischen F. Engels und K. Marx,* Bd. 4, Stuttgart, 1913

Printed according to the original

Published in English for the first time

---

[a] Wilhelm Liebknecht - [b] K. Marx, *The Eighteenth Brumaire of Louis Bonaparte.* - [c] Sigismund Borkheim - [d] Isabella II - [e] Napoleon III - [f] finished

75

MARX TO ENGELS

IN MANCHESTER

London, 23 September 1868

DEAR FRED,

From the enclosed you will see that Liebknecht wants to get rid of Schweitzer through me, just as Schweitzer wants to get rid of Liebknecht.[166] I have replied to Wilhelm[84]: No overhastiness! If he acts with tact, Schweitzer will himself SETTLE DOWN TO MORE MODERATE 'PROPORTIONS' or ruin himself. The dissolution of the General Association of German Workers[167] brings Lassalleanism *qua*[a] such to a forcible end, although it still may carry on for SOME TIME A LINGERING SECT LIFE.

I enclose Schweitzer's report in the *Social-Demokrat* on the catastrophe.[b]

I completely share your view that the Spanish revolution (it has the same significance as the Neapolitan revolution of 1848[168]) gives a new turn to European history and, in particular, like a *deus ex machina*, cuts the Gordian knot of the repulsive German-French war.

Strohn has just arrived from the continent. So, more next time.

Your

Moor

The Times paid Eccarius 2 ¹/₂ GUINEAS per column, sang hymns of praise to him, and made him advantageous proposals. Send Wilhelm[c] back to me.

First published in *Der Briefwechsel zwischen F. Engels und K. Marx*, Bd. 4, Stuttgart, 1913

Printed according to the original

Published in English for the first time

---

[a] as - [b] [J. B.] Schweitzer, 'An die Mitglieder des Allg. deutsch. Arb.-Vereins', *Der Social-Demokrat*, No. 110, 20 September 1868.- [c] Wilhelm Liebknecht's letter to Marx of 16 September 1868.

76

ENGELS TO MARX

IN LONDON

Manchester, 24 September 1868

Dear Moor,

So *that* is the reason for the sycophantic letter from Schweitzer! [a] The fellow obviously knew what was in store for him when he wrote to you. On the one hand, it may not be altogether unwelcome to him that he can drop the strict Lassallean religion, but fundamentally the loss of the 'tight' organisation and of the possibility to play at dictator is certainly fatal to him. Of course, this is the end of the Lassallean sect's self-important pretence that *it* is 'the party' in Germany, and the sect will gradually expire; it will continue to twitch the longest in the Bergisches Land, the real home of sects.

Incidentally, as Wilhelm [b] rightly guesses, his associations will also come under attack. [169] So much the better. The petty-bourgeois-people's-party-federalist fad of these fellows is not worth a penny. And it is a good thing that the government really stirs up the workers, once it sees that the workers won't let themselves be used by it against the bourgeoisie. Some form or another will surely be found.

But what a comrade Wilhelm is! Less than 4 months since he entered into a 'sort of alliance' with Schweitzer, [105] and today they are again at loggerheads, and he is too SLIPPERY for him. He knew that before, didn't he—but what about the fine lads he had 'assigned to watch him'!

What is this proclamation that you are supposed to issue by all means? [166] And these fine phrases in it about 'persons' which Wilhelm might construe against Baptist [c] and Baptist against Wilhelm! The South German democrat is impossible to get rid of, once you have him in your system. One might think Wilhelm was writing to Struve.

Schlöffel (the elder) has turned up again *in Silesia*. I am folding into the returned *Social-Demokrat* some curiosa from the *Zukunft*.

If you had only gone to Nuremberg! You would have been

---

a See this volume, pp. 105 and 107-08. - b Wilhelm Liebknecht; see this volume, p. 109. - c Baptist Schweitzer

compensated and afterwards been able to start again from the beginning with the SUFFERINGS. I tell you the fellow still can't distinguish you from Struve.

Apropos the dissolution of the General Association of German Workers [167] Wilhelm could now reprint the pertinent passages from my pamphlet,[a] in which all this was predicted for the Lassallean gentlemen. What do you think about it? I could prepare the muck for him, as I still have a few copies here.[170]

Your
F. E.

First published abridged in *Der Briefwech-sel zwischen F. Engels und K. Marx*, Bd. 4, Stuttgart, 1913 and in full in *MEGA*, Abt. III, Bd. 4, Berlin, 1931

Printed according to the original

Published in English for the first time

77

MARX TO ENGELS [80]

IN MANCHESTER

London, 25 September 1868

Dear FRED,

Can you send me £5 by Saturday[b] morning? One of the TRADESMEN just called and told me he was on the verge of bankruptcy and would have great expenses if he had not raised A CERTAIN SUM from HIS CREDITORS by Saturday.

Your
K. M.

First published in *MEGA*, Abt. III, Bd. 4, Berlin, 1931

Printed according to the original

---

a *The Prussian Military Question and the German Workers' Party.* - b 26 September

78

MARX TO ENGELS

IN MANCHESTER

London, 25 September 1868

DEAR FRED,

BY ALL MEANS do the stuff for Liebknecht [170] as quickly as feasible. Otherwise, the fellow will do it himself and, you may depend upon it, do it *badly*. It appears to me it would be a good thing if you were also to draw attention to what Bernhard Becker stole from your pamphlet [a] and endorsed, after bitter experience, in his shitty pamphlet.[b] (He cursed us so horribly when he was still 'President of Humanity'.[171]) You can have the pamphlet right away if you write immediately to Strohn, who took it with him to Bradford.

The time has now come to KICK this 'Lassalleanism' 'just for a start'. And there is no need at all to allow B. Becker's shitty pamphlet to be buried in silence.[172]

The 'appeal' the fiery Wilhelmchen speaks of [166] is this: I (i. e. in the name of the INTERNATIONAL ASSOCIATION, as its SECRETARY FOR GERMANY) must naturally address SOME GENERAL LINES to the German workers, now that their relationship to us has changed as a result of their various congress decisions. But no undue haste is necessary in so doing. In all these things 'more haste, less speed', and, as we know, our Wilhelmchen has shown no 'haste' with the matter for 6-7 years.

Quant à[c] Schweitzer, I had a sort of presentiment that some turning point WAS LOOMING SOMEWHERE. Although my reply to him had therefore been ready for some days [d] — (in which I with school-masterly reserve point out to him, in particular, the difference in conditions between a sectarian movement and a real class movement) — I have, nevertheless, held the stuff back. And I will now only answer him after the results are available of his fresh attempt to call a congress in Berlin for forming TRADES UNIONS.[164] In any case, Schweitzer has learned one thing about me, that the promptness with which I answer his letters is always in inverse proportion to their 'warmth of feeling'.

---

[a] F. Engels, *The Prussian Military Question and the German Workers' Party*. - [b] B. Becker, *Enthüllungen über das tragische Lebensende Ferdinand Lassalle's*. - [c] As for - [d] See this volume, pp. 132-35.

Wilhelm has only ONE COPY left of *The 18th Brumaire.*
How did things go with *Vogt's* LECTURES in the Schiller Institute [76]?

Your
K. M.

Blanqui was in constant attendance during the Brussels Congress.

In a BLUE BOOK [173] about the crisis of 1857,[a] *Cardwell,* CHAIRMAN of the COMMITTEE of Inquiry and the most disgusting washerwoman in the Peelite clique of old women, asks *Dixon* (MANAGING DIRECTOR of a bank which had failed in Liverpool) whether the SHAREHOLDERS of the bank had consisted largely of women, parsons and other persons with no knowledge of banking. BY NO MEANS, Dixon replied, they were mainly 'MERCANTILE MEN' but, he added very KNOWINGLY:

'THE MAJORITY OF THEM ARE PEOPLE IN BUSINESS, MERCANTILE MEN; BUT HOW FAR MERCANTILE MEN CAN BE CONSIDERED COMPETENT TO FORM AN OPINION *ON ANY OTHER BUSINESS THAN THEIR OWN,* IS *RATHER* A QUESTION.' Is that not nice?

Apropos!

Moore should send me Foster's *On Exchange* from his lending library, since it is not in the library here. I shall send it back immediately.

First published abridged in *Der Briefwechsel zwischen F. Engels und K. Marx,* Bd. 4, Stuttgart, 1913 and in full in *MEGA,* Abt. III, Bd. 4, Berlin, 1931

Printed according to the original

Published in English for the first time

79

ENGELS TO MARX

IN LONDON

Manchester, 25 September 1868

Dear Moor,

Enclosed the desired five pounds in one bank note.

The business in Spain [165] must be going well, since the government has so little good news to announce. Still, it is surprising that the telegraphs to the frontiers have not yet been

---

[a] *Report from the Select Committee on the Bank Acts; together with the Proceedings of the Committee, Minutes of Evidence, Appendix and Index. Ordered, by the House of Commons, to be Printed, 1 July 1858.*

cut. This proves that the Innocent Lady[a] *could* very well go to Madrid if she really wanted to.

Your

F. E.

First published in *MEGA*, Abt. III, Bd. 4, Berlin, 1931

Printed according to the original

Published in English for the first time

80

MARX TO ENGELS[174]

IN MANCHESTER

London, 26 September 1868

DEAR FRED,

BEST THANKS FOR £5. These lousy little SHOPKEEPERS are a wretched class. My wife immediately took the money to the house of the dun. The man himself had 'made himself scarce' for the time being (and he is in his way quite a decent fellow); his wife, dripping with tears, accepted the money for him. Many, in fact most, of these SHOPKEEPERS experience all the misery of the proletariat, plus the 'fear' and 'serfdom of respectability', and without the COMPENSATING self-esteem of the better workers.

Apropos. The squabble among the authorities of the TRADES UNIONS, which in fact paralysed them for years, has at last been settled. THE LONDON TRADES' COUNCIL (Odger et Co.), London WORKINGMEN'S ASSOCIATION (Potter et Co.) and the AMALGAMATED TRADES UNIONS (I believe the main office is at present Sheffield, it changes annually) have finally agreed on *joint action.*[175] This is the outcome of the bourgeois CAMPAIGN aganist the TRADES UNIONS.

I return the last numbers of Schweitzer,[b] since you may need them in the article for Wilhelm.[170] Keep them in Manchester, but in such a way that they can be found again if needed. I do not believe that Schweitzer had an idea of the impending blow. Had this been the case he would scarcely have clucked so triumphantly about the 'tight organisation'.[c] I believe it was the 'INTERNATIONAL

---

[a] Isabella II - [b] *Der Social-Demokrat* - [c] [J. B.] Schweitzer, 'An die Mitglieder des Allg. deutsch. Arb.-Vereins', *Der Social-Demokrat*, No. 110, 20 September 1868.

WORKINGMEN'S ASSOCIATION' that moved the Prussian government to this decisive blow. As for the 'warm fraternal' letter from Schweitzer to me,[160] this is explained simply by his fear that following the Nuremberg decision[135] I might now publicly speak up for Wilhelm[a] and against him. Such a polemic would certainly be awkward after the Hamburg affair[104] (*le bonhomme*[b] had written to me requesting me kindly to come to Hamburg in person, 'to have the well-earned laurels placed upon my brow'!).

The most essential thing for the German working class is that it should cease to agitate by permission of the high government authorities. Such a bureaucratically schooled RACE must undergo a complete course of 'self help'. On the other hand, they undoubtedly have the advantage that they are starting the movement at a period when conditions are much further developed than they were for the English and that, as Germans, they have heads on their shoulders capable of generalising. Eccarius is full of praise for the parliamentary propriety and tact that reigned at the Nuremberg congress, particularly compared with the French at Brussels.[138]

In Spain things still look doubtful; but it appears to me that the movement can be suppressed only for a short time at the most.[165] One thing I do not understand is that the LEADERS did not wait until the 'Innocent Lady'[c] had left Spain and was visiting Bonaparte. Could it be that the latter himself had a hand in the game?

Salut.

Your
K. M.

One of Schweitzer's most ridiculous operations—to which, however, he is absolutely forced by the prejudices of his army and as the president of the General Association of German Workers— is that he regularly pledges himself *in verba magistri,*[d] and each time he makes a new concession to the needs of the real workers' movement he argues timidly that this does *not* contradict the dogmas of the Lassallean faith, the only guarantee of eternal salvation. The Hamburg Congress instinctively and quite correctly recognised that the General Association of German Workers, as the specific organisation of the Lassallean sect, was endangered by the real workers' movement operating through TRADES UNIONS, etc.,

---

[a] Wilhelm Liebknecht - [b] the good man - [c] Isabella II - [d] on the words of the master (Horace, *Epistles*, Book I, Epistle I)

and that by participating in these officially it would forfeit the distinctiveness that constitutes its *point d'honneur* and *raison d'être.*

First published in *Der Briefwechsel zwischen F. Engels und K. Marx,* Bd. 4, Stuttgart, 1913

Printed according to the original

Published in English in full for the first time

81

MARX TO ENGELS

IN MANCHESTER

London, 29 September 1868

Dear FRED,

Enclosed and attached letter from Eichhoff [176] together with 2 issues of the *Social-Demokrat* [a] and the *Staatsbürger-Zeitung.*

You will see from them that 'boozy' Schulze-Delitzsch has succeeded in giving momentary importance to Schweitzer's stage-trick; that Schweitzer's whole congress consists *only* (minus 12 men) of Lassalleans [177]; and that Schweitzer believes that he can in a very simple way replace his dictatorship over the General Association of German Workers by the dictatorship over the German working class. That is very naive.

The sole practical question for us is: Should I or should I not issue an appeal *at this moment*? In view of its position, the General Council must maintain an impartial stand. Would it not therefore be better to wait until 1. the nullity of the results of Schweitzer's game has become more apparent and, 2. Liebknecht and Co. have really organised something?

It appears to me that the power of the General Council greatly depends upon its not tying itself down prematurely and never doing so without certainty of success; it should, rather, practise Russian diplomacy in its operations.

If you share this view (and you must declare yourself in 2-3 days), I can simply write to Wilhelm and Eichhoff that the majority of the General Council has declared itself against any public proclamation until the elements that have joined the

---

[a] *Der Social-Demokrat,* Nos 112 and 113, 25 and 27 September 1868.

International Working Men's Association are sufficiently organised to provide the necessary backing.

Your
K. M.

In the meantime Lassalleanism, which is already crumbling, can be further subverted UNDERHAND as, e.g., by your article.[a]

First published abridged in *Der Briefwechsel zwischen F. Engels und K. Marx*, Bd. 4, Stuttgart, 1913 and in full in *MEGA*, Abt. III, Bd. 4, Berlin, 1931

Printed according to the original

Published in English for the first time

82

ENGELS TO MARX

IN LONDON

Manchester, 30 September 1868

Dear Moor,

Once you have entered into contact with Schweitzer in your capacity as Secretary FOR GERMANY,[b] I do not see how you could do anything except observe complete neutrality between him and Wilhelmchen—at least in official conduct. As far as I know, the Lassalleans accepted your programme in Hamburg,[104] so more cannot be expected. One must simply leave it to Schweitzer to destroy himself; if we ourselves were in Germany, things would be different.

Even from the previous *Social-Demokrat* I saw that he wanted to transfer his 'tight organisation' to the TRADES UNIONS[c]; now we have to wait and see whether he succeeds, which I do not believe. TRADES BUSINESS is money business, and there dictatorship ends of itself. And the substitution won't work as easily as the *bonhomme*[d] believes.

The COUNCIL can and may only take sides when it is itself attacked directly or indirectly, or when the principles of the

---

[a] F. Engels, 'On the Dissolution of the Lassallean Workers' Association'. - [b] See this volume, p. 76. - [c] Engels presumably means the article 'Zum Allgemeinen deutschen Arbeiter-Congress. Berlin, 24. September' in *Der Social-Demokrat*, No. 112, 25 September 1868. - [d] good man

Association are infringed. This is precisely how it acted at the time with regard to the Parisians.[178]

Moreover, what is Wilhelmchen's organisation[169] so far, what has been the effect of the Nuremberg decision?[135] Have societies really affiliated, paid subscriptions, etc.? I know nothing about it. And what does Wilhelm want to do in relation to Schweitzer's STRIKE organisation?[164] What else does he want to organise? All this is still very unclear to me.

Furthermore: What practical effect would it have if you and the General Council issued a declaration against the Lassalleans? I believe very little, at most the sect as such would stick together the more firmly. And what can they be reproached with? That they do not follow W. Liebknecht? As long as the fellows have trust in Schweitzer, and as long as Liebknecht and Schweitzer squabble, all sermonising about unity is sheer folly.

To attack the Lassalle stuff in *literary* form is quite another matter. But to proscribe him, so to speak, would only consolidate a sect which is otherwise in disintegration.

I suggest you also find occasion to give Schweitzer a piece of your mind concerning his dictatorial ambitions, if you write to him at all. After all, he wanted to send you the drafts first.[160]

Apropos. The letter from *Eichhoff*[176] *was not enclosed.*

Vogt.[179] I could not write to you about this since Schorlemmer was in the LAKES, and I myself naturally asked no questions. So far, I only heard yesterday that the lecture did not cover the expenses, that Vogt, though he has always given the same lecture for the past year, nevertheless spoke very stumblingly and sloppily, often repeated himself, etc. After the lecture some people sat with him in the dining room, where the good Vogt was, however, so pressed with questions about the monkey trial by the Unitarian preacher Steinthal (brother of Weerth's[a]), by Kalisch, an old boring language teacher, and by yet another fellow, that he was absolutely overwhelmed and sneaked off at the first opportunity. He is said to have felt altogether very uneasy and uncomfortable here, while in Bradford he was very fêted and buoyant. He made a few remarks to Davisson which caused the latter to note afterwards that he must be quite a nasty fellow, capable of anything. I shall be hearing more. In any case, *he* will not come here again.

Your

F. E.

---

[a] The brother of Weerth's principal is meant.

You will probably be hearing from Borkheim shortly, otherwise from me *in re nervi rerum*.[a]

First published abridged in *Der Briefwechsel zwischen F. Engels und K. Marx*, Bd. 4, Stuttgart, 1913 and in full in *MEGA*, Abt. III, Bd. 4, Berlin, 1931

Printed according to the original

Published in English for the first time

83

ENGELS TO MARX [180]

IN LONDON

Manchester, 2 October 1868

Dear Moor,

Borkheim has done his business excellently. At the end of last month the sum of £72 was due for wine which Charles,[b] Gumpert and I had received from him. It was only at the beginning of this month, however, that I could lay my hands on the cash. So I sent it to him yesterday and asked whether he knew how to raise £100 for you or whether he could leave the wine unpaid until February. He agreed to the latter and advanced the other £28 himself. So we have, I think, peace and quiet at least for the immediate future.

But now you must get on with the 2nd volume,[41] and give your liver some exercise.

The Spanish business [165] has gone brilliantly so far. The 'dynasty' had already been wrecked in the vagina of the Innocent Lady.[c] So the minimum consequence: a change in dynasty and an elected king, plus a constituent assembly. All very nice things, even in themselves, on Mr Bonaparte's frontier. It may get better yet.

Schweitzeriana[d] back this evening, forgotten yesterday by mistake. His manner of establishing a few nice little posts for life for himself and Fritzsche is priceless. But the whole story is impracticable. In the 'Union' 3 independent powers of different origin! 1. The committee, elected by the *trades*. 2. The presidium, elected by a general vote. 3. The congress, elected by the *local organisations*. This means collisions everywhere, and that is

---

a with regard to vital (here: money) matters - b Charles Roesgen - c Isabella II - d See this volume, p. 116.

supposed to make for 'rapid action'. To be sure, the *elú du suffrage universel,*[a] as everybody's trusted agent, is in the best position. Childish of Lassalle to have taken over these idiocies from the French Constitution,[181] and of Schweitzer to treat them as eternal models to be used everywhere.[b] However it may be, the whole business will get nowhere so long as only the Lassalleans are in it, and as soon as others participate, too, the stuff will come to an end.

Have to catch the last post.

Your
F. E.

Enclosed the ceremonial RECEIPT which the illustrious Gaudissart[c] has accepted from you to prove that he is a serious businessman.

First published in *Der Briefwechsel zwischen F. Engels und K. Marx,* Bd. 4, Stuttgart, 1913

Printed according to the original

Published in English in full for the first time

84

MARX TO ENGELS

IN MANCHESTER

London, 4 October 1868

DEAR FRED,

In the package which you will receive simultaneously there are:
1. Two letters from *Eichhoff,* the *forgotten one* and one which *arrived today*[182];
2. Letter from Liebknecht[183];
3. Letter from Borkheim[184];
4. Manuscript and letter from J. Dietzgen[185];
5. Letter from the Russian Danielson in Petersburg[186];
6. Letter from Lessner.
Since most of these letters (which you must return with the exception of the manuscript) have only just arrived, in all haste the following:

---

[a] man elected by universal suffrage - [b] See also this volume, p. 135. - [c] Sigismund Borkheim

Ad No. 5. I am naturally extraordinarily pleased to hear that my book will appear in Petersburg in *Russian* translation. I shall immediately send the people what they requested[a] (as far as I can) as soon as you have returned the letter.

Ad 4. Read through the manuscript. My view is that J. Dietzgen would do best if he condensed all his ideas into *2 printed sheets* and had them printed in his name as a tanner. If he publishes them at the intended length, he will make a fool of himself because of the lack of dialectical development and the running in circles. Read it through and write your opinion.

Ad 3. To understand Gaudissart's[b] letter, briefly the following: He wanted to write about the Pan-Slav democratic movement; for this I gave him your articles about Bakunin in the *Neue Rheinische Zeitung.*[c] His plan to appear with *you* before the public is excellent, but there is no hurry because he has not turned out his 25 printed sheets by a long way yet.

Secondly, he maintained a certain correspondence, despite my warning, with Dr Crapper, alias Elard Biscamp. Now that the latter has directly attacked me and the International in the *Weser-Zeitung* and the *Augsburgerin,*[d] he proposes, as you see, to publish in Liebknecht's paper his latest exchange of letters with Biscamp. *Ce brave*[e] Gaudissart! In these letters he presents himself as *my* patron, and lets Biscamp flatter *him.* I wrote to him by return that I would have to protest tooth and nail against this sort of thing.[84] For greater security I immediately wrote to *Liebknecht* that he *must not print* the Borkheim-Biscamp correspondence *under any circumstances.*[84]

Ad 1 and 2. I have sent to Liebknecht for his political review an *entrefilet*[f] about *M. Hirsch* (because of the 'International'), and, at the same time, a few blows at Biscamp as correspondent of the *Weser-Zeitung* and the *Augsburger.*[g]

Ad 6. The £100 (of which ABOUT £35 for Laura) I have used to pay off the most urgent things and only kept as much on hand as is necessary in order not to be absolutely penniless. I still have about £100 of debts and will soon send you a list of the ITEMS so that you can see that there are no useless expenditures on my part. Now I received the enclosed note from Lessner today. His

---

[a] See this volume, pp. 123-25. - [b] Sigismund Borkheim's - [c] F. Engels, *Democratic Pan-Slavism.* - [d] [E. Biscamp,] 'London, 25. Sept.', *Allgemeine Zeitung,* No. 273, 29 September 1868 (published in the column *Grossbritannien,* signed Δ). - [e] Good old - [f] a short article - [g] K. Marx, 'Connections Between the International Working Men's Association and English Working Men's Organisations'.

wife is mortally ill, and it would be very kind of you to enable me to pay him off something.

IN ALL HASTE.

Your

K. M.

First published in *Der Briefwechsel zwischen F. Engels und K. Marx,* Bd. 4, Stuttgart, 1913

Printed according to the original

Published in English for the first time

85

ENGELS TO MARX

IN LONDON

Manchester, 6 October 1868

Dear Moor,

Enclosed Lessner's letter and bill and five pounds. I shall see to it that at least *this* bill will be paid off bit by bit.

I have scarcely been able to have a look at the other things, for I was so horribly busy today. Tomorrow I shall send you back the letters.

Best greetings to your wife and the girls, including Lafargue.

Your

F. E.

First published in *Der Briefwechsel zwischen F. Engels und K. Marx,* Bd. 4, Stuttgart, 1913

Printed according to the original

Published in English for the first time

86

MARX TO NIKOLAI DANIELSON[34]

IN PETERSBURG

London, 7 October 1868
1 Modena Villas, Maitland Park, N. W.

Dear Sir,

In reply to your esteemed letter,[186] the following:
1. You must not wait for the second volume, the publication of which will be delayed by perhaps another 6 months.[187] I cannot finish it, until certain official *enquêtes,*[a] instituted during last year (and 1866) in France, the UNITED STATES and England, have been completed or published. In any case, Volume I constitutes a whole, complete in itself.
2. Enclosed is my photogram.
3. Socialist literature does not exist in the UNITED STATES. There are only workers' papers.
4. I myself possess no collection of my works, which were written in various languages and published in various places. Most of them are out of print.

Since I am unable to meet your request in this respect—*la plus belle fille de France ne peut donner que ce qu'elle a*[b]—I shall have to confine myself to giving you some brief notes on my literary-political activity, which you might be able to use in the preface to your translation.[188]

Dr K. Marx, born 1818 in Trier (Rhenish Prussia).
1842-43: Redacteur en chef[c] of the *Rheinische Zeitung (Cologne).* This newspaper is forcibly suppressed by the Prussian government. Marx goes to Paris; publishes there, together with Arnold Ruge, the *Deutsch-Französische Jahrbücher (Paris, 1844).* At the end of 1844, Marx is expelled from France by Guizot; proceeds to *Brussels.* Together with *Friedrich Engels* publishes *Die heilige Familie, oder Kritik der kritischen Kritik. Gegen Bruno Bauer und Consorten (Frankfort on the Main, 1845).* (This work, like the essays by Marx in the *Deutsch-Französische Jahrbücher,*[d] are directed against the ideological mysticism of Hegelian and, in general, speculative philosophy.) Also published during the stay in Brussels: *Misère de*

---

[a] enquiries - [b] the most beautiful girl in France can only give what she has - [c] Editor-in-Chief - [d] *On the Jewish Question* and *Contribution to the Critique of Hegel's Philosophy of Law. Introduction.*

la philosophie. Réponse à la Philosophie de la misère de M. Proudhon (Brussels and Paris, 1847).
Discours sur le libre Échange (Brussels, 1848 [189]). Finally, at the beginning of 1848, together with *Friedrich Engels: Manifest der Kommunistischen Partei* (London).

Shortly after the outbreak of the February revolution, Marx is expelled from Belgium; receives at the same time from the French provisional government an invitation to return to France [a]; proceeds to Paris and, in April 1848, to *Cologne* (Germany), publishing there:

Neue Rheinische Zeitung (from June 1848 to May 1849). Also there:

Zwei Politische Prozesse (Cologne, 1849). (Containing the trial proceedings and Marx's defence speeches at the Assizes.[b] Marx charged on one occasion with insulting the *procureur du roi*,[c] and on the other, after the Prussian coup d'état (Manteuffel), with inciting rebellion. In both cases Marx acquitted by the jury.)

In the course of *May 1849*, the *Neue Rheinische Zeitung* is suppressed by the Prussian government and Marx expelled from Prussia.[d] Proceeds once more to Paris. Again expelled from France [e]; proceeds at the end of October *1849* to *London*, where he still resides. During his stay there, publishes:

Neue Rheinische Zeitung. Politisch-ökonomische Revue (1850, Hamburg and New York).

Der 18te Brumaire des Louis Bonaparte (New York, 1852).

Enthüllungen über den Kommunisten-Prozess zu Köln (1853, two editions, one in Basle, one in Boston, UNITED STATES).

FLY-SHEETS AGAINST LORD PALMERSTON [f] (*London, Birmingham, Glasgow,* 1853-1854).

Zur Kritik der politischen Oekonomie (Berlin, 1859).

Herr Vogt (London, 1860).

1851-1861, continuous contributions in *English* to the *New-York Tribune, Putnam's Revue* [190] and *The New American Cyclopedia*.[g]

1864: The foundation programme of the 'INTERNATIONAL WORKING-MEN'S ASSOCIATION', that is: ADDRESS TO THE WORKING PEOPLE OF EUROPE [h] and

---

[a] See 'Ferdinand Flocon to Marx in Brussels. Paris, March 1, 1848' (present edition, Vol. 6, p. 649). - [b] K. Marx and F. Engels, 'The First Trial of the *Neue Rheinische Zeitung*' and 'The Trial of the Rhenish District Committee of Democrats'. - [c] Royal Prosecutor (Zweiffel) - [d] See present edition, Vol. 9, p. 496. - [e] Ibid., pp. 526-27. - [f] K. Marx, *Lord Palmerston*. - [g] See present edition, Vols. 11-18. - [h] K. Marx, *Inaugural Address of the Working Men's International Association*. In: *Address and Provisional Rules of the Working Men's International Association...*

the *Rules* of the Association,[a] later (1866) definitively sanctioned at the congress of the International Working Men's Association at Geneva. Marx continuously, up to the present, MEMBER OF THE GENERAL COUNCIL OF THE INTERNATIONAL WORKINGMEN'S ASSOCIATION, AND ITS SECRETARY FOR GERMANY.

1867: Das Kapital etc.

Yours faithfully,

Karl Marx

First published in *Minuvshiye gody* (Bygone Years), No. 1, St. Petersburg, 1908

Printed according to the original

Published in English in full for the first time

87

ENGELS TO MARX

IN LONDON

Manchester, 8 October 1868

Dear Moor,

I have been terribly plagued with COMMERCE these days, so I can only return the letters today.[b]

Schweitzer is a special case. The fellow is more cunning and more active than all his opponents together, although this time he has certainly been *too* cunning—according to the *Kölnische Zeitung* the real workers' assemblies which are now appearing are everywhere repudiating the presidents imposed upon them by the 'Congress',[164] and these SELF-ELECTED fellows, up to and including Schweitzer, will realise that, as soon as there is real BUSINESS, these tricks and attempts to impose their sect upon the real movement as a leadership are no longer effective.

As Secretary for Germany you will of course have to correspond with the UNIONS that might be formed, as long as counter-UNIONS are not formed within the individual trades, when a choice would have to be made between the two—or could they both affiliate? In this respect, you will have English PRECEDENTS.[191] Of importance is only

---

[a] *Rules.* In: *Rules and Administrative Regulations of the International Working Men's Association* - [b] See this volume, p. 120.

the point that Schweitzer and his people should always be reminded that they are corresponding with the *Secretary for Germany,* not with *Karl Marx,* and you will see to this.

The Russian translation [a] is very gratifying; as soon as the matter has gone a little further, this should be got into the press.

I have not yet been able to look at the manuscript by Dietzgen. [185]

Gaudissart [b] becomes increasingly amusing. The 30 printed sheets are not dangerous for the time being; since they are supposed to appear simultaneously in 4 languages it will probably still take an eternity. As a Jew he simply cannot stop cheating, and it serves him right that he has burnt his fingers on Biscamp.

Wilhelmchen [c] is not bad either. Regarding the Swabians, it thus appears to be *money* matters that bind him and his people to the federalists. This should be investigated more closely, afterwards all this will fall on our shoulders. I had drawn his attention to the fact that at a moment when revolutionary action came nearer, it was absolutely *against* the interests of our Party that our people should be too closely committed to one party in the basically rotten antagonism between Greater Prussia and Austrian-Federalist Greater Germany. The unfortunate fool still cannot see that the entire antithesis with its two sides is a case of narrow-mindedness pure and simple. I thought the Spanish revolution [165] would have made him see some light, but NO GO.

I have seen no details yet about the course of the Schweitzer congress and its effects, since I only receive the *Zukunft* late.

Best greetings.

Your
F. E.

First published abridged in *Der Briefwechsel zwischen F. Engels und K. Marx,* Bd. 4, Stuttgart, 1913 and in full in *MEGA,* Abt. III, Bd. 4, Berlin, 1931

Printed according to the original

Published in English for the first time

---

[a] of the first volume of *Capital;* see this volume, p. 123. - [b] Sigismund Borkheim; see this volume, p. 121. - [c] Wilhelm Liebknecht

88

MARX TO ENGELS[174]

IN MANCHESTER

London, 10 October 1868

DEAR FRED,

THANKS FOR THE £5. I have given Lessner £8.[a] There is, incidentally, a fairly important mistake in his bill which he had, however, corrected before the intervention of my wife.

Enclosed letter from Schweitzer[192] together with a number of the *Social-Demokrat* which he sent me in the letter. You must return the letter to me by Tuesday,[b] together with your ADVICE. We cannot TEMPORISE any longer. So that you knew exactly how matters stand, the following:

For the time being, I have written to Liebknecht[84] that I COULD TAKE NO ACTION, that Schweitzer had hitherto given no official occasion, that an intervention on my part could only consolidate Lassalleanism, etc.

As TO Schweitzer, I have not yet answered his previous letter,[160] the dispatch of which he is probably now cursing. Since his TRADES UNIONS CONGRESS[164] was so near, I thought it better to await 'the course of events', and TO WATCH HIS OPERATIONS. Now I must, of course, break my silence.

As regards the letter from Schweitzer, it is clear that he does not feel quite happy in his boots. His threat of 'open war' is silly, though the phrase is 'OSTENSIBLY' only aimed against Liebknecht et Co. His claim that Mr Nobody started it, is in no way correct. His alleged identification with the International Working Men's Association stands in a certain contradiction to his HINTS in the *Social-Demokrat* after the Nuremberg affair that his association had 'not' joined the IWA. Above all it emerges from the whole letter that Schweitzer still cannot drop his fixed idea that he has 'his own workers' movement'. On the other hand, he is unquestionably the most intelligent and most energetic of all the present workers' leaders in Germany, while Liebknecht IN POINT OF FACT was only forced by Schweitzer to recall that there existed a workers' movement independent of the petty-bourgeois democratic movement.

My plan is not to use diplomacy but to tell Schweitzer the unvarnished truth about my view of his dealings, and make it clear

---

a See this volume, p. 122. - b 13 October

to him that he must choose between the 'sect' and the 'class'. If he wishes to come to a *rational* understanding with the 'Nuremberg majority',[135] I am ready as 'Secretary for Germany' to be of aid on TERMS which appear reasonable to me. If he does not desire this, I can only promise to maintain the necessary objective impartiality vis-à-vis his agitation. What I cannot promise, however, is that I will not, in my private capacity, publicly attack the Lassallean superstition as soon as I regard this as useful.[a]

Pretty and truly Lassallean is Schweitzer's notion that 'two organisations can only be harmful' and hence, since he preceded the others, they are, if not legally, then in a way morally, obliged to 'dissolve' themselves in him.

As you know, Mr Odger is standing for Chelsea, but I believe he has no chance of success. Odger has shown us the COLD SHOULDER for the whole of last year since, on my proposal, 'the *president* of the IWA' and thus also 'President' Odger were abolished once and for all.[193] Now he gives thanks for his re-election by the Brussels Congress and wishes us to support his election with a letter to his ELECTIONEERING COMMITTEE. We are only meeting his request because it is a step that is useful to the International and that recommends it in the eyes of the London WORKMEN.[194]

When you were here last,[129] you saw the Blue Book[173] on the Irish land question 1844-1845. BY ACCIDENT I found the REPORT and EVIDENCE on IRISH TENANT RIGHT 1867 (HOUSE OF LORDS) in a small second-hand bookSHOP. This was a real find. The economist gentlemen regard it purely as a question of conflicting dogmas whether rent is payment for natural differences in land, or on the other hand merely interest on the capital invested in the land; but here we have a real life and death struggle between FARMER and LANDLORD *as to how far* rent *should* include, *apart from* the payment for land differences, *also* the interest on the capital invested in the land not by the LANDLORD but by the tenant. Political economy can only be turned into a positive science by replacing the CONFLICTING DOGMAS by the CONFLICTING FACTS, and by the real antagonisms which form their concealed background.

Salut.

Your

K. M.

First published abridged in *Der Briefwechsel zwischen F. Engels und K. Marx*, Bd. 4, Stuttgart, 1913 and in full in *MEGA*, Abt. III, Bd. 4, Berlin, 1931

Printed according to the original

Published in English in full for the first time

[a] See this volume, p. 135.

89

ENGELS TO MARX

IN LONDON

Manchester, 12 October 1868

Dear Moor,

Enclosed the Schweitzeriana returned with thanks.[a] I completely share your view on the therapy in this case. But he will scarcely be ready to part with 'his own workers' movement'. His ambitions exceed his strength, or, as the Italians put it, *vuol petare più alto del culo*,[b] and on this inner contradiction he will work himself to death.

In my view, the statutes[c] are *absurd* for this purpose, but it is immaterial in the end.

And please do not omit the final sentence about the attack on the Lassallean superstition; this will be effective with the fellow, who is well aware that the whole stuff is HUMBUG.

I was unable to write to you while I was in town, and now it is nearly 8 o'clock, when the post closes out here, so I cannot add anything.

The picture of Lizzie is horrible, but still the least bad after five sittings.

Your
F. E.

First published abridged in *Der Briefwechsel zwischen F. Engels und K. Marx*, Bd. 4, Stuttgart, 1913 and in full in *MEGA*, Abt. III, Bd. 4, Berlin, 1931

Printed according to the original

Published in English for the first time

---

a See this volume, p. 127. - b he wants to fart higher up than his backside - c 'Mustersatzung für die einzelnen Arbeiterschaften' and 'Satzung für den Arbeiterschaftsverband', *Der Social-Demokrat*, No. 118, 9 October 1868 (supplement).

90

MARX TO LUDWIG KUGELMANN[29]

IN HANOVER

London, 12 October 1868
1 Modena Villas, Maitland Park

My dear Friend,

Your obstinate silence is quite incomprehensible to me. Did I perhaps give cause for it in my last letter?[a] I hope not. In any case—unintentional. I need not explain to you explicitly, you *know* that you are my most intimate friend in Germany, and I really cannot understand how, *inter amicos*,[b] people can keep such a sharp lookout, all because of some trifle. Least of all have you *such a right* with regard to me, for you know how much I owe you. Apart from everything personal, you have done more for my book[c] than all Germany put together.[195]

Yet perhaps you are so energetically silent in order to prove to me that you are not like that set of so-called friends, who are silent when things go badly, and speak when they go well. But there is no need for such a demonstration on your part.

By speaking about the 'good state of affairs' I mean, first, the propaganda made by my book and the recognition it has received from the German workers SINCE YOU WROTE ME LAST. Second, however, the wonderful progress made by the International Working Men's Association, particularly in England, too.

A few days ago a Petersburg publisher[d] surprised me with the news that a Russian translation of *Capital* is now at the printers.[196] He asked for my photogram as a vignette for the title page, and I could not deny this trifle to 'my good friends' the Russians. It is an irony of fate that the Russians, against whom I have been fighting incessantly for 25 years, not only in German, but also in French and English, have always been my 'patrons'. In 1843-1844 in Paris, the Russian aristocrats there waited on me hand and foot.[197] My book against Proudhon (1847), ditto that published by Duncker (1859),[e] have nowhere had such good sales as in Russia. And the first foreign nation to translate *Capital* is Russia. Yet not too much should be made of all this. The Russian aristocracy are educated, in their youth, at German universities and in Paris.

---

a See this volume, pp. 82-83. - b among friends - c the first volume of *Capital* - d N. P. Polyakov - e Karl Marx, *The Poverty of Philosophy...* and *A Contribution to the Critique of Political Economy*

They always yearn for the most extreme the West has to offer. It is pure *gourmandise*, like that practised by part of the French aristocracy during the 18th century. *Ce n'est pas pour les tailleurs et les bottiers,*[a] as Voltaire said at the time about his own Enlightenment. It does not hinder the very same Russians from becoming scoundrels as soon as they enter government service.

I am having plenty of 'BOTHER' JUST NOW in Germany with the leaders' squabbles, as you will see from the enclosed letters, which you will please return. On one side Schweitzer, who is appointing me Pope *in partibus infidelium,*[b] so that I can proclaim him the workers' emperor in Germany. On the other side Liebknecht, who forgets that it was, IN POINT OF FACT, Schweitzer who forced him to recall that there is a movement of the proletariat that is different from the petty-bourgeois democratic movement.

I hope you and your family are well. I hope I have not fallen into disfavour with your dear *wife.*[c] Apropos. The International Ladies' Association, *duce*[d] Mrs Goegg (READ Geck[e]), has sent an epistle to the Brussels Congress,[138] asking whether the ladies might join us.[198] The answer, of course, was a courteous affirmative. Should you, therefore, continue in your silence, I shall send your wife credentials as correspondent of the General Council.

I have been suffering rather a lot from the heat, on account of my liver, but am, at the moment, well.

Salut.

Yours

Karl Marx

P.S. I. The Spanish revolution[165] came like a *deus ex machina* to prevent the otherwise unavoidable and DISASTROUS Prussian-French war.

P.S. II. You once wrote to me that I would be receiving a book by Büchner.[f] When and how?

First published abridged in *Die Neue Zeit*, Bd. 2, Nr. 7, Stuttgart, 1901-1902 and in full in *Pisma Marksa k Kugelmanu* (Letters of Marx to Kugelmann), Moscow-Leningrad, 1928

Printed according to the original

---

[a] It is not for tailors or cobblers - [b] in parts inhabited by unbelievers—formula added to the title of Roman Catholic bishops holding purely nominal dioceses in non-Christian countries. - [c] Gertrud Kugelmann - [d] leader - [e] 'Geck' (German) means 'fop' - [f] L. Büchner, *Sechs Vorlesungen über die Darwin'sche Theorie von der Verwandlung der Arten...*

91

MARX TO JOHANN BAPTIST VON SCHWEITZER [199]

IN BERLIN

[*Draft*]

To von Schweitzer

London, 13 October 1868

Dear Sir,

A misunderstanding on my part accounts for your having received no reply to your letter of 15 September. I interpreted the letter as meaning that you would submit your 'proposals' to me for examination.[160] So I waited for them. Then came your congress,[164] and (BEING MUCH OVERWORKED) I regarded a reply as no longer urgent. Before the arrival of your letter dated 8 October, I had already *repeatedly* appealed for *peace*, in my capacity as secretary of the International for Germany. I received the answer (and with it relevant quotations from the *Social-Demokrat*) that you yourself were provoking *war*. I declared that my role must necessarily be confined to that of 'impartial referee' at a duel.[a]

In your letters you express great trust in me, and I believe I cannot respond better than to give you my opinion of the present state of affairs quite openly, without any diplomatic circumlocution. In doing so, I assume that, for you, as for myself, the cause is all that matters.

I recognise, without reserve, the intelligence and energy with which you are active in the workers' movement. I have concealed this view from none of my friends. Wherever I have to express my views in public—in the General Council of the International Working Men's Association and in the German Communist Association here[b]—I have always treated you as a man of our party, and *never* let drop *a word about points of difference.*

However, such points of difference do exist.

D'abord,[c] as regards the Lassallean Association,[104] it was formed in a period of reaction. After fifteen years of slumber, Lassalle— and this remains his immortal service—re-awakened the workers' movement in Germany. But he made great mistakes. He allowed himself to be influenced too much by the immediate circumstances

---

[a] See this volume, p. 127. - [b] the German Workers' Educational Society in London (see Note 67) - [c] First

of the time. He made the minor starting point, his opposition to the dwarf-like Schulze-Delitzsch, the central point of his agitation—state aid versus self-help.[200] In this, he merely re-adopted the slogan circulated in 1843 sqq. by *Buchez,* the leader of *Catholic* socialism, against the genuine workers' movement in France.[162] Being far too intelligent to regard this slogan as anything but a transitory *pis-aller,*[a] Lassalle was only able to justify its use on the grounds of its immediate (alleged!) PRACTICABILITY. To this end, he had to claim that it was feasible in the *immediate* future. The 'state' was, therefore, transformed into the Prussian state. He was thus forced to make concessions to the Prussian monarchy, to Prussian reaction (the feudal party) and even to the clericals. He linked Buchez's state aid for associations with the Chartist call for universal suffrage.[201] He overlooked the difference between conditions in Germany and England. He overlooked the lessons of the *bas-empire,*[b] with regard to universal suffrage in France. In addition, like everyone who claims to have in his pocket a panacea for the sufferings of the masses, he gave his agitation, from the very start, a religious, sectarian character. In fact, every sect is religious. And just because he was the founder of a sect, he denied all natural connection with the earlier movement, both in Germany and abroad. He fell into Proudhon's mistake of not seeking the real basis of his agitation in the actual elements of the class movement, but of wishing, instead, to prescribe for that movement a course determined by a certain doctrinaire recipe.

Most of what I am stating here *post factum* I predicted to Lassalle when he came to London in 1862 and called upon me to place myself, with him, at the head of the new movement.

You yourself know the difference between a sect movement and a class movement from personal experience. The sect seeks its *raison d'être* and its *point d'honneur* not in what it has *in common* with the class movement, but in the *particular shibboleth distinguishing* it from that movement. Thus when, in Hamburg, you proposed convening a congress to found TRADES UNIONS,[164] you could only suppress the opposition of the sectarians by threatening to resign as president. You were also forced to assume a dual personality, to state that, in one case, you were acting as the leader of the sect and, in the other, as the representative of the class movement.

The dissolution of the General Association of German Work-

---

[a] expedient - [b] Lower Empire (designation of the late Roman, or Byzantine Empire, and also of any empire on the decline); here, the Second Empire in France.

ers[167] provided you with an opportunity to take a big step forward and to declare, to prove *s'il le fallait*,[a] that a new stage of development had been reached and the sect movement was now ripe to merge into the class movement and end all 'eanisms'. With regard to the true content of the sect, it would, like all former workers' sects, carry this as an enriching element into the general movement. Yet instead you, in fact, demanded that the class movement subordinate itself to a particular sect movement. Your non-friends concluded from this that you wished to conserve your 'own workers' movement' under all circumstances.

Regarding the Berlin Congress,[164] the time was *d'abord* not pressing, since the Combination Law has not yet been voted.[202] You ought, therefore, to have reached an agreement with the leaders *outside* the Lassallean circle, worked out the plan together with them, and convoked the congress. Instead of this, you left them only the alternative of either publicly joining *you*, or lining up *against you*. The congress itself appeared to be only an extended edition of the Hamburg Congress.[104]

As for the draft statutes,[b] I regard them as unsuitable in principle, and I believe I have as much experience as any of my contemporaries in the field of TRADES UNIONS. Without going further into detail here, I shall merely remark that a *centralist* organisation, suitable as it is for secret societies and sect movements, contradicts the nature of the TRADE UNIONS. Were it possible—I declare it *tout bonnement*[c] to be impossible—it would not be desirable, least of all in Germany. Here, where the worker is regulated bureaucratically from childhood onwards, where he believes in authority, in those set over him, the main thing is *to teach him to walk by himself.*

Your plan is also impracticable in other ways. In the 'Union' there are to be three independent authorities of differing origin: 1. The *Committee*, elected by the *trades*; 2. the *President* (here a completely superfluous personage) {In the Rules of the International Working Men's Association there also figures a President of the Association.[d] In reality his only function was to preside at the sessions of the General Council. On my proposal, this office—which I had refused in 1866—was completely abolished in 1867, and was replaced by that of a CHAIRMAN, who is elected at each

---

a if necessary - b 'Satzung für den Arbeiterschaftsverband', *Der Social-Demokrat*, No. 118, 9 October 1868 (supplement). - c in all good faith - d Article III of the Rules. See *Rules and Administrative Regulations of the International Working Men's Association*, London, 1866.

weekly session of the General Council.[193] The LONDON TRADES' COUNCIL[175] also has simply a CHAIRMAN. Its sole permanent official is the *Secretary*, as he has a continuous business function to exercise.} {*NB*. This passage follows in the copy of the letter to Schweitzer after the end of this sentence}, elected by a *general vote*; 3. the Congress, elected by the *local branches*. Thus—collisions everywhere, and this is supposed to promote 'rapid action'! (At this point the inserted sentence.) Lassalle committed a bad mistake in borrowing the '*président élu du suffrage universel*'[a] from the French Constitution of 1852. And now this in a TRADES UNIONS movement! The latter is mostly concerned with financial issues, and you will soon discover that all dictatorialism finds its end here.

Yet whatever the shortcomings of the organisation, they can perhaps be cancelled out, to a greater or lesser degree, by rational application. As secretary of the International I am ready to act—naturally on a rational basis—as mediator between you and the Nuremberg majority,[b] which has adhered to the International directly.[135] I have written in the same vein to Leipzig.[c] I understand the difficulties of your position, and never forget that each of us depends more upon circumstances than upon his own will.

I promise you, under all circumstances, the impartiality that is my duty. On the other hand, I cannot promise that I shall not, some day, acting as a *private author*,—as soon as I feel it to be absolutely dictated by the interests of the labour movement— publicly criticise the Lassallean superstition, in the same way as I dealt, in its time, with the Proudhonist superstition.[d]

With the assurance of my best wishes to you personally,

I remain

K. M.

First published in *Die Neue Zeit*, Bd. 1, Nr. 1, Stuttgart, 1896

Printed according to the original

Published in English in full for the first time

---

[a] 'president elected by universal suffrage' - [b] See this volume, p. 128. - [c] to Wilhelm Liebknecht (see Note 84) - [d] See Marx's *The Poverty of Philosophy*... and *On Proudhon*.

92

ENGELS TO MARX

IN LONDON

Manchester, 14 October 1868

Dear Moor,

Today the *Kölnische Zeitung* states that the workers (COLLIERS) in Essen, who have just ended the STRIKE successfully,[203] have revolted against Schweitzerism and its supporters, the local bigwigs, and are demanding *strict accounting of the* STRIKE *funds.*[a] The source is suspect, but the symptom is significant. This whole agitation breaks down on money matters; the Lassallean leaders are too scoundrelly in this respect.

Further, it reports that in Gladbach the cotton *manufacturers* have recognised that the working day is too long, and are forming an association among themselves to reduce the day from 13 hours to 12 for the time being (issue of 12 October). You see that your book[b] is also having a practical effect on the bourgeoisie.

Yet another stupid issue of Wilhelm's sheet[c] this week! He interrupts your stuff about Hirsch[d] in order to publish a rubbishy article which amounts to saying that bourgeois society, or '*the* social', as he puts it, is determined by '*the* political' and not vice versa.[e] *Naturam si furca expellas,*[f] etc. Nearly every article is crawling with nonsense.

Ernest the Fox now seems to be a certainty here if you can trust the cheers with which he, in particular, is honoured everywhere among the 3 liberal candidates.[102] If things go well, this will be due neither to his cunning, nor to his STRAIGHTFORWARDNESS, but only to the instinct of the masses. The Tories can find no candidate, it is said they wish to put up here one of the Hoares (London bankers); but the man will have to have a lot of money to throw away for nothing if he lets himself in for it.

---

[a] The reports, datelined 'Essen, 8. Okt.' and 'Gladbach, 10. Okt.', appeared in the column *Vermischte Nachrichten* (Miscellaneous Reports), *Kölnische Zeitung*, No. 284, 12 October 1868. - [b] the first volume of *Capital* - [c] *Demokratisches Wochenblatt* - [d] K. Marx, 'Connections Between the International Working Men's Association and English Working Men's Organisations'.- [e] 'Der Staat und die soziale Frage', *Demokratisches Wochenblatt*, No. 41, 10 October 1868. - [f] *naturam expellas furca, tamen usque recurret*—You may drive nature out with a pitchfork, still it will return (Horace, *Epistles*, I, 10, 24).

In Berlin, as a result of the great heat last summer, afternoon lessons were completely abandoned in a number of high schools and morning lessons extended by one period. The results were quite unexpected, the boys made enormously rapid progress, and the business is now going to be tried out on a larger scale.

In Spain the rule of the generals appears to be wearing out rapidly.[165] The abolition of the Jesuits and the partial abolition of the monasteries had been long in coming and only seem to have been forced, at least in part, by financial difficulties; on the other hand, the reward for the officers and NCOs for joining the insurrectionary side came quickly enough. The disarmament of the people also appears to be only a question of time. All the same, in a movement like this the little tricks are not enough with which, after a coup, a general could edge his way through as Isabella's minister.

With best greetings.

Your
F. E.

First published abridged in *Der Briefwechsel zwischen F. Engels und K. Marx*, Bd. 4, Stuttgart, 1913 and in full in *MEGA*, Abt. III, Bd. 4, Berlin, 1931

Printed according to the original

Published in English for the first time

93

MARX TO ENGELS[34]

IN MANCHESTER

London, 15 October 1868

Tomorrow or the day after tomorrow the Lafargue FAMILY is leaving for Paris. This will greatly reduce our HOUSEHOLD EXPENSES.

I have written to A. Frank et Co. in Paris. Since I know that he has sold COPIES OF MY *Anti-Proudhon*[204] as recently as *in the past few weeks*, I asked in my letter for accounts of the whole affair, REMINDING MR Frank that he and Vogler were only my *agents de vente*[a] and that I had paid all the printing costs. Thereupon I received, a few days ago, the following reply:

---

[a] selling agents

'J'ai l'honneur, Monsieur, de vous informer que j'ai racheté la Maison A. Frank le 21 Oct. 1865, *sans* actifs et passifs.— Il y avait à cette époque 92 exemplaires de votre brochure *Misère de la philosophie* en magasin que je tiens à votre disposition.— Quant à ce qui pourrait vous revenir de solde, il faudra vous adresser soit à.Mr Vogler soit au curateur de la succession de mon prédécesseur, Mr Bassot, 58 rue de Bondy, Paris, etc. per *F. Vieweg,* propriétaire actuel de la maison A. Frank.'^a

I shall now grant Lafargue power of attorney to collect the 92 *exemplaires,* which he will sell amongst his friends. For the remainder (there were 1,500 *exemplaires*), I am granting Schily power of attorney to start legal proceedings. I do not know Vogler's whereabouts, but his former *associé* Shee still has a *librairie*^b in Brussels, where I can mobilise a handful of young lawyers belonging to our Association. It would be nice if I could still squeeze out some cash.

Attached packet of the *Social-Demokrat,* upon which you should please write me a few marginal notes (regarding the TRADES UNIONS stories) since I did not have the time to read the stuff. The letter to Schweitzer has gone off.^c Enclosed also the latest number of *Lanterne* and a pamphlet about Plon-Plon, said to be written by Charras.^d

Apropos. I had a meeting with Beesly. The SUB-EDITOR of Morley (the EDITOR for the SCIENTIFIC DEPARTMENT) declared that the argument was irrefutable. However, the article [11] was too 'DRY' for A MAGAZINE. Beesly asked me to put it in a more popular form, without sacrificing the SCIENTIFIC POINTS. This is RATHER DIFFICULT. However, I'll try. In particular, he wants a longer introduction, including personalia about MY PAST and the book's impact in Germany. This, OF COURSE, you must write. But there is time for this until I send you the BULK of the article. The whole shit is then to go into *The Westminster Review.*
Salut.

Your
K. M.

---

^a 'I have the honour to inform you, Sir, that I repurchased the Maison A. Frank on 21 Oct. 1865, *without* assets and liabilities.— At that time, 92 copies of your pamphlet *The Poverty of Philosophy* were in stock, and I hold them at your disposal.— With regard to any possible balance due to you, you should address yourself to Mr Vogler or to my predecessor's executor, Mr Bassot, 58 rue de Bondy, Paris, etc. *F. Vieweg,* current owner of the Maison A. Frank.' Marx quotes Vieweg's letter of 12 October 1868. - ^b bookshop - ^c See this volume, pp. 132-35. - ^d [J. B. A. Charras,] *Monsieur Napoléon Bonaparte (Jérôme).*

Have you read *A. Slade: 'Turkey and the Crimean War'*? It appears that 'Bosh' is a Turkish word, since Slade says: 'bosh lakerdeh' (empty words).[a]

First published in *Der Briefwechsel zwischen F. Engels und K. Marx*, Bd. 4, Stuttgart, 1913

Printed according to the original

Published in English in full for the first time

94

MARX TO HERMANN JUNG

IN LONDON

[London,] 19 October 1868

Dear Jung,

As long as there is no scandal that could implicate the International. You can be insulting if your heart demands so. But no fisticuffs.

The best thing would be to give the appearance of bringing a suit against the fellows (Besson and Le Lubez) for LIBEL because of the letter.[205] This joke could be fixed up with Merriman. You would see how the COWARDS would grovel, besides they would face the danger of being examined publicly in court about their fine gang.

Yours

K. M.

First published in: Marx and Engels, *Works*, First Russian Edition, Vol. XXV, Moscow, 1934

Printed according to the original

Published in English for the first time

---

[a] A. Slade, *Turkey and the Crimean War: A Narrative of Historical Events,* London, 1867, Glossary, p. 449.

95

ENGELS TO MARX

IN LONDON

Manchester, 22 October 1868

Dear Moor,

The little Russian Ermen,[a] whose fate you can see from the enclosed paper, has, on the pretext that he must now settle down, been living in our office for a week now, and has only emerged rather drunk to visit his betrothed. Since the whole office was turned into a pub, no sort of work could be done, and that is why I have only now got around to writing to you.

I have not yet been able to read the Congress[164] reports in the *Social-Demokrat,* which are also very boring.[b] Apart from this, Schweitzer shows that he is very serious about his sect. Not only has the General Association of German Workers been reformed, with its headquarters in Berlin[167] and with new statutes,[c] the only alterations having been made, compared to the old statutes, with an eye to the Law on Association,[206] but every detail shows that in the new TRADES UNIONS GAGW aims to play (but openly) the same role as our old secret league[118] did in the legal associations. The TRADES UNIONS are only to form an exoteric party of the Lassallean church of sole salvation, but only the latter remains the one of sole salvation. If Eichhoff forms a separate association in Berlin,[207] he is promised gracious toleration on the condition that his association takes a 'friendly' attitude towards GAGW. But Schweitzer and his Association remain "*the* party", and the others may come and join it; or else remain heretics and DISSENTERS.

Apart from this, the fellow has a much clearer grasp than all the others of the general political situation and a much clearer attitude to the other parties; and he is cleverer in his presentation than all the others. He calls 'all old parties facing us, one single reactionary mass, and their differences are scarcely of any significance for us'. He recognises that 1866 and its results are ruining the system of petty principalities, undermining the principle of legitimacy, shaking reaction, and have set the people in motion, but he has—now—also come out against the other results, the burden of

---

a Anton Ermen - b *Der Social-Demokrat,* Nos. 114, 115, 116 and 117 (with supplements); 30 September, 2, 4, 7 October 1868, *Allgemeiner deutscher Arbeiter-Congress.* - c '*Statut. Geschäfts-Reglement*', *Social-Demokrat,* No. 119, 11 October 1868.

taxes, etc., and his attitude to Bismarck is more 'correct', as the Berliners say, than e.g. Liebknecht's is, with regard to the ex-princes. You will have seen that he cites the Elector of Hesse[a] as a historical authority—on the all-too-familiar subjects—and in his last number he allows a true Hanoverian to strike up a Guelphic whimpering.[b] On this last point, couldn't you for once tell Wilhelm what is what? It is really asking a lot to expect us to support a paper in which he allows such dirty tricks.

Have at least a part of the anti-Proudhons[c] sent to London; these few remaining copies *cannot be replaced*. I myself have none. Vieweg should be asked to account for the copies sold since 1865. It is, in addition, certainly a good thing that you are following the matter up, even though only now. There is always the possibility that something may still come out of it.

The business with the *Westminster*[d] is very good. Do not allow time to slip by; the article should appear in the January issue; so send me the stuff as soon as possible, so I may do my part. It is very good that these fellows would not use a simple presentation of a new scientific development without the phraseology of their 'ESSAYS', which make the matter not only less clear, but also *drier*. I would, however, also ask Mr Beesly how many printed sheets would be available. The stuff I sent you would have made 1 sheet in the *Fortnightly*, but about $1^1/_2$ in the *Westminster*. According to space—and since only one article is possible here—we should consider whether and which parts of the book should be left out completely—for instance I do not believe it will be possible to include the chapter on accumulation[208] without cutting down the space for the main subject too much.

I've read Darwin's first volume on DOMESTICATION.[e] Only details are new, and then not much of importance.

With best greetings.

Your
F. E.

First published abridged in *Der Briefwechsel zwischen F. Engels und K. Marx*. Bd. 4, Stuttgart, 1913 and in full in *MEGA*, Abt. III, Bd. 4, Berlin, 1931

Printed according to the original

Published in English for the first time

---

[a] Ludwig III. See *Demokratisches Wochenblatt*, No. 40, 3 October 1868, *Politische Uebersicht*. - [b] *Demokratisches Wochenblatt*, No. 42, 17 October 1868 (supplement), 'Ein Hannoveraner...' - [c] K. Marx, *The Poverty of Philosophy*... See this volume, p. 138. - [d] *The Westminster Review*; see this volume, p. 138. - [e] Ch. Darwin, *The Variation of Animals and Plants under Domestication*. In 2 vols. London, 1868.

96

MARX TO ENGELS

IN MANCHESTER

[London,] 24 October 1868

Dear Fred,

Enclosed:

1. *Letter from Kugelmann.* Some interesting things in it.[209] In any case, I shall write to tell him that I *forbid pour l'avenir*[a] all his eccentric respectful outbreaks OF ESTEEM.

2. *Letter from Liebknecht.* The brute seems quite mad. Weeks ago he wrote to me saying he would let me have COPIES OF *Vogt.* And, as always with Liebknecht, there the matter rests. Not another word about it. A mass of stupid suggestions instead. I, he says, should reply to Faucher,[b] since Liebknecht *cannot* answer him, and Faucher has ADMIRERS in several Leipzig tap-rooms. He will refrain 'for the present', and against his will, from attacks on Schweitzer. As if he had not, on the other hand, asked me, in his honour, kindly to attack Schweitzer 'for the present'. I am to place at his disposal a 'selection of choice passages' from Miquel's *private correspondence* with me, since he fancies that Miquel is 'dangerous'. I am to send him Freiligrath's poem against Kinkel,[c] so he can rehabilitate Freiligrath at Kinkel's expense. Finally, I am to make a certain Stromeyer—(he means Strohn)—in Bradford the agent for Ernst Stehfest et Co., Crimmitschau (spinning and weaving partnership). WHAT ELSE? Luckily this time he has not done me the honour of asking me to *purchase* here, in the City, ENGLISH MUSTARD SPECIMENS for an alleged consumer society in Leipzig, and to *establish a 'connection' with the firm.* The UPSHOT of the whole business was—IN RETURN for the MUSTARD and the business information—the sentence: *The MUSTARD is excellent!* This is in fact what the English economists call 'CONSUMPTIVE DEMAND' *par excellence.*

Borkheim's Russophobia (with which I inoculated him as the mildest sickness for the diversion of his superfluous vital spirits) is assuming dangerous dimensions; he now has a row with OLD Philipp Becker, since the latter is on good terms with Bakunin and has written to Borkheim that he should not attack Bakunin in his letters. Borkheim regards this as a dangerous Muscovite conspiracy. He believes that his 'masterly invectives' in Wilhelm's *Wochenblatt*[d] are causing Byzantium—and therefore also Bakunin—to

---

[a] for the future - [b] See this volume, pp. 65, 86. - [c] F. Freiligrath, 'An Joseph Weydemeyer, I-II', *Die Revolution*, No. 2, 1852. - [d] [S. Borkheim,] 'Russische politische Flüchtlinge in West-Europa', *Demokratisches Wochenblatt*, Nos. 5, 6, 17, 20;

shake. In a stern letter to Becker, he has declared with his usual delicacy that he will maintain his friendship for him and his (BY THE BY negligible) pecuniary support, but—politics should now be excluded from their correspondence!

The 12 RAGAMUFFINS of the so-called FRENCH BRANCH held a PUBLIC MEETING in London last Tuesday, again under Pyat's chairman-ship[210] and with the reading of one of his melodramatic PUFFS for the revolution. There were big placards on the walls AS FOLLOWS:

République Française
La Branche française de l'Association Internationale, etc., etc. Then *Félix Pyat* in huge letters. The points for discussion, listed *in French,* included: 3. Vote d'adhésion au manifeste[a] (the manifesto of the Commune de Paris, which exists only on the moon, which was to be read by Pyat and had been fabricated by him) et protestation, contre l'indifférence en matière politique professée à Bruxelles au *dernier Congrès de l'Association Internationale.*[b] [138]

Under this, however, was the English notice (also distributed as a *HANDBILL*): *DEMOCRATS OF ALL NATIONS* ARE INVITED, etc. 'FOR THE PURPOSE OF *DECIDING* WHETHER THE WORKINGMEN'S INTERNATIONAL ASSOCIATION IS TO BE A *POLITICAL ASSOCIATION.*'

Last Tuesday[c] I was empowered to disavow the fellows immediately and publicly if the London daily newspapers should treat or mention this as a demonstration of ours. Luckily, NO NOTICE WAS TAKEN OF THEM.

This evening there is, however, to be a SUBCOMMITTEE at which witnesses are to be heard that one of this dozen was formerly a *marchand d'hommes*[d] and a brothel keeper,[e] another a gambler, a third a SPY for the MASTERS in the TAILORS' STRIKE here,[211] etc., etc. On the basis of the 'morals paragraph' of the Rules, these gentlemen will probably be kicked out. They are naturally doubly annoyed that all politics are left out in dealing with fellows like them.

Salut to MRS Burns, Jollymayer[f] and King Cole.[g]

Your

K. M.

First published abridged in *Der Briefwech-sel zwischen F. Engels und K. Marx.* Bd. 4, Stuttgart, 1913 and in full in *MEGA,* Abt. III, Bd. 4, Berlin, 1931

Printed according to the original

Published in English for the first time

1, 8 February, 25 April and 16 May 1868 (the first two articles are signed with the initials S. B.).
[a] Vote of adhesion to the manifesto - [b] and protest against the indifference in political matters displayed in Brussels during the *latest congress of the International Association.* - [c] 20 October - [d] white slave-trader - [e] Eugène Thiou - [f] Carl Schor-lemmer - [g] Samuel Moore

97

MARX TO LUDWIG KUGELMANN[29]

IN HANOVER

London, 26 October 1868

My dear Friend,

Only these few lines in reply to your letter,[212] which arrived at a moment when I am burdened with a visitor.

Kertbény's address: No. 11/III (what the III means I don't know, perhaps the floor) Behrenstrasse.

Now, permit me a word. Since you and Engels were of the opinion that it would be useful, I gave in on the question of the advertisement in the *Gartenlaube*.[a] My conviction was *decisively against* it. And now I request you *urgently finally to abandon* this joke. The only result is that fellows like Keil and the *Daheim* sort believe one to belong to the tribe of great men, literary or other, and to need or seek their protection.

I believe this sort of thing is harmful rather than helpful and *beneath* the dignity of a man of science. For instance, *Meyer's Konversationslexikon* wrote a long time ago asking me for a biography. Not only did I not send one; I did not even reply to the letter. Everybody must work out his own salvation.

As for Kertbény, he is a pompous, confused, importunate literary idler, and the less one has to do with him the better.

Salut.

Yours

K. M.

First published abridged in *Die Neue Zeit*, Bd. 2, Nr. 7, Stuttgart, 1901-1902, and in full in *Pisma Marksa k Kugelmanu* (Letters of Marx to Kugelmann), Moscow-Leningrad, 1928

Printed according to the original

98

ENGELS TO MARX

IN LONDON

Manchester, 28 October 1868

Dear Moor,

In all haste, I return the enclosures from Kugelmann[209] and Wilhelm.[b] Congratulations on the professorship. The letter from

---

a See this volume, p. 74. - b Ibid., p. 142.

A sketch of Lizzie Burns by Frederick Engels (after 4 May 1869)

Wilhelm is indeed amusing. This omnium-gatherum of instructions to you, so that you might do something too. I also congratulate Strohn on the agency for the Stehfest firm of whose commercial stability I am far from convinced.[a]

Lizzy has rushed off with her friend Mrs Chorlton (the fatty) to her relations in Lincolnshire and will return only on Friday or Saturday.[b] Naturally the maid had to pick this precise moment to fall ill, but Ellen[c] is helping us out.

Best greetings to all.

Your
F. E.

First published in *MEGA*, Abt. III, Bd. 4, Berlin, 1931

Printed according to the original

Published in English for the first time

99

MARX TO WILLIAM JESSUP[213]

IN NEW YORK

London, 28 October 1868
1 Modena Villas, Maitland Park,
Haverstock Hill

Dear Sir,

Your letter to Mr Eccarius, d.d. 3 curt. has been duly communicated by him to the General Council of the International Working Men's Association. He has been reappointed as our corresponding Secretary for America, but is at present too ill to fulfil his functions.

The General Council has appointed Mr S. Meyer and Mr August Vogt as its German-American correspondents and Mr Pelletier as its French-American correspondent. I beg to recommend you these citizens.

The General Council being itself yearly elected by the General Congress, it is self-understood that all its nominations can only be valid for the current year, if they be not renewed.

Yours fraternally
Karl Marx

---

[a] Engels puns on the name *Stehfest* and the word *Stehfestigkeit* (stability). - [b] 30 or 31 October - [c] Mary Ellen Burns

Wm. J. Jessup, Corresponding Representative for State of New York, National Labour Union, 11 Norfolk Street, New York City

First published in: Marx and Engels, *Works*, First Russian Edition, Vol. XXV, Moscow, 1934

Printed according to S. Meyer's copy of the original

Published in English for the first time

100

MARX TO SIGFRID MEYER AND AUGUST VOGT

IN NEW YORK

London, 28 October 1868

Dear Meyer and Vogt,

The enclosed credentials for Meyer (I have added the same for you [214]) will show you that your wish had already been met by 13 October. Meyer's appointment was printed in *The Bee-Hive*[a] on 3 October.[b] The GENERAL COUNCIL has resolved that the German correspondents shall correspond with me, Pelletier (for the French) with Dupont, and Eccarius with Jessup. I myself suggested the latter, as I have no time for more correspondence. You can hand the enclosed lines to Jessup[c] and, at the same time, show him your credentials.

With regard to Eccarius there is some misunderstanding. *I* have *never* quarrelled with him; on the contrary I have supported him *to this day* against the ATTACKS by the English, etc.[148] But *he*—his preponderant and often narrow-minded egoism perhaps developed as a result of his circumstances—commits unpleasant tomfooleries from time to time. I generally take no notice of this. Now and then my patience is exhausted. I give him a brain washing, and ALL IS RIGHT AGAIN for the time being. The poor devil is, at present, very ill, and he always utilises such moments to say his *pater peccavi.*[d] To what Liebknecht is referring, according to Vogt's letter, I have absolutely no idea. *I, at least,* have never written a word to anybody *against* Eccarius EXCEPT in my letter to Meyer, at a moment

---

[a] *The Bee-Hive*, No. 364, 3 October 1868, 'The International Working Men's Association'. - [b] in the original erroneously 10 October - [c] See this volume, p. 147. - [d] Father, I have sinned (Luke 15 : 21).

when I was upset by letters from our other delegates to the Brussels Congress in which they denounced Eccarius.[a] But it is quite possible that Eccarius wrote to Liebknecht without my knowledge in such a way that moved the latter to make his remarks to Vogt. This would be peculiar, since just at that time I had a big dispute with the English about and *for* Eccarius.

As far as *Sorge*[b] is concerned, no further action. My lines to Jessup explain the TEMPORARY character of the credentials.

Cards for members are no longer available, must be reprinted. Liebknecht is dabbling too much in south German patriotism, and he should not print such nonsense about 'state and society'[c] containing the exact opposite of our opinions. *Salut.* In all haste.

Yours
K. Marx

Apropos. Do you know Dietzgen? He has now returned from Petersburg to the Rhine to establish himself as a small tanner. He is one of the most gifted workers I know, I mean by correspondence. I don't know him personally.

A translation of my book is now appearing in Russian in St. Petersburg.[186] Or did I already inform you of this?

[Enclosure]

[London,] 256 High Holborn, W. C.

Citizen A. Vogt is appointed on 13 October 1868 by the General Council of the International Working Men's Association as corresponding Secretary for the year 1868-69 for the International Working Men's Association (German section in America).

13 October 1868

On behalf of the General Council

Karl Marx
SECRETARY FOR GERMANY

First published abridged in: Marx and Engels, *Works*, First Russian Edition, Vol. XXV, Moscow, 1934, and in full in: Marx and Engels, *Works*, Second Russian Edition, Vol. 32, Moscow, 1964

Printed according to the original

Published in English for the first time

---

a See this volume, p. 97. - b Ibid., pp. 61, 96. - c *Demokratisches Wochenblatt*, No. 41, 10 October 1868, 'Der Staat und die soziale Frage'.

101

MARX TO BASSOT

IN PARIS

London, 30 October 1868
1 Modena Villas, Maitland Park
Haverstock Hill

Monsieur,

I have written to the Maison A. Frank for my royalties. The new proprietor, M. Vieweg, directed me to you as the successor of M. Frank.[a] Will you please hand over to M. *Paul Lafargue*, bearer of this letter, my share of the proceeds from the sale of my brochure *Philosophie de la misère etc. contre M. Proudhon* due to me at the moment when M. Frank or the House of M. Frank were disposed of.

I have the honour to salute you,

Karl Marx

M. Bassot
58, rue de Bondy, Paris

First published in: Marx and Engels, *Works*, Second Russian Edition, Vol. 32, Moscow, 1964

Printed according to the original

Translated from the French

Published in English for the first time

102

MARX TO ENGELS

IN MANCHESTER

[London,] 4 November 1868

DEAR FRED,

On Friday[b] I have to pay the water rates and, further, Tussy's re-subscriptions with Winterbottom (gymnastics), etc. I would be

---

a See this volume, p. 137. - b 6 November.

grateful if you could send me SOME £ by the day after tomorrow.

How are things with the Russian's manuscript?[185] Have a look at it and then let me have your opinion. The poor fellow is certainly waiting anxiously for my reply.

Pyat has had a stroke of good luck. He has now got hold of *his own* German—Herr Weber[a] from the Palatinate.

In all haste.

Your
K. M.

Enclosed letters from Eichhoff.[215] He believes Schweitzer has denounced him here. NOTHING OF THE SORT. His denouncer (which he should not know) is *Borkheim.* In order to get rid of him ON THIS POINT and, at the same time, to elucidate the suspicion that could, in fact, be aroused by Eichhoff's reference to Bismarck (in his speech reported in Wilhelm's *Wochenblatt*), I have written to Eichhoff[84] that he has been denounced to the General Council here and should send me his DEFENCE.

First published in *Der Briefwechsel zwischen F. Engels und K. Marx,* Bd. 4, Stuttgart, 1913

Printed according to the original

Published in English for the first time

103

ENGELS TO MARX

IN LONDON

Manchester, 4 November 1868

Dear Moor,

You must excuse me if I do not write much now. For some time I have had nasty rheumatism not only in my right arm, but also in the 3 first fingers of my right hand; as a result, after a certain time writing becomes very burdensome for me, and in the evening almost impossible. I hope the trouble disappears; I use alcohol against it—externally that is.

If the Spaniards even now do not know where they stand, following Wilhelmchen's address, they are beyond hope.[216] Unity

---

[a] J. V. Weber

between bourgeois and worker—the bourgeois *must*, however, realise that he has to concede this and that to the worker—anything to avoid a June battle, for this is followed by 2 December.[217] It is really the crowning point of all confusion. If now the bourgeois will not 'understand', the worker will have to realise that *he* will have to make concessions to the bourgeois. This is the sole possible sense which the thing can have. Hence, the ridiculousness of measuring Spanish conditions, with the enormous beggar-proletariat, both clerical and lay, against the yardstick of conditions in *Saxony*. There is naturally not a single mention of the peasants.

Many greetings.

Your
F. E.

Moore tells me that nearly all factory workers in Vienna are Moravians and Bohemians, mainly *Czechs*. This explains much about the movement there. The real Viennese do not go into factories, they become coachmen, domestics or something like that.

First published in *MEGA,* Abt. III, Bd. 4, Berlin, 1931

Printed according to the original

Published in English for the first time

104

ENGELS TO MARX[33]

IN LONDON

Manchester, 6 November 1868

Dear Moor,

Herewith return back Eichhoff's letters[215] and Dietzgen's manuscript.[185] The latter I had placed in a *safe* place, away from the tidying females, and there it was completely forgotten.

It is difficult to pass absolutely definite judgement on the thing; the man is not a born philosopher and, in addition, half self-taught. Some of his sources (e. g., Feuerbach, your book[a] and various trashy publications on the natural sciences) can be

---

[a] the first volume of *Capital*

immediately traced partly from his terminology, but one cannot tell what else he has read. The terminology is, of course, still very confused, hence the lack of precision and frequent reiterations in new TERMS. There is also dialectics in it, but appearing more in the form of flashes than in any connected way. The presentation of the thing-in-itself as a conceivable thing [Gedankending] would be very nice and even brilliant if one could be *certain* that *he himself* had discovered *it*. There is plenty of wit in it and, despite the poor grammar, a marked talent for style. All in all, however, a remarkable instinct to think out so much that is correct on the basis of such inadequate studies.

The repetitions are, as I said, partly a result of the shortcomings in terminology, partly due to his lack of logical schooling. It will be a hard job to get rid of them all. If the man definitely wants to print his stuff, I do not know if the reduction to 2 printed sheets would be the best for him; in any case, it would be a frightful job for him, since he is not aware of his repetitions. In addition, I do not know whether 2 sheets would get any attention at all. 6-8 sheets would be more likely to do this. But he will never get it into a magazine.

Borkheim has written to ask whether I would agree that *he* should reprint my Bakunin article from the *Neue Rheinische Zeitung*[a] in Liebknecht's paper[b] and says, in this connection, that this article 'fits, for *him,* most excellently in *his* framework'. I replied[84] that we planned to publish our earlier articles, etc., jointly, that we were already negotiating with a book-dealer, but that I did not know how things stood at the moment and had therefore written to you. I don't know though which article he means; there are several and he speaks of one. Besides, he repeats his nonsense about Bakunin, Eichhoff, etc.

Eichhoff's thorough defence[c] made me laugh.

Best greetings.

Your
F. E.

First published in *Der Briefwechsel zwischen F. Engels und K. Marx*, Bd. 4, Stuttgart, 1913

Printed according to the original

Published in English in full for the first time

---

[a] F. Engels, 'Democratic Pan-Slavism', *Neue Rheinische Zeitung*, Nos. 222 and 223, 15 and 16 February 1849. - [b] *Demokratisches Wochenblatt* - [c] See this volume, p. 151.

105

MARX TO ENGELS[33]

IN MANCHESTER

London, 7 November 1868[a]

DEAR FRED,

THANKS FOR THE £5.

I (and the whole household here) are very worried because of the typhus raging in your parts. It is so contagious. Please report again soon on the *status rerum.*[b]

It will be impossible to stop that damned Borkheim, whom I shall be seeing today, printing your 2 articles[c] (those about Bakunin's manifesto to the Slavs[d]). However, I shall only tell him that you are an old personal friend of Bakunin, so that the business may under no circumstances appear in a context insulting to the latter. Borkheim takes himself completely *au sérieux*[e] and really believes he has a political mission to fulfil. He is translating for me the main passages from a Russian book about agrarian disintegration,[f] and has also given me a French book on the subject by the Russian Schédo-Ferroti.[g] The latter is very much mistaken—he is altogether a very superficial fellow—in saying that the Russian communal system came into existence only as a result of the ban on peasants leaving the land. The whole business, *down to the smallest detail*, is absolutely identical with the *primaeval Germanic* communal system. Add to this, in the Russian case (and this may be found also *amongst a part of the Indian communal systems*, not in the Punjab, but in the South), (1) the *non-democratic*, but *patriarchal* character of the commune leadership and (2) the *collective responsibility* for taxes to the state, etc. It follows from the second point that the more industrious a Russian peasant is, the more he is exploited by the state, not only in terms of taxes, but also for supplying provisions and horses, etc. for the constant passage of troops, for government couriers, etc. The whole shit is breaking down.

I regard Dietzgen's exposition,[185] in so far as Feuerbach, etc., in

---

[a] in the original erroneously 1867 - [b] state of things - [c] F. Engels, 'Democratic Pan-Slavism', *Neue Rheinische Zeitung*, Nos. 222 and 223, 15 and 16 February 1849. - [d] M. Bakunin, *Aufruf an die Slaven...*, Koethen, 1848. - [e] seriously - [f] П. Л[илиенфельд], *Земля и воля*. Спб., 1868. - [g] D. K. Schédo-Ferroti, *Études sur l'avenir de la Russie. Dixième étude: Le patrimoine du peuple.* Berlin, 1868.

short his sources, do not peep through, as entirely his own independent achievement. For the rest, I agree with everything you say. I shall have something to say to him about the repetitions; it is his bad luck that it was precisely Hegel that he did *not* study.

The great Weber[a] on behalf of 'German Association for Revolutionary Agitation, etc.' has held a meeting together with the French Mayers under Pyat's chairmanship and with other vagabonds, at which they instructed the Yankees in an address[218] to intervene *in favour of* the Spanish Republic.

Our Negro, Paul Lafargue, had the misfortune that the French would not recognise his English diploma; they want to make him run the gauntlet of five new examinations, instead of the maximum 1 or 2 as he expected.[121] MRS LAURA SENDS YOU HER COMPLIMENTS.

Salut.

Your
K. M.

First published abridged in *Der Briefwechsel zwischen F. Engels und K. Marx*, Bd. 4, Stuttgart, 1913 and in full in *MEGA*, Abt. III, Bd. 4, Berlin, 1931

Printed according to the original

Published in English in full for the first time

106

MARX TO ENGELS

IN MANCHESTER

[London,] 8 November 1868

SECOND LETTER.
Postscriptum.
I have just come from Borkheim's. To my surprise I have managed to get him *not* to print your 2 articles[b] under his patronage.

Your
K. M.

First published in *Der Briefwechsel zwischen F. Engels und K. Marx*, Bd. 4, Stuttgart, 1913

Printed according to the original

Published in English for the first time

---

a J. V. Weber - b F. Engels, 'Democratic Pan-Slavism', see also this volume, pp. 153, 154.

107

ENGELS TO MARX

IN LONDON

Manchester, 10 November 1868

Dear Moor,

Many thanks for settling things with Borkheim. From the enclosed letter, which he wrote me, you can see what a 'nincompoop' the man is.[219]

Sarah's[a] sickness is taking a very favourable course; it is a simple typhoid fever, *vulgo* gastric fever; Gumpert expects no more relapses and, by the end of this week, she should be cured. Against the contagion, which Gumpert also does not regard as dangerous, disinfection is a help.

Lizzie was in Lincolnshire, visiting a patriarchal variety of AGRICULTURAL LABOURERS who do well—they have gardens and potato land, the right of gleaning, which brings in a lot and, in addition, PASSABLE WAGES. Parallel to this, however, the GANG SYSTEM is on the increase; she described it *literally* as you depicted it in your book.[220] These patriarchal FARM LABOURERS with land are naturally a declining remnant, and are already sending their children into the GANG, while they, for their part, provide the nurseries for the babies of the women working on neighbouring GANGS.

In Jacob Grimm's Spanish romances there is one in which Conde Claros de Montalban, son of Reinolt (Rinaldo) of the Haimon family, has a love affair with the Infanta, Charlemagne's daughter; the count takes her into a thicket in the garden, where they lie down[b]:

> de la cintura en arriba (upwards) *muchos abrazos se dan,*
> de la cintura en abajo como hombre y mujer se han.[c]

Old Jacob selected a lot of naïve passages like that.
With many greetings.

Your

F. E.

First published abridged in *Der Briefwech-sel zwischen F. Engels und K. Marx*, Bd. 4, Stuttgart, 1913 and in full in *MEGA,* Abt. III, Bd. 4, Berlin, 1931

Printed according to the original

Published in English for the first time

---

[a] Sarah Parker - [b] 'Romance del conde Claros, hijo de Reynaldos de Montalvan', *Silva de romances viejos.* Publicada por Jacobo Grimm, Vienna, 1831. - [c] from the girdle upwards they gave many kisses, from the girdle downwards they behave themselves as husband and wife.

108

ENGELS TO MARX

IN LONDON

Manchester, 13 November 1868

Dear Moor,

I was really ashamed recently to send you a mere trifle of £5, but at that time I was really unable to squeeze out more; today a further five pounds follow enclosed; it was clear to me that just £5 would not help you out.

Amicus[a] Ernest Jones is now really catching it for becoming the obedient servant of Bright and Gladstone and identifying himself completely here with Bazley and Jacob Bright. This afternoon, two large posters blazed on all the walls, one black and one red, presenting a passage from *The People's Paper*, recently reprinted in the *Democrat* (WHAT IS THAT?), in which he rejects the cursing and baiting of aristocrats as a bourgeois dodge, proclaims LABOUR AGAINST CAPITAL, and slates the Manchester Liberals as the workers' worst enemies, but all in his *old* style, you know. This affair, so shortly before the election, can overthrow him.[b]

Have you got the book: Ténot, *Paris en Décembre 1851*, and can you send me it? If not, I shall order it. Everything is well at home.

Many greetings.

Your
F. E.

First published in *Der Briefwechsel zwischen F. Engels und K. Marx*, Bd. 4, Stuttgart, 1913

Printed according to the original

Published in English for the first time

---

a friend - b See this volume, p. 166.

109

MARX TO ENGELS

IN MANCHESTER

London, 14 November 1868

DEAR FRED,

BEST THANKS FOR £5.

For the past few days I have had once again the beginning of *carbunculosem.* Since this muck always starts at this time, I immediately began again with the *arsenic.* This should cut off further EVOLUTION.

I am sending you subsequently (RATHER *simultaneously*) amusing cuttings from the Paris press, supplied by Lafargue. You must send them back, since Jennychen collects the stuff.

Enclosed also a jolly cutting from *Figaro* on the people's economic conferences [221] under the LEADERSHIP of Rabbi A. Einhorn, GENERALLY KNOWN BY THE NAME OF *I. E. Horn.* This idiot (who is, incidentally, skilled in the practice of *agiotage*) published SOME TIME SINCE a book on the *banks*,[a] of which even the *Economist* said it was obviously written only for children (although the *Times* reviewed it ceremoniously).

Apropos the *Economist*, you would be surprised to hear that, following the example of *Thornton* in the *Fortnightly Review*,[b] the *Economist* declared[c] verbatim: '*No* "LAW" OF DEMAND AND SUPPLY, IN ANY SENSE WHICH HAS YET BEEN ASSIGNED TO THESE WORDS, EXISTS; NEITHER IN FACT, NOR IN TENDENCY, DO MARKET PRICES CONFORM TO THE RULE COMMONLY SUPPOSED TO GOVERN THEM.'

The great *Büchner* has sent me his '*Sechs Vorlesungen etc. über die Darwin'sche Theorie,* etc.' The book was not yet out when I was visiting Kugelmann.[77] And he (Büchner) has now already sent me the *second edition*! The way such books are made is NICE. Büchner, for instance (as everybody who has read Lange's balderdash[d] knows anyway), states that his CHAPTER *on materialist philosophy* has been copied mainly from this very Lange. And this same Büchner looks down pityingly on *Aristotle,* whom he obviously only knows by

---

a I. E. Horn, *La Liberté des banques,* Paris, [1866]. A German edition was published in 1867 in Stuttgart and Leipzig. - b W. Th. Thornton, 'A New Theory of Supply and Demand', *The Fortnightly Review,* No. XXXIV, 1 October 1866. - c J. E. C., 'The "Law" of Demand and Supply', *The Economist,* No. 1210, 3 November 1866, p. 1280. - d F. A. Lange, *Geschichte des Materialismus und Kritik seiner Bedeutung in der Gegenwart,* Bde. I-II, Iserlohn, 1866.

hearsay! What really amused me, however, was the following passage with regard to the works of *Cabanis*[a] (1798):

> '*You might almost be listening to Karl Vogt* when you read (in Cabanis) expressions like these: "The brain is intended for thinking, as the stomach is meant for digestion or the liver for secreting the bile from the blood", etc.'[b]

Büchner obviously believes that Cabanis has copied from K. Vogt. Even to imagine the opposite exceeds the critical faculties of the worthy Büchner. He appears to have first learned of Cabanis from Lange! *Ce sont des savants sérieux!*[c]

Paris is haunted. The Baudin affair is really reminiscent of the banquet movement under Louis Philippe.[222] Only today there is no National Guard, and Bugeaud (as far as brutality comes into play) is READY from the first day, while in February he was the last to be called upon and at a moment when there existed *no* ministry, that is to say, under the conditions at that time, *no government.* Moreover, barricade-building is useless. Leaving aside the Weber[d]-Pyat bulls of excommunication, I cannot see how a revolution in Paris could be SUCCESSFUL, apart from treason and defection or division in the army.

I have put a new bee into the bonnets of the Urquhartites (since *Collet* invited me and my family to visit him last Sunday week[e]: I had not seen him personally for years), a bee that is now being very *seriously* debated between Collet and Urquhart, namely that *Peel's Bank Act of 1844*[223] makes it possible for the Russian Government, under CERTAIN CONJUNCTURES OF THE MONEY-MARKET, to force the Bank of England into bankruptcy.[f] Despite my diplomacy with Collet, I could not keep silent as he driveled on about *Ireland*, and told him MOST DECIDEDLY, to his face, my VIEWS ON THIS QUESTION.

Tussy is attending private gymnastic classes. HER COMPLIMENTS TO MRS BURNS.

Salut.

Your

K. M.

First published abridged in *Der Briefwechsel zwischen F. Engels and K. Marx*, Bd. 4, Stuttgart, 1913 and in full in *MEGA*, Abt. III, Bd. 4, Berlin, 1931

Printed according to the original

Published in English for the first time

---

[a] P.-J.[-G.] Cabanis, *Considérations générales sur l'étude de l'homme...* - [b] L. Büchner, *Sechs Vorlesungen über die Darwin'sche Theorie...*, 2. Aufl., Leipzig, 1868, S. 374-75. - [c] Such are profound scholars! (an allusion to a personage in Paul de Kock's novel *L'amant de la lune*. - [d] J. V. Weber - [e] 8 November - [f] See this volume, p. 166.

110

MARX TO ENGELS[48]

IN MANCHESTER

London, 14 November 1868

SECOND LETTER. P. S.

DEAR FRED,

Since practice is better than all theory, I would ask you to describe to me *very precisely* (with examples) how you run your BUSINESS *quant à banquier, etc.*[a]

So. 1. The *method in purchasing* (*cotton*, etc.). With regard ONLY TO THE MONETARY WAY OF DOING THE THINGS; THE BILLS; TIME FOR DRAWING THEM ETC.

2. In *sales.* Bill settlement with your customers and your London CORRESPONDENT.

3. *Settlements* and OPERATIONS (CURRENT ACCOUNT etc.) with regard to your BANKER in Manchester.

Your
K. M.

Since the 2ND VOLUME[187] is largely too theoretical, I shall use the CHAPTER on credit[224] for an ACTUAL DENUNCIATION of this swindle and of COMMERCIAL morals.

First published in *Der Briefwechsel zwischen F. Engels und K. Marx*, Bd. 4, Stuttgart, 1913

Printed according to the original

Published in English in full for the first time

111

MARX TO HERMANN JUNG

IN LONDON

London, 14 November 1868

Dear Jung,

Before you went to Brussels I gave you the *secret circular* (that of Stepney) of the '*États-Unis de l'Europe*', which speaks of the

---

[a] with regard to the banker, etc.

need to make common cause with the INTERNATIONAL WORKINGMEN'S ASSOCIATION.[225] Since Gustav Vogt—i.e., that sheet—is now taking great liberties with respect to us, please send me *the thing back. I shall use it in Liebknecht's paper*[a] *against G. Vogt.*

How did it happen that, in the 2 last issues of *The Bee-Hive*, there is no word of the resolutions of the GENEVA AND BRUSSELS CONGRESS?[226]

Salut to you and FAMILY.

Yours

K. Marx

First published in: Marx and Engels, *Works*, First Russian Edition, Vol. XXV, Moscow, 1934

Printed according to the original

Published in English for the first time

112

MARX TO ENGELS

IN MANCHESTER

[London,] 18 November[b] 1868

DEAR FRED,

The LANDLORD (unfortunately he is living *pro tempore*[c] in London), wrote me the enclosed letter some time ago. Yesterday he called, but was not, of course, admitted, since I was allegedly absent. The devil of it is that, because of the OVEREND AFFAIR,[227] this fellow lives on his house rents; in addition, he will not accept bills of exchange. At other times the PRESSURE for the house has never been SO IMMEDIATE, since I only owe him for 1 QUARTER. Lessner, too, is kicking me for THE REMAINDER OF MY DEBT, his wife is DESPERATELY SICK. GENERALLY the SITUATION is bad.

Yesterday evening, on the CENTRAL COUNCIL[73] the ENGLISH TOO LATE but UNANIMOUSLY acknowledged that I had forecast *literally* for them, the, for me, HIGHLY AMUSING UPSHOT of the elections, with a criticism of the incorrect policy of the REFORM-LEAGUE.[228] The present HOUSE is the worst since the election under Pam's[d] command. The LONG PURSES have never had such an exclusive preponderance. E. Jones

---

[a] *Demokratisches Wochenblatt* - [b] In the original erroneously 18 October. - [c] for the time being - [d] Palmerston's

deserved his tumble OVER AND OVER.[102] With regard to Bradlaugh, he had boasted in too Lassallean a manner. At the last Sunday meeting of his congregation in CLEVELAND HALL, there was displayed a placard TO THIS EFFECT: FAREWELL TO THE GREAT *ICONOCLAST*, THE PEOPLE'S REDEEMER. LONG LIVE TO MR *BRADLAUGH*, THE DREAD NAUGHT OF ST STEPHEN'S! [229]

In France things look very serious, according to Lafargue's last letters too. The government wants to force the lads on to the streets so that *chassepot*[230] and RIFLED CANNON may then *laisser 'faire merveille'*[a]! Can you see any CHANCE of successful street conflicts? Defection of the army without a previous thrashing appears to me scarcely credible.

Büchner's clumsy work[b] is of interest to me in as much as it quotes most of the German research in the field of Darwinism — Prof. Jäger (Vienna) and Prof. Haeckel. According to them, the cell has been abandoned as the primaeval form; instead a formless but contractile particle of albumen is taken as STARTING POINT. This hypothesis was later confirmed by the discoveries in Canada (later also in Bavaria and SOME OTHER PLACES). The primaeval form must naturally be traced down to the point at which it may be produced chemically. And it appears that the way to this point has been found.

The conscientiousness with which Büchner has acquainted himself with the English stuff is also shown by the fact that he classifies Owen as one of Darwin's supporters.

Borkheim's letter to you,[c] which you sent me, I had the pleasure to have read to me for A SECOND TIME by him in person. This nincompoop now accuses Eichhoff of being a 'BUSYBODY'(!) and of 'writing long letters'. What self-knowledge!

Apropos the Irish elections, the only interesting POINT is *Dungarvan*, where *Burry* is presenting himself under the protection of the defector O'Donovan. (Ditto under the protection of the priest.) There is a GENERAL CRY against him amongst the Irish Nationalists since this blackguard, as government prosecutor during the first trial of the Fenians in Dublin, hurled such slanders (à la *Constitutionnel* against the June insurgents)[231] that even the London papers gave him a wigging.

Salut.

Your

K. M.

---

a work miracles - b L. Büchner, *Sechs Vorlesungen über die Darwin'sche Theorie von der Verwandlung der Arten* ... - c See this volume, p. 156.

I believe Nincompoop^a has gone to Bordeaux! Such a business trip is certainly necessary to cool his brain fever.

First published abridged in *Der Briefwechsel zwischen F. Engels und K. Marx*, Bd. 4, Stuttgart, 1913 and in full in *MEGA*, Abt. III, Bd. 4, Berlin, 1931

Printed according to the original

Published in English for the first time

113

ENGELS TO MARX [33]

IN LONDON

Manchester, 18 November 1868

Dear Moor,

What do you say about the elections in the factory districts? The proletariat has once again made an awful fool of itself. Manchester and Salford return 3 Tories^b against 2 Liberals,^c including the MILK-AND-WATER Bazley, Bolton, Preston, Blackburn, etc., almost all Tories. In Ashton it looks as if Milner Gibson has gone TO THE WALL. Ernest Jones NOWHERE, despite the CHEERING. Everywhere the proletariat are the RAG, TAG AND BOBTAIL of the official parties, and if any party has gained strength from the new VOTERS, it is the Tories. The small towns, the HALF ROTTEN BOROUGHS [232] are the salvation of bourgeois Liberalism, and roles will be reversed: the Tories will favour more members for the big towns and the Liberals will favour unequal representation.

Here the electors have increased from 24,000 to not quite 48,000, and the Tories have increased their VOTERS from 6,000 to 14-15,000. The Liberals have let slip a lot, and M. Henry did a lot of harm, but it cannot be denied that the increase in working-class VOTES has brought the Tories more than their simple percentage, and has improved their relative position. On the whole this is a good thing. As things look now, Gladstone should have a *narrow* majority and will be compelled to change the Reform Bill to stop the rolling stone; with a large majority, he would have let things take their course, as usual.

But it remains an appalling display of weakness by the English proletariat. *The parson* has shown unexpected power, and also the

---

^a Borkheim - ^b Birley, Cawley, Chorley - ^c Bazley, J. Bright

cringing before RESPECTABILITY. Not a single working-class candidate had A GHOST OF A CHANCE, but MYLORD TOM NODDY or any parvenu snob could have the workers' votes with pleasure.

The howls of the Liberal bourgeois would amuse me very much were it not for this accompanying experience. To cheer myself up properly, yesterday I made Borchardt's son-in-law, who had dutifully drudged for the Liberals, as drunk as a lord.

Your
F. E.

First published in *Der Briefwechsel zwischen F. Engels und K. Marx*, Bd. 4, Stuttgart, 1913

Printed according to the original

Published in English in full for the first time

114

ENGELS TO MARX

IN LONDON

Manchester, 20 November 1868

Dear Moor,

I shall send you some money on Sunday so that you will receive it Monday morning. The stupidity of our cashier is responsible for the fact that it did not already come today. I am sending you £20.

Militairement parlant,[a] the fellows in Paris have NOT THE GHOST OF A CHANCE, if they launch their attack at present. It is not so easy to get out of this Bonapartism. Without a military revolt, nothing can be done. In my opinion, a coup can only be attempted when at least the *garde mobile*[233] once again stands between the people and the army. It is certain and obvious that Bonaparte *wants* an attempt, and the revolutionaries would be jackasses if they gave him the satisfaction. In addition, the new rifles (1) can very easily be rendered useless (by extracting the pin) and (2) even if they fall into the hands of the insurgents in a usable state, they are valueless if you do not have the specific ammunition, which you cannot *make* like the old cartridges. And why, in fact, should they launch their attack just at this moment? The continuation of *this*

---

[a] militarily speaking

state of affairs injures Bonaparte more every day; in addition, there is no special reason for attacking. Bonaparte will also take care not to give *the sort* of reason that only the revolutionaries need.

The secret of the elections in Lancashire is the English workers'. hatred of the *Irish*. The damned Murphy cleared the way for the Tories. In the meantime, the Irish state church is finished no matter what. Otherwise things have happened as I said.[a] *The Morning Herald* has already explained that, though the Tories *seemed* to be in the minority, they were really in the majority, since they represent the majority of the people.[b]

If you have not received the £20 by Monday morning, telegraph me immediately. On Sunday I cannot register and would not consider even a registered letter safe in the hands of the post from Saturday evening to Monday morning.

Many greetings.

Your
F. E.

Send me back the letter from Nincompoop.[c] As you know I have to show him what grammatical blunders he makes.

First published in *Der Briefwechsel zwischen F. Engels und K. Marx*, Bd. 4, Stuttgart, 1913

Printed according to the original

Published in English for the first time

115

MARX TO ENGELS

IN MANCHESTER

London, 23 November 1868

DEAR FRED,

The FIRST HALF arrived this morning.

Enclosed 2 letters, ONE from Collet and the other from Jones. As regards *Collet*, I have burnt my fingers with these blasted *Urquhartites*[d]. You know—at least I think I wrote to you about

---

[a] See this volume, p. 163. - [b] Engels refers to the leading article 'London, Wednesday, November 18' in *The Morning Herald* of 18 November 1868. - [c] Borkheim; see also this volume pp. 156, 162. - [d] Ibid., p. 159.

it—that, purely for the joy of MISCHIEF-MONGERING, I set new bees in their bonnets about the Peel Act of 1844 [223] and its useful effect for Russia. (Incidentally the matter is correct WITHIN CERTAIN LIMITS.) Now Urquhart wants to print one of these letters *over my name* in his NEXT *Diplomatic Review*.[234] If I refused 'my name', I would make them mistrustful. So I am IN FOR IT. It is a consolation that not a soul reads the *Diplomatic Review* (EXCEPT A SMALL CLIQUE). The Urquhartites, however, are burning their fingers too. In order to give the affair more weight, they obviously intend to cite me as the author of *Capital*, which would be AN ABOMINATION in their eyes if they knew it.

As regards Ernest Jones, I find him EXCEEDINGLY COOL. *I* should act for him as ELECTIONEERING AGENT (for Greenwich)! I have replied [84] that I see not a GHOST OF A CHANCE for him:

1. Baxter Langley is the local candidate, and neither Mill nor Beales COULD STAND *without* his PERMISSION.

2. The GENERAL COUNCIL of the 'International' does not get mixed up in ELECTIONEERING. In no case could we act *against* B. Langley because—and this is a fact—since the Brussels Congress [138] B. Langley and his SUNDAY LEAGUE [235] have concluded an amicable agreement with us. (In fact, our sessions take place in *their* hall.)

3. He (Jones) is at present *unpopular* in London (and this is true). *Reynolds*'s ARTICLES: 'TRAITORS IN THE CAMP', etc., had damaged him.[236]

I have just received the enclosed letter from the secretary[a] of the Workers' Educational Society here.[67] This shows that the Lassalleans imported from Paris and Germany, who maintain secret contacts with Schweitzer, have made use of Lessner's absence due to his wife's sickness in order fraudulently to obtain from here a vote of confidence for *Schweitzer* against the Nurembergers.[135] As a well-known member of the Society, I would be made responsible for this—and this appears to me to be the aim of the whole operation. Thus I am writing to Speyer without delay explaining the reasons that, under these circumstances, I must announce my *resignation* from the Society.[b]

Your
K. M.

---

[a] Carl Speyer - [b] See present edition, Vol. 21, 'Statement to the German Workers' Educational Society in London'.

That damned Schweitzer is still too young to pull the wool over my eyes.

First published in *Der Briefwechsel zwischen F. Engels und K. Marx*, Bd. 4, Stuttgart, 1913

Printed according to the original

Published in English for the first time

116

ENGELS TO MARX

IN LONDON

V/J 71 968—Manchester, 7 January 1868 £10.
T/N 14 065—London, 26 February 1868 *£10.*
Second halves.
First sent with preceding post.

[Manchester,] 23 November 1868

Dear Moor,

I can send you the above only today, but give you the good news that, after a conversation today with Calico Gottfried,[a] it will *probably* be possible to prolong the contract with him for a few years.[158] I intend, if all goes well, to take 3 years, the last of which would be without any obligation on my part to work. If all this is successful, which must be more or less decided by the end of February at the latest, we are over the hill, and I shall be able without difficulty to pay off the £100 debt you still have, and in general to establish the affair properly and on a solid basis, so that this load of debts will not return, at least for the period of the contract.

Lizzie suddenly became very unwell yesterday; I thought at first it was serious, but she has slept a lot, so is now much better. She had congestions to the head. Tussy's letter gave her much pleasure, and as soon as she is better again she will answer it.

The wonderful primeval mass of the respected Büchner is still a great mystery to me. Couldn't you send us the book[b] here some time?

---

[a] Ermen. See this volume, p. 170. - [b] L. Büchner, *Sechs Vorlesungen über die Darwin'sche Theorie von der Verwandlung der Arten* ...

How ABOUT Ténot, *Paris, le 2 décembre?*
Best greetings.

Your
F. E.

First published abridged in *Der Briefwech-sel zwischen F. Engels und K. Marx*, Bd. 4, Stuttgart, 1913 and in full in *MEGA*, Abt. III, Bd. 4, Berlin, 1931

Printed according to the original

Published in English for the first time

117

ENGELS TO MARX

IN LONDON

Manchester, 25 November 1868

Dear Moor,

Enclosed returned the letters.[a] Jones is COOL INDEED, and in every sense he has counted his chickens before they are hatched. He will scarcely find another place to elect him. LIBERALS OF HIS CALIBRE there are enough, and more than enough, ever since he identified himself with this variety. Even the great Dr Borchardt asked him (if one can believe Dr Borchardt) how he could identify himself in such a way with Bright and Gladstone, since he would certainly have to attack them in 5 years time.

Nothing else new here. I have finally prevailed on Lizzie to let Gumpert treat her; so far she resisted, and said there was nothing wrong with her. He will probably have been there today. Incidentally, she was better today.

Your
F. E.

Büchner[b] received with thanks.

First published in *MEGA*, Abt. III, Bd. 4, Berlin, 1931

Printed according to the original

Published in English for the first time

---

[a] By C. D. Collet and E. Jones (see this volume, pp. 165-66). - [b] L. Büchner, *Sechs Vorlesungen über die Darwin'sche Theorie von der Verwandlung der Arten...*

118

ENGELS TO W. HOLZENHAUER[237]

IN COLOGNE

[*Draft*]

[Manchester,] 26 November 1868

Following receipt of your letter dated 18 August I inquired at home[84] about the circumstances in which you had left my brothers'[238] business and also sought to find out whether there was any prospect of your obtaining employment there again.

Now I have received the relevant information, and unfortunately it is such that I can offer you no hope whatsoever of obtaining employment there again. I am therefore returning to you enclosed the *false*, as you say, testimony of my brother-in-law.[a] In view of the information received, I must, it is true, assume this testimony does not wholly correspond to reality, a fact on which you may congratulate yourself, to be sure.

Respectfully yours,

F. E.

Published for the first time   Printed according to the original

119

ENGELS TO MARX[239]

IN LONDON

Manchester, 29 November 1868

Dear Moor,

Consider *very precisely* the answers to the enclosed questions, and answer them for me by return, so that I may have your reply on Tuesday morning.

1. How much money do you need to pay *all* your debts, so as to have a clear start?

2. Can you manage with £350 for your *usual* regular needs for a year (from this I exclude extra expenses caused by sickness and unforeseen events), i.e., so that you do not need to get into debt. If not, tell me the sum required for it. All on the assumption that

---

a Adolf von Griesheim

8–983

all the old debts have previously been paid off. This question is naturally the main one.

My negotiations with Gottfried Ermen[a] are taking the turn that, on the termination of my contract,—June 30—he wishes to *buy me out*, i.e., he offers me a sum of money if I undertake not to enter into any competing business for 5 years, and allow him to continue to manage the firm. This is exactly where I wanted to get the man. However, since in the past few years the balances have been poor, it is questionable whether this offer will place us in a position to live for a number of years without money troubles, even if we assume the probable case that all sorts of events will cause us to move again to the continent, and hence get us involved in extra expenses. The sum offered me by Gottfried Ermen (which, long before he offered it to me, I was determined to devote, if need be exclusively, to covering the necessary support for you) would put me in a position to provide you *certainly* with £350 annually for 5-6 years, and in special cases even with some more. You will, however, understand that all my arrangements would be upset if, from time to time, a sum of debts accumulated that would have to be covered out of further capital. My calculations have to be based upon the fact that our living expenses must be met not solely from *revenue*, but also—from the beginning—partly from *capital*, and for this very reason they are rather complicated and must be adhered to strictly, or we shall come to grief.

I would ask you to tell me quite frankly how these matters *really stand*, and your reply will determine how I conduct myself in the future vis-à-vis Gottfried Ermen. So, name yourself the sum you need regularly per annum, and we shall see what can be done.

What will happen after the 5-6 years mentioned above is not clear to me either. If everything remains as at present, I would no longer be in a position to send you £350 a year or even more, but still at least £150. Yet much may change by then, and your literary work will be capable of bringing something in for you.

Best greetings to your wife and the girls. Send one of the enclosed photograms to Laura.

Your

F. E.

First published in *Der Briefwechsel zwischen F. Engels und K. Marx*, Bd. 4, Stuttgart, 1913

Printed according to the original

---

[a] See this volume, p. 167.

120

MARX TO ENGELS[80]

IN MANCHESTER

London, 30 November 1868

DEAR FRED,

I am quite KNOCKED DOWN by your too great kindness.

I had my wife show me all the BILLS, and the amount of the debts is much greater than I thought, £210 (of which ABOUT £75 for the pawnshop and interest). This does not include the doctor's BILL for attendance during the SCARLATINA, which he has not yet submitted.

During the past few years we have used more than £350, but the sum is absolutely sufficient, since 1. during the past few years Lafargue was living with us, and expenses were much increased by his presence in the house; and 2., owing to the debt system, everything cost much too much. With a complete CLEARANCE of the debts, I would be able for the first time to enforce a STRICT ADMINISTRATION.

You can imagine how unpleasant conditions have been here at home over the past few months from the fact that Jennychen—behind my back—got an engagement for herself as *private governess* with an English family. The business is not due to begin until January 1869. I gave permission, after the event, on the proviso (the lady of the house, her husband is Dr Monroe, visited my wife in this connection) that the engagement should *only be binding for 1 month*, and both sides, after the month had passed, would have the *right to cancel*. Though the matter was extremely embarrassing to me (the child would have to teach small children almost all day long)—I do not need to emphasise this—I consented on this condition, since I found it favourable that Jennychen would be diverted by some sort of occupation and, in particular, get outside these 4 walls. For years now my wife has quite lost her TEMPER—understandable under the circumstances, but not thereby made pleasanter—and tortures the children mortally with her complaints and irritability and BAD HUMOUR, though no children could bear it all IN A MORE JOLLY WAY. But *sunt certi denique fines.*[a] It is naturally UNPLEASANT to write to you about this. It

---

[a] there are, after all, certain limits (Horace, *Satires*, I, 1, 106).

is easier to speak of such things. But it is necessary in order to explain to you why I did not absolutely reverse Jennychen's step.

Your

K. M.

First published in *Der Briefwechsel zwischen F. Engels und K. Marx*, Bd. 4, Stuttgart, 1913

Printed according to the original

121

MARX TO ENGELS

IN MANCHESTER

London, 5 December 1868

DEAR FRED,

Enclosed:

1. Letter from Schweitzer,
2. Mineworkers of Lugau,
3. *Russe* Serno-Solovyevich (author of the pamphlet against Goegg[a]).

So Schweitzer is determined to become king of the tailors in Germany! Good luck to him. On *one* point he is right—Wilhelm's[b] incapability! His claim that the Nurembergers[135]—on pain of high treason—should enroll under his leadership IS VERY COOL INDEED.[240]

Wilhelm becomes stupider every day. What a lousy paper![c] From the letter from Lugau[241] it emerges that he has so far done *nothing* with reference to the International. At the same time, he plays fine tricks on us. In his 'cosy' way, he announces that the *'International Working Men's Association'* costs *nothing*, so that all and sundry may join *without paying*. From Switzerland Becker complains about this absurdity.[242]

Salut.

Your

K. M.

First published in *MEGA*, Abt. III, Bd. 4, Berlin, 1931

Printed according to the original

Published in English for the first time

---

[a] [A. Serno-Solovyevich] *À propos de la grève. Réponse à M. Goegg* (signed by the pen-name A. Ébéniste). See also this volume, p. 186. - [b] Wilhelm Liebknecht's - [c] *Demokratisches Wochenblatt*

122

MARX TO LUDWIG KUGELMANN [29]

IN HANOVER

London, 5 December 1868

Dear Kugelmann,

Have you got Dietzgen's address? Quite a while ago he sent me a fragment of a manuscript on 'intellectual capacity',[185] which, despite a certain confusion and too frequent repetitions, contained much that was excellent, and—as the independent product of a worker—even admirable. I did not reply immediately after reading it through, since I wanted to hear Engels' opinion.[a] So I sent him the manuscript. A long time passed before I got it back. And now I *cannot find* Dietzgen's *letter* with his new address. He wrote me, to wit, in his last letter from Petersburg, that he would return to the Rhine and settle there. Have you perhaps received his address from him? If so, be so kind as to send it to me by return. My conscience—one never becomes completely free of this sort of thing—is pricking me for leaving Dietzgen so long without a reply. You also promised to tell me something about his personality.

I have received *Büchner's* lectures on Darwinism. He is obviously a 'book-maker' and probably for this reason is called 'Büchner'.[b] His superficial babble about the history of materialism is obviously copied from Lange.[c] The way such a whipper-snapper disposes of, e.g., *Aristotle*—quite a different sort of natural philosopher from Büchner—is really astonishing. It is also very naïve of him to say, referring to Cabanis, 'you might almost be listening to Karl Vogt'.[d] As if Cabanis copied Vogt!

Some time ago I promised to write you a few words about the FRENCH BRANCH.[72] These RAGAMUFFINS are, a half or 2/3 of them, *maquereaux*[e] and such-like rabble, and all of them—after our people had withdrawn—heroes of the revolutionary phrase, who, FROM A SAFE DISTANCE, OF COURSE, kill kings and emperors, in particular Louis Napoleon. In their eyes we are, naturally, reactionaries, and

---

[a] See this volume, pp. 119-21 and 152-55. - [b] A play on the German word *Buchmacher* (book-maker) and the name *Büchner*, derived from the word *Buch* (book). - [c] F. A. Lange, *Geschichte des Materialismus und Kritik seiner Bedeutung in der Gegenwart*, Vols. 1-2. - [d] L. Büchner, *Sechs Vorlesungen über die Darwin'sche Theorie von der Verwandlung der Arten* ... - [e] pimps

they drew up, in all due form, an indictment against us, which was, in fact, submitted to the Brussels Congress—in the closed sessions. The fury of these BLACKLEGS was heightened by the fact that they had been taken over by Felix Pyat, a failed French fourth-class author of melodramas, who, in the revolution of '48, was only used as a TOASTMASTER—(the name given by the English to the men *paid* to announce the TOASTS at public banquets, or to supervise the order of the TOASTS)—a man who has a perfect monomania 'TO SHOUT IN A WHISPER' and to play the dangerous conspirator. Pyat wanted to use this gang to convert the '*International Working Men's Association*' into his following. In particular, the aim was to compromise us. Thus, at a public MEETING which the FRENCH BRANCH announced and trumpeted by poster as a meeting of the INTERNATIONAL ASSOCIATION, Louis Napoleon, alias Badinguet,[a] was *in all due form sentenced to death*, the execution naturally being left to the nameless Brutuses of Paris.[b] Since the English press paid no attention to this farce, we also would have passed it over in silence. But one of the gang—a certain Vésinier, a circulator of *chantage*[c] literature—spread the whole muck in the Belgian paper *La Cigale*, which claims to be an organ of the 'International', a sort of 'comic' paper, the like of which certainly cannot be found anywhere else in Europe. There is, you see, nothing comic about it except its seriousness. From the *Cigale* the stuff found its way into the *Pays, Journal de l'Empire*. It was naturally grist to the mill of Paul de Cassagnac. Thereupon we—i.e. THE GENERAL COUNCIL—officially announced, in 6 lines in the *Cigale*, that *F. Pyat* had absolutely *no* connection with the '*International*', of which he was not even a member.[d] *Hinc illae irae!*[e] This frog-and-mouse war[f] ended when the FRENCH BRANCH rancorously withdrew from us, and it now goes about its business on its own, under Pyat's auspices. They have established here, in London, as a *succursale*,[g] a so-called *German Agitational Association*, consisting of a dozen and a half, headed by an old refugee from the Palatinate, the half-crazy watchmaker *Weber*.[h] Now you know all there is to know about this solemn, highfalutin and important event. Just one thing more. We had the satisfaction that Blanqui,

---

[a] The name of a stone-mason in whose clothes Napoleon III escaped from prison in 1846. - [b] See this volume, p. 62. - [c] blackmail - [d] K. Marx, 'Resolution of the General Council on Félix Pyat's Provocative Behaviour' - [e] Hence this rage! (paraphrase of the expression *Hinc illae lacrimae*—Hence these tears—from Terence's *Andria*, I, 1, 99). - [f] An allusion to the *Batrachomyomachia* (The Battle of the Frogs and Mice), an ancient Greek mock-heroic poem (attributed to Pigret) which parodies Homer's *Iliad*. - [g] annex - [h] See this volume, pp. 151, 155.

through one of his friends, writing ditto in the *Cigale,* made Pyat absolutely ridiculous, leaving him only the alternative of being either a MONOMANIAC or a police agent.[a]

Yesterday evening I received a letter from Schweitzer[240] announcing that he was off to the *cachot*[b] again, and that the outbreak of civil war—that is war between him and W. Lieb-knecht—is unavoidable. I must say that Schweitzer is right on one point, that is, Liebknecht's incompetence. His sheet[c] is really wretched. How can a man whom I crammed orally for 15 years (he was always too lazy to read) have such things published as, for instance, *Society and State,* in which '*the social*' (and that's a fine category too!) is treated as the secondary, and '*the political*' as the essential?[d] This would be incomprehensible were it not that Liebknecht is a South German, and seems always to have confused me with his old superior, the 'noble' *Gustav Struve.*

Lafargue and wife have been in Paris for 2 months. There, however, they don't want to recognise the medical qualifications he achieved in London, and demand that he take 5 new 'Paris' exams!

As the result of a SETTLEMENT, my 'economic' (not politico-economic) circumstances will take a *satisfactory* form from next year.[e]

With best greetings to your dear wife and Fränzchen.

Yours

Karl Marx

Is your wife also active in the German ladies' great emancipation campaign? I think that German women should begin by driving their husbands to self-emancipation.

First published abridged in *Die Neue Zeit,* Bd. 2, Nr. 12, Stuttgart, 1901-1902 and in full in *Pisma Marksa k Kugelmanu* (Letters of Marx to Kugelmann), Moscow-Leningrad, 1928

Printed according to the original

---

[a] G. Tridon, 'La Commune révolutionnaire de Paris, *La Cigale,* No. 29, 19 July 1868. - [b] gaol - [c] *Demokratisches Wochenblatt* - [d] 'Der Staat und die soziale Frage', *Demokratisches Wochenblatt,* No. 41, 10 October 1868 (see this volume, pp. 136 and 149). - [e] Ibid., pp. 169-70.

123

MARX TO ENGELS

IN MANCHESTER

[London,] 6 December 1868

DEAR FRED,

Please send me £3 by this Wednesday[a] (the day after tomorrow), since the gas bill, etc., are due, and I have promised to pay by then.

Salut.

Your
K. M.

So it is Lowe and Bright Co.![243]

First published in *MEGA*, Abt. III, Bd. 4, Berlin, 1931

Printed according to the original

Published in English for the first time

124

ENGELS TO MARX

IN LONDON

Manchester, 8 December 1868

Dear Moor,

Enclosed five pounds and the letters from Lugau[241] and Schweitzer[240] returned. That things would come to this pass with Schweitzer was fairly clear to me from previous practical experience. This honourable gentleman was not inclined to hand over his 'strict' organisation, headed by the nominal king of the tailors; for him the only question was whether good old Wilhelm[b] would subordinate himself to him or not. I don't exactly mind his assessing Wilhelm correctly, but he forgets that he himself, with much more brain, is, in his LINE, just such a twopenny-halfpenny

---

[a] 9 December - [b] Wilhelm Liebknecht

character as Wilhelm. His confidence that he can regularly be given ticket of leave from the *cachot*[a] also has an unpleasant ring; he should not have written this to *you* after using this method so often, and precisely during his Bismarck era, with such success.

The Lugau lads' letter does them great honour. That jackass Liebknecht has described the conditions of these workers in his sheet[b] in more than 20 articles, *yet only here* does one see clearly where the infamy lies. Incidentally, Moore says that similar conditions—though not so bureaucratically intricate ones—obtain in English coalmines.

The letter from Serno-Solovyevich[c] was *not* enclosed.

In haste.

Your
F. E.

Today in the office I was overrun, without a break, from twelve-thirty until five.

First published in *Der Briefwechsel zwischen F. Engels und K. Marx*, Bd. 4, Stuttgart, 1913

Printed according to the original

Published in English for the first time

125

MARX TO ENGELS

IN MANCHESTER [244]

London, 9 December 1868

DEAR FRED,

BEST THANKS FOR £5.

I forgot to enclose the Russian.[d] Follows herewith. In addition *Sigfrid Meyer*.[245] (The *Drury* of whom he speaks is a fishy customer who was formerly in London and who wished to push himself onto the CENTRAL COUNCIL. He impressed S. Meyer by his public appearances in New York. Meyer wrote to us that we should really appoint Drury as our agent. I replied to him[e] that Mr Drury had

---

a gaol - b *Demokratisches Wochenblatt* - c See this volume, p. 172. - d Marx means the letter of A. A. Serno-Solovyevich. - e See this volume, p. 97.

already had himself 'recommended' to us in this capacity by Cremer, Huleck, etc. We did *not* want him.)

Finally a reappearance CARD from Nincompoop.[a] This letter is very characteristic of him. Schily took him to Lafargue et Co. You know that in Paris you can only move in on the *terme*.[b] Lafargue and Laura thus lived in a *chambre garnie*,[c] high up, until about a fortnight ago (when they found lodgings, and we sent them their chests and boxes). The first thing Borkheim said when he came to visit them with Schily: 'This has put me quite out of breath. I would not like often to climb so high!' And now his marginal notes, which he sends to *me*! Incidentally, he has kept his promise about 'not-climbing'. Lafargue had bought the Ténot,[d] but since the postage to London is dear, Borkheim was supposed to bring the book here on his return journey to Bordeaux. But he was not seen again.

And this reminds me of another anecdote concerning Borkheim. Shortly before Lafargue left, Borkheim invited him and my family to dinner (Laura did not go). After the 'gentlemen' had retired to Borkheim's STUDY—the gentlemen were *Lafargue, Borkheim and myself*—Borkheim related all sorts of gossip told or published by one person or another about me. I let him have his head for a time, while Lafargue rocked crossly backwards and forwards in his chair. Finally I interrupted him and said: It was altogether extraordinary what gossip went round in the world. Engels and I could tell the best stories about this, because we possessed proper archives about the refugees. For instance, when he—Borkheim—came from Switzerland to England, we received a report that he was an agent of the Prussian Count X[e] (I cannot JUST NOW recall the name), who was himself a Prussian spy, and that it had been this count that had sent him to Switzerland, etc. Borkheim exploded like a bomb. 'He had never thought that anybody at all in London knew anything about this story, etc.' He then started to tell the story at great length and in great detail and, in his excitement, pumped too much HOT WATER and even more BRANDY into himself. In this OVERWORKED condition we then returned to the ladies for tea, and Borkheim at once burst out with the announcement that I had given him THE MOST STRANGE SURPRISE of his life. He then told the same story three times in succession, to the great annoyance of his wife, since all sorts of females play a role in

---

a S. Borkheim - b beginning of the quarter - c furnished room - d E. Ténot, *Paris en décembre 1851...*, Paris, 1868. E. Ténot, *La Province en décembre 1851 ...* Paris, 1868, See also this volume, p. 188. - e Heinemann

it. Later he wrote to me twice: I had obviously been joking, he had probably himself told me the gossip about him, etc. I, however, remained serious. (We had learned about the business from Schily, in one of his letters from Paris, at the time of the Vogt affair.) There must be punishment!

Apropos. Something that remained a mystery to me for a long time was this: during the 3 years of the cotton FAMINE, where did the English get all that cotton, even for the DIMINISHED SCALE OF PRODUCTION?[246] It was impossible to explain this from the official statistics. Despite all the imports from India, etc., there was seen to be quite an enormous deficit if you calculated the exports to the Continent (and even the occasional ones to New England). Nothing, or almost nothing, remained for HOME CONSUMPTION. The business was easily solved. It has now been proved (a fact perhaps known to you, but new to me) that, at the outbreak of the Civil War, the English had *verbotenus*[a] approximately *3 years' stock* (naturally for a DIMINISHED SCALE OF PRODUCTION). What a fine crash that would have produced if the Civil War had *not* broken out!

The EXPORTS OF YARN and MANUFACTURED GOODS in *1862, 1863* and *1864* were=1,208,920,000 lbs (REDUCED TO YARN) and the SUPPLIES (*IMPORTS*) (REDUCED TO EQUIVALENT WEIGHT IN YARN)=1,187,369,000 lbs.[b] In the first figure, the surplus of baryta hidden in the MANUFACTURED GOODS has probably been overlooked. Even so, the result roughly emerges that the entire HOME SUPPLY was met from existing stocks.

Salut.

Your

K. M.

First published abridged in *Der Briefwechsel zwischen F. Engels und K. Marx*, Bd. 4, Stuttgart, 1913 and in full in *MEGA*, Abt. III, Bd. 4, Berlin, 1931

Printed according to the original

Published in English for the first time

---

[a] literally - [b] Marx quotes the figures from the article 'A Phase of the Cotton Trade during the Civil War', published in *The Economist*, No. 1181, 14 April 1866, p. 447 (signed J. E.).

126

MARX TO ENGELS

IN MANCHESTER

[London,] 10 December 1868

DEAR FRED,

You must return the enclosed letter to me immediately after reading it, since I must send it back to Kugelmann.[247]

Kugelmann (there is nothing else worthy of notice in his letter, which I am not sending, as I wish to reply to him) has this to say about Dr Freund, the 'author' of the letter:

'Recently, in Dresden, I recruited a promising pupil for you in the shape of a very intelligent colleague, a university teacher in Breslau. He told me he had written a small study on the worker question. I recommended him to read your book[a] before publishing his study. His own reflections had led him to Malthusian ideas.— I would like to have the enclosed letter returned *quite soon*, since I still have to reply to it.—Freund is now engaged in an *epoch-making work* dealing with the development of the normal and pathological pelvis, in particular, and of the skeleton, in general. In Dresden he gave a lecture on this that created a sensation. The professors and privy councillors received his brilliant discoveries with a dignified air of superiority, which vexed me. At the close of our section meeting I said a few words in order to emphasise Freund's achievements in a complimentary manner and I asked those who agreed with me to rise. The entire section rose, but—they were perfidious enough to omit this ovation from the minutes of the meeting. When I wanted to insist on its inclusion, Freund intervened himself and said he did not wish it. I believe he now regrets this. This is to make his letter understandable. When his work appears, Engels will, in any case, have to plough through it'.

(It appears you have to plough through everything.)

Your

K. M.

First published in *Der Briefwechsel zwischen F. Engels und K. Marx*, Bd. 4, Stuttgart, 1913

Printed according to the original

Published in English for the first time

---

[a] the first volume of *Capital*

127

ENGELS TO MARX

IN LONDON

[Manchester,] 11 December 1868

Dear Moor,

I return you 2 letters, the most the ENVELOPE can hold, in all haste; I wanted to write to you from the office, but was held up, and the last post will be leaving soon out here.

Nincompoop[a] is extremely charming and tactful. This honourable gentleman appears to need to apply the SNOB-standard everywhere. When you see him, just ask him sometime if he is related to Mr *Hersch Kriminand,* and where the man lives. (This gentleman *exists* and signs himself exactly thus; he lives in Lemberg.) Then you can ask him what Lemberg *is called.* Polish Lwow, Little Russian and Great Russian Львовъ, that is to say Lvov or Löwenstadt from lev[b]=lion. The Jews translate that as Löwenberg, abbreviated *Lem*berg.

Here we have the finest crisis, and this time *pure* (though only relative) overproduction. The spinners and manufacturers have, for nearly 2 years now, on their own account, been consigning goods unsaleable here to India and China, thus doubly overloading the overloaded markets. This is no longer possible, and they are failing right and left. One of the first victims was *Knowles,* our fatty, who failed not so much because of consignments, but through general corporeal weakness—the 4 brothers had simply *gobbled up* the money.

I call this overproduction *relative* because it only becomes overproduction as a result of the cotton prices, which are still high. Two pence difference would and will suffice to absorb the whole lot lying around. Cotton Middling Orleans today 11d., before the war $6^1/_2$ d., 7d., 8d., according to season. Thus still 60 to 80% above the old price.

What you say about cotton 1860-61 is not quite so bad.[c] The harvest of 1860 was the largest ever, and the STOCK at the outbreak

---

a Sigismund Borkheim - b Engels gives the Russian word лев in Latin letters. - c See this volume, p. 179.

of the war greater than ever before. We lived on this in 1861 and even 1862, and the highest prices came only in 1863. But this also depended on other things—the effective blockade of the Southern harbours, etc., etc. But there was never any question of 3 years' reserve, that is enormously exaggerated. If you like, I can compile the things for you from the official report (i. e., the LIVERPOOL BROKER ASSOCIATION'S report), and I shall do it in any case before I abandon COMMERCE. Incidentally, you will find a lot in *Watts*.[a]

I expect any day to receive the draft contract with Gottfried Ermen.[b]

Your
F. E.

First published in *Der Briefwechsel zwischen F. Engels und K. Marx*, Bd. 4, Stuttgart, 1913

Printed according to the original

Published in English for the first time

128

MARX TO ENGELS

IN MANCHESTER

London, 12 December 1868[c]

DEAR FRED,

You will have seen that the ESTIMATE about COTTON relics on a comparison between exports and imports for 1862, 1863, and 1864. The *conclusion* regarding the *stocks of RAW COTTON + COTTON MANUFACTURES* (I believe I forgot the latter addition in the letter to you[d]) available in the *UNITED KINGDOM ON 1 JANUARY 1862* thus depends entirely on the correctness of the premisses. The data are based on the report by Messrs *ELLISON AND HAYWOOD*. The bare figures are as follows:

---

[a] J. Watts, *The Facts of the Cotton Famine*. - [b] See this volume, pp. 167 and 170. - [c] In the original mistakenly: 1866. - [d] See this volume, p. 179.

Statistics of Cotton in the United Kingdom 1862, 1863, 1864[a]

	1862	1863	1864	For 3 years
	Import			
	thousand of lbs			
Cotton Imported	533,176	691,847	896,770	
Ditto Exported	216,963	260,934	247,194	
Available to Consumption	316,213	430,913	649,576	
Waste in Spinning	53,756	64,637	90,940	
Equal to Production in Yarn	262,457	366,276	558,636	
Total				1,187,369
	Export			
	[thousand of lbs]			
Yarn	88,554	70,678	71,951[b]	
Piece goods etc.	324,128	321,561	332,048	
Total	412,682	392,239	403,999[c]	1,208,320[d]

The arsenic works excellently. You know that, ABOUT 6 weeks ago, I felt something carbuncular and then re-started imbibing arsenic, and I am still at it. In fact, nothing has appeared except constant small preliminaries, which just as constantly disappear again. For years the business always began in October, and by January was in full bloom. Now it looks as though I shall escape it this year, and that only enough *traces* of the sickness reappeared and are reappearing as were necessary to induce me to take arsenic.

In his latest speech in Edinburgh, in which Huxley again took a more materialist stand than in recent years, he opened up another loophole for himself.[248] As long as we really observe and think, we can never escape materialism. But all this is reduced to the relationship between cause and effect, and 'your great compatriot Hume' has already proved that these categories have nothing in

---

[a] The table, which Marx gives in English, is from the article 'A Phase of the Cotton Trade during the Civil War', published in *The Economist*, No. 1181, 14 April 1866, p. 447 (signed: J. E.). - [b] Marx mistakenly wrote: 171,951. - [c] Marx mistakenly wrote: 403,399. - [d] In Marx's letter and in *The Economist* mistakenly: 1,208,920.

common with the things in themselves. *Ergo*, it is up to you to believe what you will. *Q.E.D.*

Salut.

Your

K. M.

First published in *Der Briefwechsel zwischen F. Engels und K. Marx*, Bd. 3, Stuttgart, 1913

Printed according to the original

Published in English for the first time

129

MARX TO LUDWIG KUGELMANN[29]

IN HANOVER

London, 12 December 1868

Dear Friend,

I wanted to write to you at greater length, but am prevented from doing so by unforeseen external 'business'. But do not let this keep you from taking up your pen again soon.

The letter from Freund (returned enclosed, with thanks) interested me greatly.[a] It is high time for other people to come forward in Germany than the present 'pillars' of science.

I also return the portrait of Dietzgen.[249] His biography is not quite what I had thought. But I always had a feeling he was 'not a worker like Eccarius'. In fact, the sort of philosophical outlook he has worked out for himself demands a certain calmness and disposable time that the EVERYDAY WORKMAN does not enjoy. I have two very good workers living in New York, A. Vogt, a shoemaker, and Sigfrid Meyer, a mining engineer, both formerly from Berlin. A third worker who could give lectures on my book[b] is *Lochner*, a joiner (COMMON WORKING MAN), who has been here in London ABOUT 15 years.

Tell your dear wife that I never 'suspected' her of serving under Madame General Geck.[c] I queried only in jest.[d] Incidentally, the ladies cannot complain about the *'International'*, since it has appointed a lady, Madame Law, as a member of the *General Council*. Joking aside, very great progress was demonstrated at the last congress of the American *'LABOR UNION'*,[146] inter alia, by the fact that it treated the women workers with full parity; by contrast, the English, and to an even greater extent the gallant French, are

---

a See this volume, p. 180. - b the first volume of *Capital* - c Marx refers to Marie Goegg. *Geck* means *dandy*. - d See this volume, p. 175.

displaying a marked narrowness of spirit in this respect. Everyone who knows anything of history also knows that great social revolutions are impossible without the feminine ferment. Social progress may be measured precisely by the social position of the fair sex (plain ones included).

As far as the 'SETTLEMENT' is concerned, there could never, from the outset, have been any question of my taking over a business before my book was finished. Otherwise I could long have extricated myself from any embarrassing situation. The fact is simply this—but strictly **between us**—that, on the one hand, I made an arrangement with my family; on the other, Engels, without my knowledge, through agreement with his PARTNER about his own income (he is leaving the business in June), has made a SETTLEMENT for me, as a result of which, from next year, I shall be able to work in peace.[a]

With best greetings.

Yours
K. M.

First published in *Die Neue Zeit*, Bd. 2, Nr. 11, Stuttgart, 1901-1902   Printed according to the original

130

MARX TO ASHER & CO.[250]

IN LONDON

[*Draft*]

[London, not before 12 December 1868]

The only place where a few copies of *Herr Vogt* are still obtainable, is Berlin. At least, there were some to be had a few weeks ago. I shall write there and if a copy can be got, it will be forwarded to 11, Unter den Linden.

Yours truly
K. M.

First published in: Marx and Engels, *Works*, Second Russian Edition, Vol. 32, Moscow, 1964   Reproduced from the original

---

[a] See this volume, pp. 169-71.

131

ENGELS TO MARX

IN LONDON

Manchester, 13 December 1868

Dear Moor,

If the envelope holds them, I shall send back Meyer and Serno,[251] otherwise tomorrow from the office, where I have larger envelopes.

In Meyer's letter, the juxtaposition of Bohemians and Chinese amused me. Otherwise, his false Jacob-Grimm style is a bit much for me, the art of saying as little as possible with secretive circumlocutions, and putting that little unclearly.

For a Russian, Serno writes remarkably poor French; for his pamphlet[a] he must have had a lot of help. If Nincompoop[b] knew you were corresponding with a Russian! You can then tell him 1. that the name Serno, as a masculine, is impossible in Great Russian since o is a neuter ending, whereas in Little Russian male names ending in o are very frequent, thus the man is no Muscovite but a Ruthenian, a *Maloross*[c]; 2. that he is a born member of the *Brimstone Gang*[252]; *serny*—сѣрный—means sulphurous, from *sera*, sulphur; Solovyevich means son of the nightingale. I am eager to see the sheet published by these people,[d] particularly what sort of a science *he*, Serno, will propound, since he so curses the ignorance of the French. However, such a French journal is always very good, much better than the Belgian Proudhonist sheets.

The story about Nincompoop is very neat.[e]

Only now do I understand what you meant with the cotton business[f], however, you had omitted that this also included the stocks of yarn and fabrics. But then it must be noted that, to explain things rationally, you must include *1861*, when the collosal 4 million crop of 1860 gradually arrived here. How ELLISON & HAYWOOD could omit this[g] is incomprehensible to me, unless the people had a particular business purpose in their statistics. The big

---

[a] [A. Serno-Solovyevich,] *À propos de la grève. Réponse à M. Goegg* (signed with the pen-name A. Ébéniste). - [b] Sigismund Borkheim - [c] *Maloross* is the Latin translireration of the Russian *малороссъ* which means Little Russian (i.e. Ukrainian). - [d] *L'Égalité* - [e] See this volume, p. 178. - [f] Ibid., pp. 179 and 182. - [g] This refers to the item 'A Phase of the Cotton Trade during the Civil War' in *The Economist*, No. 1181, 14 April 1866 (signed: J. E.).

American crop of 1860, which came to England in [18]61, at the time of the PAPER BLOCKADE[253] is the basis of all the later production. I shall see to it that I send you the necessary data on the subject, at least regarding raw cotton. Of course, this in no way changes the fact that, without the American War, there would certainly have been, in 1861-62, an absolutely colossal collapse, this time as the result of pure, unalloyed and unconcealed overproduction.

Weighting with CHINA CLAY (this CHINA lies in Derbyshire and Staffordshire; it is fine potter's earth, and CHINA here means porcelain) has only gained ground *since* 1863-64. For some years it was the secret of a comparative few. Recently, somebody was sentenced to £1,060 DAMAGES because of this, and I hope that, as soon as I am out of the firm, they will also tackle Gottfried on account of the talc-stone he sells as cotton yarn. Tussy may well curse about the yarn when 25 to 30% of it consists of sour meal sweetened with talc-stone.

I am very glad the arsenic was and continues to be so effective.

I wish I were through with the murky business with Gottfried Ermen.[a] I cannot trust the rogue further than I can see him, and have to take all possible precautions. I still haven't even received the draft agreement; he puts the blame on the lawyer, but I blame it on the fact that he himself is still mulling over what additional chicanery for me he can get included in it. Luckily, I possess an epistle from him in which *he himself* makes the relevant proposal to me, and I myself drafted the memorandum given to the lawyer as a basis. But I already note that he is keen for me to take money out of the firm *before* I am quite in the clear with him—then he would have me in his hand and could squeeze me. But as soon as I have the draft, and find it to be FAIRLY DRAWN UP, I shall send you enough for you to pay off your debts and have some CASH IN HAND, and from the New Year the new arrangement will begin. I may come to visit you for a few days myself, but Nincompoop and his consorts must not know of this.

Best greetings to your wife and the girls.

Your
F. E.

First published abridged in *Der Briefwechsel zwischen F. Engels und K. Marx*, Bd. 4, Stuttgart, 1913 and in full in *MEGA*, Abt. III, Bd. 4, Berlin, 1931

Printed according to the original

Published in English for the first time

---

[a] See this volume, p. 170.

132

MARX TO ENGELS[174]

IN MANCHESTER

[London,] 14 December 1868

Dear Fred,

On Saturday evening[a] Ténot (*Paris* and *Provinces*)[b] and the proceedings of the Baudin trial[222] arrived. I am sending you Ténot (*Paris*) and Baudin today. The Ténot (*Provinces*) you will receive in a few days. You can bring the whole lot back yourself, for nobody in the house except me has yet read the things.

In the Ténot (*Paris*) I find little new, except a few details—I have not yet read the *Provinces*. The enormous sensation created by the book in Paris, and in France as a whole, proves a very interesting FACT, namely that the generation that has grown up under Badinguet[c] knew nothing at all about the history of the regime under which it is living. Now the fellows are rubbing their eyes and are quite thunderstruck. If one may *parva componere magnis*,[d] have we not had precisely the same experience in our own way? In Germany the story is spreading, as a remarkable novelty, that Lassalle was only one of our satellites, and that he *did not discover* the 'class struggle'.

I can discover nothing special in the speech by *Gambetta*,[e] who is now being lionised in France. His manner reminds me strikingly of Michel de Bourges. This Michel also made his name through a political trial. A few months before the February revolution he declared that he had abandoned his belief in 'democracy', since it always turned into 'demagogy'. Of course, this did not prevent him from shining as a *républicain de la veille*[f] *after* February, and rendering excellent service to Bonaparte, *nolens* or *volens*,[g] particularly in the question of quaestors.[254] He was also MORE OR LESS in contact with the republican 'Plon-Plon'.

I was really delighted to read again IN FULL the deliberations of the '*républicains modérés*', i. e., those seated in the *législative*, in the 10th Arrondissement-Mairie.[255] I believe no similar tragicomedy

_____

[a] 12 December - [b] See this volume, p. 178. - [c] Napoleon III (Badinguet is the name of the stone-mason in whose clothes he escaped from prison in 1846). - [d] compare small and great - [e] L. Gambetta, 'Plaidorie de M. Gambetta, avocat de M. Delescluze. Audience du 14 novembre 1868'. In: *Affaire de la souscription Baudin*, 3 ed., Paris, 1868. - [f] time-honoured republican - [g] willy-nilly

can be found anywhere in world history, at least not carried out in this pure form. The Frankfurt-Stuttgart Parliament [256] is nothing in comparison. The French alone understand how to put on a show, whether it be a convention or a rump parliament of thorough scoundrels.

As for the cotton, I have the import and export lists for 1861, etc., in the RETURNS of the BOARD OF TRADE.[a] The only FACT of importance to me was—and this is certainly unprecedented—that for 3 years nothing was manufactured for the home market (I mean from the *freshly-imported* raw materials during those 3 years, or those only intended *to make up stock*).

Asher, the booksellers here (a BRANCH of the Berlin one, Unter den Linden) have written to me that they need a few COPIES of *Herr Vogt* in Berlin.[b] That infernal Wilhelm,[c] as you know, never answered a very pressing letter I sent him months ago,[84] except to say that he had frittered away the 300 copies turned over to him, but that a few still existed in Berlin. I shall give him another kick today.[84]

Tussychen is enraptured at the prospect of having you here with us, and so is the WHOLE FAMILY. TUSSY IS A FANATICAL PARTISAN OF YOURS, MRS LIZZIE, AND THE 'CONVICTED' NATION.[d] But you must write when.

Salut.

Your

K. M.

In *Balzac*'s *Le Curé de Village* there is this passage:

'Si le produit industriel n'était pas *le double en valeur* de son *prix de revient en argent*, le commerce n'existerait pas.'

Qu'en dis-tu?[e]

Since Nincompoop[f] discovered Serno, he does not treat him so severely. He is only astonished that Serno turned to me instead of to him.

First published in *Der Briefwechsel zwischen F. Engels und K. Marx*, Bd. 4, Stuttgart, 1913

Printed according to the original

Published in English in full for the first time

---

[a] 'Accounts Relating to Trade and Navigation for the Year Ended December 31, 1861'. In: *The Economist*, No. 966, 1 March 1862 (supplement). As a separate edition the accounts appeared under the title *Annual Statement of the Trade and Navigation of the United Kingdom with Foreign Countries and British Possessions in the Year 1861*, London, 1862. - [b] See this volume, p. 185 - [c] Wilhelm Liebknecht - [d] See this volume, p. 79. - [e] 'If the industrial product did not have *twice the value* of its *production cost in money*, commerce would not exist.' What do you say to that? - [f] Sigismund Borkheim

133

MARX TO ENGELS

IN MANCHESTER

London, 15 December 1868
Evening, after midnight

DEAR FRED,

Would you please study the enclosed document [257] *seriously*, despite its *fadaise*.[a] *Your marginal notes* should be written for me in *French*, and the stuff itself **returned to me at the latest by** SATURDAY NEXT[b]!

Mr Bakunin—in the background of this business—is condescending enough to wish to take the workers' movement under *Russian* leadership.

This shit has been in existence for 2 months. Only this evening did OLD Becker inform the General Council about it in writing. This time Nincompoop[c] is right. As OLD Becker writes, this association should make up for the deficient '*idealism*' of our Association. *L'idéalisme Russe!*

There was great anger about the document this evening at the meeting of our *Conseil Général*, particularly among the French. I had known about the shit for a long time. I regarded it as stillborn, and out of consideration for OLD Becker, wanted to let it die a quiet death.

But the business has become more serious than I expected. And consideration for OLD Becker is no longer admissible. This evening the COUNCIL decided to repudiate this INTERLOPING SOCIETY *publicly*—in Paris, New York, Germany and Switzerland. I have been commissioned with drafting the decree of repudiation[d] (for next Tuesday[e]). I regret the whole thing, because of OLD Becker. *Mais*[f] our Association cannot commit SUICIDE because of OLD Becker.

Your
K. M.

Strohn writes to me from Düsseldorf that his brother Eugen has died suddenly in Hamburg.

---

[a] absurdity - [b] 19 December - [c] Sigismund Borkheim - [d] See this volume, p. 202. - [e] 22 December - [f] But

About the COTTON BANKRUPTCIES in Manchester, etc., can you send me *The Guardian?*

First published in *Der Briefwechsel zwischen F. Engels und K. Marx*, Bd. 4, Stuttgart, 1913

Printed according to the original

Published in English for the first time

134

ENGELS TO MARX [174]

IN LONDON

Manchester, 18 December 1868

Dear Moor,

Best thanks for the Ténot[a] and the Baudin trial.[222] As soon as I have read the latter I shall send them both back. You can keep *Province* there; I have ordered them both at the bookshop; one really must have things of this sort. The complete oblivion of revolutionary-counterrevolutionary causality is a necessary result of every victorious reaction; in Germany the younger generation knows absolutely nothing about '48, except the wretched howls of the *Kreuzzeitung*, which echoed in '49-52 in all the papers; history comes to an abrupt stop there at the end of '47.—The deliberations of the 10th *Mairie* are really exquisite; I had never read such a complete version.[255]

By chance I read E. Strohn's obituary in the *Kölnische Zeitung*. He died of articular rheumatism.

The Geneva document[257] is very naïve. Old man Becker has never been able to refrain from cliquish agitation; wherever 2 or 3 get together, he must be amongst them; yet if you had warned him in good time, he would probably have steered clear of it. Now he will be astonished by the bad effects of his well-meant efforts. It is as clear as daylight that the International cannot get involved in this fraud. Il y aurait deux conseils généraux et même deux congrès; c'est l'Etat dans l'Etat, et dès le premier moment le conflit éclaterait entre le conseil pratique à Londres et le conseil théorique, 'idéaliste', à Genève. Il ne peut y avoir deux corps internationaux (par profession) dans l'Internationale, pas plus que

---

[a] E. Ténot, *Paris en décembre 1851...* (see this volume, p. 188).

deux conseils généraux. Du reste, qui vous donne le droit de reconnaître un soi-disant bureau central sans mandataires dont les membres appartenants à la même nationalité se constituent (§ 3 du règlement on omet le '*se*' et pour cause!) en bureau national de leur pays! Ces messieurs, n'ayant pas de constituants, eux-mêmes exceptés, veulent que l'Internationale se constituât en mandataire pour eux. Si l'Internationale refuse de le faire, qui reconnaîtrait 'le groupe initiateur' autrement dit le 'bureau central' pour ses représentants? Le conseil central de l'Internationale au moins a passé par trois élections successives et tout le monde sait qu'il représente des myriades d'ouvriers; mais ces 'initiateurs'?

Et puis si nous voulons bien faire abstraction de la formalité d'élection, que représentent les noms qui forment ce groupe initiateur? ce groupe qui prétend de se donner 'pour mission spéciale d'étudier les questions politiques et philosophiques etc.'? Ce sera sans doute la science qu'ils représenteront. Nous trouverons parmi eux des hommes dont il est notoire qu'ils ont passé leur vie entière à l'étude de ces questions? Au contraire. Pas un nom dont le porteur ait, jusqu'ici, même osé prétendre à passer pour un homme de science. S'ils sont sans mandats comme représentants de la démocratie sociale, ils le sont encore mille fois plus comme représentants de la science.[a]

The rest you remarked upon in your notes. Like you, I regard

---

[a] There would be two General Councils and even two Congresses: this would be a state within the state and, right from the start, conflict would break out between the practical Council in London, and the theoretical, 'idealist', Council in Geneva. In the International there cannot be two (professional) international bodies, any more than two General Councils. Incidentally, who gives you the right to recognise a so-called Central Bureau without mandators, whose members will be of the same nationality and who constitute themselves (in paragraph 3 of the Rules this '*themselves*' is omitted, and with good reason!) the national bureau of their country! Since these gentlemen have no mandators except themselves, they wish the International to constitute itself their mandator. If the International refuses to do so, who would recognise the 'initiating group' or, in other words, the 'Central Bureau' as its representatives? The Central Council of the International has passed through at least three successive elections, and the whole world knows that it represents countless workers; but these 'initiators'?

And even if we wished to ignore the formalities of an election, what is represented by the names that make up this initiating group, this group that pretends to have been given 'the special mission to study political and philosophical questions, etc.'? No doubt it is science they will represent. Will we find among them men known to have devoted their whole lives to the study of these questions? On the contrary. There is not a name whose bearer has so far dared as much as to claim to be a man of science. If they are without mandate as representatives of social democracy, they are a thousand times more without mandate as representatives of science.

the business as a stillborn, purely Genevan local growth. It would only be viable if you were to oppose it too violently, and thus gave it importance. I think it would be best calmly but firmly to rebuff these people with their pretensions to sneaking into the International. Apart from this, we should say that they had selected a special field and one would have to wait to see what they make of it and, we should also say that, for the present, there was nothing to stop members of one association from being members of the other. Since the fellows, to put it bluntly, have no other field of activity than *chatter*, they will soon enough bore one another to death, and since it may be expected that they will have no new adherents from outside (given *such* conditions), the whole concern will certainly soon collapse. But if you violently oppose this Russian intrigue, you will unnecessarily arouse the very numerous—particularly in Switzerland—political philistines among the journeymen, and harm the International. With a Russian (and in this case there are 4,[a] not counting the females), with a Russian one must never lose one's TEMPER.

I have never read anything more wretched than the theoretical programme. Siberia, his stomach, and the young Polish woman[b] have made Bakunin a perfect blockhead.

My trip will probably not come to anything before the New Year, the damned draft contract[c] is still not ready.

Best greetings.

Your
F. E.

First published abridged in *Der Briefwechsel zwischen F. Engels und K. Marx*, Bd. 4, Stuttgart, 1913 and in full in *MEGA*, Abt. III, Bd. 4, Berlin, 1931

Printed according to the original

Published in English in full for the first time

---

[a] M. A. Bakunin, N. I. Zhukovsky, M. K. Elpidin and V. I. Bartenev - [b] A. K. Bakunina - [c] See this volume, pp. 167 and 170.

135

ENGELS TO HERMANN ENGELS

IN BARMEN

Manchester, 18 December 1868 [a]

Dear Hermann,

F. Ris in Mittlöden set himself up as N. Dürst Söhne (sons of the Cologner), and moved from there to Zurich. I believe he was formerly with Dürst, and young Dürst, who was here at the time, spoke quite well of him. According to bank information from Glarus, Ris is good for credit of 10,000 frs.

E. Burghardt is the nephew and son-in-law of the Burghardt of Burghardt, Krenels & Co. (former *associé* of Burghardt, Aders & Co.), whom you will know. He set himself up here and went bankrupt certainly once, if not twice, and virtually nothing came of it. Many years ago I sometimes met him at an inn in the evening; since he married I have scarcely seen him at all, and I know absolutely nothing of what he has been doing since then. But what do you want an agent in Munich for?

Tell Mother I still haven't received the draft contract from G. Ermen; he blames the lawyers. [b] The point is that he would like to have me withdraw large sums of money from the business at this moment; then he would have me at his mercy, but we are not as green in the eye as that.

Be so kind as to send me my current account in the course of January, since I would like to pay off the sum owed as soon as I am clear with G. Ermen. You could also say whether I should remit to Funke or there.

If I had wished to drive things with G. Ermen to extremes, that is, risk a breach, and had then had to start something else, I think I *could* have squeezed out about £750 more. But I had absolutely no interest in being tied to jolly old commerce for about another 10 years—and it wouldn't have been worth starting a new business again for a shorter period.

Enclosed—a pile of photographs, of which you could send 2 to Engelskirchen and distribute the remainder there. One of each sort is intended for Mother.

---

[a] In the original: '1866', a slip of the pen. - [b] See this volume, pp. 187 and 193.

Heartiest greetings to Mother, your wife and all my brothers and sisters, and have a good time over the holidays.

With best greetings

Your

Friedrich

First published abridged in *Deutsche Revue*, Jg. 46, Bd. II, Stuttgart-Leipzig, 1921 and in full in: Marx and Engels, *Works*, First Russian Edition, Vol. XXV, Moscow, 1934

Printed according to the original

Published in English for the first time

136

MARX TO ENGELS[174]

IN MANCHESTER

London, 19 December 1868[244]

DEAR FRED,

THANKS for your marginal notes![a] When I wrote to you that evening I was excited. But the next morning there was already a reaction and the decision to treat the matter diplomatically, quite as you advise.

Ténot's Province is much better. It contains many new details for us. Had the Parisians held out a couple of days longer, the *Empire* would have been *foutu*.[b] The movement (republican) among the rural population was much bigger than we knew.

Enclosed *Réveil*, the organ of Ledru-Rollin. Delescluze his *âme damnée, républicain de vieille roche, asinus*.[c] He is the provisional government's commissioner who led the Belgians into the *guet-àpens*[d] of Risquons Tout.[258] Thus traitor or arch-ASS. Probably the latter.

The stupid idea of the workers who wanted to give a banquet for R. Johnson has been blocked *by us*.[259] Coningsby, whose initiative it was, is a blackguard. This character was on a PLEASURE TRIP TO THE UNITED STATES and was paid by Seward for this London reception for R. Johnson. He is the same WORKMAN who wrote to *The Times* years ago, stating that the workers were politically satisfied and DID NOT WANT THE SUFFRAGE.

---

a See this volume, pp. 190 and 191-92. - b finished - c evil spirit, republican of the old guard, jackass - d ambush

If you could send me a few £ for the Christmas week now beginning, it would be very welcome.

Salut.

Your
K. M.

First published abridged in *Der Briefwechsel zwischen F. Engels und K. Marx*, Bd. 4, Stuttgart, 1913 and in full in *MEGA*, Abt. III, Bd. 4, Berlin, 1931

Printed according to the original

Published in English in full for the first time

137

MARX TO LAURA LAFARGUE[260]

IN PARIS

London, 22 December 1868

My dear child,

I wanted to send you together with Rückert[261] a truly delicious book— *Blüthen Morgenländischer Mystik by Tholuck*.[a] *Mais la plus belle fille de France ne peut donner que ce qu'elle a.*[b] The book was not to be had in all London. I have ordered it from Germany. You will get it in about 3 weeks.

Tell Lafargue that he must excuse my silence. I was really overworked during the last months, as I wanted to have done with certain studies before the beginning of the New Year. However, *aufgeschoben ist nicht aufgehoben.*[c] Meanwhile tell him that Dr Hunter, excellent as his report[d] is, knows as little as most Englishmen do of the past (social) history of his own country. The degradation of the rural labourers has nothing whatever to do with the Corn Laws of 1815.[262] If he wants to know the real causes which have brought them down to the zero of their present

---

[a] F. A. Tholuck, *Blüthensammlung aus der morgenländischen Mystik* - [b] But the most beautiful girl of France can only give what she has. - [c] postponed does not mean abandoned - [d] *Public Health, Seventh Report. With Appendix. 1864.* London, 1865. *Public Health. Eighth Report. With Appendix. 1865.* London, 1866. Marx repeatedly quotes these reports in Volume I of *Capital* (see present edition, Vol. 35).

position, you must translate him Ch. VI, Section II (Ursprüngliche Accumulation^a) of my book.[263]

Happy New Year.

Your most devoted 'Old One'

K. Marx

First published abridged in *Sotheby Parke Bernet und Co.*, 19 April 1977 and in full, in Russian, in *Kommunist*, No. 17, Moscow, 1980

Reproduced from the original in full for the first time

138

MARX TO ENGELS

IN MANCHESTER

[London,] 23 December 1868

DEAR FRED,

I simply acknowledge—since I must go to the City right away—the receipt of your brilliant CHRISTMAS present. You can imagine what jubilation there was in the house.

Salut.

Your

K. M.

First published in *Der Briefwechsel zwischen F. Engels und K. Marx*, Bd. 4, Stuttgart, 1913

Printed according to the original

Published in English for the first time

---

^a Primitive Accumulation

139

MARX TO HERMANN JUNG

IN LONDON

[London,] 28 December 1868

Dear Jung,

Scarcely had you gone when I received a letter from Bakunin[264] assuring me of his special friendship.

From his letter I see that he has once again written at length to De Paepe, in order to lure him into the *Alliance Internationale*.[265] To prevent later MISCHIEF or later complaints about the lack of timely information, you must *dispatch* to De Paepe as soon as possible a COPY of our resolution on the Alliance.[a] Of course, you must tell him, at the same time, that, because of the present state of affairs in Switzerland[266] and in order to avoid any appearance of SCISSION, we do *not* wish to have the resolution *published*, but are confining ourselves to communicating it confidentially to the respective central councils in the various countries.

Do not forget to invite *Applegarth* to the Saturday session in good time.[267] It would probably be good to do the same with *Odger*.

Yours

K. M.

First published in: G. Jaeckh, *Die Inter-nationale*, Leipzig, 1904

Printed according to the original

Published in English for the first time

---

[a] Karl Marx, *The International Working Men's Association and the International Alliance of Socialist Democracy*. See also this volume, pp. 190 and 191-92.

1869

140

MARX TO ENGELS

IN MANCHESTER

[London,] 1 January 1869

DEAR FRED,

HAPPY NEW YEAR!

From the enclosed letter from Lafargue you will see that I have received a special NEW YEAR'S GIFT—THE DIGNITY OF GRANDFATHER.[a]

From the attached 2 numbers printed *in Paris*—*Cloche* and *Diable à quatre*—you can see what an arrogant tone prevails there. It should be compared to the language used by the opposition in Prussia! This *petite presse*[b]—and its men included even Rochefort—was the Bonaparte regime's very own product. Now it is the most dangerous weapon against it.

From the enclosed issues of the *Vorbote*[c] you can learn about the scandal in Basle.[266] These bloody fellows—I mean our spokesmen over there—have a talent all their own for making the *International Working Men's Association* responsible for every local QUARREL between MASTER and MEN. At the same time, they neglect to take *any measures* for the event of war, i.e., establishing TRADES UNIONS. Instead they shout the more loudly. The petty cantonal government intervenes. The smallest incident thus becomes important. Then comes an appeal to the International Working Men's Association in general and the London General Council in particular to pay, ON THE SHORTEST NOTICE, the Swiss war costs. And then 'old man' Becker writes[d] that we should not 'compromise' ourselves again, as in the Geneva affair,[16] etc. Soon more about this and the Russian-International intermezzo.[e]

---

[a] Marx refers to the birth of Charles Étienne Lafargue - [b] little press - [c] *Der Vorbote*, No. 11, November 1868 'Zur Geschichte der Internationalen Arbeiterassociation', and No. 12, December 1868, 'Bericht über die Arbeiterbewegung in Basel'. - [d] See this volume, p. 203. - [e] Ibid., pp. 201-02.

The whole FAMILY sends the COMPLIMENTS OF THE SEASON. Tussy says POOR FRED, HE MUST FEEL RATHER SEEDY BY THIS TIME OF THE YEAR. *Addio.*

Your

K. M.

First published in *Der Briefwechsel zwischen F. Engels und K. Marx*, Bd. 4, Stuttgart, 1913

Printed according to the original

Published in English for the first time

141

ENGELS TO MARX

IN LONDON

[Manchester,] 3 January 1869

Caro Moro,[a]

Happy New Year! and my best wishes on the occasion of the Paris New Year gift. I expect you and your wife cannot look at each other without laughing about the new dignity.

The Basle business is not quite clear to me from the *Vorbote*,[b] so I am waiting anxiously for the promised additions, and also the further course of the Bakuniad. Bakunin's speeches in the *Kolokol* are very stupid.[c] The fellow does not appear to have learned anything for donkey's years. I was interested to learn from the above that he and Herzen are still in collusion with each other. Hence Herzen must be completely done for, otherwise he would not give up Колоколъ.[d][268] Incidentally, the fellow now writes *un français à lui*,[e] which is quite appalling—and this although the chap lives in a French-speaking country! Bakunin's French is much better.

Thanks for *Cloche* and *Diable à 4*; the arrogance is indeed very

---

a Dear Moor - b See the previous letter. - c [M.] Bakounine, 'Discours de Bakounine au deuxième congrès de la paix, à Berne', *Kolokol*, No. 14-15, 1 December 1868. - d Engels gives the name in Cyrillic letters. - e a French of his own

Karl Marx with his elder daughter Jenny (end of December 1868-beginning of
January 1869)

great. A few Orleanist millions scattered among the generals would now be very desirable.

Best greetings and congratulations to the whole FAMILY.

Your
F. E.

First published in *Der Briefwechsel zwischen F. Engels und K. Marx*, Bd. 4, Stuttgart, 1913

Printed according to the original

Published in English for the first time

142

MARX TO ENGELS

IN MANCHESTER

London, 13 January 1869

DEAR FRED,

THANKS for the numbers of *Zukunft*. (Thesmar and Georgios Jung!)

I put off writing to you from day to day because of a frightful cold which, for ABOUT 2 WEEKS, has been absolutely besieging my eyes, ears, nose and entire head. Since, however, this damned foggy weather still gives no hope of an early delivery from the evil, I shall wait no longer. Is it so pleasant at your place in Manchester too? Little wonder that SUICIDES are in full blossom here now. Only an Irishman, even in Seven Dials,[269] says THAT 'HE WOULD RATHER COMMIT SUICIDE ON ANY ONE THAN HIMSELF'.

Did the young Th. von Gimborn from Emmerich, manufacturer *in nuce*,[a] present himself to you? It is not quite clear to me what he wants. First, he told me he wanted to go into a factory as a technician for a certain period, SAY half a year, or as a simple worker, in order to study the organisation, etc., of English factory work. Now it is only a question of a 14-day stay in a factory supplying agricultural machinery. Does Gimborn, AFTER ALL, simply wish to discover English factory secrets? He won't find it easy.

Now a short report about the 'international incidents'.

a) '*Alliance Internationale de la Démocratie Socialiste*'[257]: On

---

[a] budding manufacturer

22 December 1868, a unanimous decision of the General Council which stated: 1. Tous les articles du Règlement de l'Alliance, etc. statuant sur les relations avec l'Association Internationale des Travailleurs, sont déclarés nuls et de nul effet; 2. l'Alliance etc. n'est pas admise comme branche de l'Association Internationale des Travailleurs.[a] The reasoning behind this decision (which I edited), is stated completely in legal form, and shows the conflict between the statutes of the planned Alliance and our Rules,[270] etc. A final considérant,[b] which must show old Becker,[c] in particular, his asininity, is that the Brussels Congress[138] already set a precedent with respect to the Ligue de la Paix et de la Liberté.[271] With regard to this organisation, which wanted to be recognised by the International Association, the Congress declared: Since the League claims to follow the same principles and to pursue the same aims as the International Association, it has no 'raison d'être' and, considérant this, stated finally, 'plusieurs membres du groupe initiateur de Genève'[d] also voted in this sense in Brussels.

In the meantime, we have received letters from Brussels, Rouen, Lyon, etc., declaring unconditional support for the General Council decision. Not one voice has been raised in support of le groupe initiateur de Genève. That this group did not act quite honestly is clear from the fact they only informed us of their establishment and their activities after they had already tried to win over the Brussels people, etc. I regard the matter as closed, though we have not yet received an answer to our 'judgement' from Geneva. The attempt has, in any case, failed.

b) Ad vocem[e] Bakunin:

To understand his enclosed letter,[264] you must know the following: D'abord,[f] this letter crossed our 'MESSAGE' regarding the 'Alliance'. Bakunin is thus still under the pleasant misapprehension that he will be allowed to go his own way. Further: The Russian Serno was, in his earlier correspondence with Borkheim, decidedly against Bakunin. In my reply to Serno[84] I wished to use this young man as an informant about Bakunin. Since I trust no Russian, I did it in this form: 'What is my old friend (I don't know if he still is) Bakunin doing, etc., etc.' The Russian Serno

---

[a] 1. All the articles of the Rules of the Alliance, etc., laying down its relations with the International Working Men's Association, are declared null and void. 2. The Alliance, etc., is not admitted as a branch of the International Working Men's Association. (Cf. K. Marx, *The International Working Men's Association and the International Alliance of Socialist Democracy*; see present edition, Vol. 21, p. 36.) - [b] consideration - [c] Johann Philipp Becker - [d] 'a number of members of the Geneva initiating group' - [e] regarding - [f] first of all

immediately informed Bakunin of this letter, and Bakunin used it for a sentimental *entrée*!

c) *Ad vocem* OLD *Becker*:

He has got himself badly stuck. *D'abord* he sends us, dated Geneva, *21 December*, a 4-page letter about the Basle business,[a] but *without a single fait précis*.[b] We should, however, act *immediately*. At the same time, he writes to Lessner that we (the General Council) had already 'compromised' ourselves in the Geneva affair, and this should not happen again. Or, he says in these precise words (in his letter to Lessner),

'does the General Council, like God, exist only in the faith of fools?' In Geneva, people only speak of us with a shrug of the shoulders, etc.

Thereupon Becker received the reply from Jung that his 4-page epistle contained *nothing*. How can he expect to receive money in London on the basis of such a vacuum?

In his letter of 21 December, Becker announced a further ELABORATE REPORT. Instead of this we receive the *Vorbote*. You saw for yourself that the *Vorbote* in fact only reported[c] on the 'concluded' LOCKOUT of the RIBBON WEAVERS,[266] and certainly did not make clear how the conflict has developed since. In short, TO THIS VERY MOMENT we know no more than is reported in *Vorbote*. Not only can no step be taken with the TRADES UNIONS on this basis, but it is impossible to publish anything about the affair on behalf of the General Council. We cannot expose ourselves to a reply from the usurers of Basle that we are shouting to the world without knowing the facts.

Summa summarum, a week ago the General Council decided to reprimand both Becker and Perret (the *French* correspondent for Geneva) for not providing us to date with the necessary information on the Basle affair. The matter will rest there for the time being. I'm sorry for OLD Becker. But he must realise that we hold the reins, although we refrain from direct intervention as long as possible.

d) STRIKES IN ROUEN, VIENNE, ETC. (COTTONSPINNING[272]):

Are ABOUT 6-7 WEEKS OLD. The interesting thing about the case is that, some time ago, the MASTER-MANUFACTURERS (and SPINNERS) in Amiens held a GENERAL CONGRESS under the chairmanship of the *maire*[d] of Amiens. Here it was decided—on the suggestion of a certain *faiseur*[e] named Vidal, who had hung out in England for a considerable time—that competition should be offered to the English in England, etc. Namely, by establishing *dépôts* for French

---

[a] See this volume, pp. 199-200. - [b] precise fact - [c] 'Bericht über die Arbeiterbewegung in Basel', *Der Vorbote*, No. 12, December 1868 - [d] mayor - [e] intriguer

yarn, etc., in England, both for sale there and to overseas merchants who trade directly with England. And this should be brought about by a *further reduction of* WAGES, after it had already been admitted that, in France itself, assuming the present tariffs, English competition was only being withstood through the low WAGES (relative to the English ones). In fact, *after* this Amiens congress, they began with wage reductions in Rouen, Vienne, etc. HENCE the STRIKES. We have let the people know, through Dupont, about the bad state of business here (especially also the COTTON TRADE), and thus the difficulty of raising money at *this time.* MEANWHILE, as you will see from the enclosed letter (Vienne), the STRIKE in Vienne has come to an end. For the present we have sent to those in Rouen, where the conflict is still going on, a draft for £20 on the Paris bronze-workers, who still owe us this money from their LOCKOUT.[18] Incidentally, these French workers act much more rationally than the Swiss and are, at the same time, much more modest in their demands.

Hoping that your head is not so sneezily and villainously idiotised as mine,

Your

K. Moro [a]

First published abridged in *Der Briefwechsel zwischen F. Engels und K. Marx*, Bd. 4, Stuttgart, 1913 and in full in *MEGA*, Abt. III, Bd. 4, Berlin, 1931

Printed according to the original

Published in English for the first time

143

ENGELS TO MARX

IN LONDON

Manchester, 19 January 1869

Dear Moor,

You must excuse me for replying so late and so briefly, but recently we have had nothing but misfortune at home. Scarcely is Sarah [b] better, than Lizzie gets violent gastric catarrh, which I treated for a long while, and scarcely is this over, and she gets, as

---

[a] Moor - [b] Sarah Parker

the result of an injury to her toe, an inflammation of the lymph ducts in her foot and leg, which could have become very unpleasant, but is now nearly over—and before she could get up, Mary Ellen[a] returns sick from her parents, where she had spent a few days. What it is I shall only find out tomorrow, since Gumpert will be coming only then: he fears scarlet fever; but, up till now, there has been no sign of a rash. In addition, there have been all sorts of stupid invitations that could not be refused—a lot of work at the office, and you will grasp that I have enough going on.

With best greetings to the ladies.

Your
F. E.

Did you get the wine that time, and also the *Social-Demokrat* and Ténot,[b] etc.?

First published in *Der Briefwechsel zwischen F. Engels und K. Marx*, Bd. 4, Stuttgart, 1913

Printed according to the original

Published in English for the first time

144

MARX TO ENGELS

IN MANCHESTER

London, 23 January 1869

DEAR FRED,

We all hope that things are better at 86 Mornington STREET. Scarlet fever is apparently raging throughout England. But perhaps Gumpert has made a mistake with Mary Ellen.[a] TUSSY SENDS HER BEST COMPLIMENTS TO HER AND MRS BURNS.

Here there is a preponderance of coughs and colds. In my case, things were so bad that, for nearly 2 weeks, I was 'puking' regularly, to use the elegant language of Frau Blind. I went out again yesterday for the first time, and today I am smoking A CIGAR *as a test.*

---

a Mary Ellen Burns - b E. Ténot, *Paris en décembre 1851...* (see this volume, pp. 188 and 191).

The enclosed photogram is sent to you by Jennychen, who is also coughing nastily. She asks for the return of Büchner,[a] since she has studied Darwin[b] and now wishes to get acquainted with the great Büchner. The cross (on the photogram of Jenny) is the Polish 1864 Insurrection Cross.[273]

Tussy has taken over sending receipts for the wine, and believes that to date she has done so.

Enclosed are 2 Borkheimiana. So that he can deposit his 'super intellect' somewhere, and not buzz my ears full, I have recommended that he write 'Russian Letters' for *Zukunft*.[274] *Nous verrons*.[c]

I have seen from *The Money Market Review* that Knowles is paying 7s.6d. in the £.[d] How is the old boy doing?

With best greetings to the whole household.

Your
Moor

First published in *MEGA*, Abt. III, Bd. 4, Berlin, 1931   Printed according to the original

Published in English for the first time

145

ENGELS TO MARX [275]

IN LONDON

Manchester, 25 January 1869
7 Southgate

Dear Moor,

In all haste, just an announcement that we are all on our feet again, and that, luckily, Gumpert raised a false alarm about scarlet fever. Today I must look carefully through the draft contract with G. Ermen, which I am now getting, so that things may be settled as soon as possible[e]; for this reason, only these few lines today. As soon as I see the way clear and everything has gone so far that no miscarriage may be feared, I shall come to London for a few days.

Best greetings to you all.

Your
F. E.

---

[a] L. Büchner, *Sechs Vorlesungen...* - [b] Ch. Darwin, *On the Origin of Species by Means of Natural Selection, or the Preservation of Favoured Races in the Struggle for Life* - [c] we shall see - [d] See this volume, p. 181. - [e] Ibid., pp. 167, 170.

Since Jenny has been coughing, you must have cancelled immediately the arrangement about giving lessons?[a]

First published in *Der Briefwechsel zwischen F. Engels und K. Marx*, Bd. 4, Stuttgart, 1913

Printed according to the original

Published in English for the first time

146

ENGELS TO MARX[275]

IN LONDON

Manchester, 26 January 1869
7 Southgate

Dear Moor,

Today, at 2 o'clock midday, Ernest Jones died of pneumonia. He had been sick since Thursday[b] and given up by the doctors since Friday.

Another of the old gang!

Your
F. E.

First published in *Der Briefwechsel zwischen F. Engels und K. Marx*, Bd. 4, Stuttgart, 1913

Printed according to the original

Published in English for the first time

147

MARX TO ENGELS

IN MANCHESTER

[London,] 28 January 1869

DEAR FRED,

The news about E. Jones naturally caused deep dismay in our household, since he was one of our few old friends.

---

[a] See this volume, p. 171. - [b] 21 January

I am sending you 1 *Vorbote* and a small pamphlet I received today from Berlin. The author, who sent it, describes himself on the envelope as a university lecturer in agricultural management.

Jennychen's cough has nearly disappeared. In the past few days I have had another bad attack, but today the business appears to me to have changed into a running cold, and thus be coming to an end.

Liebknecht writes to me that, in Switzerland and Germany, revolts are pending against Becker (OUR OLD ONE [a]) and that a public scandal can *only* be avoided if Becker breaks with Bakunin and abandons his dictatorial behaviour. People are very dissatisfied with his financial management, and his reports on it. Liebknecht wishes me to write *privatim* to Becker, since he is very STUBBORN. But the business is tricky. Wilhelm will go to Vienna in May. The last fifty copies of *Herr Vogt* have been deposited with Kugelmann, on my instructions.

The Gurney affair [227] AMUSES me immensely. I have studied this damned CASE in all the DETAILS, so I found nothing new in the PROCEEDINGS in Mansion House,[b] EXCEPT GREAT Edwards.[c]

You must notify me several days in advance when you are coming here, so I can invite Prof. Beesly for *one* evening.

Salut.

Your
Karlo Moro [d]

First published abridged in *Der Briefwechsel zwischen F. Engels und K. Marx,* Bd. 4, Stuttgart, 1913 and in full in *MEGA,* Abt. III, Bd. 4, Berlin, 1931

Printed according to the original

Published in English for the first time

---

[a] Johann Philipp Becker - [b] the official residence of the Lord Mayor of London - [c] E. W. Edwards [Speech on 23 January 1869 as a witness at the Overend, Gurney and Co. trial], *The Times,* No. 26343, 25 January 1869 - [d] Moor

148

ENGELS TO MARX

IN LONDON

Manchester, 29 January 1869

Dear Moor,

I at last have a chance to write to you at greater length.

Herr, etc. Gimborn[a] has not presented himself. According to your description, the fellow obviously wants nothing but to indulge in spying industrially.

The Bakunin group of both male and female sex (which difference Bakunin also wants to abolish, i.e., that of the sexes) has probably quietly passed away. The business was of Russian cunning, but still started stupidly; the fox tail showed too clearly and workers, in particular, cannot be caught in this way. Old Becker[b] simply cannot keep his fingers off 'organising', and was just the man to walk into the trap. I am quite ready to believe that he commits other idiocies, but I wish we had a better source than Wilhelm,[c] who simply cannot see FACTS as they really are. Apropos, Wilhelm has not sent me his sheet[d] any more since New Year; if he thinks I'm going to pay for it, he is making a big mistake. I am really glad not to be instructed every week that we may not make a revolution until the Federal Diet, the blind Guelph[e] and the honorable Elector of Hesse[f] are restored, and terrible and legitimate revenge wreaked upon Bismarck the godless.

The Basle story is very nice.[266] Altogether things are marching ahead well in Switzerland. Of course, the affair is significant only because everything which is more or less suppressed on the rest of the Continent appears there in the light of day. But that is in itself very good. And direct legislation by the people makes sense there, because the direct or indirect domination of the bourgeoisie should be countered on the legislative councils.[276] Since the Swiss workers virtually did not exist as a political party of their own until the Geneva STRIKE,[16] but were simply the tail of the radical bourgeoisie, they elected only radical bourgeois to the councils. On the other hand, the elected peasants could also be managed easily

---

a See this volume, p. 201. - b Johann Philipp Becker - c Wilhelm Liebknecht - d *Demokratisches Wochenblatt* - e George V - f Ludwig III

by the educated bourgeois. For small cantons, this may be quite satisfactory, but it naturally immediately becomes superfluous and a hindrance as soon as the proletariat enters the movement en masse and begins to dominate it.

A nice feature of the Basle strike is the contributions from Austria as far as Temesvár. It is inexcusable how old Becker has squandered this business with his wild declarations.[a]

Have only glanced at the Vogt pamphlet,[b] seen that he has the horse descended from the flea. If this is so, from whom is the jackass who wrote this pamphlet descended?

Today I am sending you back the copies of *Social-Demokrat*, etc., together with some copies of *Zukunft.*

It is very good that there are still 50 copies of *Herr Vogt* with Kugelmann. When Vogt lectures again in Berlin, Kugelmann must send some there, and *advertise it in the newspapers*. I bet that will drive him away.

Sam Moore is now busily studying the first part of your Duncker,[c] and he understands it quite well. He has completely grasped the dialectical stuff on money theory, etc., and declares it the best thing in the whole book, THEORETICALLY SPEAKING.

The business with good old Gottfried[d] is dragging on and on.[e] If I can manage it somehow, I shall come to London next Thursday[f] evening and stay until Sunday evening.

The photograph gave great pleasure.[g]

Gumpert has the Büchner[h]; I shall pick it up in the next few days; I fight shy of his wife, who is becoming increasingly philistine.

You must give it to the Lassalleans that they understand agitation in quite a different way from our good old Wilhelm and his boors of the People's Party.[277] This is very disagreeable, since they appear to outflank Wilhelm and Bebel completely, and the masses are so enormously stupid, and the leaders a bunch of blackguards.

Tomorrow Jones will be buried with an enormous procession in the same churchyard where Lupus lies. It is a real pity about the man. After all, his bourgeois phrases were simply hypocrisy, and here in Manchester there is nobody who can replace him with the workers. The people here will break up completely and trail more

---

[a] Engels is referring to the information on contributions for Basle workers, published in *Der Vorbote*, No. 1, January 1869, pp. 12-13. - [b] Ch. Vogt, *Mémoire sur les microcéphales ou hommes-singes...* - [c] K. Marx, *A Contribution to the Critique of Political Economy* - [d] Gottfried Ermen - [e] See this volume, pp. 167, 170, 206. - [f] 4 February - [g] See this volume, p. 206. - [h] L. Büchner, *Sechs Vorlesungen...*

than ever behind the bourgeoisie. Furthermore, amongst the politicians, he was the only *educated* Englishman who was, *au fond*,[a] completely on our side.

Apropos Beesly: How are things regarding the article for the *Westminster*?[b] Strike while the iron is hot.

I still have something of a cold. With weather like this, there is no end to it. I hope you are better now, too.

Best greetings to your wife and the girls. HOW IS MRS LAFARGUE AND BABY?[c]

Your
F. E.

That the Russian[d] from the start announces 'Marx, K., *Works*, Volume I',[e] is also good.

<table>
<tr>
<td>First published abridged in Der Briefwechsel zwischen F. Engels und K. Marx, Bd. 4, Stuttgart, 1913 and in full in MEGA, Abt. III, Bd. 4, Berlin, 1931</td>
<td>Printed according to the original

Published in English for the first time</td>
</tr>
</table>

149

MARX TO ENGELS

IN MANCHESTER

[London,] 29 January 1869

DEAR FRED,

Eichhoff's brother[f] wanted to reprint my '*18th Brumaire*' (and pay for it).

Accordingly, I thought it necessary to write to Meissner,[84] to ask, as it were, for his authorisation for this (he does not like pamphlets). He writes that nobody but he may print the pamphlet, since he is my publisher *ex officio*,[g] and wishes to remain such. The stuff should be sent to him direct, after minor alterations.[278]

QUESTION: can you get me a COPY of *Louis Bonaparte*? Wasn't there a copy amongst Lupus' estate?[279]

Your
K. M.

<table>
<tr>
<td>First published in Der Briefwechsel zwischen F. Engels und K. Marx, Bd. 4, Stuttgart, 1913</td>
<td>Printed according to the original

Published in English for the first time</td>
</tr>
</table>

---

a basically - b See this volume, pp. 138, 141. - c Charles Étienne - d N. F. Danielson - e See this volume, pp. 121, 123-25. - f Albert Eichhoff - g by virtue of office

150

ENGELS TO EMIL BLANK

IN ENGELSKIRCHEN

Manchester, 4 February 1869

Dear Emil,

I have just received from Mother the sad news that our dear Marie Bartels died of scarlet fever on Monday[a] evening. The news moved and shocked me deeply. I had watched her, and all your children, growing up from the start more than the children of my other brothers and sisters, accordingly my attachment to her was livelier and warmer; I saw her last at her wedding, when she was so extremely happy and could look forward to a long succession of happy years; and now all this has come to an end. What must be the feelings of you and Marien,[b] of poor Robert[c] with his two small children! For twenty years you and Marie have been so blessed by happiness, have had so little opportunity to taste the tragic face of life, that such a stroke out of a clear sky must hit you doubly hard. In such cases words of consolation are no help; one must weep oneself dry like a child, till time heals the wounds. I am not writing to console you, but only because I know that it is a comfort to receive expressions of sympathy from those from whom one may expect them. And this sympathy and this compassion I send you, please believe me, with all my heart.

Greet Marie, poor Robert, and all your children most heartily from me.

From my heart

Your
Friedrich

First published in: Marx and Engels, *Works*, First Russian Edition, Vol. XXVI, Moscow, 1935

Printed according to the original

Published in English for the first time

---

[a] 1 February - [b] Marie Blank - [c] Robert Bartels

151

MARX TO LUDWIG KUGELMANN[29]

IN HANOVER

London, 11 February 1869

Dear Friend,

The delay in this letter may be ascribed to two circumstances. First, the damned foggy weather here—NOTHING BUT MIST—has loaded me with a nearly four-week quite extraordinarily vicious influenza. Second, I had the enclosed photograms[a] taken at least 7 weeks ago but, as a result of this very weather and atmospheric darkness, the things could only be printed from the plate very recently.

The enclosed letter from A. Ruge[b] has been received by my friend Strohn in Bradford, from one of his business friends. Ruge obviously could not resist the 'negation of the negation'. You must return the letter to me immediately, since Strohn must return it to the addressee.

The TREASURER of our GENERAL COUNCIL here—Cowell Stepney, a very rich and distinguished man, but completely devoted to the workers' cause, though in a somewhat eccentric way—enquired of a friend in Bonn about literature (German) on the labour question and socialism. He sent him, *en réponse*,[c] a summary (written) made by Dr Held, Professor of Political Economy at Bonn. His comments show the tremendous narrow-mindedness of these learned mandarins. Writing about me and Engels, he (Held) states:

'*Engels. "The Condition of the Working Class"* etc., the best product of German socialist-communist literature.' 'Closely connected with Engels is Karl Marx. He is the author of the most scientific and learned work which socialism as a whole has to show, *Capital* etc. Although only recently published, this book is still an echo (!) of the movement before 1848. That is why I mention it here in connection with Engels. The work is, at the same time, (!) of great interest for the present since (!!) one may study here the source from which Lassalle drew his basic ideas.'

A nice place to find oneself!

A lecturer of political economy at a German university writes to me that I have thoroughly convinced him, but—but his position enjoins him, 'like other colleagues', *not to express* his conviction. This cowardice on the part of the specialist mandarins, on the

---

[a] The reference is to the photograph of Marx and his eldest daughter Jenny (1869). See also this volume, p. 206. - [b] Ibid., p. 542. - [c] in reply

one hand, and the conspiracy of silence of the bourgeois and reactionary press, on the other, is doing me great damage. Meissner writes that the accounts at the autumn fair are unfavourable. He is still 200 thalers *below* his costs. He adds: If only half that which Kugelmann has done for Hanover had been done in a few larger places like Berlin, we should already have a second edition.

I became a grandfather on 1 January; A LITTLE BOY [a] was the New Year gift. Lafargue has finally managed it to have himself excused 3 examinations and only has to take another two in France.

With best greetings to your dear wife and Fränzchen,

Yours

K. M.

The cross my eldest daughter Jenny is wearing in the photogram is a Polish Insurrection Cross of 1864.[273]

First published abridged in *Die Neue Zeit,* Bd. 2, Nr. 12, Stuttgart, 1901-1902 and in full in *Pisma Marksa k Kugelmanu* (Letters of Marx to Kugelmann), Moscow-Leningrad, 1928

Printed according to the original

152

MARX TO ENGELS

IN MANCHESTER

[London,] 13 February 1869

DEAR FRED,

THANKS for the copies of *Zukunft.*

Enclosed is a letter from Lugau,[280] together with the fellows' statutes, etc.[b] Since I am, at the moment, very occupied with my book,[c] and have actually started work again after a feverish-cold interruption of several weeks, it would be very good—supposing your time is not completely taken up either—if you could make me a short report on the enclosed documents[281] (if possible in English, for communication to the GENERAL COUNCIL). These good

---

[a] Charles Étienne Lafargue - [b] See this volume, p. 172. - [c] *Capital*

mineworkers in Lugau are the first in Germany to communicate with us directly, and we must take a public stand on their behalf. *Salut.*

Your
K. M.

Send me the stuff back as soon you no longer need it.

First published in *Der Briefwechsel zwischen F. Engels und K. Marx*, Bd. 4, Stuttgart, 1913

Printed according to the original

Published in English for the first time

153

MARX TO ENGELS

IN MANCHESTER

[London,] 15 February 1869

DEAR FRED,

Herewith the story about the LOANS under Westbury, etc. You can keep the booklet, but you must send me back the enclosed English letter. I told Borkheim I needed the information for an *acquaintance in Holland.*

Don't forget to let me have Foster's *FOREIGN EXCHANGES*[a] AS SOON AS POSSIBLE. I shall return it immediately after reading it. The book cannot be obtained here.

Salut.

Your
K. M.

First published in *MEGA*, Abt. III, Bd. 4, Berlin, 1931

Printed according to the original

Published in English for the first time

---

[a] J. L. Foster, *An Essay on the Principle of Commercial Exchanges...*

154

MARX TO PAUL AND LAURA LAFARGUE

IN PARIS

London, 15 February 1869

Dear Paul and beloved Cacadou,

You know Falstaff's opinion of old men. They are all of them cynics.[a] So you will not be astonished at my passing over that stubborn fact—my prolonged silence. I jump at once into *medias res*,[b] turning the back to the sins of the past.

In the first instance, I must frankly tell you that I feel much anxiety as to Laura's health. Her prolonged sequestration I know not how to account for.[c] Her invisibility to my friends, such as Dupont, stimulates my misgivings. So soon as certain arrangements permit, I shall come over for the single purpose of having a look at my child. After the publication of *The 18th Brumaire of Louis Bonaparte*,[d] I might not be quite safe at Paris. Do not, in your letters, drop any hint as to my secret plan.

I feel much obliged to little Fouchtra[e] who tries his best at keeping his Grandfather up in the literature of the day. Vermorel's book[f] has much amused me. I generally concur in his appreciation of the persons that played in 1848 a part natural selection had not meant them for. Some men he treats too seriously, f.i. Odilon Barrot, *la nullité grave*.[g] What he lacks, is the knowledge of the finer *nuances de classe* represented, more or less unconsciously, as in the case of Ledru-Rollin, by those provisional,[h] but not providential men. *Il y a quelque chose qui cloche*[i]—his continuous attempt at revindicating, and in a very clever way too, that strange mixture of the *chevalier d'industrie*,[j] the utopian, and the critic. I have named *E. Girardin*. As to his criticism, not of men, but of measures, *l'ignorance et l'arrogance Proudhoniennes* peep out at every instant.

As to the *ouvrier artiste*, he is not my man. The only thing I like,

---

a Shakespeare, *King Henry IV*, Part II, Act III, Scene 2 - b the crux of the matter (Horace, *De Arte Poetica*) - c See this volume, p. 243. - d The reference is to the second edition of Marx's *The Eighteenth Brumaire of Louis Bonaparte*. - e Marx is referring to Charles Étienne Lafargue - f A. Vermorel, *Les Hommes de 1848* - g absolute nonenty - h The reference is to Ledru-Rollin and other members of the Provisional Government of the French Republic of 1848. - i There are some things that don't go well. - j adventurer

is the portrait of Blanqui which I have sent to Beesly, to cure him of the strange prejudices he has imbibed in the book of that *vieille cocotte*, Daniel Stern.[a] When we had him at dinner, he naively asked me whether Blanqui was not one of those *irrespectable* men, like Bradlaugh. I could not but chuckle in my sleeves at this truly John Bullian appreciation of revolutionary characters. I asked him, whether his hero, Catiline,[b] had been a 'respectable' man?

The thing that amuses me most in *Le Peuple* is the circumstance—a good sample of historical irony—that these learned Proudhonians are forced to come out as *gens de lettre*,[c] a part which they despise so much, and which, nevertheless, is their only true *rôle*, the only thing they are fit for.

As to Paul's lively narration of his adventure with Mlle Royer,[282] it has tickled Engels and my humble self. I was not at all astonished at his failure. He will remember that, having read her preface to Darwin,[d] I told him at once she was a bourgeois. Darwin was led by the struggle for life in English society—the competition of all with all, *bellum omnium contra omnes*[e]—to discover competition to [...] as the ruling law of 'bestial' and vegetative life. The Darwinism,[f] conversely, considers this a conclusive reason for human society never to emancipate itself from its bestiality.

As to *La Misère de la Philosophie*, I do really not see what I can further do in this affair. The mass has been spoilt from the beginning. The books ought to have been thankfully received at once, but it is now too late to mend. I have written to Meissner[84] to look after Vogler, but we will hardly gain anything by finding out that vagabond. The worst is that Vieweg not only keeps, but sequestrates the book. If he advertises it anew, at 2 fcs per piece, he might sell it—perhaps. Lafargue ought to speak with him in that sense.[204]

I fear I cannot do much for the new paper contemplated.[283] At all events, I shall try my best. Cowell Stepney will never advance £12,000. He is a well-meaning fool who fritters away his means in a most grotesque way. The *Social Economist,* a most stupid publication by old Holyoake, who is his own Cromwell—lives upon Stepney's pocket. There is no sham philanthropical pie he has not his hand, or rather his pocket, in. So, if you want him to

---

[a] D. Stern, *Histoire de la révolution de 1848* - [b] Marx is referring to Beesly's article 'Catiline as a Party Leader', *The Fortnightly Review*, Vol. I, 15 May-1 August 1865. - [c] men of letters - [d] Ch. Darwin, *De l'origine des espèces ou des lois du progrès chez les êtres organisés...* - [e] the war of all against all (Th. Hobbes, *Leviathan...*, Ch. 13) - [f] Marx is referring to social Darwinism.

come out on a larger scale, he has neither the will nor the power to do so.

Our International makes great strides in Germany. Our new plan, proposed by myself, to allow only individual membership, and sell at 1d the cards, on whose back our principles are printed in German, French and English—works well. Jung becomes every day more and more a little master. The unction, affectation, and self-importance with which he drops his golden words and spins his long narrative yarn, grow really insupportable. So Dupont told him, adding that he (Jung) was even given, while speaking, to the habitude of putting his hands in his pockets and making jingle his purse. But he is really not so bad as that.

The old acquaintance of mine—the Russian Bakunin—had started a little nice conspiracy against the International. Having fallen out with and seceded from, the *Ligue de la Paix et de la Liberté*, on their last Berne Congress,[284] he entered the *Romande* Section of our Association at Geneva. He very soon inveigled brave old Becker,[a] always anxious for action, for something stirring, but of no very critical cast of mind, an enthusiast like Garibaldi, easily led away. Well, Bakunin hatched the plan of *L'Alliance Internationale de la Démocratie Socialiste*, which was to form at the same time a branch of our International, and a new independent International Association 'with the special mission to elaborate the higher philosophical etc. principles'[b] of the proletarian movement, and, in point of fact, would, by a clever trick, have placed our society under the guidance and supreme initiative of the Russian Bakunin. The way in which they set to business, was quite characteristic. They sent their new programme,[257] with old Becker's name at the head of the signatures—and they sent emissaries too—behind our back, to Paris, Brussels, etc. Only in the last moment, they communicated the documents to the London General Council. By a formal judgment[c] we annulled and stifled the Muscovite nursling. All our branches approved the decision. Of course, old Becker bears me now a grudge (and so does Schily on his account), but with all my personal friendship for Becker I could not allow this first attempt at disorganising our society to succeed.

Has Dupont told you that gallant Vésinier has been expelled from the illustrious French Branch as a calumniator vile and

---

a Johann Philipp Becker - b Marx is quoting *Programme et Règlement de l'Alliance internationale de la Démocratie Socialiste* (see present edition, Vol. 21, p. 207). - c K. Marx, *The International Working Men's Association and the International Alliance of Socialist Democracy* (see also this volume, pp. 190-93, 202).

base?[a] *En revanche,*[b] he has become the acknowledged hero of *La Cigale,* which has openly turned against *'l'équivoque Conseil Général à Londres et ses acolytes à Bruxelles'.*[c]

And now, my dear children, farewell, kiss little Fouchtra[d] in my name, and remember

Old Nick

First published in: Marx and Engels, *Works,* Second Russian Edition, Vol. 32, Moscow, 1964

Reproduced from the original

Published in English for the first time

155

ENGELS TO MARX

IN LONDON

[Manchester,] 17 February 1869

Dear Moor,

I shall have the report[281] READY for you by next Tuesday,[e] though I don't know what interests you mainly. Enclosed is a letter from Lugau.[280]

Best thanks for the Westbury story.[f] I return, enclosed, the letter to Borkheim. I shall ask my SHAREBROKER about it.

Enclosed is the extract made by the illustrious Gaudissart[g] about Bakunin,[285] together with annotations. You see that the main strong passages, which he quoted to us in Russian, only exist in his imagination. Still, the Pan-Slavism is really spread rather too thickly, in particular the threats against the Poles are significant. And the dissolution of the Russian Empire is qualified by the fact that Great Russia should still become the centre of the Slav confederation.

Your
F. E.

First published abridged in *Der Briefwechsel zwischen F. Engels und K. Marx,* Bd. 4, Stuttgart, 1913 and in full in *MEGA,* Abt. III, Bd. 4, Berlin, 1931

Printed according to the original

Published in English for the first time

---

[a] See this volume, p. 102. - [b] in return - [c] 'the ambiguity of the London General Council and its accomplices in Brussels' - [d] Charles Étienne Lafargue - [e] 23 February - [f] See this volume, p. 215. - [g] Sigismund Borkheim

156

MARX TO HERMANN JUNG

IN LONDON

[London,] 17 February 1869

Dear Jung,

Enclosed—the German.[a]

The letter from Lafargue to you, and letter to Stepney. I think it would be better not to deliver the latter, but do send Stepney enclosed Programme.[b] He will probably contribute something.[283]

Salut.

Your

K. M.

First published in: Marx and Engels, *Works*, First Russian Edition, Vol. XXVI, Moscow, 1935

Printed according to the original

Published in English for the first time

157

ENGELS TO MARX

IN LONDON

Manchester, 21 February 1869

Dear Moor,

Thanks very much for the pipe, which will be tried out right away this evening.

Here is the report.[281] The things themselves I shall return to you tomorrow. Such miners' guilds, taken over from mediaeval times—the humbug of the Middle Ages still clings to them in their 'accoutrements and parade rules, mining festivals and church parades'—still operate in all German mines.

Since Liebknecht's sheet[c] is, after all, the gazette for these Lugauans, you might send the report on to Wilhelm for

---

[a] See this volume, pp. 214-15. - [b] *Pour paraître le 24 février [18]69. La Renaissance. Journal politique hebdomadaire* - [c] *Demokratisches Wochenblatt*

translation, once you have read it, but on the explicit condition that it is *not* spread *over more than 2 nos.* Otherwise it is no use. He can send the original back to you if you need it again.

I hear from Wehner that the bad behaviour of the Prussian police in Hanover is becoming steadily worse; letters opened every day, particularly those of Hanoverian officers who have entered the service of Saxony. But, of course, what does one expect Stieber to do with the 400,000 thalers of secret funds that the Prussian Chamber voted him from the ex-princes' income! [36]

Your
F. E.

First published in *Der Briefwechsel zwischen F. Engels und K. Marx,* Bd. 4, Stuttgart, 1913

Printed according to the original

Published in English for the first time

158

MARX TO ENGELS

IN MANCHESTER

[London,] 24 February 1869

DEAR FRED,

BEST THANKS for the REPORT.[281] It is transparently clear. I have changed nothing, except to strike out the final sentence (or rather some words of it). Yesterday read out in the Central Council.[73] Adopted. Will be sent first to *The Times* (or rather taken there by Eccarius). If they don't take it, then to *The Daily News.* Then the English press cutting will be sent to *Zukunft, Social-Demokrat* and *Wilhelm.*[a] The POOR DEVILS of Lugau will have the great satisfaction of being mentioned in the English press.

Enclosed RESOLUTIONS,[b] etc., 6 in all. The circumstances are as follows. The resolution of the Congress (Brussels)[138] obliged us to have the Brussels resolutions printed.[226] Using the excuse that the *Geneva* resolutions form part of the PLATFORM, we have printed, at the same time, *part* of what was tabled at the Geneva congress[143] by the London Central Council and adopted by the Geneva

---

a i.e., to *Demokratisches Wochenblatt* - b *The International Working Men's Association. Resolutions of the Congress of Geneva, 1866, and the Congress of Brussels, 1868*

congress, omitting the amendments, etc., proposed by the French in Geneva and *also* adopted—rubbishy stuff. Thus, this portion is written by me. On the other hand, I had no part in drafting the 1868 RESOLUTIONS. The only phrase from me verbatim is the FIRST CONSIDERING 'ON THE EFFECTS OF MACHINERY'.[a]

That Bakunin should lay claim to the 'Slav' brothers in Courland and Livonia is great. Neither are his CLAIMS ON Silesia bad.[b]

What about Foster, EXCHANGES?[c]

Meissner is a fine fellow; I sent him, a few days *before* your visit to London,[286] a copy of *Louis Bonaparte*.[d] Asked for *immediate* notification.[84] No word yet.

Wilhelm remains unchangeably the same. He wrote to me that he had sent 50 or 60 copies[e] to Kugelmann, but Kugelmann in fact has received only 6 copies!

Salut.

Your
K. M.

First published in *Der Briefwechsel zwischen F. Engels und K. Marx*, Bd. 4, Stuttgart, 1913

Printed according to the original

Published in English for the first time

159

ENGELS TO MARX

IN LONDON

Manchester, 25 February 1869

Dear Moor,

I have just sent Borkheim a CHEQUE for £162.10, of which £100 is to pay off his advance and £62.10 is for you, which makes, together with the £25 brought to you, the sum of £87.10=1/4 of £350. At the beginning of March, or as soon as I possibly can in

---

[a] K. Marx, *Draft Resolution on the Consequences of Using Machinery under Capitalism Proposed by the General Council to the Brussels Congress* (see present edition, Vol. 21, p. 9). - [b] See this volume, p. 219. - [c] J. L. Foster, *An Essay on the Principle of Commercial Exchanges...* (see also this volume, p. 215). - [d] K. Marx, *The Eighteenth Brumaire of Louis Bonaparte* - [e] K. Marx, *Herr Vogt*

March, you will get a further £87.10, then again at the beginning of July, etc.

I *hope* the English press will take the report,[281] but I am firmly convinced that it will not, and that, in the last resort, only *The Bee-Hive* will remain. At best the fellows will make huge cuts.

I have not yet read the resolutions.[226] But at first glance one is surprised that the 1867 Lausanne resolutions are not reprinted also.

NB. about the money: I only had the choice of sending it *through Borkheim* or else in some other way, which would cause gossip here in the office; I preferred the lesser evil. In future this will naturally not happen again.

The final sentence in the report [a] was, of course, aimed only at Liebknecht's sheet [b] and the public.

Foster on *Exchanges* is being sent to you today by Globe Parcel Express, since the bookpost is not certain enough for an irreplaceable book. If you have *not* received it by Saturday [c] morning, you must immediately complain to Globe Parcel Express, 150 Cheapside or 150 Leadenhall Street. Best you should return it the same way. Even by mail train, the Globe is much the cheapest way to send *larger* consignments of books.

Regarding the copies, I would immediately haul Wilhelm over the coals, and categorically demand information. The same with Meissner. The fellow has obviously had second thoughts, but since Eichhoff is ready to print, he must decide *oui ou non.* [d]

Nothing but rain here.

Apropos, I have written to Borkheim about Bakunin [84] that *he* should raise the question as to whether it is in any way possible for us Westerners to cooperate with this Pan-Slav pack while the fellows preach their Slav supremacy; he will probably read this to you tomorrow [285] when you collect the money—but, in addition, I told him he should discuss the matter with you.

Best greetings to the household.

Your
F. E.

First published in *Der Briefwechsel zwischen F. Engels und K. Marx*, Bd. 4, Stuttgart, 1913

Printed according to the original

Published in English for the first time

---

[a] F. Engels, *Report on the Miners' Guilds in the Coalfields of Saxony* (see present edition, Vol. 21, p. 39; see also this volume, Note 281). - [b] *Demokratisches Wochenblatt* - [c] 27 February - [d] See this volume, pp. 211 and 222.

160

MARX TO ENGELS[34]

IN MANCHESTER

London, 1 March 1869
Enclosed 2 *Lanternes* and 1 *Réveil*

DEAR FRED,

THANKS for the MONEY. Paid out by Borkheim on Saturday.[a] He read me your letter[84] and then his answer. He is very proud supposedly to have been able to prove that you muddle up genders (which apparently often happens with you).

Ditto received Foster on Saturday evening. The book is indeed important for its time. First, because Ricardo's theory is fully developed in it, and better than in Ricardo—on money, rate of exchange, etc.[b] Second, because you can see here how those jackasses, BANK OF ENGLAND, COMMITTEE OF INQUIRY,[287] the theoreticians racked their brains over the problem: ENGLAND DEBTOR TO IRELAND. Despite the fact that the rate of exchange is always against Ireland, and money is exported from Ireland to England. Foster solves the puzzle for them: it is the depreciation of Irish paper money. In fact, two years earlier than him (1802), Blake had fully explained this difference between the *nominal* and the *real* rate of exchange, about which, incidentally, Petty[288] had said everything necessary—but after him this business was forgotten once again.

The Irish amnesty[289] is the paltriest of its kind ever seen. *D'abord*,[c] most of those amnestied had almost served the term after which all PENAL SERVITUDE MEN are released on TICKETS OF LEAVE. And second, the chief ringleaders have been kept inside 'because' Fenianism[86] is of 'American' origin, and thus all the more criminal. It is precisely for this reason that YANKEE-IRISHMEN like Costello are released and the ANGLO-IRISH are kept under lock and key.

If ever a mountain gave birth to a mouse, it was this ministry OF ALL TALENTS,[290] indeed in every respect.

I sent you earlier the report of Pollock and Knox[d] (the same lousy London police magistrate, a former *Times* man, who so

---

a 27 February - b Marx is referring to Ricardo's book *On the Principles of Political Economy, and Taxation...* - c firstly - d [A. Knox, G. D. Pollock] *Report of the Commissioners on the Treatment of the Treason-Felony Convicts in the English Convict Prisons*

distinguished himself in the Hyde Park affair) on the treatment of Irish 'CONVICTS' in England. One of the 'CONVICTS' has exposed, in *The Irishman*, John Bull's unprecedented infamies and the lies of that blockhead Knox.

Since Laura's health is not quite as good as we thought, I had intended to go to Paris for a few days next week. I had written to Lafargue about it.[a] As a result, an unknown man, i.e., a police agent, asked him whether Monsieur Marx had arrived yet. He had for him '*une communication à faire*'.[b] How well the inviolability of the post is preserved in Paris—still! Now I am not going.

Lafargue has been excused 3 of the 5 examinations (French), and received permission, or rather instructions, to take the 2 remaining ones in Strasbourg. Meanwhile, he appears to me to be too absorbed in POLITICS, which can become nasty, since his friends are a lot of Blanquists. I shall warn him. He should pass his examinations first.

The *coterie*[c] he keeps you can see from the enclosed prospectus.[283] What they lack is £250 security. This has a good side to it. It has emancipated Lafargue from Moilin, AS FOLLOWS:

> 'J'avais parlé à Moilin pour le cautionnement; il avait promis de le donner, mais au dernier moment il a refusé, si on ne voulait le nommer rédacteur en chef. Il n'a pas dit la chose, mais il l'a laissé entrevoir. Tridon m'a dit: Moilin est un diplomate, il a d'ailleurs la tête de Fouché; ainsi il [ne] faut jamais se fâcher avec lui: il faut le sonder, savoir ce qu'il veut, pour se tenir toujours en garde envers lui.'[d]

With regard to my book against Proudhon,[e] Lafargue writes:

> 'Blanqui en a un exemplaire et le prête à tous ses amis. Ainsi Tridon, l'a lu et a été heureux de voir de quelle façon il Moro a roulé Proudhon. Blanqui a la plus grande estime pour vous... Il a trouvé pour Proudhon le mot le plus joli que je connaisse, il l'appelle un hygromètre.'[f]

After John Bull had compromised himself so nicely with the concessions he made in the Alabama Treaty,[291] Uncle Sam has now kicked him in the behind. This is entirely the *work of the Irish* in America, as I have convinced myself from the Yankee papers.

---

[a] See this volume, p. 216. - [b] 'a communication to make' - [c] company - [d] 'I spoke to Moilin about the security; he promised to give it but, at the last moment, refused unless he were named editor. He did not say this, but allowed it to be understood. Tridon told me: Moilin is a diplomat and, incidentally, has the head of Fouché; so one should never quarrel with him: one has to sound him out, know what he wants, in order always to be on guard against him.' - [e] K. Marx, *The Poverty of Philosophy* - [f] 'Blanqui has a copy of it and lends it to all his friends. So Tridon read it, and was happy to see how il Moro had disposed of Proudhon. Blanqui has the greatest respect for you... He has found the best name I know for Proudhon; he calls him a hygrometer.'

Perhaps Prof. Beesly will realise that the Irish in the United States are not=0.

Salut.

Your
K. M.

As a comparative philologist, you may find forms of interest to you in the following extract from an early 16th[a]-century Scottish chronicle [292] about the death of the DUKE OF Rothesay (son OF KING Robert III):

'Be quhais deith, succedit gret displeseir to hir son, David Duk of Rothesay: for, during hir life, he wes haldin in virtews and honest occupatioun: eftir hir deith' (namely Queen Annabella) 'he began to rage in all maner of insolence: and fulyeit virginis, matronis, and nunnis, be his unbridillit lust. At last, King Robert, informit of his young and insolent maneris, send letteris to his brothir, the Duk of Albany, to intertene his said son, the Duk of Rothesay, and to leir him honest and civill maneris. The Duk of Albany, glaid of thir writtingis, tuk the Duk of Rothesay betwix Dunde and Sanct Androis, and brocht him to Falkland, and inclusit him in the tour theirof, but ony meit or drink. It is said, ane woman, havand commiseratioun on this Duk, leit meill fall daun throw the loftis of the toure: be quhilkis, his life wes certane dayis savit. This woman, fra it wes knawin, wes put to deith. On the same maner, ane othir woman gaif him milk of hir paup, throw ane lang reid; and wes slane with gret cruelte, fra it wes knawin. Than wes the Duk destitute of all mortall supplie; and brocht, finalie, to sa miserable and hungry appetite, that he eit, nocht allanerlie the filth of the toure quhare he wes, bot his awin fingaris: to his gret marterdome. His body wes beryit in Lundonis, and kithit miraklis mony yeris eftir; quhil, at last, King James the First began to punis his slayaris: and fra that time furth, the miraklis ceissit.'

The Times does not seem to be publishing the REPORT. [281] But as *dernière instance*[b] there is *The Morning Advertiser*, which publishes everything out of stupidity.

First published abridged in *Der Briefwechsel zwischen F. Engels und K. Marx*, Bd. 4, Stuttgart, 1913 and in full in *MEGA*, Abt. III, Bd. 4, Berlin, 1931

Printed according to the original

Published in English in full for the first time

---

a The original mistakenly has '15th'. - b last resort

161

MARX TO ENGELS

IN MANCHESTER

[London,] 2 March 1869

DEAR FRED,

You must either send me the booklet from Lugau—or, better still, send me *in German* the paragraphs of the rules that you quote.[281]

I shall translate the stuff myself, since I do not regard Wilhelm[a] as competent and also because I do not wish to hand over the affair to him alone.[b]

Your
K. M.

Apropos. A PAMPHLET, WRITTEN BY A PUBLIC ACCOUNTANT, ADDRESSED TO MR Gladstone[c] states that at least 1/10 of the LIFE ASSURANCE CO'S (the whole BUSINESS IN LIFE ASSURANCE has a nominal capital of £100 million) is *bankrupt* and IS NOT WORTH THE PAPER UPON WHICH THEY PRINT THEIR ADVERTISEMENTS.

What will the bourgeois gentlemen say to this, those gentlemen who were so very very delighted about the PROSPECTIVE BANKRUPTCY (in 20 years or so) of the TRADES UNIONS?

They will keep their mouths shut.

First published in part in *Der Briefwechsel zwischen F. Engels und K. Marx*, Bd. 4, Stuttgart, 1913 and in full in *MEGA*, Abt. III, Bd. 4, Berlin, 1931

Printed according to the original

Published in English for the first time

---

a Wilhelm Liebknecht - b See this volume, pp. 220-21. - c *An Actuary. Life Assurance Companies: their Financial Condition. Discussed, with Reference to Impending Legislation, in a Letter Addressed to the Right Hon. W. E. Gladstone, M. P., First Lord of the Treasury*, p. 6.

162

MARX TO ENGELS

IN MANCHESTER

London, 3 March 1869

DEAR FRED,

Iterum Crispinus![a]

Our valued Wilhelm [b] has his own PROCEEDINGS.

First, he reprints from the *Revue der Neuen Rheinischen Zeitung* Eccarius' article about 'Tailoring in London',[c] without asking Eccarius and without quoting the *Revue* as his source. Then he writes to Eccarius that he would like to print the article as a pamphlet. Therewith Eccarius replies that, in this case, a 2nd CHAPTER is necessary, since the conditions have changed completely over the last 19 years, something that Wilhelm had absolutely overlooked in his copying craze.

Then a second move by Wilhelm:

He writes to Eccarius: he should send him the issue of the *Revue* containing your article on the 'German Peasant War'.

So Wilhelm wanted to reprint your article *without your prior knowledge* and once again *without citing the Revue.*

Luckily, Eccarius informed me yesterday evening at the Central Council.[73] I told him I would write to you about the case and, in the meantime, Eccarius should send him nothing.

With regards to the stuff itself, I have a SPARE COPY I could send to Wilhelm. And I believe—even supposing we should later publish our assorted articles together—that publication in Wilhelm's sheet would do us no harm and the immediate effect of the publication would be very good.

But, UNDER ALL CIRCUMSTANCES, Wilhelm should not be allowed to publish the article as an original contribution for him, instead of as a reprint from the *Revue.*

Write me without delay your *arbitrium.*[d]

Another curiosity. You may have seen in the Augsburg

---

[a] *Ecce iterum Crispinus*—again Crispinus (Juvenal, *Satires,* IV, 1); fig. 'again the same'. - [b] Wilhelm Liebknecht - [c] J. G. Eccarius, 'Die Schneiderei in London oder der Kampf des großen und des kleinen Capitals', *Demokratisches Wochenblatt,* Nos. 2-5, 7; 9, 16, 23, 30 January and 13 February 1869 (reprinted from *Neue Rheinische Zeitung. Politisch-ökonomische Revue,* No. 5/6, May-October 1850). - [d] decision

Allgemeine Zeitung that both of us figure as contributors to a workers' paper to be published by Oberwinder in Vienna.[a]

The facts are as follows:

About 4 weeks before New Year's Day, Oberwinder had Wilhelm write to me that he wanted to publish an almanac and needed my biography for it. I should send what was necessary to Oberwinder. I sent *simplement*[b] the FACTS and a few DOCUMENTS (Cologne Trial,[c] etc.).[84] Heard nothing further of the matter.

Now, SOME WEEKS SINCE, Oberwinder writes to me that nothing has come of the almanac, but he will place the stuff in a paper he is going to publish. About 6-7,000 subscribers are already assured. Requested me as contributor. *I forgot to answer him*; shall do it today.[d]

Incidentally I would regard it as a good thing if we had a footing in Vienna.

Salut.

Your
K. M.

Apropos. What do the German commercial oxen understand by:
1. PRIMAGE?
2. *Courtage* for the *rembours?*[e]

First published in *Der Briefwechsel zwischen F. Engels und K. Marx*, Bd. 4, Stuttgart, 1913

Printed according to the original

Published in English for the first time

163

ENGELS TO MARX

IN LONDON

Manchester, 3 March 1869

Dear Moor,

You see how right I was to dissuade you from taking a trip to Paris under any circumstances. It would be madness to put oneself in the hands of those scoundrels, particularly since nobody

---

[a] *Die Volksstimme* - [b] simply - [c] K. Marx, *Revelations Concerning the Communist Trial in Cologne* - [d] See this volume, pp. 233-34. - [e] Ibid., p. 238.

enquires about you and the *lois de sûreté*[293] are still in force. Let Lafargue go to Strasbourg as soon as possible and take his examinations; once that is over, he will be able to take some liberties. The fact that he has emancipated himself from Moilin is of enormous value; this Jesuit would certainly have got him into trouble. What Lafargue writes about Blanqui is very nice.[a]

Moore tells me that Beesly has written an article on the social question in the new *Fortnightly* which reaches the maximum confusion.[b]

The only thing linguistically new for me in the old Scottish passage[292] was the *participium praesentis* havand, having,—showing that this form still existed in Scotland at the beginning of the 16th[c] century, when it had long disappeared in England.

I really did make the blunder in Russian. I have pretty well forgotten the Russian declensions.[d]

The Lugau material[281] will be returned today by BOOK POST. Since I no longer know which passages I quoted, I cannot indicate them for you; however, I made a sort of index to the pamphlets, which is attached, and you may be able to see from this where the passages might be.

What is the pamphlet against the LIFE ASSURANCE Co., called?[e] We really must get hold of it.

So Wilhelmchen appealed to you against Schweitzer.[294] This will make a fine story, since Schweitzer cannot be caught so easily. The row is going to be fun; don't you get the *Social-Demokrat* any more? Just now, Eichhoff should keep us properly *au courant*.[f] In the next few days I shall send you some articles that he (certainly nobody else) wrote in the *Zukunft*.[g]

In the meantime, in Essen the Social-Democrat Hasenclever, also supported by Liebknecht, has been elected with a majority of 960 votes over what the *Landrat*[h] and the National-Liberal candidate[i] *received together*, and in Hanover (I believe Celle) there are also prospects for getting someone in.[295]

Incidentally, Wilhelm appears to be bestirring himself more and to be having some success in Saxony. If the jackass would only abandon his stupid South-German-federalist and his Guelphic concerns,[j] he could accomplish something despite his thick-

---

a See this volume, p. 225. - b E. S. Beesly, 'The Social Future of the Working Class', *The Fortnightly Review*, Vol. V, No. XXVII, 1 March 1869 - c The original mistakenly has '15th'. - d See this volume, p. 224. - e Ibid., p. 227. - f informed - g 'Die Gewerksgenossenschaften', *Die Zukunft*, Nos. 32, 35, 37, 40 and 47; 7, 11, 13, 17 and 25 February 1869 (see also this volume, p. 239). - h Keßler - i Dr Hammacker - j See this volume, p. 141.

headedness, in view of the mistrust of Schweitzer that rules amongst the leaders of the Lassalleans; for Schweitzer's bad conscience disarms him too, when things come to a climax. But with his People's Party[38] and his mania for restoring thrones, he'll have no success in dangling carrots before north German workers.

The odd thing is that he suddenly wants to go to Berlin, that is to say, admits that he *can*, without danger.

Incidentally, I cannot see how you, as the GENERAL COUNCIL, could declare yourselves competent on this question—even if both parties agreed—unless they both also declared themselves willing to subject themselves to the arbitration verdict against the organisation and management of the TRADES UNIONS, etc.

Your
F. E.

First published abridged in *Der Briefwechsel zwischen F. Engels und K. Marx*, Bd. 4, Stuttgart, 1913 and in full in *MEGA*, Abt. III, Bd. 4, Berlin, 1931

Printed according to the original

Published in English for the first time

164

MARX TO LUDWIG KUGELMANN[29]

IN HANOVER

London, 3 March 1869

Dear Kugelmann,

The damned photographer[a] has once again been leading me by the nose for weeks, and has still not supplied additional COPIES. But I shall not delay this reply longer because of this.

With regard to *Herr Vogt*, I wished to make sure of those copies which could still be saved from Liebknecht's hands (I had sent him 300 from London to Berlin, i.e., all those still left) in case they were needed. I therefore took the liberty of ordering them to be stored at your place. But Örindur, solve for me this mystery of nature![b]

Liebknecht sent you just 6 COPIES, but announced to me that he had sent 50 COPIES. Will you please ask him for the answer to this riddle![c]

---

[a] Fehrenbach - [b] paraphrase of the well-known words from Müllner's drama *Die Schuld*, Act II, Scene V - [c] See this volume, pp. 106, 142, 189, 208.

Quételet is now *too old* for one still to make any sort of experiment with him.[296] He rendered great services in the past by demonstrating that even the apparently casual incidents of social life possess an inner necessity through their periodic recurrence and their periodic average incidence. But he was *never* successful in interpreting this necessity.[297] And he made no progress, but simply extended the material for his observations and calculations. He is today no further on than he was *before* 1830.

It will probably take until the summer before I am finished with Vol. II.[41] Then—with the manuscript—I shall come to Germany with my daughter[a] and see you then. Or, to be more precise, shall descend on you.

In France—a very interesting movement in progress.

The Parisians are once again really studying their recent revolutionary past, to prepare themselves for the pending new revolutionary business. First, the *origin of the Empire*—then the *coup d'état of December.* This had been entirely forgotten, just as the reaction in Germany has been able to wipe out memories of 1848/49 completely.

That is why *Ténot's* books about the coup d'état in Paris and the provinces[b] aroused such enormous interest that they rapidly went through 10 editions. They were followed by dozens of other books on the same period. *C'était la rage,*[c] and this soon became a speculative business for the publishers.

These writings came from the *opposition*—Ténot is an *homme du Siècle* (I mean the liberal bourgeois paper, not our century). All the liberal and illiberal rogues belonging to the official opposition promoted this *mouvement.* Also the republican democrats, people like *Delescluze,* for example, who was formerly Ledru-Rollin's adjutant and now, as republican patriarch, edits *Réveil* in Paris.

Until now everybody has been indulging in these posthumous revelations, or rather reminiscences—everybody who was not Bonapartist.

But then came *le revers de la medaille.*[d]

First, the French Government itself got the renegade Hippolyte Castille to publish *Les Massacres de Juin 1848.* This was a blow in the face for Thiers, Falloux, Marie, Jules Favre, Jules Simon, Pelletan, etc., in short, the chiefs of what is called in France '*l'Union Libérale',*[298] who wish to perform a sleight of hand with the next elections, the infamous old rogues.

---

[a] Jenny Marx - [b] E. Ténot, *Paris en décembre 1851...* and *La province en décembre 1859...* - [c] This was all the rage - [d] the other side of the medal

Then came the Socialist Party, which 'unmasked' the opposition and the old-style republican democrats.

Including *Vermorel: Les Hommes de 1848* and *L'Opposition.*

Vermorel is a Proudhonist.

Last came the Blanquists, for example, *G. Tridon: Gironde et Girondins.*

So the whole historic witches' brew is simmering.

When shall *we* have got this far?

To show you how well the French police are served:

I intended to go to Paris next week to see my daughter.

Last Saturday[a] a police agent enquired of Lafargue whether Mons. Marx had arrived yet. He had a commission for him.[b]

FOREWARNED!

My heartiest greetings to your dear wife and Fränzchen.

How is Madame Tenge?

Yours

K. M.

First published abridged in *Die Neue Zeit,* Bd. 2, Nr. 13, Stuttgart, 1901-1902 and in full in *Pisma Marksa k Kugelmanu* (Letters of Marx to Kugelmann), Moscow-Leningrad, 1928

Printed according to the original

165

MARX TO HEINRICH OBERWINDER

IN VIENNA

[*Draft*]

London, 3 MARCH 1869
1 Modena Villas, Maitland Park,
Haverstock Hill, N.W.[c]

Dear Sir,

You must forgive my delayed reply to your letter of 14 February, resulting from my indisposition.[d]

I do not need to assure you that I am greatly interested in the workers' movement in Vienna.[e] If I could dispose freely of my

---

a 27 February - b See this volume, pp. 216 and 225. - c in the original: W.C. - d See this volume, p. 229. - e deleted in the original: 'and thus in your paper', i.e. *Volksstimme*

time and my strength, I would immediately stand at your disposal as a contributor to your paper. My ability to work is, however, continually interrupted by illness. The little leisure left me after completing the second volume of my work *Capital*[41] is absorbed by the business of the International Working Men's Association.

Thus, I cannot offer the prospect of contributions from me in the *near future*.

I remain, with best respects[a]

Karl Marx

First published in: Marx and Engels, *Works*, First Russian Edition, Vol. XXV, Moscow, 1934

Printed according to the original

Published in English for the first time

166

ENGELS TO MARX

IN LONDON

Manchester, 4 March 1869

Dear Moor,

I must leave it quite up to you to do what you think best about the article.[b] For my part, I do *not* think that the article would have any sort of effect in Liebknecht's paper[c] in instalments of 1 or 2 columns, since it would thus be spread over *two years*. On the other hand, if he wanted to print it *cheaply for* the workers, this would be different and could have an impact. Since he is now involved in a row with Schweitzer,[294] I would suggest to him that he publish the last section of my pamphlet on military questions[d] in his sheet, or ask Meissner the price at which he would allow him to sell the remainder (he once asked me about this through Moore, but as I have had no occasion to write to him since, this too has remained unanswered). If, however, he should reprint the article, he must

---

[a] deleted in the original: 'You cannot, therefore, expect contributions from me in the near future, but I can assure you of such in the long view.—Yours faithfully' - [b] See this volume, p. 228. - [c] *Demokratisches Wochenblatt* - [d] F. Engels, *The Prussian Military Question and the German Workers' Party*

indicate the source. I myself have *not got* a copy and you cannot part with yours either; we must keep one, after all!

Your
F. E.

First published in *Der Briefwechsel zwischen F. Engels und K. Marx*, Bd. 4, Stuttgart, 1913

Printed according to the original

Published in English for the first time

167

MARX TO ENGELS [33]

IN MANCHESTER

[London,] 5 March 1869

DEAR FRED,

The enclosed little document arrived *yesterday* (though dated 27 February).[299] You must send it back as soon as you have read it, since I have to lay it before the COUNCIL on TUESDAY NEXT.[a] The gentlemen of the 'Alliance' have taken a long time to produce this opus.

In fact, we would rather they had kept their 'unnumbered legions' in France, Spain and Italy to themselves.

Bakunin thinks: if we approve his '*programme radical*' he can trumpet it forth and compromise us *tant soit peu.*[b] If we declare ourselves against it, we shall be denounced as counter-revolutionaries. Moreover: If we admit it, he will see to it that, at the Congress in Basle, he is seconded by some RIFF-RAFF. I think the answer should be along the following LINES:[300]

According to para. 1 of the Rules, every workers' society that is 'AIMING AT THE SAME END; VIZ., THE PROTECTION, ADVANCEMENT AND *COMPLETE EMANCIPATION OF THE WORKING CLASSES*', is to be admitted.[c]

As the stage of development reached by different sections of the workers in the same country and by the working class in different countries necessarily varies considerably, the actual movement also necessarily expresses itself in very diverse theoretical forms.

---

[a] 9 March - [b] however little - [c] *Rules of the International Working Men's Association. Founded September 28th, 1864*, p. 4 (see also present edition, Vol. 20, p. 442).

10*

The community of action the International Working Men's Association is calling into being, the exchange of ideas by means of the different organs of the sections in all countries and, finally, the direct discussions at the general congresses would also gradually create a common theoretical programme for the general workers' movement.

With regard to the programme of the 'Alliance', therefore, it is not necessary for the General Council to submit it to an *examen critique*.[a] The Council does not need to examine whether it is an adequate scientific expression of the workers' movement. It has only to ask whether the *general tendency* of the programme is in opposition to the general tendency of the International Working Men's Association—the COMPLETE EMANCIPATION OF THE WORKING CLASSES!

This reproach might apply to only one phrase in the programme, para. 2: 'elle veut avant tout l'égalisation politique, économique et sociale *des classes*.[b] *'L'égalisation des classes'*, interpreted literally, is simply another way of saying the *'Harmonie du capital et du travail'*[c] preached by bourgeois socialists. The final aim of the International Working Men's Association is not the logically impossible *'égalisation des classes'*, but the historically necessary *'abolition des classes'*. From the context in which this phrase appears in the programme, however, it seems to be merely A SLIP OF THE PEN. The General Council has little doubt, therefore, that this phrase, which might lead to serious misunderstanding, will be deleted from the programme.[301]

On this assumption, it is the principle of the International Working Men's Association to leave each section the responsibility for its own programme. There is, therefore, no obstacle to the transformation of the sections of the Alliance into sections of the International Working Men's Association.

As soon as this has taken place, the General Council must, in accordance with the Rules, be supplied with a *dénombrement*[d] of the newly adhering sections, according to country, residence and numbers.

This last point—the census of their legions—will, of course, upset the gentlemen. When you return the letter, tell me what you want changed in this draft reply.

Quoad[e] *Liebknecht*, I have given further thought to the matter[f]. Publication in the lousy little sheet must not be allowed.

---

a critical examination - b 'above all, it desires the political, economic and social equalisation of *the classes*' - c harmony of capital and labour - d listing - e with regard to - f See this volume, p. 234.

Publication as a pamphlet by Wilhelm is a DELUSION. Should I write to Eichhoff asking whether his brother[a] would publish it at a reasonable price? Could you, in this case, bestow your fee upon the GENERAL COUNCIL, which is greatly in need of money? I still have a copy of the 6th issue containing the *Peasant War* (*apart* from my bound *Revue*,[b] which is complete). I could send this to Berlin.[302] Please reply by return.

Moreover, Wilhelm should reprint the last section of the pamphlet on military questions.[c] The transaction with Meissner (in which Wilhelm would have to show his cash!—anyway Meissner is very TICKLISH UPON SUCH POINTS) is impossible.

Salut.

Your

K. M.

First published in *Der Briefwechsel zwischen F. Engels und K. Marx*, Bd. 4, Stuttgart, 1913

Printed according to the original

Published in English in full for the first time

168

ENGELS TO MARX

IN LONDON

Manchester, 7 March 1869

Dear Moor,

The answer[300] for the Russian[d] and his retinue is exactly as it should be. Even in their own *sommation*,[e] the fellows do not dare to call upon you to make the programme your own; they simply wish indirectly to induce you to make a theoretical criticism. A stupid Russian trap into which people in this country will surely not fall. Apart from this, the people's retreat is complete, and nothing more could be desired. The about-face by which the fellows are being compelled to allow you to review their forces is very amusing, and will act like a bucket of cold water over their phrase-mongering heads.

As for the *Peasant War* it must, I believe, be offered first to Meissner[f] for decency's sake; and if he is not interested in

---

[a] Albert Eichhoff - [b] *Neue Rheinische Zeitung. Politisch-ökonomische Revue* (see also this volume, p. 234). - [c] F. Engels, *The Prussian Military Question and the German Workers' Party* (see also this volume, pp. 234-35) - [d] Mikhail Bakunin - [e] challenge - [f] See the previous letter.

printing it as a popular, cheap pamphlet, there will still be time with Eichhoff. You will have to write to him about *The 18th Brumaire*, which you could do at the same time. If Meissner does not get on with *The 18th Brumaire*, or is scared, then steps must be taken and the thing given to Eichhoff.[a] Otherwise time will be wasted and the opportunity lost.

I discovered a copy of *The 18th Brumaire* at Charles',[b] and immediately confiscated it. I read it through again and immediately saw that the book must appear *in French without delay*.[303] That will have quite a different effect from just German, and will immediately make you a name amongst the French, which will at once ensure the translation of your book.[c] See who you might get to do this and, in any case, take steps along these LINES. Printed in Brussels, it would get to France en masse.

Before the *Peasant War* is sent off, send me the copy so that I can correct the misprints, see whether a preface, etc., is necessary, or some notes for the philistines. I am not quite sure whether the Spanish Bergenroth is Frau Jung's Bergenroth. I think I heard the latter had gone to America.

Ad vocem[d] Oberwinder[e]: did you ever write to the Angerstein who approached us previously?[304] The fellow still has some sort of paper[f] in Vienna. It would be good to avoid an unnecessary squabble with Oberwinder; Wilhelm will have to inform us of the relations between these two and what Angerstein, who was also recommended by him, is now doing.

PRIMAGE is unknown to me in exchange rates and exchange practice. In freightage, it is a supplement to the usual freight, i.e., you pay 36s.—per ton freight and 10% PRIMAGE, that means 39s.6d. If you quote me the context, I can probably explain.

Courtage for the *rembours* is also a very sloppily-worded phrase, so the whole passage would be useful here, too. It probably means *courtage*, i.e., BROKERAGE for calling in from the drawer the sum of a bill that has gone to protest.[g]

The Augsburg [*Allgemeine Zeitung*] is again full of the information on the International in Geneva. Clossmann appears to have approached Becker.[h] Quite useful.

How are things in Basle? Becker has written 3-4 pamphlets about all these things, but apparently never sends any here.[305]

---

a See this volume, p. 211. - b Charles Roesgen - c the first volume of *Capital* - d regarding - e See this volume, pp. 229, 233-34. - f *Allgemeine Volkszeitung* - g See this volume, p. 229. - h See 'Genf, 21 Febr.' (in the section *Neueste Posten*), *Allgemeine Zeitung*, No. 55, 24 February 1869 (supplement); 'Genf, 28 Febr.' (in the section *Schweiz*), *Allgemeine Zeitung*, No. 63, 4 March 1869.

For a change, Schorlemmer has once again burned his face; a bottle of bromic-phosphorus he was preparing exploded in front of his nose. He looks good, but has otherwise suffered no damage.

Your
F. E.

First published abridged in *Der Briefwechsel zwischen F. Engels und K. Marx*, Bd. 4, Stuttgart, 1913 and in full in *MEGA,* Abt. III, Bd. 4, Berlin, 1931

Printed according to the original

Published in English for the first time

169

MARX TO ENGELS[180]

IN MANCHESTER

London, 14 MARCH 1869

DEAR FRED,

From the enclosed letter from Meissner you can see how things look with the Louis Bonaparte.[306] Since Meissner told me directly (personally) that he only publishes pamphlets occasionally, now and then, *in order to oblige,* something of which *you need not be aware,* I would prefer you to write to him direct about the *Peasant War.* If nothing emerges, I shall write to Eichhoff[a], with whom I maintain 'international' relations.

Liebknecht has the gift of gathering the *stupidest people* in Germany around him. *Exempli causa*[b] the author of 'Die demokratischen Ziele und die deutschen Arbeiter'[c]. This stuff can only be read, even to oneself, in south German patois. This dunderhead requests the workers to rid him of Bismarck and then promises to provide them with '*full freedom of movement*' and *other* socialist achievements! *Horreur!*[d]

The man from *Zukunft*[e] is infinitely more cunning and sharp in the north German way. But with him, too, the UPSHOT is that the workers should pull the chestnuts out of the fire for the

---

[a] Wilhelm Eichhoff - [b] for example - [c] 'Die demokratischen Ziele und die deutschen Arbeiter', *Demokratisches Wochenblatt*, Nos. 34, 36, 47 and 48; 22 August, 5 September, 21 and 28 November 1868, No. 10, 6 March 1869. - [d] ghastly - [e] 'Die Gewerksgenossenschaften', *Die Zukunft*, Nos. 32, 35, 37, 40 and 47; 7, 11, 13, 17 and 25 February 1869 (see also this volume, p. 230).

democratic gentlemen and should not, for the time being, indulge in such pursuits as TRADES UNIONS. If these gentlemen are such hot-headed friends of direct *revolutionary* action, why don't *they* set the example, instead of writing careful and reserved articles for *Zukunft*! Do they expect such stuff to awaken revolutionary passion? That won't catch anybody!

The reply to the Genevans[a] has been sent off. In the French text I kept the tone still icier and *passablement ironique*.[b] Luckily, this was not noticed by the English, who naturally only know my English translation.

Apart from the official communication [299] about which I told you, the gentlemen also sent a 4-page *private letter* to Eccarius, according to which a *direct breach* had only been avoided thanks to the EFFORTS of Becker, Bakunin, and Perret, author of the document. Their 'revolutionary' programme had had more effect in some weeks in Italy, Spain, etc., than that of the International Working Men's Association had in years. If we should reject their 'revolutionary programme', we would [produce] a *separation* between the countries with a '*revolutionary*' *workers*' *movement* (these are listed as *France*, where they have all of 2 correspondents, *Switzerland*(!), *Italy*—where the workers, apart from those who belong to us, are simply a tail to Mazzini—and *Spain*, where there are more clerics than workers) and those with a *more gradual development* of the working class (viz., England, Germany, the United States and Belgium). Thus, a separation between the volcanic and plutonic workers' movement on the one hand, and the AQUEOUS movement on the other.

That the Swiss should represent the revolutionary type is really amusing.

Old Becker must have become very stupid if he really believes that Bakunin has invented a 'programme'.

Your

K. M.

First published abridged in *Der Briefwechsel zwischen F. Engels und K. Marx*, Bd. 4, Stuttgart, 1913 and in full in *MEGA*, Abt. III, Bd. 4, Berlin, 1931

Printed according to the original

Published in English in full for the first time

---

[a] K. Marx, *The General Council of the International Working Men's Association to the Central Bureau of the International Alliance of Socialist Democracy* (see also this volume, pp. 235-36). - [b] passably ironic

170

ENGELS TO MARX

IN LONDON

[Manchester,] 15 March 1869

Dear Moor,

Enclosed, Meissner returned.[306] Today only the following:

Even in the past I considered that *Bonaparte*[a] really ought to be printed together with your 3 articles in the *Revue* about the period from February 1848 to 1850[307]; but I thought that it would cause too much loss of time. Since, however, Meissner *himself* is delaying, I would *still do* this *now*. This will make the whole thing more voluminous—ca. 10-12 printed sheets—and more complete.

If you write to Meissner right away, I am sure there will be enough time.

More tomorrow.

Your
F. E.

Lizzie is in bed with bronchitis and a bad cold; somewhat better today.

First published in *Der Briefwechsel zwischen F. Engels und K. Marx*, Bd. 4, Stuttgart, 1913

Printed according to the original

Published in English for the first time

171

ENGELS TO MARX[180]

IN LONDON

Manchester, 18 March 1869

Dear Moor,

I am writing to Meissner about the *Peasant War*.[b]

Even according to *Social-Demokrat* (which I'll send you back in a

---

[a] K. Marx, *The Eighteenth Brumaire of Louis Bonaparte*. - [b] F. Engels, *The Peasant War in Germany* (see also this volume, p. 238).

couple of days), Wilhelm[a] appears to have kept ahead in Saxony.[b] On the other hand, you have to grant the Lassalleans that they are developing quite a different sort of activity and know how to make ten times more out of the limited means than the People's Party does.[38] Even when Schweitzer was imprisoned, the *Social-Demokrat* did not publish such idiocies as Wilhelm does.

I wonder what Wilhelm will say about the fact that, in Celle the *Hanoverian particularists*, defeated in the first round of polling, voted in the second round for Planck, the *National-Liberal* Bismarckian, and thus got him into the Reichstag *instead* OF Yorck, the worker. But that does not matter to Wilhelm.

Huxley's famous article in the *Fortnightly*[248] in fact contains almost nothing except the joke about Comtism. The Comtists are said to be very furious about this, and intend to publish a thunderous reply, as a geological friend[c] in London writes to Moore.

What do you think of my suggestion about printing the articles from the *Neue Rheinische Zeitung*[307] before *Bonaparte*? And about the French version?[d]

Many thanks for the Castille.[e] Only yesterday was I able to start reading it. Clearly a crypto-Bonapartist factional publication. However, it is enormous progress that the June insurrection is now generally seen for what it was.[217]

Tony Moilin[f] is really charming. This *homme de*[g] 1869, who cheerfully declares that nobody should earn less than 2,400 fr.! I laughed myself half sick over this naïve doctor with extraordinary pretensions. If Lafargue were still to think anything of him, his wife would laugh at him.

I wanted to write to you about quite a long story, but can't recollect it at the moment. I have to go home now to hear what Gumpert has said about Lizzie, who has been in bed since Sunday.[h]

Your
F. E.

First published abridged in *Der Briefwechsel zwischen F. Engels und K. Marx*, Bd. 4, Stuttgart, 1913 and in full in *MEGA*, Abt. III, Bd. 4, Berlin, 1931

Printed according to the original
Published in English in full for the first time

---

[a] Wilhelm Liebknecht - [b] 'Zur Agitation in Sachsen', *Social-Demokrat*, Nos. 21, 22, 24, 25 and 30-32; 17, 19, 24 and 26 February, 10, 12 and 14 March 1869. - [c] apparently Dakyns - [d] See the previous letter. - [e] H. Castille, *Les massacres de juin 1848* - [f] T. Moilin, *La liquidation sociale*. - [g] man of - [h] 14 March

172

MARX TO ENGELS[56]

IN MANCHESTER

[London,] 20 March 1869

Dear Fred,

We all hope that, in your next letter, you will be sending us better news about Mrs Lizzie's state of health. Tussy especially asks you to extend our deepest sympathy to her. It's damned awful weather. Jennychen can't get rid of her cold, and for the past few days I have been cold-wild and cough-confused.

Next week (Friday or Saturday[a]) the children are going to Paris to the Lafargues. The business with Laura was this: she *had a fall* 2 or 3 weeks *before* her accouchement. As a result of this fall, she had to keep to her bed until 1-2 weeks ago and only with difficulty avoided danger.

I intend to have myself *naturalised* as an Englishman,[308] so I can travel to Paris safely. Without such a journey the French edition of my book[309] will never materialise. My presence there is absolutely necessary. Under Palmerston's law you can, if you wish, slough off the Englishman again after 6 months. The law provides no protection for the naturalised person with regard to illegalities committed in his country of birth *before* naturalisation, if he should return to that country. With this exception, a naturalised person is on the same footing as any Englishman vis-à-vis foreign GOVERNMENTS. I really cannot see why I should not visit Paris *without the permission* of M. Bonaparte, if I have the means to do so.

My best thanks to Schorlemmer for the 2ND EDITION of *Chemie*.[b] Tomorrow, as a Sunday recreation, I shall start re-reading the 2nd part, the organic chemistry (and assume that this is where the changes are to be sought).

As regards *Louis Bonaparte*, I am not in favour of printing the series from the *Revue* up to 1850 as an introduction[c]. On the one hand, I don't wish to give Meissner new excuses for delay. On the other, it would be very easy, by patching in FACTS that emerged later, to revise this section, but there is no hurry. In Brussels, De

---

[a] 26 or 27 March - [b] H. E. Roscoe, *Kurzes Lehrbuch der Chemie nach den neuesten Ansichten der Wissenschaft.* Deutsche Ausgabe, unter Mitwirkung des Verfassers bearbeitet von Carl Schorlemmer. - [c] See this volume, p. 241.

Paepe has sought in vain for a French publisher for *Louis Bonaparte*. For such operations, these gentlemen demand *money* from the author.

Blanqui, *who is now in Paris*, made very good jokes at Lafargue's about Moilin's[a] real QUACK NOSTRUM. France, he said, is always ungrateful to its great men. Moilin, for instance, has solved the problem of the century in an unprecedentedly simple manner — and Paris goes about its business as though nothing had happened.

Castille was a June insurgent, was transported as such to Cayenne, and returned after the general amnesty. He wrote the first edition of his book[b] *de bonne foi.*[c] In the meantime, the government bought him, and staged this second edition as the antithesis to Ténot's writings. The changes made are: 1. the tone has become more bourgeois, sometimes smart-alecky. 2. Passages against the men of December[d] have been removed. 3. A few quietly apologetic phrases for Bonaparte have been patched in. Despite all this, the *fonds*[e] unchanged, and it remains as you say, a very satisfactory work. It is a very good thing when M. Bonaparte pushes back the writing of history to the period before 2 December. The struggle of the various parties, their mutual: *Et tu Brute!*[f] will help put a stop to the 'revolutionism' of the old scoundrels of 1848 and earlier.

I sent to Beesly, by city post, WITH A FEW RANDOM NOTES for him to read, Vermorel's pamphlet[g] that I also sent you (with the Castille). He sent it back to me with the *enclosed* note, which is as stupid as it is MAGISTERIAL and arrogant. It appears to me that positive philosophy may be equated with ignorance about everything positive. The other sheet enclosed was sent me by Borkheim for my 'DUTCH RELATIONS'.[h]

Yesterday I found the report on the 'miners' guilds',[i] printed in full in the *Social-Demokrat* of last Wednesday. Whether the *Zukunft* has taken it I do not know.[281] Possibly the report does not stand at that lofty stage of wisdom that alone can satisfy social policy. I have not yet received Wilhelm for this week.[j]

Apropos. In the very near future there will be a demonstration here for E. Jones. The business is sponsored by the Clerkenwell

a See this volume, p. 242. - b H. Castille, *Le massacres de juin 1848...* - c in good faith - d This refers to the coup d'état of 2 December 1851 - e basis - f Cf. Shakespeare, *Julius Caesar*, III, 1, 77. - g A. Vermorel, *Les hommes de 1848*. - h See this volume, p. 215. - i F. Engels, 'Bericht über die Knappschaftsvereine der Bergarbeiter in den Kohlenwerken Sachsens', *Der Social-Demokrat*, No. 33, 17 March 1869. - j The reference is to *Demokratisches Wochenblatt*.

branch of the *quondam* Reform League.[228] Their leaders, Weston, Lucraft, etc. are members of our General Council. The festival committee offered me one of the 5 presidential chairs in Trafalgar Square, from which the masses are to be harangued. I refused the courtesy very politely. What I could not refuse, however, was to promise a small contribution to the demonstration costs on behalf of myself and friends. It must be paid Tuesday next[a] If you and Moore want to take a share, it must be done by then.

Addio.

Your

Moor

who every day resembles more a 'white' washed Moor.

First published abridged in *Der Briefwechsel zwischen F. Engels und K. Marx*, Bd. 4, Stuttgart, 1913 and in full in *MEGA*, Abt. III, Bd. 4, Berlin, 1931

Printed according to the original

Published in English in full for the first time

173

ENGELS TO MARX

IN LONDON

Manchester, 21 March 1869

Dear Moor,

Lizzie's case was pleurisy, which, however, took a remarkably quick course—not till last Tuesday[b] was the exudation on the right lung evident, and by this morning it had already vanished completely. She is getting up again today for the first time. Through a remarkable piece of divination, I diagnosed pleurisy for Gumpert on Sunday,[c] he examined her, found nothing, declared it was bronchitis (which was also present), in addition to catarrh in the lungs, and it was naturally rather annoying for him when the pleurisy declared itself after all. I naturally do not claim that it was present when he could not find it.

Poor Löhrchen[d] must have had a hard time of it. Ten weeks in

---

a 23 March - b 16 March - c 14 March - d Laura Lafargue

childbed is no joke, and it is good that it is over. When they get there, Tussy and Jenny must give her and Lafargue too my hearty greetings.

The explanation about Castille was very useful to me. The wisdom of Solomon Beesly returned herewith.[a] It is the greatest nonsense. In time, this Comtism will confirm an even stronger version of that remark made by that man from Bonn about the Hegelians: they do not need to know about anything in order to write about everything.

In Germany the conversion of the natural forces, for instance, heat into mechanical energy, etc., has given rise to a very absurd theory, which incidentally follows with a certain inevitability from Laplace's old hypothesis, but is now displayed, as it were, with mathematical proofs: that the world is becoming steadily colder, that the temperature in the universe is levelling down and that, in the end, a moment will come when all life will be impossible and the entire world will consist of frozen spheres rotating round one another. I am simply waiting for the moment when the clerics seize upon this theory as the last word in materialism. It is impossible to imagine anything more stupid. Since, according to this theory, in the existing world, more heat must always be converted into other energy than can be obtained by converting other energy into heat, so the original *hot state*, out of which things have cooled, is obviously inexplicable, even contradictory, and thus presumes a god. Newton's first impulse is thus converted into a first heating. Nevertheless, the theory is regarded as the finest and highest perfection of materialism; these gentlemen prefer to construct a world that begins in nonsense and ends in nonsense, instead of regarding these nonsensical consequences as proof that what they call natural law is, to date, only half-known to them. But this theory is all the dreadful rage in Germany.

I've not yet seen the *Zukunft.*

Tomorrow I shall send you STAMPS for one pound for the E. Jones demonstration.

Best greetings.

Your
F. E.

First published abridged in *Der Briefwech-sel zwischen F. Engels und K. Marx,* Bd. 4, Stuttgart, 1913 and in full in *MEGA,* Abt. III, Bd. 4, Berlin, 1931

Printed according to the original

Published in English for the first time

---

[a] See this volume, p. 244.

174

ENGELS TO MARX

IN LONDON

Manchester, 28 March 1869

Dear Moor,

You must really have a foul cold, since even the usual Sunday letter did not arrive today. Enclosed a cheque on the UNION BANK OF LONDON for £87.10 for March-June and a pound in STAMPS for the cost of the meeting, which I forgot to send you on Monday.[a]

This week I read myself fairly well into Dutch-Frisian, and have discovered some quite nice philological things there. Can you discover what *snieuntojowns* means? It is odd, that, today, the West Frisians in many cases *speak* as the English *write*, e.g. GREAT, *hearre* (hear), etc. However, in most cases this is accidental and of more recent date, and Old Frisian from the same area generally differs from this.

Lizzie is on her feet again.

Best greetings—have the girls gone to Paris, and what do they write about Löhrchen[b]? And are you already a BRITON NEVER SHALL BE SLAVES[c]?

Your
F. E.

First published in *Der Briefwechsel zwischen F. Engels und K. Marx*, Bd. 4, Stuttgart, 1913

Printed according to the original

Published in English for the first time

---

[a] 22 March - [b] Laura Lafargue - [c] Words from the British song *Rule, Britannia...* An allusion to Marx's attempts to acquire British citizenship (see also this volume, p. 243).

175

MARX TO ENGELS

IN MANCHESTER

[London,] 29 March 1869

Dear Fred,

Best thanks for the CHEQUE and the STAMPS. I paid Lucraft last Tuesday.[a] Have you seen the short report about the demonstration in *The Times* OF SATURDAY LAST[b]? It states that a German group ('of our people!') carried a red flag inscribed *Proletarier aller Länder, verunreiniget Euch!*, which they said in English, means 'RAGAMUFFINS OF ALL REGIONS, BEFOUL YOURSELVES!'

As you correctly assume, I am cold-maddened and cold-stupefied.

The children left on Friday[c] evening (to the horror of the English, on GOOD FRIDAY). We received a letter from them this morning. They arrived safely in Paris, but had a stormy crossing.

I am not yet a FREEBORN BRITON. One resists such a step as long as one can.[308]

Nothing could be more gallant than the way Wilhelm the Honourable is extracting himself from the affair of the *Vogt* copies.[d] At my INSTIGATION, Kugelmann wrote to him about it. No reply to the first letter, and to another letter he received the enclosed screed, which may be summed up as follows: If *I* (Liebknecht) announced [the despatch of] 60 copies, but only 6 arrived, you should be aware that *I always lie*, so there the matter must rest. If, however, C. Hirsch of Berlin advised you of the number (he naturally does not know that *I* advised Kugelmann), it is a different matter and must be investigated.

The sort of artful dodges the fellow gets up to is displayed in a letter from Hirsch to Kugelmann. Hirsch writes to Kugelmann[310]:

'Liebknecht probably hopes for nothing more than that you should circulate the books IN QUESTION in Hanover, in order to enlighten the Democratic Party there about the doings of Herr Vogt, etc.'

Thus Wilhelm kept it secret from Hirsch that *I* had demanded information about the state of affairs, and an assured place for storing those copies still available.

Kugelmann writes:

---

a 23 March - b 'The Demonstration in Trafalgar Square', *The Times*, No. 26396, 27 March 1869. - c 19 March - d The reference is to K. Marx, *Herr Vogt* (see this volume, pp. 208 and 231).

'The coming clash of words between Liebknecht and Schweitzer reminds me less of Luther and Eck than of Pater José and Rabbi Juda....' 'But it seems to me, as well, that the rabbi and the monk, both of them to heaven smell'[a]

With regard to this clash of words, I received (today) the enclosed letter from *Bebel*.[311] Since the 60-copy letter,[84] Wilhelm himself does not dare write to me—until more water has flowed under the bridge.

They are amazing fellows! First they wilfully get themselves into a situation where they are bound to get a drubbing. Then I am supposed to intervene as *deus ex machina* and elegantly reject Schweitzer's resolution on the acceptance of the programme of the International, should Schweitzer's general meeting pass it![312] And all this after Wilhelm and Co. have not taken *one single step* about the International *since the Nuremberg Congress*,[135] have done absolutely *nothing* so that those poor devils in Lugau found it necessary to turn directly to London.[b] I believe Bebel to be useful and able. He only had the particular misfortune to find his 'theoretician' in Mr Wilhelm.

Something else demonstrates the fellows' carelessness and sloppiness: to date they have not informed me of a single FACT to prove the charges of high treason, etc., levelled against Schweitzer. Fine businessmen.

Lloyd's Paper, in the Sunday number a week ago,[c] carried long hymns of praise about our RESOLUTIONS and the INTERNATIONAL ASSOCIATION in general.

I have received a letter from Dietzgen, who is a prosperous tanner in Siegburg.[313] I shall send it to you as soon as it is answered. Dietzgen's ideas will be published by Meissner, for whom he has guaranteed the printing costs, under the title: *Die Kopfarbeit, dargestellt von einem Handarbeiter usw.*

Salut. Greetings to MRS Lizzie and the two accomplices[d].

Your

K. M.

First published in part in *Der Briefwechsel zwischen F. Engels und K. Marx*, Bd. 4, Stuttgart, 1913 and in full in *MEGA*, Abt. III, Bd. 4, Berlin, 1931

Printed according to the original

Published in English for the first time

---

a Personages from Heinrich Heine's 'Disputation', (Romanzero, III). - b See this volume, p. 172. - c 'International Labour Laws', *Lloyd's Weekly London Newspaper*, 21 March 1869. - d Samuel Moore and Carl Schorlemmer

176

ENGELS TO MARX

IN LONDON

Manchester, 2 April 1869

Dear Moor,

I cannot write much to you today, since for some time I have had a chronically inflamed eye (mild), and can only do the most essential work.

L'homme propose et la femme dispose.[a] Yesterday evening I laid out for you a pile of copies of *Zukunft*, and also B. Becker on Lassalle,[b] but this morning the room was being swept out, so I forgot them. *Die Zukunft*, incidentally, has carried the Lugau story as a feature article.[314]

Wilhelm's stupidities exceed everything. Bebel's cry of alarm was really touching.[311] As you will see from *Zukunft*,[c] his friends in Hanover, the particularists, voted in the Lüneburg election *against* Yorck (Lassallean) and *for* the National-Liberal.[d] The rabble are all united against the workers but this does not disturb Liebknecht. I look forward to the dread debate with great eagerness.

About *Vogt*[e]: if I were you I would write directly to the Berlin Hirsch. Then you will finally reach the proper quarter.

Lizzie is better, but does not go out yet and is on a strengthening diet. How is Mrs Lafargue?

Best wishes.

Your

F. E.

First published abridged in *Der Briefwechsel zwischen F. Engels und K. Marx*, Bd. 4, Stuttgart, 1913 and in full in *MEGA*, Abt. III, Bd. 4, Berlin, 1931

Printed according to the original

Published in English for the first time

---

[a] Man proposes and woman disposes. - [b] B. Becker, *Enthüllungen über das tragische Lebensende Ferdinand Lassalle's.* - [c] 'Bei der in engerer Wahl vollzogenen Ersatzwahl ...', *Die Zukunft*, No. 60, 12 March 1869, in the column 'Berlin, 11. März'. - [d] Gottlieb Planck - [e] K. Marx, *Herr Vogt.*

177

ENGELS TO MARX

IN LONDON

Manchester, 4 April 1869

Dear Moor,

What are Applegarth and Odger thinking of, lending themselves to Lloyd Jones as partners and directors of the planned *Citizen Newspaper*?[315] And how has Lloyd Jones suddenly managed to establish his position as a LEADER? For he is supposed to become the editor of this 'oh-so educated'[a] worker-petty-bourgeois paper. The sooner I get information about this, the better, as that jackass Kyllmann is hawking the prospectus around here.

Yesterday we finally achieved the long-planned transfer of my official headquarters from Dover STREET to 86 Mornington STREET,[316] to the great pleasure of Lizzie, who also went out again for the first time yesterday.

You have not told me what news you have about Löhrchen's[b] health.

Best greetings.

Your
F. E.

Since you obviously have not discovered what *snieuntojown* means, I shall tell you: Saturday evening.[c] But how? That is now the question.

First published in *Der Briefwechsel zwischen F. Engels und K. Marx*, Bd. 4, Stuttgart, 1913

Printed according to the original

Published in English for the first time

---

[a] 'jebildeten' in the original (Berlin dialect) - [b] Laura Lafargue - [c] See this volume, p. 247.

178

ENGELS TO FRIEDRICH LESSNER

IN LONDON

Manchester, 4 April 1869
86 Mornington Street

Dear Lessner,

I was very pleased to have word from you, and enclose the photograph requested. The Becker story[a] together with other material I expressly placed ready a week ago, in order to send it to Marx, but the womenfolk put the stuff somewhere else each morning, so I forgot it day after day. Tomorrow I shall take the package into town, and send Becker directly to you.

The compliments you have so undeservedly paid me shame me all the more since, unfortunately, in the last 18 years, I have been able to do as good as nothing *directly* for our cause, and have had to devote all my time to bourgeois activities. I hope this will soon change, I expect in a few months once again to be master of my time, and I shall then surely do my part to earn your compliments; it will always be a pleasure for me to bash the same enemy on the same battlefield together with an old comrade like you. You are right; the cause goes better than ever before; years ago, at a time when the stupid democratic mob complained about reaction and the people's indifference to them, we, Moor and I, were right in foreseeing in the period of this reaction the enormous industrial development of the last 18 years and declared this would result in a sharpening of the contradictions between labour and capital, and more acute class struggle. It would make a donkey laugh to see how these stupid democrats have now really been duped, so that there is not even a decent little place for them in any other corner of the world. The Party of Progress in Germany,[317] republicans in France, radicals in England, all of them equally rotten. There is nothing funnier than the sweet-sour compliments they have to make to the social movement, though they know full well that, one fine day, this social movement will have its foot on their necks.

In old friendship

Your
F. Engels

First published in: Marx and Engels, *Works*, First Russian Edition, Vol. XXVI, Moscow, 1935

Printed according to the original

Published in English for the first time

---

[a] B. Becker, *Enthüllungen über das tragische Lebensende Ferdinand Lassalle's.*

179

MARX TO ENGELS

IN MANCHESTER

London, 5 April 1869

DEAR FRED,

I can't make anything of your *snieunt* (I can't read the following letters) *jown*.[a] According to the etymology, I can only explain *lucus a non lucendo*[b] that in Danish *snoe* means turn, and *jeon* means EVEN.

I congratulate you on the energy with which you have cut the umbilical cord with Dover Street.[c]

Laura is quite well again. Jenny will be coming home tomorrow or the day after 'for business reasons'. Tussy will stay in Paris for at least 2 months. As you will note from the enclosed letter, she is absolutely delighted with Fouschtra,[d] the YOUNGSTER of the Lafargue FAMILY.

The Wilhelm-Bebel-Schweitzer clash of words has not really been so bad; after all, when of 11,000 voters, 4,500 abstained from voting *for* Schweitzer, this was not exactly a triumph for this gentleman.[318]

With regard to the *Citizen*,[315] the contributors to which include Dr Engel of Berlin and Dr Brentano of the same, this appears to be stillborn or, as OLD Werner says, 'laid out'. Lloyd Jones is an old tailor by trade, who figured in a STRIKE back in 1824. For a long time now he has been an apostle of cooperation, and a lazy-bones. Odger and Applegarth are both possessed by a mania for mediation and a longing for respectability. On the CENTRAL COUNCIL, we ticked off Mr Applegarth properly.[319] With regard to Odger's *collaboration* in particular, it never went further than the prospectus, and here people simply laugh at such PROMISSORY BILLS on his part.

In 2 issues the Bonapartist *Peuple* (directly edited *with* Boustrapa[320]) denounces our International because of the recent

---

a See this volume, pp. 247, and 251. - b Literally: 'a grove from not being light'. The expression, first used by Quintilian in *De institutione oratoria* (I, 6, 34), illustrates the practice ascribed to ancient Roman etymologists of deriving words from their semantic opposites, as *lucus* ('grove') from *lucere* ('to shine, be light') because a grove is not light. - c See this volume, p. 251. - d Charles-Étienne Lafargue

exercises of terrorism in Geneva[a] (on the occasion of the typographers' STRIKE[321]), and, at the same time, makes mocking remarks about our impotence. It would naturally be very good to keep the volcanic explosion on such a small but conspicuous stage, *if the means were available.* But to drag in the International so directly, as Becker[b] and Co. are doing, without preparation, without thinking about a war-chest, without taking into consideration the good or bad state of business in Europe—this is simply compromising. I shall send you the relevant numbers of *Peuple* after I have presented them to the COUNCIL tomorrow.

Oberwinder has sent me the prospectus of his paper[c] for subscription. It appears twice a month, and costs 45 kreuzer per quarter. If I send the list back with subscriptions, 1 copy for you, 1 copy for Moore, 1 for Borkheim and 1 for me, we shall have to send the total sum of 3 gulden. You can't send the money individually, I mean for one COPY.

Enclosed *Lanterne* and *Cloche* and *Werker.*

Do send me copies of *Zukunft,* so that I can see something about the Reichstag.

And also, if possible, Manchester papers containing arguments about the price of cotton. The Liberal M.P. from Manchester[d] is supposed to be agitating or spreading agitation amongst the workers in Stockport so that they should demand, directly from the GOVERNMENT, *cotton production* in India, that is, PROTECTION IN ANOTHER FORM.

COMPLIMENTS to MRS Lizzie ON RESTORATION OF HEALTH. *Salut.*

Your
Moor

I hope your eye inflammation has passed.

First published in *Der Briefwechsel zwischen F. Engels und K. Marx,* Bd. 4, Stuttgart, 1913

Printed according to the original

Published in English for the first time

---

[a] Ch. Gaumont, 'La grève à Genève', *Le Peuple,* 29 and 30 March 1869. - [b] Johann Philipp Becker - [c] *Die Volksstimme* - [d] Thomas Bazley

180

ENGELS TO MARX[124]

IN LONDON

Manchester, 6 April 1869

Dear Moor,

Liebknecht has again had the good luck of fools. The vote of 6,500 against 4,500 was a tremendous defeat for Schweitzer,[318] even if it was not a direct victory for Wilhelm. The *Kölner Zeitung* says that Schweitzer was frightfully dismayed, and though he had declared earlier that he would resign if any sort of considerable minority were to vote against him, he has taken a lot of care not to do so.[322]

In any case, Schweitzer's campaign for the kingdom of the tailors has failed, and his position in his own association has been shaken severely. *N'est pas dictateur qui veut.*[a] The process of the disintegration of specific Lassalleanism has thus begun, and is bound to continue rapidly. The figures 6,500:4,500 mean either a split or abandonment of the 'strict' organisation and Schweitzer's personal leadership. So far Liebknecht's foolhardiness has had a good effect. And under *these* circumstances I shall not take it amiss that he has let himself in for a new armistice,[323] although this is the third case between the two of them of 'cad's fighting, when ended, is very soon mended'.

The copies of *Zukunft* follow enclosed. Unfortunately, the Reichstag debate on industrial legislation is very poorly reported in them. There is nothing more comical than Schweitzer's lecture on the socialist demands, culminating in the declaration that he favours trades freedom[b] up to Wagener, Miquel et Co.[c] Simply childish babble. Best by far was *Bebel*.[324]

I am sending the B. Becker[d] to *Lessner* today. I hear that the latest *Fortnightly* has an article on it.[e]

---

[a] Not everyone who wishes is a dictator. A paraphrase from Victor Hugo's *Napoleon le petit.* - [b] J. B. Schweitzer, [Speech in the North German Diet, 17 March, 1869], *Die Zukunft*, No. 66, 19 March, 1869. - [c] H. Wagener, [Speech in the North German Diet, 17 March, 1869], *Die Zukunft*, No. 66, 19 March, 1869; J. Miquel, [Speech in the North German Diet, 18 March 1869], *Die Zukunft*, No. 67, 20 March, 1869. - [d] B. Becker, *Enthüllungen über das tragische Lebensende Ferdinand Lassalle's...* - [e] J. M. Ludlow, 'Ferdinand Lassalle, the German Social-Democrat', *The Fortnightly Review*, Vol. V, No. XXVIII, 1 April 1869.

I shall send you the *Zukunft* on Schweitzer and Liebknecht, and immediately if there is anything more in it; I assume that Liebknecht sent them a report straight away.

Your

F. E.

First published abridged in *Der Briefwechsel zwischen F. Engels und K. Marx*, Bd. 4, Stuttgart, 1913 and in full in *MEGA*, Abt. III, Bd. 4, Berlin 1931

Printed according to the original

Published in English in full for the first time

181

MARX TO ENGELS

IN MANCHESTER

[London,] 7 April 1869

DEAR FRED,

Enclosed letter from Wilhelmchen.[325] Return after reading. What shall I write him about the *Peasant War*[a]?
Strohn is at the door, so *addio*.

Your

K. M.

First published in *MEGA*, Abt. III, Bd. 4, Berlin, 1931

Printed according to the original

Published in English for the first time

182

ENGELS TO MARX

IN LONDON

Manchester, 7 April 1869

Dear Moor,

The letters from Tussy and Wilhelmchen[325] returned enclosed. The latter remains true to his principle of greatly scorning all

---

[a] F. Engels, *The Peasant War in Germany*.

facts. Anybody who regards facts as important, who 'takes them into consideration', is someone who idolises success, a Bismarckian. So even if Schweitzer's 'dirty deeds' were as cheap as blackberries, he would not give us any facts about them, since, according to the principles of the People's Party,[38] the only important thing about all these facts is that Wilhelm declares them to be 'dirty deeds'. It follows that, as Schweitzer's dirty deeds become enormous, the friction with him disappears. The fellow's logic is as amusing as the anticipation with which he still hopes for a proclamation from you, declaring him to be the angel of light, and naming Schweitzer as Satan.

It is also amusing that he wants to sell an essay[a] of *at least 4 or 5 printer's sheets* for *1½ groschen*, and emphasises: not at a profit. *'Le représentant a dit: avec du fer et du pain on va jusqu'en Chine. Il n'a pas parlé de chaussures.'*[b] And Wilhelm has not mentioned who will meet the loss when you sell things at $^1/_3$ to $^1/_4$ of cost price.

I have not yet written to Meissner, and I really cannot expect him to do the wondrous things that Liebknecht boldly ventures. Once Wilhelm has spoken with an *expert* about the printing costs, determined a rational price and made sure that he can raise the printing costs, I am not disinclined to let him print the stuff; tell him to write to me as soon as he can fulfil these conditions, then we shall arrange further steps.

Snieuntojown is sun-jovn-to-jovn — sun-eve-to-eve.[c] The word has caused me to rack my brains; there really are some very difficult things in West Frisian.

The Bazleyite agitation in favour of state aid for cotton cultivation has not yet become so public here that there has been anything substantial in the newspapers. However, I shall soon send you some cuttings about the STRIKE in Preston,[326] which the MASTERS directly provoked in order to bring about a general shut-down of the factories there. Since they cannot agree amongst themselves on SHORT TIME or complete closure, as some would then go on working and the others would be vexed at this, the sole form to bring about joint action amongst them is a STRIKE, since *no manufacturer opposes* the proposal to reduce wages. The cream of the thing is that these fellows, who admit that, for 2 years, they have been losing 1 to 2d. per 1b of yarn or cloth, and still did not want to close down or work SHORT TIME, now declare that a 10% wage

---

[a] F. Engels, *The Peasant War in Germany.* - [b] 'The commercial traveller said: with iron and bread you can get as far as China. He did not mention boots.' - [c] See this volume, pp. 247, 251, 253.

reduction, i.e., a saving of $\frac{1}{10}$ to $\frac{1}{6}$ *penny* per £, is a matter of life or death!

Best greetings

Your

F. E.

First published abridged in *Der Briefwech-sel zwischen F. Engels und K. Marx*, Bd. 4, Stuttgart, 1913 and in full in *MEGA*, Abt. III, Bd. 4, Berlin, 1931

Printed according to the original

Published in English for the first time

183

MARX TO ENGELS

IN MANCHESTER

[London,] 8 April 1869

DEAR FRED,

I wrote to Wilhelmchen immediately today, as you suggested.[84] I added that it would be good if the price could be fixed, even at a minimum, *above* the cost, so that this surplus could be used to pay for INDIVIDUAL CARDS OF MEMBERSHIP (ld. each). According to the Lausanne[143] and Brussels[138] decisions, representatives cannot be admitted to congress if their *committants*[a] have not contributed to the national levy.[b]

The thing I liked best in *Zukunft* was the decision of the *High Court of Justice* on the freedom of assembly of the Prussian subjects.[c] This beats the French courts *holo*.[d] And this scurvy Kirchmann with his scurvy critics,[e] is fine and successful. This is the same Kirchmann who, a few years ago, proved the immortality of the soul.[f] His works, in any case, are not immortal.

---

[a] mandataries - [b] 'Procès-verbaux du congrès de l'Association Internationale des Travailleurs réuni à Lausanne du 2 au 8 septembre 1867', p. 37. 'Troisième Congrès de l'Association Internationale des Travailleurs...' Supplément au journal *Le Peuple belge*, 24 septembre 1868. - [c] 'In Bezug auf das Vereins und Versammlungs-Gesetz ist vom Obertribunal folgender Rechtsgrundsatz angenommen worden...', *Die Zukunft*, No. 61, 13 March 1869. - [d] completely - [e] 'V. Kirchmann's Aesthetik', *Die Zukunft*, Nos. 71 and 72; 25 and 26 March 1869. (Anonymous review of J. H. v. Kirchmann's *Aesthetik auf realistischer Grundlage*, in two vols.) - [f] J. H. Kirchmann, *Ueber die Unsterblichkeit. Ein philosophischer Versuch.*

The enclosed letter[327] shows the frame of mind of the workers in the Rhine province about the Barmen-Elberfeld Congress. Schweitzer had forgotten that Robespierre did not answer accusations only when he was sure of his cause, or when he could answer with the guillotine. But the CORRUPTIBLE should not take the INCORRUPTIBLE as their model.

Salut.

Your
K. M.

First published in *Der Briefwechsel zwischen F. Engels und K. Marx*, Bd. 4, Stuttgart, 1913

Printed according to the original

Published in English for the first time

184

MARX TO JOHN MALCOLM LUDLOW[328]

IN LONDON

[London,] 10 April 1869
1 Modena Villas, Maitland Park,
Haverstock Hill, N. W.

Dear Sir,

Being aware of your services to the working class, I should before this have given myself the pleasure of sending you my last work: *Das Kapital* (2nd and 3d volumes not yet published[41]), if I had known you to be a German reader.

In your article on Lassalle in the *Fortnightly*[a] you say first that Lassalle propagated my principles in Germany and say then that I am propagating 'Lassallean principles' in England. This would indeed be what the French call '*un échange de bons procédés*'.[b]

In the volume I send you, you will find (Preface, p. VIII, note *1*) the plain facts stated viz. that 'Lassalle has taken from my writings almost literally *all his general theoretical developments*', but that I 'have nothing whatever to do with *his practical applications*'.[c]

---

[a] J. M. Ludlow, 'Ferdinand Lassalle, the German Social-Democrat', *The Fortnightly Review*, Vol. V. No. XXVIII, 1 April 1869. - [b] exchange of good manner - [c] See present edition, Vol. 35.

His practical nostrum, government aid to co-operative societies, I call by courtesy *his*. It belongs in fact to, and was zealously preached, at the time of Louis Philippe, by *Monsieur Buchez*, Ex-St. Simonian, author of the *Histoire Parlementaire de la Révolution Française*, glorifying Robespierre *and* the Holy Inquisition.[162] M. Buchez put forward his views, f.i. in the journal *L'Atelier*, in *opposition* to the radical views of the French communism of that time.

Since you quote my reply to Proudhon: *Misère de la Philosophie*, you cannot but be aware from its last chapter that in 1847, when all the political economists and all the socialists concurred on one single point—the condemnation of *trades' unions*, I demonstrated their historical necessity.

Yours truly
Karl Marx

J. M. Ludlow, Esq.

First published in: Marx and Engels, *Works*, First Russian Edition, Vol. XXVI, Moscow, 1935

Reproduced from the original

185

ENGELS TO MARX

IN LONDON

Manchester, 14 April 1869

Dear Moor,

Enclosed the Solingen letter[329] returned, which is also significant because it clarifies Liebknecht's boasts about the 'establishment of associations in Solingen and Bourscheid'. The one in Solingen was already there,[330] and the Solingen people established the one in Bourscheid.

The article on the Cretan insurrection[331] in *The Diplomatic Review*[a] is the best thing they have published for a long time; ditto Urquhart's letter to Fuad Pasha.[b] But, as always, the source is not given for Brunnow's statement in the Greek dispatch,[c] i.e.,

---

[a] 'The "Eastern Question" Closed. Summary from the Blue-Books', *The Diplomatic Review*, 7 April 1869. - [b] D. Urquhart, 'Au grand Vizir, 16 août, 1867', *The Diplomatic Review*, 7 April 1869, in the column 'Insurrection en Candie. M. Urquhart à Fuad Pasha'. - [c] 'Le Ministre Grec à Londres à son Gouvernement', 29 December 1868, [extract] *The Diplomatic Review*, 7 April 1869.

whether this dispatch is published in one of the official publications, which is not easy to believe (unless a Greek book), or whether it found its way into Urquhart's hands along private channels. It would be interesting to know this, in case it is quoted later. The statement coincides completely with my constant claim that Russia will not unleash a war before 2 railways are completed to the Black Sea and the Pruth. They are now building like mad, and borrowing money like crazy—in the past 3 years—about £47,000,000! A major part of this represents the future costs of war.

However, in the light of these negotiations, Beust appears to be the Austrian Palmerston, and here too there could be a motive that would favour a speed-up of the action.

Doesn't Eichhoff still send you the *Social-Demokrat*? It would be very important to see how Schweitzer is conducting himself at the moment in his own paper.

You will have read the article about Lassalle in the *Fortnightly*,[a] and will have seen that you are regarded therein as the real papa of Lassallean and other socialism. Who is this Ludlow? If he could be prevailed upon to write an article in the *Fortnightly* about your book,[b] this would be better than nothing after all.—Congreve's reply to Huxley is the DULLEST, most stupid and most confused thing I have ever seen[c]; if this is the supreme wisdom of the Comtists, they can let themselves to be buried without further ado.

I still must not strain my eye too much, and I feel it a little again today, since I read too much by lamplight yesterday evening; so I am closing. On Saturday[d] we received a very jolly letter from Tussy.

Best greetings to your wife and Jenny.

Your
F. E.

First published abridged in *Der Briefwechsel zwischen F. Engels und K. Marx*, Bd. 4, Stuttgart, 1913 and in full in *MEGA*, Abt. III, Bd. 4, Berlin, 1931

Printed according to the original

Published in English for the first time

---

[a] J. M. Ludlow, 'Ferdinand Lassalle, the German Social-Democrat', *The Fortnightly Revue*, 1 April 1869. (See this volume, p. 259.) - [b] the first volume of *Capital* - [c] R. Congreve, 'Mr. Huxley on M. Comte', *The Fortnightly Revue*, Vol. V, No. XXVIII, 1 April 1869. - [d] 10 April

186

MARX TO ENGELS[174]

IN MANCHESTER

London, 15 April 1869

Dear Fred,

Jennychen arrived safely on Wednesday.[332] During the return journey they had such fog at sea that the ship had a hair's-breadth escape from running aground.

From Wilhelm[333] the enclosed note. You will see, *d'abord*[a] his first answer to my query[84] about the 'knavish tricks' of which he accuses Schweitzer. 'Political' amongst this—only two enclosed ELECTIONEERING things. You must send them back to me, for Wilhelm asks for them back, and they appear to constitute his entire political 'evidence for the prosecution'.

Lafargue has sent me his French translation of the *Communist Manifesto* for us to revise. I am sending you the manuscript by post today. For the moment, the business is not urgent. I certainly do not want Lafargue to burn his fingers prematurely. However, if the stuff is eventually to be published in France, certain parts, such as those on German or 'True' Socialism, should be reduced to a few lines, since they are of no interest there.

To get back to the negotiations with Wilhelm. *I* write to him[84] about the conditions on which you are ready to give him the *Peasant War.*[b] *He* writes to you that *Eccarius* (who knew nothing about the matter) had informed him you would send him the stuff, and that he would *not* fulfil the conditions you laid down. He further writes to me that he has owed Eccarius 30 thaler for 2 quarters, and that *I* should advance it, since he would, 'on his word of honour', repay it at an—unspecified—date. I certainly feel no inclination towards this transaction, since I have already loaned somewhat more than this sum to my friend Dupont.

Ludlow is BARRISTER AT LAW, a leading contributor to the *Spectator*, a co-operator, devout, a determined enemy of the Comtists. He resigned publicly from our *Commonwealth* because Beesly, Harrison, etc., were contributors. He had sent me a few of his little pamphlets at an earlier date, and is a friend of Jones Lloyd or Lloyd Jones, or whatever the tailor's name is. A few days ago,

---

[a] first - [b] See this volume, p. 256.

after I had seen the relevant issue of the *Fortnightly*, I sent him MY LAST AVAILABLE COPY OF *Capital*. (Note of receipt enclosure No. I.) I naturally knew he read German. At the same time, I sent him a letter in which I made a few JOKES about his article, in which he first stated that Lassalle disseminated *my principles in Germany* and then that I disseminated *Lassalle's principles in England*.[a] (Reply in No. 2.) I hope by this means still to achieve a review of my book in an English paper.[334] Ludlow is, ditto, a great admirer of Ricardo, something exceptional today, after Mill mucked everything up.

I discovered BY ACCIDENT today that we had two *Neveu de Rameau*[b] in our house, and so am sending you one. This unsurpassed masterpiece will once again give you a treat.

Referring to it, OLD Hegel said: 'The mocking laughter at existence, at the confusion of the whole and at itself, is the disintegrated consciousness, aware of itself and expressing itself, and is, at the same time, the last audible echo of all this confusion.... It is the self-disintegrating nature of all relations and their conscious disintegration... In this aspect of the return to self, the *vanity* of all *things* is the self's *own vanity*, or the self is itself vanity ... but as the indignant consciousness it is aware of its own disintegration and, by that knowledge, has immediately transcended it... Every part of this world either gets its mind [sein Geist] expressed here or is spoken of intellectually [mit Geist] and declared for what it is.—The *honest consciousness*' (the role Diderot allots himself in the dialogue) 'takes each element as a permanent entity and does not realise, in its uneducated thoughtlessness, that it is doing just the opposite. But the disintegrated consciousness is the consciousness of reversal and indeed of absolute reversal; its dominating elements is the concept, which draws together thoughts that, to the honest consciousness, lie so wide apart; hence the brilliance [geistreich] of its language. Thus, the content of the mind's speech of and about itself consists in the reversal of all conceptions and realities; the universal deception of oneself and others and the shamelessness of declaring this deception is, therefore, precisely the greatest truth... To the quiet consciousness, which in its honest way goes on singing the melody of the True and the Good in even tones, i.e., on a monotone, this speech appears as "a farrago of wisdom and madness", etc.'[c] (a passage from Diderot follows).

More amusing than Hegel's commentary is that by Mr Jules Janin, which you will find in the form of an excerpt in the postscript to the little volume. This *'cardinal de la mer'*[d] deplores the absence in Diderot's *Rameau* of the moral point, and consequently sets things in order by discovering that Rameau's entire absurdity arises from his resentment at not being a 'born *gentilhomme'*.[e] The Kotzebue-like muck he has heaped upon this cornerstone is being melodramatically presented in London.[335]

---

a See this volume, pp. 259-60. - b D. Diderot, *Le neveu de Rameau*... - c G. W. F. Hegel, *Phänomenologie des Geistes, Werke*, Bd. II, S. 393-97 - d 'cardinal of the sea' - e gentleman

From Diderot to Jules Janin must be what the physiologists call a regressive metamorphosis. French intellect *before* the French Revolution and *under* Louis Philippe!

I shall ask Collet about the source of Brunnow's maxim.[a] I would not be at all surprised if it were to be found in the English BLUE BOOK,[173] in an English legation letter from Athens. I found similar things from Brunnow in a 1839 BLUE BOOK about the SYRIAN-EGYPTIAN AFFAIRS.[b]

Eichhoff always sends me the Schweitzer[c] in great masses. So he must be coming soon.

Mr Thornton has written a thick book about CAPITAL AND LABOUR. I haven't seen it yet, only extracts in *The Daily News*, to the effect that capital, as a force separate from labour, will fade away in the distant future.

Take care with your eye.

Salut.

Your

K. M.

First published in part in *Der Briefwechsel zwischen F. Engels und K. Marx*, Bd. 4, Stuttgart, 1913 and in full in *MEGA*, Abt. III, Bd. 4, Berlin, 1931

Printed according to the original

Published in English in full for the first time

187

ENGELS TO MARX [180]

IN LONDON

Manchester, 16 April 1869

Dear Moor,

Enclosed returned the 2 Ludlows[336] and the 2 'knavish tricks'.[d] From Wilhelm you sent only the few lines for me, not those to you to which you refer.[333] If Wilhelm can't do more than this, then it is a miracle he did not do even worse in Barmen.[318] In a few days I shall send you reports in *Zukunft* about the general assembly,[e] which

---

[a] See this volume, p. 260. - [b] *Correspondence, 1839-1841, relative to the affairs of the East, and the conflict between Egypt and Turkey*, in 4 parts. - [c] *Der Social-Demokrat* - [d] See this volume, p. 263. - [e] *Die Zukunft*, Nos. 76, 79, 80 and 86; 2, 6, 7 and 14 April 1869.

appeared very late and show that the ground had already been well prepared in Schweitzer's association, and that the rebellion would have broken out even without Wilhelm.

The Ludlow correspondence very useful.

Many thanks for the *Rameau*,[a] which will give me much pleasure. At the moment I am reading almost nothing, in order finally to get my eye back on the right track; I have also cut down on my work at the office.

Wilhelm is badly mistaken if he thinks I would send him the *Peasant War*[b] on the basis of such vague promises, so he could subsequently pop up and yell that, if I did not send the sum of umpteen pounds, it would be impossible to print the final sheets. His letter is real twaddle, and his calm assumption that you should pay his fees is impudent.

Fowler, the STIPENDIARY MAGISTRATE here, who had the Fenians brought into court shackled to one another, has relinquished his post. Leaving behind his wife and 2 children, he has eloped with the wife of Milne, the CHAIRMAN OF QUARTER SESSIONS (daughter of the late Brooks, the rich BANKER, and WORTH £80,000 IN HER OWN RIGHT), who, for her part, left 5 children with her beloved husband. Great consternation amongst the philistines.

Salut.

Your
F. E.

This final story can only be explained etymologically; FOWLER from FOWL=Vogel.[c]

First published in part in *Der Briefwechsel zwischen F. Engels und K. Marx*, Bd. 4, Stuttgart, 1913 and in full in *MEGA*, Abt. III, Bd. 4, Berlin, 1931

Printed according to the original

Published in English in full for the first time

---

[a] D. Diderot, *Le neveu de Rameau...* - [b] F. Engels, *The Peasant War in Germany*. - [c] This may be an allusion to the German word 'vögeln' ('have it off with').

188

MARX TO ENGELS

IN MANCHESTER

[London, 16 April 1869]

E.=Eichhoff — B.=Borkheim.[337] I had written to Wilhelm[84] saying he should cease his malicious chatter and scribbling directed against Eichhoff, since Borkheim himself has now recognised his error. Wilhelm, of course, does not know that I know *his own* insinuations against Eichhoff from Kugelmann and OLD Becker.[a][61]

Did you receive the Lafargue manuscript?[b] It is not noted in today's letter from you.

Apropos: *Hermann* is now Stieber's official organ. Juch was forced to sell it, because of his 'diverse' creditors. In today's issue, Stieber starts right away by printing, on the first page, warrant notices, e.g., against the so-and-so Jaeger for illicit abortion of the foetus. Stieber is naturally represented here by a National-Liberal 'sub-Stieber'. I shall hunt out the carefully 'hushed-up' name.[c]

With regard to the eye: try washing it with alcohol. This helped me. To begin with it hurts a bit. For the FIRST attempt, dilute the alcohol a bit with water. That will show you how much you can stand it. Anyway, trying can't hurt.

Salut.

Your
K. M.

First published in: Marx and Engels, *Works*, First Russian Edition, Vol. XXIX, Moscow, 1946

Printed according to the original

Published in English for the first time

---

a Johann Philipp Becker - b See this volume, p. 262. - c Heinemann

189

ENGELS TO MARX

IN LONDON

Manchester, 19 April 1869

Dear Moor,

Enclosed Liebknecht returned. I wrote to him in a strictly BUSINESSLIKE [84] way about the *Peasant War*,[a] and I shall hear how he reconciles the gushing of funds for printing pamphlets with the newspapers'[b] deficit.

Lafargue's manuscript[c] is here; I have not yet been able to take a look at it, and I think he should take his exams *avant tout*.[d]

The great Thesmar from Cologne is now here, has introduced himself to Gumpert and also Borchardt under the name Themar, but has already accepted Thesmar. If you can send me the number of *Zukunft* that mentioned the warrant out against him for embezzlement, then do so; otherwise I shall have to write to Schneider.

Your
F. E.

Another curious subject[e] greeted Borchardt as 'editor of the *Neue Rheinische Zeitung*'; Borchardt himself will write to you about him.

First published in *Der Briefwechsel zwischen F. Engels und K. Marx*, Bd. 4, Stuttgart, 1913

Printed according to the original

Published in English for the first time

---

[a] F. Engels. *The Peasant War in Germany* (see this volume, pp. 262, 265). - [b] *Demokratisches Wochenblatt* - [c] See this volume, p. 262. - [d] first of all - [e] Gromier (see this volume, p. 275).

11*

190

MARX TO ENGELS [180]

IN MANCHESTER

London, 24 April 1869

DEAR FRED,

For ABOUT 12 days I have been suffering dreadfully with my old liver complaints. I am swigging the old medicine from Gumpert, but so far without success. As a result, I am completely paralysed mentally. This condition appears every spring. If I do not pass through it SAFELY, the CARBUNCLES come next. So please ask Gumpert if he knows of anything new for me. I have not smoked for a week. *Ça suffit*[a] to make clear to you my state.

It will take me a few days to get the information for Borchardt from Dupont. I cannot find the copies of *Zukunft*.

Apropos. The new 'sub-Stieber' who now edits *Hermann* is named, or calls himself, 'Dr' Heinemann, and claims to come from Manchester. Do you know anything about him?

The worthy 'Hillmann' from Elberfeld has written to me. I'll send you his letter on Monday.[b] He attacks Liebknecht on account of his renewed armistice with Schweitzer, as a result of which the fruits of victory have been lost. Hillmann the Honorable was, in 1867, the rival worker candidate to Schweitzer.[338] *Hinc illae lacrimae.*[c]
Salut.

Your
K. M.

First published abridged in *Der Briefwech-sel zwischen F. Engels und K. Marx*, Bd. 4, Stuttgart, 1913 and in full in *MEGA*, Abt. III, Bd. 4, Berlin, 1931

Printed according to the original

Published in English in full for the first time

---

[a] that suffices - [b] 26 April - [c] Hence these tears (Terence, *Andria*, Act 1, Scene 1).

191

ENGELS TO MARX[239]

IN LONDON

Manchester, 25 April 1869

Dear Moor,

Most useful for your liver would be a change of air and a change of your set habits. So do the right thing straight away: take a train immediately, and come here for a week or two. I have made myself quite a lot of spare time, and we shall be able to take vigorous walks together. Then you will be able to have Gumpert examine and treat you and, out of deference for your 'condition', you will be able to turn down invitations to 'tea'. You will then be fresh and ready for work in a short time again, to do more work in a few weeks than you can in months in your present condition. So telegraph me tomorrow to the WAREHOUSE which train you are coming on, and be here by the evening. That is the simplest and will *certainly* cure you.

Your
F. E.

First published in *Der Briefwechsel zwischen F. Engels und K. Marx*, Bd. 4, Stuttgart, 1913

Printed according to the original

192

MARX TO ENGELS[239]

IN MANCHESTER

[London,] 26 April 1869

DEAR FRED,

BEST THANKS FOR THE INVITATION. But it is quite impossible for me TO LEAVE AT THIS MOMENT. My wife is coughing badly, and I am waiting that out; as soon as she can travel, she will go to Paris TO FETCH TUSSY.[332] I shall perhaps come up with the latter.

In addition there are some things to put in order in the
International this week, which won't get going without me.[339]

And finally, however bad I might feel, I have to complete
CERTAIN SLIPS OF PAPER, since it is always difficult to continue, not with A
NEW SUBJECT, but in the middle of a certain topic.

WITH ALL THAT, if I don't get better, I shall naturally have to go
away.

More tomorrow.

Your
K. M.

First published in *Der Briefwechsel zwischen
F. Engels und K. Marx*, Bd. 4, Stuttgart,
1913

Printed according to the original

193

MARX TO ELEANOR MARX

IN PARIS

[London,] 26 April 1869

My dear little Quoquo,[a]

You must really excuse my long silence. I am just head over
heels immersed in work.

Now first as to your animals. Sambo has become almost
inseparable from me, to make some way or other up for the
absence of his supreme master. Blacky behaves always like a
gentleman, but a very dull one, too. Tommy has again done
everything in her power to prove the truth of the Malthus theory.
Helen[b] will to-day, I suppose, murder the new offspring of that
old hag. Whiskey, that great and good personage, was at first like
Calipso not to be consoled, desperate at your departure. He
declined the finest bones, never left your bedroom, and altogether
exhibited all symptoms of the deep sufferings of a '*schöne Seele*'.[c]
Still, when your name is uttered, he gets into a fit.—Dicky has
turned out a very fine singer, and we both encourage our
respective musical talents by mutual 'exercises'. Sometimes, how-

---

[a] Eleanor Marx was called in the family by a humorous nickname of Chinese
Prince Quo-Quo. - [b] Demuth - [c] 'beautiful soul'

ever, when I commence whistling, Dicky treats me as Luther treated the devil—he turns his ... upon me. Jocko has come out again, but its temper is as bad as possible. Having ascertained that you are absent, it gave vent to every sort of spleen and baffled all Helen's attempts at coaxing. Another source of annoyance for Jocko, was the arrangement of the little garden—a world Jocko considered justly as its own station and domain—by the gardener. Jocko misses its little hills, caves, rents, and all that lively disorder it delighted in.

As to the other 'animals'—as they belong not to the dumb sort, but are rather of a most talkative kind, and perfectly able to account for their own doings—I shall just now not lose one syllable upon them.

On Friday evening,[a] I was at dinner at Beesley's. Besides myself, there was Crompton, a barrister, and Jung and Dupont. Jung related his own doings. He told them what '*happy* (literal!) *speeches*' he made here, and what 'cutting hits' he made there. In this world of '*Weltschmerz*',[b] discontent, and restlessness, it gladdens your heart to be acquainted with an individual that is 'happy' and, moreover, possesses not only one shirt, but Sarah and other good things into the bargain.

The Irishman I send you tomorrow.

Many thanks to Cacadou[c] for her letter.

Many kisses to Fouschtra.[d]

And compliments to the African.[340] It will give him great pleasure to hear—if he has not already seen from the French papers, that the first 'black' ambassador of the United States has been appointed by Grant.[341] *Adio* my little Quoquo.

Your
Old Nick

First published in Russian in *Voinstvuyuzhchy materialist*, Book 4, Moscow, 1925

Reproduced from the original

Published in English for the first time

---

[a] 23 April - [b] weariness of life - [c] Laura Lafargue - [d] Charles Étienne Lafargue

194

MARX TO ENGELS

IN MANCHESTER

[London,] 1 May 1869

DEAR FRED,

Enclosed letter to our Belgian secretary [a] [342] will become comprehensible to you from the attached *Cigale*, the organ of the FRENCH BRANCH,[72] one analogue of which has formed itself in Brussels [b] and one (*Comité de l'avenir* [c]) in Geneva; ALL TOGETHER a few dozen men under Pyat's leadership.

My wife is still not well at all, but thinks she will be able to leave for Paris on Tuesday.

Once again it is just before Thomas, i.e., close of post. I think that tomorrow I shall at last be able to write more fully to you.

Salut!

Your
K. M.

First published in *MEGA*, Abt. III,
Bd. 4, Berlin, 1931

Printed according to the original

Published in English for the first time

195

ENGELS TO MARX

IN LONDON

Manchester, 2 May 1869

Dear Moor,

I would have written long since if you had not left me waiting for the 'more tomorrow'.

I hope your wife is improving with the fine weather; the

---

[a] Marie Bernard - [b] 'Association Internationale des Travailleurs. Formation d'une nouvelle section à Bruxelles', *La Cigale*, No. 16, 18 April 1869. - [c] Committee of the Future

journey will scarcely do her any harm; a change of air generally has a very favourable effect upon such coughs resulting from irritation of the larynx.

You can imagine the jubilation awakened here by the news that , you would bring Tussy with you, YOU ARE NOW IN FOR IT and must bring her with you whatever happens. And if she can only come a few days *after* you, that doesn't matter, we could meet her at the station. You might come rather earlier for health reasons. You do not write how you are doing; if I were in your shoes, I would put everything aside and come here, the sooner the better; why let the business become chronic and torment you for so long when the cure is at hand any day.

Your
F. E.

Best greetings to your wife and Jenny.
The *Cigale* did not arrive.

First published in *Der Briefwechsel zwischen F. Engels und K. Marx*, Bd. 4, Stuttgart, 1913

Printed according to the original

Published in English for the first time

196

ENGELS TO MARX

IN LONDON

Manchester, 7 May 1869

Dear Moor,

Your liver must be raging, since we neither see nor hear anything of you. How are things, and when are you coming? And is your wife well again?

No answer from Wilhelm.[a] I wrote to him in a BUSINESSLIKE manner to stop him indulging in any more dodges. If he does not reply soon, we shall have to see to it that Eichhoff prints the stuff.[b] He, i.e., W.,[c] apparently doesn't give any sign of life either.

A few numbers of *Zukunft* by post today, and enclosed the Belgian

---

a Wilhelm Liebknecht - b F. Engels, *The Peasant War in Germany*; see also this volume, p. 262. - c Wilhelm Eichhoff

letter,[a] returned with thanks. It is curious how, everywhere on the Continent, the people, relying on the International, simply launch strikes, and apparently have not the faintest intention of filling the general war-chest.

Tomorrow will, I hope, finally be that more lively 'tomorrow' when you will 'at last' get down to letting us have more news of you.[b]

In the debate on the trade regulations[324] Wilhelm played a quite deplorable role. All the motions came either from Schweitzer or from Bebel, and Wilhelm wisely kept his mouth shut, since positive knowledge was called for in this case. Schweitzer was also a treat when he tried to prove that the ban on Sunday work=increased consumption by the worker=wage rise.

Best greetings.

Your
F. E.

First published abridged in *Der Briefwech-sel zwischen F. Engels und K. Marx*, Bd. 4, Stuttgart, 1913 and in full in *MEGA*, Abt. III, Bd. 4, Berlin, 1931

Printed according to the original

Published in English for the first time

197

MARX TO ENGELS

IN MANCHESTER

[London,] 8 May 1869

Dear FRED,

In the main you had the right explanation for my obstinate silence: it came *from the liver*. However, there were several other additional INCIDENTS. *D'abord*,[c] my wife was very unwell. As soon as the business had got a bit better, last Tuesday,[d] she went to Paris, but arrived there quite benumbed. Paris has adopted the unmannerly custom of conforming to the London weather. When it rains here, it does there too, etc. Second, Eichhoff[e] arrived here, and is still here. And he arrived with a trio, a Berlin engineer, ditto

---

[a] See this volume, p. 272. - [b] Ibid., pp. 272-73. - [c] Above all - [d] 4 May - [e] Wilhelm Eichhoff

merchant, and ditto banker. Their task here, and it seems to be succeeding, is to find names for the prospectus of a bank in East Prussia, which has already received a concession. Finally, there were the *massacres belges*.[343] After addresses had streamed in from all quarters, as you will see from the enclosed papers, it finally became necessary for the CENTRAL COUNCIL[73] to speak on this really important issue. I was appointed to edit the ADDRESS.[a] If I had refused, the business would have fallen into the hands of Eccarius, who would be a square peg in a round hole for a vital document like this. So I accepted. In view of the present state of my liver, it was very awkward to do it in English—since such things call for a certain rhetorical style—but then, in addition, the agony afterwards TO DO THIS IN FRENCH! But necessity knows no law, and I DID IT IN FRENCH. To start with, I wanted to send the thing to the Belgians in the original English, but our Belgian secretary Bernard (French by birth) declared to the assembled *patres conscripti*[b] (last Tuesday[c]) that it would be better to abandon the project altogether if the translation was going to be left to the Belgians, who only half knew English and absolutely no French. So I HAD TO GIVE WAY. You will be able to enjoy the thing in both languages. However, I left the German translation, which does not interest me, to Mr Eccarius, who also has a monetary interest.[344]

But writing French, with or without liver, is dead easy if you give the public the sort of French used by Mr Urquhart in the *Diplomatic Review* which is travelling to you today. Astonishing double Dutch—even the original sample given by the *grand* and *illustre* Gaudissart[d] was nothing compared to this!

After my wife left I would have been able to come to your place right away; and I would certainly have gained time by restoring the proper operation of this damnable sack of flesh earlier. But Jennychen was looking forward to my wife's short absence in Paris, to have me entirely at her disposition and be able to let herself go. So I stay here! Apropos Jennychen, she claims that you know everything, and therefore wants to know from you: WHY DID MR 'EXCELSIOR',[e] OF THE ALPINE CLUB, NOT MARRY 'LADY CLARA VERE DE VERE'[f]?

About the FRENCHY[g]—Borchardt had his daughter II ask me

---

a K. Marx, 'The Belgian Massacres'. - b members of the General Council (originally collective title of Roman senators) - c 4 May - d Sigismund Borkheim - e the main character of Henry Longfellow's poem 'Excelsior' - f the main character of Alfred Tennyson's poem by the same name - g M. Gromier. See also this volume, p. 267.

about him [345]— I have only learned after a considerable waste of time that he is a *lumpacius vagabundus*,[a] who, however, held a SUBORDINATE post on the *Glowworm,* a very SUBORDINATE lousy sheet. Communicate this to the doctorly priest or the priestly doctor.

Don't forget to report to me on that Dr Heinemann OF Manchester, the sub-Stieber on *Hermann.*

As TO Wilhelm[b]: Eichhoff brought Eccarius a gratification of £10 (I believe Eichhoff paid it out of *his own* private pocket) for 'my Mill', but told me, in confidence, that 'my Mill'[346] had been printed but now lay firmly aground with the Leipzig printer,[c] who demanded exactly *double* the printing costs stated by Mr Wilhelm. Your steps were, therefore, prophetically correct. Meissner wrote to me more than a fortnight ago that he would start,[347] but NOTHING OF THE SORT! This is really too much.

According to Eichhoff's report, credit swindling and the FINANCING game are at present so dominant in Germany that everything else is absorbed by them, as far as the upper classes are concerned. As for the workers in Berlin, he declares they are the most contemptible specimens in the whole of Germany. Even the imported ones are soon totally corrupted by the city's atmosphere, and the 'low-priced' minor amusements. Bismarck, Duncker, Schulze-Delitzsch and Dr Max Hirsch compete for ascendancy in this sphere.

The old Hatzfeldt's Scurvy-Mende used to be an itinerant improviser and declaimer, a brute who belongs through and through to the lumpenproletariat.

Hasenclever has allowed himself to be captured by Schweitzer. Eichhoff praises Bebel greatly.

Harney—today under-secretary or SOMETHING OF THE SORT in the HOME DEPARTMENT of the COMMONWEALTH OF Massachusetts (they still say officially 'COMMONWEALTH' and not 'REPUBLIC')—in Boston, has sent £1 membership fee to the INTERNATIONAL COUNCIL,[d] ditto a letter in which he asks after you very affectionately. Ditto, he says I should send him A COPY OF *Capital.* He hopes to find a translator and publisher in New York.

A Frenchman who has translated various volumes of Hegel and Kant has written to Lafargue stating that he wants to Frenchify the book,[e] but—and what a visionary idea—for an honorarium of £60, for which sum he will also provide the bookseller.

The *International,* the Bonapartist organ here, had the impu-

---

[a] a vagabond rascal - [b] Wilhelm Liebknecht - [c] Otto Wigand - [d] the General Council - [e] the first volume of *Capital*

dence to state that the GENERAL COUNCIL of the '*Internationale*' no longer presides in London; that the leadership has now passed into the hands '*d'un personage très haut placé*'ᵃ in Paris.ᵇ

For the subscription list for the Belgians it would be very good if you could also send us SOMETHING from Manchester, and quickly.

Apropos. In the report on the EMPLOYMENT OF AGRICULTURAL CHILDREN (only 2 volumes out yet, Report I and EVIDENCE), the COMMISSIONERS, in their preliminary resumé, present a variety of facts about the expropriation of the workers from common land, quite in my sense.

My best greetings to MRS LIZZY, KING COLE or COAL,ᶜ and JOLLYMAYER.ᵈ

Your

Moor

First published abridged in *Der Brief-wechsel zwischen F. Engels und K. Marx*, Bd. 4, Stuttgart, 1913 and in full in *MEGA*, Abt. III, Bd. 4, Berlin, 1931

Printed according to the original

Published in English for the first time

198

ENGELS TO MARX

IN LONDON

[Manchester, 10 May 1869]

Dear Moor,

Letter and 2 consignments received. Best thanks. Enclosed with speed for tomorrow's meeting £1 in STAMPS from us here for your Belgian subscription. The Irish pamphlet caused a great sensation here. Ask Eichhoff if he can get the *Peasant War*ᵉ printed by his brother.ᶠ Meissner is obviously frightened.

Here we are in a lovely industrial crisis, and despite the SHORT TIME, too much is still being produced. The only means the manufacturers have of agreeing among themselves on SHORT TIME and a shutdown is—a STRIKE by the workers. They have been working towards this in a planned way for 2 months now. The one

---

ᵃ of a very high-ranking person - ᵇ 'Berlin', *L'International,* 22 April 1869 (in the column *Dernières nouvelles*). - ᶜ Samuel Moore - ᵈ Carl Schorlemmer - ᵉ F. Engels, *The Peasant War in Germany*. - ᶠ Albert Eichhoff

in Preston [a] was the first attempt, now followed by the 5% wage reduction in East Lancashire.[326] If the workers accept this, it will be followed by a new one, and so on, *until they strike,* for this is the sole aim. The honest Watts did not even mention this type of strike in his pamphlet,[b] *et pour cause.*[c]

When will you be coming?

Your
F. E.

First published in *MEGA*, Abt. III, Bd. 4, Berlin, 1931

Printed according to the original

Published in English for the first time

199

MARX TO LUDWIG KUGELMANN [29]

IN HANOVER

London, 11 May 1869

Dear Kugelmann,

You must excuse my PROTRACTED SILENCE. First, I suffered for many weeks from the *liver complaint* that always afflicts me in the months of spring, which is all the more vexatious since it lays me almost completely fallow for intellectual work. Second, I was waiting impatiently from day to day for the photogram you want, which Mr Fehrenbach, a German clot, has still not delivered.[d]

My wife and my youngest daughter [e] are, at the moment, on a visit to the Lafargues in Paris, so we are very lonely here.

The Palmerston PAMPHLETS (mine)[f] I could not find for you with the best will in the world. Urquhart's PUBLICATIONS against Russia and Palmerston,[348] though they contain a good deal that is correct, spoil everything again because of the CROTCHETS of the great 'David'.[g]

---

[a] See this volume, p. 257. - [b] J. Watts, *Trade Societies and Strikes.* - [c] and for good reasons - [d] See this volume, pp. 213 and 231. - [e] Eleanor Marx - [f] K. Marx, *Lord Palmerston.* - [g] an ironic allusion to David Urquhart

Your article sent to Engels.[a] As we are completely isolated from the RESPECTABLE PRESS, it will be difficult for us to act for you in this field, BUT WE SHALL TRY.

I intend to descend on you ABOUT the end of August with my daughter,[b] and to lodge with you until the end of September wherever you want in Germany[349]; even at the risk of suspending the completion of my manuscript.[c] No longer period is, of course, at my disposal.

I have read your letter to Borkheim. You note quite rightly that the St Bartholomew chatter about the BELGIAN MASSACRES WILL NOT DO. Yet you, for your part, overlook the importance and particular meaning of these events. Belgium, you should know, is the sole country where sabres and muskets *regularly*, year in, year out, have the last word in every STRIKE.[350] The matter is made clear in an address of the GENERAL COUNCIL here, which I have written in French and English.[d] It should be printed (in English) by tomorrow. I shall send it to you immediately.

In addition, I have just written an English address for the GENERAL COUNCIL of the International Association here to the NATIONAL LABOR UNION in the UNITED STATES[e] regarding the war with England,[351] which the bourgeois Republicans over there want to stage JUST now.

Mr Meissner has had the (printed and corrected) manuscript of the *18th Brumaire* since the end of January, but to date he has repeatedly delayed publication. This is pleasant too! He is waiting until the time for a possible effect has passed, for stupid bookselling reasons.

With best wishes to your dear wife and Fränzchen.

Yours
K. Marx

First published abridged in *Die Neue Zeit,* Bd. 2, Nr. 13, Stuttgart, 1901-1902 and in full in *Pisma Marksa k Kugelmanu* (Letters of Marx to Kugelmann), Moscow-Leningrad, 1928

Printed according to the original

---

[a] See this volume, p. 314. - [b] Jenny Marx - [c] the second volume of *Capital* - [d] K. Marx, 'The Belgian Massacres'. - [e] K. Marx, 'Address to the National Labour Union of the United States'.

200

ENGELS TO HERMANN ENGELS

IN ENGELSKIRCHEN

Manchester, 13 May 1869

Dear Hermann,

My best congratulations on the increase in the family, which pleases me all the more since this finally breaks the spell that caused you so much concern. YOU WILL NOW HAVE TO MAKE UP FOR LOST TIME.

The current account is so far correct, but I cannot calculate how interest at 5% on 27,924.29.4 thalers should come to 1,396.25.5 instead of 1,396.7.6 thalers. But since this does not amount to more than a bottle of moselle wine it is not worth altering much.

Not a step further contractually with Gottfried.[a] The lawyers are protracting the matter excessively; my lawyer advises me not to hurry, since Gottfried has more interest in coming to a conclusion than I have, which I believe too, because as soon as I have my money I can, if the worst came to the worst, always start up a business again and compete with him; to do this I don't need to start by collecting lots of samples and notes; I've got all that in my head. In the meantime, I have already taken the greater part of my money out of the business and invested in shares, and this in such a way that he himself is now short of money, and I have purchased shares from him for about £2,400; at first he encouraged me to draw funds liberally, but he got out of his depth when I drew about £7,500, and so he had to sell me these shares himself, as he held just the sort I needed.

I am very sorry that I was so deceived by the business with the reform of weights[352] at your end. I thought that such a measure would not be introduced if it were not to be carried out *absolutely* and be made valid for *all.* This, however, would have meant completely excluding yourselves from the market outside Germany, and I concluded that you were not very interested in business outside Germany. Had this not been the case, I would, as I mentioned to Adolf[b] 2 years ago, and to mother last year, have

---

[a] Gottfried Ermen - [b] Adolf von Griesheim

first asked you whether you would like to go into business outside Germany, and if so, to what extent we could come to an arrangement. But I had to assume the contrary, and therefore arranged my business with G. Ermen, and now, after this was arranged, mother writes to me that you have made this weight reform for Germany *only*. In this case I, in your place, would not have done it at all, since in Holland, Switzerland, Austria, Italy, etc., they want anything except dutiable weight, and when you expand your business outside Germany you will have just as much trouble and entanglement as before.

Mother writes to me that 4,000 thalers were credited to me there on 1 April. This will have reduced my account to about 17,000 thalers, which will be further reduced by the COPS, which have been bought cheap and will soon be ready. This I shall remit to you *in thalers* at the beginning of July, since it is high time that I also finally profited from the rate of exchange. If you would prefer STERLING, that's all right too, providing we share equally, you half and I half, the whole rate-of-exchange profit you have made since 1860 on my remittances, and also the 35-38% discount you stuck on me then.

Regarding the COPS, there can be no question of obtaining them directly from the spinners, since these people don't know anything, and don't *want* to know anything, about forwarding and advices. You will have to pay the $1^1/_2\%$ brokerage of some commission house, which will be well worth while, as differences of quality arise at the spinners, of which you know nothing, etc. For instance, for years I purchased the 45 from Samuel Taylor & Son in Oldham, but now suddenly the same yarn from John Wagstaffe & Co. in Stalybridge, which you and we used to utilise, has suddenly become much cheaper, so I am buying it again. The 55s and finer yarns are all from John Knowles in Bolton (formerly J. & G. Knowles), and you will have to stick to this yarn, or to that of his brother G. Knowles & Son, Bolton. Will you select a commission agent or shall I suggest one? As soon as you have chosen one, I can explain everything to the man, face to face. Incidentally, I always had the name of the spinners placed on the invoices.

Among my papers I found the original contract with Peter Ermen of 1862, and wanted to send it to you; but I discover that it is the one dealing only with the business *here*, so it would be of no use to you. So I shall keep it here, but if you should ever need it, you now know where it is. The arrangement about *there* you have there.

G. Ermen said recently to his nephew Heinrich[a]: 'There is really nothing to be done with Anton,[b] his head is completely worn out.' I calculate that the fellow has damaged us here, directly and indirectly, to the tune of between £1,000 and £2,000 per year.

Heartiest greetings to Emma and the little ones; the same to mother.

Your
Friedrich

The COPS cost $\dfrac{45}{16\,^3/_4}$, $\dfrac{55}{21\,^3/_4}$d.

First published abridged in *Deutsche Revue*, Jg. 46, Bd. II, Stuttgart-Leipzig, 1921 and in full in: Marx and Engels, *Works*, First Russian Edition, Vol. XXVI, Moscow, 1935

Printed according to the original

Published in English for the first time

201

MARX TO ENGELS

IN MANCHESTER

[London,] 14 May 1869

DEAR FRED,

My wife will come back only sometime next week, so I cannot be in Manchester AT THE OPPORTUNE TIME.

Eichhoff left yesterday. His proposal — *quant à*[c] the *Peasant War* — is that his brother[d] should publish the stuff and that he pay out the balance ON BEHALF of the 'International' at the next Book Fair, after subtracting his commission and costs.[e] He says: as far as his brother is concerned, you may regard the proposal as *definitive*.

With regard to *Herr Vogt*: When Liebknecht was arrested in Berlin, he left everything in confusion and, ditto, he did not clear up at the time of his EXPULSION. So 'he cannot remember' what happened to *Vogt*.[f] Eichhoff finally discovered that a second-hand bookseller had been advertising the book for 2 years in his sales catalogue. He visited the fellow, named Kampfmeyer. He had sold them all, and 'ditto cannot remember' *how* the books came into his hands. So everything Liebknecht told *us* was — fiction, to put it mildly.

---

[a] Henry Ermen - [b] Anton Ermen - [c] regarding - [d] Albert Eichhoff - [e] See this volume, pp. 211 and 237. - [f] Ibid., pp. 106, 142, 189.

The press here is lousy. First, they have suppressed like *one* man every word of our *Belgian* MISSIVE[a] (after deliberately publishing last week some stupid lines in the sense of Cherval, probably written by the '*police member*' of the Brussels special committee); and not only that, they have ditto like *one* man suppressed our Address to the AMERICAN LABOR UNION[b] (written by me, approved last Tuesday[c]), although this is *against* war between the UNITED STATES and England.[351] But there are things in it that these blackguards do not like.

Salut.

Your

K. M.

First published abridged in *Der Briefwechsel zwischen F. Engels und K. Marx*, Bd. 4, Stuttgart, 1913 and in full in *MEGA*, Abt. III, Bd. 4, Berlin, 1931

Printed according to the original

Published in English for the first time

202

ENGELS TO MARX

IN LONDON

Manchester, 19 May 1869

Dear Moor,

I must congratulate you on not having come here last week in this lousy weather. But this time you should really come.

About the *Peasant War* when we meet.

The address about Belgium is very good, and that for the Americans even better.[d] I saw them in the *Bee-Hive.*

Please bring with you the two numbers of the Prussian General Staff Report of 1866;[e] I must compare them with the Austrian ones,[f] which show up some pretty Prussian exaggerations.

---

[a] K. Marx, 'The Belgian Massacres'. - [b] K. Marx, 'Address to the National Labour Union of the United States'. - [c] 11 May - [d] K. Marx. 'The Belgian Massacres' and 'Address to the National Labour Union of the United States'. - [e] *Der Feldzug von 1866 in Deutschland.* Redigirt von der kriegsgeschichtlichen Abtheilung des Großen Generalstabes; *Der Feldzug der preußischen Main-Armee im Sommer 1866.* - [f] *Österreichs Kämpfe im Jahre 1866.* Nach Feldacten bearbeitet durch das k. k. Generalstabs-Bureau für Kriegsgeschichte, Bd. I-V.

Let me know as soon as possible when you will be coming. Your liver must have got somewhat better in the meantime.

Close of post.

Your

F. E.

First published in *Der Briefwechsel zwischen F. Engels und K. Marx*, Bd. 4, Stuttgart, 1913

Printed according to the original

Published in English for the first time

203

MARX TO ENGELS

IN MANCHESTER

[London,] 21 May 1869

Dear Fred,

Tussy and my wife returned from Paris on Wednesday,[a] and I intended to come to Manchester with Tussy tomorrow. In the meantime, this has been made impossible by an economic obstacle.

The various Paris journeys by Jenny, Tussy and Madame, and the purchases connected therewith, have naturally entailed extra expenditure for me. Second, there were borrowings to a sum of £14, which I absolutely could not avoid, by an unhappy coincidence of circumstances. Dupont, the soundest of the people here, has not only *chômage*,[b] but his wife is hopelessly ill. He is such a discreet man that he borrows from nobody, except in extreme need, and he is so conscientious that he always pays back. So I loaned him £6. Then along came Lessner, put into difficult circumstances by his wife's long and finally fatal illness. I could deny him all the less since I was myself his debtor for a long time. Thus £5. Finally the worthy Liebknecht (after writing to me *in vain* on the subject) writes to Eccarius himself, asking him to approach me for an advance. I told Eccarius that I had already turned Wilhelm down. But Eccarius wailed—and this is a fact—that he would be turned out of the house if I did not advance him at least £2 for rent owing. I thus did this, but at the same time wrote to Wilhelm that he should return it to me. So £14

---

[a] 19 May - [b] unemployment

OUT OF POCKET. All this left me with £15 lying *in petto*. But then, yesterday, A CERTAIN Drengler (*nomen omen*[a]) arrived from the City with a letter from Mr Zitschke in New York, who *13 years ago* loaned me £15, and then suddenly disappeared from London because of embezzlement (he dispatched emigrants to New York). TURNS NOW UP AGAIN with the old loan, which I had thought settled by his defection with the cash. I had to deal with the matter all the more because, in the meantime, he has become friendly with Mr Heinzen; in the event of a refusal to pay, he would have been able to 'Pioneer me out'.[b] Thus cleaned out.

Fox has died in Vienna after a 5-day pulmonary disease. His family left in poverty. Letters on this have reached me from Vienna. Fox's mother (Peter Fox *nom de plume*,[c] real name Peter Fox André) is a rich woman, who, however, left him completely in the lurch, partly because he married her abigail (now old), and partly because of his atheism. I have now approached her, *threatening* that if she does not give something, public collections will be held for her son in London.

Meissner sent me, 1 week ago, the 1st sheet of the *18th Brumaire*, and wrote that things should now go 'quickly'. But sheet 2 is not here yet. He appears to be dragging the matter out as long as possible.

Salut.

Your
K. M.

First published abridged in *Der Briefwech-sel zwischen F. Engels und K. Marx*, Bd. 4, Stuttgart, 1913 and in full in *MEGA*, Abt. III, Bd. 4, Berlin, 1931

Printed according to the original

Published in English for the first time

---

[a] The name says it (the name *Drengler* derives from the German verb *drängen*—to press). - [b] Marx refers to the possibility of this material being published in Heinzen's newspaper *Pioneer*. - [c] literary pseudonym

204

ENGELS TO MARX

IN LONDON

Manchester, 23 May 1869

Dear Moor,

Enclosed the promised first halves of 3 fivers, the other halves follow in a letter I shall put in the letter-box after close of post, which will thus arrive by the next post. Be so good as to let me know which train you will be coming on on Tuesday,[353] so I can pick you up.

From Euston Square	leaves	9	arrives	2	o'clock
"	"	10	"	3	"
"	"	12	"	5.35	"
" King's Cross Great Northern					
"	"	10	"	3.10	"
"	"	12	"	6	"
" St. Pancras, Midland	"	9	"	2.40	"
"	"	10	"	3	"

I hope you arrive at the latest by 3 pm, so we can still dine together. The weather has already changed and is nice and warm, and instead of sitting by the fire I am sitting with the window open for the first time today.

Best greetings to your wife and the girls.

Your
F. E.

First published abridged in *Der Briefwechsel zwischen F. Engels und K. Marx*, Bd. 4, Stuttgart, 1913 and in full in *MEGA*, Abt. III, Bd. 4, Berlin, 1931

Printed according to the original

Published in English for the first time

205

MARX TO P. LE NEVE FOSTER, ESQ.[354]

Manchester,[355] 28 May 1869

I have to thank You for your letter offering me to be proposed as a member of the Society of Art [356] and beg to say in reply that I shall feel obliged if You will be kind enough to do so at an early opportunity.

I am, Sir,
Your obedient servant

Karl Marx [357]

First published in *The Royal Society of Arts Journal*, Vol. CXXIX, No. 5296-5297, London, March 1981

Reproduced from a photocopy of the original

206

MARX TO PAUL LAFARGUE

IN PARIS

Manchester, 2 June 1869

My dear Paul,

You can, of course, *dispose of my name as you like*. Still, there are some objections. In the first instance, what you want, is work which, for the present, I am unable to perform, while Engels still suffers from an inflammation of the eyes which for some time is sure to debar him from writing. Of course, if a very urgent question arose, we should address ourselves to the *Renaissance*,[283] but this could be done without my name figuring amongst the *rédacteurs*. A merely nominal co-editorship would prove of no possible avail. However, my most serious objection is of an exclusively private nature, and I leave it to your discretion to decide the case. The intended paper will probably involve you and your friends in judicial conflicts with the government, and your father,[a] becoming sooner or later aware of my name figuring among

---

[a] François Lafargue

the *rédacteurs* of that paper, would be likely to draw the conclusion that I had pushed you to premature political action, and prevented you from taking the steps necessary (and which I am continuously urging you to take [a]) to pass your medical examinations and establish you professionally. He would justly consider such presumed influence on my part as running counter to our express mutual engagement.

As to the misgivings of Le Petit,[b] they are altogether unfounded. To make ready for an invasion of France, Prussia would, *under the most favourable circumstances,* want instead of 8 days at least one month. But the circumstances are now anything but favourable to her. There exists, in point of fact, *no German unity.* It could only be founded by a German Revolution, sweeping away the Prussian dynasty, which was, is, and must always be, the man-servant of the Muscovite. It is only by the overthrow of 'Prussia' that Germany can become really centralised.

Prussia has not merged into Germany. It has, on the contrary, conquered a part of Germany, and treats it—the directly annexed provinces as well as those pressed into the Northern German Confederation—as a conquered land. Hence the greatest disaffection prevails in her new acquisitions. In case of an *offensive* (*not defensive*) war against France, Prussia would be forced to employ a large part of its army for the purpose of keeping down these provinces, the more dangerous since her means of communication with France, such as railways, telegraphs etc. run through them, and the Prussian lines of retreat from the Rhine pass through them. As to the military contingents raised from Hanover, Schleswig-Holstein, Saxony, Kurhessen, Nassau etc., they could not be relied upon, and would prove a source of weakness instead of strength.

Apart from these provinces, either directly annexed or pressed into the Northern German Confederation, there is *Southern Germany* (Baden, Württemberg, Bavaria, Hessen-Darmstadt) numbering 9 millions. Here the popular masses are Anti-Prussian to the core. In case of a war against France, Prussia would, therefore, have to detach another part of her army in order to make sure of that part of Southern Germany which, on a long-stretched line, borders upon France.

And last, not least, Prussia would be bound to concentrate a strong army of observation against Austria. Do not forget that the Hapsburg Dynasty is sorely smarting under the recent humilia-

---

[a] See this volume, pp. 224-25.- [b] Louis Auguste Blanqui

tions and losses [358] inflicted upon it by the Prussian upstart.[a] Admit even *the quite absurd hypothesis*, that the Hapsburg Dynasty was ready to condone for the past, it would still be unable to support Prussia. The Austrian Emperor[b] has no longer any control over international affairs. The Hungarian diet has now to decide, and it would decide for France against Prussia. So would the Vienna diet. Thus, however friendly the apparent attitude of the Vienna Cabinet might be, Prussia could and would not rely upon it, but find herself always obliged to detach a strong army of observation against the army which Austria would be sure to concentrate in Bohemia.

Hence you see *de prime abord*,[c] that of the seemingly formidable military power of Prussia a very large part would not be available against France, but, on the contrary, would have to be frittered away in different directions.

Prussia would have no ally except Russia who is not able to dispose of her army on a *sudden emergency*. Before her contingents had been mobilised and had entered Prussia the whole campaign would have been decided.

The very idea that Prussia, under such circumstances, would venture *single-handed*, as she must do, upon an invasion of France, and revolutionary France too, is incorrect.

I have till now considered only the strictly military and diplomatic aspect of the question but there is not the least doubt that in case of a Revolution in France, Prussia would have to act now as in 1848. Instead of throwing her forces abroad, she would be forced to absorb them in *expeditions à l'intérieur*.

If, in 1848, the movement in Germany paralysed the Prussian Government, what would the case be now, when the popular masses in Prussia and the other parts of Germany, are much more developed, and, simultaneously, the Prussian government as well as the other German governments have ceased to be absolute and been weakened by the trammels of a mock constitutionalism?

As to the German working classes, they are, in my opinion, better organised than the French ones. Their ideas are more *international* than in any other country. Their *atheism* is more pronounced than in any other country. Their predilection for France, is general.

Prussia can *do nothing* in case of a French Revolution. (One working men's representative *in the North German Diet*[d] recently *threatened them* with the approach of a French Revolution.[359]) Only

---

[a] Bismarck - [b] Francis Joseph I - [c] at first sight - [d] Johann Baptist von Schweitzer

in the case of an *Imperial Invasion of 'Fatherland'*, Prussia could become a dangerous antagonist of France.
    Addio.

Old Nick

First published in: Marx and Engels, *Works*, Second Russian Edition, Vol. 32, Moscow, 1964

Reproduced from the original

Published in English for the first time

207

MARX TO HIS DAUGHTER JENNY[360]

IN LONDON

[Manchester,] 2 June 1869

My dear Emperor,

The thing under the arm was no carbuncle, but another sort of abscess, which bothered me much but, since yesterday, is quickly healing. It was a fortune I was at Manchester. Otherwise, it might have turned out a troublesome affair. I am now quite in good health.

I hope to be with you in the course of next week. Tussy will probably somewhat prolong her stay at Manchester.[353] After the restraint at Paris,[361] she feels here quite at her ease like a new-fledged bird.

I hope Lessner's departure to Brazil is not yet definitively decided upon. I regret very much being not able to do something for him. With your usual kindness you seem to have sacrificed yourself in the interminable tête-à-tête of Sunday last. As to Lafargue's paper,[283] I feel rather uneasy. On the one hand, I should like to oblige Blanqui. On the other hand, my other occupations will not allow me to do much for them, but, above all things, I fear lest *old* Lafargue[a] should suspect me to push his son to premature political action and make him neglect his professional duties.[b] As it is, he has not much reason to delight in his connexion with the Marx family.

---

[a] François Lafargue - [b] See this volume, pp. 287-88.

And now, dear By-Bye, good-by and my compliments to all.

Your retainer

Old Nick

First published, in English, in *Annali dell'Istituto G. G. Feltrinelli*, an. 1, Milano, 1958

Reproduced from the *Annali*

208

MARX TO HIS DAUGHTER JENNY

IN LONDON

Manchester, 10 June 1869

My dear child,

I was firmly resolved to leave Manchester yesterday. But on the pretext, that, during the first week of my stay, I had been an invalid, Engels insisted so much upon my remaining here till Monday next, that I had to give way.[353] He is really too kind towards me to seriously oppose such a whim on his part.

On our three days' trip to the Devonshire Arms, near the Bolton Abbey, I made the acquaintance of a most strange fellow, Mr Dakyns, a geologist, who lives transitorily in that part of Yorkshire in order to make a geological survey. *En passant,* you ought to know that a geological map is taken up of all England, under the orders of government, and under the leadership of Professor Ramsay, of Jermyn street. Moore is himself a geologist. By him Engels and Schorlemmer became acquainted with Dakyns who lives in a farmer house, in midst of a Yorkshire wilderness. That farmer's house was also an old abbey, and the lower part of it still serves as a chapel. It was to see Dakyns that we set out for that part of the world. Dakyns looks much like a German peasant of stunted side, with a face always grinning a broad smile, something monkeyish in the formation of his head, nothing British about him save the protruding upper set of teeth which reminded me of the late Mrs Seiler. His dress is about that of a slovenly and '*under*dressed' farm servant, of utmost negligence. Cravat and such paraphernalia of civilisation he is a stranger to. The first impression he makes upon you is that of a boorish clown whose good heart leaps through his eyes and grins on his lips, but you would give him no credit for intellect. Still, this is a highly scientific man, even an enthusiast for his science and whose name begins already to pierce through a big valley of rivals. He is naive like a child; without the least pretention always ready to communicate his scientific discoveries to the first comer wanting to pump him out. There is in fact always a couple of other geological surveyors swarming to and from him for the express purpose to beat money out of him, or fame, by appropriating his researches. In fact, we found him in the company of two such fellows, one of whom, named Ward, was a timid youth and the other, named Green, a bold, pushing man. We had a dinner on his farm—on Sunday last—in the room directly lying over the chapel. The room had evidently formerly served as an assembly room of the monks, big walled (*ich meine, mit dicken Mauern umgeben*[a]), with a look out to magnificent trees, and to an amphitheatrical group of mountains, the one overtopping the other, and wrapt in that blue veil Currer Bell[b] is so delighted with. During the very merry, and in spite of its rusticity comfortable dinner, the singsong of the youth in the chapel, coming from the depth, intercepted by the big walls, and sounding as from a far-away place, reminded me somewhat of the Christian Song in *Faust.*[c]

Well, our friend Dakyns is a sort of Felix Holt,[d] less the affectation of that man, and plus the knowledge (by the by, the Tories here say 'Felix Holt, the rascal', instead of the 'radical'). He invites once a week the factory lads, treats them to beer and tobacco, and chats with them on social questions. He is a '*naturwüchsiger*'[e] communist. I could of course not forbear making a little fun of him and warning him to fight shy of any meeting with Mrs Eliot who would at once lay hold of him and make literary property out of him. He had already written to Moore that he wanted to enter the International. So I brought him a card and he made a donation, as his entrance fee, of 10 sh., which is a sum for him. These men get only 150 £ a year, and have very hard work, mentally and bodily. The Government could not afford to get these men at such a price, if it was a mere matter of competition, but most of them are full of 'geological'

---

[a] I mean, surrounded by thick walls - [b] pseudonym of Charlotte Brontë - [c] Apparently the reference is to the angels' chorus in Gounod's opera *Faust*. - [d] the main character of George Eliot's novel *Felix Holt, the Radical* - [e] natural

zeal and improve this opportunity afforded them of making researches. They are provided with cards which bind every landowner, farmer and so forth, to allow them to walk over their estates, and farms and look into the formation of the soil. Dakyns, who has a good deal of farcical humour about himself, often enters into a farm, takes out his instruments, and sets at working, when the farmer comes up, growls at the impudent intruder, and bids him to pack himself off, lest he want to become acquainted with the teeth of his dog or the momentum of his flail. Dakyns affects not to mind him, proceeds in his business, and provokes the boor by some bad jokes. When the comedy has been approaching to a certain climax, he pulls out his card, and the cerberus is softened. During our stay he gave me to read in the nick of time the last number of *The Fortnightly Review*—an article of Huxley[a] where he merrily thrashes old Congreve. Dakyns is also a declared enemy of the Comtists or Positivists. He is of my opinion that there is nothing positive about them except their arrogance. As to my friend Beesly, he mentioned him amongst the 'doctrinaires' who mistake their fanciful crotchets for science.—In the same number of the *Fortnightly* is the second article of Mill[b] on Thornton's Capital and Labour. I saw from the criticism that both are equally small fry.—Dakyns is a neighbour of ours. That is to say, he lives at Kilburn (when in London) with his father, a lawyer.

Yesterday evening I had the unavoidable tea at the Gumperts. Mrs Gumpert has been much affected by the teeth of time. I have never before witnessed a more rapid change. The hypocrisy of a Greek nose has given way to the true Jewish type, everything about her looks rather shrivelled and dried up, and the voice has that guttural sound which the selected people is to some degree cursed with. Speaking of the disagreeableness to be in an omnibus, or at public firework, or in the theatre even near to the pit—all this because of the bad smells of the vile multitude, she said: 'I like the clean million, but not the dirty million'. I affected to have understood, clear million, and said that it was a very common predilection with mankind to prefer a clear million of pounds sterling to any million of men, whether washed or unwashed.

And now my dear child *addio*. Give my best wishes to all. On

---

[a] T. H. Huxley, 'The Scientific Aspects of Positivism', *The Fortnightly Review*, Vol. V, No. XXX, 1 June 1869. - [b] J. S. Mill, 'Thornton on Labour and its Claims', Part II, *The Fortnightly Review*, Vol. V, No. XXX, 1 June 1869.

Monday[a] I shall positively leave. As to Tussy, she looks quite blooming, and a little longer stay at Manchester will do her good.

Yours
Old Nick

First published in *Voinstvuyushchy materialist*, Book 4, Moscow, 1925

Reproduced from the original

Published in English for the first time

209

MARX TO ENGELS

IN MANCHESTER

[London,] 16 June 1869

DEAR FRED,

Arrived safely the day before yesterday[a] after 5 hours rail travel. From Manchester (by the railway line on which I travelled) you have to take a ticket to KENTISH TOWN STATION. Then you are near my house. St. Pancras is one station further, more in the town.

Was in the International yesterday evening. Letter from Paris. 3-4 of our people (Murat, Varlin, etc.) arrested. They write that the GAMINERIES, DEVASTATION of the *kiosques*, etc., were carried out *by police agents*, who were allowed to do what they liked; then bystanders were attacked. The aim was to produce something 'bloody'.

Your trunk will be sent back today. You will find in it a wallet of yours that travelled with me, while a notebook of mine remained in Manchester.

Best greetings to all.

Your
Moor

First published in *Der Briefwechsel zwischen F. Engels und K. Marx*, Bd. 4, Stuttgart, 1913

Printed according to the original

Published in English for the first time

---

[a] 14 June

210

ENGELS TO MARX[180]

IN LONDON

Manchester, 22 June 1869

Dear Moor,

I don't know whether you have such fine weather there as we have here, but daylight has been so exhausted that, on the longest day, we had to turn the gas on at 4 o'clock in the afternoon. And it is devilish to read or write when you don't know whether it is day or night.

Tussy is very jolly. This morning the whole family went SHOPPING; tomorrow evening they want to go to the theatre. She has read right through *Hermann und Dorothea*,[a] not without difficulty because of the idyllic philistines' twaddle. Now I have given her the younger *Edda*, which contains several nice stories; then she can read from the elder one[362] the songs of Sigurd and Gudrun. She also plays the piano sedulously. I have also read Danish *Kjämpeviser*[b] with her.

So that is Wilhelm's entire success: that the male-female line and the all-female line of the Lassalleans have united![363] He really has achieved something there. Schweitzer will naturally be re-elected — in view of the precipitacy with which the business has been conducted — and then he will, once again, be the chosen one of general suffrage. Wilhelm is also preserving an obstinate silence about this event.

The *Urning*[c] you sent me is a very curious thing. These are extremely unnatural revelations. The paederasts are beginning to count themselves, and discover that they are a power in the state. Only organisation was lacking, but according to this source it apparently already exists in secret. And since they have such important men in all the old parties and even in the new ones, from Rösing to Schweitzer, they cannot fail to triumph. *Guerre aux cons, paix aus trous-de cul*[d] will now be the slogan. It is a bit of luck that we, personally, are too old to have to fear that, when this party wins, we shall have to pay physical tribute to the victors. But

---

[a] by Goethe - [b] epics - [c] K. H. Ulrichs, '*Argonauticus*'. *Zastrow und die Urninge des pietistischen, ultramontanen und freidenkenden Lagers.* - [d] War on the cunts, peace to the arse-holes

the younger generation! Incidentally it is only in Germany that a fellow like this can possibly come forward, convert this smut into a theory, and offer the invitation: *introite*,[a] etc. Unfortunately, he has not yet got up the courage to acknowledge publicly that he is 'that way', and must still operate *coram publico* 'from the front', if not 'going in from the front' as he once said by mistake. But just wait until the new North German Penal Code recognises the *droits du cul*[b]; then he will operate quite differently. Then things will go badly enough for poor frontside people like us, with our childish penchant for females. If Schweitzer could be made useful for anything, it would be to wheedle out of this peculiar honourable gentleman the particulars of the paederasts in high and top places, which would certainly not be difficult for him as a brother in spirit.

At the end of the week, Schorlemmer will be going to Germany for 4 weeks via Grimsby and Rotterdam.

The STRIKES here in the cotton factories[326] have been over since this morning, when the Oldhamites went back. So overproduction has no restraints any more.

Close of post. Best greetings.

Your
F. E.

First published in *Der Briefwechsel zwischen F. Engels und K. Marx*, Bd. 4, Stuttgart, 1913

Printed according to the original

Published in English in full for the first time

211

MARX TO ENGELS

IN MANCHESTER

[London,] 26 June 1869

DEAR FRED,

With THANKS I notify the £90, first half-notes.

Enclosed for Tussy 2 LETTERS. She must reply to tight-fisted Collet.

---

[a] enter - [b] rights of the arse-hole

The enclosed letter from Eichhoff shows, unfortunately, that his brother has become skittish.[364] Write me what should happen now.

The last proof-sheets finally arrived and have been returned, ditto preface sent.[a] It now turns out that the procrastination was for two reasons: 1. Mr Wigand in Leipzig is the printer, and 2. Mr Meissner, for his part, does not keep a watch on the Leipziger. He really believed that I had received the last sheets direct from Leipzig several weeks ago. German sloppiness!

The honourable Wilhelm [b] is maintaining a deep silence.

Today the weather finally TURNS to the better.

I have received an invitation from the SOCIETY OF ARTS [356] for a *conversazione* in Kensington Museum on 1 July. This takes place only once a year, and is attended by the entire London aristocracy, from the court down to, etc. So Jennychen will have a chance to see this rabble.[365]

Addio.

Your

K. M.

While re-arranging my bookshelves a small old edition of Rochefoucauld's *Réflexions etc.* fell into my hands again. Leafing through it, I found:

'La gravité est un mystère du corps, inventé pour cacher les défauts de l'esprit' [c] [56].

Thus, pinched *by Sterne* from Rochefoucauld [366]!

And these are nice too:

'Nous avons tous assez de force pour supporter les maux d'autrui' [5].

'Les vieillards aiment à donner de bons préceptes, pour se consoler de n'être plus en état de donner de mauvais exemples' [20].

'Les rois font des hommes comme des pièces de monnaye; ils les font valoir ce qu'ils veulent; et l'on est forcé de les recevoir selon leur cours, et non pas selon leur véritable prix' [126].

'Quand les vices nous quittent, nous nous flattons de la créance que c'est nous qui les quittons' [39].

'La modération est la langueur et la paresse de l'âme, comme l'ambition en est l'activité et l'ardeur' [63].

· 'Nous pardonnons souvent à ceux qui nous ennuyent, mais nous ne pouvons pardonner à ceux que nous ennuyons' [65].

'Ce qui fait que les amants et les maîtresses ne s'ennuyent point d'êtres ensemble, c'est qu'ils parlent toujours d'eux-mêmes' [d] [67].

---

[a] K. Marx, *The Eighteenth Brumaire of Louis Bonaparte.* - [b] Wilhelm Liebknecht - [c] 'Gravity is a secret of the body, invented to hide the defects of the mind.' - [d] 'We are all strong enough to bear the sufferings of others.'—'The elderly like to give good precepts, to console themselves for no longer being able to set bad

I attended the TRADES UNIONS MEETING LAST WEDNESDAY,[a] in Exeter Hall.[367] Beesly delivered a really fine, very impudent SPEECH, recalling the June days (it was 24 JUNE).[368] The newspapers naturally KILLED, i.e., SUPPRESSED, him. In addition, he committed the crime of speaking very contemptuously of English journalists.

<table>
<tr><td>First published abridged in Der Brief-wechsel zwischen F. Engels und K. Marx, Bd. 4, Stuttgart, 1913 and in full in MEGA, Abt. III, Bd. 4, Berlin, 1931</td><td>Printed according to the original

Published in English for the first time</td></tr>
</table>

212

ENGELS TO MARX

IN LONDON

Manchester, 27 June 1869

Dear Moor,

Enclosed the other halves of the notes in all haste. Thank Jenny in my name and Tussy's for her two letters. I shall write you more tomorrow or Tuesday, and also return Eichhoff.[b] But it is a crying shame that when the German workers have found a publisher, he cannot even hold on.

Best greetings from all of us to all of you. Sam Moore has been sentenced to be fed by Tussy at tea this evening, and she plans to

---

examples.'—'Kings stamp men like money; they determine their worth as they will; and one is forced to accept them at their exchange-rate and not at their real price.'—'When vices abandon us, we flatter ourselves with the belief that we have abandoned them.'—'Moderation is the indifference and indolence of the soul, as ambition is its activity and ardour.'—'We often pardon those who bore us, but we cannot pardon those whom we bore.'—'Lovers and mistresses never bore one another when together, because they always speak of themselves.' - [a] 23 June - [b] See the previous letter.

give him bread and butter and TREACLE, and to smear the syrup in his beard. This is the latest.

Your

F. E.

First published abridged in *Der Brief-wechsel zwischen F. Engels und K. Marx,* Bd. 4, Stuttgart, 1913 and in full in *MEGA,* Abt. III, Bd. 4, Berlin, 1931

Printed according to the original

Published in English for the first time

213

ENGELS TO MARX[180]

IN LONDON

Manchester, 1 July 1869

Dear Moor,

Hurrah! Today *doux commerce*[a] is at an end, and I am a free man.[369] All the main points I settled with dear Gottfried[b] yesterday; he gave way on everything. Tussy and I celebrated my first free day this morning with a long walk in the fields. In addition, my eye is considerably better, and with a bit of gentle treatment should soon be completely back to normal.

The accounts and the lawyers will keep me on the run for another few weeks, but this will not be anything like the time lost so far.

Beesly really seems to be improving.[c] Just think what respect he still had for the English press that evening when he visited you.

Eichhoff returned enclosed.[364] Wilhelm[d] now appears to be pushing him forward in order to beg forgiveness. In the meantime, war has been declared again between Schweitzer and Wilhelm, and there is rebellion in the General Association of German Workers. But always the bold expectation that *we* should take the side of Wilhelm and the People's Party.[38] Wilhelm would do well to read the *Manifesto*[e] on the attitude of the workers' party, if reading or anything else would do any good! I am very anxious to see how this brawl develops; in any case, it will produce

---

[a] sweet business - [b] Gottfried Ermen - [c] See this volume, p. 298. - [d] Wilhelm Liebknecht - [e] K. Marx and F. Engels, *Manifesto of the Communist Party.*

some amusing scandal. Schweitzer really showed colossal presumption towards his gang in expecting them to allow themselves to be bartered off like a herd of sheep.[363]

I assume you received the 2nd halves of the notes on Monday.

The Irish MEMBERS behaved wretchedly again in connection with Moore's motion, and Mr Bruce made a happy laughing-stock of himself once again.[370]

From Eichhoff's information, it appears very questionable to me whether one should write to Meissner at all about popularising your book.[a] What do you think? In any case, if books for 5 silver groschen don't sell, then one for 8 to 10 silver groschen will circulate even less. The only thing that would help here would be a small pamphlet of 1-2 sheets at $2^1/_2$ silver groschen, but this needs work and is nothing for Meissner. What do you think of this? Or will you reserve it for personal discussion, since you will certainly visit Meissner in Germany?

I suppose Jenny has gone to the seaside with her honourable Monroes.[371]

Best greetings from all to all.

Your
F. E.

First published abridged in *Der Brief-wechsel zwischen F. Engels und K. Marx*, Bd. 4, Stuttgart, 1913 and in full in *MEGA*, Abt. III, Bd. 4, Berlin, 1931

Printed according to the original

Published in English in full for the first time

214

ENGELS TO ELISABETH ENGELS

IN ENGELSKIRCHEN

Manchester, 1 July 1869
86 Mornington Street, Stockport Road

Dear Mother,

Today is the first day of my freedom, and I cannot use it better than by immediately writing to you. Yesterday I finally reached a

---

[a] the first volume of *Capital*

settlement with Gottfried Ermen on all the main questions. The draft contract, drawn up by his lawyer, was such that I would never have signed it *in that form*. I obliged myself not to compete with him in the next five years, i.e., neither to make nor sell bleached, coloured or dressed cotton cloth. That was all right. But his lawyer had set this out in such a way that, if I breached any stipulation, I was obliged, in advance, to pay a penalty rising from £100 to £1,000 for each single instance, so that, in these monetary penalties, I would have had to pay back to G. Ermen *more* than the £1,750 paid to me, not counting the legal costs. My lawyer advised me strongly not to agree, so we struck out the whole business, nearly half the whole draft. Then there was another point, about the continuation of the firm Ermen & Engels by Gottfried. My lawyer told me that if I *explicitly* allowed him to do this, then, in the case of insolvency, I could still be regarded as *associé*[a] and be held liable. I therefore demanded that my *explicit* agreement to this should also be limited to 5 years, and this only so long as he himself was an active *associé* in the firm.

My Gottfried, who was originally very pressing with the negotiations, soon started dragging things out, and once even left the draft at home for 3 weeks without saying anything about it, so only about 3 weeks ago did I receive the 2nd draft contract (which is between G. Ermen, Anton Ermen and me, and governs the arrangement when I leave), and because of the usual lawyers' formalities could only begin to negotiate 8 days ago. In the past few days G. Ermen appeared frequently to avoid me, as though he wished to delay the matter until I was out of the business, when he might hope to deal with me more easily. Only yesterday morning did we get down to negotiations, and then Gottfried gave way *on all points*, while, for my part, I conceded him that, for 5 years, I would not spin and twine any cotton yarn *under No. 40*; I would remain free to trade in such yarn as long as it was in the *raw* condition. This concession has no sort of practical importance for me, and I thus obliged him.

Thus the matter has now been concluded, with the exception of a few legal matters of form, and I think everything *could* be finished in three weeks; but I am resigned that it might last in to August, since the accounts must be completed, and the lawyers always drag things out so.

Yesterday afternoon I went to the mill with Gottfried and inspected the stores and the reception; afterwards we went to his

---

[a] partner

house, where he served me a bottle of very good Scharzhofberger. He is as glad as I am that the matter is finished, that he is now the sole master of the firm, and that he is not going to have a row with me, since 1. as my lawyer tells me, if I had gone into partnership with my brothers, we would have been able to conduct the firm of Ermen & Engels *here too*, and we could prohibit him from doing so; 2. he is anyway very much afraid of competition; and 3. it now emerges that he still needs me very much for a time if bad blunders are to be avoided in the business; for this reason, he has invited me to come to the office as often as I like, and has requested me to give the people information from time to time, to which I naturally agreed. He has engaged a young Stuttgarter as correspondent, but he has only been there for 3 weeks and is naturally still very green. He'll have a heavy enough load.

Gottfried is not finished with Charles[a] either; his notice runs out in 8 days. I am curious whether they will reach an agreement. Five years ago Charles obtained from him a promise to make him managing clerk, but has never received the post; now he is demanding £1,000 compensation for this, but Gottfried will never give it to him.

Neither does he seem to want to keep on Anton as an *associé*. At least the 2nd draft contract dissolves the partnership with him in just the same manner as with me, and Gottfried would not go to this trouble if he did not intend it that way. On the one hand, Gottfried has realised that Anton is worth absolutely nothing in practical business, i.e., in earning money and, on the other, Anton continually draws so much money behind Gottfried's back, and sends it to his Julie[b] that Gottfried is apprehensive that he might some day start drawing money directly from the bank as long as he—Anton—has the right to sign. When Anton joined, Gottfried advanced him £500, which represented Anton's capital, but Monsieur Anton, who should leave £250 yearly standing from his emoluments, has not only not done this, but has also squandered the £500 long-ago.

My new freedom is just the thing for me. Since yesterday I have been quite a new man, and ten years younger. This morning, instead of going into the gloomy city, I walked in this wonderful weather for a few hours in the fields; and at my desk, in a comfortably furnished room in which you can open the windows without the smoke making black stains everywhere, with flowers on the windowsills and trees in front of the house, one can work

---

a Charles Roesgen - b later Anton Ermen's wife

quite differently than in my gloomy room in the WAREHOUSE, looking out on to the courtyard of an ale-house. I live ten minutes walk from my club, just far enough away from the German and lodging-house quarters to be sure that I am not overrun. At 5 or 6 in the evening I dine at home, the cooking is really quite good, and then generally go for a few hours to the club to read newspapers, etc. But I shall only be able to organise this properly when I no longer have to go to the city because of the accounts, etc.

But now *adieu*, dear Mother; give my heartiest greetings to all, and if you have plans to travel let me know, so that I can, if possible, adjust to them; as I am situated at the moment, you should not take me into consideration.

From my heart, your son

Friedrich

First published in *Deutsche Revue*, Jg. 46, Bd. II, Stuttgart-Leipzig, 1921

Printed according to the original

Published in English for the first time

215

MARX TO ENGELS [124]

IN MANCHESTER

[London,] 3 July 1869

DEAR FRED,

Best congratulations upon your escape from Egyptian bondage [a]! In honour of this event, I drank 'one glass too many', but late in the evening, not before sunrise like the Prussian gendarmes.

Enclosed a momentous letter from Wilhelm,[372] from which you will see that he has suddenly appointed himself my *curator*, and lays down this and that which I '**must**' do.

I *must* come to their August congress,[373] *must* show myself to the German workers; *must* send the International cards *immediately* (after *they* had *not* replied to two queries on the subject in 3 months), *must* muck the *Communist Manifesto* about; *must* come to Leipzig!

---

[a] Exodus 13:14; see also this volume, p. 299.

It is really very naive that, in the same letter in which he complains that he *cannot* pay back the £2 (which I gave to Eccarius for him), he offers *me my fare* to Germany. *Toujours le même!*[a]

He appears to be morally indignant about you. I have already replied to him that he has misinterpreted your letter. The fellow simply cannot grasp that convictions and business management are not poles apart, as he assumes in his newspaper administration, and as others have to assume if they do not wish to become SUSPECTS.

Our Wilhelm has a sanguine nature and is a liar. So there are probably, once again, exaggerations in his description of the victory over Schweitzer. Still, there must be something in it. Schweitzer would not have returned to the Church of Hatzfeldt had he not been shaky in his own association. On the other hand, he speeded up the general dissolution by the doltish management of his latest *coup d'état*.[363] I hope that, as a result of this business, the German workers' movement will finally leave the stage of Lassallean infantile disorders behind, and that the Lassallean residue will decay in sectarian isolation.

As for Wilhelm's various 'absolute commandments', I have answered him TO THIS EFFECT:

I feel absolutely no need to show myself to the German workers, and will *not* go to their congress. Once they have really joined the International and given themselves a proper party organisation—and the Nuremberg Congress[135] showed how little trust can be put in just promises, tendencies, etc.—then there will be an opportunity BY AND BY. In addition, it must be CLEARLY understood that the new organisation must be, for us, neither People's Party[38] nor Lassallean church—as little the one as the other. If we went now we would have to speak *against the People's Party*, and that would not please Wilhelm and Bebel! And if they—*mirabile dictu*[b]—would themselves admit this, we would have to throw *our weight* directly onto the scales against Schweitzer and Co., instead of having the change-over appear as a free action by the workers.

As far as polishing up the *Manifesto*[c] is concerned, we would consider this as soon as we have seen the decisions of their congress, etc.

He should hang on to his £2 and not worry about my fare. I praise their action against Becker.[d]

a Always the same! - b strange to say - c K. Marx and F. Engels, *Manifesto of the Communist Party*. - d Johann Philipp Becker

That's all on that.

About Meissner it is probably best if I speak to him. Incidentally, if you have time (that is, if it doesn't bother your eye) to finish something, it is easier to negotiate *with* a manuscript rather than *without* one. I know enough to know that Meissner prefers 5 sheets to 2. The shorter the pamphlet, the harder to sell, as he told me himself.

What do you say about the way that the virtuous Gladstone and puritanical Bright acted with regard to Overend, Gurney, *et* Co.?[227]

Remarkable, also, was Bruce's declaration on the Mold shooting,[374] which was not so INNOCENT as the Manchester papers reported. So the RIOT ACT[375] need *not be read*. It is enough for some fox-hunting UNPAID MAGISTRATE to whisper in the ear of an officer, and the peppering starts. Yet even this is not necessary. The soldiers may use their RIFLES IN SELF-DEFENCE (and they themselves judge whether this is necessary). But then, shouldn't the ARMS ACTS[376] be repealed, so everybody would be able to use his own RIFLE in SELF-DEFENCE against the soldiers?

The Gurney business, or rather the attitude of the Ministry towards it, ditto the Mold affair, finally the ministerial trickery with Lamuda and other scoundrels against the TRADES-UNIONS-BILL[377]—have made a mighty big dent in the fascination held by the names Gladstone and Bright amongst the workers here in London.

Laura was ill and bed-ridden for 14 days, but is said to be better now. They have given notice on their rooms, and in October will move to a more airy locality (Montmartre or some such).

BEST COMPLIMENTS TO ALL.

El
Moro

First published abridged in *Der Briefwechsel zwischen F. Engels und K. Marx*, Bd. 4, Stuttgart, 1913 and in full in *MEGA*, Abt. III, Bd. 4, Berlin, 1931

Printed according to the original

Published in English in full for the first time

216

MARX TO P. ST. KING

IN LONDON

3 July 1869
1 Modena Villas, Maitland Park

Dear Sir,

Will you send me

1) *Report of Commission on Bombay Bank,* issued this session;
2) *Agricultural Statistics. Ireland* f. 1867, issued this session (not the *General Abstract* for 1867 which I have already);
3) *Statistical Abstract for the U. Kingdom, f. 1868.* <******> Sixteenth Number.
4) *Report of Committee of H. o. Commons of July, 1843, on results of the allotment system etc.*[378]

Yours truly
K. Marx

First published in *Marx-Engels Jahrbuch,*   Reproduced from the original
No. 8, Berlin, 1985

217

ENGELS TO MARX [33]

IN LONDON

Manchester, 6 July 1869

Dear Moor,

Enclosed returned Wilhelm.[372] In fact, it is amazing, what he says you *must, **must, must*** do. But always the same old story. When he gets involved in a squabble with Schweitzer, you **must** always be called in to help. This will happen again, too.

With regard to the Basle congress,[379] I hope you have not minced words with him over the fact that only representatives *of those who have really joined* can be accepted. It would be vexing if he and Bebel had to be excluded on a technicality.

As far as my letter is concerned, his moans about 'reproaches instead of money' are the exact counterpart of Bismarck's complaint: 'Gentlemen, we ask for bread, and you give us stones',[a] when his taxes were rejected. The point that so 'upset' Mr Wilhelm was the question as to how he could tell me, *in one and the same letter*, that he did have the money to print the *Peasant War*, but at the same time had none for the sheet.[b] Further, how is it that the sheet was already 'guaranteed' $1\frac{1}{2}$ years ago, yet today it still doesn't pay? On this point, Monsieur Wilhelm is completely silent and is morally indignant that I should remind him of the shares he promised at that time *to send voluntarily and by return*; naturally I shall not get them now either, since Wilhelm says I shall 'naturally receive' them. The shares were only mentioned in order to prompt Wilhelm to remark upon the status of the sheet; it is fairly clear to me that Wilhelm and his consorts have managed things so sloppily that the printer or some other creditor can take over the sheet, and turn them out *as soon as it does pay*. In this case, it might be very agreeable for Mr Wilhelm if he had a few shareholders sitting here, who could exercise their legal claims in his favour. If the idiot had given me a satisfactory answer (which, however, would scarcely have been possible), he would have got the money; but simply to send a demand, and this self-contradictory, and without excuse either for his earlier dawdling or a word on the condition of the sheet—I wouldn't think of it. We don't want Wilhelm to get into the habit of things *like that.*

The extent to which his shouts of victory are premature is shown by the 4 numbers of *Social-Demokrat* that you sent me today. Certainly Schweitzer is also a big liar, but, *for the moment*, he appears to have saved the mass of the RANK AND FILE. However, things with him are going quickly downhill and, if he had any other opponent than Wilhelm, the process would be speeded up greatly. But, of course, the sultry waffle Wilhelm is now having printed as his 'speech'[c] will not help much. But Bebel is pressing Schweitzer hard, and cites some points that are very vexing to him, which would suggest the possibility that Schweitzer received his share of the Guelph funds surrendered to Stieber.[380]

In any case, nothing can be done with Wilhelm until he has

---

a Matthew 7:9 - b *Demokratisches Wochenblatt* (see also Note 372). - c W. Liebknecht, 'Ueber die politische Stellung der Sozial-Demokratie...', *Der Social-Demokrat*, No. 27 and supplement to No. 32, 3 July, and 7 August 1869.

quite definitely separated his organisation from the People's Party[38] and placed himself, at most, in a loose cartel relationship with it. Charming, too, is his intention of putting the International on the title of his sheet, which would then, *at one and the same time,* be the organ of the People's Party *and* of the International Working Men's Association! The organ both of the German petty bourgeoisie *and* of the European Workers!

Another fine idea of Wilhelm's is that concessions to the workers should neither be accepted nor *extorted* from the 'present state'. He'll get a long way with the workers like this.

I can't possibly prepare anything for you for Meissner in time. Until the accounts have been balanced, I have to go into town at least 2-3 times weekly, and probably even more often over the next few weeks, since I have to check the stuff carefully. My eye is much better, but still needs to be spared, since I don't want to make it worse again. In addition, I must put a mass of other money matters, my private accounts, etc., once and for all in order, and this is occupying me a lot too. Also, and particularly in this special case, I would like to hear Meissner's views first, since you say he is rather sensitive on such matters.

Tell Jenny I shall reply to her as soon as the beer in question puts in an appearance here, which so far is not the case.

Tussy says she will write tomorrow. She is now reading the Serbian folk songs in the German translation, and she appears to like them a lot; she has replaced me in giving piano lessons to Mary Ellen,[a] to the latter's great advantage. When the weather is good and I don't have to go to town, we go for a walk for a few hours every morning, otherwise in the evening, WEATHER PERMITTING.

The pamphlet by Tridon[b] was mainly of interest to me because of the second part, since I am not familiar with the newer material about the first revolution. The first part is, however, very confused, particularly about centralisation and decentralisation; it's a good thing that the *Renaissance* has been adjourned for the time being[283]; the people would have soon fallen foul of one another. It's a comic idea that the dictatorship of Paris over France, which led to the downfall of the first revolution, could be accomplished without more ado today once again, and with a quite different result.

Bruce's statement about Mold[374] has indeed proved that previous ideas about the English laws in this connection were quite

---

[a] Mary Ellen Burns - [b] G. Tridon, *Gironde et Girondins. La Gironde en 1869 et en 1793.*

wrong, and that people take an entirely Prussian point of view. Useful, too, for the workers to know this.

I hope you will soon be able to give me better news about Laura's health. In any case, to move lodgings is sensible.

Best greetings.

Your
F. E.

First published abridged in *Der Briefwechsel zwischen F. Engels und K. Marx*, Bd. 4, Stuttgart, 1913 and in full in *MEGA*, Abt. III, Bd. 4, Berlin, 1931

Printed according to the original

Published in English in full for the first time

218

MARX TO FRANÇOIS LAFARGUE

IN BORDEAUX

London, 7 July 1869

My dear friend,

Your letter decided me to leave immediately for Paris.[381] There I shall be able to judge the state of affairs and to act in the sense indicated by you. I quite share your views. I shall write to you from Paris, where I shall stay for two or three days.[a] The news of the state of your health has deeply pained me and all my family, who love you sincerely.

Please, pass my compliments to your wife.

Yours
Karl Marx

First published in *Annali dell'Istituto G. G. Feltrinelli*, an. 1, Milano, 1958

Printed according to the original

Translated from the French

Published in English for the first time

---

[a] See this volume, pp. 314-15.

219

ENGELS TO JENNY MARX (DAUGHTER)[382]

IN LONDON

Manchester, 9 July 1869

*Dear Jenny,

*My best thanks for your two kind letters[383] and for the beer which arrived safely on Wednesday and was tried on Thursday after a day's settling. I have just been into the cellar to fetch another bottle up, it is very nice, and Lizzie[a] especially likes it because it reminds her more of her beloved 'Bavarian' than the regular Vienna beer. There is no doubt, it will soon be emptied, and the more so as I am afraid it will not keep very long in hot weather, being lighter than the common Vienna beer, so that there will be plenty of pretexts for taking frequent 'headers' into the cellar and fetching up a bottle or two of 'that same'.

*I, and indeed all of us, were very much amused with your description of that highly aristocratic *soirée*. That little bit of a printed caution about mobbing, and the fact of its being sent round with the invitations,[384] is more than characteristic of 'that lot', as we say here in Lancashire. Very good, too, on the part of these Britishers, to describe this, their own darling 'vulgar habit' as one 'common throughout Europe'—common, indeed, wherever the British snob—and the snob and the flunkey is at the bottom of all of them—puts his foot!* I'd like to see any place on the Continent where such a circular would be issued on such an occasion. To be sure, it clearly follows from the entire story that the admixture of rich UPSTARTS has also begun winning the upper hand in aristocratic areas, AND IN FACT, IS NOW SWAMPING 'SOCIETY'. So much the better. Your description, like the circular, fits our Manchester MOCK-'SOCIETY' completely, and the more the smart mob in London Manchesterises, the more gratifying for us.

I am just now in the honey-moon of my newly-recovered liberty, and you will not require to be told that I enjoy it amazingly.[369] As my eye, although very much better, still requires a little careful treatment, *I have not yet settled down to regular work and indeed shall not be able to do so until all my business

---

[a] Lizzy Burns.

affairs are regularly settled, which will take about a month. In the meantime I walk about a good deal with Tussy and as many of the family, humane and canine, as I can induce to go with us. We have just come back from a long walk through the fields to Heaton Chapel, about 5 or 6 miles the way we went, Tussy, Lizzie, Mary Ellen,[a] myself and two dogs, and I am specially instructed to inform you that these two amiable ladies had two glasses of beer *a-piece* (this is the vernacular Lancashire in which I got my orders). No wonder I had to bring them home by the train (we have a station about seven minutes' walk from our house), but no sooner arrived, than they walked, in common with me, into your Lager-Beer. Now they are getting their tea ready, or getting themselves ready for it, I don't know which, and after that there will be a reading of Irish novels which is likely to last till bedtime or nearly so, unless relieved by a bit of talk about the 'convicted nation'.[b] Anyhow, they seem to like it, and so it's all right to me.*

Meanwhile they all send you the heartiest greetings, and I'll do the same.

Your with all my heart

F. Engels

If you and Moor don't go to Germany before the end of this month or if you don't return before the end of September, *I* may possibly meet you there somewhere.[c]

First published in *Friedrich Engels. 1820-1970. Referate, Diskussionen, Dokumente,* Hanover, 1971

Printed according to the original

Published in English in full for the first time

---

a Mary Ellen Burns - b Irish - c See this volume, pp. 341-42.

220

ENGELS TO LUDWIG KUGELMANN[385]

IN HANOVER

Manchester, 10 July 1869
86ª Mornington Street, Stockport Road

Dear Kugelmann,

As the enclosures show, I do keep my word, and I would have done so a long time ago, had it not been for the following: 1. I still had the enclosed photograph of Lupus,[b] but none of me, and only after frequent sittings last winter did I get a bearable one; 2. then I found that the Lupus photo had been mislaid and, despite all the searching, could not be found. So, 3. I got the photographer who had the negative to make 24 more copies of Lupus, but they turned out miserably, since it was very faded, and I wouldn't like to send any of them. Finally, 4. I found the original one and *les voici*[c] both.

I regretted to hear through Marx that you had to undergo an operation and that, now, for the summer, you want to live healthily, which is certainly very useful, and here and there also probably pleasant. I hope this will put you properly on your feet again, but will probably have the result that our friend Schorlemmer, who has been in Germany for 14 days, and who wanted to go via Hanover and visit you in about 10-12 days, will not find you there. Marx will probably be coming to Germany with his daughter Jenny at the end of this month or the beginning of next,[349] how things will be with me I don't know yet, for the following reasons:

On 30 June this year my agreement with my present *associé*[d] expired.[369] According to my original calculations, at the beginning of the agreement I had expected that, on its expiry, I would have made enough money out of noble COMMERCE to live on, though very modestly by standards here, and be able to bid *adieu* to trade. This did not ensue completely, but after various negotiations with my *associé* we finally agreed that I would allow him to use my name in the firm for 5 years, and I would promise during these 5 years not to go into competition with him, for which he paid me quite a nice round sum, so that I have, in fact, reached the point

---

a In the manuscript: 89 - b Wilhelm Wolff - c here are - d partner at which I aimed. Since the 1st inst. I have been out of the business, and my time is finally my own again—that is, for the time being, purely theoretically since I cannot leave here until the balance has been drawn and the necessary documents have been arranged by the lawyers; and I shall still have to waste a lot of time to put these matters in order. I expect, however, to be finished during next month, and if you would let me know where you will be about that time, it might be possible for all of us to meet somewhere in Germany. I don't need to tell you how happy I am to be rid of that damned commerce, and to be able to work for myself again. Particularly, too, since this was possible just now, when events in Europe are taking an increasingly critical turn and when, one fine day, the thunder may clap quite unexpectedly.

The Lassallean sect appears, not without dialectical irony, to seek its effective dissolution precisely in its nominal reunification.[386] Schweitzer may, for the moment, still hold the majority of the people together, but no party or sect can endure the repeated expulsion of its leaders. And this time the dirty washing of this extremely unclean clique will produce all sorts of *curiosa*, which can only harm Schweitzer. The dissolution of the Lassallean sect and, on the other hand, the severence of the Saxon and South German workers from the leading-strings of the 'People's Party'[38] are the two fundamental conditions for the new formation of a genuine German workers' party. The Lassalleans will now play their part themselves and devour one another, but it will be far more difficult to get rid of the South-German-republican philistine narrow-mindedness systematically drummed into the workers by Liebknecht. Just take the stupidity of inscribing on his sheet[a] 'Organ of the People's Party', i.e., of the South German philistines! If Bebel only had some theoretical knowledge, something like this could not happen; he seems to me to be quite a capable fellow, who simply has this one shortcoming. Then along comes Liebknecht and demands that we should come out on his side and that of his People's Party against Schweitzer! Whereby it is obvious that 1. we have far less in common with the People's Party, as a bourgeois party, than we have with Schweitzer's Lassalleans, who are after all a workers' sect; and 2. that Marx, in his capacity as Secretary of the International Working Men's Association for Germany, is *obliged* to treat decorously *every* leader whom a sufficient number of workers place at their head and elect to parliament.

---

[a] *Demokratisches Wochenblatt*

I would ask you from now on always to send your letters to my home address, given above.

Recently Marx sent me your study on the treatment of exanthematous disorders by means of ventilation. In my opinion you still apply the ventilation much too moderately. Here the window of the bedroom is kept open between 3 and 12 inches without further ado, without a screen, etc., and care is only taken that the patient is not lying in a *direct draught*—and this summer or winter. In addition *extractum carnis*[a] and port in big doses, otherwise practically no medicine. My servant-girl was treated thus last November for typhoid fever, and Marx's two unmarried daughters last summer for scarlet fever. I thought that this method of treatment had long been generally adopted in Germany too but, according to your account, the old keeping-warm and stink-hole method still seems to predominate.

Hoping to hear from you soon. With best wishes

Yours
F. Engels

First published in: Marx and Engels, *Works*, First Russian Edition, Vol. XXVI, Moscow, 1934

Printed according to the original

Published in English in full for the first time

221

MARX TO FRANÇOIS LAFARGUE[80]

IN BORDEAUX

Paris, 10 July 1869

My dear friend,

I arrived here on Thursday[b] evening and I shall return to London on Monday.[381]

In your letter, which I have reread, you seem to believe that Madame Marx is also here. That is a mistake.[c]

The first thing that struck me is that Laura is still suffering greatly, and her health is very delicate.

---

[a] meat extract - [b] Marx wrote *Thursday* instead of *Tuesday*. See this volume, p. 315. - [c] See this volume, p. 284.

I begin with this remark because it explains the apparent apathy of our Paul. He has not interrupted his studies, but he has neglected to take the necessary measures to pass his examinations.

To my reproaches on this subject he replied—and I must say had every right to reply—the following: 'Before I think of the future, I must occupy myself with the present. The state of Laura's health demanded a great deal of care on my part. It did not even permit me to be absent for any length of time. In order not to cause anxiety to you or to my family, I wanted to conceal all this. Laura and myself, we even did our best not to rouse the suspicions of Madame Marx.'

I have talked to a very good doctor whom Paul invited to the house. He told me that it was absolutely necessary for Laura to go to the seaside, and he suggested Dieppe because a prolonged voyage would do her harm.

Besides, Paul has promised me that on his return from Dieppe he will do his best to cut short the time necessary to pass his doctorate.

I must tell you frankly that the state of my daughter's health is a matter of serious concern to me.

Our grandson[a] is a charming boy. I have never seen a better shaped child's head.

My compliments to Madame Lafargue.

Accept, my dear friend, the most sincere compliments of your

Karl Marx

First published in: Marx and Engels, *Works*, Second Russian Edition, Vol. 32, Moscow, 1964

Printed according to the original

Translated from the French

222

MARX TO ENGELS

IN MANCHESTER

[London,] 14 JULY 1869

DEAR FRED,

Arrived in Paris last Tuesday evening, left again Monday (12 July).[381] I managed to remain completely *incognito*; on landing

---

a Charles Étienne Lafargue

at Dieppe I passed first the *douaniers*[a] and police without them intervening, though, curiously enough, several innocent people (including a YANKEE with very black hair, who was taken for an Italian) were asked for their passports and, in accordance with the latest regulations, the Frenchmen had to give their names. I lodged as A. Williams in Paris, Rue St Placide, *maison meublée*[b] (next street to Lafargue).

Laurachen has been suffering from a really serious illness. She is now convalescing, and is going tomorrow with Paul, etc., to Dieppe, where they will spend a month at the seaside, and will perhaps come over to England later. My BUSINESS in Paris was to have a look at the *status rerum*,[c] following a letter from Lafargue senior, and then write to the senior (from Paris), after consultations with the junior.[d] Because of Laura's state of health, Lafargue has naturally been completely absorbed by domestic worries, but has promised most solemnly to take the necessary steps as soon as Laura is completely restored. The senior also put his foot in it in his letters to Paris. I shall see what he writes to me in his reply.

Le petit[e] has left Paris (where he was present *incognito* at all the crowd-gatherings, etc.) for Brussels and, under the circumstances, his absence was by no means unpleasant for me. Because of this, the paper has been 'postponed'.[283]

I saw neither Schily nor ANYBODY ELSE, but confined myself entirely to the FAMILY, with whom I sauntered through more or less the whole of Paris. The bank where they live (Faubourg St Germain, etc.), has not changed much and is not Haussmannised.[387] Then, as now, narrow stinking streets. However, things look much changed on the other bank of the Seine, where the CHANGE already starts with the front of the Louvre.

The females appear to have become much uglier.

The heat was unbearable, particularly in the train.

The biggest sensation, to the great annoyance of the democratic opposition (including the *irréconciliables*), was caused by Raspail's *short* SPEECH,[388] in which he demanded the release of his election committee. He spoke of the *injustice de la justice*. Thereupon INTERRUPTIONS. He continued: *Niez-vous les injustices commises contre moi par la Restauration? Par ce ridicule Louis-Philippe?*[f] etc. He wanted no *peines*,[g] was ready *à brûler le code civil* and *le code*

---

a customs officials - b furnished house - c state of affairs - d See this volume, p. 309. - e Louis Auguste Blanqui - f Do you deny the injustices committed against me by the Restoration? By *this ridiculous Louis Philippe?* - g punishments

pénal[a]; in the meantime, the punishments of officials should be converted into *fines* (i.e., *deductions from salary*) and should begin with *M. le préfet de la police*, namely because of the '*orgies infernales de casse-tête*'.[b] The language of the old man was in violent contrast to the ROUNDABOUT prattle of the *faux jeunes hommes*.[c] And the next day, the government released his *Comité*.

The sessions of the *Corps législatif* were relatively very stormy. For this reason, Bonaparte has adjourned.

Tussychen must also write to me about her plans for staying in Manchester. Schnaps,[d] a charming little lad, sends heartiest greetings.

Addio, OLD BOY.

Il
Moro

MY COMPLIMENTS TO MRS[e] BURNS.

First published abridged in *Der Briefwechsel zwischen F. Engels und K. Marx*, Bd. 4, Stuttgart, 1913 and in full in *MEGA*, Abt. III, Bd. 4, Berlin, 1931

Printed according to the original

Published in English for the first time

223

MARX TO LUDWIG KUGELMANN[29]

IN HANOVER

London, 15 July 1869

Dear Kugelmann,

Your letter of 2 June arrived here while I was in Manchester.[353] They forgot to send it on to me, and later completely forgot about its existence. I have *only just* put my hands on it, after my attention was drawn to it by your letter of 6 July. The latter letter I also received yesterday since, owing to the indisposition of my Laura, I had been for a week *incognito* in Paris[f] where, BY THE BY, a growing movement is manifest. Otherwise, I should have hastened to write to you in your time of suffering.

---

[a] to burn the civil code and the penal code - [b] 'hellish orgies of bludgeoning' - [c] hypocritical young men - [d] Charles Étienne Lafargue - [e] Here the MS is damaged. - [f] See the previous letter.

As for the *18th Brumaire,* Meissner's assurances are sheer prevarications.[389] He has had the stuff since the end of January. Naturally, he did not get the preface because he didn't send the last 2 proof sheets. I finally received the latter on 23 June, and sent them back, corrected, the same day, together with the preface. Thus, once again, more than three weeks lost, so we shall be launched right into the off season in the book trade!

I shan't be coming to Germany before September.[349] I am making the journey mainly because of my daughter.[a] But, in any case, I would come to see you in Helgoland (I am travelling via Hanover).

Regarding Engels' biography,[b] be so kind as to return it to me.[390] He must revise it, since it is now intended for a different audience.

With hearty greetings to your dear wife and Fränzchen,[c]

Yours

K. M.

First published in *Pisma Marksa k Kugelmanu* (Letters of Marx to Kugelmann), Moscow-Leningrad, 1928

Printed according to the original

224

ENGELS TO HERMANN ENGELS

IN ENGELSKIRCHEN

Manchester, 15 July 1869

Dear Hermann,

You really are a fine chum. It stands to reason that I wrote about the exchange-rate matter to you simply as *our mother's business manager.*[d] But just *because* you are her business manager, you can't get out of it like that and tell me that I should approach mother directly about the matter. It would be a fine state of affairs if you always resigned as business manager as soon as the other party's opinion differed from yours, or when your arguments were exhausted. No, my lad, you've got to stick to it now.

To get to the point: what do you mean, we agreed to calculate

---

[a] Jenny Marx - [b] F. Engels, *Karl Marx.* - [c] Kugelmann's daughter Franziska - [d] See this volume, pp. 280-82.

everything at 6 thalers 20 silbergroschen? Nothing more nor less than that both parties, our mother and I, should waive making an exchange profit on these £10,000. Since, however, a considerable exchange profit *has* been made by mother on the £7,000 paid back by me, I felt it to be absolutely in order that I should also make my profit on the small remainder. You solve the pattern much more simply, by claiming offhandedly that mother alone has a right to the exchange profit.

In addition, you have not considered that, in presenting mother quite correctly as the only interested party, you are sawing off the bough on which you sit with regard to the discount business. I repay mother £1,000 and, on enquiry, receive the reply that this should be sent to R. Funke & Co. in bills *at any sight*. I did this, and was thus entitled to have these bills credited to me at full value per date of maturity. What Funke later did with the bills as a result of some agreement—of which I know nothing, and which is no business of mine—between R. Funke & Co. and Ermen & Engels, Barmen (2 firms which, as you say, do not concern me in the slightest), is no longer my concern, any more than what the bank did at which Funke discounted them. This should now at last be clear to you.

There can be absolutely no question of 'trickery'. But those who are merchants by profession, just like lawyers by profession, easily accustom themselves to regard the matter in hand solely from the most advantageous angle from their own point of view; when one is dealing with scientific questions this habit is the one which must be broken first. The discount business gave me the impression that your viewpoint on this matter was not entirely unprejudiced, so I have felt since then that I should myself pay rather more attention to my own interests.

I have no recollection at all that *I expressed the desire* to keep the accounts in thalers for *your* convenience. But you overlook the fact that your entire chain of evidence, which is based simply upon the fact the £10,000 stayed here in Manchester to *my* advantage, also demonstrates that, if the exchange rate had remained at 6 thalers 12 silbergroschen, I would have been obliged to remit in *thalers*, since nobody would wish mother to lose money on it. And you must admit yourself what sort of value an argument has that demands that, when the rate is high, I must cover in sterling, and when low, in thalers.

I should also like to ask you, with regard to the COPS AND SEWINGS I purchased for you, whether you have charged them to mother at the current exchange or at 6 thalers 20 silbergroschen, although I do not doubt at the former, in view of your zeal for mother's profit on the exchange rate.

But that's enough. As your patience appears to be coming to an end, and the matter is not worth the trouble, I'll oblige you and cover in sterling. Under my agreement with Gottfried,[a] the sum of £1,000 is payable on 1 August, and then every 2 months, and I shall devote the first instalments, as far as possible, to cover mother. It is, however, probable that Gottfried will hold back the first instalment until the accounts are completed and the contracts signed, which could take 14 days longer, so I would ask you not to depend on it as a certainty and to the day. Be so good, therefore, as to send me my current account, made up as of 30 June; my account here is so lengthy, as a result of many money withdrawals, that I would prefer not to depend upon it, since I have not yet received my statement, and can only check it superficially in the office. The whole approximate balance you will receive: 1. in August circa £800-900, 2. in October £1,000, and in December—the remainder; I would request you to let me know in good time where and how you would like the remittances.

Your letter of the 13th just arrived; I shall sign the thing as soon as I go to town and meet the vice-consul, probably tomorrow. But be so kind as to enquire what I should do in order to be spared any further communications from the Royal District Court in Bochum with regard to the Vereinigte[b] Engelsburg. From time to time a fat epistle arrives here, written on heavy, poor-quality scribbling paper, with a seal as big as a two-thaler piece, addressed to me as 'Official Business, Post Free'; whereupon the English Post Office, which doesn't give a damn for the District Court of Bochum, charges me between 3 and 5s. postage. A week ago I received a packet like this, with the names of all the shareholders in the Vereinigte Engelsburg and the draft of the amalgamation, and the request that I should make my declaration on it. I learned from this that I may some day have the pleasure of possessing $3 \frac{601}{672}$ mining shares divided by 8, but feel that it is a little too dear to pay 4s. 8d. postage for this information. If I could only read the name of the worthy district judge appended to this, I would write him a very polite epistle, praying him to leave me in peace with the Vereinigte Engelsburg; but the Prussian officials purposely write their signatures so illegibly, in order to avoid the danger of receiving replies. Be so good as to inform this illegible

---

[a] Gottfried Ermen - [b] United

gentleman that the unstamped post of the Dortmund and Bochum District Court is not recognised here and that I'll be grateful to him, if he, in accordance with the power of attorney, sends all communications to mother.

The situation with the firm is this: Gottfried attaches importance to keeping it as long as *you* keep it, since otherwise you would have been able to take over part of the legacy of Ermen & Engels, Manchester. I regarded it as not only superfluous, but also harmful, for me to interfere on your behalf, since you had 1. P.[a] Ermen's promise, which covers you *here*, and 2. the expert opinion of the lawyers, which I took for gospel truth. For as long as P. Ermen *lives* you are safe from G. Ermen; had I known that your rights were not quite bomb-proof, I would certainly have avoided drawing Gottfried's attention to this by making proposals; and G. Ermen would not have entered into an engagement not to challenge your rights *after* P. Ermen's death. Meanwhile we have him in our hands, because I have given him the rights of the firm for only 5 years, and although I promised him that after that period I would make no difficulties for him, this depends, together for instance with my discretion about business secrets, completely upon his conduct, particularly vis-à-vis yourselves, and I have made this plain to him.

On the £10,000 that I have already invested in shares, I had earned at least £170 net in market appreciation by 30 June. They bring me in an average of $5^7/8\%$ of my investment capital. They are mostly gas, WATERWORKS and railway shares, all English companies.

My freedom pleases me more and more from day to day. Unfortunately, I have still too much running about to do to be able to start any particularly thorough studies, but this will soon be settled.

I have spoken about the COPS with Schuncks' buyer, and have sent him a memorandum, a copy of which I enclose for your use. With regard to the SEWINGS, the qualities have changed so much since my last purchases that it would be best for you to order them from samples if you still need some. Likewise with the COPS, it would be best for you to *bind* Schuncks to the yarns named in the memorandum; they are those we have been using here for 20 years, and they are *indispensable for you* as long as they don't change the quality.

---

a Peter

Best regards to Emma, the little ones, and all brothers and sisters. Enclosed 2 lines for E. Blank.

Your
Friedrich

First published abridged in *Deutsche Revue*, Jg. 46, Bd. II, Stuttgart-Leipzig, 1921 and in full in: Marx and Engels, *Works*, First Russian Edition, Vol. XXVI, Moscow, 1935

Printed according to the original

Published in English for the first time

225

MARX TO ENGELS

IN MANCHESTER

[London,] 17 July 1869

Dear Fred,

The heat here is killing. With you too?

Enclosed a mass of stuff from Eichhoff, Wilhelm,[a] Fritzsche.[391]

Dear old Wilhelm—as always happily disposing of what is not his—naturally refers Fritzsche to me, in order to touch the trades unions here for £300, and *he* guarantees repayment! And quite pointlessly puts me in the embarrassing position of having to turn down Fritzsche!

In addition, he doesn't even seem to read properly the letters sent him. I sent him 900 cards and told him the annual subscription was ld. per card. Of these 900, I placed 500 gratis at his disposition, so the fellows would at least be eligible for representation at the congress.[379] And now he asks me whether fixed annual dues must be paid.

The tough conditions under which Schweitzer returned to the bosom of Hatzfeldt are shown very vividly by the fact that he has been forced to allow Mende to start a row with the International[392] in the *Social-Demokrat*. He himself knows best how dangerous this operation is for him!

---

[a] Wilhelm Liebknecht

Incidentally, that old jackass Becker[a] had no need to involve the International officially in this dissolution process of the Lassallean church, instead of maintaining objective reserve. The old brute does a lot of damage with his longing for action.

Freiligrath, the family poet, gave me much amusement with his 'robber' and 'corsair'[b]—Viennese mannikin.

Best greetings to all.

Your
Moor

First published considerably abridged in *Der Briefwechsel zwischen F. Engels und K. Marx*, Bd. 4, Stuttgart, 1913 and in full in *MEGA*, Abt. III, Bd. 4, Berlin, 1931

Printed according to the original

Published in English for the first time

226

ENGELS TO MARX

IN LONDON

Manchester, 18 July 1869

Dear Moor,

Glad the journey went off so well.

Many thanks for what you sent. The letters will be returned tomorrow.[c]

If Schweitzer attacks the International, we should consider whether to oblige him.

Frightful muck is developing as the Lassallean swindle putrefies. Fritzsche wanted 1,800 thalers from Schweitzer and, when he turned him down, then you should get him 3,000 thalers. The fellow is obviously just as big a blackguard as Schweitzer. From the beginning, Lassalle introduced venality, and this has grown. But where did Schweitzer get the money from, if not the Prussians?

The calm assumption that the English workers should provide £450 for Fritzsche, even before he and his consorts have joined the IWA, is really good. I truly believe that Wilhelm *absolutely* incited Fritzsche to saddle you with himself.

---

[a] Johann Philipp Becker - [b] Apparently the reference is to Freiligrath's poems *Banditenbegräbnis* and *Piratenromanze*. - [c] See the previous letter.

You long ago read the renowned letter sent me 2 years ago.[393] Naked assertion was the only argument to the effect that he could not and should not have acted otherwise. He also said he and his consorts had nothing in common with the People's Party[38] except the name! That's a good one! He is past all remedy.

Heat? Terrible. Yesterday I lay on the floor half the night because it was simply too hot to go to bed. It is so hot that even these few lines have bathed me in sweat.

Enclosed Kugelmann.[394] What do you think of his plans? Karlsbad[a] would be *quite excellent* for you, but Jenny meanwhile in Hanover? What do you say?

Your
F. E.

Fragment of this letter first published in *Der Briefwechsel zwischen F. Engels und K. Marx*, Bd. 4, Stuttgart, 1913 and in full in *MEGA*, Abt. III, Bd. 4, Berlin, 1931

Printed according to the original

Published in English for the first time

227

ENGELS TO MARX

IN LONDON

Manchester, 21 July 1869

Dear Moor,

The whole family including Tussy, has gone to see the PRINCE OF WALES[b] drive past. Congratulations to them in such heat.

How dare Wilhelm assure Schweitzer publicly that 'the General Council of the IWA' takes exactly the same attitude to the said Schweitzer as he, Wilhelm does?[395] This is rather much, particularly if, as I assume, he did so without your permission.

That Schweitzer has lost a lot of support among the masses is shown by the fact that he has not dared to proclaim the voting figures.[c][396] Incidentally, he remains—as a DEBATER—superior to all his opponents. The joke about the 'red' republic was very good, and his exploitation of Wilhelm's 'People's Party', ditto that

---

[a] Karlovy Vary - [b] Albert Edward - [c] F. Mende, 'An die Mitglieder des Allgem. deutschen Arbeiter-Vereins', 5 July 1869, *Der Social-Demokrat*, No. 79, 9 July 1869.

Wilhelm is betraying the workers to the bourgeois democrats; Wilhelm is taking care not to answer both points, and altogether he appears even more incapable than usual in this polemic. How absurd, for instance, *just at the moment,* to reprint from Schwaben-mayer's [a] *Demokratische Correspondenz* the glorification of the *bourgeois* American Republic because of the Pacific Railway.[b]

And how can Wilhelm announce to Schweitzer that he will be shown the door at the Basle Congress [379]?

Monsieur Bonaparte appears to have gone right out of his mind. One cropper after another. First his message with its apparent concessions, then the sudden adjournment, now this droll ministry.[388] If he had set out to show even the stupidest Frenchman that he wants to expose France to worldwide derision, he couldn't have done it better. This is just the way to shake the confidence his majority, his ministers and prefects, his judges and officers have in him. And since all the loyalty has been purchased and was conditional on his future success, they will desert him much earlier than the Senate and *Corps législatif* deserted the old Napoleon in 1814 and 1815.[397] Really not much is needed to lose respect for Mr Louis.

What has happened to the *18th Brumaire?* I see and hear nothing of it.[c] Apropos! You must send me a copy for Charles,[d] whom I relieved of his copy (old edition) on this pledge.

What state are your travel plans in? Jenny writes that she will be returning on Saturday, and then a decision will, I suppose, soon be taken as to when you will go. Here the balancing of accounts is dragging on. Yesterday they said at least 14 days, which I translate as: at least 3 weeks. I'm afraid I'll be stuck here until about 20 August.

I shall cut to length and send to Kugelmann for the *Zukunft,* for its feuilleton, the biography[e] he returned to me. If you want to see it first, let me know.

I close because of the heat; with best greetings.

Your

F. E.

First published abridged in *Der Briefwech-sel zwischen F. Engels und K. Marx,* Bd. 4, Stuttgart, 1913 and in full in *MEGA,* Abt. III, Bd. 4, Berlin, 1931

Printed according to the original

Published in English for the first time

---

a Karl Mayer - b 'Was Bürger drüben können und hüben könnten', *Demokratisches Wochenblatt,* No. 29, 17 July 1869, supplement. - c The reference is to the second edition of Marx's work *The Eighteenth Brumaire of Louis Bonaparte.* See this volume, p. 297. - d Charles Roesgen - e F. Engels, *Karl Marx.* See also this volume, p. 318.

228

MARX TO ENGELS [398]

IN MANCHESTER

[London,] 22 July 1869

DEAR FRED,

Wilhelm really has colossal impudence, issuing bulls of excommunication on behalf of the General Council of the International.[a] I had written to him that I, personally, was keeping myself out of this scandal [399] (Hatzfeldt, the old trollop, would like nothing better than to drag me in), particularly since I am just as decidedly against the Lassalle clique as against the People's Party. I added that Wilhelm could give notice (to Schweitzer) that (in accordance with the resolutions of the Brussels Congress) only *real* members will be admitted at Basle. And this he did in a paragraph in the issue *before last*.[400]

After soliciting me in vain to take official steps against Schweitzer, he has had the impudence to involve me in this scandal! I wrote him an extremely rude letter immediately upon receipt of the last *Wochenblatt*,[b] in which I reminded him how often he had already compromised me, and declared frankly that I would *publicly disavow* him as soon as he showed such impudence again.[401] (Impudence which, in addition, is a *lie*, since the General Council has never discussed the Schweitzer affair, etc., let alone passed a resolution.)

It depends on how Schweitzer, *who has been badly provoked*, now acts. I shall 'cast off' Mr Wilhelm if he should get me caught up in dirty work for the third time. The fellow does not even have the excuse that he marches with us through thick and thin. He commits his stupidities on his own behalf, betrays us when he sees fit, and identifies us with him as soon as he sees no other way out.

For about 6 days now I have had a large carbuncle on my left arm which, in 'this heat', is not pleasant.

I have another 'family' unpleasantness. I have noticed for some time that my wife was not able to manage on the money I give her every week, although there has been no increase in expenditure. Since I am anxious not to run into debt again, and since the

---

[a] See the previous letter. - [b] 'Man schreibt uns...', *Demokratisches Wochenblatt*, No. 29, 17 July 1869.

money I gave her last Monday had already 'run out', I asked for an explanation. And the daftness of females then emerged. In the list of debts she had made me for you[a] she had suppressed ABOUT £75, which she was now trying to pay back BY AND BY out of the housekeeping money. Why, I asked? Reply: she would have been afraid to admit to the full sum! Females obviously need to be under constant tutelage!

Jennychen returned yesterday. Although half a year has passed now, Mrs Monroe has not yet paid her. The Scots hold tight to their CASH![371]

I don't know what to do about the journey. You know that my only aim in this business is to provide Jennychen with the recreation that is practically indispensable for her. But Kugelmann's illness has changed everything. I would not go to Karlsbad[b] to be his comrade-in-sickness, even if I had needed the trip for myself. And now to leave the child as companion with Frau Kugelmann.[394] Nothing at all can come of this. I expect you will write to tell me your opinion.

Mr Schweitzer's discovery that the Geneva committee consists mainly of workers is good![392] Bakunin and Schweitzer state councillors!

Bonaparte's rickety ways will soon lead to defections amongst his generals.

Between Prussia and Russia there is a row that does not seem completely 'play-acting'.

On Monday I wrote to Meissner, tersely and rudely.[402]

Laura and Lafargue and son are now in lodgings in Dieppe. My letter from Paris[c] to Lafargue senior had the desired effect.

Salut.

Your
Moor

Both Liebknecht's and Fritzsche's[391] letters indicate clearly that the delightful Wilhelm had directed the latter to me on the money issue.

The ideas the Germans in general hold about our financial means you will see from the enclosed letter from Kugelmann, *voce*[d] Bracke.[403] The fellows never sent a pfennig here. The General Council owes 5 weeks rent, and is in debt to its secretary. Peculiar conceptions!

---

[a] See this volume, pp. 169-70. - [b] Karlovy Vary - [c] See this volume, pp. 314-15. - [d] regarding

I do not need to see the biography business.[a][390] This appears to be a sort of mania with Kugelmann.

First published abridged in *Der Briefwechsel zwischen F. Engels und K. Marx*, Bd. 4, Stuttgart, 1913 and in full in *MEGA*, Abt. III, Bd. 4, Berlin, 1931

Printed according to the original
Published in English in full for the first time

229

MARX TO ENGELS

IN MANCHESTER

[London,] 24 July 1869

Dear Fred,

I can only write you a few lines today. The thing is in full suppuration, so very painful, but will also soon be over. The swilling of arsenic will have to begin again.

This morning I received the enclosed screed from Liebknecht.[404] Which is the more extraordinary, the stupid impudence or the impudent stupidity? This honest fellow regards *official lies*, such as that about non-existent resolutions of the General Council, as permissible in his own mouth, but as highly reprehensible in Schweitzer's. And why did *he* achieve a *reconciliation* with Schweitzer the Monster in Lausanne? And his theory of action! This consists of giving Mr Wilhelm the right to make 'arbitrary' use of my name and that of the General Council wherever he considers appropriate. And the courage of this honest fellow! He claims to be against Lassalle, and so takes the part of the 'true' Lassalleans against the 'false' Lassalleans! Bracke, his man, after all accuses Schweitzer of declaring Lassalle's theory of state credit to be simply an agitational tool, and of not believing in panacea. He had involved me in 'battles'! In 'scandals', I wrote to him.[405]
Salut.

Your
K. M.

I regret that I did not know the book *Die Werkzeuge und Waffen, ihre Entstehung und Ausbildung, von Dr Gustav Klemm*, 1858, before

---

a F. Engels, *Karl Marx*. See this volume, p. 325.

the publication of my first volume.[a] What I indicated in the section 'Labour Process' and later 'Division of Labour'[406] is here proved with abundant material.

First published considerably abridged in *Der Briefwechsel zwischen F. Engels und K. Marx*, Bd. 4, Stuttgart, 1913 and in full in *MEGA*, Abt. III, Bd. 4, Berlin, 1931

Printed according to the original

Published in English for the first time

230

ENGELS TO MARX[398]

IN LONDON

Manchester, 25 July 1869

Dear Moor,

Don't go grey-haired over the £75[b]; as soon as Gottfried[c] pays me my next INSTALMENT, i.e., as soon as the accounts are balanced and the contracts signed, I shall send you the sum. Just make sure that nothing like this happens again; you know our calculations are very tight, and allow absolutely no MARGIN for extravagances. Thus, since 1 July, I have been noting all expenditures in order to see what all the stuff costs, and in order to find out where something can be cut if necessary.

The new carbuncle proves you must immediately swill arsenic again. Do not delay for a day longer. You should have taken the case under your arm here as warning, and started. Drinking arsenic doesn't hinder you in your ordinary way of life in any manner, so just go on taking it for 3-4 months in order to get rid of the business finally.

As regards your journey, if I were you I would pack my things as soon as Jenny is ready and your carbuncle has healed. You can then adjust your plans for the journey as you like, and also visit worthy Kugelmann. If this way—by ensuring that the period of your journey and his cure do not coincide, or only partly—you will best avoid the Karlsbad[d] business. *Amicus*[e] Kugelmann is, with regard to his health, certainly a considerable hypochondriac, and

---

[a] of *Capital* - [b] See this volume, p. 327. - [c] Gottfried Ermen - [d] Karlovy Vary - [e] Friend

would certainly be a rather doleful cure-companion in Karlsbad. Since I shall not be free before 15-20 August in any case, it would be madness for us to consider anything combined. If I should be free earlier, we can still see what can be done.

I should certainly come to serious grips with Mrs Monroe. Jenny should go to her and tell her frankly that she needs the CASH. Perhaps Mrs Monroe is waiting to receive a formal bill: MRS MONROE TO MISS MARX. TO ONE HALFYEAR'S TUITION, etc. And if Jenny's visit does not help, I would, in your place, write a polite but firm letter. You have to show these Scots that you know what BUSINESS is, and they then respect you all the more.

The impudence of old Wilhelm exceeds the possible.[a] Trying to convince you that, with his lying, he had remained 'within the bounds of your letter'! Just how lazy his conscience is in this connection is shown by the fact that he uses the phrase 'take into consideration' which he otherwise abhors, and by his closing, touching appeal to your good heart. The simpleton demands that we and the whole International should undergo all his metamorphoses *in re* Schweitzer, concluding peace when he concludes peace, thrashing Schweitzer when he thrashes him, and allowing him to lie to his heart's content in the name of the International whenever he thinks it 'necessary'. And *he* wants to prescribe to the Congress[b] who should be admitted and who not.

Also rather strong that, in the Vogt business[407] *he* has left the defence 'up to you!' and this 'for the sake of the Party'. He really takes himself what might be called seriously.

And how lame is the business with the factory inspectors! The government has flatly decided to introduce them, but Liebknecht has *prevented* this, naturally in the interests of the workers, so that they shall not be bribed by them. Bismarck prevented by Liebknecht! Quite something! Not to mention the craftiness of such a policy.

The *18th Brumaire* received yesterday with thanks. The book reads much better in a decent binding and without the misprints. The introduction is very good. This, and the book itself, will bring Wilhelm no pleasure. The manner in which democracy, and even more Social-Democracy, is treated is by no means grist to his mill, but rather on his head. Incidentally, he can no longer say he has no agitational material: we shall see what he does with it.

I am now on the *Journals, Conversations and Essays on Ireland* by

---

[a] See the previous letter. - [b] The reference is to the Basle Congress of the International Working Men's Association.

Mr Senior (1843-58). Some FACTS and a few nice admissions, but generally only of special interest because they are stated by such a 'respectable' man. Therefore valuable for me, 2 volumes, 1868. I don't think there will be anything new in it for you.[408]

If Schweitzer had not got such a bad conscience, and if he had not committed the stupidity recently of *threatening* the International, then he would certainly have responded to Liebknecht's bull of excommunication[395]; he would have challenged the General Council on the question and then you would *have had* to disavow Monsieur Wilhelm. Instead of excommunicating Schweitzer in the name of the IWA, why does Wilhelm not grab Schweitzer because of this threat, and with this help put the General Council in a position in which it must say something in response to Schweitzer's threat? The fellow really is too clumsy.

The business with Bracke is also good.[403] These Lassallean menials are always shouting for money, just money. In my opinion, it would be very ill-advised of the IWA to send the Germans *even one pfennig* before they have paid regular dues for a period. The demoralisation that has prevailed since Lassalle and through him must be firmly removed.

Enclosed Kugelmann and Wilhelm returned. You will certainly be writing to Kugelmann yourself about your journey. Send me back Kugelmann's letter so that I can reply to him; without a bit of medical chat he won't release me.

Tussy is reading *Götz von Berlichingen*, and afterwards I'll give her *Egmont*.[a] Walks have almost ceased in this heat; today it will be somewhat cooler.

Best greetings from all to all.

Your
F. E.

First published abridged in *Der Briefwechsel zwischen F. Engels und K. Marx*, Bd. 4, Stuttgart, 1913 and in full in *MEGA*, Abt. III, Bd. 4, Berlin, 1931

Printed according to the original

Published in English in full for the first time

---

[a] Goethe's works

13*

231

MARX TO ENGELS

IN MANCHESTER

[London,] 27 July 1869

DEAR FRED,

Amongst the enclosed PAPERS, look at the *Vorbote* and especially what I marked on pp. 105, 106.

You will see that OLD Becker[a] cannot give up making himself important.[409] With his *language group system* he casts aside our whole Rules and the spirit of the statute, and alters our organic system into an artificial construction of *arbitrary language relations* instead of *real state and national relations.* Extremely reactionary business, fitting for the pan-Slavists! And all this because we allowed *him provisionally* to remain the centre for his former correspondents, until the '*International*' in Germany *gets stronger.*

I immediately put a spoke in his wheel when he attempted at the Eisenach Congress[373] to promote himself as centre for Germany.

Bebel has sent me 25 thalers for the Belgians from his Workers' Educational Association.[410] Today I ACKNOWLEDGED this gift, and took the opportunity to write to him about Becker's fantasy plans.

I drew his attention to *Article 6 of the Rules,*[b] which only recognises *national central committees in direct contact* with the General Council and, where this is impossible because of the police, obliges the *local groups in each country* to correspond directly with the General Council. I explained to him the absurdity of Becker's pretensions and finally stated that if the Eisenach Congress— *quoad*[c] THE *INTERNATIONAL*—accepted Becker's suggestion, *we* would immediately and publicly *quash* it as *contrary to the Rules.*

Incidentally Bebel and Liebknecht had written to me *earlier,* SPONTANEOUSLY, that *they* had written to Becker telling him they did *not* recognise him but corresponded directly with London.

Becker himself is not dangerous. But, as we have been informed from Switzerland, his secretary Remy was pressed upon him by Mr Bakunin and is Bakunin's TOOL. This Russian obviously wishes

---

[a] Johann Philipp Becker - [b] *Rules and Administrative Regulations of the International Working Men's Association* (see present edition, Vol. 20, pp. 441-46). - [c] regarding

to become the dictator of the European workers' movement. He should be careful. Otherwise he will be officially excommunicated.

Your
Moor

As soon as I receive copies[a] from Meissner I shall send them to my friends in Manchester and Charles Roesgen.

First published in *Der Briefwechsel zwischen F. Engels und K. Marx*, Bd. 4, Stuttgart, 1913

Printed according to the original

Published in English for the first time

232

ENGELS TO LUDWIG KUGELMANN

IN HANOVER

Manchester, 28 July 1869

Dear Kugelmann,

Enclosed the biography suitably adapted for *Zukunft*,[390] and drawing attention to the *18th Brumaire*. I would be grateful if you had it copied there, since it would be better for Weiss *not* to know it is by me.

Marx will be writing to you, or will have already written, about the journey. You certainly will not get him to go to Karlsbad,[b] and as far as I am concerned, the business with the final accounts, etc. is dragging on so much that I have no idea *when* I shall be able to get away; it's as good as certain that this will *not* be before 15-20 August. It's very unpleasant, but since this is the last time that COMMERCE will burden me so, I should not grumble too much. This means that I shall scarcely get to see you this year, as I shall hardly get as far afield as Karlsbad.

In order to get the biography off today I must close now—so until next time, and let Karlsbad do some good to your gall-stones.

---

a K. Marx, *The Eighteenth Brumaire of Louis Bonaparte*, 2nd edition. - b Karlovy Vary

One of my sisters-in-law in Barmen also had some once, but she is happily rid of them, and once again round, fat and jolly.

Yours
F. E.

First published in: Marx and Engels, *Works*, First Russian Edition, Vol. XXVI, Moscow, 1935

Printed according to the original

Published in English for the first time

233

MARX TO ENGELS

IN MANCHESTER

[London,] 29 July 1869

Dear Fred,

Enclosed the letter from Kugelmann.[394]

Things are better with the arm. Started with the arsenic.

The *Bee-Hive* is now under the control of Samuel Morley, since when everything too anti-bourgeois in the REPORTS on our sessions is crossed out. For instance my entire exposition about Roman and German testate and intestate inheritance law at the last session of the General Council.[411]

During my stay in Paris[a] the fellows committed some stupidities, i.e. admitting 5 MEMBERS of the Bronterre O'Brien Society,[412] fellows who are just as dumb and ignorant as they are quarrelsome and conceited about their sectarian secret wisdom.

Salut.

Your
K. M.

Jennychen has received her 'little fortune'.[b] The dear child feels very happy about her 'own income'.

First published in *Der Briefwechsel zwischen F. Engels und K. Marx*, Bd. 4, Stuttgart, 1913

Printed according to the original

Published in English for the first time

---

[a] in the original: London - [b] See this volume, pp. 327 and 330.

234

ENGELS TO MARX

IN LONDON

Manchester, 30 July 1869

Dear Moor,

Old Becker must have gone completely off his head. How can he decree that the TRADES UNION *must* be the real workers' association and the basis of all organisation, that the other associations *must* only exist provisionally alongside, etc.[409] And all in a country where real TRADES UNIONS still do not yet even exist. And what a complicated 'organisation'. On the one hand each TRADE centralises itself in a national leadership, on the other hand the various TRADES in each locality centralise themselves again in a local leadership. If one wanted to make the eternal squabbling permanent, this would be the arrangement to adopt. But it is *au fond*[a] nothing but the old German journeyman's desire to preserve his 'inn' in every town, and takes this to be the unity of the workers' organisation. If many more such proposals come to light, the time at the Eisenach Congress[373] will be nicely debated away.

The international plans have naturally no other purpose than to ensure the leadership for Becker as far as the German tongue is heard (he has already annexed Mulhause in Alsace, see *Vorbote*, p. 109 under 'Basle'). In practice this fine organisation, with its leadership in Geneva, must come to grief on the German laws, since Becker has, as usual, made out the bill without the waiter. Generalising the idea of central committees based upon language, in other words putting the Genevan workers under Paris and the Antwerpers under Amsterdam (if Geneva is not intended to rule the whole of France and Walloon-Belgium, which those in free Geneva have very probably assumed), is presumably only designed to strengthen his claim to regency over the German language.[b] But it is very good that the *Eisenach* Congress and *not* the international *Basle* Congress[379] should settle these matters.

Incidentally, I would never claim to have understood Becker's plan properly; given the German and the logic which rule there, sense and understanding come to a complete stop.

It's quite clear that fat Bakunin is behind it. If this damned

---

a basically - b See this volume, p. 332.

Russian really thinks of intriguing his way to the top of the workers' movement, then the time has come to give him once and for all what he deserves and ask the question whether a pan-Slavist can be a member of an international workers' association. The fellow can very easily be tackled. He should not imagine that he can play a cosmopolitan communist for the workers, and a burning national pan-Slavist for the Russians. A few hints to Borkheim, who is just dealing with him now, would be quite in order; Borkheim will undoubtedly understand a broad hint.

You will have seen that the worthy Swiss want to have 'direct legislation by the people'[413] discussed at the congress. That will be nice.

It really is a disgrace that after nearly 40 years of political workers' movement in England, the only workers' paper[a] in existence can be bought up by a bourgeois like S. Morley.[b] But unfortunately it appears to be a law of the proletarian movement that everywhere a part of the workers' leaders necessarily become corrupted, though it has happened nowhere else in the general fashion to which Lassalle developed it in Germany.

Tussy is now reading Firdusi[c] in the very good version by Schack; so far she likes it very much, but whether she will work right through the enormous volume is something different.

At the end of next week I think I shall finally be through with honest Gottfried,[d] and then I shall have about 14 days of freedom ahead of me. So if you want to make a plan for a journey, then make it and let me know; we could meet somewhere in Germany or in Holland too if you like, or we could leave London together. At the end of August I must meet my mother in Ostend, about the 20th or 25th. Can Tussy stay here in the meantime and keep Lizzie company? What do you think?

Your
F. E.

You will get money as soon as I am in order with Gottfried Ermen, possibly earlier, *id est* IF HE FORKS OUT BEFORE. Send the

---

[a] *The Bee-Hive* - [b] See this volume, p. 334. - [c] Firdusi, *Heldensagen.* In deutscher Nachbildung nebst einer Einleitung über das Iranische Epos von Adolf Friedrich von Schack. - [d] Gottfried Ermen

enclosed to Tussy in a disguised hand; she will wonder where-from.

First published abridged in *Der Briefwech-sel zwischen F. Engels und K. Marx,* Bd. 4, Stuttgart, 1913 and in full in *MEGA,* Abt. III, Bd. 4, Berlin, 1931

Printed according to the original
Published in English for the first time

235

MARX TO LUDWIG KUGELMANN [29]

IN HANOVER

[London,] 30 July 1869

Dear Friend,

I had (not yet quite healed) for ABOUT 12 days an abscess (carbuncular) on my left arm, which I had DITTO during my stay with Engels in Manchester,[353] under the armpit of my left arm. This is not, however, the reason that so far I have delayed my reply to your letter of 17 inst.

Since I would certainly not like to clash with your plans, and since I am personally interested in enjoying your company, I have taken various steps in order to arrange things in your sense. But this is *positively impossible.* I *must* be in *Holland* at the end of August with my relatives,[a] where all sorts of matters of interest and importance to me have to be settled. My proposal to transfer this *rendezvous* to another date has been turned down flatly, as the people whom I am meeting are all tied up by their business, and only have a certain time free for the meeting in Bommel.[b]

I shall, therefore, be leaving London at the end of August.[349] You should write and tell me when you will be back in Hanover. I shall then see to what extent I can adjust my further PROGRESS accordingly.

With best greetings to your dear wife and Fränzchen,[c]

Yours
K. M.

---

[a] the Philips family - [b] Zalt-Bommel - [c] Kugelmann's daughter Franziska

P.S. In addition, during August Lafargue, wife and little son are coming to London.

First published in *Pisma Marksa k Kugelmanu* (Letters of Marx to Kugelmann), Moscow-Leningrad, 1928

Printed according to the original

236

MARX TO ENGELS

IN MANCHESTER

[London,] 2 August 1869

DEAR FRED,

Because of Kugelmann my whole travel plan has been thrown to the winds.

If I visited him *before* he went to Karlsbad,[a] he would move heaven and earth to take me with him to this boring and expensive place — *or* I would hinder him in carrying out his own plan, which he must carry out for the sake of his health.

I have therefore written to him[b] that I *must* go to Holland on family business *at the end of August,* and from there I would perhaps have the opportunity to see him in Hanover *after* his return. I really knew no other way of arranging things. Other reasons for delaying the journey:

Firstly: the Lafargue FAMILY may be coming to London soon.

Secondly: If I left here now, the General Council would be completely at a loss with the necessary work with regard to the Basle Congress.[379]

Tussy appears to want to stay on in Manchester. During the 14 days of your absence the excuse for this is plausible. Your drawing will be sent to her from a local (English) seaside resort.[c]

Enclosed letters from Bebel and Wilhelm.[414]

You will I hope also be coming to London on your journey.

Your
Moor

---

a Karlovy Vary - b See the previous letter. - c See this volume, p. 336.

So far I have not seen that Meissner has announced the *18th Brumaire*. His motto: *Chi va piano va sano.*[a]

First published in *Der Briefwechsel zwischen F. Engels und K. Marx*, Bd. 4, Stuttgart, 1913

Printed according to the original

Published in English for the first time

237

ENGELS TO MARX

IN LONDON

Manchester, 3 August 1869

Dear Moor,

Enclosed, returned, Wilhelm and Bebel[414] and, in addition, a draft on the UNION BANK OF London for £100, with which I hope the debts are done with for ever.

Since, as Tussy tells me, Jenny has September free too, you can of course postpone your journey until that month. I always thought that, because of Jenny, you were limited to only four weeks during which you *had to* travel.

The row between Schweitzer and the Leipzig people is getting jolly. The accusations that Bebel has been bribed by the Guelphs, and the threat of the Schweitzerians that they will impose their victory upon the congress by muscle power, point to a fine show.

How stupid it was of Wilhelm to allow Goegg to be co-signatory of his congress manifesto, and thus expose himself to the attacks of the *Social-Demokrat*.[415] But Wilhelm simply can't get along without his philistine republicans.

My documents should now be signed today week, if the lawyers are ready. I shall certainly not get away before Wednesday, 11th inst. In any case I shall see you in London on the way there or back.

Best greetings to all.

Your

F. E.

---

[a] Who goes slowly goes surely.

So far I have watched in vain for the announcement of the *18th Brumaire*.

First published in *Der Briefwechsel zwischen F. Engels und K. Marx*, Bd. 4, Stuttgart, 1913

Printed according to the original
Published in English for the first time

238

MARX TO ENGELS

IN MANCHESTER

[London,] 4 August[a] 1869

DEAR FRED,

£100 received with BEST THANKS. I SHALL NOW WATCH THE PROCEEDINGS SO CLOSELY THAT SIMILAR MISTAKES, etc.

I am by no means in top form. The arm business is in the last stage of healing. I attribute my further indisposition to the weather, and I gulp Gumpert's liver medicine against it.

Yesterday there was a tragicomical meeting of the General Council. Dunning letters for cards, rent, arrears of secretary's salary, etc. In short, INTERNATIONAL BANKRUPTCY, so we can't yet see how we can send a delegate.[b] *On the other hand*, a letter from Geneva, FRENCH SIDE, in which the General Council was politely requested to issue a circular in the 3 languages advising all the members to collect money (and this immediately) for the purchase of a building in Geneva (for MEETINGS), which would cost only £5,000 and should become the property of the 'International'. Is this not a modest presumption on the part of these fellows, who have not yet paid their 1d. per man!

Becker, the chief of the German tongue,[c] sends 280d for his 'myriads'.

The gist of the story is this: the local committees (including central committees) spend too much money and tax their people too highly for their national or local needs, and leave nothing over for the General Council. Money is always there to print idiotic addresses to the Spaniards[416] etc., and for other FOLLIES. We shall be forced to declare to the next congress, either in written or

---

a 3 August in the original - b to the Basle Congress - c See this volume, p. 335.

spoken form, that we cannot continue to run the General Council in this way; but that they should be so kind, before they give us successors, to pay *our debts*, which would reach a much higher figure if most of our secretaries did not personally cover *correspondence costs.*

If only I could somewhere see people who would not involve us in stupidities, I would greet with the greatest pleasure the exit of the Central Council [73] from here. The business is becoming *ennuyant*.[a]

Salut.

El
Moro

Beesly married on 24 July.

First published in *Der Briefwechsel zwischen F. Engels und K. Marx*, Bd. 4, Stuttgart, 1913

Printed according to the original

Published in English for the first time

239

ENGELS TO JENNY MARX (DAUGHTER) [417]

IN LONDON

Manchester, 8 August 1869

Dear Jenny,

I have received Lizzie's orders to thank you, in her name, for the very handsome and very considerate present you made her in the volume of Moore's *Irish Melodies*.[b] You could not have made her a greater pleasure. She knows, from her childhood, most of the tunes, but scarcely one of them completely, and so now she can refresh her rather broken-down memory from the book.

Next Sunday[c] there is to be a grand Irish concert in which the whole Fenian and non-Fenian company, convicted and unconvicted, will have to join. I only regret that the whole musical talent of our house will be unable to take full advantage of the book when Tussy will have left us; but then, Mary Ellen *will* have to learn as much as is required for that.

When are you and Moor going to Holland and Germany[d]? I

---

[a] boring - [b] Thomas Moore, *Irish Melodies.* - [c] 15 August - [d] See this volume, p. 354.

have now, at last, made my arrangements. I shall have to be in Ostend on the evening of the 17th or morning of the 18th August and intend to stay there for about a week.[418] Probably I shall come over to London on Monday the 16th and spend a day with you, and to see whether I cannot make arrangements to meet you and Moor somewhere in Germany. If not, I shall very likely come straight home again from Ostend. I hope, however, that you will, in the meantime, bring your plans to some state of maturity so as to enable us to have a bottle of hock together in its native country.

With kind regards to Moor and your Mama, I remain

Yours faithfully
F. Engels

First published in *Friedrich Engels. 1820-1970. Referate, Diskussionen, Dokumente,* Hanover, 1971   Reproduced from the original

240

MARX TO ENGELS[33]

IN MANCHESTER

[London,] 10 August 1869

DEAR FREDDY,

I am in a great dilemma with Tussy. The Lafargues have written that they will be arriving here next Tuesday or Wednesday.[a] If I do *not* inform Tussy that Fouchtra,[b] whom she loves fanatically, is coming, she will reproach me later. If I do inform her, there will be a tragic collision between her wish to stay with Mrs Lizzie as promised, and the wish to see Fouchtra. I shall leave it to you to deal with the matter as you judge best.

In *L'International,* the French police sheet, an article 'La Dictature Universelle' against the INTERNATIONAL WORKING MEN'S ASSOCIATION, evoked by the STRIKES in France, which follow blow upon blow. This article by Jerusalem[c] concludes as follows:

'Quoi qu'il en soit, on sait maintenant qu'il dépend de la Ligue de faire cesser la vie sociale là où il entrera dans ses vues de tout arrêter d'un seul mot. S'il se trouvait un ministre ambitieux qui sût gagner ses bonnes grâces, on comprend ce qu'il pourrait

---

[a] 17 or 18 August - [b] Charles Étienne Lafargue - [c] [Jerusalem,] 'La Dictature universelle', *L'International,* 3 August 1869.

contre des rivaux qui le gêneraient. Nous sommes parfaitement convaincu que ce même ministre, une fois arrivé à son but, n'aurait rien de plus pressé que de détruire la Ligue par des procédés radicaux; nous ne savons pas s'il y réussirait; mais, pour l'instant, nous déclarons que la Ligue internationale est véritablement la Dictature universelle. Attendons le moment où ses [caisses[a]] seront pl[eines].[a' b]

If the fellow wants to wait until then he will have a long wait.

The part of Wilhelm's speech (delivered in *Berlin*[c]) printed in the supplement demonstrates, beneath the stupidity, an undeniable cunning in arranging the affair suitably. By the way, this is very nice. *Since* the Reichstag may *only* be utilised as a *means of agitation,* one may *never agitate* there for something sensible and directly affecting the workers' interests! The worthy Wilhelm's illusion that, since Bismarck 'is fond of' turns of speech friendly to the workers, he would not oppose *real workers' measures* is REALLY CHARMING! 'As though'—as Bruno Bauer would say—Mr Wagener would not declare himself theoretically in the Reichstag *in favour* of the Factory Acts, but *in practice* against them 'since they would be useless under Prussian conditions'! 'As though' Mr Bismarck, if he really would and *could* do something for the workers, would not force the *implementation* of the existing legislation *in Prussia itself*! Merely because this occurred in Prussia, liberal 'Saxony' etc. *would have* to follow. What Wilhelm does not grasp is that the present governments flirt with the workers, but know full well that their only support lies with the bourgeoisie, and that they therefore scare the latter with phrases friendly to the workers, but are never *really able* to take steps against the bourgeoisie.

The brute believes in the future '*state* **of democracy**'! Secretly that means sometimes constitutional England, sometimes the bourgeois United States, sometimes wretched Switzerland. '*It*' has no conception of revolutionary politics. Copying Schwabenmayer,[d] he quotes as proof of democratic activity: the railway to California was built by the bourgeoisie *awarding* itself through Congress an

---

a paper damaged - b 'Be this as it may, today one is aware that it depends upon the League to bring the life of society to a halt at that moment when it intends stopping everything with one word. If an ambitious minister were to be found who knew how to win their good graces, it may be understood what he would be able to undertake against rivals uncomfortable to him. We are perfectly convinced that this same minister, his goal once achieved, would find nothing more urgent to do than to take radical measures to destroy the League; we do not know whether he would be successful; but at present we declare that the International League is, in truth, the universal dictatorship. Wait until their cash-boxes are filled.' - c W. Liebknecht, 'Ueber die politische Stellung der Sozial-Demokratie...', *Demokratisches Wochenblatt,* No. 27 and supplement to No. 32, 3 July and 7 August 1869. - d Karl Mayer

enormous mass of 'public land', that is to say, *expropriating* it from the workers; by importing Chinese rabble to depress wages; and finally by instituting a new off-shoot, the 'financial aristocracy'.

Incidentally, I find it a cheek on Wilhelm's part to introduce our names *ad vocem*[a] Brass.[419] I declared myself *outspokenly* against his tippling with Brass and, at the same time,— *viva voce*[b]—declared: if this led to a scandal *we would publicly disavow him*.

The following passages from *Daniel Defoe's 'Memoirs of a Cavalier'* [c] may interest you.

1. Speaking of Cardinal Richelieu's army parade in Lyons, he states:

* 'The *French foot*, compared to the infantry I have since seen in the German and Swedish armies, were not fit to be called soldiers. On the other hand, considering the Savoyards and Italian troops, they were good troops.'*

2. Speaking of the beginning of Gustav Adolf's intervention in the German muck:

* 'First, they' (the German Protestant princes) 'were willing to join him, at least they could not find in their hearts to join with the emperor, of whose powers they had such just apprehensions; they wished the Swedes success and would *have been very glad to have had the work done at another man's charge; but like true Germans they were more willing to be saved, than to save themselves,* and therefore hung back and stood on terms.'*

I hope to see you next Monday.[d]
Salut.

Il
Moro

Do not forget the small note-book I left with you. There are a few notes in it. Ditto regarding the worthy Dühring.

First published abridged in *Der Briefwechsel zwischen F. Engels und K. Marx*, Bd. 4, Stuttgart, 1913 and in full in *MEGA*, Abt. III, Bd. 4, Berlin, 1931

Printed according to the original

Published in English in full for the first time

---

a regarding - b orally - c [D. Defoe], *Memoirs of a Cavalier or a Military Journal of the Wars in Germany and the Wars in England from the Year 1632, to the Year 1648*, London [1720], pp. 19, 36. - d 16 August

241

ENGELS TO MARX

IN LONDON

Manchester, 12 August 1869

Dear Moor,

I have cut the Gordian knot regarding Schnaps [a] by simply informing Tussy of the FACT; whether this has plunged her into a natural conflict I do not know. Unfortunately, however, she now has something else to do, for, since last Friday, she has continuously had horrible toothache in the same tooth that gave her a lot of trouble earlier. So far she has borne the thing with astonishing heroism, but shortened sleep and the long nervous tension have had an effect, and today she looks somewhat exhausted. She said you didn't want the tooth to be pulled out; but I sent her today, since things could not continue thus, together with Lizzie to one of the leading dentists here, and told her she should submit to his judgement. After a long examination he said he hoped to save the tooth, but if the pain did not cease by Saturday morning, the tooth would have to come out. At all events, the child cannot stand this constant and nerve-racking pain every 6 months; her general health suffers far more from this than the whole tooth is worth. But I think I shall soon be able to give better news.

I must just call in at the Schiller Society,[76] and see what has happened in Eisenach.[373] On Saturday the two parties seem to have parted in peace, so they have at least avoided *general* fisticuffs.

The stupidity and meanness of the Urquhartites is demonstrated by the fact that they never mention:

A RESIDENCE IN BULGARIA BY St. Clair, LATE CAPTN. 28. REGT. AND Ch, Brophy, 1869.

The book is written by two fellows, of whom St. Clair, a former Crimean officer who knows Turkish, Polish, Russian and Bulgarian, lived 3 years in the country, and the other $1^1/_2$ years, and they are still there. The thing is written in a very lively and graphic style, and is worth more than any other book I know on the subject. For Englishmen the fellows are remarkably free of prejudices, though they have their blind-spots IN ECONOMICS and also

---

[a] Charles Étienne Lafargue; see this volume, p. 342.

IN POLITICS. But they can *see*. They arrived—at least Brophy did—as friends of the Christians, and changed their views completely in favour of the Turks. But since they *also find their blind-spots* in the Turkish governmental system (though here, too, they have something in common with Urquhart), the Urquhartites *are* not *allowed* to mention a book that is worth more than their entire *Free Press*, even from their own point of view. The FACTS in it are worth more to me than all the chatter by the Urquhartites, and SHORT-ARMED Collet can envy the two their description of Russian and French policy in Constantinople. The business is so described that you can read it, moreover with interest, and will be more useful here than 10 years of the *Free Press* with its oracular announcements.

Finished with Gottfried Ermen the day before yesterday.[a] Everything signed.[b] Finally *completely* free from the honorable gentleman.

Best greetings to all.

Your
F. E.

First published abridged in *Der Briefwechsel zwischen F. Engels und K. Marx*, Bd. 4, Stuttgart, 1913 and in full in *MEGA*, Abt. III, Bd. 4, Berlin, 1931

Printed according to the original
Published in English for the first time

242

MARX TO HERMANN JUNG

IN LONDON

[London,] 13 August [1869]

Dear Jung,

Your letter just received (2 o'clock).

Go at all events.[420] The sending of Applegarth by his own Union will show to the continentals that the English workmen are not so indifferent in regard to the International as their ill-wishers say. It is only a pity that Applegarth does not even take part at our present discussions, so as to be able to represent our views.

---

a 10 August - b See this volume, p. 320.

If care be not taken, the asses of Denmark street may work mischief. A letter ought also to be written to our Pole[a]—I have not his address.

Yours truly
K. M.

First published in Russian in *Bazelsky kongress I Internatsionala 6-11 sentyabrya 1869*, Moscow-Leningrad, 1934

Reproduced from the original

Published in English for the first time

243

ENGELS TO MARX

IN LONDON

Manchester, 16 August 1869

Dear Moor,

Yesterday I received a telegram informing me that my mother will not be getting to Ostend until Wednesday evening. Since I must now wait for a letter from home providing me with more detailed information and since yet another reason requires that I still be here tomorrow, I telegraphed you today that I will not be coming until Wednesday.[b] Also, I am worried that if in the meantime the Lafargues should come I may not find night quarters in your doubtless full house and, this being the case, would like to know whether I might find lodging somewhere near you.

Tussy's tooth is out; the dentist found that since one of the three roots was inflamed the only solution was to extract. The pain is now gone.

I am planning to take the 3:30 Midlands train that arrives in London at 8:50.

Best greetings.

Your
F. E.

First published in *Der Briefwechsel zwischen F. Engels und K. Marx*, Bd. 4, Stuttgart, 1913

Printed according to the original

Published in English for the first time

---

[a] Anton Zabicki - [b] 18 August

244

ENGELS TO MARX

IN LONDON

Manchester, 16 August 1869

Dear Moor,

CONFUSION WORSE CONFOUNDED [a]! A fresh telegram from home that my mother, because of a slight indisposition, will not be in Ostend tomorrow either, and that I shall only get more information on Thursday.[b] Since this means that the Ostend business has become uncertain, I have decided to go to Ireland with Tussy and Lizzie on Thursday evening, if nothing intervenes, and spend 10-14 days there.[421] The business could only be altered by a letter arriving from my mother on Thursday at the latest, but I cannot see, as things now stand, that this is in any way probable.

Best greetings.

Your
F. E.

More on Thursday.

Nearly forgot the main thing. Enclosed—£10 BANKNOTE, of which 5 from Moore and 5 from me as a contribution to the International. Send Moore his RECEIPT direct, S. MOORE, 25 DOVER STREET, OXFORD ROAD, MANCHESTER.

Y/D 69 237, Manchester, 30 January 1868.

First published abridged in *Der Briefwechsel zwischen F. Engels und K. Marx*, Bd. 4, Stuttgart, 1913 and in full in *MEGA*, Abt. III, Bd. 4, Berlin, 1931

Printed according to the original

Published in English for the first time

---

[a] J. Milton, *Paradise Lost*, Book II, 996. - [b] 19 August

245

MARX TO ENGELS

IN MANCHESTER

[London,] 17 August 1869

DEAR FRED,

Everything is READY here for your arrival.

Don't forget, either, to take a TICKET only to KENTISH TOWN STATION (just near us), or, if you take it to ST. PANCRAS STATION, at least to get out at KENTISH TOWN STATION.

Mr Lafargue, in principle, never announces the day of his arrival, on the basis that anxiety will thus be avoided should chance delays occur. That's a PRINCIPLE too!

I hope POOR Tussychen is ALL RIGHT again now.

I send, enclosed, Schweitzeriana,[a] for you to enjoy on the journey.

Your
K. M.

Enclosed—COPIES (Bonaparte)[b] for 1. Charles,[c] 2. Schorlemmer, 3. Moore, 4. Gumpert.

First published in *MEGA*, Abt. III, Bd. 4, Berlin, 1931

Printed according to the original

Published in English for the first time

246

MARX TO ENGELS[174]

IN MANCHESTER

[London,] 18 August 1869

DEAR FRED,

Rather disappointed by YOUR LETTER, since all had hoped to see you here this evening. The plan about Ireland is very good (Lizzie

---

[a] This apparently refers to a series of articles: 'Der Congress zu Eisenach', *Der Social-Demokrat*, Nos. 93, 94 and 95, 10, 13 and 15 August 1869. - [b] K. Marx, *The Eighteenth Brumaire of Louis Bonaparte*, 2nd edition. - [c] Charles Roesgen

and Tussy will be able to admire the 'CONVICTED' *in natura*) if nothing new intervenes. This evening the Lafargue FAMILY arrives, leaving Dieppe today at 10 o'clock.

The £10 received, but can't send RECEIPT *before Saturday*,[a] on which day there is a meeting of the sub-committee. The money is very welcome just before closing time.[b]

Yesterday Dupont announced that the French (or Paris) TRADES UNIONISTS (BRONZE WORKERS) had paid back £45, i.e., sent it to him to pay back.[422] This money was partly loaned and partly given to them years ago by the UNIONS here through our mediation. (Even earlier, £20 was sent on our instructions from Paris to Rouen.) I have arranged that *députés* shall wait upon the UNIONS here to appeal to their consciences when they pay in the money.— Incidentally, the Paris UNIONISTS have behaved very decently. Ditto, a letter arrived yesterday from Ludwig Neumayr, *de dato* Eisenach, with the following purport[423]:

> 'At the congress in Eisenach, it was resolved that the workers of Germany should be called upon to join the International Working Men's Association by taking out cards as central members. Since I have now been appointed by Joh. Ph. Becker in Geneva as the agent of the German-language sectional groups of the International Working Men's Association for *Wiener-Neustadt* and surroundings, I would request exact instructions as to how I should now act. With social-republican fraternal greetings, etc. Address: Ludwig Neumayr, editor of the *Wiener-Neustädter Wochenblatt* in *Wiener-Neustadt*, Austria.'

This is a blow to OLD Becker and also, in particular, to the 'language-group *cash-box*'. But the matter itself may not be mucked about because of private friendship.

You will recall *Werner* (bookbinder) of Leipzig, to whom I wrote from Manchester. Since then he has worked for us diligently.

Yesterday the adherence of an (Italian) group from Trieste arrived. Ditto from *Barcelona*; I enclose a COPY of the *organ*[c] of this new group.

In Posen—as Zabicki reported—the *Polish* workers (joiners, etc.) have victoriously ended a STRIKE with the assistance of their colleagues in Berlin.[424] This struggle against *Monsieur le Capital*— even in the minor form of a STRIKE—will deal with national prejudice differently from the peace declamations made by bourgeois gentlemen.

---

[a] 21 August 1869 - [b] See this volume, p. 348. - [c] *Federacion*

I HOPE TO RECEIVE SOME LINES FROM TUSSY AS TO HER STATE OF HEALTH. MY BEST COMPLIMENTS TO MRS LIZZIE.

El
Moro

Much to be regretted is the sudden death of Sylvis (aged 41), President of the American Labor Union,[146] just *before* the meeting of the LABOR UNION CONGRESS, for which purpose he travelled across the United States agitating for nearly a whole year. Part of his work will thus be lost.

First published abridged in *Der Briefwechsel zwischen F. Engels und K. Marx,* Bd. 4, Stuttgart, 1913 and in full in *MEGA,* Abt. III, Bd. 4, Berlin, 1931

Printed according to the original

Published in English in full for the first time

247

ENGELS TO MARX

IN LONDON

Manchester, 5 September 1869

Dear Moor,

Got back here again midday yesterday[a] from Ostend. I arrived in London at 6.15 in the morning, found a train going here at 7.30, and journeyed on through, since I had scarcely slept all night, and was good for nothing else. I also thought you were away with Jenny,[b] and only here heard the contrary. This delay in your departure looks a little queer to me; I can't think that the Basle Congress[379] is alone to blame, and I am forced to ask myself whether it is not a money matter. When you asked for the £75 I sent you 100, imagining you could use the rest for the journey; since, however, I did not state this in so many words, you perhaps found another use for it; if this is so, *telegraph* me *tomorrow morning* (before 10 o'clock if possible), saying *how much you need.* We shall, you see, be leaving for Dublin tomorrow evening,[421] and I shall be going into town around 11-12 to look after money matters, so I could deal with this at the same time.

---

a 4 September - b See this volume, pp. 353-54.

I was in Engelskirchen[418] for a few days. People in Germany are becoming increasingly stupid. It is true that the workers' movement is closing in upon them threateningly, and they all flirt with it and have NOSTRUMS of all sorts, but their intelligence has not become any sharper; the opposite is true. My brother,[a] for instance, wanted to solve the social problem by 'redeeming labour', just as he redeems factory installations, buildings, machinery etc., by, for instance, putting a groschen *on the price* of each pound of yarn, and thus paying off the workers who have become old, sick and disabled! The *bonhomme*[b] was very surprised when I explained to him how hopelessly naive and absurd this idea was, and he finally promised to read your book.[c] Concerning the Prussian journeymen's provident funds, he gave me an article in Engel's statistical journal; the most blatant infamies of the statutes of Saxony are *not* present there, but otherwise everything similar.[425]

The greatest man in Germany is undoubtedly Strousberg. The fellow will soon become German Kaiser. Everywhere you go people talk of nothing but Strousberg. Incidentally, the fellow is not as bad as all that. My brother, who had negotiations with him, has described him very vividly to me. He has a lot of humour and some brilliant qualities, and, in any case, is immeasurably superior to Hudson the RAILWAY KING. He is now buying up all sorts of industrial establishments, and immediately cuts the working time to 10 hours everywhere, without reducing wages. He also has the clear knowledge that he will end up a really poor wretch. His main principle is: only swindle share-holders, but deal fairly with contractors and other industrialists. In Cologne I saw his portrait on exhibition; not bad at all, jovial. His background is completely dark: some say he is a qualified lawyer; according to others he kept a brothel in London.

Wilhelmchen[d] has now fallen so low that he may no longer say that Lassalle cribbed from you, and wrongly at that. This has emasculated the whole biography, and only he can know why he continues to print it.[426]

And he has declared the miserable *Felleisen*, not even the *Vorbote*, the journal of the bumpkins in Switzerland.[427] They are a fine bunch. Cf. the debate about social-democratic, democratic-social, or social-democratic + democratic-social workers' party at the Eisenach Congress. And Rittinghausen their prophet![428]

Wilhelm still makes no mention of the *18th Brumaire*. Here, too,

---

[a] probably Rudolf Engels - [b] honest fellow - [c] the first volume of *Capital* - [d] Wilhelm Liebknecht

he would have to 'omit' various things that 'might upset' him and others!

With best wishes from all of us to all of you.

Your
F. E.

Enclosed—a picture for transmission to the zoologist Vogt. Liebknecht can arrange this through his friend Goegg. It is democratic in front and socialist behind, thus completely orthodox and democratic-socialist.

First published abridged in *Der Briefwech- sel zwischen F. Engels und K. Marx*, Bd. 4, Stuttgart, 1913 and in full in *MEGA*, Abt. III, Bd. 4, Berlin, 1931

Printed according to the original

Published in English for the first time

248

MARX TO ENGELS[33]

IN MANCHESTER

Hanover, 25 September 1869

Dear FRED,

I had two unpleasant pieces of news from home today. Little Schnappy[a] is in a very bad way, and during our short absence has lost 1 $^1/_2$ pounds. Kugelmann insists—and is writing in this sense to London today—that Dr West in London, a famous children's doctor and, he believes, professor at Lafargue's hospital (St Bartholomew's) should be consulted. Second, Laura is again IN INTERESTING CIRCUMSTANCES, which is equally bad luck for herself and for Lafargue.

We have been here for 8 days. We stayed for several days in Belgium (Bruges and Liège), then on to Cologne. From there a visit to Dietzgen the thinker in Siegburg. From there to Bonn, and from there by steamer to Mainz. This journey delighted Jennychen. Unfortunately, afflicted by an importunate guest. In Bonn I had paid a call on Hagen in the evening. Not at home. Appeared next morning at the moment of our departure. Announcing that he

---

[a] Charles Étienne Lafargue

would accompany us to Rolandseck, we were saddled with him until Mainz. In Mainz we spent one day with Stumpf, who has a most delightful family (daughter and sister). Used the opportunity for a side trip to Wiesbaden. Omitted Ems. One day in Aachen with Karl Philips.

During this tour through Belgium, stay in Aachen, and journey up the Rhine, I convinced myself that energetic action must be taken against the clerics, particularly in the Catholic areas. I shall work in this vein in the International. Where it appears suitable, the rogues are flirting with workers' problems (e.g., Bishop Ketteler in Mainz, the clerics at the Düsseldorf Congress, etc.).[429] In fact we worked for them in 1848, but they enjoyed the fruits of the revolution during the period of reaction.

Everywhere I went people knew nothing about my *Louis Bonaparte*. On this point I sent Meissner a note that was by no means courteous. He has not so far replied.[430]

Liebknecht has written to me again about your *Peasant War*,[a] which is to be printed as a propaganda piece. As, this time, the thing is appearing under the auspices of the Eisenach Central Authority, I would advise you to make the necessary corrections, and to *send the thing in without delay*.[431] Since I shall probably have a rendezvous with Wilhelm in a few days,[b] write to me *by return* about your INTENTIONS.

Feuerbach has written to Kapp in New York in a sense similar— *mutatis mutandis*—to that in which Ruge[c] wrote about my book,[d] and Kapp for his part has informed our Meyer[e] in St Louis about the matter.

Jennychen has still not received an *ordre de retour*[f] from her EMPLOYERS.[g] The business is unpleasant. On the one hand, it is difficult to get away from here quickly. On the other, the CHANGE does the child a lot of good. She is looking really splendid.

Heartiest greetings to Mrs Burns and Tussychen.

Salut

Your

K. M.

First published abridged in *Der Briefwechsel zwischen F. Engels und K. Marx*, Bd. 4, Stuttgart, 1913 and in full in *MEGA*, Abt. III, Bd. 4, Berlin, 1931

Printed according to the original

Published in English in full for the first time

---

a F. Engels, *The Peasant War in Germany*. - b See this volume, p. 358. - c Ibid., pp. 542-43. - d K. Marx, *Capital*, Volume I. - e Sigfrid Meyer - f summons to return - g the Monroe family

249

MARX TO LAURA LAFARGUE[80]

IN LONDON

Hanover, 25 September 1869

My dear Cacadou,[a]

I regret that I cannot celebrate at home the birthday of my dear clear bird's eye, but Old Nick's[b] thoughts are with you.[432]

Du bist beslôzen
In mînem Herzen.[c][433]

I was happy to see from Möhmchen's[d] letter (written in her usual amusing way, she is a real virtuoso in letter-writing) that your health is improving. Our dear little Schnappy,[e] I hope, will soon get better. At the same time, I fully share Kugelmann's opinion that Dr West ought to be consulted *at once* (or another medical man if he be absent). I trust you and Lafargue will in this case yield to my paternal authority, a thing, you know full well, I am not in the habit of appealing to. Nobody is more difficult to treat than a baby. In no case more immediate action is wanted, and any delay more hurtful. You must under no circumstances accelerate your departure from London. It would be really dangerous to the child and do no good to yourself. On this point, every medical man will give you the same advice.

I am glad the Basle Congress[379] is over, and has, comparatively speaking, passed off so well. I am always fretting on such occasions of public exhibition of the party '*mit allen ihren Geschwüren*'.[f] None of the actors was *à la hauteur des principes*,[g] but the higher class idiocy effaces the working class blunders. We have passed through no little German town the *Winkelblatt*[h] of which was not full of the doings of 'that formidable Congress'.

We are here in a sort of fix. The Kugelmanns will not hear of an early leave-taking. At the same time, Jenny is much improving in health consequent upon the change of air and circumstances.

With Liebknecht I am likely to meet, within a few days, at Brunswick. I decline going to Leipzig, and he cannot come to

---

[a] Laura's nickname used by her family - [b] Marx's nickname used by his family - [c] Thou art enclosed in mine heart (Middle-High German). - [d] Marx's wife Jenny - [e] Charles Étienne Lafargue - [f] with all its ulcers - [g] highly principled - [h] local rag

Hanover, since the Prussians would probably give him the advantages of free lodging during the present prorogation of the Reichstag.[434]

My best thanks to Paul for his elaborate letter.[435] Meine herzlichsten Grüsse an das ganze Haus und[a] hundred kisses to yourself and my dear little Schnappy.

Adio, my dear child!

Ever yours
Old Nick.[b]

First published in *Die Neue Zeit*, Bd. 1,   Reproduced from the original
Nr. 2, Stuttgart, 1907-1908

250

ENGELS TO MARX

IN HANOVER

Manchester, 27 September 1869

Dear Moor,

Since there is nothing doing with Eichhoff[c] it would be better if Wilhelm were to print the *Peasant War* than for it not to be printed at all. So I shall go through the piece right away. Incidentally, Wilhelm can write to me himself about it; he still has not replied to my last letter, and I don't see why I should make advances to him.[431]

Lafargue is madder with his doctoring than I expected. You must really take energetic steps, otherwise there might really be a misfortune.[d]

We returned safely from Ireland[e] last Thursday[f]; were in Dublin, the Wicklow mountains, Killarney and Cork. Greatly enjoyed ourselves, but both females returned even *hiberniores*[g] than when they departed.[421] Weather fine on the whole. According to the papers the weather with you is now even worse than here.

Learned from Trench's *Realities of Irish Life* the whole secret of why Ireland is so 'overpopulated'. The worthy gentleman proves with examples that, on average, the land is worked by the Irish peasants to such degree that an outlay of £10-15 per ACRE, which is

---

[a] My heartfelt greetings to the whole family and - [b] On the inside of the letter: 'To Laura'. - [c] See this volume, pp. 282 and 297. - [d] Ibid., p. 353. - [e] Ibid., pp. 348 and 351. - [f] 16 September - [g] more Irish

completely paid off in 1-4 years, *raises* the rental value from 1s. to 20s., and from 4s. to 25-30s. per ACRE. *This* profit has to be brought into the pockets of the LANDLORDS.

Mr Trench, in return, is nicely checked by his own statements to Senior, which the latter has had published.[a] Trench tells the liberal Senior that, were he an Irish peasant, he too would be a RIBBONMAN[436]!

I would have visited Dietzgen from Engelskirchen,[418] but the highway to Siegburg had just been washed away and communications almost broken off.

Can't Jenny write to the Monroes, I should have thought the matter could be arranged.[b]

Ireland's trade has grown enormously over the last 14 years. Dublin port was unrecognisable. On Queenstown Quay I heard a great deal of Italian, then Serbian, French and Danish or Norwegian. THERE ARE INDEED A GOOD MANY 'ITALIANS' IN CORK, as the comedy has it. The country itself really looks depopulated, however, and you immediately get the idea that there are far too few people. Everywhere you are faced by the state of war. The ROYAL IRISH rush about everywhere in squads, with sheath-knives and sometimes revolvers at their belts, and unsheathed police batons in their hands; in Dublin a horse-drawn battery drove right through the centre of town, something I have never seen in England, and there are soldiers literally everywhere.

The worst thing about the Irish is that they become CORRUPTIBLE as soon as they cease to be peasants and fall into bourgeois ways. Of course this is true of most peasant nations. But in Ireland it's particularly bad, so the press is also particularly scurvy.

Moore is in the Tyrol; will probably return next week.

I expect you'll be going to Hamburg and seeing Meissner.[437] IF SO, you may mention to him that I am working on something about Ireland, and will offer it to him in due time.[438]

Hearty greetings to Jenny and Kugelmann.

Tussy and Lizzie also send greetings.

Your
F. E.[c]

First published abridged in *Der Briefwechsel zwischen F. Engels und K. Marx*, Bd. 4, Stuttgart, 1913 and in full in *MEGA*, Abt. III, Bd. 4, Berlin, 1931

Printed according to the original

Published in English for the first time

---

[a] N. W. Senior, *Journals, Conversations and Essays Relating to Ireland*, Vol. 2, London, 1868, p. 208. - [b] See this volume, p. 354. - [c] On the inside of the letter: 'To Dr Marx'.

251

MARX TO ENGELS

IN MANCHESTER

Hanover, 30 September 1869

DEAR FRED,

Your letter arrived yesterday evening.

Better news today from London on Schnappy's health.[a] Laura and Lafargue intend to leave London as soon as the little one's condition makes it possible. Under these circumstances, Tussy's IMMEDIATE RETURN to London appears necessary. Laura will hold it against her very much if she should leave for Paris without Tussy attempting to see the Lafargue family first.

I have *just* gossiped away an hour with a deputation of 4 Lassalleans sent to me by the local branch of the German General Workers' Association.[104] I naturally conducted myself with great reserve and diplomacy, but *sub rosa*[b] I informed the people of the necessary.[439] We parted good friends. I naturally rejected their invitation—extended in the name of the Association—to lecture to them.

On Sunday another delegation arrives from Brunswick: Bracke, Bonhorst, Spier.[440] This is less agreeable to me.

Liebknecht writes that he can't come because of the Prussians.[434]

But: 1. In this way, to Hamburg 2 days instead of 4 hours. 2. Simply for travelling expenses—extra expenditure of ABOUT 40 thaler. I NEITHER LIKE NOR AM ABLE TO AFFORD.[c]

I must close, since the mail is only open until 1.15 (the first) and now it is 10 MINUTES PAST ONE.

Shall speak to Meissner about your book.[438]

Your

K. M.

First published abridged in *Der Briefwechsel zwischen F. Engels und K. Marx*, Bd. 4, Stuttgart, 1913 and in full in *MEGA*, Abt. III, Bd. 4, Berlin, 1931

Printed according to the original

Published in English for the first time

---

[a] See this volume, pp. 353 and 356. - [b] confidentially - [c] See this volume, pp. 355-56.

252

MARX TO LUDWIG KUGELMANN [29]

IN HANOVER

London, 12 October 1869

Dear Kugelmann,

In all haste, as Tussychen and Engels have just arrived. You will see from these lines that we arrived safely in England during yesterday.[349] We had several marine and other adventures, about which Jennychen will write you more.

In the meantime, our heartiest greetings to the whole family.

Your
K. M.

Special greetings to *Madame la comtesse*[a] and Käuzchen[b]! Ditto greetings from Engels, Lafargue, Mrs Marx, etc. The little one[c] is well again.

First published in *Pisma Marksa k Kugel-*   Printed according to the original
manu (Letters of Marx to Kugelmann),
Moscow-Leningrad, 1928

253

MARX TO PAUL AND LAURA LAFARGUE

IN PARIS

London, 18 October 1869

My dear Paul and Laura,

I send you to-day the manuscript of Mr Keller.[441] I cannot find his address. So you must through the aid of Schily get it out from M. Hess.

Tell Mr Keller that he shall go on. On the whole, I am satisfied with his translation, although it lacks elegance and is done in too negligent a way.

---

[a] Gertrud Kugelmann - [b] Franziska Kugelmann - [c] Charles Étienne Lafargue

He will do best to send me every chapter *through you*. As to chapter IV I shall subdivide it.[442]

The changes I have made in this chapter II need not be maintained, but they show the direction in which I want the corrections to be made.

As to the word '*Verwertung*'[a] see my note p. 12 of his manuscript. He must make a note on it for the French reader.

I doubt whether the frequent *large printing of words* will do for French printers.

In German we use the word 'Process' (procès) for economical movements, as you say chemical procès, *si je ne me trompe pas*.[b] He translates by 'phenomena' which is nonsense. If he can find no other word, he must always translate by 'mouvement' or something analogous.

Kiss dear Schnappy on my behalf.

Yours

Old Nick

I have received a letter from St Petersbourg. A Russian sends me his work (in German[c]) on the situation of the peasantry and the working class generally in that benighted country.[443]

[In Lafargue's handwriting]

Faire remarquer à Keller que les mots pointillés sont maintenus dans le texte.[d]

First published in *Annali dell'Istituto G. G. Feltrinelli*, an. 1, Milano, 1958   Reproduced from the original

---

[a] increase of value - [b] if I am not mistaken - [c] should be 'in Russian' - [d] Let Keller retain the words underlined by dots.

254

ENGELS TO MARX

IN LONDON

Manchester, Friday, 22 October 1869

Dear Moor,

In all haste have enclosed the photographs, of which Jenny should select one. I have a bad grippe because of the great change in temperature, but it is starting to get better.

The book by Wakefield [a] is cited by Butt [b] as *A View of Ireland* and also *An Account of Ireland*, 2 volumes, 1812 or 1813.

Young's book is called: *A Tour in Ireland*, 2 volumes, date not given.

Ranc's novel [c] is very nice.

Best greetings.

Your
F. E.

First published in *Der Briefwechsel zwischen F. Engels und K. Marx*, Bd. 4, Stuttgart, 1913

Printed according to the original

Published in English for the first time

255

MARX TO ENGELS

IN MANCHESTER

[London,] 23 October 1869

Dear Fred,

Best thanks for the photograms.

I am also suffering from a bad grippe.

I have already ordered the A. Young, and will write to the same man (Adams) about the Wakefield. [d]

---

[a] E. Wakefield, *An Account of Ireland, Statistical and Political*. - [b] I. Butt, *The Irish People and the Irish Land: a Letter to Lord Lifford*. - [c] A. Ranc, *Le Roman d'une conspiration*. - [d] See the previous letter.

According to Lafargue's letter, great excitement rules in Paris.

I have been sent from St Petersburg a thick 500-page Flerovsky volume on the condition of the Russian peasants and workers.[443] Unfortunately in *Russian.* The fellow worked on the book for 15 years.

The great Bakunin is now off to Naples, as DELEGATE to an atheists' congress being held there in opposition to the oecumenical consilium.[444]

Salut.

Your

K. M.

First published abridged in *Der Briefwechsel zwischen F. Engels und K. Marx,* Bd. 4, Stuttgart, 1913 and in full in *MEGA,* Abt. III, Bd. 4, Berlin, 1931

Printed according to the original

Published in English for the first time

256

ENGELS TO MARX[33]

IN LONDON

Manchester, 24 October 1869

Dear Moor,

My grippe has happily—in the main—been conquered by limiting beer consumption, staying at home in the evening and consuming linseed tea with lemon and honey.

I was happy to discover the Wakefield[a] here in my SUBSCRIPTION LIBRARY—that is to say, in the catalogue, for in reality it was not to be found. They are trying to track it down; I shall write to you about it again. It consists of *2 fat quarto volumes.* In fact, I find that quite a number of the things I have here are very useful, particularly for the 1500-1800 period, and some very important, so if Wakefield comes to light and Young[b] can be flushed out, I would need virtually only quite modern things. Sadler[c] is here too.

About the Flerovsky[d]—the name is non-Slav and, in particular,

---

a E. Wakefield, *An Account of Ireland, Statistical and Political.-* b A. Young, *A Tour in Ireland...,* Vols. I-II.- c M. Th.Sadler, *Ireland; Its Evils and Their Remedies.-* d The reference is to Н. Флеровскій, *Положеніе рабочаго класса въ Россіи.-*

un-Russian, not a single Russian word starts with *fl*, apart from flangovy, flot, flankirovat,[a] etc.—you will probably need Gaudissart[b]; for although one can learn enough Russian in 3 months to read such a book, you have no time for this at the moment. Let Gaudissart look at it, and if it is worth something, I may be able to read myself to some extent into Russian again with it, as soon as I am finished with Ireland. From Ireland to Russia *il n'y a qu'un pas.*[c]

Enclosed envelope of your 2nd letter from Hanover,[d] which shows signs of Prussian attention, though I fail to grasp how the people found the time, since you only posted the letter 10 minutes before the close of post. Between then and the time when the train left, however, they may have found the time for a *tête-à-tête*.

Irish history shows what a misfortune it is for one nation to subjugate another. All English abominations have their origin in the Irish PALE.[445] I still have to bone up on the Cromwellian period, but it appears clear to me that things in England would have taken another turn but for the necessity of military rule in Ireland and creating a new aristocracy.

Your
F. E.

First published abridged in *Der Briefwechsel zwischen F. Engels und K. Marx*, Bd. 4, Stuttgart, 1913 and in full in *MEGA*, Abt. III, Bd. 4, Berlin, 1931

Printed according to the original

Published in English in full for the first time

257

MARX TO ENGELS[446]

IN MANCHESTER

London, 30 October 1869

DEAR FRED,

Please return to me after reading the enclosed letters from Bonhorst and the Goeggiana.[447]

That Serno should have expedited himself from life into death is only natural, but that Bakunin, with whom he stood on bad

---

[a] flank man, fleet, flanking - [b] Sigismund Borkheim - [c] it is only one step - [d] See this volume, p. 358.

terms right to the end, should immediately have seized his papers, is an unnatural discovery.[448]

Apropos. The secretary[a] of our French Genevan committee[b] is utterly fed up with being saddled with Bakunin, and complains that he disorganises everything with his 'tyranny'. In the *Égalité*, Monsieur Bakunin indicates that the German and English workers have no desire for individuality, so accept our *communisme autoritaire*. In opposition to this, Bakunin represents *le collectivisme anarchique*.[c] The anarchism is, however, in his head, which contains only one clear idea—that Bakunin should play first fiddle.

For a complete understanding of Goegg's and Bonhorst's letters, you should know that the bumpkins' (or rather their representatives') party in Switzerland, Austria and Germany, are screaming blue murder about the resolution of the Basle Congress on *propriété foncière*.[d]

The foolishness and weakness (exploited by the cleverer Schweitzer) with which Wilhelm and his consorts reply to the howls by Schwabenmayer[e] and the rest of their anti-People's Party supporters,[449] make one's hair stand on end. It has not even occurred to one of these jackasses to ask the liberal howlers if there does not, perhaps, exist in Germany, side by side with small peasant property, also large landed property, which forms the basis of the surviving feudal economy; whether it will not be necessary to put an end to this in the course of a revolution, if only to put an end to the present economy of the state; and whether this can be done in the antiquated manner of 1789[450]? *Quod non*.[f] The jackasses believe Schwabenmayer's statement that the land question is only of direct practical interest for England!

The creation of the LAND AND LABOUR *League*[451] (incidentally, directly inspired by the General Council) should be regarded as an outcome of the Basle Congress[379]; here, the workers' party makes a clean break with the bourgeoisie, NATIONALISATION OF LAND [being] the STARTING POINT.[g] Eccarius has been appointed active secretary (in addition to Boon as HONORARY ONE), and is being paid for it.

I have been instructed by the GENERAL COUNCIL to write a few words to the ENGLISH WORKING CLASS about the IRISH PRISONERS' DEMONSTRATION LAST SUNDAY. Being so busy, I have no inclination to do it, BUT

---

a Henri Perret - b The Federal Council of Romance Switzerland - c See 'Nouvelles de l'étranger. France, Lyon, le 1er octobre 1869; Paris, le 21 vendémiaire, an 78 (12 octobre 1869)', *L'Égalité*, No. 39, 16 October 1869. - d landed property - e Karl Mayer - f But no. - g See [Resolution of the Basle Congress on landed property], *Report of the Fourth Annual Congress...*, p. 26.

MUST BE DONE. The demonstration was quite incorrectly reported in the London papers. It was capital.[452]

Best greetings to Mrs Lizzie and the Sunday guests.

Your
K. M.

The Prussians closed my letter to you from Hanover[a] so badly partly out of shortage of time, and partly out of anger at finding nothing in it.

First published in *Der Briefwechsel zwischen F. Engels und K. Marx*, Bd. 4, Stuttgart, 1913

Printed according to the original

Published in English in full for the first time

258

ENGELS TO MARX[446]

IN LONDON

Manchester, 1 November 1869

Dear Moor,

The resolution on landed property[b] has worked real wonders. It forces the fellows in Germany to think, for the first time since Lassalle started his agitation, something hitherto regarded as completely superfluous. This can be seen plainly in the letter from Bonhorst.[453] In other respects, too, I find the letter not bad; despite the affectation and semi-education, it contains a certain healthy popular humour and, with the mortgage, he has hit the nail on the head. Incidentally, the people forget that, apart from the main business with big landed property, there are also various sorts of peasant: (1) the tenant farmer to whom it is immaterial whether the land belongs to the state or to the big landowner; (2) the owner, first the big peasant, against whose reactionary existence the day-labourers and farm-hands should be incited; second the middle peasant, also reactionary and not very numerous; and third, the debt-laden small peasant, who can be got at through his mortgage. In addition it may be said that, for

---

a See this volume, p. 358. - b Ibid., p. 364.

the time being, the proletariat has no interest in raising the question of *small* land-holding.

It is delightful that that simple soul Goegg has now been sacked by his own people for being too communist! The worthy Ladendorff is behind this. Beust[a] may be a communist on paper, but can easily be caught if he is told that the money was not given for that reason, but only to revolutionise Germany in general. Now *we* are supposed even to keep alive the unhappy *Felleisen*, though all that can be said is that, the sooner it goes to the devil, the better.

You could send me some characteristic specimens of the German stuff so that I might remain a little *au courant*.[b]

The Prussians have once again produced a wonderful Prussian trick by destroying the Langensalza memorial in Celle. Never has anything been more grovelling than Mr Miquel's interpellation on this point. Roon took the opportunity to conclude that, in Prussia, an official order from above is sufficient for the military to trample on any court decision.[454]

I am sorry about Serno[c]; he seems, for a change, to have been a decent Russian.[448] But I am still sorrier for Goegg with his opinion about Serno's classical French,[d] of which we have also seen samples.

It is a real stroke of luck that the *Bee-Hive* is now flaunting the bourgeois colours both insolently and stupidly. I have never seen such a filthy issue as that of yesterday.[455] This cringing to Gladstone and the whole bourgeois-patronising-philanthropic tone must break the back of the sheet, and make the need felt for a real workers' paper. It is a very good thing that, just at the moment when the workers sober up from their liberal intoxication, their only paper should become more and more bourgeois. But Sam Morley should not be so stupid as to put such stupid chaps there, and to allow them to spread the bourgeois varnish so thickly and so obviously.

The Fenian demonstration in London[e] simply proves once again the value the press attaches to public opinion. About 100,000 assembled in the most imposing demonstration seen in London for years and, since it is in the interests of RESPECTABILITY, the entire London press, with no exception, manages to depict this as a shabby FAILURE.

In connection with the present STRIKE by the spinners in

---

a Friedrich von Beust - b in the know - c Serno-Solovyevich - d See this volume p. 186. - e Ibid., pp. 364-65.

Bolton,[456] a MASTER SPINNER told Sam Moore quite frankly: WE DON'T CARE AT ALL ABOUT THE 5% REDUCTION OF WAGES, WHAT WE WANT AND INTEND TO HAVE IS A REDUCED PRODUCTION (that is to say a STRIKE).

The Wakefield [a] has still not been found here. But before I need it, I must check the basis more thoroughly, that's to say, the history of 1600-1700.

So that my Irish sources should not lack a comic side, I have found here in the FOREIGN LIBRARY *Irland* by Jacobus Venedey!

Best greetings. Lousy weather here.

Your
F. E.

First published in *Der Briefwechsel zwischen F. Engels und K. Marx*, Bd. 4, Stuttgart, 1913

Printed according to the original

Published in English in full for the first time

259

MARX TO ENGELS

IN MANCHESTER

London, 6 November 1869

DEAR FRED,

I send you 1 *Pionier*, 1 *Volksstaat*, and various copies of *Social-Demokrat*.

You will see from the *Pionier* that Heinzen believes I only wrote *Capital* so that *he* should not understand it.[457]

Schweitzer—utilising Liebknecht's anxiety with regard to his democratic friends[b]—is behaving as though polemics against landed property were the first word in the Lassallean creed! *Quelle impudence!* Incidentally, Bonhorst did him good service in an issue of the *Volksstaat* that I cannot find.[458] I don't know whether you receive the *Volksstaat*.

Bonhorst's arrest is good.[459]

There could be nothing more ridiculous than the respectable people's fear concerning the Queen's procession today.[460] Every-

---

[a] E. Wakefield, *An Account of Ireland, Statistical and Political.* - [b] See this volume, p. 364.

where overrun by police as in France. The whole alarm was produced by a HOAX. A few agitators have had their fun in the past few weeks, circulating HANDBILLS calling on the starving workers of the East End to present themselves *en masse* to the Queen, and *de ne pas laisser passer la reine*.[a]

My family has just returned from the spectacle. Icy coldness amongst the public. Madame is said to have stared fuming-mad and ultra-crabby.

I shall send you, in the next few days, a volume I happened to pick up, which contains all sorts of pamphlets on Ireland. Those by Ensor (whom I also quoted in *Capital*) contain many piquant points.[b] Ensor was a political economist of English origin (his father still lived in England when Ensor was born), Protestant and, despite all this, one of the most resolute REPEALERS[461] before 1830. Being himself indifferent to religious things, he can defend Catholicism with wit against the Protestants. The first pamphlet in the book is by Arthur O'Connor. I had expected rather more of it, since this O'Connor played an important role in 1798,[462] and I have found good articles by him about Castlereagh's administration in Cobbett's *Political Register*. Tussy should sometime look through Cobbett, for something there about Ireland.

This week Tussy and I lost 3 days putting my workroom in order. It had become jumbled to the frontiers of possibility.

Salut.

Your
K. M.

TUSSY SENDS HER BEST COMPLIMENTS TO THE FAMILY.

First published in *Der Briefwechsel zwischen F. Engels und K. Marx*, Bd. 4, Stuttgart, 1913

Printed according to the original

Published in English for the first time

---

[a] not let the Queen pass - [b] G. Ensor, *An Inquiry Concerning the Population of Nations: Containing a Refutation of Mr. Malthus's Essay on Population* and *Anti-Union. Ireland as She Ought to Be*.

260

ENGELS TO MARX [33]

IN LONDON

Manchester, 9 November 1869

Dear Moor,

That is quite a bit of impudence with the vaudeville about the *Régence*.[a] I would scarcely have expected the EMPIRE to put up with something like this. But we see what can be done with pluck, though of course, our Guidos and Wilhelms[b] will not take this as their example.

The *Réforme*, just like *Réveil* and *Rappel*, is rather weak, though a certain amount of declamation can be excused at the moment. The fellows are confused, however. Among them, particularly Raspail. The idea of selecting a provisional government at this very date is as good as a joke against Bonaparte, but otherwise, naturally, nonsense. Bonaparte is supposed to be ill again; things appear to be drawing to an end for him physically, too.

Schweitzer's turnabout immediately to adopt the Basle decision on landed property and to behave as though he and Lassalle had always preached this, is extraordinarily bare-faced,[458] but very ingenious vis-à-vis the simple souls *à la* Wilhelm. But what should they do when confronted by this blackguard, who has enough brains always to behave correctly as far as theory is concerned, and who knows that they are completely at a loss as soon as a theoretical point comes up. Incidentally, I did *not* see the *Volksstaat* here.

I did not expect Monsieur Carey[c] to be such an amusing bit of reading. I find his cock-and-bull stories of natural sciences read very well and provide plenty of occasions for laughter. I would not have dared consider the man so stupid and uninformed. For instance, he has disintegrated carbon, and it consists of carbonic acid and CINDERS! Ditto, water disintegrates into vapour. Geology proves that plants and even ferns were in existence long before any animal! The disintegration of metals is a mere trifle for him—in voltaic batteries the tin and copper of which they consist are disintegrated! And a hundred other things. Ditto, his historical

---

a Apparently, *La Régence de Decembrostein*, Paris, 1869. - b reference to Guido Weiss and Wilhelm Liebknecht - c H. Ch. Carey, *Principles of Social Science*. First edition was published in 1858-59. Engels used the 1868-69 edition.

fables. The fellow imagines that, in South Lancashire, among other places the Forest of Rossendale (a dense industrial district), the rental is so high only because the ground here is extremely productive of corn! I am making you a whole pile of marginal notes, etc., and as soon as I have read the rent theory I shall write my opinion of it and return the book to you. He naturally explains the origin of rent with just such a nonsensical cut-throat theory as Ricardo, and also his idea *of how it took place* is as absurd as the way all economists imagine such things. Yet this does not affect the theory of rent itself. What Carey means by the 'best land' can be seen from the fact that, according to him, even today in the Northern States it is *only profitable in exceptional cases* to cultivate the so-called best land!

Post closing. Best greetings to all.

Your
F. E.

Vaudeville to be returned tomorrow.

First published abridged in *Der Briefwechsel zwischen F. Engels und K. Marx*, Bd. 4, Stuttgart, 1913 and in full in *MEGA*, Abt. III, Bd. 4, Berlin, 1931

Printed according to the original
Published in English in full for the first time

261

MARX TO ENGELS

IN MANCHESTER

[London,] 12 November 1869

DEAR FRED,

This week something suspicious has displayed itself in my left arm-pit (as in Manchester[353]), and on my leg. Arsenic again immediately. Additionally, Tussy forces me to take long walks with her after 1 or 2 o'clock every day. Finally, today introduced surreptitiously *for the first time* a flannel vest, since a cold in this state is not pleasant.

You are surprised by the pluck of the French,[a] and speak SOMEWHAT SNEERINGLY of us upright Germans. What risks we take you will see from the enclosed extravaganza.

In Stuttgart, in accordance with his habit, Freiligrath once again had himself photographed in several dozen poses, decked out as a statue, etc. The most successful holy picture of this Classen-Kappelmann-hero [463] is—*verbotenus*[b]—a scene in which he *as a lion* rides on a *camel*. This is probably a back-hander for Heine's camel who defeats the lion.[c]

Liebknecht will be taking off next week for 3 months in prison, and has sent Borkheim a desperate plea for money.

What scares me about the French is the terrible confusion in their heads. Ledru-Rollin's circular letter is quite that of a pretender.[464] He really appears to take *au sérieux*[d] the dictatorship over France offered him by Heinzen. On the other hand, *Zukunft* has been good enough to offer Mr Acollas, whom nobody in Paris knows, a post in the provisional government, because he had called the French to accept Dr J. Jacoby's programme instead of the antiquated human and *citoyen*[e] rights of 1793. One good turn deserves another. I find that OLD Jacoby himself is not playing properly the role he dictated for himself. Grasping the opportunity of the Hanoverian event,[454] should he not call on the Prussian sergeant-major-government—since Prussia is, after all, a 'military state'—also to lay aside those useless and, at the same time, expensive decorations, such as chambers, civil courts and the like? Wrapping oneself up silently in the depths of one's own moral indignation does not lure a soul from his hearth.

A while ago, the Russian gentlemen bombarded an island near Korea just for amusement, as Borkheim discovered in a Moscow newspaper.[f] Not a word about it in the English papers. If things go on like this, these fine fellows will soon be in possession of Japan.

The latest MEETINGS in Ireland were very nice; the clerics were seized by their collars and removed from the speaker's stand. Instead of the programme on Ireland,[g] for which there is no proper motive, I have had (in order to adopt resolutions) the following placed on the agenda for next Tuesday.[h]

1. Proceedings of the English ministry on the Irish amnesty question!

---

[a] See this volume, p. 369. - [b] literally - [c] See H. Heine, *Atta Troll*. - [d] seriously - [e] citizen - [f] «Бомбардированіе корейской крепости винтовой лодкой *Соболъ*», *Московскія вѣдомости*, No. 207, 23 September 1869. - [g] See this volume, p. 364. - [h] 16 November

2. The attitude of the English working class to the Irish question.
Salut.

Your

K. M.

First published abridged in *Der Briefwechsel zwischen F. Engels und K. Marx*, Bd. 4, Stuttgart, 1913 and in full in *MEGA*, Abt. III, Bd. 4, Berlin, 1931

Printed according to the original

Published in English for the first time

262

MARX TO SAMUEL DAVENPORT [465]

London, 12 November 1869
1 Modena Villas, Maitland Park,
Haverstock Hill, N. W.

Sir,

I have the honour to enclose a post office order for 2 guineas as my yearly subscription for the Society of Arts.[356]

Yours obediently

Karl Marx

First published in Russian in *Kommunist*, No. 3, Moscow, 1983

Printed according to the photocopy of the original

Published in English for the first time

263

ENGELS TO MARX [180]

IN LONDON

Manchester, 17 November 1869

Dear Moor,

I hope the arsenic and the exercise will have thundered a rapid retreat to that certain 'suspicious' matter. But I also hope that these constant relapses will finally lead you to the conclusion that you must commence a more rational way of life. You poison your blood yourself by making regular digestion impossible. And you certainly don't then produce the same quantum (and *quale*[a]) of work as you would under normal circumstances.

The idyllic drama *Familienglück coram Philistaco* is really enchanting.[b] One does not know what to admire more, the *fadaise*[c] of the speeches and the poets (only interrupted by the nasty-sounding nonsense of boozy Karl Beck), or the importunity of the family, which has something like this printed as 'manuscript for friends' (that is PUBLIC *for non-friends*). But it is not quite clear to me how the noble Freiligrath can have printed the intrepid words of the tender-hearted Walesrode: that the poet Freiligrath has also achieved something in the way of worldly possessions (by begging[6]). I would like to have seen the faces in his family when these words were uttered.

Monsieur Ledru-Rollin is certainly reckoning on nothing other than a dictatorship. The little fellow Louis Blanc also re-emerged as though nothing had happened—why not the others? At a moment like this, the bourgeois press does not tell us anything about what is really happening, and even the revolutionary press does not suffice to enlighten one. The confusion is certainly great, but it is equally certain that the crisis is not yet really close. But a general in Paris has said: *Nous avons encore un Empereur, mais l'empire n'existe plus.*[d]

The Russians are having a rare old time of it in Asia. They are now happily waging war with the Khan of Kashgar,[e] formerly subject to the Chinese, but who has now made himself independent. If they subdue *him*, they will run directly up against countries already under English dominion (Ladekh, Kashmir), about 200 miles from the English frontier. You will have seen Vámbéry's news (taken over by English papers from the Augsburg *Allgemeine Zeitung*[f]) about the trickery in Bukhara (where, under treaty, Russian goods pay 3% customs, English 40%!), Afghanistan, etc. John Bull's stupidity is becoming ever greater, as a result of his bumptiousness.

Isn't it the best joke of the Irish to propose O'Donovan Rossa as candidate for Tipperary? If this succeeds, Gladstone will find himself in a fine fix. And now, again, an amnesty in Italy.[466]

---

a quality - b See this volume, p. 371. - c rubbish - d We still have an Emperor, but the Empire no longer exists. - e Mohammed Jakub Beg - f H. Vámbéry, 'Eine neue Wendung in der central-asiatischen Frage', *Allgemeine Zeitung*, No. 308, 4 November 1869. See also *The Times*, 8 November 1869.

I hope to read at length about the debates, etc., in the International[a] next Sunday in the *Bee-Hive*. Be sure to send me any documents there may be. Last Sunday the *Bee-Hive* had nothing about the International but, instead, something about the wedding of the Duke of Abercorn's daughters.

Prendergast's *Cromwellian Settlement* is OUT OF PRINT. You would, therefore, oblige me greatly if you *order it second-hand* immediately. Butt's *Irish People*: NONE in London. Other Irish pamphlets, e.g., those of Lords Rosse and Lifford: CANNOT FIND. These are the answers my bookseller received from his London agent, and he told me the English book trade could not, in any case, occupy itself with obtaining publications appearing in Ireland, since it is not usual to have a correspondent in Dublin, but only in London. Now I shall write direct to Duffy in Dublin.

I have found here a number of very useful things about Ireland. Wolfe Tone's *Memoirs* etc., that is, in the *catalogue*. As soon as I ask for these things in the library, they cannot be found, like, for instance, Wakefield.[b] Some old fellow must have had all the stuff out together and returned it *en masse*, so the whole pile is lying hidden somewhere. In any case, these things must be found.

Goldwin Smith in *Irish History and Irish Character* is quite the wise bourgeois thinker. Ireland was intended by providence to be GRAZING LAND, the prophet Léonce de Lavergne[c] foretold it, *ergo pereat*[d] the Irish people!

I wanted to write about Carey[e] today, but was interrupted. Soonest.

Best greetings to all the LADIES.

Your
F. E.

First published abridged in *Der Briefwechsel zwischen F. Engels und K. Marx*, Bd. 4, Stuttgart, 1913 and in full in *MEGA*, Abt. III, Bd. 4, Berlin, 1931

Printed according to the original

Published in English in full for the first time

---

[a] See this volume, pp. 371-72, 375-76, 386-87, 392-93. - [b] E. Wakefield, *An Account of Ireland, Statistical and Political*. - [c] L. de Lavergne, *The Rural Economy of England, Scotland and Ireland*. - [d] so perish - [e] H. Ch. Carey, *Principles of Social Science*.

264

MARX TO ENGELS[467]

IN MANCHESTER

[London,] 18 November 1869

DEAR FRED,

I am sending you today a parcel by BOOKPOST, containing 1. the volume of Irish pamphlets[a] (especially *Ensor* OF SOME VALUE,[b]) 2. *Social-Demokrat* and *Volksstaat*, 3. 3 COPIES for you, Moore and Schorlemmer of the *Report on the Basle Congress*. I don't know if I have already sent it. In this case, the COPIES can be given to other people.

I'll look after your commissions.[c]

The *Bee-Hive completely suppressed* the report (by Eccarius) on the latest session,[d] on the *pretext* that it had received it too late. The real reason was that:

1. it did *not* wish to *announce* that the GENERAL COUNCIL would open a discussion on the Irish question at its next meeting;

2. in the report, unfavourable references were made to it (i.e., to Mr Potter), about the LAND AND LABOUR LEAGUE.[451] The fact is that Mr Potter *failed* glaringly as a candidate for the COMMITTEE of the LEAGUE.

Last Tuesday[e] I opened the discussion on point 1: *the attitude of the British Ministry to the IRISH AMNESTY QUESTION*. I spoke for ABOUT an hour and a quarter, MUCH CHEERED,[468] and then proposed the following resolutions ON point No. 1:

* Resolved,

that in his reply to the Irish demands for the release of the imprisoned Irish patriots—a reply contained in his letter to Mr O'Shea etc. etc.—Mr Gladstone deliberately insults the Irish Nation;

that he clogs political amnesty with conditions alike degrading to the victims of misgovernment and the people they belong to;

that having, in the teeth of his responsible position, publicly and enthusiastically cheered on the American slaveholders' Rebellion,[469] he now steps in to preach to the Irish people the doctrine of passive obedience;

---

[a] See this volume, p. 368. - [b] G. Ensor, *An Inquiry Concerning the Population of Nations...* and *Anti-Union. Ireland as She Ought to Be.* - [c] See the previous letter. - [d] of the General Council on 9 November 1869 - [e] 16 November

that his whole proceedings with reference to the Irish Amnesty question are the true and genuine offspring of that '*policy of conquest*', by the fiery denunciation of which Mr Gladstone ousted his Tory rivals from office;

that the *General Council* of the '*International Working Men's Association*' express their admiration of the spirited, firm and highsouled manner in which the Irish people carry on their Amnesty movement;

that these resolutions be communicated to all branches of, and working men's bodies connected with, the '*International Working Men's Association*' in Europe and America.* a

Harris (an O'Brien-MAN) declared TO SECOND. But the President (Lucraft) pointed to the clock (we may only stay until 11); HENCE, adjourned until next Tuesday. However, Lucraft, Weston, Hales etc., IN FACT the whole COUNCIL, tentatively declared their agreement IN INFORMAL WAY.

Milner, another O'Brienite, declared that the language of the RESOLUTIONS was too weak (i.e., not declamatory enough); furthermore he demands that everything I said in support of the case should be included in the RESOLUTIONS. (A fine kettle of fish!)

Since the debate will continue on Tuesday, NOW THE TIME FOR YOU to tell, rather to write, me anything you might wish to *amend* or **add** to the RESOLUTIONS. In the latter case, if you, for example, wish to add a paragraph about the amnesties all over Europe, ITALY for example, write it at once in resolution form.

INCIDENT OF LAST COUNCIL'S SITTING. Mr Holyoake—BE EVERY MAN HIS OWN CROMWELL—appears and, after leaving, has himself proposed by Weston. Tentatively declared that he should first take out a card as a member of the INTERNATIONAL WORKING MEN'S ASSOCIATION, otherwise he cannot even be *proposed*. His aim is SIMPLY to make himself important—and to figure as a DELEGATE at the next GENERAL CONGRESS. The debate on his ADMISSION will be stormy, since he has many friends among us and, as an offended intriguant, could play some nasty tricks on us. What are your ideas about the tactics to be followed?

Enclosed—screed from Liebknecht,[470] who has also complained bitterly in his letter to Borkheim that we do not support him, either morally or materially. RETURN the 2nd enclosed letter from Wilhelm, which is addressed to Borkheim.

---

a K. Marx, *Draft Resolution of the General Council on the Policy of the British Government Towards the Irish Prisoners*

Marx's membership card of Land and Labour League (30 November 1869)

A BRANCH ESTABLISHMENT of the International founded in Dundee, ditto—new branch in Boston. (New England.)

Carbunculosa not yet quite vanquished.

Salut.

Your
K. M.

Apropos L. Blanc: When Reclus[471] was here he also visited L. Blanc and told me after the visit: the little fellow is filling his trousers at the mere thought of having to return to France. He feels devilish well here as the *'petit grand homme'*[a] removed from danger, and he has—as he frankly told Reclus, lost absolutely all confidence in the French.

First published in *Der Briefwechsel zwischen F. Engels und K. Marx*, Bd. 4, Stuttgart, 1913

Printed according to the original

Published in English in full for the first time

265

ENGELS TO MARX[472]

IN LONDON

Manchester, 19 November 1869

Dear Moor,

I hope Eccarius will force Potter to publish the report belatedly,[b] particularly because of the LAND AND LABOUR LEAGUE.[451]

I think an addition on the amnesties in the rest of Europe would only weaken the resolution[c] since, apart from Russia (which would be very good *on its own*[473]), Russia would have to be excluded because of those sentenced in the Guelphic conspiracy.[474] I would, however, polish up the language somewhat in: *Alinéa*[d] 2 I would insert IMPRISONED or something of the sort before VICTIMS, to make it EVIDENT at first sight who is meant.

Alinéa 3, it is questionable whether one can speak of THE TEETH OF A POSITION, and instead of STEPS IN I would say TURNS ROUND.

Alinéa 4. WITH REGARD TO appears to me *more direct* than WITH REFERENCE TO.

---

[a] little grand man - [b] See this volume, p. 375. - [c] Ibid., pp. 375-76. - [d] paragraph

Lizzie immediately passed a VOTE OF THANKS to you for the resolution, and is vexed that she will not be able to be there on Tuesday.

The business with Holyoake is vexatious.[a] The fellow is simply a GO-BETWEEN for the radical bourgeoisie with the workers. The question is this: is the composition of the GENERAL COUNCIL such that a SWAMPING by such rabble is to be feared or not? If you accept Holyoake, then others might follow, and they will do so as soon as the affair becomes more important. Moreover, if the times become more tempestuous, these gentlemen will certainly also visit the sessions, and try to grasp the leadership. And as far as I know, Mr Holyoake has never done the slightest thing for the working class *as such*. *A priori*, everything against his acceptance, but if his rejection would lead to splits in the COUNCIL, while his acceptance would, in practice, make little difference to the constitution of the GENERAL COUNCIL, *eh bien*[b]! Despite this I cannot well envisage a workers' COUNCIL with this fellow on it.

Before the receipt of yours of yesterday, I had sent Wilhelm[c] £5 with a few frosty lines. The fellow really is too brazen-faced. First he insults me in every way, then I should give moral and material support, and send him articles for his sheet,[d] which he has ceased sending me without saying a word. If you should write to him, you would be doing me a favour if you let him understand that, if he wants articles from me, he should pray write directly to me. To act as bootblack to Mr Wilhelm—that crowns it all! Enclosed, the letter returned.

Best thanks for the Irish PAMPHLETS and REPORTS,[e] I shall deliver the two for Moore and Schorlemmer.

When was Reclus in London[471]? And how is the French translation of your book going[441]? Since I have been back here I haven't heard a word about it.

And now for *Carey*.[f]

The entire point at issue does not seem to me to be directly connected with political economy as such. Ricardo says that rent is the surplus yield of the more productive plots of land over that of the least productive. Carey says exactly the same.

Continuation by 2nd post.

Your
F. E.

They are agreed upon what RENT is. But, how and by what agency

---

a See this volume, p. 376. - b very well - c Wilhelm Liebknecht - d *Der Volksstaat* - e See this volume, p. 375. - f H. Ch. Carey, *Principles of Social Science*.

rent materialises, is a matter of dispute. Now, Ricardo's description of the process by which RENT originates (Carey, p. 104), is just as unhistorical as all such historical travesties by the economists, and Carey's own great Robinson-Crusoe-story about Adam and Eve (p. 96 et seq.). With regard to the older economists, including Ricardo, this is still excusable to some extent; they do not wish for historical knowledge; they are just as unhistorical in their whole conception as the other apostles of the 18th-century Enlightenment, for whom such alleged historical digressions are always only a *façon de parler*[a], enabling them to represent the origin of this or that in a rational manner, and in which primitive men always think and behave as if they were 18th-century French philosophers. But when Carey, who wants to propound an historical theory of his own, proceeds to present Adam and Eve to us as Yankee backwoodsmen, then he cannot demand that we believe him, for he lacks the same excuse.

The entire point at issue would be nil, had not Ricardo, in his naïvety, simply called the more productive land 'FERTILE'. According to Ricardo, THE MOST *FERTILE* AND *MOST FAVOURABLY SITUATED* LAND is cultivated first. Just the way a thoughtful bourgeois, on land cultivated for centuries, must picture things. Now Carey clings to the 'FERTILE' and foists upon Ricardo the assertion that the lands that are *in themselves* the most productive are those first cultivated, and states: No, on the contrary, the lands *in themselves* the most capable of production (the Amazon valley, the Ganges delta, tropical Africa, Borneo and New Guinea, etc.) are not cultivated even today; the first settlers, because they cannot do otherwise, always commence cultivation on *self-draining land*, that is to say, strips situated on hills and slopes, and these are by nature *poorer*. And when Ricardo says: FERTILE *AND THE MOST FAVOURABLY SITUATED*, he is saying the same thing, without noticing that he is expressing himself *LOOSELY* and that a contradiction can be seen between these two qualifications connected by AND. But when Carey gives a sketch on p. 138 and claims that Ricardo places his first settlers in the valley, while Carey puts them on the heights (in the sketch on bare crags and impracticable slopes of 45 degrees) he is simply falsely imputing this to Ricardo.[b]

Carey's historical examples, as far as they apply *to America*, are the only useful things in the book. As a Yankee, he himself lived through the process of SETTLEMENTS, could follow it from the

---

[a] manner of speech - [b] The reference is to D. Ricardo, *On the Principles of Political Economy, and Taxation*. See also present edition, Vol. 31.

beginning, and is well posted about it. Nevertheless, there is undoubtedly a lot of uncritical stuff mixed up in it, which would have to be sifted. When he speaks of Europe, however, the structures and the untenableness get under way. And that Carey is not unprejudiced with regard to America is shown by the eagerness with which he attempts to prove the worthlessness, indeed the NEGATIVE value-quality of the uncultivated land (that the land is, so to speak, worth minus 10 dollars an ACRE) and praises the self-sacrifice of societies that, to their own certain ruin, make waste land serviceable for mankind. Related in the country of colossal land jobbery, this becomes ludicrous. Incidentally, he never mentions *prairie land* here, and elsewhere it is touched upon very lightly. The whole story of the negative value-quality of the waste land, and all his calculated proofs are best contradicted by America itself. If the story were true, America would not only be the poorest of countries, but would become *relatively* poorer every year, because more and more labour would be thrown away on this worthless land.

Now, as for his definition of RENT: THE AMOUNT RECEIVED AS RENT IS INTEREST UPON THE VALUE OF LABOUR EXPENDED, *MINUS* THE DIFFERENCE BETWEEN THE PRODUCTIVE POWER (THE RENT-PAYING LAND) AND THAT OF THE NEWER SOILS WHICH CAN BE BROUGHT INTO ACTIVITY BY THE APPLICATION OF THE SAME LABOUR THAT HAS BEEN THERE GIVEN TO THE WORK (pp. 165, 166), this may have a certain amount of validity here and there, within certain limits, especially in America. But RENT is, in any case, such a complicated thing, to which so many other circumstances contribute, that even in these cases it can apply only *ceteris paribus,*[a] only when 2 pieces of land lie *side by side*. Ricardo knew as well as he that INTEREST FOR THE VALUE OF LABOUR EXPENDED is also included in RENT. If Carey declares land as such worse than worthless, then RENT *must* naturally be INTEREST UPON THE VALUE OF LABOUR EXPENDED or theft, as it is called on p. 139. Carey still owes us an explanation of the transition from theft to interest.

It seems to me that the *origin* of rent in different countries, and even in one and the same country, is by no means such a simple process as both Ricardo and Carey imagine. In Ricardo, as I said, this is excusable; it is the history of the fishers and hunters in the sphere of agriculture. It is not, in fact, an economic *dogma,* but Carey wants, furthermore, to make a dogma out of his theory and prove it to the world as such, for which, indeed, historical studies of a very different sort from Mr Carey's are necessary.

---

[a] other things being equal

There may even have been localities where RENT originated as Ricardo suggests, and others where it originated in Carey's way, and yet others where it had quite different origins. To Carey one may also remark that, where fever has to be reckoned with, in particular tropical fever, economics more or less come to an end. Unless his theory of population can be thus interpreted: with the increase in population, the surplus people are forced to cultivate the most fertile, i.e., the most unhealthy stretches of land, in which they either succeed or perish; in this way he would successfully establish harmony between himself and Malthus.

In northern Europe, RENT originated neither in Ricardo's nor in Carey's way, but simply from the feudal burdens, later brought by free competition to their correct economic level. In Italy it was different again, *vide*[a] Rome. To calculate what part of the RENT in the long civilised countries is really original RENT and what part is interest on labour invested is impossible, since it differs in each case. Moreover, it is of no importance, once it has been shown that RENT can also increase without labour being put into land. The grandfather of Sir Humphrey de Trafford at Old Trafford near Manchester had such a load of debts on his back that he had no idea what to do. His grandson, after paying off all the debts, has an income of £40,000 a year. If we subtract about £10,000, which comes from building sites, £30,000 remains as the yearly value of the agricultural ESTATE, which 80 years ago brought in perhaps £2,000. Further, if £3,000 be taken as the interest on invested labour and capital, and that's a lot, there remains an increase of £25,000, which is five times the former value, including IMPROVE-MENTS. And all this, not because labour is contained in it, but because labour was put into something else nearby, since the ESTATE lies close to a city like Manchester, where good prices are paid for milk, butter and garden produce. The same happens on a big scale. From the moment when England became a corn- and cattle-importing country, and even before then, population density became a factor determining or increasing RENT, quite indepen-dently of the labour invested generally in the land of England. Ricardo, with his MOST FAVOURABLY SITUATED LANDS, also considers the relation *to the market*, but Carey ignores this. And if he were then to say: the land itself has only a negative value, but the *location* has a positive value, he would thereby admit what he denies—that land, just because it can be monopolised, has, or *can* have, a value independent of the labour invested. But on this point Carey is as quiet as a mouse.

---

[a] see

It is equally a matter of indifference whether the labour invested in land in civilised countries pays regularly or not. I asserted more than 20 years ago that in today's society no instrument of production exists that could last 60-100 years—no factory, no building, etc.—that, by the end of its existence, has covered the cost of its production.[475] All in all, I still believe this is perfectly true. And if Carey and I are both right, this proves nothing either about the rate of profit or the origin of rent, but simply that bourgeois production, even measured by its own standards, is rotten.

These random comments on Carey will no doubt be enough for you. They are very mixed, because I made no excerpts. As for the historic-materialist-scientific trimmings, their entire value=those two trees, the tree of life and the tree of knowledge, which he has planted in his paradisiacal work, not indeed for his Adam and Eve who have to drudge in the backwoods, but for their descendants. His ignorance and slovenliness are only equalled by the impudence that allows him to present such nonsense publicly.

You will not expect me to read the other chapters. It is pure blather, and the grammatical errors are no longer strewn so closely. I'll send you the book as soon as I go up to town; out here no pillar-box is large enough to take it. Monday or Tuesday.

Wilhelm's sheet is really disgraceful. I am not referring to the free-church-clerical babble,[476] but all the news from their associations, etc., is always 8-14 days old before it is printed. Schweitzer holds a meeting on the *9th* in *Leipzig,* and dispatches triumphal telegrams, which are printed on the *10th* in *Social-Demokrat.*[a] On the *12th* the *Social-Demokrat* states that Liebknecht receives 1,000 thaler from Fränkel the banker.[b] Up to the *17th no reply*!! And we are supposed to take the responsibility for such stupidity and sloppiness.

Tussy will be getting a letter soon.

With best greetings.

Your
F. E.

First published abridged in *Der Briefwechsel zwischen F. Engels und K. Marx,* Bd. 4, Stuttgart, 1913 and in full in *MEGA,* Abt. III, Bd. 4, Berlin, 1931

Printed according to the original

Published in English in full for the first time

---

[a] 'Aus Leipzig geht uns folgendes Telegramm zu...', *Der Social-Demokrat,* No. 132, 10 November 1869 (signed: Petzoldt). - [b] 'Wir constatieren...' (in the column 'Vermischtes'), *Der Social-Demokrat,* No. 133, 12 November 1869.

266

MARX TO ENGELS[477]

IN MANCHESTER

[London,] 26 November 1869

Dear Fred,

This week I have not been really on my feet, and the business under my arm is still a bother. That's why I didn't thank you earlier for the notes on Carey, whose VOLUME I also received yesterday.[a]

In my book against Proudhon, in which I still fully accepted *Ricardo's* theory of RENT, I already explained the fallacies, even from his (Ricardo's) own point of view.[b]

'Ricardo, after postulating bourgeois production as necessary for determining rent, applies the conception of rent, nevertheless, to the landed property of all ages and all countries. This is an error common to all the economists, who represent the bourgeois relations of production as eternal categories.'

Mr Proudhon naturally converts Ricardo's theory into an expression of egalitarian morals at once, and thus discovers in the rent determined by Ricardo:

'an immense *land valuation* which is carried out contradictorily by the proprietors and the farmers ... in a higher interest, and whose ultimate result must be to equalise the possession of the land, etc.'

To this I remarked, *inter alia*:

'For any land valuation based upon rent to be of practical value, the conditions of present society must not be departed from. Now we have shown that the *rent*[c] paid by the farmer to the landowner expresses the *rent*[d] with any exactitude only in the countries most advanced in industry and commerce. Moreover, this rent often includes *interest* paid to the landowner on capital incorporated in land. The location of the land, the nearness of towns, and many other circumstances influence the farm rent and modify the land rent... On the other hand, rent could not be the *invariable* index *of the degree of fertility of the land*, since every moment the modern application of chemistry is changing the nature of the soil, and geological knowledge is just now, in

---

a See this volume, pp. 378-82. - b K. Marx, *The Poverty of Philosophy. Answer to the 'Philosophy of Poverty' by M. Proudhon* (see present edition, Vol. 6, pp. 202-04). Marx quotes in French. - c in the original: le fermage (lease money) - d in the original: la rente

our days, beginning *to revolutionise all the old estimates of relative fertility* ... fertility is not so natural a quality as might be thought; it is closely bound up with the *social relations* of the time.'

As far as the development of cultivation in the UNITED STATES is concerned, Mr Carey ignores even the most familiar facts. For instance, Johnston, the English agricultural chemist, shows in his *Notes* on the UNITED STATES [a]: the agricultural migrants from New England to New York State left worse for better land (better not in Carey's sense of land, which still had to be made first, but in the chemical and also economic sense); the agricultural migrants from New York State who first settled beyond the Great Lakes, SAY IN MICHIGAN FOR INSTANCE, left better for worse land, etc. The settlers in Virginia exploited so abominably the land so suitable both in *location* and *fertility* for tobacco, their main product, that they had to move on to Ohio, where the land was worse for this product (if not also for wheat, etc.). The nationality of the immigrants also made itself felt in their settlements. The people from Norway and from our timber forests selected the rugged northern forest land of Wisconsin; the Yankees in the same territory kept to the prairies, etc.

Prairies, both in the UNITED STATES and Australia, are, IN FACT, a thorn in Carey's flesh. According to him, land not absolutely overgrown with forest is infertile by nature, that is all natural grasslands.

The joke of it is that Carey's two great final conclusions (with regard to the UNITED STATES) directly contradict to his dogma. *First*, as a result of England's diabolical influence, the inhabitants, instead of socially cultivating the good model lands of New England DISSEMINATED to the poorer (!) lands of the West. Thus, a move from better land to worse. (Besides, BY THE BY, Carey's DISSEMINATION, in opposition to association, is all copied from Wakefield.[b]) *Second*, in the south of the UNITED STATES we have the misfortune that the slave-owners (whom Mr Carey, as a harmoniser, defended in all his previous works) take the better land under cultivation too soon and skip the worse. Thus, just what should not happen: starting with the better land! If, with this example, Carey convinces himself that the real cultivators—in this case the slaves—are induced neither by economic reasons, or other reasons OF THEIR OWN, but by *external constraint*, he should have been able to

---

[a] J. F. W. Johnston, *Notes on North America, Agricultural, Economical and Social.* - [b] [E. Wakefield,] *England and America. A Comparison of the Social and Political State of Both Nations.*

count on his own 5 fingers that this occurs in other countries too. According to his theory, cultivation in Europe should have originated in the mountains of Norway and proceeded from there to the Mediterranean countries, instead of marching in the other direction.

Carey tries, by means of an extremely absurd and fantastic theory of money, to conjure up anyway the very disgusting economic fact that, in contrast to all other improved machinery, the *always better* earth-machine, *increases* the cost of its product—at least for a period—instead of *cheapening* it. (This was one of the circumstances that struck Ricardo; but he poked his nose no further than the history of corn prices in England from ABOUT 1780 to 1815.)

As a harmoniser, Carey first proved there was no ANTAGONISM between capitalist and wage labourer. The second step was to show the harmony between landowner and capitalist, and this is done by showing land-ownership *as* being *normal* where it has *not yet* developed. The fact that may, under no circumstances, be mentioned is the great and decisive difference between a colony and an old civilised country: that, in the latter, the mass of the population is excluded by *landed property* from the soil, whether it be fertile or infertile, cultivated or uncultivated; while in the colonies, the land can, RELATIVELY SPEAKING, still be appropriated by the cultivator himself. This may play absolutely no part in the rapid development of the colonies. The disgusting '*property question*', and that in its most disgusting form, would of course put a spoke in the wheel of harmony.

As regards the deliberate distortion that, because in a country with developed production the natural fertility of the soil is an important factor in the production of surplus value (or, as Ricardo says, affects the rate of profit), it follows conversely that the richest and most developed production will be found in those areas most fertile by nature, so it should be higher in Mexico, for example, than New England; I have already answered this in *Capital*, p. 502 et seq.[a]

Carey's only merit is that he asserts, just as one-sidedly, the movement from worse to better land as Ricardo asserts the opposite. In fact, however, soil-types of differing grades of fertility are always cultivated simultaneously, and for this reason the Germans, the Slavs and the Celts very carefully distributed scraps

---

[a] Marx refers to the first German edition of *Capital*, Vol. I (see present edition, Vol. 35).

of land of different types amongst the members of the community; it was this that later made division of the community lands so difficult. As for the development of cultivation in the course of history, this—depending on the circumstances—takes place in both directions simultaneously, and one direction or the other dominates according to the epoch.

The factor that makes the *interest* on the capital invested in the land a component part of *differential rent* is precisely the fact that the landowner receives this interest from capital which not *he,* but the *tenant-farmer* has invested in the land. This FACT, known throughout Europe, is claimed to have no economic existence, because the tenant-farmer system has *not yet* developed in the UNITED STATES. But this fact presents itself in another form there. The LAND JOBBER and not the tenant-farmer is ultimately paid in the *price* he gets for the land, for the capital expended by the tenant-farmer. Indeed, the history of the PIONEERS and the LAND JOBBERS in the UNITED STATES is reminiscent of the worst horrors taking place, for instance, in Ireland.

BUT NOW DAMN CAREY! *VIVAT* FOR O'DONOVAN ROSSA!

Last Tuesday's meeting was very fiery, lively, vehement.[478] Mr MUDDLEHEAD,[a] or the devil knows what he's called—a Chartist, an old friend of Harney's—had foresightedly brought Odger and Applegarth along. On the other hand, Weston and Lucraft were absent, attending an Irish ball. *Reynolds's* had published my RESOLUTIONS[b] in its Saturday issue, together with an ABSTRACT of my SPEECH[c] (as well as Eccarius could do it; he's no stenographer) and *Reynolds's* printed it right on the front page of the paper following opening editorial. This seems to have scared those who are flirting with Gladstone. HENCE the appearance of Odger and A LONG RAMBLING SPEECH OF Mottershead, who got it in the neck badly from Milner (himself an Irishman). Applegarth sat next to me, so did not dare to speak *against*; on the contrary he spoke *for,* obviously with an uneasy conscience. *Odger* said that, if the VOTE were forced, he would have to vote for the RESOLUTIONS. But unanimity was surely better and could be obtained by a few minor MODIFICATIONS etc. Then I declared—since it is precisely *him* I wish to push into a corner—that *he* should present his modifications at the next session! At the last session, although many of our most reliable

---

a Thomas Mottershead - b See this volume, pp. 375-76. - c [Record of Marx's Speech on the Policy of the British Government with Respect to the Irish Prisoners. From the Minutes of the General Council Meeting of 16 November 1869]

mentors were absent, we would thus have declared the resolution against *one single* vote. On Tuesday we shall be IN FULL FORCE. *Salut.*

Your
K. M.

First published in *Der Briefwechsel zwischen F. Engels und K. Marx*, Bd. 4, Stuttgart, 1913   Printed according to the original

267

ENGELS TO MARX[33]

IN LONDON

Manchester, 29 November 1869

Dear Moor,

It is very amusing that Carey is also worthless in the only field in which one might expect that he *must* have a certain knowledge, in the history of the colonisation of the UNITED STATES.[a] After this, *au fond*,[b] the fellow is left with nothing.

The election in Tipperary is an event.[466] It launches the Fenians from empty conspiracies and the fabrication of coups on a path of action that, even if legal in appearance, is still far more revolutionary than what they have done since their abortive INSURRECTION.[479] IN FACT, they are adopting the methods of the French workers, and this is an enormous advance. If only this business is carried on as intended. The fear this new turn has produced amongst philistines, which is now screeching through the whole liberal press, is the best proof that, this time, the nail has been hit on the head. The *Solicitors' Journal* is typical noting with horror that the election of a political prisoner is *unprecedented* in the British realm! *Tant pis*,[c] show me the country *except* England where this doesn't happen every day! The worthy Gladstone must be terribly annoyed.

But you really should look at *The Times* these days. *Three* LEADERS in 8 days either urging the Government to end the excesses

---

[a] See the previous letter. - [b] basically - [c] So much the worse.

of the Irish national press, or in which the Government itself urges this.[a]

I long to hear about your debate tomorrow evening, and about the result, of which there can be no doubt.[b] It would be fine to get Odger into a pickle. I hope that, apart from him, Bradlaugh will stand for Southwark, and it would be much better if he were elected.. Incidentally, if the English workers can't take an example from the peasants of Tipperary, then they are in a bad way.

Here, in the FREE LIBRARY, and the CHETHAM LIBRARY (which you know)[480] I have discovered a mass of very valuable sources (besides the books with SECOND-HAND-INFORMATION), but unfortunately neither Young nor Prendergast,[c] nor the English edition of the Brehon LAW[481] commissioned by the English Government. Wakefield,[d] on the other hand, has put in an appearance again. Also, various things by old Petty. Last week I ploughed through the TRACTS of old Sir John Davies (ATTORNEY GENERAL FOR IRELAND under James)[482]; I don't know whether you've read them, they are the main source, but you've certainly found them quoted 100 times. It's downright shame that the original sources are not everywhere available; one gets infinitely more out of them than from the compilers, who make everything that is clear and simple confused and intricate. The tracts show clearly that, in *Anno 1600,* common ownership of land still *existed IN FULL FORCE* and was cited by Mr Davies in his pleas on the forfeited land in Ulster as evidence that the land did not belong to the individual owners (peasants), and thus [belonged] either to the LORD, who had forfeited it or, from the outset, to the Crown. I've never read anything finer than this plea. Re-allotments were made every two or three years. In another PAMPHLET he describes the income of the chief of the clan in exact detail. I've *never* seen these things quoted, and if you can use them, I'll send you them in detail. At the same time, I've caught out Monsieur Goldwin Smith beautifully.[e] The fellow never read Davies, so makes the most ridiculous assertions to exonerate the English. But I shall catch the fellow.

Today I have not yet been able to set my eyes on the oration of the noble Louis-Napoleon, but only the sweet hopes of the worthy Prévost-Paradol,[483] who imagines he is living once again under

a Apparently the reference is to the leading articles in *The Times* of 23, 25 and 29 November 1869: 'From Our Own Correspondent', Dublin, Nov. 24; Dublin, Nov. 25; Dublin, Nov. 26. - b See this volume, pp. 392-93. - c A. Young, *A Tour in Ireland*; J. P. Prendergast, *The Cromwellian Settlement in Ireland*. - d E. Wakefield, *An Account of Ireland, Statistical and Political*. - e See this volume, p. 374.

Louis-Philippe and that the constitutional millennium will dawn today. INCORRIGIBLE! I wanted to get good old Dido[a] to reply to Tussy's letter this evening, which only arrived today; but the cur has run out into the rain and snow to avoid this duty, and now it is close of post, so Tussy will have to be patient until tomorrow. But she is certainly thinking more about O'Donovan Rossa in Chatham PRISON than about HER OWN OLD CHAP, who has just come in cold and filthy and is also locked up like a CONVICT in the BACK CELLAR.

Best greetings to all.

Your
F. E.

First published abridged in *Der Briefwech-sel zwischen F. Engels und K. Marx*, Bd. 4, Stuttgart, 1913 and in full in *MEGA*, Abt. III, Bd. 4, Berlin, 1931

Printed according to the original

268

MARX TO LUDWIG KUGELMANN[484]

IN HANOVER

London, 29 November 1869

Dear Kugelmann,

ABOUT 5 weeks ago Jennychen sent you a letter[b]—in fact two letters, one to you and one to Madame the Countess.[c] With it she enclosed a portrait of *G. Weerth*—and as this is difficult to replace, and no second one can be sent, Jennychen would like to know as soon as possible whether you received the letter or not.

Some doubts about the inviolability and safety of the postal services have certainly been awakened here because a letter I wrote to Engels from Hanover[d] was undoubtedly opened and then reclosed very CLUMSILY. Engels retained the envelope, so that I could convince myself by ocular inspection.

My long and, to some extent, criminal silence may be explained by the fact that I had to catch up with a mass of work, not simply for my scientific studies, but also *quoad*[e] *International*; in addition to have to grind at *Russian*, as the result of a book sent me from

---

[a] Engels' dog - [b] See this volume, pp. 545-47. - [c] Kugelmann's wife Gertrud - [d] See this volume, pp. 358 and 363. - [e] regarding

St Petersburg on the situation of the working classes (OF COURSE, PEASANTS INCLUDED) in Russia,[a] and, finally, my state of health is by no means satisfactory.

You will probably have seen in the *Volksstaat* the resolutions I proposed regarding Gladstone on the Irish amnesty question.[b] I have now attacked Gladstone—and this has attracted attention here—just as I attacked Palmerston[c] earlier. The demagogic REFUGEES here love to attack the continental despots from a safe distance. I find this only attractive if it is done *vultu instantis tyranni*.[d]

Yet both my appearance on this Irish amnesty issue and, further, my proposal to the GENERAL COUNCIL that it should discuss the attitude of the English working class to Ireland and adopt a resolution on the subject,[e] naturally had other grounds than simply to speak out loudly and decidedly for the OPPRESSED IRISH against their OPPRESSORS.

I have become more and more convinced—and the thing now is to drum this conviction into the English working class—that they will never be able to do anything decisive here in England before they separate their attitude towards Ireland quite definitely from that of the ruling classes, and not only make common cause with the Irish, but even take the initiative in dissolving the UNION[461] established in 1801, and substituting a free federal relationship for it. And this must be done not out of sympathy for Ireland, but as a demand based on the interests of the English proletariat. If not, the English people will remain bound to the leading-strings of the ruling classes, because *they* will be forced to make a common front with them against Ireland. Every movement of the working class in England itself is crippled by the dissension with the Irish, who form a very important section of the working class in England itself. The *primary condition* for emancipation here—the over-throw of the English landed oligarchy—remains unattainable, since its positions cannot be stormed here as long as it holds its strongly-entrenched outposts in Ireland. But over there, once affairs have been laid in the hands of the Irish people themselves, as soon as they have made themselves their own legislators and rulers, as soon as they have become autonomous, it will be infinitely easier there than here to abolish the landed aristocracy (to a large extent *the same persons* as the English LANDLORDS) since in

---

Н. Флеровскій, *Положеніе рабочаго класса въ Россіи.* - [b] K. Marx, *Draft Resolution of the General Council on the Policy of the British Government Towards the Irish Prisoners*; see also this volume, pp. 375-76. - [c] K. Marx, *Lord Palmerston* (see present edition, Vol. 12). - [d] in the face of the tyrant - [e] See this volume, pp. 371-72.

Ireland it is not just merely an economic question, but also a *national* one, as the LANDLORDS there are not, as they are in England, traditional dignitaries and representatives, but the mortally-hated oppressors of the nationality. And not only does England's internal social development remain crippled by the present relationship to Ireland, but also her foreign policy, in particular her policy with regard to Russia and the United States of America.

Since, however, the English working class undoubtedly throws the greatest weight on the scales of social emancipation generally, this is the point where the lever must be applied. It is a fact that the English Republic under Cromwell met shipwreck in— Ireland.[485] *Non bis in idem*[a]*!* The Irish have played a capital joke on the English government by electing the CONVICT FELON O'Donovan Rossa as member of Parliament.[b] Government newspapers are already threatening a renewed suspension of the Habeas Corpus Act,[486] a renewed system of terror! In fact, England never has and never *can* rule Ireland any other way, as long as the present relationship continues—only with the most abominable reign of terror and the most reprehensible corruption.

In France things are going well so far. On the one hand, the outmoded demagogic and democratic bawlers of all shades are compromising themselves. On the other, Bonaparte has been driven along a path of concession on which he is bound to break his neck.

Yesterday's *Observer* (this weekly belongs to the *Ministry*), referring to the Eulenburg scandal[487] in the Prussian Chamber, remarks: 'Napoleon said: "*Grattez le Russe, et vous trouverez le Tartare*"'.[c] With regard to a Prussian it isn't even necessary to scratch—to find a *Russian*.

Apropos. Reich, Dr Med., has the Christian name of Eduard, and appears, from the preface to his book, to live in Gotha.[488] My best wishes to Madame the Countess and Fränzchen.[d]

Your
K. Marx

Couldn't we have the Bielefeld *Freiligrath-Fest-Broschüre?*

First published abridged in *Die Neue Zeit*, Bd. 2, Nr. 13, Stuttgart, 1901-1902 and in full in *Pisma Marksa k Kugelmanu* (Letters of Marx to Kugelmann), Moscow-Leningrad, 1928

Printed according to the original

---

[a] This shall not happen twice! - [b] See this volume, pp. 373, 387-88. - [c] 'Scratch a Russian and you find a Tartar.' - [d] Kugelmann's daughter Franziska

269

MARX TO ENGELS[489]

IN MANCHESTER

[London,] 4 December 1869

DEAR FRED,

The RESOLUTIONS UNANIMOUSLY CARRIED[a] despite Odger's incessant VERBAL AMENDMENTS. I gave in to him on only one point, to omit the word 'DELIBERATE' before 'INSULTS' in para. 1.[b] I did this ON PRETENCE, THAT EVERYTHING A PRIME MINISTER PUBLICLY DID, MUST BE PRESUMED *eo ipso* TO BE *DELIBERATE.* The real reason was that I knew, as soon as the first para. was accepted in substance, all further opposition would be in vain. I'm sending you 2 *National Reformers* containing reports on the 2 first sessions, not yet on the latest. This report, too, is poor, and much is quite wrong (due to misunderstanding), but better than Eccarius' reports in *Reynolds's.* They are by Harris, whose *currence panacea* you will also find in the latest number of the *National Reformer.*[490]

With the exception of Mottershead, who appeared as John Bull, and Odger, who as always acted the diplomat, the English delegates have behaved excellently. The general debate on the attitude of the ENGLISH WORKING CLASS to the IRISH QUESTION begins on Tuesday.[491]

One has to struggle here not only against prejudices, but also against the stupidity and wretchedness of the *Irish* spokesmen in Dublin. *The Irishman* (Pigott) cannot know of the proceedings and RESOLUTIONS solely from *Reynolds's,* to which he subscribes and from which he often quotes. They (the RESOLUTIONS) had already been sent him directly by an Irishman on 17 November.[c] Till today, *deliberately not a word.* The jackass behaved in a similar way during our debate and petition for 3 MANCHESTER MEN.[492] The 'IRISH' QUESTION must be treated as something quite distinct, excluding the outside world, and it must be *concealed* that *English* workers sympathise *with* the Irish! What a dumb ox! And this with regard to the *International,* which has press organs all over Europe and the UNITED STATES! This week he has received the RESOLUTIONS officially, signed by the FOREIGN SECRETARIES. The material has also been sent to the '*People*'.[d] *Nous verrons.*[e] Mottershead subscribes to *The*

---

[a] See this volume, pp. 371-72. - [b] Ibid., p. 375. - [c] In the original: 'December'. - [d] probably *The New-York Irish People* - [e] We shall see.

Irishman and will not fail to use this opportunity to POKE FUN AT THE 'HIGHSOULED' IRISHMEN.

But I'll play a trick on Pigott. I'm writing to Eccarius today, asking him to send the RESOLUTIONS with the signatures, etc., to Isaac Butt, the President of the IRISH WORKING MEN'S ASSOCIATION. Butt is not Pigott.

The following explains to you the enclosed letter from Applegarth:

After the end of the last session, in which he behaved very well, he took me aside and told me the following: AN EMINENT MEMBER OF THE HOUSE OF COMMONS[a] had written to him that he had been commissioned BY AN EMINENT MEMBER OF THE HOUSE OF LORDS (LORD Leachfield!) to ask him whether he had voted for the abolition OF ALL PRIVATE PROPERTY at Basle.[379] His answer was decisive for the attitude towards him of Applegarth's parliamentary patrons. He (Applegarth) wanted to give the fellows a decisive answer, I should write down briefly the '*reasons*', and this the following day. I was very busy, as well as still SUFFERING under the arm; cold made worse by the frightful FOG after the session on Tuesday evening. Thus, wrote to Applegarth on Wednesday[b] that I had been prevented, but READY TO SUPPORT HIM when he received a reply.[493] With English obstinacy he did not accept; wrote enclosed letter.[494] So I was WILLY-NILLY forced to write him 8 closely-written pages, which will give him a lot to pore over about LANDED PROPERTY and the NECESSITY OF ITS ABOLITION.[495] The fellow is very important since, ON THE PART OF BOTH HOUSES OF PARLIAMENT he is the officially recognised representative of the English TRADES UNIONS.

Enclosed, also, a letter from Bracke.[496] I have nothing against Bonhorst; I had only told Kugelmann that I regarded him as a rather revolutionary character. Kugelmann, with his usual tact, informed Bracke of this in amplified form.

Tussy thanks Dido[c] very much for his letter, and sends greetings to all.

Salut.

Your
Moor

First published abridged in *Der Briefwechsel zwischen F. Engels und K. Marx*, Bd. 4, Stuttgart, 1913 and in full in *MEGA*, Abt. III, Bd. 4, Berlin, 1931

Printed according to the original

Published in English in full for the first time

---

[a] apparently A. J. Mundella - [b] 1 December - [c] See this volume, p. 389.

270

ENGELS TO MARX [489]

IN LONDON

Manchester, 9 December 1869

Dear Moor,

In the reports in the *National Reformer*[490] a certain amount of nonsense is, however, attributed to you. They can't get along without something like that. I see, the *Bee-Hive* is ignoring the whole debate. This is called publicity, just like the dear old *Didaskalia für Geist, Gemüt und Publizität.*

I half expected what happened with *The Irishman.* Ireland still remains the *sacra insula,*ᵃ whose aspirations may not be lumped together with the profane class struggle of the rest of the sinful world. Partly, this is certainly an honest madness of these people, but equally certainly it is partly a calculated policy on the part of the spokesmen in order to maintain their domination over the peasants. In addition, a nation of peasants is always forced to take its literary representatives from among the bourgeoisie of the towns and its ideologists, and here Dublin (I mean *Catholic* Dublin) is approximately to Ireland what Copenhagen is to Denmark. For these gentry, however, the whole labour movement is pure heresy, and the Irish peasant must not be allowed to find out that the socialist workers are his sole allies in Europe.

In other respects, too, the *Irishman* is very scurvy this week. If it was ready to retreat *in this way* at the first threat of SUSPENSION of the Habeas Corpus Act,[486] then the sabre-rattling was absolutely misplaced from the start. And now even the fear that still more political prisoners might be elected! On the one hand, the Irish are warned, quite rightly, not to let themselves be inveigled into any illegalities; on the other, they should be held back from doing the only lawful thing that is opportune and revolutionary in character, the only thing that might successfully break with the established practice of electing place-hunting lawyers and might impress the English liberals. Pigott is obviously afraid that others could outstrip him here.

Of course you will remember how O'Connell, also, always incited the Irish against the Chartists, although—or just because— they had inscribed REPEAL[497] on their banner.

ᵃ sacred isle

The question put to Applegarth is delicious. One sees how these trumpery lords and M.P.s imagine that the whole labour movement is already in their pockets because Odger and Potter flirt with them and the *Bee-Hive* has been sold. The gentlemen are in for a surprise. In the meantime, it's a good thing that a new election is not, apparently, in the immediate offing; the gentlemen have to make fools of themselves first. Applegarth[494] and Bracke[496] returned enclosed.

From the enclosed query from Solingen you will see all the things I'm supposed to afford.[498] What should be done in this case? If I send the people 50-100 thaler it will not help them, and I can't risk more for them since, in the long run, it will certainly be throwing money away. What is your opinion?

The worthy gentlemen from *tiers parti*[a] believe they already occupy the ministerial chairs, and have already made wonderful fools of themselves. They vote gaily for the vindication of the prefects of Monsieur de Forcade Laroquette.[499] In this way I cannot see why any sort of ministerial change is necessary, if everything the present ministers have done is ALL RIGHT. On the other hand, Louis[b] certainly believes that he has now once again so frightened the bourgeois with the red spectre that he can get away with phrases. The business is entangling itself quite nicely.

What scurvy knaves the Prussians are. Scarcely has an apparently constitutional wind begun to blow from Paris, when they immediately start making small concessions. Eulenberg takes over, in the state budget, the proxy costs of the deputies who are state officials, etc. And for this Camphausen diddles the Chamber out of $8^2/_3$ million annually, which previously, by law, *had to be* devoted to eliminating debts, and on the other hand he now abolishes the *amortissement*, except where the *Government* and the Chamber decree that there should be redemption. The stupid Liberals *themselves demanded* this earlier and must now vote for it.

China, with the steady expansion of her market, appears to wish to save the COTTON TRADE once again, at least for a while. The reports from there are considerably better, though much has been consigned there, and since then there has again been a veering-round here, and once again work is going swingingly. This will naturally drive up the cotton price again, and the whole profit will go into the pockets of the importer. But at least they are working here without losses.

With Gottfried[c] I am now completely in the clear. Yesterday he

---

[a] the third party - [b] Napoleon III - [c] Gottfried Ermen

paid me the last remainder of my money,[a] and we shall now probably more or less show each other our backsides.
Best greetings.

Your
F. E.

How anxious Bracke is not to give an opinion about people whom he should know very well. Also appears to have more good nature than resolution.

First published abridged in *Der Briefwechsel zwischen F. Engels und K. Marx*, Bd. 4, Stuttgart, 1913 and in full in *MEGA*, Abt. III, Bd. 4, Berlin, 1931

Printed according to the original

Published in English in full for the first time

271

MARX TO ENGELS[489]

IN MANCHESTER

London, 10 December 1869

Dear Fred,

D'abord,[b] about the Solingen business.[498] (Are £2 necessary here? I think only one.)

These people have BOTHERED *me*, the CENTRAL COUNCIL,[73] the *Basle Congress* etc., with their APPEALS. They themselves admit that their productive cooperative is only of *local* interest. How can they expect foreign countries to contribute a SINGLE FARTHING to them, in view of the *international* sacrifices that the STRIKES, etc., cost, and of the tribulations of hundreds of French and English production cooperatives? They have seen what benefit they have gained from *Becker's enthusiastic appeals*.[c]

On the other hand: these Solingen people are supporters for *you and me* in the Rhine Province. They belonged (THE LEADERS) to the

---

^a See this volume, p. 299. - ^b First of all - ^c Marx has in mind the appeals for aid to the Solingen cooperative issued by the Central Committee of the German language sections: 'Rundschreiben des Zentralkomite's der Sektionsgruppe deutscher Sprache an die Sektionen und mitgenössischen Gesellschaften', *Der Vorbote*, No. 11, November 1868; 'Mahnruf. An unsere Bundesgenossen und die Arbeiter und Arbeitervereine aller Länder', *Der Vorbote*, No. 10, October 1869.

League.[118] Under Lassalle's lordly sway, when Marquis Izzy[a] was in Cologne, the same Karl Klein announced a TOAST for us,[500] the editors of the *Neue Rheinische Zeitung*, and Izzy was forced *de faire bonne mine à mauvais jeu*.[b] Further, their cooperative was solid and maintained itself for years. The stupidity of the Prussian legislation forced them to *fix* their capital and thus reduce their *working capital*. Then the Rhenish bourgeois became irritable and decided to break them up, partly *by selling their* OBLIGATIONS, and partly by *withdrawing all* COMMERCIAL ADVANCES (not based on OBLIGATIONS).

Thus, the business is of general importance and, for us, personal importance.

What I suggest is this:

You send the fellows 50 *thaler for* OBLIGATIONS, and tell them, at the same time, that they must themselves see you can do *nothing* for them among the English bourgeois in Manchester. Tell them as well—and this is a FACT—that *I* in London have made *all possible efforts on their behalf, but in vain*. Finally, tell them—and I shall try this *immediately*—that I shall try to raise money for them among the *German bourgeois*. I shall—naturally you will *not* tell them this—write immediately to Menke in Hamburg to this end. It is possible that Menke (who is a millionaire, and has read *Capital*[c] from beginning to end, and furnished it with 'correcting notes', which he himself showed me) will do something. 2,000 thaler are nothing to such people. They would naturally, *d'abord*, SEND SOMEBODY TO Solingen to look at how the thing works. If the business is *not capable of surviving*, it *should not and may not* receive support. If the contrary, then *I am certain* that these people (Menke *et* Co.) will provide the money.

A d   v o c e m[d]: IRISH QUESTION. I did not attend the CENTRAL COUNCIL last Tuesday.[e] My 'FAMILY' did not allow me to go in this FOG and in my PRESENT STATE OF HEALTH, although I had undertaken TO OPEN THE DEBATES.

With regard to the report in the *National Reformer*,[f] not only has nonsense been attributed to me, but even what is *rightly* reported is *incorrectly* reported. But I didn't want to complain. *D'abord*, I would, thereby, offend the REPORTER (Harris). Second, as long as I don't interfere, all these reports are in no way official. If I correct something, I admit the rest is right—yet everything is wrong the

---

[a] Ferdinand Lassalle - [b] to grin and bear it - [c] K. Marx, *Capital*, Vol. I (see present edition, Vol. 35). - [d] As to - [e] 7 December - [f] See this volume, pp. 392 and 394.

way it is reproduced. BESIDES, *I have reasons* not to convert these reports into *legal EVIDENCE against me,* which happens the moment I *correct details.*

The way I shall express the matter next Tuesday is: that, quite apart from all 'international' and 'humane' phrases about *JUSTICE FOR IRELAND*—which are taken for granted on the *INTERNATIONAL COUNCIL*—it is in *the direct and absolute interests of the ENGLISH WORKING CLASS TO GET RID OF THEIR PRESENT CONNEXION WITH IRELAND.* I am fully convinced of this, for reasons that, in part, I can*not* tell the English workers themselves. For a long time I believed it would be possible to overthrow the Irish regime by ENGLISH WORKING CLASS ASCENDANCY. I always took this viewpoint in the *New-York Tribune.*[501] Deeper study has now convinced me of the opposite. The English WORKING CLASS will *never accomplish anything* BEFORE IT HAS GOT RID OF IRELAND. The lever must be applied in Ireland. This is why the Irish QUESTION is so important for the social movement in general.

I have read a lot of *Davies*[a] in extracts. The book itself I have only glanced through superficially in the Museum,[b] so you would oblige me if you would copy out for me the passages relating to COMMON PROPERTY. You *must* get hold of *Curran's 'Speeches' edited by Davies (London: James Duffy, 22 Paternoster Row).* I meant to give it to you when you were in London. It is now circulating among the English MEMBERS OF THE CENTRAL COUNCIL, and God knows when I shall see it again. For the period 1779-1800 (Union[461]) it is of decisive importance, not only because of *Curran's 'Speeches'* (namely *in court;* I regard *Curran* as the *sole great lawyer* (people's advocate) of the 18th century, and the *noblest personality,* while *Grattan* was a parliamentary rogue), but because you find *all the sources* about the *UNITED IRISHMEN.*[462] This period is of the greatest interest, SCIENTIFICALLY AND DRAMATICALLY. First, the dirty infamies of the English in 1588-89 repeated (perhaps even intensified) in 1788-89. Second, class movement is easily shown in the Irish movement itself. *Third,* the infamous policy of Pitt. *Fourth,* which very much irks Messrs the English, the proof that Ireland came to grief because IN FACT, FROM A REVOLUTIONARY STANDPOINT, *the Irish were too far advanced for the ENGLISH KING AND CHURCH MOB,* while, on the other hand, English reaction in England (as in Cromwell's time) had its roots in the subjugation of Ireland. *This period* must be described in at least one chapter[502]: a pillory for John Bull!

Enclosed something French—and, as a contrast, Freiligrath-ish!

---

[a] J. Davies, *Historical Tracts.* - [b] the British Museum Library

I would be glad if you would send the money for the next quarter as *soon as possible.*

Apropos. Tussy has undertaken A FOOLISH WORK, embroidering a sofa cushion for you for Christmas. I don't believe she will be finished before the New Year. She allows neither Mama, nor Jennychen, nor Lenchen to sew a single stitch, so she has done *nothing* else for weeks. This is, however, *a great secret,* and you must naturally *not give the slightest* hint that you know about it. Tussy would eat me alive.

COMPLIMENTS TO MRS LIZZY.

Your

K. Moor

Of the French stuff I am sending you, *Gaulois*—half Bonapartist, half opposition—is STUPID. *Père Duchêsne* will astonish you by its impudence. And in such a STATE OF THINGS the bitch Eugénie dares to push herself forward [503]? She really wants to get hanged.

Apropos. The translation of *Capital* GOES ON.[441] Keller has now interrupted it, however. He wants to publish *18th Brumaire*[a] first, believing this possible under the present circumstances and important for France.

As for the current *Irish movement,* 3 important factors: 1. opposition to lawyers and TRADING POLITICIANS and BLARNEY; 2. opposition to the dictates of the priests who (*the higher ones*) are TRAITORS, as in O'Connell's time, just as in 1798-1800; 3. the emergence of the AGRICULTURAL LABOURING CLASS against the FARMING CLASS ON THE LAST MEETINGS.[b] (Similar phenomenon from 1795 to 1800.)

The *Irishman* only made its way owing to the suppression of the FENIAN PRESS. For a long time it stood IN OPPOSITION TO Fenianism. Luby, etc., OF THE *Irish People* were educated people who treated religion as a bagatelle. The government cast them into prison, and then came the Pigotts *et* Co. The *Irishman* will only continue to amount to anything until those people come out of prison. He knows this, though he is now squeezing POLITICAL CAPITAL out of declarations on behalf of the 'FELON CONVICTS'.

First published abridged in *Der Briefwechsel zwischen F. Engels und K. Marx,* Bd. 4, Stuttgart, 1913 and in full in *MEGA,* Abt. III, Bd. 4, Berlin, 1931

Printed according to the original

Published in English in full for the first time

---

[a] K. Marx, *The Eighteenth Brumaire of Louis Bonaparte* - [b] 'From Our Correspondent. Dublin, November 30' (in the 'Ireland' column), *The Times,* 1 December 1869; 'Great Excitement' (from the Belfast papers), *The Irishman,* 4 December.

272

MARX TO ENGELS

IN MANCHESTER

[London,] 12 December 1869

DEAR FRED,

Just before the close of post I saw the letter from the Solingen people lying next to me; so I had forgotten to enclose it for you yesterday, which I do herewith.[a]

Also a proof, sent me by Beesly, but the continuation of it is missing. The page with the portraits— *Paris*—belongs to Jennychen, so you must return it after PERUSAL.

Salut.

Your
Moor

Various resolutions will be taken about the *Bee-Hive, d'abord*[b] in order to register them in our Minutes Book, and then to publish them *when there is an opportunity.*[c]

First published in *MEGA*, Abt. III, Bd. 4, Berlin, 1931

Printed according to the original

Published in English for the first time

273

ENGELS TO MARX

IN LONDON

Manchester, 13 December 1869

Dear Moor,

Enclosed—what I have discovered from Davies[d] and otherwise about Irish land ownership ABOUT 1600. The post will be closing immediately, so I must keep things short today.

---

[a] See this vólume, pp. 395, 396-97. - [b] first - [c] See this volume, pp. 497-98. - [d] J. Davies, *Historical Tracts.*

About the Solingen people—ALL RIGHT. From the start it was my opinion that *both of us* had a special interest in the people.[a] I shall probably go to Barmen next week, as my mother simply insists I spend a Christmas at home again, and this time it is very possible that I shall travel to Solingen and see the people myself. Correction of incorrect reports would naturally be of no help.[b] It would have to be done every week.

I have the Curran[c] here, in an edition that is probably much more complete, but I suppose I shall be glad also to acquire the new edition. For the time being I have enough to do with the early history up to 1660, and as soon as I'm finished with that, the period 1782-1800 will naturally be my main interest. First of all, however, I want to finish off the old stuff, particularly since I have found that the original positions between 1172-1600 are everywhere represented completely falsely, and I am only slowly discovering the original sources.

Not heard anything about Prendergast yet[d]? This book will soon be indispensable to me, or its lack will become very *gênant.*[e] More tomorrow.

Your
F. E.

First published in *Der Briefwechsel zwischen F. Engels und K. Marx*, Bd. 4, Stuttgart, 1913

Printed according to the original

Published in English for the first time

274

ENGELS TO MARX[504]

IN LONDON

Manchester, 16 December 1869

Dear Moor,

Enclosed—the desired remittance. This time I have been able to make it one hundred pounds, since a minor error to my

---

[a] See this volume, pp. 395, 396-97. - [b] Ibid., pp. 397-98. - [c] J. Ph. Curran, *The Speeches of the Right Honorable John Philpot Curran*, 2nd edition, Dublin, 1855. - [d] J. P. Prendergast, *The Cromwellian Settlement of Ireland.* - [e] painful

disadvantage was found in the last accounts, and Sir Godfrey[a] had to make it good to me subsequently—IT WILL COME IN FOR CHRISTMAS.

That damned Giraldus Cambrensis dances before me like a will-o'-the-wisp. I must get the fellow, since he is the first foreign, that is to say first authentic, source on the state of Ireland on the arrival of the English, and the quotations I have seen lead me to believe that I shall find something more. The book, called *Hibernia expugnata,*[b] is nowhere to be found, but the first part, which interests me, is in the *Frankfurt* (!) edition of Camden's *Britannia,*[c] I don't know whether in another edition. This edition is naturally *not* here; an English edition in the FREE LIBRARY does not contain Giraldus[505]; the third volume of another edition in the lending library which *might* contain it is lost, and thus my only hope is the Chetham LIBRARY,[480] to which I shall go tomorrow. Incidentally, this hunt for sources is quite a different sort of pleasure than it was to hunt for customers on the blasted stock exchange.

Are Petty's *Political Anatomy of Ireland* and *Political Survey of Ireland* two different works, or only different editions? For the latter is here.

I have here a later edition of Kane's book; the one from you is unfortunately of little use because of its age (1846).[506]

I am making a written record of each period as soon as I have fairly finished my studies. Then you have the interrelations more clearly in your head and, altogether, a more vivid idea of the business, and can still make corrections. That is why, on the whole, I am keeping so strictly to the historic periods in arranging the order in which I plough through sources. I am nearly finished up to 1600.

On the side, I am reading Grant's CAMPAIGN AGAINST Richmond by Cannon.[d] Grant is a self-willed jackass who had so little confidence in himself and his army that he never dared undertake the simplest flanking manoeuvre against Lee, who was weaker by half, before he had weakened him by several days of frontal attack and had nailed him down in his original position. He relied upon the simple calculation that if he lost three men for every one of Lee's, then Lee would run out of people before he did. Nowhere else have there been such brutal butcheries as on that occasion. It was

---

[a] Gottfried Ermen - [b] Giraldus Cambrensis, *Topographia hibernica et expugnatio hibernica.* In: *Giraldi Cambrensis Opera,* Vol. V. - [c] G. Camdenus, *Britannia, sive florentissimorum regnorum Anglioe, Scotœ, Hiberniœ, et insularum adiacentium ex intima antiquitate.* - [d] J. Cannon, *History of Grant's Campaign for the Capture of Richmond (1864-1865).*

the day-long skirmishes in the forests that cost so many lives; the wooded terrain made detours very difficult, and this is Grant's only excuse.

Best greetings to the LADIES.

Your
F. E.

First published in *Der Briefwechsel zwischen F. Engels und K. Marx*, Bd. 4, Stuttgart, 1913

Printed according to the original

Published in English in full for the first time

275

MARX TO ENGELS

IN MANCHESTER

London, 17 December 1869

DEAR FRED,

BEST THANKS for £ 100.[a] Yesterday I couldn't acknowledge because of the sudden appearance of Strohn. The poor fellow had his blood relapse again in May. Because of his health, he has had to hang around since then in Switzerland, etc.; looks very poorly and is very peevish. The doctors recommend him to marry. Strohn will be returning from here to Bradford, and desires you to return him the *Urnings* or whatever the paederast's book is called.[b]

As soon as he goes (on Monday) I shall myself buzz around town to raise the *Prendergast.*[c] I couldn't do it last week because of the filthy weather, which I couldn't risk TO UNDERGO in my not-yet-restored state of health. I remember vaguely that, in his introduction, *Prendergast* depicts the Anglo-Norman period, it seems to me, in fantastic-uncritical-optimistic radiant colours. The book must be obtained for you also to consult for the first period. Our Irish resolutions[d] have been sent to all TRADES UNIONS that maintain ties with us. Only one has protested, A SMALL BRANCH OF THE CURRIERS, saying they are political and not WITHIN the sphere of action of the COUNCIL. We are sending a deputation to enlighten

---

[a] See the previous letter. - [b] K. H. Ulrichs, 'Argonauticus'. *Zastrow und die Urninge des pietistischen, ultramontanen und freidenkenden Lagers.* - [c] J. P. Prendergast, *The Cromwellian Settlement of Ireland.* - [d] See this volume, pp. 375-76.

them. Mr Odger has now noticed how useful it was for him to vote *for* the RESOLUTIONS despite all sorts of diplomatic objections. As a result, the 3-4,000 Irish electors in Southwark have promised him their votes.

From the enclosed *Égalité,* which I must have back, you'll see how impudent *il Signor* Bakunin is becoming.[507] This fellow now has control over 4 organs of the *International* (*Égalité, Progrès* in Locle, *Federacion,* Barcelona, and *Eguaglianza,* NAPLES). He is trying to gain a foothold in Germany through alliance with *Schweitzer,* and in Paris through flattery for the newspaper *Le Travail.* He believes the moment has come to start an open squabble with us. He is playing himself up as the guardian of real proletarianism. But he's in for a surprise. Next week (luckily the Central Council[a] has adjourned until the Tuesday[b] after New Year's Day, so we on the SUBCOMMITTEE are free to work without the *cosy* intervention of the English) we shall be sending a threatening MISSIVE to the Romance Federal Committee[c] in Geneva, and since the gentlemen know (incidentally a major part, perhaps the greater part are *against* Bakunin) that, according to the resolutions of the last Congress, we can *suspend* them if necessary,[508] they will consider the matter twice.

The main point on which our MISSIVE turns is this: the only representation with regard to us of the *branches romandes en Suisse*[d] is the *Federal Committee* there. They have to dispatch their *demandes* and *reprimandes* to us PRIVATELY, through their secretary, *Perret.* They have absolutely no right TO ABDICATE THEIR FUNCTIONS INTO THE HANDS OF THE *Égalité* (a NON-EXISTENCE *for us*), and to expect the Central Council to get involved in public explanations and polemics with this *remplaçant.* Whether or not the *rejoinders* of the General Council are published in the organs of the international branches, the whole thing depends on the decision of the General Council, which alone is *directly* responsible to the Congress. At this opportunity, blows will fall upon certain intrigants who are usurping undue authority, and who wish to subject the *International* to their private control.

Regarding the tumult of the Cossacks[e] about the *Bulletin,* the matter is as follows:

It was decided at the Brussels Congress[138] that we should publish 'IN THE SEVERAL LANGUAGES' bulletins on STRIKES etc., '*AS OFTEN AS ITS*

(*THE GENERAL COUNCIL*) *MEANS PERMIT*'.[509] But on the condition that we, for our part, received reports, documents, etc., from the FEDERAL *comités* at least every 3 months. Since we have received neither these reports nor the MEANS to print reports, this resolution naturally remained a dead letter. In fact, it became superfluous as a result of the founding of numerous international newspapers, which exchange with one another (*Bee-Hive* as register of English STRIKES, etc.).

At the Congress in Basle,[379] the question was raked up again. The Congress treated the Brussels resolutions on the *Bulletin* as NON-EXISTENT. Otherwise, it would simply have charged the Central Council with carrying them out (which would, once again, without the provision of MEANS, have remained a *lettre morte*[a]). At issue was a bulletin in a different sense (not, as before, a *resumé* of STRIKES, etc., but RATHER GENERAL REFLEXIONS ON THE MOVEMENT). The Congress *did not*, however, *come to a vote* on this point. There is, therefore, at present *no* resolution IN THIS QUESTION. But what a marvellous policy it would be to inform the public, through an open reply to *Égalité* that, at an earlier date, the Brussels resolutions remained *unfeasible*, 1. because the MEMBERS did not pay their PENCE, and 2. because the FEDERAL *comités* did not perform their functions!

With regard to Schweitzer, Mr Bakunin, who understands German, knows that Schweitzer and his gang *do not* belong to the International. He knows that Schweitzer *publicly rejected* Liebknecht's offer to appoint the General Council as arbiter.[294] His interrogation is all the more villainous since his friend Ph. Becker, the president of the German language groups,[510] sits on the Geneva *FEDERAL COUNCIL*, in order to give them the necessary information there. His aim is simply to gain a grip on Schweitzer. *Mais il verra!*[b]

I have written fully to De Paepe[c] about the affair (to lay before the Brussels Central Committee).

As soon as a Russian gets a foothold, there is the devil to pay.

Borkheim has now plunged into Turkish.

Will you be going to Germany?

Salut.

Your
K. M.

First published in *Der Briefwechsel zwischen F. Engels und K. Marx*, Bd. 4, Stuttgart, 1913

Printed according to the original
Published in English for the first time

---

[a] dead letter - [b] But he will see! - [c] See this volume, pp. 406 and 413-14.

1870

276

MARX TO HERMANN JUNG

IN LONDON

[London,] 8 January 1870

My dear Jung,

First Shaw's[511] *funérailles*, afterwards other incidents have prevented me from sending you earlier the 'missive' to Geneva.[a]

There are *des changements*[b] in the text—I have struck away, I have added some sentences, and very often corrected the phraseology.

Hence you must copy the thing anew (as quickly as possible) so that the text I send to day to Bruxelles be conform with that sent to Geneva. As soon as you have done, put the thing into the hands of Dupont.

With compliments to your family

Yours truly
Karl Marx

I have, besides the copy of the Geneva 'missive', made a full report to the Bruxelles Comité[512] '*pour les encourager*' *et aussi un peu*[c] to show them the theoretical nonsense preached at Geneva.

First published in: Marx and Engels, *Works*, First Russian Edition, Vol. XXVI, Moscow, 1935

Reproduced from the original

---

[a] K. Marx, *The General Council to the Federal Council of Romance Switzerland*. -
[b] changes - [c] 'to encourage them' and also partly

277

ENGELS TO MARX

IN LONDON

Manchester, 9 January 1870

Dear Moor,

A Happy New Year!

I arrived back here at midday on Thursday, after thoroughly wrecking my stomach in Barmen with innumerable guzzlings.[513] The people there are overjoyed, that is, the philistines are. The danger of war has now been finally overcome; Louis-Napoleon has once again finely maintained his superior wisdom through prudent compliance.[514] Bismarck is once again able to work, confidence is returning, COMMERCE *must* improve, and so 1870 must be an extremely blessed year for the honest German duffers. I cannot grasp how these people manage to take leave of more of their senses every year.

Hühnerbein, the old tailor and general of the revolution, was very pleased to see me. He still has a complete set of the *Neue Rheinische Zeitung* bound in red, which is good to know. He sends greetings; he has two very pretty daughters.

I did not go to Solingen [a] for the following reasons:

1. It would have been very difficult for me to get away for a day at HOLIDAY time;

2. I could not very well have asked for a closer look at the business without contributing a larger sum myself, which was not possible and

3. as a Party friend, I would have been forced to take the people's word for some things, and not to have insisted so strictly, like a *complete stranger*, on the presentation of all documents and SECURITIES; and Menke, as a result of *my* report, would perhaps refrain from sending anyone, and thus load me with a responsibility I would prefer to decline.

Now I shall wait for your reply and then write to the people.[b]

If I hadn't been so wrecked and, in addition, worried about Lizzie, whom I left unwell, and from whom I heard nothing all the time, I would have dropped in on you on the return journey.

Read practically no newspapers the whole time, but I see that

---

[a] See this volume, p. 401. - [b] Ibid., pp. 420-21.

the Hatzfeldt, through Mende, has laid an interdict on Schweitzer[515]; things must be all over for Schweitzer soon. I shall presumably get details through you from the papers.

In Cologne I visited Klein[a] for a few moments. Was very cool; these people become so philistinised that we appear to really bother them. They now have an anti-ultramontane association, naturally including Cherethites and Pelethites[b] (which means Cretans and Philistines according to Ewald's translation).

Best greetings.

Your
F. E.

First published abridged in *Der Briefwechsel zwischen F. Engels und K. Marx*, Bd. 4, Stuttgart, 1913 and in full in *MEGA*, Abt. III, Bd. 4, Berlin, 1931

Printed according to the original
Published in English for the first time

278

ENGELS TO MARX[180]

IN LONDON

Manchester, 19 January 1870

Dear Moor,

I hope you are having a better time with the infamous carbuncle following the lancing.[c] It's a ghastly business. Keep on with the arsenic till all the symptoms have disappeared, and *then for at least another 3 months.* I shall go to Gumpert in the next few days and ask him for his opinion,[d] but be so good as to let me know first for how long you stopped taking the arsenic, and when you began again, so I can answer his very first question.

I would have thought you really must realise that in the interests of your 2nd volume,[41] too, you need a change of life-style. If there is a constant repetition of such suspensions, you will never get finished; with an increase in movement in fresh air, which will keep off the carbuncles, then sooner or later.

---

[a] Johann Jacob Klein - [b] 2 Samuel 8:18; 15:8 - [c] See this volume, pp. 551, 552. - [d] Ibid., p. 551.

Unfortunately, now that I can no longer call upon the packers in the WAREHOUSE I haven't such opportunities for sending wine as formerly. I must wait, as with Brauneberger, until I find a ready-packed crate, or depend somehow or other on chance. That is why the small crate of port I am sending you today, has proved so slim. It is an old butter crate from Renshaws; I could not get more than 5 bottles in the narrow space, and the thin boards would not have stood more weight. It should keep you going for a while, however.

The Peter Bonaparte business is a bang-up inauguration for the new era in Paris.[516] Louis[a] is *décidément*[b] unlucky. For the bourgeois a very rude awakening from the illusion that the whole foundation of corruption and dirty work, carefully and slowly constructed over eighteen years, would disappear immediately noble Ollivier took over the helm. Constitutional Government with such a Bonaparte, such generals, prefects, police and Decembrists! The anxiety of the fellows, I mean the bourgeois, is nowhere more clearly expressed than in Prévost-Paradol's letter in Monday's *Times*.[517]

The worst part of this business is that Rochefort thereby acquires a quite exaggerated nimbus. To be sure, though, the official Republicans are also a miserable lot.

John Bright deserves congratulations. The poor fellow is so helpless in his new and elevated situation that, despite all discretion, he promises the Irish FREE LAND and OPENING OF THE PRISON DOORS.[518] The latter naturally only to revoke it the following day, as soon as the slightest attempt is made to take him at his word. As far as FREE LAND is concerned, this was already—in Bright's sense, *à la* FREE TRADE—introduced by the ENCUMBERED ESTATES COURT.

I have at last discovered a copy of Prendergast[c] in a local library, and hope to be able to obtain it. To my good or bad fortune, the ancient Irish laws[481] are now also appearing, and I shall have to wade through these as well. The more I study the subject, the clearer it becomes to me that, as a result of the English invasion, Ireland was cheated of its whole development, and thrown back centuries. And this ever since the 12th century; neither should it be forgotten, of course, that 300 years of invasion and plunder by the Danes had already dragged the country considerably backwards; but this had ceased more than 100 years earlier.

---

[a] Napoleon III - [b] decidedly - [c] J. P. Prendergast, *The Cromwellian Settlement of Ireland.*

In recent years there has been rather more criticism in Irish research, particularly in Petrie's antiquarian studies[a]; he also forced me to read some Celtic-Irish (naturally with a parallel translation). It doesn't seem all that difficult, but I shan't delve deeper into the stuff; I'm already hobbled with enough philological nonsense. In the next few days, when I get the book, I'll see how the ancient laws have been dealt with.

I congratulate you on your progress in Russian. You will charm Borkheim, and it is also a good thing because mine has nearly all become very rusty again, and if you let yours become rusty again, then I shall have to start once more.

Best greetings to your wife and the girls. Lafargue is in a really frightful hurry.[b]

Your
F. E.

First published abridged in *Der Briefwechsel zwischen F. Engels und K. Marx*, Bd. 4, Stuttgart, 1913 and in full in *MEGA*, Abt. III, Bd. 4, Berlin, 1931

Printed according to the original

Published in English in full for the first time

279

MARX TO ENGELS

IN MANCHESTER

[London,] 22 January 1870

Dear Fred,

I am only writing you THESE FEW LINES today, since my left arm is under bandages and POULTICES, that is to say, not under my command.

The business was an ABSCESS connected with the GLANDS. In addition, a few other little things, which were put in order yesterday by being lanced. Today, everything in best progress; the doctor was fully satisfied.

The port, which arrived yesterday, is doing me a great service.

You should not imagine that I have learned so much Russian IN A

---

[a] G. Petrie, *The Ecclesiastical Architecture of Ireland, Anterior to the Anglo-Norman Invasion*. In: *The Transactions of the Royal Irish Academy*, Vol. XX. - [b] See this volume, p. 551.

FEW WEEKS; I won't say as much as you have forgotten, but as much as would remain to you had you forgotten three times as much. I am still a beginner.

So Herzen is dead. Just about time I finished *Тюрьма* etc.[519] Plenty of things have happened in the 'International', especially with regard to Bakunin's intrigues.[507] But too long to write about now.

The Paris MOVEMENTS are amusing.[a] Since Ollivier is also a FREE TRADER, he is naturally a man after the heart of the English philistine, who always forgets that what suits him must be, *prima facie*,[b] DISGUSTING to French Frenchmen.

MY COMPLIMENTS TO MRS Lizzie AND ALL OF THEM.

Your
Moor

What do you say to the clever-clever stuff in *Zukunft*, by means of which they attempt to push themselves out of the purely political camp!

Apropos. I still have a little note from Liebknecht[520] which arrived for you during your absence from England. But I can't look it out now amongst the mess of papers. Next time.

First published abridged in *Der Briefwechsel zwischen F. Engels und K. Marx*, Bd. 4, Stuttgart, 1913 and in full in *MEGA*, Abt. III, Bd. 4, Berlin, 1931

Printed according to the original

Published in English for the first time

280

MARX TO CÉSAR DE PAEPE[48]

IN BRUSSELS

London, 24 January 1870

Dear citizen De Paepe,

I am writing to you WITH SOME DIFFICULTY, as my left arm is bandaged. At the end of last month, an abscess of the gland began to form near the armpit. I neglected the thing, and I am punished for my sin. Several days after I sent the letter to Brussels,[512] the

---

[a] See this volume, p. 409. - [b] immediately

pain became intolerable and I fell into the hands of doctors. I underwent two operations, and I feel better, but I am still being treated and must stay at home.

In the first place, I am writing this letter to ask you a personal favour. You probably know that a part of the English bourgeoisie has formed a sort of LAND LEAGUE[521] against the workers' LAND AND LABOUR LEAGUE.[451] Their ostensible purpose is to transform English landed property into small-lot property, and to create a peasantry for the greater benefit of the people. Their real purpose is an attack against landed aristocracy. They want to throw land in free circulation in order to transfer it in this way from the hands of LANDLORDS into those of capitalists. To this effect, they published a series of popular tracts under the title of *Cobden Treaties*, in which small-scale property is painted in rosy colours. Their great battle-horse is *Belgium* (principally the *Flemings*). It would appear that in that country the peasants live under paradisiacal conditions. They established contact with Mr Laveleye who provides them with facts for their rhetoric. In the meantime, as I treat of landed property in Volume Two of *Capital*,[187] I believe it useful to go into some detail there on the structure of landed property in Belgium and of Belgian agriculture.[522] Will you have the goodness to send me the *titles of the principal books* which I must consult[523]?

My illness has naturally prevented me from attending the General Council[a] in the last weeks. Yesterday evening, the subcommittee (the executive committee) of which I am a member visited me. Among other things, they communicated to me the content of a letter sent by Mr Hins to Stepney. As Stepney believed that I would be able to attend the session of the General Council (on 25 January), he did not communicate to me any extracts from that letter. I do not know any of it except from hearsay.[524]

In the first place, it is probably believed in Brussels that the catastrophe of Geneva, the change in the staff of *L'Égalité*,[525] was produced by resolutions of the General Council.[b] That is an error. Jung was so busy with his work as watchmaker that he did not find the time to copy the resolutions and dispatch them to Geneva *before 16 January*. In *the interval*, he received two letters from H. Perret, secretary of the Romance Committee. The first letter, dated *4 January*, is official. It is a communication of the Romance Committee to the General Council stating that some editors of

---

[a] See this volume, p. 471. - [b] K. Marx, *The General Council to the Federal Council of Romance Switzerland*.

L'Égalité convened to wage a public campaign against the General Council *and* the Swiss Committees with which they were not in accord, but that they acted *against* the will of the Romance Committee.

The second letter, of a later date but arriving also *before* the resolutions of the General Council were dispatched by Jung, is a confidential letter sent by Perret to Jung. I am giving you literal extracts from it to put you in the picture. As the letter is private, I need not tell you that these extracts must not be communicated to the Belgian Committee or that the name of the writer must remain a secret.[526]

'...Bakunin has left Geneva. So much the better. Those kind of people bring discord among us. He was the head of the *Alliance*.[257] These democrats are authoritarians, they do not want any opposition; such are Bakunin, Perron and Robin; these three were at the head of *L'Égalité*. Bakunin, with his personal attacks, cost us 200 or 300 subscribers in Geneva. Robin is even more authoritarian, his ambition was to change everything here; he has not succeeded, we do not wish to allow ourselves to be dominated by these gentlemen who believe themselves to be indispensable. They attempted to bring pressure to bear on the Federal Committee, and that did not succeed; we do not want to engage in adventures with them or to bring discord in our sections. Please believe me that *l'Alliance* is dangerous for us, especially now. As for their plan in Geneva, I guessed it a long time ago: to let the men of *l'Alliance* move to the top of all the societies in order to dominate the Federation. If you knew their mode of action— *denigrating* at the sections the people who do not let themselves be dominated by them; they did everything to push my candidature out of the way in Basle, the same thing in Grosselin... You see the manoeuvre—sending to Basle no one but members of the *l'Alliance*, Heng, Brosset, Bakunin. That did not succeed at all. Besides, he[a] worked on the delegations at Lyons, at Naples; these methods are not ethical. They left for Basle before us to prepare their intrigues... Here is something that happened at the Congress,[379] something I guessed about but had no certain proof of. Martinaud, delegate of the Neuchâtel section, had a mandate signed by the brother of Guillaume,[527] a forged, false mandate— *we have proof of that in our hands*. The Neuchâtel section was not yet definitively constituted, and the provisional committee wrote to us not to recognise either Guillaume or Martinaud. These are the morals of the apostles of *l'Alliance*, for Guillaume and some others from Locle are their friends. Besides, the creation of *Progrès* has lured away subscribers to *L'Égalité*, although our journal was founded by all and we must support it.

'The last bit of news: the cut-throats of *l'Alliance* have just handed in their resignation from *L'Égalité*—Perron, Robin and some others, more or less capable ones. A little coup d'état *à la* Bakunin and *à la* Robin. *They wanted to force the hand of the Federal Committee, that it might dismiss* from the staff a member[b] who offered opposition and who condemned attacks made against various committees and the General Council. We do not wish to increase the authority of these gentlemen, we are going to have a quiet fight with them yet, but it seems that *l'Alliance* loses many of its members; it is diminishing—so much the better.'

---

a Mikhail Bakunin - b Pierre Waehry

So much for the extracts from Perret's letter.

If Mr Hins has not yet communicated my letter (and the resolutions of the General Council) to the Belgian Council,[512] *it would be better to suppress entirely the paragraph about Bakunin.* I have no copy of it, but I know that I wrote it in irritation brought on by physical suffering. Thus I do not doubt that Mr Hins justly blames me for the form of that paragraph. As to the substance and the facts, they are independent both from my bad manner of expression and the good opinion of Mr Hins about Bakunin. The fact is that *l'Alliance,* of which Bakunin is the creator and which has not been dissolved except *nominally,* is a danger to the *International Association* and an element of disorganisation.

In the paragraph concerning Bakunin, I am told that Mr Hins again picks up the phrase '*le bonhomme Richard*'.[a] That is a SLIP OF THE PEN, which I regret all the more as Richard is one of the most active members of the Association. I used the phrase only to say that, in the correspondence cited here, he accepts with a great deal of simple-mindedness opinions which he never fathomed. Besides, when I wrote those words, Richard had just given a fresh proof of his thoughtlessness. He had sent to the Council a letter in which a judgement was expressed declaring certain persons belonging to a would-be schismatic Lyons branch to be *infamous traitors expelled* from the Association. We are asked to copy this judgement, to stamp and sign it, and to return it by post. And that without proof, without documents, without giving those condemned the right to defend themselves.

I am also told that Mr Hins reproaches the English Report on the Basle Congress[b] for having suppressed everything related to the question of heritage. That is obviously a misunderstanding. On pages 26-29 we find the report of the General Council,[c] the report of the committee appointed at Basle, and a summary of the discussion on this question. Moreover, the English Report on the transactions of the Congress was written by Eccarius. The Council appointed a commission to examine that report. Although I was appointed a member of this commission, I refused to take part in its work as I had not been present at the Congress and was thus not competent to judge the exactness of the report. My entire collaboration was restricted to purely stylistic improvements.

Finally, if the resolutions passed by the General Council were

---

[a] that simpleton Richard - [b] *Report of the Fourth Annual Congress of the International Working Men's Association held at Basle, in Switzerland* - [c] K. Marx, 'Report of the General Council on the Right of Inheritance'.

not good enough to satisfy Mr. Hins, they obviously satisfied the Romance Committee, for two weeks after their adoption it passed the resolution to free itself from the dictatorship of *l'Alliance*.

Yours very truly,

K. M.

First published abridged in *Bazelsky kongress Pervogo Internatsionala, 6-11 September 1869,* Moscow-Leningrad, 1934 and in full in: Marx and Engels, *Works,* First Russian Edition, Vol. XXVI, Moscow, 1935

Printed according to the original

Translated from the French

Published in English in full for the first time

281

ENGELS TO MARX

IN LONDON

Manchester, 25 January 1870

Dear Moor,

It was a great RELIEF to learn that, this time, it was only a glandular abscess, not a carbuncle. In view of your decisively anti-lymphatic temperament, the involvement of the gland (*axillaris*) can only be secondary and not mean anything. This state of affairs is fully explained by the prolonged neglect that arose from you treating the thing as a carbuncle.

Prendergast [a]—finally received, and, as always happens, two copies at once; W. H. Smith & Sons have also got hold of one. I shall be finished with it tonight. The book is important because of the many excerpts from unpublished documents. No wonder it is OUT OF PRINT. Longman & Co. must have been furious at having been induced to put their name on *such* a book, and since there was certainly little demand for it in England (Mudies have *not a single copy*), they will have sold the edition for pulping as soon as possible, or, also possible, have sold the edition to a syndicate of Irish LANDLORDS (for the same purpose), and will certainly not print a 2nd. What the author says about the Anglo-Norman period is correct in so far as those Irish and Anglo-Irish who lived at some distance from the Pale,[445] continued during that period to live

---

[a] J. P. Prendergast, *The Cromwellian Settlement of Ireland.*

roughly the same old casual life which preceded the settlement; and that the wars, too, in this period were more easy-going in character (with a few exceptions), and had not the distinctly devastating character they assumed in the 16th century, and which became the rule thereafter. But his theory that the enormous amiability of the Irishmen, and particularly Irishwomen, *immediately* disarms every immigrant, however hostile, is just THOROUGHLY IRISH, since the Irish way of thinking lacks all distinction of degree.

A new edition of Giraldus Cambrensis has been published: *Giraldi Cambrensis Opera, edidit J. S. Brewer*, London, Longman & Co. 1863, *at least* 3 volumes; could you find out the price for me, and whether it would be possible to get cheaply, SECOND HAND, the whole work, or at least the volume containing 'Topographie Hiberniae', and possibly also 'Hibernia expugnata'.[528]

In order not to make a fool of myself over Cromwell, I shall have to mug up considerably more on the English history of the period. This will do no harm, but will steal a lot of time.

I am reading the French papers with thanks and interest, and will return them tomorrow with several numbers of *Zukunft*. This paper is becoming more and more depressing and difficult for both readers and writers.

It is close of post, so *adieu*. Best greetings to all.

Your
F. E.

First published abridged in *Der Briefwechsel zwischen F. Engels und K. Marx*, Bd. 4, Stuttgart, 1913 and in full in *MEGA*, Abt. III, Bd. 4, Berlin, 1931

Printed according to the original

Published in English for the first time

282

MARX TO ENGELS[180]

IN MANCHESTER

[London,] 27 January 1870

DEAR FRED,

I am still UNDER TREATMENT and confined to my room. The business was complicated to some degree by small carbuncles near the abscess, nearly the size of an egg. But IN A FEW DAYS ALL WILL BE QUITE RIGHT.

It is curious how doctors have differing opinions. Dr Maddison, who was employed in Edinburgh in a hospital for skin diseases, and still works in this branch, in addition to his practice in a London hospital, states that in both hospitals they are completely *against arsenic* for carbuncles, though use arsenic for rashes. As long as I am in his care, which comes to an end this week, I naturally take *his* medicine. As soon as this finishes, I shall take arsenic regularly for 3 months for *il faut en finir.*[a]

Enclosed—the announced note from Wilhelm.[520] If you write to him, do inform him, in passing (referring to the screed he sent you for me) that 1. if all newspapers write as much about the *18th Brumaire* as his,[b] that is to say, not at all, it is not surprising that nobody hears of it; and 2. that if this material cannot be obtained in Leipzig (which I regard as humbug), he should not write to me, but to *Meissner direct.*

Enclosed—letter from Dr J. Jacoby to Kugelmann, and note from Kugelmann. The matter is as follows: Kugelmann saw in supplement No. 18 of *Zukunft* (22 January) a SPEECH by Jacoby, in which the latter avows socialism and, in the main part of the same issue, the story of the meeting at which this happened, when Schweitzer seized the presidency with the help of his bullyboys and, after the end of Jacoby's speech, accused him, *inter alia,* of borrowing arguments from me. Kugelmann wrote with his usual fervour to Jacoby on this, congratulating him and, at the same time, dressing him down for quoting all sorts of people, but precisely not me, who had supplied him with his real matter. HENCE JACOBY'S REPLY.[529]

The odd thing is only that Jacoby—during the meeting, in answer to Schweitzer—said that I myself 'utilise in my works the labours of my predecessors on countless occasions'. Since I conscientiously cite everybody who contributed as much as a comma to the exposition, this means that Jacoby can take the substance of his new beliefs from me, without citing me. In addition, I am not a '*predecessor*' of 70-year-old Jacoby. A mere populariser and superficialiser has no 'predecessors'. Yet despite all this, it is very fine that Jacoby, like Arnold Ruge, has been converted to *communism.*[c] 'Liberty' no longer suffices!

I am sending you the latest issue of the *Democratic News.* The sheet is no good, but it is in the hands of our own chaps, and

---

a it must be ended - b *Der Volksstaat* - c See this volume, pp. 542-43.

could be made into a *counterbalance* to the *Bee-Hive*, particularly since it only costs 1 HALFPENNY. You and Moore should both subscribe to 12 COPIES, since a similar subscription has also been imposed upon members of the General Council. In addition, one or the other of you could send me quite short reports about Lancashire etc., weekly or bi-weekly, for the sheet.

Salut

Your
K. M.

<table>
<tr><td>First published abridged in *Der Briefwechsel zwischen F. Engels und K. Marx*, Bd. 4, Stuttgart, 1913 and in full in *MEGA*, Abt. III, Bd. 4, Berlin, 1931</td><td>Printed according to the original

Published in English in full for the first time</td></tr>
</table>

283

ENGELS TO MARX [33]

IN LONDON

[Manchester,] 1 February 1870

Dear Moor,

I only received the relevant *Zukunft* yesterday evening, so I can only return the Jacobyana[a] today. It is very clear why the old Yid did not name you; he was sheepishly ashamed of himself, but he should at least have known that, once Schweitzer had been elected president, or was simply present, the plagiarism would certainly be rammed down his throat; but an old wiseacre like he always thinks, in his stupidity, that things might go well. If conversions continue like this, we shall soon dislodge old almighty God from the Rhenish proverb which states that he 'keeps curious company'.

I shall try to raise subsidies for the *Democratic News*. 12-fold subscriptions can lead to nothing, as we have simply no use here for the piles of waste paper. And I don't know, either, what could be reported from here.

I shall inform Wilhelm suitably; I presume he has *never* spoken in his sheet[b] about the *18th Brumaire.* That not a single copy can be obtained in Leipzig is certainly a lie, unless the whole edition has

_____
a See the previous letter. - b *Der Volksstaat*

been sold out. Apropos, *how do things stand with the French translation* of it, and of your book [530]?

I shall send Wilhelm the *Peasant War*, but shall only write the introduction for the *complete* publication. There is no sense in writing an introduction for a serial publication that might drag on for 6 months or more.[486]

It is a real stroke of luck that, despite G. Flourens, *no* blow was struck at Noir's funeral. The fury of *Pays* shows the Bonapartists'[a] great disappointment. They could not wish for anything better than to catch all the revolutionary masses of Paris *en flagrant délit*[b] on the open field *outside* Paris, even *outside the fortifications*, which only have a few passages. Half a dozen cannon at the posterns, an infantry regiment in skirmishing order, and a brigade of cavalry to lay about and pursue—and, in the space of half-an-hour, the entire unarmed crowd—the few revolvers some might carry in their pockets would not count—would be routed, cut down or captured. Since they have 60,000 soldiers, they could even let them enter the fortifications, occupy these, shoot down with grapeshot and ride down the crowd in the open terrain of the Champs Elysées and on the Avenue de Neuilly. Delightful! 200,000 unarmed workers should, from the open field, conquer Paris occupied by 60,000 soldiers!

The French newspapers arrived this morning. Best thanks.

Have you read a full translation of *Land and Freedom* (the Russian thing)[531]? I now have one; you can have it.

Best greetings to your wife, Jenny and Tussy.

Your
F. E.

First published abridged in *Der Briefwechsel zwischen F. Engels und K. Marx*, Bd. 4, Stuttgart, 1913 and in full in *MEGA*, Abt. III, Bd. 4, Berlin, 1931

Printed according to the original

Published in English in full for the first time

---

[a] See this volume, p. 553. - [b] red-handed

284

ENGELS TO KARL KLEIN AND FRIEDRICH MOLL

IN SOLINGEN

Manchester, 8 February 1870
86 Mornington Street, Stockport Road

Dear Friends,

I must apologise very much for having left your letter of 3 December unanswered until today.[498] My only excuse is that I wanted to write something really nice, so I had to look around first, also in the interests of the cooperative. If I now have no very good news, this is, as you will see, not my fault.

I remember Solingen well from anno 48 and 49. Not only were the workers of Solingen at that time the most developed and most determined in the Rhine Province, as was also shown by the Elberfeld affair; I have a reason to be personally grateful to them, since the Solingen column, with which I marched to Elberfeld, supported me and guarded me there against the cowardly and treacherous Committee of Public Safety of the bourgeois 'radicals'. Had it not been for the Solingers, these bourgeois would have bunged me into jail, where I would probably have been left as an expiatory sacrifice for the Prussian gentlemen.[532] And I know full well that, during the whole period of the Lassallean triumphal processions, the Solingers did not behave as disciples of the new teaching, but as people who had belonged to the socialist movement for many years, who could, of course, join the new Association,[104] but did not need to learn anything from it. And I know very well, how, when Lassalle was being idolised as a new messiah, Friend Klein had the courage to remind him and the workers that the people round the *Neue Rheinische Zeitung* had already contributed something towards the independence of the workers.[466]

Thus, it is doubly painful to me that my own means do not permit me to give the cooperative a helping hand in a way that would be of special use to it. The little money I have is so tied up that, with the best will in the world—and certainly for the next few years at least—I cannot get at it, not even for my personal ends. I can thus only dispose of my income, which is not brilliant in the circumstances here. But to show my good will, at least, I enclose *50 thaler* in one Prussian banknote I. Lit. C. N. 108,126; I would ask you to send me the relevant bond title; the interest, however, should be credited not to me, but to the reserve fund of the cooperative.

Together with Marx, with whom I have discussed the matter,[a] I have looked around to see whether we might drum up money for the cooperative in some other way. Marx knows some people who have means, and who can be assumed to have good will. But the man [b] through whom we would have to manoeuvre this is away for a number of months, and *until then* nothing can be done. We intend to do the following: if we succeed in interesting these people in the matter, we shall ask them to send somebody to Solingen to inspect the state of the cooperative himself. It would then be necessary for this person to be shown all the books and records and be provided with all the necessary explanations with the greatest frankness. Otherwise, you cannot ask people to put money into a business and, if I were myself in a position to advance a larger sum, then I would come to Solingen and ask for the same. In business matters everybody has the duty to look out for himself, since anybody can make a mistake, particularly somebody who is interested in a certain thing. In addition, such a person—who naturally would be a complete stranger to Solingen—would have to give his word of honour that he would make no use of the information thus obtained. And when this person has convinced himself of the reliability of the business and the trustworthiness of the management, we hope a decent sum will be taken up in bonds.

I naturally give you this simply as our plan of operations, and would not like you to set great hopes in it already, as it is clear that we cannot just dispose of other people's money. I would not for the world wish the cooperative, basing itself upon such prospects, which might come to fruition at the earliest in months, or perhaps not at all, let itself in for transactions that would tie up its means, and get it into difficulties. I can only promise that we shall do our best in this matter, and remain, with best wishes for the success of the cooperative and the prosperity of all members, with greetings and a handshake

Frederick Engels

My address is now as above.

First published abridged in *Borba klassov*, No. 5, Moscow, 1931 and in full in: Marx and Engels, *Works*, First Russian Edition, Vol. XXVI, Moscow, 1935

Printed according to the original

Published in English for the first time

---

a See this volume, pp. 395, 396-97. - b presumably Menke

285

ENGELS TO MARX

IN LONDON

Manchester, 9 February 1870

Dear Moor,

Either you are sick, or you once again cramming yourself into sickness; otherwise one would hear from you.

The blasted:

Ancient Laws of Ireland.—Senchus Mor.—PART I AND II, DUBLIN, PRINTED FOR HER MAJESTY, STATIONERY OFFICE,[a] the 2nd part of which appeared 3-4 weeks ago, are said to be '*REPRINTING*', and lay me completely by the heels. QUERY, can one get something of this sort SECOND HAND in London?

So Rochefort has quietly been put in quod. Ollivier obviously wants a collision; the barricade attempts will presumably turn out to be 'white smock'[533] pranks. And if Ollivier doesn't want a collision, then Bonaparte, behind his back, does.

Best greetings.

Your
F. E.

First published abridged in *Der Briefwechsel zwischen F. Engels und K. Marx*, Bd. 4, Stuttgart, 1913 and in full in *MEGA*, Abt. III, Bd. 4, Berlin, 1931

Printed according to the original

Published in English for the first time

286

MARX TO ENGELS[534]

IN MANCHESTER

[London,] 10 February 1870

DEAR FRED,

I first went out again last Saturday, but as a result of this damned foggy weather immediately contracted a sort of inflamma-

---

[a] See this volume, pp. 409-10.

tion of the tonsils. The body is naturally sensitive after some weeks of SEQUESTRATION. A north-east wind is howling here and, under the circumstances, prolongs imprisonment. But I hope to have my throat ALL RIGHT again in the course of this week.

On Sunday, LITTLE Dakyns (the geologist) visited me. I invited him for next Sunday. His Scottish cap was the sole MEMENTO of his costume as Felix Holt, THE RASCAL.[a] He was as sprightly as ever, and Tussy was DELIGHTED to see him.

As far as new things are concerned—such as the Irish Laws, etc.[b]—it is very difficult to get them here SECOND HAND.

Laura writes to us today, inter alia, that since last June the excitement in Paris has been steadily rising. Since the Victor-Noir[c] tragic balladry,[516] the females in the working strata have gone daft, and you know what that means in Paris.

Flourens, the CRACK-BRAINED youngster, is the son OF LATE Flourens, *secrétaire perpétuel de l'Académie,* who always adhered to the existing government throughout his nearly 100 years of life, and who was, in turn, Bonapartist, legitimist, Orleanist and again Bonapartist. During the last years of his life he still made himself noticeable with his fanaticism against Darwin.

Apropos, about Napoleon I. In one of the copies of *Cloche* that you have, there is, in one of the memoirs—I no longer remember which—a passage about the wretched behaviour of the hero.[535] Jennychen wants to have the quotation. She has had a squabble at the Monroes' about it, where they wished to deny the FACTS.

I have read the first 150 pages of *Flerovsky*'s book[d] (taken up with Siberia, North Russia and Astrakhan). This is the first work to tell the truth about Russian economic conditions. The man is a determined enemy of what he calls 'Russian optimism'. I never held very rosy views about this communist El Dorado, but Flerovsky surpasses all expectations. It is, in fact, rum, and at any event sign of a change, that something like this can be published in Petersburg.

'У насъ пролетаріевъ мало, но зато масса нашего рабочаго класса состоитъ изъ работниковъ, которыхъ участь хуже чѣмъ участь всякаго пролетарія.'[e]

The method of presentation is quite original; sometimes it reminds you most of Monteil.[f] You can see that the man has

---

[a] A personage from George Eliot's *Felix Holt, the Radical.* - [b] See this volume, pp. 409-10 and 422. - [c] in the original: Louis Noir - [d] Н. Флеровскій, *Положеніе рабочаго класса въ Россіи.* - [e] 'We have few proletarians, but the mass of our working class consists of working people whose lot is worse than that of any proletarian.' - [f] A. A. Monteil, *Histoire des français des divers états aux cinq derniers siècles.* Volumes I-X.

travelled about everywhere and observed things for himself. Blazing hatred of LANDLORD, capitalist and official. No socialist doctrine, no mysticism about the land (although he favours the form of communal property), no nihilistic extravagance. Here and there a certain amount of well-meaning twaddle, which is, however, suited to the stage of development of the people for whom the book is intended. At all events, it is the most important book published since your work on the *Condition of the Working-Class*. And the family life of the Russian peasants is also well depicted—with the awful beating-to-death of their wives, the drinking, and the concubines. It would, therefore, be very opportune if you would send me the fantasy-lies of Citizen Herzen.[a]

You will recall that *Égalité*, inspired by Bakunin, attacked the GENERAL COUNCIL, made all sorts of interpellations publicly, and threatened more.[b] A communication[c]—which I composed—was, thereupon, sent to the *Comité Romand* in Geneva, and ditto to all the other *Comités* of French tongue corresponding with us. Result: The entire Bakunin gang has quit *Égalité*. Bakunin himself has taken up residence in Tessin, and will continue intriguing in Switzerland, Spain, Italy and France. Now the armistice is at an end between us, since he knows that I attacked him heatedly and inveighed against him on the occasion of the latest Geneva *événements*.[d] The brute really imagines that we are '*too bourgeois*' and, therefore, incapable of grasping and esteeming his lofty concepts about 'inheritance right', 'equality', and the replacement of the present state systems by '*l'Internationale*'. Nominally, his '*Alliance* de la Démocratie Socialiste'[257] has been dissolved, but, in fact, continues. From the enclosed copy of a letter (which you must return to me) from H. Perret, *secrétaire du Conseil Romand*, to Jung,[536] you will see that, in fact, the catastrophe in Geneva took place before they received our communication there. This, however, strengthened the new *status rerum*.[e] The Belgian '*Conseil*' (Brussels) has officially declared itself completely in favour of our stand against *Égalité*, but the *secrétaire* of the Belgian COUNCIL, Hins (brother-in-law of De Paepe, but fallen out with him), has sent a letter to Stepney[524] in which he takes Bakunin's side, accuses me of supporting the reactionary party amongst the Geneva workers, etc., etc.

Did you notice, in one of the copies of *Marseillaise* sent to you, that Mr K. Blind had inserted an advertisement for K. Blind in the aforesaid sheet, according to which the aforesaid Blind was sent to Paris as 'ambassador' with General Schurz (*Schütz* does not sound good enough), was exiled from Paris by Bonaparte, and still is! and also was previously *member of the German National Assembly*[537]!

MY COMPLIMENTS TO MRS LIZZIE AND FRIENDS.

K. M.

[Postscript from Eleanor Marx]

MY DEAR Engels,

I AM *VERY* MUCH OBLIGED TO YOU FOR SENDING ME THAT ADVERTISEMENT. THE SITUATION IS ONE THAT WILL SUIT ME VERY WELL, SO I SHALL LOSE NO TIME IN APPLYING FOR IT. YOU WILL I AM SURE GIVE ME A REFERENCE.

WITH THANKS AND BEST LOVE TO ALL.

GOOD BYE.

TUSSY.

First published abridged in *Der Briefwechsel zwischen F. Engels und K. Marx*, Bd. 4, Stuttgart, 1913 and in full in *MEGA*, Abt. III, Bd. 4, Berlin, 1931

Printed according to the original

Published in English in full for the first time

287

ENGELS TO MARX [180]

IN LONDON

Manchester, 11 February 1870

Dear Moor,

Your tonsil business, following the abscess in your auxillary gland, doesn't make me very happy. In any case, it shows that something is not quite kosher about your lymphatic system. If the business does not clear up soon, I would ask Allen, who made such a correct prognosis about my glandular business. Yours, however, is obviously chronic, whilst mine was extremely acute; but better is better.

I am sending you, enclosed, what I've written for Liebknecht [520] as an introduction to the *Peasant War*.[a] Since, in this connection, it

---

[a] F. Engels, *Preface to the Second Edition of 'The Peasant War in Germany'*

is not possible to steer clear of the year 1866, which has hitherto been avoided, we shall have to reach an agreement on what to say about it. Other remarks would also be welcome.

Further, Wilhelmchen's reply.[538] Totally Wilhelm. He didn't *know* at all that the *18th Brumaire* had been published. On the other hand, *I* should *immediately* send him my address. Since *he* had no longer sent me his sheet, his excuse is that *I* must have left my address. And now this penance—belatedly throwing the whole *Volksstaat* from 1 October onwards at my head!

I would ask for the earliest return of these two documents, so I might send Wilhelmchen what he wants and have him leave me in peace.

Today I returned to you, per Globe Parcel Co., all copies of *Cloche, Lanterne, Marseillaise, Figaro,* etc. that I had here. The relevant number of *Cloche* is among them.[535] Since Jennychen collects these things, it is best if she has them all together. I have only kept one *Marseillaise* here, containing the business about the guncotton[539]; I wish to examine Chlormeier[a] further about it.

Dakyns wanted to visit you before Christmas, and wrote to Moore for your address. He, whose insight into character and sense of judgement is not, however, always unexceptionable, gave him such a picture of your inaccessibility at home that I said immediately that poor Dakyns would be quite unnecessarily intimidated. So I wanted to give you Dakyns' address last time, but forgot; but I told Moore immediately that he should not put such nonsense into Dakyns' head.

The sentence quoted from Flerovsky[b] is the first Russian sentence I have understood *completely* without a dictionary. What is the Russian title of the book? I shall acquire it for myself. What I wanted to send you was not *Herzen,* but the German translation of Земля и воля, *Land and Freedom,* by the aristocrat *Lilienfeld,*[c] which also describes the bad results of freedom for the peasants, and the resulting decay of agriculture.[531] I wrote to you about this more than a year ago,[d] and since then Borkheim has also acquired it and, I believe, translated passages from it for you. As soon as I have read it through, I'll send you it.

Perret's letter[536] also returned, enclosed. It's a good thing Bakunin has gone to Tessin. He won't create much trouble there, and it proves the business in Geneva is over. Since there are simply such ambitious vain incompetents in every movement, it is *au*

---

[a] Carl Schorlemmer - [b] See this volume, p. 423. - [c] In the original: Lilienthal. - [d] See this volume, pp. 55-56.

fond[a] good that they join together in their own way, and after that move into the public eye with their cosmic whimsies. Then it soon becomes possible to demonstrate to the world that it is all gas. And this is better than if the struggle stays in the field of private gossip, in which people who have something to do are never a match for those who have the whole day for forming cliques. But an eye must be kept on the fellows, so they do not manage to occupy the field somewhere or another without resistance. Spain and Italy will have to be left to them, of course, at least for the time being.

It would be a very good thing if Mr Rochefort, or as Lizzie says RUSHFORTH, were to go missing in prison for a while.[533] The *petite presse* is quite a good thing, but when it supplants everything else I lose my taste for it. It still has in its bones the whole quality of its origins in the *bas-empire*.[b] And when Rochefort preaches unity of the bourgeois and the worker, it is even funny. On the other hand, the 'serious' leaders of the movement are, for their part, really comically serious. It is truly marvellous. The SUPPLY of *heads*, which, until '48 the proletariat obtained from other classes, appears to have dried up completely, and in all countries. The workers seem to be increasingly constrained to do it *themselves*.

What is *l'illustre* Gaudissart[c] up to? I hear and see nothing of him. Hasn't he got any business again yet?

Best greetings.

Your
F. E.

First published abridged in *Der Briefwechsel zwischen F. Engels und K. Marx*, Bd. 4, Stuttgart, 1913 and in full in *MEGA*, Abt. III, Bd. 4, Berlin, 1931

Printed according to the original

Published in English in full for the first time

---

[a] basically - [b] Lower Empire (designation of the late Roman, or Byzantine Empire, and also of any empire on the decline); here, the Second Empire in France. - [c] Sigismund Borkheim

288

MARX TO ENGELS[174]

IN MANCHESTER

[London,] 12 February 1870

DEAR FRED,

Allen visited me yesterday. Nothing but a simple chill. He advised me, however, to continue my house arrest until the Russian wind 'WHICH BLOWS NO GOOD TO ANYBODY' ceases.

Your introduction[a] is very good. I know of nothing that should be altered or added. I agree *verbotenus*[b] with your treatment of 1866. The double thrust at Wilhelm[c] of the People's Party[38] and Schweitzer, with his bodyguard of ruffians, is very pretty.

Regarding the EXCUSES made by Wilhelm,[538] one never knows whether he is lying intentionally, or whether everything is revolving in confusion like a mill-wheel in his head. The FACT is that I wrote to Meissner from Hanover that he should send COPIES[d] to Wilhelm, *Zukunft* and Schweitzer, and the latter *immediately* published a detailed announcement.[e] Additionally: Wilhelm's friends—Bonhorst and Bracke—*saw* the new edition when they visited Hanover,[f] *and* told me that they had reached agreement with Meissner on the publication of a cheaper, popular edition. Meissner wrote to me about it. I agreed this edition should consist of 2,000 copies, of which 1,000 should be supplied to Bonhorst, etc., at cost price. They pledged themselves to see to the placing of this 1,000. I've heard nothing about the matter since. We should now put Wilhelm to the test. Write to him that he should write to Meissner, asking how it is that he has not advertised the *18th Brumaire* either in *Volksstaat* or in *Zukunft,* and ditto, despite my instructions from Hanover, why he has sent neither him nor Weiss of *Zukunft* COPIES? The reply from Meissner would, at the same time, give me an opportunity to have a serious word with the latter about his sloppiness.

I agree entirely with your marginal notes on the FRENCH RADICAL

---

[a] F. Engels, *Preface to the Second Edition of 'The Peasant War in Germany'.* - [b] word for word - [c] Wilhelm Liebknecht - [d] of the second edition of K. Marx, *The Eighteenth Brumaire of Louis Bonaparte* - [e] [The announcement of the publication of the second edition of K. Marx, *The Eighteenth Brumaire of Louis Bonaparte,*] *Der Social-Demokrat,* No. 117, 6 October 1869 (the 'Literarisches' column). - [f] See this volume, p. 358.

PRESS.[a] Not for nothing was Proudhon the socialist of the Imperial period. I am firmly convinced that, although the first blow will come from France, Germany is far riper for a social movement, and will grow far over the heads of the French. It is a great error and self-deception on their part that they still regard themselves as the 'chosen people'.

Apropos. Jennychen heard whispers yesterday at Monroe's that Mr John Bull Bright is *not in the country* as the papers report, but in town in the care of a *mad-doctor.* Softening of the brain HAS AGAIN SET IN. On the occasion of Castlereagh's suicide, Cobbett noted, that England DURING ONE OF ITS MOST CRITICAL EPOCHS, WAS GOVERNED BY A MADMAN.[b] And the same again today, during the Irish crisis.

It's extremely amusing that Bouverie, THIS INCARNATION OF PURE WHIGGISM, should find the proceedings *quoad*[c] O'Donovan to be illegal.[540] Bouverie is furious that he was given the COLD SHOULDER in the distribution of offices.

The title of the book by *Н. Флеровскій:*
'*Положеніе рабочаго класса въ Россіи*', *С.-Петербургъ. Изданіе Н. П. Полякова. 1869.*[443]

One of the things that amuses me very much in Flerovsky is his polemic against the peasants' *direct dues.* It is a complete reproduction of Marshal Vauban and Boisguillebert.[d] He also feels that the situation of the country people has its analogy in the period of the old French monarchy (since Louis XIV). Like Monteil,[e] he has a great feeling for national characteristics—'the straightforward Kalmyck', 'the Mordvinian, poetic despite his dirt' (whom he compares to the Irishman), the 'agile, epicurean, lively Tartar', the 'talented Little Russian', etc. Like a good Russian, he tells his fellow-countrymen what they should do to turn the *hatred* all these races feel for them into the opposite. As an example of the hatred, he cites, for instance, a genuinely *Russian* colony from Poland which moved to Siberia. These people know only Russian, not a word of Polish, but they regard themselves as Poles, and foster a Polish hatred of the Russians, etc.

His book shows incontestably that the present conditions in Russia are no longer tenable, that the emancipation of the serfs OF

---

a See this volume, p. 427. - b W. Cobbett, 'To the Boroughmongers', *Cobbett's Weekly Register,* Vol. 43, No. 8, 24 August 1822. - c concerning - d An allusion to S. Vauban, *Projet d'une dime royale* and [P.] Boisguillebert, *Dissertation sur la nature des richesses, de l'argent et des tributs...* . In: *Economistes financiers du XVIII-e siècle.* - e See A. A. Monteil, *Histoire des français des divers états aux cinq derniers siècles.*

COURSE only hastened the process of disintegration, and that fearful social revolution is at the door. Here, too, you see the real roots of the schoolboy nihilism that is now the fashion among Russian students, etc. In Geneva, BY THE BY, a new colony of exiled Russian students has grown up with a programme proclaiming opposition to pan-Slavism, which should be replaced by the 'International'.[541]

In a special section, Flerovsky demonstrates that the 'Russification' of alien races is a sheer optimistic delusion, *even in the East*.

You don't need to send me Lilienfeld.[a] Gaudissart[b] has it in Russian and German. He announced his return to me the day before yesterday. According to an earlier communication from his wife to mine, he had found a new post. But it surprises me that he doesn't mention this in his latest epistle.

Enclosed, it must be returned, *a copy of the letter from Hins to Stepney*.[c] In my reply[d] I gave the fellow a thorough dressing down. The exact manner in which he informs himself is shown by the following points, amongst others. He says that, in our *Report on the Basle Congress*,[e] we *suppressed* the discussion on the *right of inheritance*. Bakunin probably palmed this off on him, and he believes it, although he has our Report in his hands and knows enough English to read it! He speaks of '*my*' letter to Geneva, though I have not addressed a line there! My expostulation about Bakunin's goings-on is in my letter to Brussels, in which—apart from communicating the missive of the GENERAL COUNCIL to Geneva[f]—I had to give a general report and communicate the appointment of a new secretary for Belgium (Serraillier, *ouvrier bottier*[g] from Marseilles). He accuses us of having provoked the crisis in Geneva which —as *Égalité* shows—*ended* more than a week before our MISSIVE arrived there, etc. The Belgian *Conseil Général*[h] has, despite Hins, declared its full agreement with us.

Curious that OLD Becker[i] announced his withdrawal from the editorial committee of *Égalité*[525] together with the other Bakunin-

---

a In the original: Lilienthal (see also this volume, p. 426). - b Sigismund Borkheim - c See this volume, pp. 411-15. - d The reference is to Marx's letter to De Paepe of 24 January 1870 (see this volume, pp. 411-15). - e *Report of the Fourth Annual Congress of the International Working Men's Association, held at Basle, in Switzerland.* - f K. Marx, *The General Council to the Federal Council of Romance Switzerland.* - g shoemaker - h The Belgian Federal Council - i Johann Philipp Becker

ists. At the same time, he publishes in his *Vorbote* the exact opposite of what Bakunin did in *Égalité*.[542] The old confusionist! *Salut.*

Your

K. M.

First published abridged in *Der Briefwechsel zwischen F. Engels und K. Marx*, Bd. 4, Stuttgart, 1913 and in full in *MEGA*, Abt. III, Bd. 4, Berlin, 1931

Printed according to the original

Published in English in full for the first time

289

ENGELS TO MARX

IN LONDON

Manchester, 17 February 1870

Dear Moor,

I have written the necessary to Wilhelm.[a] I'm now eager to hear how he will extricate himself.

For a long time I have seen nothing more ridiculous than Flourens' letter about his heroic deeds in Belleville, where he 'had possession of a whole *faubourg*[b] for 3 hours'. The start is wonderful, where he calls on the people to follow him, but only 100 go along, and these soon melt away to 60, and then these evaporate, until he, finally alone 'with one lad',[543] is beaten in the theatre.

The story about Bright is very odd.[c] He has had one such attack already, and had to go to the country for 2 years fishing.

The story about the Russians changed into Poles is absolutely Irish. I must have Flerovsky[d]; unfortunately, I won't, for the time being, have any time to plough through it.

Hins returned—enclosed. The letter is obviously only written for you.[524]

Yesterday I was at a fine blow-out, twelve of us, *nothing but Tories*, merchants, manufacturers, calico-printers, etc. The fellows all agreed that:

---

[a] See this volume, p. 428. - [b] suburb - [c] See this volume, p. 429. - [d] Ibid., p. 429.

1. for the past 3 years here in Lancashire THE HANDS HAD BEEN ALWAYS IN THE RIGHT AND THE MASTERS ALWAYS IN THE WRONG (SHORT TIME VERSUS REDUCTION OF WAGES);

2. the BALLOT WAS NOW NECESSARY TO PROTECT THE CONSERVATIVE VOTERS, and

3. England would be a republic in 25 years, and even earlier unless the Prince of Wales,[a] makes himself *very* popular.

It's amusing how people gain insight as soon as their party is OUT OF OFFICE, and how quickly they lose it as soon as they are IN.

Apropos. You probably know that, in LADY Mordaunt's DIVORCE TRIAL, the '*SOME OTHER PERSON*' with whom she had a CRIMINAL CONNECTION is the Prince of Wales.

So Gladstone the mountain has successfully been delivered of his Irish mouse.[544] I really don't know what the Tories could have against this BILL, which is so indulgent with the Irish LANDLORDS, and finally places their interests in the tried and trusty hands of the Irish lawyers. Nevertheless, even this slight restriction of the eviction right will result in an end to the excessive emigration, and will put a stop to the conversion of arable land into pasture. But it is very jolly if the worthy Gladstone should think that he has abolished the Irish question by means of this new prospect of endless procedure.

Is it possible to get a copy of the BILL? It would be very important for me to be able to follow the debates on the individual clauses.

You in London can have no idea of the way the telegraph has broken down since it was taken over by the Government. Only the first third of Gladstone's speech was published in yesterday's papers here, and even this was *pure nonsense.*[b] The LATEST TELEGRAMS are all 24 hours later than before, so that, if you want to know something, you have to wait for the London newspapers to arrive. A telegram from here to Nottingham, handed in on Thursday, arrived Monday.

You know that, for the past 3-4 years, there has been a big squabble between Prussian and Austrian historians about the Peace of Basle,[545] because Sybel claimed that Prussia was forced to conclude it because it had been betrayed by Austria in Poland.[c] Now Sybel once again has a long story about it, from the Austrian

---

a Albert Edward - b Gladstone's speech in the House of Commons on 15 February 1870 was published in *The Times,* 16 February and in *Manchester Daily Examiner and Times,* 17 February 1870. - c H. Sybel, *Oestreich und Deutschland im Revolutionskrieg. Ergänzungsheft zur Geschichte der Revolutionszeit 1789 bis 1795.*

archives, in his *Historische Zeitschrift*.[a] Every line proves how Russia set Prussia and Austria at each other's throats and, at the same time, drew them into the 1792 war against France, exploited, cheated and dominated both; but stupid Sybel notices nothing of this; instead searches in this whole filthy murk of cheating, treaty-breaking and infamy, in which they were all equally involved, for only one thing: proof that Austria was even more rascally than Prussia. Never have there been such blockheads. His wrath is not directed against Russia, no, solely against Austria, and he explains Russian policy, which is displayed here quite openly and clear as day, with childish motives, such as annoyance at Austrian double-dealing.

From Flerovsky's account[b] it apparently emerges that Russian power is bound to collapse very shortly. Urquhart will, of course, say that the Russians had the book written in order to throw dust in the eyes of the world.

To Tussy my best thanks for the Prussian Minister of Public Worship, sent me as a VALENTINE.

Your
F. E.

First published abridged in *Der Briefwechsel zwischen F. Engels und K. Marx*, Bd. 4, Stuttgart, 1913 and in full in *MEGA*, Abt. III, Bd. 4, Berlin, 1931

Printed according to the original

Published in English for the first time

290

MARX TO LUDWIG KUGELMANN[29]

IN HANOVER

London, 17 February 1870

Dear Kugelmann,

Yesterday I was out in the fresh air again for the first time in a long period.

First to business: be so good as to send *immediately* a copy of

---

[a] H. Sybel, 'Polens Untergang und der Revolutionskrieg', *Historische Zeitschrift*, Vol. 23, Munich, 1870, pp. 66-154. - [b] Н. Флеровскій, *Положеніе рабочаго класса въ Россіи.*

Vogt[a] to Asher & Co., Unter den Linden 11, Berlin. I would prefer it if you were to obtain a confirmation of posting certificate when you send the book off, and *send* me same. You would also oblige me if you would let me know roughly *when* C. Hirsch wrote to you about *Vogt.*

The pamphlet you sent me is one of the appeals currently being made by the privileged estates of the German-Russian-Baltic provinces to German sympathies. These *canaille,* who have always distinguished themselves with their zeal in the service of Russian diplomacy, army and police, and who, since the transfer of the provinces from Poland to Russia, have happily bartered their nationality for the legal right to exploit their peasantry, are now clamouring because they see their privileged position endangered. The old system of rank and estate, orthodox Lutheranism and bleeding the peasants—that is what they call *German culture,* to defend which Europe should now mobilise. Hence, too, the last words of this pamphlet— *landed property as the basis of civilisation,* and landed property, moreover, as the wretched pamphleteer himself admits, consisting mainly of directly manorial estates or *tributary* peasant estates.

In his quotations—in as far as they refer to Russian communal property—the fellow displays both his ignorance and CLOVEN FOOT. Schédo-Ferroti[b] is one of the fellows who (naturally IN THE INTERESTS OF LANDLORDISM) attribute the miserable situation of the Russian peasantry to the existence of communal property, just as, formerly, the *abolition of serfdom* in Western Europe, instead of the serfs' loss of their land, was decried as the cause of pauperism. The Russian book *Land and Freedom* is of the same calibre. The author is a Baltic country squire *von Lilienfeld.*[c] The Russian peasantry is thrown into misery by the same thing that made the French peasantry miserable under Louis XIV, etc.— *state taxation and the obrok*[d] *to the big landowners.* Instead of producing the misery, communal property alone diminished it.

It is, further, a historical lie that this *communal property* was *Mongolian.* As I have indicated at various points in my writings,[546] it is of *Indian* origin, and may, therefore, be found among all European peoples at the beginning of their development. The specific *Slav* (not Mongolian) form of the same in Russia (which is also repeated amongst the *non-Russian South Slavs*) even re-

---

a K. Marx, *Herr Vogt.* - b D. K. Schédo-Ferroti, *Études sur l'avenir de la Russie*; see also this volume, p. 154. - c in the original: Lilienthal - d quit rent

sembles most, *mutatis mutandis*,[a] the *Old German* modification of Indian communal property.

The Pole *Duchiński* in Paris declared the Great Russian race to be *Mongolian* and *not Slav*, and attempted to prove this with a great expenditure of scholarship; and from the standpoint of a Pole, this is in order. Even so, it is wrong. Not the Russian peasantry, but only the Russian aristocracy, is strongly mixed with Mongol-Tartar elements. The Frenchman *Henri Martin* has taken over the theory from Duchiński, and the 'enthusiastic Gottfried Kinkel' translated Martin [547] and set himself up as a Polish enthusiast, in order to make the Democratic Party forget his servile homage to Bismarck.

On the other hand, the fact that the Russian state represents *Mongolianism* in its *policy* towards Europe and America is naturally a truth that has today become a platitude, and thus accessible even to people like Gottfried and Baltic country squires, philistines, clerics and professors. Despite everything, therefore, the Baltic-German cries of dismay must be exploited, since they place *Prussia*, the German great power, in a 'ticklish' position. Everything that arouses antipathy on our side towards these 'representatives of German culture' in Prussia's eyes is bound to make it appear worth protecting!

Another example of the crass ignorance of the pamphleteer: he sees the cession of Russian North America as no more than a diplomatic ruse by the Russian Government, which incidentally WAS VERY HARD PRESSED FOR COSTS.[548] But the main point is this: the American Congress recently published the documents about this transaction. They include, among other things, a report by the American envoy, in which he writes explicitly to Washington: the acquisition is at the moment not worth a cent *economically*—but England is, thereby, cut off from the sea on one side by the Yankees, and the reversion of the whole of British North America to the UNITED STATES thus accelerated. There's the rub!

I approved of the substance of your correspondence with Jacoby,[b] but I was *absolument* shocked by the exaggerated praise of my activities. *Est modus in rebus!*[c] If you must praise, Old Jacoby himself is worth praising. Which other OLD RADICAL in Europe has had the sincerity and courage to align himself so directly with the proletarian movement? It is quite unimportant that his transitional measures and detailed proposals are not worth much. Between

---

[a] with alterations of details - [b] See this volume, p. 417. - [c] All has its measure! (Horace, *Satires*, I, 1.)

ourselves—TAKE ALL IN ALL—I expect more for the social movement from Germany than from France.

I had a big row with Bakunin, that intriguer. But more about that in my next letter.

My best compliments à Madame la Comtesse[a] and Fränzchen.[b]

Your
K. M.

First published abridged in *Die Neue Zeit,* Bd. 2, Nr. 13, Stuttgart, 1901-1902 and in full in *Pisma Marksa k Kugelmanu* (Letters of Marx to Kugelmann), Moscow-Leningrad, 1928

Printed according to the original

291

MARX TO ENGELS[180]

IN MANCHESTER

[London,] 19 February 1870

DEAR FRED,

Although it is still very inopportune to go out in the evenings in such weather, nevertheless I visited Gaudissart[c] yesterday evening. He had, you see, written to me that he had something very important to tell me, and could not really drag the files to me. And what was it? A giant letter about *Russica,* an impossible omnium-gatherum rambling on from one thing to another, with which he had honoured *Zukunft,*[274] and which this had not printed; neither had he received an answer to his furious letter requesting 'an explanation' of such methods. Further: a letter from the publisher[d] of *Hermann* here, requesting him to write against Russia for his paper. It would thus appear that Bismarck is very cross about Katkov's attacks.

Finally, an article in Katkov's paper[e] in which he 1. makes[n] insinuations against Bakunin concerning various money matters; 2. describes him as his Siberian correspondent; 3. charges Bakunin with having written an *extremely humble letter to Emperor Nicholas,* from Siberia or shortly before being sent there—I don't re-

---
[a] Gertrud Kugelmann - [b] Kugelmann's daughter Franziska - [c] Sigismund Borkheim - [d] Heinemann - [e] Московскія вѣдомости

member exactly.[549] Gaudissart will send me a COPY of this, which I shall then communicate to you.

Gaudissart has business again, but not yet a new OFFICE in the CITY. He also has to get the BUSINESS going again.

This evening—although yesterday evening did me no good—I must go into town again. I have been SUMMONED to the SUBCOMMITTEE. It is, in fact, an important matter, since the people in Lyons have thrown Richard out of their society, though the GENERAL COUNCIL must make the decision. Richard, hitherto LEADER in Lyons, a very young man, is very active. Apart from his INFEODATION to Bakunin and a super-wisdom linked with this, I don't know what reproaches can be made against him. It appears that our last circular letter[a] caused quite a sensation and that a hunt for Bakuninists has started in both Switzerland and France. But *est modus in rebus*,[b] and I shall see to it that there is no injustice.[550]

The best bit of Gladstone's speech[c] is the long introduction, where he states that even the 'BENEFICENT' laws of the English always have the opposite effect in practice. What better proof does the fellow want that England is not fit to be lawgiver and administrator of Ireland!

His measures are a pretty piece of patchwork. The main thing in them is to lure the LAWYERS with the prospect of lawsuits, and the LANDLORDS with that of 'state aid'.

Odger's election scandal was doubly useful: the lousy Whigs have seen, for the first time, that they must let workers into Parliament, or Tories will get in. Second, the lesson for Mr Odger and consorts. Despite Waterlow,[551] he would have got in *if part of the Irish workers had not abstained,* because he had behaved so TRIMMING during the debate in the GENERAL COUNCIL, which they found out from *Reynolds's.*[d]

You'll receive the Irish Bill[544] next week.

Salut.

Your
K. M.

Apropos. Mr Siebel or Sybel,[e] or whatever the fellow is called, appears to forget that the Prussians had already left the Austrians

---

[a] K. Marx, *The General Council to the Federal Council of Romance Switzerland.* - [b] all has its measure (Horace, *Satires,* I, 1). - [c] Gladstone's speech in the House of Commons on 15 February 1870 was published in *The Times,* 16 February and in *Manchester Daily Examiner and Times,* 17 February 1870. See also this volume, p. 432. - [d] See this volume, pp. 386-87, 392. - [e] Ibid., pp. 432-33.

in the lurch, in order to participate *in the second partitioning* of Poland excluding them. The filthy behaviour of the Prussians on that occasion was already disclosed in a Polish publication of 1794, which I have read in German translation, and the very clumsy way in which Russia made the two great German powers into its TOOLS and FOOLS in the anti-Jacobin war is very well set out in a Polish pamphlet, written in French in 1848.[a] The *names* of the two authors quoted escape my memory, but they are in my notebooks.

First published abridged in *Der Briefwechsel zwischen F. Engels und K. Marx*, Bd. 4, Stuttgart, 1913 and in full in *MEGA*, Abt. III, Bd. 4, Berlin, 1931

Printed according to the original

Published in English in full for the first time

292

MARX TO CHARLES DOBSON COLLET [552]

IN LONDON

London, 19 February 1870

My dear Sir,

When I received your last letter, I was dangerously ill and, therefore, unable to answer.

The very *minimum* of the Russian Railway Loans amounts to 100 mill. £St. This sum has been mainly raised in Holland, Frankfort on the Main, London, Berlin, and Paris.

As appears from the Moscovite public journals, the Russian government intends raising, if possible, *in the course of the next two years, no less than 50 mill. £St.*

In regard to the *last* Railway Loan of 12 mill. £St., its history comes to this:

As you will be aware, the Russian government had successively, but vainly tried to raise money, first by Thompson and Bonar, then by Baring. Being hardly pressed for money, it succeeded at last to get from *Rothschild*, acting through his agent *Bleichröder* at Berlin, a loan of something like two millions £St.

With a view to get further securities for the repayment of this loan, Rothschild undertook to bring out the last Railway Loan.[553]

---

[a] L. L. Sawaszkiewicz, *Tableau de l'influence de la Pologne sur les destinées de la Révolution française et de l'Empire.*

He stipulated

1) 4 per cent commission for himself—which, on 12 mill. £St., amounts to the nice round sum of 480,000 £St.;

2) another 5,000£ to be annually paid to him for 80 years for his trouble of paying out the coupons.

Rothschild proceeded very cautiously. He limited the *English* share of the loan to but 4 mill. £St., part of which he took up on his own account, while the rest was placed exclusively with confederate stockjobbers and City friends. Thus, when the loan was thrown on the open market, it was mere child's play to push it quickly to 4 per cent premium.

Still Rothschild's anticipations were quite surpassed. So floated was he with applications that he expressed his regret of not having at once issued a loan of 20 mill. £St.

The present financial distress of the Russian government may be inferred from the following facts:

About a year ago the Russian government issued a 'series' of paper money to *be refunded* after a certain term of years, and amounting to 15 mill. roubles. The official pretext of this new issue was that by this operation 15 mill. roubles of the *old paper assignats* should be withdrawn from the market and replaced by a more solid sort of currency. But hardly had the 'series' been issued in the way of state payments, when the *Petersburgh Official Gazette*[a] declared in a short, dry note that, for the present, *no* paper assignats would be withdrawn.

During *the few last months*, the Russian government has again issued no less than 12 new 'series' of that new sort of paper money, amounting together to 36 mill. roubles.

The Russian Exchange on London is now 28-29d. per rouble, while the *par of exchange* would be 40d. per rouble.

One reason of this state of things is *avowed by the Russian press itself*, viz. that, consequent on several bad harvests in the North-Eastern provinces, and still more on *revival of American competition*, the Russian corn exports have fallen by $^1/_3$.

Yours truly
Karl Marx

First published in: Marx and Engels, *Works*, First Russian Edition, Vol. XXIX, Moscow, 1948

Reproduced from the original

ª *С.-Петербургскія вѣдомости*

293

MARX TO ENGELS [554]

IN MANCHESTER

[London,] 21 February 1870

DEAR FRED,

Enclosed—Borkheim's extract from Katkov's article.[a] At the same time, you will see from Gaudissart's letter, *on the reverse side,* the shameless claims he makes on me as a result of a passing remark I made to him—on the evening I visited him[b]—about Flerovsky. How should I respond to this thirst for action?

Also enclosed—a letter from Imandt.[555] To me, the Prussian claim appears superannuated. What do you think? Doesn't it depend on the form of the counter-bill he drew up for the university professors[c]?

I wrote to De Paepe today about the foul deeds of the English Government against the Fenian PRISONERS. This business absolutely must get into the Continental press.[556]

Salut.

Your
K. M.

First published in *MEGA*, Abt. III, Bd. 4, Berlin, 1931

Printed according to the original

Published in English for the first time

294

ENGELS TO MARX

IN LONDON

Manchester, 22 February 1870

Dear Moor,

If Imandt had gone immediately to a SOLICITOR, just like the

---

[a] «Москва, 5 января», *Московскія вѣдомости*, No. 4, 6 January 1870 (see also this volume, p. 436). - [b] See this volume, pp. 436-37. - [c] Ibid., pp. 443-44.

North German consul, he would most probably have learned that a debt contracted abroad is not recoverable by legal action in Scotland—or should Scotland be an exception to all other countries? On superannuation, the *Code Civil* states, Article 2262, that *all plaints* are superannuated after 30 years; Article 2265: who acquires something in *good faith*—superannuation in 10, respectively 20 years [557]; Article 2271: the plaint of masters and teachers of sciences and arts regarding instruction given *monthly*, superannuates in *6 months*. Since this last article does not correspond to the case, the plaint has obviously been filed simply in order to *interrupt* the superannuation in Rhenish Prussia, or also to see if Imandt can be browbeaten by fear of showing himself up, and will thus pay. His counter-bills are possibly made out on word of honour, in which case he could be shown up badly, in his position. Under Article 2244 a *court summons* interrupts the superannuation.

Katkov's elucidations about Bakunin are not worth much.[a] He does not say to *whom* the repentant letters were supposedly sent. Borrowing money is such a normal Russian means of sustenance that no Russian should reproach another on the subject. And that Bakunin should have used the 6,000 roubles lent him in order to flee, instead of paying the *otkupschtschik*,[b] is really ludicrous. And that somebody banished to Siberia should once turn to Katkov, although otherwise he has no time for him—one can't make much of that either. It will annoy Bakunin, but I can't see that Gaudissart[c] will dig much capital out of it.

You can tell Gaudissart concerning his plan regarding Flerovsky that, if an English publisher is interested, he will find himself a translator who will translate AT THE MARKET RATE, which differs considerably from what Gaudissart calls 'paying well', and who will finish it in 2-3 months, and not take a whole year. Gaudissart should not think that he is the only person who knows Russian. There will still be time to return to the other points when he has really found a publisher. Incidentally, it won't hurt at all if Gaudissart makes enquiries amongst the London PUBLISH-ERS. If he should find somebody, which I hardly believe, this contact could be utilised at a later date. You can easily refuse the preface, saying it would be arrogant of you to wish to introduce a foreign book to English literature, before you yourself

---

a See this volume, p. 436. - b tax agent (the Russian word is written by Engels in Latin letters in the original) - c Sigismund Borkheim

had been *introduced* to it by an English edition of your own book.[147]

Apropos, why don't you put Eccarius on to tackling the foul prison deeds in *Volksstaat?*

Sybel, of course, does mention the second partitioning of Poland behind Austria's back,[a] but, at the same time, he tries to prove once again that Prussia was entitled to do this, on account of some sort of previous Austrian treachery. His entire reasoning is this: when Prussia allies itself with Russia *against* Austria, this is in order, but if Austria attempts to ally itself with Russia against Prussia, this is treachery. The Pan-Germans and Austrians—Arneth, Vivenot and consorts—claim the opposite; so the two schools of history-mutilators today behave just as stupidly with regard to Russia as the two German powers did then.

I still haven't got hold of the damned Irish laws.[481] I have discovered Giraldus Cambrensis[b]; it can be had from Bohn, translated, for 5s. At the moment I'm going through Wakefield,[c] who has a lot of good things on climate, soil, etc., with all sorts of omnium-gatherum in between. The fellow considers himself very learned, and is partial to quoting German, Dutch, Danish, etc., trash.

Yesterday I laughed more than I have for ages when I read Moses' Paris letter in *Volksstaat* about Flourens[d] and the other new 'forces' that are replacing and supplanting old Blanqui, etc. The old blockhead never changes. Wilhelm[e] ditto: his latest reports on *19 February* are: Hanover, *13 January,* Lörrach, 23 January, Munich, 25 January, Ernstthal, 17 January!

Incidentally, things are moving quickly in France. Jules Favre could do nothing better than to declare himself so vehemently against all violence, and in favour of peaceful progress, though limited.[558]

My move to London late in summer has now been decided. Lizzie has told me that she would like to leave Manchester, the sooner the better; she has had some rows with relations, and she is fed up with the whole business here. We shall get rid of our house

---

a See this volume, pp. 432-33, 437-38. - b *Ancient Laws of Ireland. Senchus Mor.* Vols I-II; Giraldus Cambrensis, *Topographia hibernica et expugnatio hibernica.* In: *Giraldi Cambrensis Opera,* Vol. V. - c E. Wakefield, *An Account of Ireland, Statistical and Political.* - d [M. Hess,] 'Die Woche, welche...', *Der Volksstaat,* No. 15, 19 February 1870 (the 'Aus Frankreich' column). - e Wilhelm Liebknecht

in September, so everything must be arranged between July and September.

Best greetings.

Your

F. E.

First published abridged in *Der Briefwechsel zwischen F. Engels und K. Marx*, Bd. 4, Stuttgart, 1913 and in full in *MEGA*, Abt. III, Bd. 4, Berlin, 1931

Printed according to the original

Published in English for the first time

295

MARX TO PETER IMANDT

IN DUNDEE

[London,] 23 February 1870

Dear Imandt,

As far as I am aware, debts contracted abroad are not recoverable by legal action in Scotland. I expect any old SOLICITOR there would confirm this for you.

On superannuation the *Code Civil* states,[a] Article 2262, that *all plaints* are superannuated after 30 years; Article 2265: who acquires something in *good faith*—superannuation in 10, respectively 20 years; *Article 2271*: the plaint of masters and teachers of sciences and arts regarding instruction given *monthly*, superannuates in *6 months.*

The whole officiousness of the Prussians is obviously *simply an attempt to browbeat you*, and you can just laugh in the fellows' faces. It would only be inconvenient if the counter-bills are made out *on word of honour*. This would not alter things legally, but would be compromising. But this is surely not the case?

As you perhaps know, Dronke went bankrupt in a big way, then disappeared. According to some he is again haunting Liverpool; according to others, however, he is knocking about in Paris or Spain. In any case, you can get the most certain and reliable news about him *from Schily*.

---

[a] See this volume, p. 441.

17*

That scamp Biscamp continues to send his inspirations to the *Augsburg Allgemeine Zeitung* and the *Weser-Zeitung,* ditto, also, the *Post,*[a] published here by Juch since the New Year (*Hermann* has passed into Bismarckian hands[b]). I read nothing of all this, and still less do any personal relations exist. As far as I know, the Hesse Cassel man[c] is hanging out SOMEWHERE in the London area, and is once again 'husband'. Since you...[d]

First published in: Marx and Engels, *Works,* Second Russian Edition, Vol. 32, Moscow, 1964

Printed according to the original

Published in English for the first time

296

MARX TO ENGELS

IN MANCHESTER

[London,] 5 March 1870

DEAR FRED,

Last week we received the news that the youngest Lafargue child has died.[559] The extraordinary coldness in Paris contributed to this. The child was STINTED FROM THE BEGINNING.

In the meantime, all sorts of things have happened in FENIAN AFFAIRS. A letter I wrote to the *'Internationale'* in Brussels, censuring the FRENCH REPUBLICANS for their narrow-minded nationalist tendency, has been printed, and the editors have announced that they will publish their remarks *this* week.[560] You should know that, in the letter of the Central Council to the *Genevans*[e]—which was communicated to the Brussels people[f] and the main International centres in France—I propounded, in detail, the importance of the Irish question for the working-class movement in general (owing to its repercussions in England).

A short while later, Jennychen flew into a rage at that disgusting article in *The Daily News,* the private organ of Gladstone's ministry,

---

[a] *Londoner Deutsche Post* - [b] See this volume, p. 266. - [c] Elard Biscamp - [d] The end of the letter is missing. - [e] K. Marx, *The General Council to the Federal Council of Romance Switzerland.* - [f] See this volume, pp. 406, 411-15, 430.

in which this wretched rag addresses itself to its 'liberal' brothers in France, and warns them not to lump the CASES OF Rochefort and O'Donovan Rossa together. The *Marseillaise* really fell into the trap, saying *The Daily News* was right, and in addition published a wretched article by that prattler Talandier, *exprocureur de la République*, now a teacher of French at the military school in Woolwich (and also ex-private tutor at Herzen's, about whom he wrote a glowing obituary); in this article he attacks the Irish because of their Catholicism, and accuses them of causing Odger's defeat—because of his participation on the Garibaldi committee.[561] Besides, he adds, they still support Mitchel although he has sided with the SLAVEHOLDERS, as though Odger did not continue to side with Gladstone, despite his much more important support for the SLAVEHOLDERS [435]!

Jennychen— *ira facit poetam*[a]—therefore wrote, in addition to a private letter, an article for *Marseillaise*, which was *printed*.[562] And she received, from the *rédacteur de la rédaction*, a letter, a copy of which I enclose. Today she'll be sending another letter to the *Marseillaise* which, referring to Gladstone's reply (this week) to questions about the treatment of the PRISONERS, contains extracts from O'Donovan Rossa's letter (see *The Irishman, Feb. 5, 70*). According to Rossa's letter Gladstone is here presented to the French as a monster (insofar as Gladstone is, IN FACT, responsible for the entire treatment of the PRISONERS, under the Tories, too) and also as a ridiculous hypocrite, as author of the *Prayers, The Propagation of the Gospel, The Functions of Laymen in the Church*, and *Ecce Homo*.

With these two papers—the *Internationale* and *Marseillaise*—on the Continent we shall now unmask the English. If you should happen, ONE DAY OR THE OTHER, to find something suitable for one of these papers, you, too, should take part in our good work.

The state of my health has not permitted me to take part in the meetings of the CENTRAL COUNCIL.[73] so far. But I shall, next Tuesday,[b] if it doesn't rain. The discussions in the American HOUSE OF REPRESENTATIVES about the FENIAN PRISONERS[563] have, as far as I could see, been most carefully suppressed by the English press.

Mr W. Liebknecht displays himself this time in his full glory. First, he is in a great hurry to have your *Peasant War*. Now procrastination and, instead, he prints, in No. 17 of the *Volksstaat*, *de dato*[c] Hamburg, an article against the idea of 'class' differences, which comes from *Heinzen*'s propaganda clique.

---

[a] ire makes a poet (Juvenal, *Satirae*, I) - [b] 8 March - [c] dated from

Quant à Meissner and the *18th Brumaire, il observe un silence significatif.*[a]
Salut

Your
K. M.

First published abridged in *Der Briefwech-sel zwischen F. Engels und K. Marx*, Bd. 4, Stuttgart, 1913 and in full in *MEGA*, Abt. III, Bd. 4, Berlin, 1931

Printed according to the original

Published in English for the first time

297

MARX TO LAURA AND PAUL LAFARGUE[56]

IN PARIS

London, 5 March 1870

Dear Laura and Paul,

You feel certainly great and just indignation at my prolonged silence, but you ought to excuse it as the natural consequence, first, of illness, then of extra work to make up for the time lost.

The sad news Paul communicated to us, did not take me by surprise.[b] The evening before the arrival of his letter I had stated to the family my serious misgivings as to the little child. I have suffered myself too much from such losses to not profoundly sympathise with you. Still, from the same personal experience I know that all wise commonplaces and consolatory thrash uttered on such occasion irritate real grief instead of soothing it.

I hope you will send us good news of little Schnappy,[c] my greatest favourite. The poor dear little fellow must have suffered severely from the cold so adverse to '*la nature mélanienne*'.[d] [340] Apropos. *Un certain M. de Gobineau*, has published, *il y a à peu près dix ans*,[e] a work in 4 volumes *Sur l'Inégalité des races humaines*, written for the purpose to prove in the first instance that '*la race blanche*'[f] is a sort of God amongst the other human races and, of course, the noble families within the '*race blanche*' are again *la*

---

[a] As for Meissner and the *18th Brumaire*, he observes a significant silence. - [b] See this volume, p. 444. - [c] Charles Étienne Lafargue - [d] dark-skinned creature - [e] some ten years ago - [f] white race

London. 5 March, 1870.

Dear Laura and Paul,

You feel certainly great and just indignation at my prolonged silence, but you ought to excuse it as the natural consequence, first, of illness, then of extra work to make up for the time lost.

The sadness Paul communicated to us, did not take me by surprise. The evening before the arrival of his letter I had stated to the family my serious misgivings as to the little child. I have suffered myself too much, from such losses to not profoundly sympathise with you. Still, from the same personal experience I know that all well-meant commonplaces and consolatory trash uttered on such occasion irritate real grief instead of soothing it.

I hope you will send us good news of little Schnappi, my greatest favourite. The poor dear little fellow must have suffered severely from the cold so adverse to la nature méridionale. À propos. Uncertain M. de Gobineau has published — il y a à peu près dix ans, a work in 4 volumes "Sur l'Inégalité des races humaines" written for the purpose to prove in the first instance that la race blanche is a sort of god amongst the other human races and of course, the noble families within the "race blanche" are again la crème de la crème — I rather suspect that M. de Gobineau, dans ce temps là, premier secrétaire de la légation de France en Suisse, to have sprung himself not from an ancient Frank warrior but from a modern French huissier. However that may be, and despite his spite against the "race noire" — to such people it is always a source of satisfaction to have somebody they think themselves entitled to mépriser] — he declares "excepté"

crème de la crème.[a] I rather suspect that M. de Gobineau, *dans ce temps là 'premier secrétaire de la légation de France en Suisse',*[b] to have sprung himself not from an ancient Frank warrior but from a modern French *huissier.*[c] However that may be, and despite his spite against the '*race noire*'[d]—(to such people it is always a source of satisfaction to have somebody they think themselves entitled to *mépriser*[e])—he declares '*le négre*' ou '*le sang noir*'[f] to be *la source matérielle de l'art,*[g] and all artistic production of the white nations to depend on their mixture *avec 'le sang noir'.*

I have been much delighted by the last letter I received from my sweet ex-secretary,[h] and much amused by Paul's description of Moilin's soirée.[564]

Ce 'grand inconnu'[i] seems at last to have found the secret of catching that '*gloire*'[j] which till now always slipped so treacherously out of his fingers when he had just laid hold of its tail. He has found out that to be successful with the world everything depends upon the circumstance of circumscribing the world within one's own four walls, where one may nominate himself president and have such an audience as will swear in *verba magistri.*[k]

Here, at home, as you are fully aware, the Fenians' sway is paramount. Tussy is one of their head centres.[565] Jenny writes on their behalf in the *Marseillaise* under the pseudonym of J. Williams.[562] I have not only treated the same theme in the Brussels *Internationale,*[l] and caused resolutions of the Central Council[73] to be passed against their gaolers.[452] In a circular, addressed by the Council to our corresponding committees, I have explained the merits of the Irish Question.[m]

You understand at once that I am not only acted upon by feelings of humanity. There is something besides. To accelerate the social development in Europe, you must push on the catastrophe of official England. To do so, you must attack her in Ireland. That's her weakest point. Ireland lost, the British 'Empire' is gone, and the class war in England, till now somnolent and chronic, will assume acute forms. But England is the metropolis of landlordism and capitalism all over the world.

What is Blanqui about? Is he at Paris?

---

a the upper crust - b at that time 'the first secretary of the French legation in Switzerland' - c usher - d black race - e to despise - f 'the Negro' or 'black blood' - g the material source of art - h Laura Lafargue - i This 'great stranger' - j glory - k by his tutor's words (Horace, *Epistles,* I. 1) - l K. Marx, *The English Government and the Fenian Prisoners.* - m K. Marx, *The General Council to the Federal Council of Romance Switzerland,* Point 5 (see present edition, Vol. 21, pp. 87-90).

You have of course heard nothing of my translator, M. K.[a] I am in the same predicament.[441]

The book of Flerovski on 'the situation of the labouring classes in Russia',[b] is an extraordinary book. I am really glad to be now able to read it somewhat fluently with the aid of a dictionary. This is the first time that the whole economical state of Russia has been revealed. It is conscientious work. During 15 years, the author travelled from the West to the confines of Siberia, from the White Sea to the Caspian, with the only purpose of studying facts and exposing conventional lies. He harbours of course some delusions about *la perfectibilité perfectible de la Nation Russe, et le principe providentiel de la propriété communale dans sa forme Russe.*[c] But let that pass. After the study of his work, one feels deeply convinced that a most terrible social revolution—in such inferior forms of course as suit the present Muscovite state of development—is irrepressible in Russia and near at hand. This is good news. Russia and England are the two great pillars of the present European system. All the rest is of secondary importance, even *la belle France et la savante Allemagne.*[d]

Engels will leave Manchester and, at the beginning of August next, settle definitely down in London.[e] It will be a great boon to me.

And now farewell my dear children. Don't forget to kiss brave little Schnappy on behalf of his

Old Nick

First published in: Marx and Engels, *Works*, Second Russian Edition, Vol. 32, Moscow, 1964

Reproduced from the original

Published in English in full for the first time

---

[a] Keller (see this volume, p. 359). - [b] Н. Флеровскій, *Положеніе рабочаго класса въ Россіи.* - [c] the perfectible perfectibility of the Russian Nation and providential principle of *communal property* in its Russian form - [d] Splendid France and learned Germany - [e] See this volume, pp. 442-43.

298

ENGELS TO MARX

IN LONDON

Manchester, 7 March 1870

Dear Moor,

Your letter arrived here yesterday[a] in a very suspicious state and, what is even more suspicious, *a full hour* after time. Since, on Sunday, there is only *one* POST DELIVERY here, this looks very odd. Is the very honourable Mr Bruce taking an interest in our correspondence?

When I read on Saturday afternoon in the 'Irishman in Paris' the story about the *Marseillaise*, I knew immediately in which part of the world Mr Williams was to be found, but stupidly enough could not explain the Christian name.[566] The business is very fine, and the naïve letter, with Rochefort's naïve suggestion that O'Donovan Rossa should be asked to contribute to the *Marseillaise*, gives Jenny an excellent opportunity to establish a link with the treatment of the prisoners, and to open the eyes of the *bons hommes*[b] over there.

Why don't you publish the General Council's letter to the Genevans[c]? The central sections in Geneva, Brussels, etc., read these things, but they do not penetrate to the masses unless they are published. And they should also be published in German in the papers in question. *You don't publish anything like enough.*

Please send me the relevant copies of *Marseillaise* and *Internationale* for a few days.[d] Jennychen's success has been greeted with a general hurrah here, and Mr J. Williams' health has been drunk with ALL DUE HONOURS. I am very eager to hear how the matter develops. The stupid correspondent of the 'Irishman in Paris'[e] should try some time to get such things into his friend Ollivier's papers.

A couple of days ago my bookseller suddenly sent me the *Senchus Mor*, the ancient Irish laws,[481] and what's more, not the new edition but the *first.* So, with a lot of pushing, I have

---

[a] 6 March. A reference to Marx's letter of 5 March 1870. - [b] simple souls - [c] K. Marx, *The General Council to the Federal Council of Romance Switzerland.* - [d] See this volume, pp. 445, 453. - [e] An allusion to the anonymous article printed in the 'Irishman in Paris' column of *The Irishman*, No. 36, 5 March 1870.

succeeded in *that.* And such difficulties with a book carrying *Longmans* as the London firm on its title page, and published by the government! I haven't been able to look at the stuff yet, since, in the meantime, I have started on various modern things (about the 19th century) and must finish them first.

I have concluded with Meissner on the basis of sharing the profits.[567]

I have just received a semi-incomprehensible telegram from Barmen, undated, from which it can only be seen that my mother is seriously ill. I don't know whether a letter is on its way, or whether an earlier telegram got lost.[568] I didn't get Liebknecht's sheet[a] today, either. It is very possible that I shall have to go to Germany in a few days, IF SO I shall see you on my way there. But I hope everything will still go well.

Your
F. E.

First published abridged in *Der Briefwechsel zwischen F. Engels und K. Marx,* Bd. 4, Stuttgart, 1913 and in full in *MEGA,* Abt. III, Bd. 4, Berlin, 1931

Printed according to the original

Published in English for the first time

299

ENGELS TO RUDOLF ENGELS

IN BARMEN

Manchester, 8 March 1870

Dear Rudolf,

I received your telegram today a few minutes before 5, which means it took scarcely 3 hours, since it was dated 1.52 p.m. So far your news is good, and I hope it remains so.

Hermann's letter from Saturday[b] I received only this morning; the storms must have delayed the Sunday boat from Ostend. In the regular run of things I should have received it yesterday afternoon, some hours *before* Hermann's telegram,[c] and then your information would have accorded properly. The matter seems to

---

[a] *Der Volksstaat* - [b] 5 March - [c] See the previous letter.

me extremely serious, and the worst is that it can drag on for a very long time and cause mother, at her age, a great deal of suffering, even if everything goes well this time. That the doctor is quite satisfied I understand to mean under the prevailing circumstances; a haemorrhage lasting from Wednesday until the following Tuesday appears to me to be certainly something serious. But we should hope for the best, namely that, when this is past, this does not re-occur.

I am ready to leave at any moment and, if my presence is desirable, I can, depending on the time at which I receive your telegram, either leave here at midday and arrive there the following evening, or leave late in the evening, per day-boat to Ostend, and get to Cologne the same day, where I would surely have to lie up for the night.

Try to keep mother as cheerful and in as good heart as possible.

Best greetings.

Your
Frederick

First published in *Deutsche Revue,* Jg. 46, Bd. II, Stuttgart, 1921

Printed according to the original

Published in English for the first time

300

MARX TO ENGELS

IN MANCHESTER

[London,] 9 March 1870

Dear FRED,

Enclosed—2 copies of the *Internationale.* You don't need to return them, since they have sent me 5 COPIES OF EACH NUMBER.

In No. II there is nothing by me, except for translation of the FACTS from *The Irishman.*[569]

As TO No. I, I had written it quickly to De Paepe as a private letter for him to work up into an article. Instead, he published it verbatim,[a] adding nonsensical clauses, e.g., that the BODILY punish-

---

a K. Marx, *The English Government and the Fenian Prisoners.*

ment of O'Donovan should be understood as—lashes with a whip!

Have you read the stuff by Huxley about the lack of difference between ANGLO-SAXON (*vulgo* ENGLISHMEN) and CELT?[570] He is giving his 2nd lecture on the subject next Sunday. LITTLE Dakyns has sent us TICKETS for this.

We are much DISTURBED here about the silence of the Parisians[a] since the notice of death.[b] Let's hope there has been no new misfortune.

Strohn was here the day before yesterday, and left for the Continent the same day.

Salut.

Your
K. M.

First published in *Der Briefwechsel zwischen F. Engels und K. Marx*, Bd. 4, Stuttgart, 1913

Printed according to the original

Published in English for the first time

301

MARX TO ENGELS

IN MANCHESTER

[London,] 10 March[c] 1870

DEAR FRED,

Since I know this stuff amuses you, the following with all haste (post just closing): in addition to a few introductory marginal notes on Gladstone's latest declaration in the House of Commons about the PRISONERS, Jennychen sent the *Marseillaise* an extract from an older letter by O'Donovan Rossa, published in *The Irishman* on 5 February (I believe that was the date). The *Marseillaise* (in a truly French way it gives this letter as from 'Newgate') proceeds to publish this in a special issue on Tuesday evening, containing only articles by '*prisonniers politiques*' and costing 50 centimes.[571] This has now been reprinted (re-translation into English) this evening in *The Echo*, etc. Levy's *Telegraph* also refers to it in its Paris correspon-

---

[a] Paul and Laura Lafargue - [b] See this volume, p. 444. - [c] In the original 9 February is corrected to 10 March by Engels.

dence. *The Irishman* may well complain that it is not quoted as the source. But Jennychen will use this to demonstrate *how* the English press suppresses the FACTS published in the Irish press, and only publishes them as such when they come from Paris in some extraordinary manner. The English press will soon note that the idyllic days of systematic lying and hushing up the FACTS are over.

Pays remarks that the increase in the price of the *Marseillaise* to 50 c. is against all the rules, since 'prison goods are always sold cheaper than others'.

Salut.

Your
K. M.

First published in *Der Briefwechsel zwischen F. Engels und K. Marx*, Bd. 4, Stuttgart, 1913

Printed according to the original

Published in English for the first time

302

ENGELS TO MARX

IN LONDON

Manchester, 13 March 1870

Dear Moor,

Mʀ J. Williams[a] has certainly had a bang-up and well-earned success. The dodge by the *Marseillaise* in printing the letter as an original[b] has got the whole English press into a fine pickle, and has finally forced *The Irishman* to admit its debt to the *Marseillaise* and the *Internationale.* The hushing-up is at an end, and Mʀ Bruce—although in the lousy *Daily News* he again has O'Donovan Rossa described as 'ORDINARY CONVICT AND NOTHING ELSE'—will probably sing quite a different tune in answering the interpellations that are to come. Bravo Jenny! Lizzie is particularly grateful to you for the articles in the *Internationale,*[c] which pleased her enormously.

The two letters enclosed came to me from Solingen. I had

---

[a] Marx's daughter Jenny - [b] See the previous letter. - [c] K. Marx, *The English Government and the Fenian Prisoners*.

addressed this Moll[a] as 'thou', assuming him to be the brother of Jupp,[b] and an old member of the League[c]; thus the intimate tone. You will also note that we have also fallen prey to myth-formation. I know nothing about either the Schapper business, which looks very fuddled, or the business with my old man.[d] My old man would have taken care not to let me pay out wages or anything like that; for this, I could not count well enough for his taste.[572] Since I have to answer the fellows soon, you might let me know whether you have heard anything concerning Menke in the meantime.

The whole week I have been standing ready to have to go away because of my mother, but luckily things are getting better.[e]

The following passage suffices to characterise gentle old Gladstone's whole long LAND BILL[544] as pure muck:

'THE LEASES IN QUESTION' (namely, as they are given today, now and then, in Ireland by the LANDLORDS to the TENANTS) '*ARE QUITE AS PRECARIOUS AS TENANCIES AT WILL. THEY HAVE NO EFFICACY WHATEVER IN REMOVING THE SENSE OF INSECURITY. A LEASE TO BE OF ANY AVAIL FOR THAT PURPOSE, SHOULD, SAVE IN THE PARTICULARS OF SUBDIVIDING AND SUBLETTING, BE FREE AND UNFETTERED—ABOVE ALL, IT SHOULD PUT NO OBSTACLE TO THE SALE OF THE TENANT'S INTEREST. BUT MODERN LEASES ARE THE REVERSE OF THIS—THEY ARE ENCUMBERED WITH CLAUSES AND COVENANTS PRESCRIBING THE MODE OF CULTIVATION AND THE DISPOSAL OF THE PRODUCE, NEGATIVELY AND AFFIRMATIVELY REGULATING THE ACTION OF THE TENANT AND ENTIRELY FORBIDDING THE ESSENTIAL POWER OF FREE ALIENATION. EVERY LINE IN THESE DOCUMENTS MAY WITHOUT MUCH EXAGGERATION BE SAID TO CONTAIN A LEGAL PITFALL FOR THE UNWARY AND THERE ARE FEW, INDEED, IF ANY, WHO CAN ESCAPE THE EFFECT OF THE LAST CLAUSE WITH WHICH THEY WIND UP, MAKING VOID THE LEASE IN CASE OF THE BREACH OF ANY OF THE FOREGOING COVENANTS. SUCH LEASES AFFORD NO SECURITY. THEY ARE QUITE AS PRECARIOUS AND MORE DANGEROUS THAN TENANCIES AT WILL.*'

And who says this? MR Gallwey, *AGENT (!!)* OF THE Kenmare ESTATE, AT THE Killarney BOARD OF GUARDIANS, 4 November, 1869. And the Kenmare ESTATE belongs to MARQUIS OF Landsdowne, whose general agent for all his Irish ESTATES is the honourable 'REALITY' *Trench!*[f] One could not hope for a better authority. And these LEASES are the contracts BY WHICH, AFTER THE PASSING OF THIS BILL, EVERY IRISH TENANT IS TO BE HELD BOUND according to the noble Gladstone.

Have you had news from the Lafargues?

Best greetings to all of you.

Your

F. E.

First published in *Der Briefwechsel zwischen F. Engels und K. Marx*, Bd. 4, Stuttgart, 1913

Printed according to the original

Published in English for the first time

[a] Friedrich Moll - [b] Joseph Moll - [c] the Communist League - [d] Frederick Engels' father—Friedrich Engels, Senior - [e] See this volume, pp. 452-53. - [f] an allusion to Trench's *Realities of Irish Life*; see this volume, p. 356.

303

ENGELS TO JENNY MARX (DAUGHTER)

IN LONDON

Manchester, 17 March 1870

Dear Jenny,

I congratulate you on your well-earned success.[573] That Mr Bruce had to stammer his apologies in yesterday's *Daily News* is priceless.[574] It will now be necessary to show up the hollowness of these apologies, and that is not difficult. Here is some material, as I do not know whether you still have a copy of the *Pollock and Knox Report*[a] about THINGS NOT GENERALLY KNOWN.

Bruce says:

'WITH REFERENCE TO THE COMPLAINT THAT HE WAS COMPELLED TO BATHE IN UNCLEAR BATHS, THE COMMISSIONERS, AFTER FULL INQUIRY INTO THE PRACTICE OF THE PRISON, SAY "IT WOULD BE IDLE TO DWELL UPON SUCH ABSURDITIES."'

What do the Commissioners say? PAGE 23:

'AT BATHING HOURS, HE STOOD NO. 1 OF A PARTY OF 30, *HE WAS NOT CALLED FIRST TO THE BATH*. IT TURNED OUT THAT THE WARDER IN CHARGE ON ONE OCCASION BEGAN WITH NO. 1, NEXT WEEK WITH NO. 30; THE 3RD WEEK HE TOOK NO. 16 AND 17 FIRST AND WORKED ROUND TO THE FLANKS *SO AS TO GIVE EACH HIS PRIORITY*, WITHOUT WHICH THERE WOULD HAVE BEEN UNIVERSAL DISCONTENT. *IT WOULD BE IDLE TO DWELL ON SUCH ABSURDITIES.*'[b]

THUS, THE ABSURDITY does not consist in fact that it is stated that Rossa[c] had to bathe in the dirty water of criminals. No, but *in the fact that he complains about it.* Bruce changes the fact (admitted by the COMMISSIONERS) in such a way as if they had treated it 'as an absurdity'. That's the way Bruce treats the truth.

On the fact itself, the CONVICT of Clonmel explains (THINGS NOT GENERALLY KNOWN, p. 9)[575]:

'IT IS NOT GENERALLY KNOWN THAT WE HAD TO BATHE IN THE SAME WATER IN WHICH SEVERAL OF THESE CRIMINALS BATHED OR WERE BATHING AT THE TIME.'

I might further remark that PENAL SERVITUDE is similar to the French *travaux forcés* or the so-called *galères*, and a CONVICT PRISON of this sort = the French *bagne*, and CONVICT = *galérien*.

The enclosed clipping is a LEADER from the local John Bright's paper.[d] The *Manchester Guardian* also has a leader on the subject,

---

[a] This refers to [A. A. Knox and G. D. Pollock,] *Report of the Commissioners on the Treatment of the Treason-Felony Convicts in the English Convict Prisons*. - [b] italics by Engels - [c] O'Donovan Rossa - [d] *Manchester Daily Examiner and Times*, leader, 17 March 1870

aping that of yesterday's *Times*,[a] but also with the comment that political prisoners have a claim to some CONSIDERATION.

Nota Bene: if you do not have the above report or the THINGS etc., I can send them to you immediately.

You should see the pleasure which this whole thing gave my wife. She is infinitely grateful to you for bringing all these infamies to light, and sends you the enclosed twig of SHAMROCK, for today is St Patrick's day and we don't know if you have any there.[576] There is also a SHAMROCK for Tussy.

Give my affectionate greetings to Moor, your Mama, Tussy and Ellen.

Your

F. Engels

First published in *Friedrich Engels. 1820-1970. Referate, Diskussionen, Dokumente*, Hanover, 1971

Printed according to the original

Published in English for the first time

304

MARX TO ENGELS[577]

IN MANCHESTER

London, 19 MARCH 1870

DEAR FRED,

Enclosed, the *Marseillaise*, which should, however, be returned with the previous ones. I haven't read it myself yet. The article was written jointly by Jennychen and myself,[562] as she hadn't got SUFFICIENT TIME available. This is also why she hasn't answered your letter, and why she is sending MRS Lizzie her thanks for the SHAMROCK[576] PROVISIONALLY through me.

From the enclosed letter from Pigott to Jenny you will see that MRS O'Donovan, to whom Jenny sent a private letter, together with 1 *Marseillaise*,[b] took her for a GENTLEMAN, although she signed it Jenny Marx. I answered Pigott today on Jennychen's behalf, and took the opportunity to explain to him briefly MY VIEWS OF THE IRISH QUESTION.[578]

---

[a] 'The Fenian Convict O'Donovan Rossa', *The Times*, 16 March 1870. - [b] Apparently carrying the second article by Jenny Marx from the Irish question series.

Your HINT about Bruce's falsification[a] has already been used in the letter Jenny sent yesterday to the *Marseillaise*.[b] We have Knox' *et* Pollock's Report[c] (but did not consult it) and ditto 'THINGS NOT GENERALLY KNOWN'. On the other hand, you would oblige me if you would send *by return*: 1. *Lassalle*'s publication against Schulze-Delitzsch, and 2. the book by 'Clement', the crazy Frisian.[d]

The sensation caused in Paris and London by Jennychen's second letter (containing the CONDENSED TRANSLATION of O'Donovan's LETTER) has robbed Talandier of his sleep; he is loathsome and importunate (but very FLUENT with gob and pen). In the *Marseillaise* he had denounced the Irish as CATHOLIC IDIOTS. Now, equally FULLMOUTHED, he is taking their side in a review of what *The Times, The Daily Telegraph* and *The Daily News* have said about O'Donovan's letter.[579] Since Jennychen's second letter was left unsigned (BY ACCIDENT), he obviously flattered himself with the idea that he would be taken for the secret sender. This was frustrated by Jennychen's third letter. The fellow is, *du reste*, TEACHER OF FRENCH AT THE MILITARY SCHOOL OF Sandhurst.

Last Tuesday[e] I was back again, for the first time, at a meeting of the GENERAL COUNCIL.[580] With me—Felix Holt, THE RASCAL.[f] He had a very good time since, for a change, there was really something interesting going on. As you know, the *prolétaires 'positivistes'* in Paris had sent a deputy[g] to the Basle Congress. There was a discussion as to whether he should be admitted, since he represented a philosophical society and not a workers' society (although he and his consorts all belong 'personally' to the WORKING GLASS). Finally, he was admitted as a delegate of personal MEMBERS of the '*Internationale*'. These fellows have now constituted themselves in Paris as a *branche* of the *Internationale*—an event about which the London and Paris Comtists have made a great FUSS. They thought that they had driven in THE THIN WEDGE. The GENERAL COUNCIL, being informed by the '*prolétaires positivistes*' of their affiliation, reminded them politely that the COUNCIL could only permit their admission after examining their programme. So they sent a programme—real Comtist-orthodox—which was discussed last Tuesday. In the chair was Mottershead,[h] a very intelligent (though anti-Irish) old Chartist,

---

a See this volume, p. 455 - b The fourth article by Jenny Marx from the Irish question series. - c [A. A. Knox and G. D. Pollock,] *Report of the Commissioners on the Treatment of the Treason-Felony Convicts in the English Convict Prisons*. - d F. Lassalle, *Herr Bastiat-Schultze von Delitzsch, der ökonomische Julian, oder: Capital und Arbeit*; K. J. Clement, *Schleswig, das urheimische Land des nicht dänischen Volks der Angeln und Frisen und Englands Mutterland, wie es war und ward*. - e 15 March - f Dakyns (see this volume, p. 423.). - g Gabriel Mollin - h See this volume, p. 386.

and a personal enemy of, and expert on, Comtism.[581] After a longish debate: Since they are workers they may be admitted as a simple branch. Not, however, as '*branche positiviste*', since the principles of Comtism directly contradict our Rules. And anyway, it was their own affair how they reconciled their philosophical private views with those of our Rules.

About the screeds from Solingen soon.

Salut.

Your

Moro

First published abridged in *Der Briefwechsel zwischen F. Engels und K. Marx*, Bd. 4, Stuttgart, 1913 and in full in *MEGA*, Abt. III, Bd. 4, Berlin, 1931

Printed according to the original

Published in English for the first time

305

ENGELS TO MARX

IN LONDON

Manchester, 21 March 1870

Dear Moor,

Your letter of the day before yesterday[a] was *only* delivered to me *today*, and the state of the envelope (enclosed) leaves no further doubt that the scoundrel Bruce is keeping an eye on our correspondence. I am, therefore, *not* sending these lines by post and, at the same time, a few lines, in which Pigott's letter[b] is returned, are going off to you by post.[582]

Close your envelopes carefully, and seal them with sealing-wax *over* the glue so that the signet-print touches *all four flaps* of the envelope. Your present envelopes are not suitable; the 4 flaps have to come quite close together so that this can be done. This makes things more difficult, so that, in the short time the fellows have they are forced to leave visible evidence, and then one can denounce them publicly. In the meantime, write *important things* to

_____

[a] 19 March - [b] See this volume, p. 458.

me under the address: Schorlemmer, Owens College, Manchester, or 172 Brunswick Street, Manchester, or S. Moore, 25 Dover Street, Oxford Street, Manchester, and don't write the address yourself. For *very secret* things, the best way is some sort of packet per Globe Parcel Co. like this one. In this way you could also let me have another address; it must *not* be that of your house. It's a good thing that I am soon moving to London, then this will come to an end. I have just given notice on my house. In fact, the beastly government could wish for no better medium than our correspondence in order to keep informed of the activities of the entire proletarian party; the government will also find things in our correspondence that they can utilise with their continental colleagues. At least because of this we must take all precautions. We must not correspond for Stieber's sake.

Jenny can shout: *victoire sur toute la ligne!*[a] If it were not for her, the honourable Gladstone would *never* have granted the new *enquête*.[b] How Moore[c] allowed himself to be diddled again by Gladstone concerning this enquiry can be shown by comparing the hopeful NOTE on P. 608 of *The Irishman*, which obviously proceeds from Moore, with Gladstone's Thursday speech, in which he reserved for himself the composition, procedures, etc.[583]

An attempt was also made, probably in Cologne, to open the letter from Solingen[d] to me, but it was unsuccessful, owing to proper use of sealing-wax.

Hearty greetings.

Your

F. E.

In their haste, the fellows laid together the four flaps of the envelope *incorrectly*, the proof is therefore absolute.

First published in *Der Briefwechsel zwischen F. Engels und K. Marx*, Bd. 4, Stuttgart, 1913

Printed according to the original

Published in English for the first time

---

[a] victory along the whole line! - [b] enquiry - [c] George Henry Moore - [d] See this volume, p. 455.

306

MARX TO ENGELS[174]

IN MANCHESTER

[London,] 24 March 1870

Dear Fred,

Enclosed, 2 copies of *Marseillaise* (1 J. Williams[a] in it), and *Het Volk*, more about which in the course of this letter.

The fellows here should look out with their letter-opening. The times of the worthy Graham are past.[584] As soon as I have any completely striking, certain proof, I shall write directly to the Postmaster General. *Il ne faut pas se gêner.*[b] ·

I thought I was properly back on my feet, was working away gaily again for the past 2 weeks, but then there appeared, *d'abord*,[c] a lousy cough from the March east wind—I'm still suffering from it—and then, since the day before yesterday, once again unpleasant manifestations on my right thigh, which for two days now have made walking and the seated position difficult. *À tous les diables!*[d]

Enclosed, a letter from the *Russian colony* in Geneva. We have admitted them; I have *accepted* their commission to be their representative on the General Council, and have also sent them a short reply (official, apart from *lettre privée*) with permission to publish it in their paper.[e][541] *Drôle de position*[f] for me to be functioning as the representative of *jeune Russie*[g]! A man never knows what he may achieve, or what STRANGE FELLOWSHIP he may have to suffer. In the official reply I praise Flerovsky[h] and emphasise that the chief job of the Russian *branche* is to work for Poland (i.e., to free Europe from Russia as a neighbour). I thought it safer to say no word about Bakunin, either in the public or the confidential letter. But what I shall never forgive these fellows is that they turn me into a *vénérable*. They obviously believe I am between 80 and 100 years old.

The letter from the publisher of *Volk*[i] enclosed herewith—was addressed to me without a particular address on the envelope, but instead: 'Her Karl Marx, *Algemeen Correspondent voor Nederland der*

---

[a] Jenny Marx's fourth article on the Irish question - [b] One should not constrain oneself. - [c] first - [d] The devil take it! - [e] *Народное дѣло* - [f] Odd position - [g] young Russia - [h] The reference is to Н. Флеровскій, *Положеніе рабочаго класса въ Россіи.* - [i] *Het Volk.*

Internationale Arbeiders Vereeniging, London.'ᵃ This post of an *'Algemeen Correspondent voor Nederland'* was completely unknown to me hitherto. But before I get mixed up in any way with 'Herr Philipp von Roesgen von Floss', I thought it safer to write *d'abord* to our Flemish *branche* in Antwerp to request information about this long name.ᵇ

Best greetings to Mrs Lizzy.

Your
Moor

Apropos. Old Beckerᶜ has finally written to Jung (also a few lines to me,[585] which I shall answer tomorrow). He presents all the stupidities he committed as deep and intentional machiavellianism. *Le bon homme!*ᵈ Thereby, the interesting datum that Bakunin, who hitherto, as Becker states, shouted blue murder about Herzen, began to sing hymns of praise as soon as he was dead.[586] *Thereby he achieved his aim*, that the propaganda money, about 25,000 frs annually, which the *rich* Herzen had paid to himself from Russia (his party there), is now transferred to Bakunin. Bakunin appears to love this type of '*inheritance*',[587] despite his antipathy *contre l'héritage*.ᵉ [379]

The *Napoleon* race has fallen pretty low when they, *à tort et à travers*,ᶠ attempt to *prove* that they are being treated to *boxed ears*.[588]

First published abridged in *Der Briefwechsel zwischen F. Engels und K. Marx*, Bd. 4, Stuttgart, 1913 and in full in *MEGA*, Abt. III, Bd. 4, Berlin, 1931

Printed according to the original

Published in English in full for the first time

ᵃ Mr Karl Marx, general correspondent of the International Working Men's Association for the Netherlands, London. - ᵇ See this volume, pp. 464-65. - ᶜ Johann Philipp Becker - ᵈ The good fellow! - ᵉ against inheritance -ᶠ so imprudently

307

MARX TO WILHELM BRACKE[589]

IN BRUNSWICK

[London, 24 March 1870]

Dear Friend,

Yesterday[a] I send you 3,000 CARDS OF MEMBERSHIP addressed to *von Bonhorst*.[590]

I have information for you, which is not uninteresting, about the internal affairs of the Internationals. This will reach you by an indirect route.[b] In accordance with the Rules, all national committees in contact with the General Council must send it three-monthly reports on the situation of the movement. When I remind you of this, I would ask you to consider that this report is *not* written for the public, and should, therefore, present the facts completely factually, without make-up.

From Borkheim and from the latest letter from Bonhorst I know that the finances of the Eisenachers are in a bad state.[591] As a consolation, the information that the finances of the General Council are below zero, steadily growing *negative* dimensions.

First published in: W. Bracke, *Der Braunschweiger Ausschuss der socialdemokratischen Arbeiter-Partei in Lötzen und vor dem Gericht*, Brunswick, 1872

Printed according to the book

Published in English for the first time

308

MARX TO PHILIPPE COENEN[592]

IN ANTWERP

London, 24 March 1870
1 Modena Villas, Maitland Park,
Haverstock Hill, London

Citizen,

Yesterday I received the *proefblad*[c] of *Het Volk* published at Rotterdam and a *letter* from its editor, Philipp von Roesgen von Floss,[d] in which he asks, among other things, for a card as a

---

[a] 23 March - [b] See this volume, p. 470. - [c] specimen number - [d] See this volume, pp. 462-63.

member of the *International*. I know neither Mr Philipp von Roesgen von Floss nor the state of our affairs at Rotterdam. I suppose that you are better informed, and I am asking you to please write to me on these two points: (1) What is the state of affairs of the *International* at Rotterdam? (2) Can the General Council establish relations with Mr Philipp von Roesgen von Floss?

Greetings and fraternity.

Karl Marx

First published in: Marx and Engels, *Works*, First Russian Edition, Vol. XXVI, Moscow, 1935

Printed according to a copy of the original

Translated from the French

309

MARX TO ENGELS

IN MANCHESTER

[London,] 26 March 1870

Dear Fred,

Returned, enclosed, the letter from the 'wrong' Moll.[a] I have heard nothing from Menke yet. When you write to the lads, please tell them, also, 1. that Lessner has written repeatedly to them that the *Central Council*[b] can do nothing on this matter; 2. that they can work it out on their own 5 fingers that their cooperative society is of absolutely no interest to the English; and 3. that the Central Council is bombarded from all parts of Europe with demands for money, without receiving financial contributions from anybody on the continent.

I don't understand your lines of this morning. This is probably due to the fact that my head, as a result of physical infirmity, is not at its most lucid.

I would appreciate it if you could send me, tomorrow evening (if there is a post on Sunday, which is not the case here), £5 as an advance on the coming quarter. My wife informed me too late, i.e. at a moment of EXHAUSTED EXCHEQUER, that the gas bill has to be paid at 2 o'clock on Monday.

---

[a] Friedrich Moll (see this volume, pp. 455-56). - [b] General Council

I think I left behind in Manchester [353] the number of the *Queen's Messenger* containing the biography of Clanricarde. Since this brute is putting on great airs in connection with the Irish COERCION BILL, [593] it is high time for J. Williams [a] to introduce to the French a counterpart for Pierre Bonaparte. [562]

Have you ever seen such filthy weather as this winter and autumn? No wonder that one can't get back on one's feet.

Salut.

Your

K. M.

First published abridged in *Der Briefwechsel zwischen F. Engels und K. Marx*, Bd. 4, Stuttgart, 1913 and in full in *MEGA*, Abt. III., Bd. 4, Berlin, 1931

Printed according to the original

Published in English for the first time

310

MARX TO LUDWIG KUGELMANN [29]

IN HANOVER

[London,] 26 March 1870

Dear Kugelmann,

I am only writing you a few lines today, since a Frenchman has arrived, just at the moment when I was getting ready to correspond again with you after such a long period. I shall not get rid of the fellow this afternoon, and the post goes at 5.30.

Tomorrow, however, is Sunday, when a good Christian like myself is allowed to interrupt his work and write to you at greater length, particularly about the Russian *casus,* which has taken a pretty turn.

Jennychen, OUR ILLUSTRIOUS J. Williams, [562] has quite a good edition of Father Goethe. [594] BY THE BYE, she was recently invited to Madame Vivanti's, the wife of a rich Italian merchant. There was a great *assemblée,* including a number of English people. Jennychen had a *furibundus* [b] success with a Shakespeare declamation.

Je te prie de saluer Madame la comtesse [c] *de ma part et de la remercier*

---

[a] Marx's daughter Jenny - [b] furious - [c] Kugelmann's wife Gertrud

des lignes aimables qu'elle a bien voulues m'adresser. Elle n'a pas la moindre raison de regretter d'avoir préféré le latin au français.[595] *Cela ne révèle pas seulement un goût classique et hautement développé, mais explique encore pourquoi Madame ne se trouve jamais au bout de son latin.*[a]

And best greetings to Fränzchen.

The
Moor

First published in *Pisma Marksa k Kugel-manu* (Letters of Marx to Kugelmann), Moscow-Leningrad, 1928

Printed according to the original

311

ENGELS TO MARX

IN LONDON

Manchester, 27 March[b] 1870

Dear Moor,

If you did not understand my few lines of the day before yesterday, then the enclosure must have been missing. You wrote on the 24th that you would take steps as soon as you had in your hands completely striking certain proof that our letters had been opened. The envelope of this letter was the most striking proof: the sealing-wax had been loosened with a hot iron and afterwards spread just as sloppily back on the envelope, so that every trace of the imprint was blotted out, and the unfastened flaps were not even properly covered again. So I immediately sent you *this* envelope, wishing thus to put you in a position to take immediate steps. If it was not enclosed, it had been taken out. But if it was in the same state in which you dispatched it, then you obviously need not put any sealing-wax on the letters, and might just as well send them completely open. Since this case interests me, please tell me how things stand.

---

[a] I would ask you to greet Madame la comtesse from me, and thank her for the friendly lines she wrote me. She has not the slightest reason to regret preferring Latin to French. This not only displays a classical and highly-developed taste, but also explains why Madame is never non-plussed. - [b] In the original: 29 March.

Luckily, I have money at home, and I send you enclosed £5, S/7, 29,808, Manchester, 16 January 1869, BANK OF ENGLAND NOTE. Unfortunately, because of Sunday I cannot register the letter; the rogues who open our letters are equally capable of stealing the money. I wanted to get the rest yesterday, but the bank closes so early on Saturday that I wouldn't have got into town in time. I'll get it tomorrow.

I don't remember seeing the *Queen's Messenger* with Clanricarde's biography.[a] As far as I know, I sent back to you all the *Queen's Messengers*, etc., which you did not take with you personally, in the parcel with the *Cloches* and *Lanternes*; but I'll take another look.

Mr Philipp von Roesgen von Floss has also spread himself in the *Werker* several times; the really Dutch, precise handwriting suggests a come-down notary's clerk. Caution is suggested before he be granted the *personeel diploma as lid*[b] of the International.[c]

If your friend Collet only knew that you also have now become a *bona fide* and frank RUSSIAN AGENT.[d] But it's really quite nice of the fellows, who certainly seem to be a different sort of Russians from those we have previously encountered. They can be left with their project of playing patron to the other Slavs until a firm footing has been gained in Austria and Hungary, and then this will cease of itself. They also have a good picture of the Servian Omladina; it is a sort of student society with tendencies about as clear as those of the old *Burschenschaft*.[596]

The explanation about Bakunin very good. Thus he is also rendered harmless, since the Russian paymasters will not permit him to go further than Herzen.

You must be having worse weather than us; here it's fairly cold, and the wind veers between northwest and east, but otherwise it's mostly fine, and I can take a decent walk every day. But 8 days ago, when it was once warm, I got a frightful grippe, which I drove out with 3 days of linseed tea.

I shall send you back the Dutch and Russian letters with the second post, so you'll get them tomorrow afternoon.

I have been looking through our correspondence of last year, and have discovered that roughly from July-August onwards your letters first individually, and later all without exception, show

---

a See this volume, p. 466. - b member - c See this volume, pp. 462-63, 464-65. - d Ibid., pp. 462-63.

more or less clear signs of MANIPULATION. The one I received this morning was, if it had been opened, at least decently closed.

Best greetings.

Your

F. E.

First published abridged in *Der Briefwechsel zwischen F. Engels und K. Marx*, Bd. 4, Stuttgart, 1913 and in full in *MEGA*, Abt. III, Bd. 4, Berlin, 1931

Printed according to the original

Published in English for the first time

312

ENGELS TO MARX

IN LONDON

Manchester, 28 March 1870

Dear Moor,

Yesterday I sent you, in a letter that was not registerable because it was Sunday, a £5 NOTE, S/7, 29,808, Manchester, 16 January 1869, which I hope you received together with the letter. Enclosed now follow £82.10—DRAFT ON DEMAND ON UNION BANK OF LONDON, DRAWN BY MANCHESTER AND COUNTY BANK TO ORDER OF F. ENGELS AND ENDORSED TO YOU, and, further, the various Dutch and Russian letters. The Roesgen here[a] claims that he is certainly not a relative of the Rotterdam one.[b] The latter is quite something in his confusion— the divine right of the *king* and the people—the protest against *hedendaagsche*[c] Communism, the defence of constitutional monarchy against the republic (though in this there is *in Holland* an atom of historical idea) and, finally, protective tariffs. In such a case one may well be called Philipp von Roesgen von Floss. And it is also rather cool that he accuses the bourgeoisie that they first want *hunne eigene beurs vullen*[d] and then *het door her uitgezogen land*

---

[a] Charles Roesgen - [b] Philipp von Roesgen von Floss - [c] contemporary - [d] to fill their own purses

aan den daarop vlammenden Pruis verkoopen.[a] This should be sent to Bismarck.

Your

F. E.

First published in *Der Briefwechsel zwischen F. Engels und K. Marx*, Bd. 4, Stuttgart, 1913

Printed according to the original

Published in English for the first time

313

MARX TO LUDWIG KUGELMANN[597]

IN HANOVER

London, 28 March 1870

Dear Kugelmann,

Since an abscess on my right thigh makes sitting for any time impossible, I send you, enclosed, a *letter for the Brunswick Comité, Bracke and Co.*, instead of writing twice. It would be best if you delivered it personally, after reading it through, and reminded them again that this information is confidential, not intended for the public.[b]

First published in *Die Neue Zeit*, Bd. 2, Nr. 15, Stuttgart, 1901-1902

Printed according to the magazine

Published in English in full for the first time

---

[a] sell the land they have sucked dry to *Prussia*, which ardently desires it. - [b] Marx enclosed *Confidential Communication* written by him.

314

MARX TO SIGFRID MEYER AND AUGUST VOGT[174]

IN NEW YORK

London, 9 April 1870

Dear Meyer and dear Vogt,

So here you have me in all postures, one time together with my eldest daughter Jenny. Kugelmann had all these things printed from earlier photograms.[a] *Je ne suis pas l'auteur responsable de ces folies.*[b]

First of all, with regard to my long letter-debt to you, you will see from the enclosed note from Eccarius that the General Council has *passiert*[c] a *votum* OF CONDOLENCE[598] because of the state of my health. (You see, I am practising Pennsylvanian German.) In fact, because of repeated relapses, I have only been able to attend the meetings of the General Council twice since the beginning of December, so, for all important discussions, the SUBCOMMITTEE came *to my place.* Under these circumstances (and I am still not completely restored), my free moments have literally been so absorbed by work that my correspondence has been limited to the completely unavoidable.

First, ad vocem[d] *Sorge*: he has written two letters to Eccarius as General Secretary. Eccarius informed the General Council of this. The latter instructed Eccarius to deliver the letters to me for answering, as I was Secretary for the German branches in the UNITED STATES. I tarried intentionally, as I knew that Meyer was on a trip to the West Indies, and could not find Vogt's private address.

I do not know Sorge's private letters to Eccarius. They probably deal simply with the money question, payment to Eccarius for his contributions to the *Arbeiter-Union.* Eccarius regards his position as General Secretary too much as a means of *making money,* and in a way that compromises *us Germans* in the eyes of the French and English. See, for instance, the enclosed note to me from Lessner.[599] This is also the reason that I shall not communicate Meyer's letter to Eccarius,[600] since it conveys the information, irresistible to Eccarius, that Sorge has '*pecuniary resources*'.

---

[a] See this volume, p. 213 - [b] I am not the author responsible for these follies. - [c] An unidiomatic use of the German verb *passieren* (to happen, take place, pass by), on which Marx comments in the parenthesis. - [d] regarding

With regard to Sorge's two official letters, they are written in the name of the General German Workers' Association 'LABOR UNION' No. 5, and *signed* Corresponding Secretary.

One letter contains orders for the reports of the General Council, and various other commonplace stuff.

The other letter contains nothing essential except for the notification that the association has joined the 'International'.

I shall write a few lines to Mr Sorge today, sending him the 15 COPIES of the latest report he requests.[a]

A certain *Robert William Hume* (*Astoria, Long Island, New York*) sent us a detailed letter some time ago, on the occasion of the decisions of the General Council concerning the Irish amnesty[b]— a letter better than anything we had so far received from English-American circles. On my recommendation, he was named American-English correspondent, and has accepted this. I would, therefore, request you to get into contact with this man, and for this purpose I enclose a few lines addressed to him.

From the enclosed cutting from the *Marseillaise* of 2 April, you will see that F. Carl and F. Jubitz—persons unknown to us here—have sent an address to Paris in the name of the German workers.[601] I would like to know whether these people belong to you. What was regarded as dubious here—on the General Council—was the fact that the *International* was not mentioned at all, but rather treated as non-existent.

General *Cluseret* has offered himself from New York to the General Council as French correspondent. Whether he was accepted I cannot say, believe I have heard so, however. He is a flighty, superficial, officious, boastful fellow. For instance, in one of his latest letters to the *Marseillaise*[c] he presents himself as a recognised representative of the workers of New York. But the man is of a certain importance for us just because of his links with the *Marseillaise*. In case you should wish to get to know this 'hero', even if only to sound him out, I enclose for you *a* CREDENTIAL, which might also be OF USE elsewhere.

The money Meyer sent to Stepney has been delivered to the General Council. Stepney is a very pedantic, but honest Englishman. He sent me the letter from Meyer with enclosures, so I had to send the stuff back to the General Council.

---

[a] *Report of the Fourth Annual Congress of the International Working Men's Association, held at Basle, in Switzerland.* - [b] K. Marx, *Draft Resolution of the General Council on the Policy of the British Government Towards the Irish Prisoners* (see also this volume, pp. 375-76). - [c] G. P. Cluseret, 'Aux travailleurs américains', *La Marseillaise*, No. 103, 2 April 1870.

The day after tomorrow (11 April) I shall send you what International things I have at hand. (It is too late for the mail today.) I shall, ditto, send more of the 'Basle'.[a]

Amongst the stuff sent, you will also find a few copies of the RESOLUTIONS of the General Council of *30 November* on the *Irish amnesty*, which you already know, and which I initiated[b]; ditto an Irish pamphlet on the treatment of FENIAN CONVICTS.[c]

I had intended to submit further RESOLUTIONS on the necessary transformation of the present Union [461] (i.e., enslavement of Ireland) IN A FREE AND EQUAL FEDERATION WITH GREAT BRITAIN. Further progress on this matter has been temporarily suspended AS FAR AS PUBLIC RESOLUTIONS GO because of my enforced absence from the General Council. No other member of it has enough knowledge of Irish affairs or sufficient prestige with the *English* members of the General Council to be able to replace me on this matter.

Time has not passed uselessly, however, and I would ask you to pay particular attention to the following:

After studying the Irish question for years I have come to the conclusion that the decisive blow against the ruling classes in England (and this is decisive for the workers' movement ALL OVER THE WORLD) can*not* be struck *in England*, but *only in Ireland*.

On 1 January 1870[d] the General Council issued a secret circular, written by me in French[e]—{for repercussions in England, only the French papers are important, not the German}—on the relationship of the Irish national struggle to the emancipation of the working class, and thus on the attitude the International Association must take towards the Irish question.

Here I give you, quite shortly, the salient points. Ireland is the BULWARK of the *English landed aristocracy*. The exploitation of this country is not simply one of the main sources of their material wealth; it is their greatest *moral* power. They represent, IN FACT, the *domination of England over Ireland*. Ireland is, thus, the *grand moyen*[f] by which the English aristocracy maintains *its domination in England* itself.

---

[a] *Report of the Fourth Annual Congress of the International Working Men's Association, held at Basle, in Switzerland.* - [b] K. Marx, *Draft Resolution of the General Council on the Policy of the British Government Towards the Irish Prisoners.* - [c] Apparently Marx refers to the first five articles on the Irish question written by Jenny Marx and published by that time in the *Marseillaise.* - [d] the original has: 1 December 1869 - [e] *The General Council to the Federal Council of Romance Switzerland.* - [f] cardinal means

On the other hand: if the English army and police were withdrawn from Ireland tomorrow, you would immediately have AN AGRARIAN REVOLUTION IN IRELAND. But the overthrow of the English aristocracy in Ireland would entail, and would lead immediately to, its overthrow in England. This would bring about the prerequisites for the proletarian revolution in England. In Ireland, the *land question* has, so far, been the *exclusive form* of the social question; it is a question of existence, a *question of life or death* for the immense majority of the Irish people; at the same time, it is inseparable from the *national* question: because of this, destruction of the English landed aristocracy is an infinitely easier operation in Ireland than in England itself—quite apart from the more passionate and more revolutionary character of the Irish than the English.

As for the English *bourgeoisie*, it has, *d'abord*,[a] a common interest with the English aristocracy in turning Ireland into simple pastureland to provide meat and wool at the cheapest possible price FOR THE ENGLISH MARKET. It has the same interest in reducing the Irish population to such a low level, through EVICTION and forced emigration, that *English capital* (leasehold capital) can function with 'SECURITY' in that country. It has the same interest IN CLEARING THE ESTATE OF IRELAND as it had IN THE CLEARING OF THE AGRICULTURAL DISTRICTS OF ENGLAND and SCOTLAND. The £6,000-10,000 ABSENTEE and other Irish revenues that at present flow annually to London must also be taken into account.

But the English bourgeoisie also has much more important interests in the present Irish economy. As a result of the steadily-increasing concentration of leaseholding, Ireland is steadily supplying its SURPLUS for the English LABOUR MARKET, and thus forcing down the WAGES and material and moral position of the ENGLISH WORKING CLASS.

And most important of all! All industrial and commercial centres in England now have a working class *divided* into two *hostile* camps, English PROLETARIANS and Irish PROLETARIANS. The ordinary English worker hates the Irish worker as a competitor who forces down the STANDARD OF LIFE. In relation to the Irish worker, he feels himself to be a member of the *ruling nation* and, therefore, makes himself a tool of his aristocrats and capitalists *against Ireland*, thus strengthening their domination *over himself.* He harbours religious, social and national prejudices against him. His attitude towards him is roughly that of the POOR WHITES to the

---

[a] in the first place

NIGGERS[a] in the former slave states of the American Union. The Irishman PAYS HIM BACK WITH INTEREST IN HIS OWN MONEY. He sees in the English worker both the accomplice and the stupid tool of *English rule in Ireland*.

This antagonism is kept artificially alive and intensified by the press, the pulpit, the comic papers, in short by all the means at the disposal of the ruling class. *This antagonism is the secret of the English working class's impotence*, despite its organisation. It is the secret of the maintenance of power by the capitalist class. And the latter is fully aware of this.

But the evil does not end here. It rolls across the ocean. The antagonism between English and Irish is the secret basis of the conflict between the UNITED STATES and England. It renders any serious and honest cooperation impossible between the working classes of the two countries. It enables the governments of the two countries, whenever they think fit, to blunt the edge of social conflict by MUTUAL BULLYING and, IN CASE OF NEED, by war between the two countries.

England, as the metropolis of capital, as the power that has hitherto ruled the world market, is for the present the most important country for the workers' revolution and, in addition, the *only* country where the material conditions for this revolution have developed to a certain state of maturity. Thus, to hasten the social revolution in England is the most important object of the International Working Men's Association. The sole means of doing so is to make Ireland independent. It is, therefore, the task of the 'INTERNATIONAL' to bring the conflict between England and Ireland to the forefront everywhere, and to side with Ireland publicly everywhere. The special task of the Central Council[73] in London is to awaken the consciousness of the English working class that, *for them, the national emancipation of Ireland* is not a QUESTION OF ABSTRACT JUSTICE OR HUMANITARIAN SENTIMENT, but THE FIRST CONDITION OF THEIR OWN SOCIAL EMANCIPATION.

These are roughly the main points of the circular letter, which, at the same time, gave the *raisons d'être* for the resolutions of the Central Council on the Irish amnesty. Shortly afterwards I sent a strongly-worded anonymous article on the English treatment of the FENIANS etc., and against Gladstone etc., to the *Internationale*[b] (organ of our Belgian Central Committee[c] in Brussels). In this article I also pilloried the FRENCH REPUBLICANS—(the *Marseillaise* had

---

[a] See p. XXXVIII of the Preface.— *Ed.* - [b] K. Marx. *The English Government and the Fenian Prisoners*. - [c] Belgian Federal Committee

published some stupid nonsense about Ireland, written here by the wretched Tallandier[a])—for saving, in their national egoism, all their *colères*[b] for the Empire.

This worked. My daughter Jenny wrote a series of articles for the *Marseillaise* under the name J. Williams (she signed herself Jenny Williams in her private letter to the editors), and published, among other things, O'Donovan Rossa's letter. HENCE IMMENSE NOISE. After many years of cynical refusal, *Gladstone* was *thereby* finally compelled to authorise a *parliamentary enquête*[c] into the treatment of the FENIAN PRISONERS. She is now REGULAR CORRESPONDENT ON IRISH AFFAIRS for the *Marseillaise*. (*This is naturally a secret between us.*) The British Government and press are furious that the Irish question has thus been placed on the *ordre du jour*[d] in France, and that these blackguards will now be watched and exposed all over continent, via Paris.

A second bird was hit by the same stone. We have, thereby, forced the Irish leaders, journalists, etc. in Dublin to establish contact with us, something the *General Council* had hitherto failed to achieve!

You have a wide field in America for work along the same lines. *A coalition of the German workers with the Irish workers* (naturally, also, with the English and American workers who wish to join in) is the greatest thing you could undertake now. This must be done in the name of the 'International'. The social significance of the Irish question must be made clear.

Next time, several special things about the position of the English workers.

Salut et fraternité!

Karl Marx

First published abridged in *Die Neue Zeit*, Bd. 2, Nr. 33, Stuttgart, 1906-1907 and in full in: Marx and Engels, *Works*, First Russian Edition, Vol. XXVI, Moscow, 1935

Printed according to the original

Published in English in full for the first time

---

a See this volume, p. 445. - b wrath - c investigation - d agenda

315

ENGELS TO MARX

IN LONDON

Manchester, 13 April 1870

Dear Moor,

Best thanks for the *parlamentaires*.[a] Some of them anticipated my wishes; others were new to me and very handy. I am sending you several numbers of *Zukunft* to give you an opportunity to admire the infinitely foul methods used by the National Liberals in the debate on political crimes (Criminal Code). This excels everything. The cowardly rogues believe they have performed such a deed of heroism with the abolition of the death sentence for *common* crimes—and that, too, only on paper—that political offenders may now be calmly imprisoned in convict jails and treated as COMMON CONVICTS.[602] For *political* crimes, powder and lead will continue to exist, through the agency of martial law.

Enclosed—a jolly letter from Wilhelm, which I request returned for the sake of answering. You will see that the fellow acts as though *I* were copying from *him*. He has not yet firmly established his Leipzig sheet,[b] and already wants to start a *daily* in Berlin.[603] The fellow always sees the heavens filled with melodious violins,[c] but the strings are missing and the sounding-board is smashed.

After various interruptions I am finally finished with Wakefield[d]—16-1700 pages quarto.

The book is gruesomely written and still more gruesomely printed—nearly all figures and dates are wrong—but, as far as the material is concerned, unequalled in my practice. I have never before seen something so complete about a country. And the fellow has eyes and is fairly honest. The anxiety of the English concerning Ireland from 1808 to 1812 is priceless. Dispatches sent to India in which Lord W. Bentinck declared that Ireland was *lost* for England, were intercepted by the French and published.

---

[a] parliamentary materials - [b] *Der Volksstaat* - [c] The German 'ihm hängt der Himmel voller Geigen' corresponds to the English 'he sees everything in rosy colours'. - [d] E. Wakefield, *An Account of Ireland, Statistical and Political.*

It is striking 8 o'clock; I must run to catch the post.
Best greetings.

Your
F. E.

First published abridged in *Der Briefwechsel zwischen F. Engels und K. Marx*, Bd. 4, Stuttgart, 1913, and in full in *MEGA*, Abt. III, Bd. 4, Berlin, 1931

Printed according to the original

Published in English for the first time

316

MARX TO ENGELS [34]

IN MANCHESTER

[London,] 14 April 1870

DEAR FRED,

Enclosed, Wilhelm returned.[a] From the attached letter from Borkheim,[604] you will see what ill-mannered things Wilhelm says about me. I don't like such churlish sentimentality, and since Wilhelm is a born Darmstadt man and so has not, at least, the excuse that he is a born Westphalian, I have sent him a rather blunt reply.

In your article[b] he has intentionally overlooked the fact that the People's Party [38] and the 'National Liberals' are treated as the two poles of *the same* narrow-mindedness.

On Tuesday[c] I was at the Central Council[d] for the first time once again, and took the opportunity to muster Pfänder, who had entered as a member once more (re-elected), but had not yet presented himself.[605] He informed me that he had been called a week before to *Schapper*, who is very dangerously ill. Schapper wanted to see me; Pfänder did *not* inform me of this, *because* I could not walk well as a result of the business on my thigh. But I would have driven there if he had notified me. On the same evening (Tuesday), Lessner reported that Schapper was *in articulo mortis*.[e] I hope it is not as bad as that.

---

[a] See the previous letter. - [b] F. Engels, *Preface to the Second Edition of 'The Peasant War in Germany'*. - [c] 12 April - [d] General Council - [e] dying

While I am on medical matters, just this: I regard the latest outbreak simply as after-effects, which arrive with some regularity, and then disappear as the warm weather proceeds. I believe, therefore, that I am finished with it for this year. As always, however, the arrival of warmer weather has produced the liver complaint (or whatever it is), and for this I am gulping Gumpert's medicine. Kugelmann claims that the only way to put me properly on my feet is to take the cure at Karlsbad[a] at the end of the summer. The whole thing derives from poor nourishment, this from poor digestion, and this is connected with the fact that my liver doesn't function properly. I would, therefore, ask you to question Gumpert about this. But it would be better if you said that the Karlsbad proposal came from my English doctor, for the very name Kugelmann might induce him not to judge the case objectively, contrary to his inclination and conscience. I feel that, in fact, some sort of decisive preventive measures must be taken, since one gets a year older every year, and this sort of infirmity is not helpful, either for ONE SELF or for ones outside effectiveness.

Did you know that Meyen had died?

The copies of *Zukunft*[b] give, I must say, a fine picture of the Prussian-Liberal present. But the *Future*[b] will convert itself into the *Present*. As *Future* the paper is really bankrupt. In its new form, it comes under the sway of Sonnemann in Frankfort (with Weiss, as previously, as editor *en chef*). It should represent, purely politically, the *People's Party* in Berlin. *Quelle imbécilité!*[c] By abandoning its flirtation with the 'social question', it will completely lose its little bit of influence and circulation among the workers, and it will certainly not win over the Prussian, and especially Berlin bourgeois by a stronger South German coloration.

I enclose for you 2 Vienna workers' papers[d] and 1 *Égalité*, and request the return of all three after reading.

In the *Volkswille* the 'structure' is 'fine' which the little Jew Leo Frankel (Schweitzer's Paris correspondent, I don't know whether still?) constructs from my explanation of the components of value. *Par exemple*: (labour power+wage labour−wage=independent worker).[e]

From the *Égalité* you will gather that, at the Congress of the *Suisse Romande*[f] in La Chaux-de-Fonds, it came to open warfare between the Bakuninists led by Guillaume (the brute calls himself

---

a Karlovy Vary - b A pun: *Zukunft*—the title of the newspaper—means 'future'. - c What stupidity! - d *Volkswille* - e L. Frankel, 'Ein belauschtes Zwiegespräch. VIII', *Volkswille*, No. 10, 2 April 1870. - f Romance Switzerland

professór, is editor of *Progrès* in Locle, Bakunin's personal paper), and the *Conseil Romand*[a] (Geneva).[606] The presentation is very confused. On Tuesday evening Jung informed us of the official report of the Geneva COUNCIL,[b] written by the Russian Utine, who holds the function of secretary of the Romance Congress. The anti-Bakuninists, 2,000 persons, were outflanked and thereby forced to *secessio*,[c] by the Bakuninists, consisting of 600 persons, who, however, *per fas et nefas*,[d] including forged mandates, made sure of a larger number of delegates. There were stormy declarations about Bakunin's activities, which were exposed by Utine, among others. The COUNCIL *Romand* now demands, on the basis of the resolution of the last (Basle) Congress,[508] that the Central Council decide. We have *replied*: all FACTS, with the *minutes of the meetings*, must be sent here. Ditto, we have commissioned Jung to write to Guillaume, so that he may, ditto, submit his vouchers.

Recently also we had to rule on a dispute in Lyons.[550] And finally, in Basle, one clique (under State Attorney Bruhin) has laid charges with us against the other (more proletarian one). We have, however, referred the latter case, as *completely local*, to J. Ph. Becker as arbitrator.

In Paris Lafargue got to know a very learned Russian lady[e] (a friend of his friend Jaclard, an excellent young man). She told him: *Flerovsky*—although his book[f] passed censorship at the time of the LIBERAL FIT—has been, if you please, banished to Siberia for the same. The translation of my book has been confiscated and prohibited before being published.[196]

You will receive, this week or at the beginning of next: *Landlord and Tenant Right in Ireland. Reports by Poor Law Inspectors. 1870,* ditto *Agricultural Holdings in Ireland. Returns. 1870.*

The REPORTS of the POOR LAW INSPECTORS are interesting. Like their *Reports on Agricultural Wages*, which are already in your hands, they show that the conflict between LABOURERS ON THE ONE HAND, FARMERS and TENANTS on the other, began after the FAMINE.[607] As regards the *Reports on Wages*—assuming the present figures on wages are correct, and that is probable, considering other sources—the *former wage rates* are either quoted *too low*, or those in the earlier PARLIAMENTARY RETURNS, which I'll look out for you in my PARLIAMENTARY PAPERS, were *too high*. On the whole, however,

---

a Romance Council - b Federal Council of Romance Switzerland - c to split - d by fair means and foul - e A. V. Korvin-Krukovskaya - f *Положеніе рабочаго класса въ Россіи*

what I stated in the section on Ireland[608] is confirmed: that the rise in wages has been more than outweighed by that in food prices, and that, with the exception of the autumn period, etc., the RELATIVE SURPLUS of LABOURERS is properly established despite emigration. Also important in the *Landlord and Tenant Right Reports* is the FACT that the development of MACHINERY has turned a mass of HANDLOOM WEAVERS into PAUPERS.

You would oblige me if you would tell me, quite shortly, about the BOGS, PEATS etc., of Ireland. In all the BLUE BOOKS I have read, the BOG is sometimes situated on the mountain, that is on the mountain slope, but also sometimes on the plain. What is the situation? What do the IRISH understand by TOWNLANDS[a]?

It is clear from the two REPORTS of the POOR LAW COMMISSIONERS that 1. since the FAMINE the CLEARING of the ESTATES of LABOURERS has begun *as in England* (not to be confused with the SUPPRESSION of the 40s. FREEHOLDERS after 1829[609]).

2. that the ENCUMBERED ESTATES PROCEEDINGS have put a mass *of small usurers* in the place of the TURNED OUT prodigal LANDLORDS (the CHARGE OF LANDLORDS $^1/_6$ according to the same REPORTS).

I would appreciate it if you and Moore could send me a few £s *for Dupont.* His wife is in hospital with consumption. He himself has been TURNED OUT of his old trade. The *excuse*: his political opinions; the *real cause*: he made *all the inventions*, which his manufacturer appropriated. For this reason, he has been *persona ingrata*[b] for a long time for him (he thinks he has sucked him completely dry). But the Manufacturer has cut his own throat, so FAR as Dupont has made a quite new invention, which solves a problem that has existed for a long time in piano manufacture. I have already given Dupont a few £s; since, together with his 3 small girls, he had been condemned to just dry bread. It's only a matter of helping for a few weeks until he finds a new position. Who can write the story of WORKINGMEN EVICTED because of *inventions*!

And, in addition, the poor devil is also being HARASSED by the jealousy of the Paris people, and the slanders of the FRENCH BRANCH,[72] who naturally immediately cornered Flourens.

Salut.
                                                    Your
                                                    K. M.

Apropos. Stirling (Edinburgh), the translator of Hegel's *Logic*,[c] and heading the British SUBSCRIPTION for the Hegel monument—has

---

a See this volume, p. 483. - b an uncomfortable person - c An allusion to J. H. Stirling, *The Secret of Hegel: Being the Hegelian System in Origin, Principle, Form, and Matter.*

written a small pamphlet against *Huxley* and his *protoplasm*.[a] As a Scotsman, the fellow has naturally adopted Hegel's false religion and Idea-istic mysticism (so induced Carlyle to declare publicly his conversion to Hegelianism). But his knowledge of Hegel's dialectic allows him to demonstrate Huxley's weaknesses—where he indulges in philosophising. His business in the same pamphlet against Darwin comes to the same as what the Berliner Blutschulze[b] (Hegelian OF THE OLD SCHOOL) said some years ago at the natural scientists' meeting in Hanover.[610]

First published abridged in *Der Briefwechsel zwischen F. Engels und K. Marx*, Bd. 4, Stuttgart, 1913 and in full in *MEGA*, Abt. III, Bd. 4, Berlin, 1931

Printed according to the original

Published in English in full for the first time

317

ENGELS TO MARX[34]

IN LONDON

Manchester, 15 April 1870

Dear Moor,

Enclosed, returned, Borkheim.[604] Good old Wilhelm[c] did not expect his bragging about you would be communicated to you *ipsissimis verbis*.[d] Remains a blockhead all his life.

The papers will be returned to you on Sunday evening. I shall try to see Gumpert tomorrow, but since he has himself been suffering with his nerves for some time because of 'over-work' (of what sort?), it's possible he'll be away during the holidays. In the meantime, I suggest you try taking strenuous walks—3-4 hours together—for several consecutive days and, WEATHER PERMITTING, walk at least 1-2 hours daily, and then every week such a long walk at least 1-2 times. Now I can no longer work properly until I have walked for an hour or more; it has a wonderful effect and will certainly also get your liver more or less going again. In addition, I quite agree with Kugelmann's view.[e]

---

[a] J. H. Stirling, *As Regards Protoplasm in Relation to Prof. Huxley's Essay on the Physical Basis of Life*; T. H. Huxley, 'On the Physical Basis of Life', *The Fortnightly Review*, Vol. V, No. XXVI, 1 February 1869. - [b] Franz Eilhard Schulze - [c] Wilhelm Liebknecht - [d] verbatim - [e] See this volume, p. 479.

Fränkelche[a] is a real yiddisher lad. He learned '*la formule*' in Paris, and delivers good wares.[b] It's delicious that he understands the *frais généraux*[c] as part of surplus value, including wear and tear of machinery, lubrication, coal (if this is not raw material), ground rent, etc.

Bogs are simply peat bogs or marshes, which occur in 2 main sorts of locality: 1. on the plains, in valleys (old lake beds) or depressions, the exit from which has become blocked; 2. on heights with a flat or mildly-rolling summit, as a result of deforestation, where the moss, grass, heather, etc., become matted, and the water flows off, on average, more slowly than it rains in. A marsh in the plains sometimes even has a big river flowing through it, which, however, does not dry it out (various places on the Shannon, Donaumoss in Bavaria, etc.). Very usually such bogs are also the source reservoirs of rivers (the Bog of Allen, from which there flowed, in its original but now very reduced size, the Boyne, the Barrow, various tributaries of these two, and the Shannon). Chat Moss, between Liverpool and Manchester, which you know, is a real, typical Irish bog, as Wakefield[d] confirms. It lies at least 30-40 feet above the Mersey and Irwell, which flow around it in a semicircle, so drainage very easy, yet this is only about $1/3$ done, and they've been at it since 1800. This is because of the landlords; such an object can naturally only be drained systematically and compulsorily. They have them in Holland too—peat bogs are the same all over Europe. The Irish name those on the *plain* RED BOG and the mountain [bog] BLACK BOG. Water trickling down can produce on the slopes—even very steep, 30-40 degrees—similar marshy places which, in time, produce peat. On steep slopes it's naturally only thin; on flatter ones it can get thicker and thicker. The thickest, naturally, is on the flat summits.

TOWNLANDS are the lowest administrative divisions in Ireland, which are everywhere based on the old Irish CLAN divisions, and in the north and the west these have mostly been retained unchanged. The counties represent the local dukedoms (Donegal, the realm of THE O'Donnell, who then had others under him, e.g., THE Mac Swine and his people. Tyrone is that of THE O'Neill, Fermanagh that of THE Maguire, etc.). The baronies represent the individual CLANS, and in these the *ballybetaghs* (as Davies writes it[e]) or, translated into English, TOWNLANDS, the individual village bounds,

---

held jointly by the inhabitants. In Ulster, for example, these have been completely retained in their old boundaries; in other parts more or less. The PARISH, the POOR LAW UNION and other special English divisions, were later inserted between BARONY and TOWNLAND.

Your conclusions from the PARLIAMENTARY REPORTS[a] agree with my results. It should not, however, be forgotten that, in the first period after 1846, the process of CLEARING the 40SH. FREEHOLDERS[609] was mixed up with the CLEARING OF LABOURERS, the reason being that, up to 1829, in order to produce FREEHOLDERS, LEASES FOR 21 or 31 YEARS AND A LIFE (if not longer) had to be made, since a man could only become a FREEHOLDER if he *could not be turned out* during his lifetime. These LEASES almost never excluded SUBDIVIDING. These LEASES were partly still valid in 1846, respectively the consequences, i.e., the peasants were still on the ESTATE. Ditto, on the estates then in the hands of MIDDLEMEN (who mostly held LEASES for 64 years AND THREE LIVES, or even for 99 years); these estates often only reverted between 1846 and 1860. Thus, these processes ±[b] ran mixed up, respectively the Irish LANDLORD was never, or seldom, in a situation of having to decide whether particularly LABOURERS, rather than other traditional small TENANTS should be cleared. Essentially it comes to the same thing in England as in Ireland: the land must be tilled by labourers who live in *other POOR LAW UNIONS*, so that the landlord and his tenant might be spared the pauper-rate.[611] This is stated by Senior, or rather by his brother Edward, POOR LAW COMMISSIONER in Ireland: THE GREAT INSTRUMENT WHICH IS CLEARING IRELAND IS THE *POOR LAW*.

Land sold since the ENCUMBERED ESTATE COURT amounts, according to my notes, to as much as $^1/_5$ of the total; the purchasers were indeed largely usurers, speculators, etc., *mainly Irish Catholics*. Partly, also, GRAZIERS who had become rich. Yet even now there are *only about 8-9,000 landowners* in Ireland.

What do you say to the way the whole European bourgeoisie has made itself a laughing-stock, by pledging itself to the *empire libéral*, and lately awarding laurels to Louis Bonaparte for his sincere transition to constitutionalism? And now it comes to light that he means this so sincerely that he *explicitly reserves* for himself, for the suitable moment, the right to a coup d'état, *vulgo* a plebiscite.[612] Nobody should be able to say that he had overthrown the constitution for a 2nd time. This is also a commentary on '*gouvernement direct par le peuple*',[c] which the Swiss are now

---

[a] See this volume. pp. 480-81. - [b] more or less - [c] direct government by the people

introducing[613] and the French frankly don't want. What is a plebiscite called in Swiss—veto or referendum? This question should be put to Wilhelm. *Ad vocem* Wilhelm—have you seen the marvellous advertisement in No. 27 of *Volksstaat*: *Who borrowed from me 'Kolb's Statistik'*[a]? *W. Liebknecht.* Not enough that he is sloppy; he has to advertise the fact too.

Zukunft—very amusing.[b] The jackasses!

Best greetings.

Your
F. E.

First published abridged in *Der Briefwechsel zwischen F. Engels und K. Marx*, Bd. 4, Stuttgart, 1913 and in full in *MEGA*, Abt. III, Bd. 4, Berlin, 1931

Printed according to the original

Published in English in full for the first time

318

MARX TO PAUL LAFARGUE[614]

IN PARIS

[London,] 18 April 1870

Dear Paul-Laurent,[615]

I send enclosed credentials for Mr H. Verlet.[616] Let him give to the new section he is about to establish no *sectarian 'name'*, either Communistic or other. *Il faut éviter les 'étiquettes' sectaires dans l'Association Internationale.*[c] The general aspirations and tendencies of the working class emanate from the real conditions in which it finds itself placed. They are therefore common to the whole class although the movement reflects itself in their heads in the most diversified forms, more or less phantastical, more or less adequate. Those who interpret best the hidden sense of the class struggle going on before our eyes—the Communists are the last to commit the blunder of affecting or fostering sectarianism.

Mr Verlet would do well to put himself in communication with our friend Jules Johannard, 126 rue d'Aboukir.

---

[a] G. F. Kolb, *Handbuch der vergleichenden Statistik der Völkerzustands- und Staatenkunde.* - [b] See this volume, p. 479. - [c] Sectarian 'labels' must be avoided in the International Association.

One thing which ought to be done as quickly as possible, and which might be done by Paul-Laurent, is to publish in the *Libre pensée* a true and literal translation of the *International Rules*.[a] The French current translation, emanating from our first Paris Committee, Tolain *et* Co., is full of *intentional* mistakes. They suppressed everything which they did not like. If a true translation was made, it would be well to send it me *before* its publication.[617]

In Germany people would much wonder at Verlet's appreciation of Büchner.[b][618] In our country he is only considered, and justly so, as a *vulgarisateur*.

You know how much I admire le 'Roman de Conspiration'.[c] I was, therefore, truly delighted to see it so well appreciated by Paul-Laurent.

I am now forced to say a few words which Paul-Laurent will a little fret at, but I cannot help doing so.

Your father wrote me a letter to Hanover which I have not yet answered, because I did not know what to say.

I feel quite sure that Paul has discarded all notion of finishing, or occupying himself with, his medical studies. When at Paris I wrote to his father in a different sense, and I was warranted in doing so by Paul's own promises.[d] Thus I am placed in quite a false position towards M. Lafargue *aîné*.[e] I cannot remain in that fix. I see no other prospect of getting out of it but by writing to him that I have as little influence with his beloved son as himself. If you see any other way of escape for me, any other means of clearing my position, please communicate it to me.

In my opinion, which however I neither pretend nor hope to see accepted and acted upon, Paul-Laurent *cum figlio*[f] ought to pay a visit to their parents at Bordeaux and try to coax them by the many means personal intercourse permits of.

Yours truly...[g]

First published in *Annali dell'Istituto G. G. Feltrinelli*, an. 1, Milano, 1958   Reproduced from the original

---

[a] See this volume, p. 557. - [b] L. Büchner, *Kraft und Stoff*. - [c] This refers to Paul Lafargue's article 'Le Roman d'une conspiration par A. Ranc', *La Libre pensée*, No. 13, 16 April 1870, signed Paul-Laurent Lafargue. - [d] See this volume, p. 315. - [e] senior - [f] and son - [g] The signature is torn off.

319

ENGELS TO MARX

IN LONDON

Manchester, 19 April 1870

Dear Moor,

I forgot to write to you on Friday[a] that I had no money in the house and could, therefore, enclose nothing for that poor devil Dupont.[b] Enclosed S/6 11,916, Leeds, 15 July 1869—£5 for him. I hope it will suffice him until he has found a place again.

About Schapper, write to me, too, how things are going.

I have not yet seen Gumpert. I am, however, firmly convinced that plenty of exercise during the present marvellous weather will do you a lot of good, and will constitute an excellent pre-cure to Karlsbad.[c] Yesterday, with Schorlemmer, I walked some 17-18 miles; you do the same, and you will soon forget you have a liver.

Today I am returning you 2 issues of *Marseillaise* and *Égalité* and the Vienna newspaper,[d] and enclose a few cuttings from the *Examiner and Times* on Ireland, which are particularly remarkable since they come from a Methodist who, as a result of his isms (TEETOTALISM), etc., hangs out with the *Ism*ists here; otherwise, the *Examiner* would certainly not have accepted them. I shall need them later, so send them back sometime.[e]

Apropos, what is Mr Williams[f] doing? Tussy writes that he is still working, but I see no results.

I ordered Flerovsky[g] some time ago, but have heard nothing further, so I assume it has been confiscated and is no longer available.

Best greetings.

Your

F. E.

First published in *Der Briefwechsel zwischen F. Engels und K. Marx*, Bd. 4, Stuttgart, 1913

Printed according to the original

Published in English for the first time

---

[a] 15 April - [b] See this volume, p. 481. - [c] Karlovy Vary - [d] *Volkswille* - [e] J. Fourlong, 'The Irish Roman Catholic Bishops on the Land Question', *Manchester Daily Examiner and Times*, 30 March 1870. - [f] Marx's daughter Jenny - [g] Н. Флеровскій, *Положеніе рабочаго класса въ Россіи*.

320

MARX TO ENGELS

IN MANCHESTER

[London,] 19 April 1870

IN ALL HASTE

DEAR FRED,

I am sending you 2 PARLIAMENTARIES ON IRELAND, and the latest *Égalité, ditto La Solidarité.* From the enclosed letter from Perret,[619] ex-secretary of the *Fédéral Comité* in Geneva—which I must have back *by Friday*—you will see how the Muscovite beast[a] is acting. He was naturally forced to appeal also—which he did—to the CENTRAL COUNCIL[73] through his *sécrétaire général* Robert. I also enclose this letter.[620] What do you think we should do about these fellows?

MR WILLIAMS SENDS YOU HIS COMPLIMENTS. ONE OF HIS ARTICLES HE HAD SENT TO *Reynolds's.* HE WENT TO TOWN TO FIND ANOTHER COPY FOR YOU, BUT IT WAS NOT TO BE GOT. Two further ARTICLES[b] together with OTHER *Marseillaises* HE SHALL FORWARD YOU THIS WEEK.[562]

My wife took the £5 to Dupont this morning. BEST THANKS FOR IT. HIS WIFE IS DYING IN THE HOSPITAL.

I have visited Schapper. Bad inflammation of the lungs, very emaciated, but perhaps he can still be saved.

Salut.

Your
K. M.

We shall put a spoke in Bakunin's wheel in the *Marseillaise* through *Flourens*, who has seen through the 'FRENCH BRANCH'[72] and annexed himself to us. HE IS A MAN OF VERY GREAT RESOLUTION. LEARNED. TOO SANGUINE.

First published in *Der Briefwechsel zwischen F. Engels und K. Marx*, Bd. 4. Stuttgart, 1913 and in full in *MEGA*, Abt. III, Bd. 4, Berlin, 1931

Printed according to the original

Published in English for the first time

---

[a] Mikhail Bakunin - [b] the sixth and seventh articles by Jenny Marx from the Irish question series

321

MARX TO PAUL LAFARGUE

IN PARIS

London, 19 April 1870

Dear Paul-Laurent,[615]

I shall have you proposed by Dupont on Tuesday next.[621] Meanwhile I call your attention to the presence in your committee[a] of *Robin, Bakunine's agent* who, at Geneva, did all in his power to *discredit the General Council* (he attacked it publicly in the *Égalité*)[507] and to prepare *la dictature de Bakounine sur l'Association Internationale*.[b] He has been expressly sent to Paris there to act in the same sense. Hence this fellow must be closely watched without becoming aware of having a surveillant at his side.[622]

In order *de vous mettre au courant*[c] I must give you a succinct review of Bakunine's intrigue.

Bakunine does not belong to the *International* but for about 1¹/₂ years. *C'est un nouveau venu.*[d] At the Berne[e] Congress (*September 1868*) of the *Ligue de la Paix et de la Liberté*[f][271] (he was *one of the executive committee* of this International middle-class Association founded in opposition to the proletarian International) he played one of the mountebank parts he delights in. He proposed a series of propositions, stupid in themselves, but affecting an aim of swaggering radicalism calculated to frighten *les crétins bourgeois*.[623] In that way, being outvoted by the majority, he made his noisy exit from the League and had this great event triumphantly announced in the European press. He understands *la réclame*[g] almost as well as Victor Hugo *qui, comme Heine dit, n'est pas simplement égoïste, mais Hugoïste*.[h]

Then he entered our Association—its Geneva *branche Romande*.[i] His first step was a conspiracy. He founded *l'Alliance de la Démocratie Socialiste*. The Programme of that society[257] was nothing else but the series of resolutions proposed by Bakunine on the Berne Peace League Congress.[j] The organisation was that of a sect with its head-center at Geneva, constituting itself as an

---

[a] the Paris Federal Council - [b] Bakunin's dictatorship in the International Association - [c] to acquaint you with the matter - [d] a novice - [e] Here and below Marx erroneously wrote 'Lausanne'. - [f] League of Peace and Freedom - [g] publicity - [h] who, as Heine put it, is not merely an egoist but Hugoist. - [i] Romance branch - [j] [M.] Bakounine, 'Discours de Bakounine au deuxième congrès de la paix, à Berne', *Kolokol*, No. 14-15, 1 December 1868 (see also this volume, p. 200).

International Association which was to have General Congresses of its own, which was to form an independent international body, and, *at the same time*, to be an integral member of our *Internationale*. In one word, our Association was by this interloping secret society by and by to be converted into an instrument *du Russe*[a] Bakounine. The pretext was, that this new society was founded for the special purpose '*à faire la propagande théoretique*'.[b] Very funny indeed, considering that Bakunine and his acolytes know nothing of theory. But Bakunine's programme was '*the theory*'. It consisted, in fact, of 3 points.

1) That the first requirement of the social Revolution was—*the abolition of inheritance, vieillerie St Simoniste*,[624] *dont le charlatan et l'i g n o r a m u s Bakunine se faisait l'éditeur responsable*.[c] It is evident: If you have had the power to make the social Revolution in one day, *par décret plébiscitaire*,[d] you would abolish at once landed property and capital, and would therefore have no occasion at all to occupy yourselves with *le droit d'héritage*.[e] On the other hand, if you have not that power (and it is of course foolish to suppose such a power), the proclamation of the *abolition of inheritance* would be not a serious act, but a foolish menace, rallying the whole peasantry and the whole small middle-class round the reaction. Suppose f.i. that the Yankees had not had the power to abolish slavery by the sword. What an imbecility it would have been to proclaim the *abolition of inheritance in slaves*! The whole thing rests on a superannuated idealism, which considers the actual jurisprudence as the basis of our economical state, instead of seeing that our economical state is the basis and source of our jurisprudence! As to Bakunine, all he wanted was to improvise a programme of his own making. *Voilà tout. C'était un programme d'occasion*.[f]

2) *L'é g a l i t é des différentes c l a s s e s*.[g] To suppose on the one hand the continued existence of *classes*, and on the other hand the *égalité* of the members belonging to them, this blunder shows you at once the shameless ignorance and superficiality of that fellow who made it his 'special mission' to enlighten us on 'theory'.

3) The working class must not occupy itself with *politics*. They must only organise themselves by trades-unions. One fine day, by means of the *Internationale* they will supplant the place of all existing states. You see what a caricature he has made of my doctrines! As the transformation of the existing States into

---

[a] of the Russian - [b] to carry on theoretical propaganda - [c] old St Simonist rubbish, of which Bakunin, a charlatan and *ignoramus*, was the responsible publisher - [d] by plebiscite - [e] right of inheritance - [f] That's all. This was a makeshift programme. - [g] *Equality* of different *classes*.

Associations is our last end, we must allow the governments, these great trade-unions of the ruling classes, to do as they like, because to occupy ourselves with them is to acknowledge them. Why! In the same way the old socialists said: You must not occupy yourselves with the wages question, because you want to abolish wages labour, and to struggle with the capitalist about the rate of wages is to acknowledge the wages system! The ass has not even seen that every class movement *as* a class movement, is necessarily and was always a *political* movement.

This then is the whole theoretical baggage of Mahomet-Bakunine, a Mahomet without a Koran.

His conspiracy he went secretly on with. He had some affiliates in Spain and Italy, a few dupes at Paris and Geneva. Good old Becker was foolish enough to allow himself to be put forward somewhat in a leading character by Bakunine. He regrets his blunder at present.

The General Council was only informed and called upon to sanction the statutes of the '*Alliance*' after Bakounine considered that concern as *fait accompli*. However he was mistaken. In an elaborate document the General Council declared the 'Alliance' to be an instrument of disorganisation, and rejected every connexion with it. (I shall send you the document.)[a]

A few months later, the *Comité Directeur* of the 'Alliance' addressed a letter to the General Council to the effect: The great men were willing to dissolve their organisation and merge it into the *Internationale*, but on the other hand, we were to declare categorically, *Oui ou Non!*,[b] whether we sanctioned their principles? If not, there would be a public secession on their part, and we would be responsible for such a misfortune[c]!

We answered that the General Council was not the Pope, that we allowed every section to have its own theoretical views of the real movement, always supposed that nothing directly opposite to our Rules was put forward. We hinted in a delicate way that we considered their 'theory' to be a sham. We insisted that '*l'égalité des classes*'[d] be changed for '*l'abolition des classes*',[e] what they did.[301] We requested them to give us the *dénombrement*[f] of their members, what they have never complied with. (You will also get this second document.[g])

---

[a] K. Marx, *The International Working Men's Association and the International Alliance of Socialist Democracy*. - [b] yes or no - [c] See this volume, p. 235. - [d] equality of classes - [e] abolition of classes - [f] the number - [g] K. Marx, *The General Council of the International Working Men's Association to the Central Bureau of the International Alliance of Socialist Democracy*

Thus the Alliance was *nominally* dissolved. In fact, it continued to form an *imperium in imperio.* Its branches had no connexion at all with the General Council, but that of conspiring against it. It acted under Bakunine's dictatorship. He prepared everything to *frapper son grand coup au Congrès de Bâle.*[a] On the one side, he made the Geneva Committee[b] propose *la question d'héritage.* We accepted the challenge.[625] On the other side, he conspired everywhere to discredit us and to have the seat of the General Council transferred from London to Geneva. At that congress, *ce saltimbanque figurait comme 'délégué de Naples et de Lyon'*[c] (at that latter place, *Albert Richard,* otherwise a very active and well-meaning youngster, is his acolyte). Where the fellow got the money for all his secret machinations, travels, missions of agents etc. remains to this moment a secret. Poor like a church mouse, he has never in his life earned a farthing by his own work.

At the Congress he was baffled. After the Congress he commenced to attack us publicly by his private *moniteur, Le Progrès* (de Locle), edited by his valet James Guillaume, a Swiss schoolmaster, and by the *Égalité* (de Genève).[507] We allowed this to go on for some time, and then sent a missive to the Federal Council of Geneva. (This document—copy of it—is in the hands of *Varlin.*) But before our circular arrived, the Federal Council of Geneva, never friendly to Bakunine and the *Alliance*, had broken loose from him. Robin *et* Co. were expulsed from the Editorship of the *Égalité.* The Federal Council of the Swiss *Romand* Section made his *pronunciamento* against the intrigues of the Alliance and its Muscovite dictator.

Meanwhile Bakounine had left Geneva to reside at Tessin. His circumstances were changed. Herzen died suddenly. Bakounine, who had attacked him fiercely during the latter times (probably because he found Herzen's purse shut against him), all at once became the fiery apologist of Herzen in the French etc. press.[586] Why? Because Herzen (although a millionaire) received annually for his *Cloche* and *'propagande Russe'* a rather large sum from the *Panslavistes démocrates* in Russia.[587] Although a fierce enemy *de l'héritage* Bakounine wanted to inherit Herzen's position and salary. He succeeded by his panegyrics of the dead man. He had the *Cloche,* the subvention etc. transferred to himself.[626]

On the other hand there had grown up at Geneva a colony of Russian émigrés,[541] enemies of Bakunine, because they knew the

---

a to deal a decisive blow at the Basle Congress - b the Federal Committee of Romance Switzerland - c this charlatan acted as the 'delegate of Naples and Lyons'

mere personal ambition of this very mediocre man (although an accomplished intriguer) and because they knew that in his '*Russian*' writings he propagates doctrines quite contrary to the principles of the *Internationale.*

The late *Swiss Romand Congress* at La Chaux de Fonds (5 April this year) was seized upon by Bakunine and his *moutons*[a] to bring about an open split.[606] The Congress was split into two Congresses, on the one hand a Congress of Bakunites, proclaiming abstention from all politics, representing about 600 men; on the other hand the Congress of the *Federal Comité* of Geneva, representing 2,000 men. Outine (*c'est un des jeunes Russes*) *dénonça publiquement les intrigues de Bakounine.*[b] His men have constituted themselves as a 'Federal Central Council' *pour la Suisse Romande,*[c] and have founded their own organ *La Solidarité*, edited by Bakounine's *valet de chambre*, James Guillaume. The '*principle*' of that paper is 'Bakounine'. Both parties have appealed to the General Council.

Thus this damned Muscovite has succeeded to call forth a great public scandal within our ranks, to make his personality a watchword, to infect our Working Men's Association with the poison of sectarianism, and to paralyse our action by secret intrigue.

He hopes to be strongly represented at our next Congress. To direct to himself the attention of Paris, he has opened a correspondence with the *Marseillaise.* But we have spoken with Flourens, who will put a stop to this.

You are now sufficiently informed to counteract Bakounine's movements within our Paris branches.

My thanks to Laurent[d] for her letter.[627] Another time try to find an envelope for your missives which is not so easily opened.

Apropos. Look whether you possess still the article of the *Queen's Messenger* on Lord Clanricarde.[e] We want it here and can get it from nowhere else.

Yours

Old Nick

First published in *Annali dell'Istituto G. G. Feltrinelli*, an. 1, Milano, 1958

Reproduced from the original

---

a sheep - b (a young Russian) publicly denounced Bakunin's intrigues - c of Romance Switzerland - d Laura Lafargue - e See this volume, pp. 466, 468.

322

ENGELS TO MARX

IN LONDON

Manchester, 21 April 1870

Dear Moor,

Enclosed, returned, the Swiss letters. The Genevans are, at all events, rather sluggish, otherwise they would not have got into this unfortunate position with the Bakuninists formally having the rules on their side with regard to them. This does not, of course, alter the fact that the Genevans must remain in the right; but, for the time being, the General Council has no reason to intervene, since the Genevans have appealed for a ballot in the *sections*, and you will have to wait for the result of this, one way or the other, before making a decision. The Bakuninists will probably not let themselves in for this referendum, since their *règlement fédéral*[a] probably makes no mention of it, and they will, thereby, expose their weak point in wishing to sacrifice the unity of the International, and the International itself into the bargain, to their empty formalism. Then there would be reason enough to intervene. On the other hand, the Genevans themselves must see to it this time that they gain the majority in their plebiscite. Till then, the General Council could, at the most, suspend *both* central committees, and replace them by a neutral provisional one (Becker,[b] etc.).

In the matter itself it is clear that the Alliance, even if tolerated by the General Council, has no place in a local organisation like the *Suisse Romande*,[c] since it wishes to correspond with all countries and maintain sub-sections there. Thus it should either stay out of it, or abandon its international character. Whereas, if the business in Switzerland continues to develop, the result will be either that it leaves the International completely, or can be thrown out. But it must be impressed on the Messrs Genevans that they cannot be helped unless they help themselves. If Bakunin were to get a majority of the workers of the *Suisse Romande* on his side, what could the General Council do? The only conceivable point is that of the total abstinence from all politics, but even this action would not be so certain.

---

[a] *Statuts pour la Fédération des Sections Romandes adoptés par le Congrès Romand...* -
[b] Johann Philipp Becker - [c] Romance Switzerland

The Messrs Genevans might have kept their *God* in the bag too![628]

Your
F. E.

First published in *Der Briefwechsel zwischen F. Engels und K. Marx*, Bd. 4, Stuttgart, 1913

Printed according to the original

Published in English for the first time

323

MARX TO ENGELS

IN MANCHESTER

[London,] 28 April 1870

DEAR FRED,

I visited Schapper again yesterday. I FEAR HE IS FAST SINKING. He himself spoke of his death as settled, even told me he had instructed his wife to have him buried next Sunday. It is consumption of the lungs. Schapper spoke and acted really *d'une manière distinguée*.[a] As long as his wife and eldest son were in the room he conducted the conversation (he can only speak with difficulty) in French. *Je ferai bientôt la dernière grimace*.[b] He poked fun at old Oborski, who in the past few months has become a Catholic and says his prayers; ditto at Ruge, who once again believes in the immortality of the soul. In this case, he said, Schapper's soul would play rough with Ruge's soul in the hereafter. It gives him pleasure to make jokes about the old stories, meetings with Louis Bonaparte, Dr Conneau, Persigny, General Cavaignac etc., later Willich, etc. It comforts him that his daughter is married, his eldest son Karl is independent (a bookbinder), and each of the two younger ones already earning £1 PER WEEK (as goldsmiths). He hopes his brother (Nassau) will take in his youngest. He has left all his scant possessions to his wife, and she will live with the two younger boys. 'Tell all our people that I have remained true to our principles. I am no theoretician. During the period of reaction I had my hands full bringing up my

---

[a] in a very composed manner - [b] I shall soon pull my last face.

family. I have lived as a HARD WORKING worker, and die a proletarian.' I gave him your greetings, and said that, had you believed the business was dangerous, you would have come up to see him. This obviously pleased him. Schapper is 57 years old. The true manliness of his character emerged once again clearly and strikingly.

Leaving Schapper, I had to make a second sick-bed visit. Borkheim wrote me a few lines the day before yesterday, that he had been at home sick the whole week, would probably have to stay in bed another week, then to the country, etc. From the way his wife received me, I saw immediately that the matter was *sérieux*. He had had typhoid fever; seems now on the road to improvement. His lungs have certainly been affected. The English doctor—one of the hospital doctors here—predicted all this, and repeats now that he hopes, and is virtually sure, that he will get away with it this time, but that if Borkheim does not abandon his mad life, he has not as much as a year before him.

The fact is that Borkheim studies Russian etc., with frenzy from 4.30 or 5 in the morning until 9, then again from 7 in the evening until 11. You know he writes polemical letters to everybody under the sun and, since he came into possession of a considerable library, has wished to make himself a scholar by brute force.

The doctor demands that he should chuck up everything *except business* for at least two years, and devote his leisure to light reading and *other relaxations*. Otherwise he is lost, and *this inevitably*. He has not the physical strength to do the work of two people.

I saw him for ABOUT 10 MINUTES. He looked damnably *fatigué* and thin. I told him that, as long as you were tied to business, you had engaged yourself only VERY MODERATELY in other things. I did this on purpose, since I know he respects you very much. When I came downstairs to his wife in the PARLOUR I recounted the conversation to her. She said—and I promised to do what I could to this end—that *you* would do her the greatest favour by writing to her husband. First of all, it would cheer him up greatly—such a sign of attention on your part—and second, he would take it to heart if you advised him not to ruin himself by EXTRA WORK.

It is my FEELING that Borkheim is, at the moment, *hors de danger*,[a] but he must watch out like the devil. Apropos. He is very annoyed with Liebknecht, for first printing the Bakunin letter[629] and then writing to him (Borkheim) that he (Borkheim) *must* now answer.

---

[a] out of danger

Good old Wilhelm, always READY to make BLUNDERS so that others *must* work! *C'est un imbécile.*[a]

Flourens has already visited me at home several times. He is a very nice fellow. His predominant characteristic is AUDACITY. But he is very well educated in the natural sciences. For a year he gave lectures on ethnology[630] at Paris University, and was all over the place in Southern Europe, Turkey, ASIA MINOR, etc. Full of illusions and revolutionary impatience, BUT A VERY JOLLY FELLOW WITH ALL THAT, not one of the 'damned serious' school of men. His name has been proposed for our COUNCIL, where he has twice assisted as a guest. It would be a very good thing if he were to stay here longer. It is WORTH WHILE working on him. If, however, Bonaparte grants an amnesty after the plebiscite, he will return to Paris. Yesterday evening, he and Tibaldi were given a banquet by the FRENCH Freemasons' lodge, the FRENCH BRANCH,[72] etc. L. Blanc, Talandier, etc., also wanted to[b] take part. All the French revolutionary riff-raff here are courting him, but he is already PRETTY WELL informed about these gentry.

My best thanks for your explanation about the IRISH BOG.[c] For fun I got hold of the RETURN on *GAME LAWS CONVICTIONS (ENGLAND AND WALES)* for 1869. Total number of CONVICTIONS: 10,345. These are thus the specific AGRARIAN CRIMES of the English and Welsh. Why does not Mr Gladstone also suspend the constitution in England?

You were right to smell a rat in Pigott's letter. From the enclosed *Flag of Ireland* (LETTER of the Paris correspondent of *The Irishman* in it) one can see the fellow Pigott's *mauvaise foi*[d]—since he knows *we* take *The Irishman* here—has the muck printed in the *Flag*.

I am sending you, with the *Flag*, 5 numbers of Spanish organs of the International, viz. 2 *Federacion*, 1 *Obrero* and 1 *Solidaridad.*

I shall only send off the copies of *Marseillaise* on Saturday. First, I must make some notes from them about the Creuzot case, etc. for the CENTRAL COUNCIL.[631]

Last Tuesday[e] the Central Council[73] unanimously adopted my proposal (SUPPORTED BY Mottershead[f]): TO SEVER OUR CONNEXION WITH THE *Bee-Hive* AND TO *PUBLISH* THAT RESOLUTION. Mr Applegarth sat opposite me while I was giving the reasons for my proposal, with A DIMINISHED HEAD. He and Odger on editorial committee of *Bee-Hive.* I denounced the paper as being sold to the bourgeois (S. Morley, etc.), mentioned particularly its treatment of our Irish resolutions

---

[a] He is an idiot. - [b] in the original: will - [c] See this volume, p. 488. - [d] bad faith - [e] 26 April - [f] See this volume, p. 386.

and debates, etc.[a] I should introduce the *formal* motion[b] on the decision of the CouncIL next Tuesday.[c]

Salut.

Your

Moor

First published abridged in *Der Briefwechsel zwischen F. Engels und K. Marx*, Bd. 4, Stuttgart, 1913 and in full in *MEGA*, Abt. III, Bd. 4, Berlin, 1931

Printed according to the original

Published in English for the first time

324

ENGELS TO WILHELM BRACKE[632]

IN BRUNSWICK

[Manchester, 28 April 1870]

I was very pleased by the detailed and precise financial statement.[633] Here, in England, in front of my very eyes, so many attempts to found workers' movements and organisations have failed because of bad treasurer's work and book-keeping, and the resultant recurrent justified and unjustified charges of embezzlement and so on, that in this case I can consider myself competent to deliver judgement on the importance of this point. The workers have to deprive themselves for every farthing, so have the fullest right to know where every farthing goes, as long as they do not need and are not putting aside *secret* funds. And I believe that this is of special importance, particularly in Germany, since there, too, exploitation of the workers by knavish agitators has become the fashion. It is a hollow pretext to say that, by publishing such financial statements, you betray the weakness of your own party to the enemy. If the enemy wishes to judge the strength of a workers' party according to its specifically weak side — the state of its funds — it will, in any case, be out in its reckoning. And the damage done in *one's own* ranks by keeping such things secret is far greater than that which can arise from publication.

---

[a] *Record of Marx's Speech on 'The Bee-Hive'. From the Minutes of the General Council Meeting of April 26, 1870.* - [b] K. Marx, *Resolution of the General Council on 'The Bee-Hive'.* - [c] 3 May

Bonhorst bewails the apathy of the workers [634]—but I find that things are going unexpectedly swimmingly in Germany. The individual successes naturally entail a hard struggle, and those involved naturally think things are going too slowly. But compare 1860 and 1870, and compare the present state of affairs in Germany with that in France and England—and recall the head start that these two countries had over us! The German workers have got half a dozen of their people into parliament; the French and the English *not a single one.* Allow me to remark, in this connection, *that all of us here* regard it as of the greatest importance that as many worker candidates stand as possible in the coming elections, and that as many are elected as possible.[a]

First published in *Der Volksstaat,* No. 39,
14 May 1870

Printed according to the newspaper

Published in English for the first time

325

ENGELS TO MARX

IN LONDON

Manchester, 29 April 1870

Dear Moor,

I wrote immediately to Borkheim,[635] addressed to 10 Brunswick Gardens, Kensington W.[b] If that is not correct, be so good as to notify him.

I would, in fact, have been glad to come over to see Schapper, and would still do so, had not your letter led me to assume he was already dead. There was always something so elementally revolutionary about him, and even if the poor fellow .has to go sometime, I am pleased at least that he is behaving so finely to the end. If, as the result of the pleurisy, he has contracted consumption, then there is nothing to be done, and it will happen very quickly.

Bakunin's letter is really very naïve.[629] What hard luck for the world, were it not a ghastly lie, if there were 40,000 revolutionary students in Russia, without a proletariat or even a revolutionary

---

[a] See this volume, p. 500. - [b] Ibid., p. 496.

peasantry behind them, and with any career ahead of them except the dilemma: Siberia, or emigration to Western Europe. If there were anything that could ruin the West European movement, it would be the importation of these 40,000±[a] educated, ambitious, hungry Russian nihilists; all of them officer cadets without an army, which we should provide them; a marvellous piece of impertinence that, in order to bring unity to the European proletariat, it must be commanded in Russian! Yet however greatly Bakunin exaggerates, it is as clear as day that the danger exists. Святая Русь[b] will spit out a certain number of these 'careerless' Russians every year, and, with the excuse of the *principe international*, they will creep in everywhere amongst the workers, swindle their way into leading roles, carry their private intrigues and brawls—unavoidable amongst the Russians—into the sections, and then the GENERAL COUNCIL will have its work cut out. It has already struck me that Utine has already found a way to obtain a position with the Genevans. And these Russians moan that, back at home, all positions are occupied by Germans!

I have had it out in all friendship with Wilhelm on various points, both about his previous attitude and also about his present attitude in the Reichstag. Bonhorst was arrested in Eschweiler because he lacked legitimation papers, after *the Reichstag* had passed the Passport Abolition Law, yet Monsieur Liebknecht misses the chance to interpellate the government about flagrant illegality and to force it to confess that such laws are in no way intended to apply to workers. And the jackasses expect the workers to re-elect them. Incidentally, I have also written to Bracke, who approached me for money for the 'Party', saying how necessary it is that they should nominate worker candidates and force them through everywhere.[c] Wilhelm is capable of saying that this is not necessary at all.

The Spanish papers and the *Flag*[d]—received with thanks. When I travelled past Majorca in 1849 I would not have dreamed that, in 20 years, we would have a paper[e] there. At the time that hole was regarded as a Corsican wilderness.

Pigott remains the same ambiguous figure. In Ireland they must have a 'Republic', but the French should remain under Bonaparte. They will pass over my book[f] in silence when it appears, just as they do now with the Irish articles in the *Marseillaise*.[g]

---

a more or less - b Holy Russia - c See this volume, p. 499. - d *The Flag of Ireland* (see this volume, p. 497) - e *El Obrero* - f F. Engels, *The History of Ireland* - g Jenny Marx's articles on the Irish question.

The ancient laws of Ireland,[a] through which I am at present rummaging, are a bitter mouthful. First, the text itself is not very clear, since it assumes a knowledge of *all* ancient Irish law, which no longer exists. 2. It is very garbled. 3. The translation is bad, and in places definitely wrong, but it is clear that the agrarian conditions were not quite as simple as good old *Davies*[b]—with interest—described them. The laws insofar as published, give only the complicated side, not the simple one. Incidentally, I am not yet through with the stuff; from time to time I am forced to refer to the Celtic text, too, and since I don't even have a grammar, I don't get along very fast. But so much is clear: the editors, for all their knowledge of Celtic, don't understand the contents any more than I do.

These things have been published at state cost by the COMMISSIONERS FOR THE PUBLICATION OF THE ANCIENT LAWS AND INSTITUTES OF IRELAND.[636] It is obviously a gruelling job. *In which PARLIAMENTARY PAPER can one find out how much these fellows cost annually?* They have been in session since 1852, do nothing except engage WORKING UNDERSTRAPPERS, and these two volumes are all that has appeared so far.

Best greetings to you all.

Your
F. E.

First published abridged in *Der Briefwech-sel zwischen F. Engels und K. Marx,* Bd. 4, Stuttgart, 1913 and in full in *MEGA,* Abt. III, Bd. 4, Berlin, 1931

Printed according to the original

Published in English for the first time

326

MARX TO ENGELS

IN MANCHESTER

[London,] 29 April 1870

Dear FRED,

POOR Schapper died yesterday morning at 9 o'clock.

Enclosed, 3 issues of *Marseillaise* containing J. Williams.[c][562] I

---

[a] *Ancient Laws of Ireland. Senchus Mor.* Volumes I-II. - [b] J. Davies, *Historical Tracts.* - [c] Jenny Marx, see this volume, p. 503.

must *have them back* (with the Swiss *Égalité* and *Solidarité*) because of notes for the GENERAL COUNCIL,[a] for which I have not yet found time. (*Don't* send back the *Spanish papers.*) Ditto, latest *Vorbote.* You will see from this that Becker[b] has broken openly with Bakunin.[c] (*Don't* send back.)

Finally, ONE COPY of the *Russian translation* of our *Communist Manifesto* for you. I saw in the *Werker*, etc., that the *Kolokol* publishing house, which was willed to Bakunin, also includes 'this stuff', so ordered 6 copies from Geneva.[637] It's very interesting for us.

Addio OLD BOY. COMPLIMENTS TO MRS Lizzy, Jollymeyer[d] AND Moore.

Old
Nick

First published in *Der Briefwechsel zwischen F. Engels und K. Marx*, Bd. 4, Stuttgart, 1913

Printed according to the original

Published in English for the first time

327

ENGELS TO MARX

IN LONDON

[Manchester,] 1 May 1870

Dear Moor,

POOR Schapper! The toll amongst our old comrades is getting very high.[e] Weerth, Weydemeyer, Lupus, Schapper—but, all the same, *à la guerre comme à la guerre.*[f] Couldn't you get me a photograph of him? Or, if possible, two, you know the Solingen people also want one.

Thanks for the papers. Everything requested goes back tomorrow. I would have sent *Égalité* and *Solidarité* long ago, but I thought the GENERAL COUNCIL would have received *several* copies. In the Spanish things, which certainly still betray a rather Spanish standpoint, you can see how Bakunin's phraseology shines through.

---

a See this volume, pp. 497-98. - b Johann Philipp Becker - c 'Zur Geschichte der Internationalen Arbeiterassociation', *Der Vorbote*, No. 4, April 1870. - d Carl Schorlemmer - e See the previous letter. - f war is war

I saw Gumpert yesterday. When he asked after you, and I told him your liver complaints were flaring up again, he blew up without waiting for anything further: *Why doesn't he go to Karlsbad?* There you have the answer.[a] He thinks it would be best early in the summer, or only towards autumn, since it is very full there in July-August, and horribly hot. The Crown Prince of Prussia[b] is there at the moment, wouldn't you like to keep him company? He is an 'edicated'[c] man.

The resolution on *Bee-Hive*[d] will please Sam Moore greatly; he has taken *Bee-Hive* up to now, and been very annoyed at the lousy sheet. I shall tell him he should take *Reynolds's*, or do you know something better? Does the *Democratic News* still exist?

Enclosed, the latest from Wilhelm.[e] He very much favours Prussia being the *only serious* opponent of the revolution in Germany, but is very much against it being a *serious* opponent.[638] *Pauvre hère!*[f]

Lizzie, for whom I immediately made a quick translation of the 3 Williams,[g] is absolutely enthusiastic about them, and thanks Mr Williams warmly.

Best greetings.

Your

F. E.

For some time now your letters have been arriving in an unobjectionable condition. At least they have become more careful.

Steps have presumably been taken for a decent obituary on Schapper in the press? I don't know whether Eccarius is the man to do justice to this best type of old conspirator.

First published abridged in *Der Briefwechsel zwischen F. Engels und K. Marx*, Bd. 4, Stuttgart, 1913 and in full in *MEGA*, Abt. III, Bd. 4, Berlin, 1931

Printed according to the original

Published in English for the first time

---

[a] See this volume, p. 479. - [b] Frederick William - [c] In the original 'jebildeter' (Berlin dialect). - [d] K. Marx, *Resolution of the General Council on 'The Bee-Hive'*. - [e] Wilhelm Liebknecht - [f] Poor devil - [g] the sixth, seventh and eighth articles by Jenny Marx from the Irish question series

328

MARX TO ENGELS

IN MANCHESTER[577]

[London,] 7 May 1870

DEAR FRED,

All sorts of interesting things have happened here this week. But the English post is too INQUISITIVE at the moment, and I don't feel the call to SUPPLY it indirectly with news. So, about this, later by word of mouth.[639]

The *Marseillaise* did not arrive today. Possibly it has been confiscated. Last Wednesday[a] we informed them by telegraph that they would receive the General Council resolution[b] on Thursday in the original French; they should not translate it from English. This telegram naturally came immediately to the attention of the Paris police, and Pietri does not, perhaps, want our proclamation one day before the plebiscite.

The absurd Reuter-Havas telegrams have finally given us the long-awaited opportunity to declare publicly in the Paris press that the SO-CALLED LONDON FRENCH BRANCH does *not* belong to the *International*.[640]

Yesterday and the day before *The Standard* published two lousy articles against the *International*, dictated directly from the French Legation, as, ditto, the article in the London French paper *L'International*.

All London papers have received instructions from *Bruce*—and naturally obey them like the born dogs they are—not to mention a word in their columns about the steps the *English police* have taken very quietly in past weeks with regard to *Flourens* and the *International* GENERAL COUNCIL (they make a HODGE PODGE out of the two).

Ten thousand COPIES of *The Standard* mentioned have been sent to France. Is this, also, a method of payment, or has the *Société du 10 Décembre*[641] suddenly learned English?

Last Tuesday the rumour was spread in London that we were going to be arrested in our meeting room. As a result PRESS REPORTERS, for once hungry for news, were in attendance.

---

a 4 May - b K. Marx, *Concerning the Persecution of the Members of the French Sections. Declaration of the General Council of the International Working Men's Association* (present edition, Vol. 21).

In England, at a moment of panic the fellows immediately forget their own laws, and allow themselves to be carried away by the press, which is partly ignorant, and partly lies with intent.

To be nice to the police, let us assume that everything reported by Grandperret, Reuter and the *Journal officiel* is gospel truth. Even so, the English Government could do *nothing*, apart, at the most, from making fools of themselves.

There can, *d'abord*,ᵃ be no question of the *extradition* of Flourens—*Gaulois* says it has been demanded.[642] There is only *one* Extradition Treaty between France and the UNITED KINGDOM, that of 1843. In 1865 the French Government declared it would denounce it after 6 months, since it was practically unworkable because of the ENGLISH LAWS OF EVIDENCE. As a result, in 1866 some of the formalities regarding EVIDENCE were changed, without any change in the content of the treaty. This specifies very precisely the crimes that lead to extradition, including murder (PARRICIDE, INFANTICIDE, and murder by poison) and attempted murder, notabene, attempts in the sense *qu'il y avait un c o m m e n c e m e n t d' e x é c u t i o n*,ᵇ 'THE DIRECT CONSEQUENCE OF WHICH WOULD PROBABLY BE THE DEATH OF THE INDIVIDUAL WHOSE LIFE WAS ATTACKED'.

Under *this* treaty Beaury, for instance, could *not* be extradited had he fled to England, let alone Flourens.

The only question is whether a FOREIGNER *here* could be sentenced by an English court for COMPLICITY IN A CONSPIRACY TO COMMIT THE CRIME OF MURDER ABROAD.

Before 1828 nobody—Englishman or FOREIGNER—could be prosecuted here for MURDER COMMITTED OUT OF THE UNITED KINGDOM. English duellists made use of this. SECT. 7 OF 9, GEO. IV stipulated,

'THAT IF ANY OF H. M.'S "SUBJECTS" SHOULD BE CHARGED WITH MURDER OR WITH ANY ACCESSORY TO MURDER COMMITTED ON LAND OUT OF THE UNITED KINGDOM HE SHOULD BE TRIABLE FOR SUCH OFFENCES IN THE UNITED KINGDOM'.

The law was, in fact, made to fit English duellists, and therefore applies only to 'HER MAJESTY'S SUBJECTS'.

At Dr Bernard's TRIAL´ in 1858 he therefore pleaded 'THAT THE COURT HAD NO JURISDICTION'. The SERVILE COURT reserved this point, without taking a decision, and ruled that, for a start, A PLEA OF NOT GUILTY SHOULD BE RECORDED. His ACQUITTAL prevented any further decision on this LEGAL POINT.

Immediately after the Orsini PLOT of 1858, Palmerston introduced the CONSPIRACY BILL into the HOUSE OF COMMONS,[643]

ᵃ for the time - ᵇ in which a *deed was commenced*

'WITH THE OBJECT OF MAKING *CONSPIRACY* TO COMMIT MURDER EITHER WITHIN THE UNITED KINGDOM OR WITHIN THE TERRITORY OF ANY FOREIGN STATE A *FELONY*'.

This BILL was justified by the following in

1. 'CONSPIRACY WAS ONLY A *MISDEMEANOUR*' and that, under English LAW, a CONSPIRACY TO MURDER is nothing more nor less than A CONSPIRACY TO BLACKEN A MAN'S CHARACTER.

2. And this was shown very emphatically by the ATTORNEY GENERAL Sir R. Bethell—

'THAT THE 9 GEO. IV SECT. 7 ONLY APPLIED TO *NATIONAL BORN BRITISH SUBJECTS*, AND THAT *FOREIGNERS RESIDENT IN THIS UNITED KINGDOM COULD CONSPIRE TO COMMIT MURDER ABROAD WITH IMPUNITY*'.

The CONSPIRACY BILL, as everyone knows, was rejected, and Lord Palmerston fell FOR THE TIME BEING, together with the bill.

The whole commotion in the English and French press is, therefore, complete nonsense. If the worst comes to the worst, Flourens could be prosecuted for a MISDEMEANOUR in order, finally, to obtain a DEFINITIVE JUDICIAL DECISION on 9 GEO. IV SECT. 7 and certainly to fail thereby, and be forced to table the CONSPIRACY BILL. Gladstone will tempt the devil where Palmerston failed.

If this PLOT—for the ASSASSINATION of Badinguet [a]—is not simply a police invention, then it is the biggest possible bit of tomfoolery open to man. Luckily, the EMPIRE can no longer be saved even by the stupidity of its enemies.

Bakunin's agent *Robin*, now in Paris and a member of the Paris *Fédération* (*Internationale*),[644] immediately proposed a resolution there recognising the new *Conseil Romand* as the genuine one, and making a public announcement in the *Marseillaise* that only its supporters are really MEMBERS of the *Internationale*. But we had advised our people in Paris.[b] Robin thus failed gloriously with his resolution. It was decided that the *Fédération Parisienne* had absolutely no *autorité* to intervene; the matter was something for the *Conseil Général* in London. This business is, however, characteristic of the *modus operandi* of Gospodin[c] Bakunin.

The Paris PLOT brings to a sorry end the well-advanced plan to hold the *Congress in Paris*, and to take this opportunity also to transfer the General Council there.

I have received from Bakunin the 5 first Nos. of *Kolokol* and its French *supplément*. Even the Russian programme is very characteristic.[645] The paper should be in no way the expression of an

---

[a] a nickname of Napoleon III (the name of a stonemason in whose clothes he fled from the prison in 1846) - [b] See this volume, p. 489. - [c] Mr

exclusive party (выраженіе какой-либо исключительной партіи) but of all decent people (честныхъ людей)[a] who desire the 'liberation of Russia' and who are 'dissatisfied with the present conditions'. No pedantry, above all *practical*! For our part, we, Western Europe and the UNITED STATES, should confine ourselves *exclusively* to propaganda of the *theory* of Mr Bakunin (i.e., the absence of all theory), and this in such a manner as though all nations had already been abolished. He thus bans us from any intervention, in either domestic or foreign policy. What an artful dodger!

Things are going slowly with Borkheim, but he is improving. I visited him again last Thursday[b] (on this trip I caught a frightful cold, which is almost driving me mad). He was delighted with your letter.[635] From his 'enclosure' you will see his need to make a fool of himself.[646] The gentility with which he—a born figure of fun[c]—delivers his estimate of Lever, was so patronising—he laughs now and then, and excuses this with his sickness—and the naïvety with which he believes one can supply him with *Harry Lorrequer par douzaines*[d] like blackberries[e]! After this I sent him *Peter Simple*[f] and, in fact, he finds this 'much better'.

Schapper was buried last Wednesday.[g] Write down for me any biographical notes about him you have in your head. We shall have to compose a short obituary.

COMPLIMENTS TO MRS LIZZY, Moore, Jollymeyer.[h]

El Moro
(My beard becomes whiter daily.)

You will receive with this: two numbers of *Égalité*, and of the *pamphlets plébiscitaires*:

Aux Electeurs, Par Alceste (finely written),

Le Plébiscite Impérial par *Rogeard* (very bad),

Le Plébiscite de Boquillon par *A. Humbert* (one of the **Marseillaise** editors, fine burlesque) (in the style of Offenbach's music).

First published in *Der Briefwechsel zwischen F. Engels und K. Marx*, Bd. 4, Stuttgart, 1913

Printed according to the original

Published in English for the first time

---

[a] The words in brackets are given in Russian by Marx. - [b] 5 May - [c] In the original: *Kladderadatsch*—the title of the Berlin satirical journal - [d] by the dozen - [e] Paraphrased Falstaff's words (see Shakespeare, *King Henry IV*, Part I, Act II, Scene 4). - [f] F. Marryat, *Peter Simple.* - [g] 4 May - [h] Carl Schorlemmer

19*

329

ENGELS TO MARX [180]

IN LONDON

Manchester, 8 May 1870

Dear Moor,

With his plot-comedy, Mr Pietri appears to me to have far overshot the mark. In the end the policemen don't even believe one another's buffoonery. It's really too fine. This scurvy Bonaparte has a fixed remedy for every sickness; in case of a plebiscite, the *populus* must be given a dose of assassination, just as every quack begins every bigger treatment with a strong laxative. I am longing to hear the result of the treatment; so far I know only about the Paris vote, which was so good that all forgeries by officials could not falsify it completely.[612]

The *Daily News* and *Observer* virtually announced that the English police had obtained the necessary and telegraphed it to the French police. With the FENIAN SCARE the English police have completely dropped their disguise and are baser than any other. NB. Do use thinner paper for your envelopes; I could open these thick envelopes without leaving a trace.

You really should publish in France and Germany the heroic deeds of the English police regarding the International and Flourens.[a]

10,000 COPIES=£40 is damned cheap; I would have expected *The Standard* to sell itself dearer. This manner of bribery has, however, long been common here.

Flerovsky[b] does not appear to have been confiscated; there are copies at least in Leipzig. My bookseller, the jackass, did not order the Russian text but a non-existent English translation. Hence the non-arrival.

So *Колоколъ* [Kolokol] will be even finer under Bakunin than it was under Herzen.[626]

Monsieur Wilhelm[c] is no longer to be borne. You will have seen that 'owing to the absence of the printer' (who is, thus, the real editor), the *Peasant War*[d] was printed in a mix-up that Grandperret could not have managed better and, at the same time, the

---

[a] See this volume, pp. 504-06. - [b] Н. Флеровскій, *Положеніе рабочаго класса въ Россіи.* - [c] Wilhelm Liebknecht - [d] F. Engels, *The Peasant War in Germany.*

dunderhead has the impudence to affix marginal notes that are complete nonsense, without any note as to authorship, and *everyone will ascribe them to me*. I have already forbidden him to do this once before, and he was piqued; but the nonsense is laid on so thick that it is no longer bearable. *Ad vocem*[a] Hegel, the fellow glosses: known to the general public as the discoverer (!) and glorifier (!!) of the royal Prussian *state concept* (!!!). I have retorted to him suitably, and have sent him, for publication, a declaration as mild as was possible under the cricumstances. This dunderhead, who has been jogging around helplessly for years on the ridiculous contradiction between right and might, like an infantry man placed upon a horse with the staggers and locked in the riding-school—this ignoramus has the insolence to wish to dispatch a man like Hegel with the word 'Preuss'[b] and, at the same time, suggests to the public that *I* had said it. I have now had enough of the whole thing. If Wilhelm doesn't publish my declaration, I shall turn to his superiors, the 'Committee',[c] and if they also get up to tricks, I shall prohibit any further publication. I would rather not be published than let Wilhelm proclaim me a jackass thereby.[647]

Borkheim, returned enclosed. The fellow is gracious enough to wish to find Lever[d] jocose. 'Boquillon'[e] is very nice; I haven't yet read the other things.[f]

I can tell you nothing about Schapper[g] that you do not know yourself or you could not get much better from *Pfänder*.

The *Kölnische Zeitung* has been gammoned into writing that the floor of the Atlantic Ocean is covered with protoplasm—'a moving slime that nourishes itself'.[h]

In LONDON CLAY, Owen has found the skull of a giant bird, similar to the great wingless birds of New Zealand.

The jolliest point about old Irish law[481] is the family law. Those must have been free-and-easy times. Polygamy existed, was at least *tolerated*, and the concubines here were divided into 6-7 classes, including one, the *imris*, 'WHOM HE (THE MAN) HAS WITH THE CONSENT OF HER HUSBAND'. Very naïve, too, is the regulation about the disposition of property. If they both have the same amount, the husband and (the first or main) wife dispose of it jointly. If the husband has everything and the wife nothing, the husband disposes. Has the

---

a Regarding - b disparaging form of 'Prussian' - c to the Brunswick Committee of the Social-Democratic Workers' Party - d Ch. Lever, *Harry Lorrequer*. See this volume, p. 507. - e A. Humbert, *Le Plébiscite de boquillon.* - f See this volume, p. 507. - g Ibid. - h 'Die Tiefsee-Untersuchungen', *Kölnische Zeitung*, No. 122, 3 May 1870.

wife all and the husband nothing, then 'the wife takes the position of the husband, and the husband that of the wife'. Yet still more civilised than the modern English laws.

The legal position of *hommes entretenus*[a] is also defined.

Best greetings.

Your
F. E.

Don't talk about grey hairs. They are growing thickly enough in my beard, but the corresponding *dignitas* simply won't appear.

First published abridged in *Der Briefwechsel zwischen F. Engels und K. Marx*, Bd. 4, Stuttgart, 1913 and in full in *MEGA*, Abt. III, Bd. 4, Berlin, 1931

Printed according to the original

Published in English in full for the first time

330

MARX TO LUDWIG KUGELMANN

IN HANOVER

[London, about 8 May 1870]

Dear Kugelmann,

As a filthy cough has made me incapable of writing for the moment, herewith only MY BEST THANKS FOR THE FINE BIRTHDAY PRESENTS.[b]

YOURS TRULY
Karl Marx

First published in: Marx and Engels, *Works*, First Russian Edition, Vol. XXV, Moscow, 1935

Printed according to the original

Published in English for the first time

---

a kept men - b See this volume, pp. 512 and 558.

331

MARX TO ENGELS[56]

IN MANCHESTER[577]

[London,] 10 May 1870

DEAR FRED,

Yesterday I received the enclosed screed from Wilhelm.[a] An incorrigible South German bumpkin.

You will see from it, *d'abord*, that the blockhead *never* wrote to Meissner[b] and attended to *all my commissions* in the same way. And, for precisely this reason, I should now write to him 'regularly', and you should go to 'Stuttgart', in the same way as he wished to propose *you* as a MEMBER of the North German Reichstag[648]!

I had written to him[649] that if, when he wrote about Hegel, he knew nothing better than to repeat the old Rotteck-Welcker muck, then he would do better to keep his mouth shut.[c] He says that this would be 'making rather informally short work, etc.' of Hegel, and when he writes stupidities beneath Engels' articles, then 'Engels can of course (!) say something *at greater length* (!!)'. The fellow really is too stupid.

The circular,[d] which reached him in such a '*romantic*' manner, states that the General Council reserves the right to speak about Schweitzer, etc., '*publicly*' *as soon as* it considers suitable. This Wilhelm converts into us wanting to make a 'public declaration'— for Wilhelm!

With regard to the next congress, what do you think of Bebel's suggestion about Mainz or Mannheim[650]? Better Mainz. The business would be a good thing, insofar as Mr Bakunin *et Co.* would be totally powerless in Germany.

Shameless Wilhelm, who thought my *Bonaparte*[e] scarcely worth a note in his sheet,[f] demands my permission to publish my articles on the French Revolution[g]!

From the *Marseillaise* of last *Sunday*[h] you will see that *Opinion nationale*, the Plon-Plon[i] sheet, has discovered that the *French*

---

[a] Wilhelm Liebknecht - [b] See this volume, p. 428. - [c] Ibid., p. 509. - [d] K. Marx, *Confidential Communication.* - [e] K. Marx, *The Eighteenth Brumaire of Louis Bonaparte.* - [f] *Der Volkstaat* - [g] K. Marx, *The Class Struggles in France, 1848 to 1850.* - [h] Marx refers to *Une Dénonciation*, written by A. de Fonvielle and published in *La Marseillaise*, No. 139, 8 May 1870. - [i] Jérôme Charles Paul Bonaparte

original of our declaration,[a] written by me, was certainly written *in Paris*! Incidentally, I am pleased that this sheet is finally abandoning the patronage it has hitherto granted us, which we found very distasteful.

The ancient Irish business with women quite pales compared to what the Celts in WALES allowed themselves in that field. This was (up until the 11th-12th century) quite Fourier's fantasy *mise en pratique*.[b]

For my birthday, Kugelmann sent me two pieces of wallpaper from Leibniz's study, which amused me very much. It appears Leibniz's home was pulled down last winter, and the stupid Hanoverians—who could have made good business in London with the relics—threw everything away. Each of these two pieces depicts something mythological, one Neptune in his waves, etc., the other Venus, Amor, etc., all in poor Louis XIV style. On the other hand the quality (solidity) of the hand manufactory of those days compares well with today's. I have hung the two pieces up in my study. YOU KNOW MY ADMIRATION FOR Leibniz.

I am still suffering so much from the nose stoppage resulting from my last visit to Borkheim that my daughters have *forbidden* me to go to the GENERAL COUNCIL this evening, and threaten, if I disobey, to send to FRED Engels A SAVAGE DENUNCIATION OF MY CONDUCT. My presence there is really very necessary just now. *Enfin, nous verrons!*[c]

Apropos. I recently purchased a 14-volume edition of *Swift* (of 1760) for all of $4^{1}/_{2}$ shillings. So, as soon as you need to look at Swift's things about *Irish subjects*, the necessary will be sent to you.

Has not the time nearly come for us to look around for a house for you here, and for you to give instructions IN THAT LINE?

Salut.

Your
K. M.

The elections in France—so far as they make sense—have produced a grand result. A great and ever repeated tomfoolery of the Republicans to persuade the poor devils of soldiers to vote 'no'. *A quoi bon?*[d] That the government should repeat the old trick, get to know and to root out the unreliable elements. Very

---

[a] K. Marx, *Concerning the Persecution of the Members of the French Sections. Declaration of the General Council of the International Working Men's Association.* - [b] put into practice - [c] Well, we shall see! - [d] Who profits?

soon, the 4,000 military NO VOTERS of Paris will have vanished, partly to Algeria, partly to distant provincial punitive garrisons.[612]

First published abridged in *Der Briefwechsel zwischen F. Engels und K. Marx*, Bd. 4, Stuttgart, 1913 and in full in *MEGA*, Abt. III, Bd. 4, Berlin, 1931

Printed according to the original

Published in English in full for the first time

332

ENGELS TO MARX[56]

IN LONDON

Manchester, 11 May 1870

Dear Moor,

The relevant Liebknecht stuff was missing; I suppose it will turn up tomorrow.[648]

Holding the congress in Germany would present some difficulties, since one simply does not know what laws rule there, though one does know which police practices prevail. But it is fairly certain that a *dissolution* of the congress by the police would be the worst to be expected; the people would be safe, with the exception of a possible 24-hour detention; but it would have to be determined *now* where the congress should reassemble if dissolved—in Belgium or Switzerland. Otherwise, Mainz would be quite a good place, and Mannheim, too; the Baden Government is so harassed by the People's Party[38] and the ultramontanists that it would scarcely take any action.

Since Wilhelm mucked about my *Peasant War* in such a manner,[647] think what he will do with your articles[a]!

Could you get together for me that material for a note, with citation of the sources, on the Welsh phanerogamic being[b]? I could use it just now, in a few days I shall be writing about this.

The bourgeois vandalism with regard to Leibniz's house is very common. In any case, I congratulate you on the relics.

I shall hardly likely be needing Swift before I move to London.

The decision in the large towns in France is very fine. The remainder is faked and doesn't count. Regarding the way the

---

[a] K. Marx, *The Class Struggles in France, 1848 to 1850.* - [b] See this volume, pp. 512, 515-16.

Republicans urged the army about *non*, this would only have been useful if immediate action had been intended, but it is agreed that this was *not* the case. As things have now turned out, the soldiers will have to suffer, and 'more reliable' regiments will be sent to Paris.[612]

If you and your family wish to reconnoitre the surrounding district for a house for me, this would be very agreeable for us here. I have my house here until the end of September, so if I move at the end of August there is time enough. In addition, I have enough material to made through here, and it's easier here than in London. You know the sort of house I need: at least 4, if possible 5 bedrooms (since Pumps[a] is growing up), and apart from a study for me, two living rooms and kitchen, etc. If possible without a close dominant *vis-à-vis*. It would be desirable that it should not be much higher up than you live, since Lizzie has an asthmatic reluctance about hill climbing. If you find something, then I can come over. It doesn't need to be as big as your house, and smaller rooms would suffice for me.

Best greetings to all.

Your
F. E.

Your letter appeared to have been opened again, and badly stuck down with too much gum, so that the excess of gum made it adhere to another letter, and traces remained.

Do you know of an Irish grammar, or is one to be had second-hand? I would very much dislike to quote a Celtic word incorrectly, perhaps in the genitive or nominative plural—instead of nominative singular.

First published abridged in *Der Briefwechsel zwischen F. Engels und K. Marx*, Bd. 4, Stuttgart, 1913 and in full in *MEGA*, Abt. III, Bd. 4, Berlin, 1931

Printed according to the original

Published in English in full for the first time

---

[a] Mary Ellen Burns

333

MARX TO ENGELS [56]

IN MANCHESTER

[London,] 11 MAY 1870

DEAR FRED,

I only noted from your letter today that I had forgotten to enclose the Wilhelm.[a] It follows herewith, ditto, letter from Bracke, etc., which I must have back before Tuesday, when I intend to be on my feet again. Mainz, Darmstadt, Mannheim [650]? Wouldn't Mannheim be best? Mainz is a Prussian fortress city.

With regard to the Welsh, I *don't* find the main thing in my notebooks. But this much:

The community of goods was accompanied by Celtic looseness of the marriage tie, already known in antiquity, at the same time, however, *voting rights for women* in the tribal assembly.' (*W. Wachsmuth, 'Europäische Sittengeschichte', Zweiter Teil, Leipzig, 1833.*)

Wachsmuth bases his description specifically on the laws of King Dyonwall Moelmud and Howel Ddas.[b] '*Leges Molmutinae*. Translated by *William Probert*: '*THE ANCIENT LAWS OF CAMBRIA*, CONTAINING THE INSTITUTIONAL TRIADS OF D. MOELMUD, THE LAWS OF HOWEL THE GOOD, TRIADICAL COMMENTARIES, CODE OF EDUCATION, AND THE HUNTING LAWS OF WALES", London, 1823', and: '*Edward Davies*, "Celtic Researches", London 1804'.

I find noted in my notebooks, as curiosities:

'Precepts on ascertaining virginity. The testimony of one person suffices, e.g., that of a girl on her virginity.' 'A man who has got rid of one bed-companion because of another atones with as many *denarii* as are necessary to cover the bottom of the complainant. A woman who lays a plaint against a man for rape clasps his member with her left hand, lays her right upon reliquaries, and thus swears her testimony.'

'*Fornication with the queen* costs the double mult to the king.'

The first chapter of the book on common law deals with the women.

'If his wife lay with another man and *he beats her*, he sacrifices his claim to indemnification... What a wife might *dispose of*—differing according to station—is exactly specified. The wife of a peasant (*taeawgh*) might only dispose of her neck-band, and might *lend* only her sieve, and this not further than her voice could be heard when demanding its return. The wife of a nobleman (*uchelwr*) could dispose of cloak, shirt, shoes, etc., but *lend* all her household utensils. *Sufficient grounds for divorce for a wife were* the man's impotence, scabies and *bad breath*.'

---

a Liebknecht's letter (see this volume, p. 513) - b the Good

Quite some lads, these Celts. But born dialecticians, everything being composed in *triads*. When I leave the house again I shall look up Wachsmuth on phanerogamy in the Museum.[a]

At this opportunity I have also found in my notebooks quotations from various writings on Ireland, but which you have certainly seen, or are superfluous because of better sources. One book, the title of which I cannot read properly, *Cgygia* or *Ogygia* by *R. O'Flaherty*, London, 1685.

Dr Charles O'Conor: Scriptores Rerum Hibernicarum. Buckingham (1814-1826, 4 volumes).

The antiquities and history of Ireland, by Jam. Ware, London, 1705; Ware, Two books of the writers of Ireland. Dublin, 1709.[651]

In the case of Bakunin, either the transaction *has broken down*, or it has been arranged thus *pour sauver les apparences*.[b] Looking at things more closely, I discover, that Ogarev is the editor.[626] In the first numbers Bakunin has only *one* letter,[c] in which he acts like a stranger, attacks the editors for lack of principles, etc., puts on airs as a socialist and internationalist, etc. Yet, WITH ALL THAT, what his letter amounts to is that, in theory, all coalitions are to be condemned, but in practice, to be sure, Ogarev is right. The main thing now is to overthrow Tsarism, and for this the unification of all parties hostile to it is necessary, etc., etc. Later they will be able to scuffle with one another, etc. Thus, 'politics' are permissible for socialists in Russia, but not for the world in Western Europe!

The Russian things I am sending you today you may keep, since I have duplicate copies.

Salut.

Your

K. M.

I shall look around for the Irish grammar as soon as I can go out again.

The state of my last letter was *not* the fault of the post.

First published abridged in *Der Briefwechsel zwischen F. Engels und K. Marx*, Bd. 4, Stuttgart, 1913 and in full in *MEGA*, Abt. III, Bd. 4, Berlin, 1931

Printed according to the original

Published in English in full for the first time

---

[a] the British Museum Library - [b] to save appearances - [c] М. Бакунинъ, 'Редакторамъ *Колокола*', *Kolokol*, No. 2, 9 April 1870.

334

ENGELS TO MARX

IN LONDON

Manchester, 15 May 1870

Dear Moor,

Mainz is not so bad, the Hessian Government is always at loggerheads with the Prussian Governor, and the Prussians have to declare a state of siege in the city before they can do anything. Darmstadt has too small a proletariat and, in addition, a *small court*, so one cannot count on anything. Mannheim, also, has a smaller proletariat than Mainz, and altogether I think it would be good to hold the congress under the noses of the Prussian soldiers. If it is broken up, then the whole show can move to Brussels; even those compromised in Prussia can get there via Strasbourg, Metz and Luxembourg in 24 hours; the others via Cologne or Saarbrücken-Luxembourg. Apropos, the International should try to obtain a footing in Luxembourg; there are many miners, tanners, etc., there. This must be done from Saarbrücken or Aachen; the committee[a] should be charged with this.

Best thanks for the Celtica.[b] I shall take a few hours to look up further details in the Chetham LIBRARY, where I shall probably find something.

Ogygia[651] is a horribly uncritical thing; here and there there are notes of some value, since the fellow had at his disposal old writings now lost, but in order to discover this you would have to plough through Irish *Codices* for at least 3 years. Dr Ch. O'Conor's *Scriptores* are ±[c] good sources, but mainly later ones; but he also published the *Annals of Ulster* with a Latin translation and, ditto, the first volume of the *Annals of the 4 Masters*, and I don't know whether this is included there. But the *Annals of the 4 Masters*, the main work, was edited and translated by Dr O'Donovan in 1856, and I have it here; I went through the first volume yesterday.[652]

Ware (Sir Jam. Ware, I think judge or something of the sort under Charles I) is by far the best of the older ones; he also had available to him, in translation, old writings now lost; he wrote in Latin (Waraeus), I have him in English and Latin.

---

[a] the Brunswick Committee of the Social-Democratic Workers' Party - [b] See this volume, pp. 515-16 - [c] more or less

The continuous reading of Irish books, i.e., the parallel English translation, could not be stood without at least a superficial knowledge of the phonetic and inflexional laws of the language. I have discovered here a frightful Irish grammar from Anno 1773,[a] and ploughed through it the day before yesterday, thereby learning *something*, but the man himself had no idea of the real laws of Irish. The only *good* grammar is that by Dr John O'Donovan, mentioned above, the best Irologist of this century. When you go to the Museum[b] you should take it out in order to see what it would cost approximately (O'Donovan has the habit of publishing nothing except fat expensive quarto volumes): O'Donovan's *Irish Grammar*. In addition you might also look at:

Genealogies, Tribes and Customs of Hy-Fiachrak, PRINTED FOR THE IRISH ARCHAEOLOGICAL SOCIETY 1844 (presumably by O'Donovan), and

Tribes and Customs of Hy-Many (ditto), to find out whether there is anything in them about *social* conditions, and whether these are fat expensive books: if not, and there is something in them, I shall acquire them.

There exists, further, an edition (by O'Donovan) of *Leabhar nag-Ceart* (BOOK OF RIGHTS), and if you could find an opportunity to take a look at it and tell me whether there is any prospect of results in it—NB. *only* for *social* conditions, everything else is of no interest to me—and whether it is an expensive de luxe edition, I would be very much obliged. On the basis of the quotations I have, there is not much in it for my purpose.

But this, I think, fairly well exhausts the relevant *old* literature, insofar as it has been published.

Ogarev was already an editor of *Kolokol* with Herzen, and is quite an ordinary bourgeois and poet. If Bakunin should really receive the money, and not Ogarev, then Ogarev will certainly be fettered to him as a controller.

In the last few days I have often been sitting at the quadrilateral desk in the small bow-window where we sat 24 years ago; I like this place very much; because of its coloured window the weather is always fine there.[480] Old Jones the librarian is still around, but he is very old and does nothing more; I haven't yet seen him there again.

Best greetings.

Your
F. E.

---

[a] Ch. Vallancey, *A Grammar of the Iberno-Celtic, or Irish Language.* - [b] the British Museum Library

The letter from Wilhelm[648] (which is returned, enclosed, together with the Brunswick one) is really the silliest thing I have ever read. What a dumb ox! Now I am wondering what reply he will give me. At the end I advised him[653] to consider whether it were not fitting to first study something if you want to teach it.

In which PARLIAMENTARY PAPER can one see how much money is thrown away annually on the COMMISSIONERS FOR THE PUBLICATION OF THE ANCIENT LAWS AND INSTITUTES OF IRELAND[636]? This is a simply colossal job (in miniature). It would also be important to know how much of this money is allocated 1. as remuneration for the inactive commissioners, 2. as salaries for the actually-working UNDERSTRAPPERS, printing costs, etc. This must be given in some PARLIAMENTARY PAPER. The fellows have been drawing emoluments *since 1852*, and until now *2 volumes* have been published! 3 LORDS, 3 judges, 3 priests, 1 general, and *1* professional Irologist, now long dead.[481]

First published abridged in *Der Briefwechsel zwischen F. Engels und K. Marx*, Bd. 4, Stuttgart, 1913 and in full in *MEGA*, Abt. III, Bd. 4, Berlin, 1931

Printed according to the original

Published in English for the first time

335

MARX TO ENGELS[180]

IN MANCHESTER

[London,] 16 MAY 1870[654]

Dear FRED,

Enclosed—a very well-behaved screed from Wilhelm[655]!

The old fool is beginning to take fright. In my last letter,[649] I told him that Borkheim was very sick; the Dr had forbidden him to do literary work for a long time even *after* his recovery; the continuation of Bakunin's twaddle,[629] which should never have been started, must now be stopped, etc.!

And what does the brute do? In the issue of *Volksstaat* that arrived today he published a personally defamatory article against Borkheim, written by the vagabond Nechayev.[656] I am really afraid this will excite Borkheim in a dangerous manner. Borkheim wrote to me the day before yesterday; he wanted to see me. I could not go because of my very foul cold and cough. But my wife was there yesterday. He is still very weak, and all excitement has specifically been prohibited by the Dr! The arrival of *Volksstaat* today will have caused an awful scene!

I wrote immediately to Wilhelm, the silly blockhead, and fittingly hauled him over the coals. At the same time, I mentioned that his effusions about you were 'too childish' to be answered, but he could rely upon it that his (Wilhelm's) 'private views about Hegel or ANYTHING ELSE' were a matter of indifference to you,[a] ditto the circumstance 'which' and 'what assortment of studies' he (Wilhelm) 'rather despises'. The fellow's claim that he has led 'for 22 years a restless life, with no time for any leisure' is delicious. We know he spent ABOUT 15 years of the 22 in idleness.

I am sending you the *Echo*, which you must preserve, because of the disavowal of the *FRENCH BRANCH,*[b] also published in the *Marseillaise*, *Internationale* (Brussels), and our other organs. Circumstances were finally so favourable that we had an opportunity to give an official kick to the rabble.

Mayence! soit![c]

It is *un peu indiscret*[d] for Bracke to have had extracts from your private letter to him[e] published in *Volksstaat*. But the intention is good, and I even believe this operation was politically correct. They obviously wished thereby to take a kick at Schweitzer.

There has already been a lot in *The Irishman* about the scurvy IRISH LAWS COMMISSION.[636] I shall try to find out the necessary about it.

If my condition *doesn't quickly* change so that it no longer disturbs my work, I might come for 8-14 days to Manchester.[639] If nothing else helps, perhaps a change of air will.

Your

K. M.

First published in *MEGA*, Abt. III, Bd. 4, Berlin, 1931

Printed according to the original

Published in English in full for the first time

---

a See this volume, pp. 509-10. - b K. Marx, *Draft Resolution of the General Council on the 'French Federal Section in London'*. -c Mainz! for all I care! - d a little indiscreet - e See this volume, pp. 498-99.

336

ENGELS TO MARX

IN LONDON

Manchester, 17 May 1870

Dear Moor,

Liebknecht will hardly send you my letter, since it is just the opposite of what Wilhelm says it is. I took special care not to use any insulting expression, but the whole letter naturally centres on the bitter FACT that Wilhelm writes under *my* signature on subjects about which he knows nothing (as now admitted). And this must of course 'insult him'.

Even now it is incomprehensible how he could publish Nechayev's filthy letter,[656] which consists of a series of curses, and nothing else but the very stupidest Russian Herzenite platitudes. Something like this can only be explained by his enormous indolence, which makes him struggle as hard as he can to fill up his paper[a] without working himself.

To bring your 'condition' to an end, the best thing for you would be to come in the course of this week, and with Tussy. A change of air has always been good for you, and we shall see to it that you get better exercise here than there. Then, if things are bad, you can also consult Gumpert. But bring Tussy with you. Lizzie has already baked CURRANT BREAD against her arrival, and the whole house has been *in jubilo* since I announced I would ask you to bring her with you. If you can come tomorrow, *tant mieux*[b]; just telegraph, no more notice is needed to have you rooms ready. Otherwise on Thursday.[c] It will do both of us good to march through the fields, and to laugh about the assorted humbuggery that has been abroad since I was last in London.[657] Lizzie has promised to go to bed unhesitatingly with Tussy at 11 o'clock every night—SUNDAYS ALWAYS EXCEPTED—so that this point will make no trouble either. And, finally, I feel that my 1857 Rüdesheimer is now just at the stage when it should be drunk, and for this I need your help.

Thus, either a telegram tomorrow and *'han selv'*[d]—not with

---

[a] *Der Volksstaat* - [b] all the better - [c] 19 May - [d] himself

22,000 men as '*han selv*' said, but still with Tussy—or then the day after tomorrow.

Best greetings.

Your
F. E.

Bracke queried me about publication of the letter,[a] and set a term for my prohibition, which I allowed to pass, since I attached no importance to it.

First published abridged in *Der Briefwech-sel zwischen F. Engels und K. Marx*, Bd. 4, Stuttgart, 1913 and in full in *MEGA*, Abt. III, Bd. 4, Berlin, 1931

Printed according to the original

Published in English for the first time

337

MARX TO ENGELS[446]

IN MANCHESTER

[London,] 18 May 1870

DEAR FRED,

On Monday[b] we shall be travelling to join you for 14 days, not longer, since Tussy is interrupting all her lessons. It's no go this week, since SWEET Jennychen has holidays until Monday, and we should not leave her alone for this period.

The enclosed muck from Heinzen discloses at the tail-end—the false story about my relationship with Lassalle—who is prompting Heineke, the doughty bondsman.[658] It is OLD Hatzfeldt, probably operating through Weber junior, who deliberates in New York. Incidentally, Heineke is making a grievous mistake if he expects me to honour him with a word of rebuttal. He has been working to this end for years—to no avail!

Our French MEMBERS are demonstrating *ad oculos*[c] the French Government the difference between a political secret society and a genuine workers' association. No sooner had the government jailed all the members of the Paris, Lyons, Rouen, Marseilles etc., COMMITTEES[642] (some of them fled to Switzerland and Belgium) than committees *twice as numerous* announced themselves in the newspapers as their successors with the most daring and defiant

---

declarations (and, as an added touch, with their *private addresses* as well). The French Government has finally done what we so long wanted it to do: transform the political question—EMPIRE or Republic—into a question *de vie ou de mort*[a] for the working class! Altogether, the plebiscite is dealing the final blow to the EMPIRE! Because so many voted 'yes' for the *empire avec la phrase constitutionelle*,[b] Boustrapa[320] believes he can now unceremoniously restore the *empire sans phrase, c'est à dire le régime du Décembre*.[c] In Paris—according to all private information—*la société du 10 Décembre*[641] has been fully restored and is fully active.
Salut.

Your
K. M.

The transfer of the congress to Mainz—UNANIMOUSLY VOTED yesterday—will give Bakunin a fit.

First published abridged in *Der Briefwechsel zwischen F. Engels und K. Marx*, Bd. 4, Stuttgart, 1913 and in full in *MEGA*, Abt. III, Bd. 4, Berlin, 1931

Printed according to the original

Published in English in full for the first time

338

ENGELS TO MARX

IN LONDON

Manchester, 19 May 1870

Dear Moor,

So Monday.[d] Had you come yesterday you could just as well have brought Jennychen with you; she could have slept with Tussy for the few days until Sunday, and she ought to see Manchester once before we leave here.

Bonaparte really is an incorrigible jackass. The blockhead has no conception of any sort of historic movement; all history is a JUMBLE of unconnected chance events, in which the little dodges of the old trickster play the decisive role—and what dodges! Always the same old recipe for every EMERGENCY. That he is once again organising his December 10 gang is [...][e]

---

[a] of life or death - [b] Empire with the constitutional phrase - [c] Empire without phrase, that's to say the December regime - [d] 23 May - [e] The manuscript is damaged here.

Old Heinzen is really entertaining. For twenty years and even longer the same old tune, but literally, it's really moving. You only need to say: Communist, and up jumps Heinzen, like a frog in strychnine-tetanus leaps when you touch the table on which it is lying. Old Hatzfeldt's hand is unmistakable here, and the thing was certainly made in America,[658] since nobody in Germany knows Heinzen's tune, the one you must whistle to make OLD Heinzen dance. The myths about Lassalle's attempted revolution, which we caused to fail in Cologne, are just too stupid.

The behaviour of the French workers is grand. The people are now active again and are in their element; there they are masters.

Best greetings.[a]

The extant part of the letter was first published abridged in *Der Briefwechsel zwischen F. Engels und K. Marx*, Bd. 4, Stuttgart, 1913 and in full in *MEGA*, Abt. III, Bd. 4, Berlin, 1931

Printed according to the original

Published in English for the first time

339

MARX TO HIS DAUGHTER JENNY

IN LONDON

Manchester, 31 May 1870

My dear child,

We were beginning to fret somewhat at the obstinate London taciturnity, but your letter[659] has again cleared up the horizon. I think not that we shall stay longer than to the beginning of next week.

My cold is not yet quite gone, but the general state of health has [been] wonderfully improved consequent upon the change of air. I see Gumpert almost daily and his advice is the more valuable the less he gets paid for it.

Here things are going on pretty much in the old track. Fred is quite jolly since he has got rid of '*den verfluchten*[b] Commerce'. His book on Ireland[c]—which by the by costs him a little more time than he had at first supposed—will be highly interesting. The

---

[a] The signature is missing, the manuscript is damaged. - [b] damned - [c] F. Engels, *The History of Ireland*.

illustrious Doppelju[a] who is so much up in the most recent Irish history and plays so prominent a part in it, will there find his archeological material ready cut.

Lange's book[b] differs from an 'Irish stew' in that particular point that it is all sauce and no substance. This muddled meddler evidently intends to fish out some compliments from me in return for *his* 'sweets', but he is woefully mistaken. How much he has understood of the *Capital* is clearly shown by his discovery that my theory of 'value' has nothing whatever to do with the developments on the *Arbeitstag*[c] etc.

Our friend Gumpert settles more and more down into a liberal, town-talk speaking, commonplace sort of fellow. What with his self-produced and with his 'inherited' family, this is hardly to be wondered at. It is too much of a good thing.

Tussy looks very blooming and is quite merry. She has happily found the live stock at Mornington Palace[660] increased by a new supply of kittens and so forth. She crossexamined Fred of course as to the 'threatening letters'; he considered it dangerous to allude to such a thing in letters conveyed by post and possibly falling under the eye of some Stieber. The true Stieber, who, I see, is eagerly busying himself at Paris to hatch a new complot, in which the 'Intern. W. Ass.' is to play the principal part and where I, as his old protégé, and *'wirklicher geheimer Oberhauptchef'*[d] must of course put[e] in my appearance.

While I write these lines, damned Fred is bothering me by continual 'fragmentary' communications from the old Norse Sagas. Apropos of Norse Sagas, has Möhmchen[f] not assisted at K. Blind's poetical lecture Sunday last?

Little Dakyns came over Saturday evening and stayed here on Sunday. This his visit was paid to Tussy and myself. This brave gnome was horselaughing all the time over. His costume was faster than ever before—*papierne Vatermörder ohne Kravatte,*[g] a dirty white hat instead of the Scotch cap, and *eine Sorte weisser Schuhe wie man sie* at the seaside *trägt.*[h] At our Sunday walk— Schorlemmer and Moore belonging of course to the party—his success with the general public was more than a *succès d'estime.* He created quite a sensation.

---

[a] The reference is to Jenny Marx's pseudonym: J. Williams. - [b] F. A. Lange, *Die Arbeiterfrage. Ihre Bedeutung für Gegenwart und Zukunft* (see also this volume, pp. 527-28). - [c] working day - [d] 'real secret leader' - [e] In the original: set - [f] Marx' wife, Jenny - [g] a paper stand-up collar without a tie - [h] a kind of white shoes such as one wears at the seaside

And now, illustrious Doppelju, give my best compliments to Möhmchen and Lehnchen.[a] I miss here very much the *Marseillaise* and all news from Paris. At the Schiller Club[76] they keep *Le Temps*, about the dullest of all the French papers. Also its editor-in-chief is one Nefftzer, an Alsacian.

Addio, illustrious one.

Old Nick

First published in *Voinstvuyushchy materialist*, Book 4, Moscow, 1925

Reproduced from the original

Published in English for the first time

340

MARX TO VICTOR LE LUBEZ[661]

IN LONDON

Manchester, 14 June 1870
86 Mornington Street, Stockport Road

[*Draft*]

Sir,

Yours dd. 11 June has been sent me from London. I want now to be informed by you who is the informer that gave you the *absurd* information that I am the London Correspondent of the *Volksstaat* and the author of an Article on your person. Allow me to observe that my time is spent on subjects of a more general interest.

I am
Sir

Yours etc.
K. M.

Mr Le Lubez.

First published in: Marx and Engels, *Works*, First Russian Edition, Vol. XXVI, Moscow, 1935

Reproduced from the original

Published in English for the first time

---

[a] Helene Demuth

341

MARX TO LUDWIG KUGELMANN [29]

IN HANOVER

London, 27 June 1870

Dear King Wenceslaus,[a]

I returned here this week after a stay of one month in Manchester, and found your letter waiting.[662]

In fact I can give you no reply as to the date of my departure, and not even to the question—which you have not asked—namely, *whether I shall travel at all.*

Last year I anticipated that, after the Easter Fair, I would have a second edition of my book,[b] and CONSEQUENTLY the *takings* from the first edition. You will see, however, from the enclosed letter from Meissner,[c] which arrived today, that all this is still a long way off.[663] (Be so kind as to send me the letter back.)

Messieurs the German professors have recently found themselves obliged to take note of me now and then, even if in a very silly way; for example, A. Wagner in a pamphlet on landed property, and Held (Bonn) in a pamphlet about the rural loan banks in the Rhine Province.[d]

Mr Lange (On *the workers' question,* etc., 2nd edition)[e] pays me great compliments, but with the object of increasing his own importance. Mr Lange, you see, has made a great discovery. All history may be subsumed in one single great natural law. This natural law is the *phrase* (—the Darwinian expression becomes, in this application, just a phrase—) 'STRUGGLE FOR LIFE', and the content of this phrase is the Malthusian law of population, or RATHER over-population. Thus, instead of analysing this 'STRUGGLE FOR LIFE' as it manifests itself historically in various specific forms of society, all that need be done is to transpose every given struggle into the phrase 'STRUGGLE FOR LIFE', and then this phrase into the Malthusian 'population fantasy'. It must be admitted that this is a very rewarding method—for stilted, mock-scientific, highfaluting ignorance and intellectual laziness.

---

[a] Kugelmann's nickname - [b] the first volume of *Capital* - [c] See this volume, pp. 529-30. - [d] A. Wagner, *Die Abschaffung des privaten Grundeigenthums*; A. Held, *Die ländlichen Darlehenskassenvereine in der Rheinprovinz und ihre Beziehungen zur Arbeiterfrage.* - [e] F. A. Lange, *Die Arbeiterfrage. Ihre Bedeutung für Gegenwart und Zukunft.*

And what this Lange has to say about the Hegelian method and my application of the same is simply childish. First, he understands *rien*[a] about Hegel's method and, therefore, second, still less about my critical manner of applying it. In one respect he reminds me of Moses Mendelssohn. That prototype of a windbag once wrote to Lessing asking how he could possibly take 'that dead dog Spinoza'[664] *au sérieux*[b]! In the same way, Mr Lange expresses surprise that Engels, I, etc., take *au sérieux* the dead dog Hegel, after Büchner, Lange, Dr Dühring, Fechner, etc., had long agreed that they—POOR DEAR—had long since buried him. Lange is naïve enough to say that I 'move with rare freedom' in empirical matter. He has not the slightest idea that this 'free movement in matter' is nothing but a paraphrase for the *method* of dealing with matter—that is, the *dialectical method*.

My best thanks to Madame la comtesse[c] for her kind lines. This really does one good at a time 'when more and more of the better ones are disappearing'. But, *sérieusement parlant*,[d] I am always pleased when a few lines from your dear wife remind me of the happy times I spent in your circle.

Regarding Meissner's pressure for the second volume,[41] I was not only held up by illness throughout the winter. I found it necessary to mug up on my Russian, because, in dealing with the land question, it has become essential to study Russian land-owning relationships from primary sources. In addition, in connection with the Irish land question, the English Government has published a series of BLUE BOOKS (soon concluding) about the land relations IN ALL COUNTRIES. Finally—*entre nous*—I would like the second edition of Vol. I first. It would simply be disturbing if this came in the middle of the ULTIMATE finalisation of Vol. II.

BEST COMPLIMENTS ON JENNY'S PART AND MY OWN TO ALL THE MEMBERS OF THE Kugelmann FAMILY.

Your

K. M.

First published abridged in *Die Neue Zeit*, Bd. 2, Nr. 17, Stuttgart, 1901-1902 and in full in *Pisma Marksa k Kugelmanu* (Letters of Marx to Kugelmann), Moscow-Leningrad, 1928

Printed according to the original

---

[a] nothing - [b] seriously - [c] Gertrud Kugelmann - [d] speaking seriously

342

MARX TO ENGELS

IN MANCHESTER

[London,] 5 July 1870

DEAR FRED,

You must excuse the interruption in our correspondence since my return to London.[639] THERE WAS SO MUCH INTERNATIONAL AND OTHER BUSINESS PRESSING UPON ME.

Dupont, whose one child (BABY) is, for the time being, staying with his brother-in-law, the second with Serraillier, the third with him[a]—all small girls—has in the meantime received two OFFERS as sort of MANAGER or chief OVERLOOKER (in wind-music-instrument factories), one in Paris, the other in Manchester. I advised against No. I, since there he would not only soon be arrested, but also become completely absorbed IN QUARRELS with the various cliques. I strongly advised, on the other hand, No. II, despite his aversion to it. He has, therefore, accepted the offer of J. Higham, 131 Strangeways, Manchester (BRASS MUSICAL INSTRUMENTS).

The difficulty is that he will have to take one child, No. II, with him immediately, and will have the two others follow him in a few weeks, so he needs a little house in Manchester, and some sort of reliable female person to look after the children and for DOMESTIC MANAGEMENT. His income for a start will be £3 WEEKLY. Could LIZZY do something directly or indirectly on this matter?

Dupont is politically a character, but *privatim* enormously weak. *D'abord*[b] he can stand very little liquor without getting very EXCITED. SECONDLY he is easily dominated and exploited by his company.

He will perhaps go to Manchester in the course of this week. In any case, I shall write in advance about his day of arrival.

From the enclosed letter from Meissner[663] you will see how things are there. I had a pressing letter from Kugelmann, who will be leaving for Karlsbad[c] on 12 August, and is waiting for my declaration before renting accommodation, to which I replied with Meissner's letter. I reminded him that Meissner had spoken in his presence of certain prospects for a second edition,[d] and payment for the Easter Fair; and I added that, UNDER PRESENT CIRCUMSTANCES, I

---

a See this volume, p. 487. - b Firstly - c Karlovy Vary - d of the first volume of *Capital*; see also the previous letter.

could not say either when I would go to Karlsbad, or whether I would go at all. HENCE his enclosed letter. I have not yet replied, since we are still awaiting an answer from Dublin concerning O'Donovan Rossa's photograph.

Lafargue had notified me that a young Russian, Lopatin, would bring a letter of introduction from him. Lopatin called on Saturday[a]; I invited him for Sunday (he was with us from 10 o'clock until 12 at night),[665] and he returned on Monday to Brighton, where he is living.

He is still very young, was two years in the lock-up, after this 8 months fortress confinement in the Caucasus, from which he escaped. He is the son of an impoverished nobleman, and had to earn his living at the University of St Petersburg by private tutoring. Today is living very meagrely from translations for Russia. Lives in Brighton, since there he can bathe in the sea 2-3 times a day, gratis, at a certain distance from the official bathing beach.

A very wide-awake *critical* brain, cheerful character, stoical, like a Russian peasant who simply accepts what he gets. Weak point: *Poland.* Here he talks just like an Englishman—SAY AN ENGLISH CHARTIST OF THE OLD SCHOOL—does about Ireland.

He told me the whole story about Нечаевъ[b] (23 years) is an abominable lie. Нечаевъ has *never* been in a Russian prison; the Russian Government never undertook an *assassinat* against him, etc.

The story is this. Нечаевъ (one of Bakunin's few agents in Russia) belonged to a secret society. Another young man, X,[c] rich and enthusiastic, supported this society with money via Нечаевъ. ONE FINE MORNING X tells Нечаевъ that he will not give another kopeck, since he does not know what is being done with the money. Whereupon, Mr Нечаевъ suggested to his secret society (perhaps because he could not account for the money) that X be murdered, since he might change his views *at a future date*, and could become a traitor. *He really did murder him.* He is thus sought by the government simply *as a murderer vulgaris.*

In Geneva, Lopatin *d'abord* took Нечаевъ personally to task (about his lies), and he excused himself with the sensational political usefulness for the so-called cause. Lopatin then told the story to Bakunin, who told him that as a '*bon vieillard*'[d] he had believed it all. Bakunin then challenged Lopatin to repeat the story in the presence of Нечаевъ. Lopatin immediately went with Bakunin to Нечаевъ where the scene was repeated. Нечаевъ

---

[a] 2 July - [b] S. G. Nechayev - [c] Ivan Ivanov - [d] 'good old man'

remained silent. All the time Lopatin was in Geneva, Нечаевъ remained very unobtrusive, no longer saying a word. Scarcely had Lopatin left for Paris, and the whole buffoonery started again. Shortly after this, Lopatin received an insulting letter from Bakunin about the affair. He replied in even more insulting terms. Result: Bakunin wrote a *Pater-peccavi*[a] letter (in Lopatin's possession *here*), but— *il est un bon vieillard crédule*[b]! (*En passant*:[c] Lopatin says that whole sentences written by Borkheim are completely unintelligible and make complete nonsense in Russian, not only grammatically wrong but 'nothing at all'! And that fool Borkheim has, in the meantime, as he told me before my meeting with Lopatin, sent his bungling work through our friend Eichhoff in Berlin to a German there—who is used by the Berlin police as a Russian interpreter—in order to obtain from him a certificate that *he* can write Russian. The talent of our Gaudissart for unconscious comedy is really UNRIVALLED!)

Чернышевскій,[d] I learned from Lopatin, was sentenced in 1864 to 8 years *travaux forcés*[e] in the Siberian mines; so he still has two years to slave. The first court was decent enough to declare that there was absolutely *nothing* against him, and that the alleged intriguing, plotting secret letters were obvious FORGERIES (which they were). But the *Senate*, on the Tsar's orders, most graciously reversed this verdict, and sent off to Siberia this cunning man who, as the judgement said 'was so clever that he cast his writing in a legally unexceptionable form, but nevertheless publicly dispensed poison therein'. *Voilà la justice russe.*[f]

Flerovsky is in a better situation. He is only in administrative exile in a miserable little hole between Moscow and Petersburg!

You suspected rightly that *Flerovsky* is a *pseudonym*. But Lopatin says that the name, although not originally Russian, occurs quite frequently amongst Russian clerics (namely MONKS, who think it is the Russian translation of Fleury, and who are just as keen on sweet-scented names as are the German Jews). Lopatin was originally a naturalist by professional training. He has also been concerned in commercial business, and it would be a good thing if one could find something for him in this line.[g] I shall speak about it with Borkheim and Pohl. About Paris, etc., very soon.

Your
Moor

---

a Father, I have sinned - b he is a credulous good old man - c by the way - d N. G. Chernyshevsky - e forced labour - f Such is Russian justice. - g See this volume, p. 535.

Apropos. Jennychen would like to know whether she should not rather name you as the author of the NOTE.[a]

And—she is very obstinate—she will not allow me to change a few words in the manuscript without your special permission!

MY BEST COMPLIMENTS TO MRS LIZZY.

[Postscript by Marx's daughter Jenny]

5 July 1870

DEAR Engels,

THANK YOU VERY MUCH FOR YOUR LETTER AND THE MOST INTERESTING NOTES. I ONLY HOPE MR RISSÉ WOULD INTERLARD THEM WITH THE Judenkirschen[b] OF WHICH HE SEEMS TO HAVE A PLENTIFUL STOCK ON HAND. FOR O'DONOVAN ROSSA'S PORTRAIT I HAVE WRITTEN TO Pigott. IN CASE A GOOD PHOTOGRAPH IS NOT TO BE HAD, OF COURSE, I CAN AS YOU SAY, SEND Kugelmann THE PRINT WHICH APPEARED IN THE IRISHMAN. WITH MANY THANKS, I REMAIN

AFFECTIONATELY YOURS

Jenny

First published abridged in *Der Briefwechsel zwischen F. Engels und K. Marx*, Bd. 4, Stuttgart, 1913 and in full in *MEGA*, Abt. III, Bd. 4, Berlin, 1931

Printed according to the original

Published in English for the first time

343

ENGELS TO MARX

IN LONDON

Manchester, 6 July 1870

Dear Moor,

Your instructions regarding Dupont[c] are so uncertain that I can do absolutely nothing. I should rent him a COTTAGE—but furnished or unfurnished? You say nothing on this point, but this is the main thing. In addition, a reliable housemaid is damned difficult to drum up in a hurry and, third, Lizzie cannot leave the house because of her knee which, as a result of her unrest and impatience, is not getting better as quickly as it should.

Under the circumstances, Dupont's plan to come here with one child right away appears to me completely impracticable. I should

---

[a] F. Engels, *Notes for the Preface to a Collection of Irish Songs*. - [b] Jewish wit - [c] See this volume, p. 529.

think that his brother-in-law or Serraillier would be able to accommodate the 3rd child, too, for 8-14 days; in this case it would be better for him to come here *alone* right away, then I could immediately go round *with him* and get a house and, in the meantime, we could make enquiries about a woman. Since he will have to bring the children here, or have them brought by somebody, it makes no difference if there are 2 or 3 of them.

If this is agreed, write to me immediately, so that I can get him quarters near his workshop, LODGINGS for a week with board if he wants it—I assume he will only want a BEDROOM without the expense of a SITTING ROOM?—and when he will be coming. On this I expect an immediate reply, so I know what I have to do. But, as I said, to bring the child with him right away would be absolute nonsense; it *would cost him much more money,* and would be in his way everywhere during the first few days. Where should a woman spring from all of a sudden, if he doesn't simply take the first one to offer?

Quoad[a] Karlsbad,[b] I am, as I said, in favour of you going there this summer. I can make £40 available to you for the journey. The cure is absolutely essential for you, even if you cannot completely avoid Kugelmann and his fervent fire thereby. C. Roesgen was also there, I saw him yesterday; he said it is not expensive there, particularly since 'there is no opportunity to spend money' during the cure; the cure did a lot of good to his liver (which is in a fine state compared to yours), and he looks rather thinner but much healthier. So make up your MIND; apart from Kugelmann you will certainly find other interesting liver patients there, and on your way back you will travel via Hamburg and put pressure on Meissner. So take a quick decision and leap with eyes closed into the hot springs of Karlsbad, and the equally warm admiration of Kugelmann. NB. Because of possible passport difficulties on the Austrian frontier, it might be a good thing if you were to travel in the company of your personal physician.

Lopatin's stories about the other русскія дѣла[c] are very interesting and it is very useful to know them. That Нечаевъ[d] should turn out to be just a common blackguard is quite desirable.

Jennychen does not need to name me as the author of the note[e] since Kugelmann knows my handwriting quite well; but she can deal with it as she will, and as far as alterations are concerned, do

---

a Regarding - b Karlovy Vary - c Russian affairs - d S. G. Nechayev - e F. Engels, *Notes for the Preface to a Collection of Irish Songs.*

what you like with it. There will probably be no refuge from the Jewish wit to which she refers.

Apropos Dupont. Lizzie has her eyes on somebody quite suitable for him if only we can get hold of her, but I fear we shall have no information on this before Sunday or Monday. It is her cousin Anna Kane, a person who is not young, not pretty, but honest to the backbone. Tussy knows her; but we shall scarcely discover before Friday where she is at the moment, and will probably not be able to see her before the end of this week or the beginning of next.

I found and looked through the old Welsh laws[a] in the official RECORD COMMISSION edition. There are quite jolly things in it. If a man discovers, on his nuptial night, that his wife is not a virgin, but lies with her until the morning, then nothing of hers falls to him, sed si, postquam illam vitiatam deprehenderit, surrexerit ad pronubos, pene erecto, et testaretur eis se illam vitiatam invenisse, et non concubuerit cum illa ad crastinum usque; illa nihil ab eo in crastinum habebit. Si mammae et crines et menses apparuerint, tunc lex pronuntiat neminem posse certe scire num virgo sit necne[b] and thus she must produce 7 compurgators, including her parents and brothers and sisters. If she will not or cannot do this LET HER SHIFT BE CUT OFF AS HIGH AS HER HIP, AND LET A YEARLING STEER BE PUT IN HER HAND, HAVING HIS TAIL GREASED WITH TALLOW, AND IF SHE CAN HOLD HIM BY HIS TAIL, LET HER TAKE HIM IN LIEU OF HER SHARE OF THE *argyvreu* (PARAPHERNALIA), AND IF SHE CANNOT HOLD HIM, LET HER BE WITHOUT ANYTHING.—

Now we have 'To BE LET' in the window. Haven't you found anything yet?

What is the catalogue of the London LIBRARY like? This is very important for me, so that I know what I can leave unread here.

Best greetings to you all.

Your
F. E.

First published abridged in *Der Briefwechsel zwischen F. Engels und K. Marx,* Bd. 4, Stuttgart, 1913 and in full in *MEGA,* Abt. III, Bd. 4, Berlin, 1931

Printed according to the original

Published in English for the first time

---

[a] *Ancient Laws and Institutes of Wales,* volumes I-II. - [b] but if, as soon as he discovers she is damaged, he goes to the marriage arrangers with erect penis, and it is testified by them that he found her damaged and did not lie with her until the morning, she will on the next day receive nothing from him. If breasts, hair and menstruation are present, the law proclaims that nobody can know with certainty whether she is a virgin.

344

MARX TO HERMANN LOPATIN [666]

IN BRIGHTON

[London, 6 July 1870]

The occupation of a translator is abominable; commerce will give you a great deal. A greater chance to use your free time for the study and propaganda...

First published in *Istoriya SSSR*, No. 6, Moscow, 1959

Printed according to the letter of Hermann Lopatin to Pyotr Lavrov of 6 July 1870

Translated from the French

Published in English for the first time

345

ENGELS TO MARX

IN LONDON

Manchester, 7 July 1870

Dear Moor,

I had to write to you yesterday about Dupont[a] in all haste, and without being able to consider the case properly with Lizzie; I had been busy in town the whole day, and in the evening there was a BALLOT at the club, so I could only discuss the business properly with Lizzie later; and it thus turned out that there is no reason to burden either Serraillier or Dupont's brother-in-law with the girl, for it will be hard enough for them to look after the other children; the child can sleep perfectly well with Mary Ellen[b] and will not inconvenience us in any way. Dupont can also stay with me for the first few days, until we have got him fixed up to some extent, and it will be much better if I do this together with him, rather than alone, without having him along. Lizzie says she has bedding enough, without that used by Mary Ellen during her scarlet fever, which I naturally would not like to have used yet.

---

a See this volume, p. 532. - b Mary Ellen Burns

When I wrote to you yesterday morning I had no way of knowing this yet, but so that you might receive today other news in addition to yesterday's letter, I telegraphed you this morning:

Dupont's LITTLE GIRL WELCOME TO STAY WITH US, DIRECT THEM BOTH TO MY HOME, ADVISE TIME OF ARRIVAL.

I hope you received this telegram *before* further consultations with Dupont. You must persuade him that he should not hesitate to accept my offer (if it is necessary, i.e., the persuasion), he is making things easier not only for himself but for *me* too, by coming to me right away with the little one. So request him in my name to do as I suggest, and just let me know when he will be arriving so I can meet him at the station.

Best greetings.

Your
F. E.

First published abridged in *Der Briefwechsel zwischen F. Engels und K. Marx*, Bd. 4, Stuttgart, 1913 and in full in *MEGA*, Abt. III, Bd. 4, Berlin, 1931

Printed according to the original

Published in English for the first time

346

MARX TO ENGELS

IN MANCHESTER

[London,] 8 July 1870
Damn heat!

DEAR FRED,

After receipt of your telegram I informed Dupont of the necessary. He is leaving on Monday,[a] 11 o'clock, from Euston STATION.

I would recommend you to let the child sleep with him for the short time he'll be there. Since the sickness and death of the mother there has been a certain neglect and, owing to school attendance, the possibility of creepy-crawlies on her head. At least it appears so to the female section here.

Tomorrow I'll send you the FRENCH PAPERS with the trial proceed-

---

[a] 11 July

ings.[667] I must have them *back as soon as possible.* Little Jew Frankel[a] has won laurels. Both with the *accusés*[b] and in the newspapers etc., you will note the tendency to claim for themselves (Paris) the invention of the *Internationale.*

I'll go and see Beesly about the London catalogue tomorrow. *Salut.*

Your
K. M.

(*Verte*)[c]

Jenny has still had no reply from Ireland, apart from the enclosed letter from Pigott.[d] The fellow writes as if he were replying to an ADVERTISEMENT. Jennychen is TOO *gentille* for him. *Il lui faut*[e] THE FEROCIOUS IRISH GIRL. If FOREIGNERS here are, in general, prejudiced against the Irish, aren't narrow-minded nationalists like Pigott responsible?

First published abridged in *Der Briefwechsel zwischen F. Engels und K. Marx*, Bd. 4, Stuttgart, 1913 and in full in *MEGA*, Abt. III, Bd. 4, Berlin, 1931

Printed according to the original

Published in English for the first time

347

MARX TO HERMANN JUNG[668]

IN LONDON

[London,] 14 July 1870

* Dear Jung,

Enclosed the Programme. The questions are *arranged* in such an order as will *facilitate the business* of next Congress. You'll understand my meaning.

Yours truly *
K. M.

---

a Leo Frankel - b accused - c Turn over - d See this volume, p. 562. - e He needs

20–983

(1) On the necessity of abolishing the public debt. Discussion on the right of indemnity to be accorded.

(2) The relations between political action and the social movement of the working class.

(3) Practical measures for converting landed property into public property (*see the note*).

(4) On the conversion of currency banks into national banks.

(5) Conditions of cooperative production on a national scale.

(6) On the necessity for the working class to keep *general statistics of labour* in accordance with the resolutions of the Geneva Congress of 1866.

(7) Reconsideration by the congress of the question of measures to abolish war.

Note to point (3): The *General Council of Belgium* has proposed this question:

'Practical measures to set up *agricultural sections* within the *International* and to achieve solidarity between the proletarians in agriculture and the proletarians in other industries.'

The *General Council of the International Association* believes that this question is inherent in point (3).

* The following must *not be published* but only communicated by letter to the different sections.*

Confidential notice to the different sections.

(1) The General Council requests that the different sections give their delegates formal instructions on the opportunity of changing the seat of the General Council for the year 1870-71.

(2) In the event that the change were to be decided upon, the General Council would propose Brussels as the seat of the General Council for the same year.

First published abridged in *Kommunistichesky Internatsional*, No. 29, Moscow, 10 October 1934 and in full in: Marx and Engels, *Works*, Second Russian Edition, Vol. 32, Moscow, 1964

Printed according to the original

Translated from the French

Published in English for the first time

APPENDICES

Your favourite virtue   Jollity
… in man   quality in man   to mind his own business
… woman —   in woman   not to mislay things
— chief characteristic   knowing everything by halves
Idea of happiness   Château Margaux 1848.
— — misery   to go to a dentist
The vice you excuse   excess of any sort
—   detest   Cant
Your aversion   affected, stuck-up women
The character you   } Spurgeon
most dislike
Favourite occupation   chaffing & being chaffed
—   Hero   none
—   Heroine   too many to name one
Poet   Reinecke de Vos, Shakespeare, Ariosto etc
Prose writer   Goethe Lessing, Dr. Samelson.
Flower   Blue Bell
Colour   any one not Aniline
Dish   cold: Salad, hot: Irish Stew
Maxim   not to have any.
Motto — take it easy.

F. Engels

A page from the album of Marx's daughter Jenny with Frederick Engels'
'Confession'

1

FREDERICK ENGELS[669]

CONFESSION

[London, early April 1868]

Your favourite virtue	
in man quality	jollity
in man	to mind his own business
in woman	not to mislay things
Chief characteristic	knowing everything by halves
Idea of happiness	Château Margaux 1848
" misery	to go to a dentist
The vice you excuse	excess of any sort
" detest	Cant
Your aversion	affected stuck up woman
The characters you most dislike	Spurgeon
Favourite occupation	chaffing and being chaffed
— Hero	none
— Heroine	too many to name one
— Poet	Reineke de Vos,[670] Shakespeare, Ariosto, etc.
— Prose writer	Goethe, Lessing, Dr Samelson
— Flower	Blue Bell
— Colour	any one not Aniline
— Dish	Cold: Salad, hot: Irish Stew
— Maxim	not to have any
— Motto	take it aisy

F. Engels

First published in: Marx and Engels,
Works, Second Russian Edition, Vol. 32,
Moscow, 1964

Reproduced from the original

2

ARNOLD RUGE TO STEINTHAL[671]

IN MANCHESTER

Brighton, 25 January 1869
7 Park Crescent

Dear Mr Steinthal,

At the same time as this letter, I am sending you Marx on capital by book-post.

Many thanks! This book has given me constant food for thought, though I had to work on all sorts of other things at the same time.

It is an *epoch-making work* and throws a shining and often scorching light on the development of the social periods, with the declines, the birth-pains, and the frightful days of agony.

The proofs of *surplus value* through unpaid labour, of the expropriation of the workers *who* had worked *for themselves*, and of the coming *expropriation of the expropriators*, are classical.

On the latter, p. 745[a]: 'The capitalist mode of production and appropriation, hence *capitalist* property, is the first negation of *individual private property, as founded on the labour of the proprietor.* The *negation of this negation* therefore again gives the producer individual property, but based on the acquisitions of the capitalist era: i.e., *on the co-operation of free labourers and their possession in common of the land and of the means of production produced by labour itself.*'

Marx is a man of broad erudition and with a brilliant dialectical talent. His book is above the level of many people and newspaper writers; but it will quite certainly make its way, and exercise a powerful influence, despite its broad scope; yes, precisely because of this.

With regard to religion, the author states very accurately: 608: 'As, in religion, man is governed by the products of his own brain, so in capitalistic production, he is governed by the products of his own hand.'

And to liberate him, it by no means suffices to shine a light in the owl's eye; in fact, whenever he loses his master, like the Frenchman or the Spaniard, then he himself installs one over himself again.

---

[a] The following quotation, slightly modified by Marx, is from *Capital*, Vol. I (1867), pp. 744-45.

But still all the best for 1869! May it stand the test like its predecessor! My best greetings to Mrs Steinthal and Mr Heydemann.

Yours sincerely

Dr A. Ruge

First published in *Die Neue Zeit*, Bd. 2, Nr. 12, Stuttgart, 1901-1902

Printed according to the original

Published in English for the first time

3

JENNY MARX TO LUDWIG KUGELMANN

IN HANOVER

London, 15 September 1869[a]

Dear Mr Kugelmann,

I would have replied long since to your friendly lines from Karlsbad,[b] had I not been hoping day by day for more definite news from our dear travellers. Since their first and last letter from Liège, we have completely lost track of them. But I expect they will move in on you this week, probably after a bit of tacking hither and thither,[672] so I am sending for your joint reading today's *Times* and an older number of *The Pall Mall Gazette*. There is a deathly silence in the press here about the Congress,[c] apart from the quite confused twaddly article in *Pall Mall*, which I enclose. Today *The Times* has broken the ice for the first time with a very favourable factual and concise article,[d] which will arouse great interest here, and particularly in France, because of the speech by the American delegate.[e] I believe I can smell out our 'George',[f] in various turns of phrase, expressions and 'Eccariads', if it is possible to ascribe so much tact to him.[673]

A real arsenal of newspapers and letters has accumulated here in the meantime; and I really don't know whether they are worth the trouble and cost of sending overseas; their contents are mostly

---

^a The year is in Kugelmann's hand. - ^b Karlovy Vary - ^c The 1869 Basle Congress of the International Working Men's Association. See Note 379. - ^d [J. G. Eccarius,] 'The International Working Men's Congress', *The Times*, No. 26543, 15 September 1869. - ^e Andrew Cameron - ^f Georg Eccarius

now so antiquated. Lessner wrote 3 very pleasant detailed letters about the Congress and Liebknecht 2 wishy-washy ones that would be better left unread.[674] Eccarius conveys the curious fact that an American told him that he had heard from Mr Slack, the correspondent of the *New-York Tribune* in London, that 'Bright had written to all London newspaper offices and requested them to publish *no* reports on our deliberations'. This would provide some explanation for the silence of the press.

But if *The Times* publishes a few more reports, the other bell-wethers will follow, and then the success of the Congress will be assured. In any case, it will have more success than that of the Eisenachers,[373] the only effect of which seems to be to have helped 'our great master Ferdinand'[a] to obtain, in addition to his official '*moniteur*',[b] the *Social-Demokrat*, a semi-official one in the form of Liebknecht's sheet.[c] Even in Basle they tried to push the wretched Schweitzer scandal into the foreground, so that one might have thought that the 'Internationals' had no other mission but to *internationalise* the principles of the 'Man of Iron'[d] without the *strict organisation.*[675]

I shall send some private letters of interest to Hanover immediately, as soon as I hear that our dear 'wanderers' have reached you. Laura, with her husband and their delightful little chap,[e] have been with us here just 4 weeks to the day; now they are beginning to prepare for their return to Paris. Unfortunately, mother and son are not as well as I might wish. The sweet little lad is suffering from the break-through of his first teeth, with all the usual symptoms. His friendly face has grown so narrow and small, and his shining little eyes stare out of his pale face twice as large and rich as usual. He is a cheerful, gentle lad, and we shall sorely miss the little monkey.

Please give my heartiest respects to your dear wife,[f] give Fränzchen[g] a kiss, and accept friendliest greetings from

Yours

Jenny Marx

First published in *Movimento Operaio*, No. 2, Milan, 1955

Printed according to the original

Published in English for the first time

---

[a] Ferdinand Lassalle - [b] organ - [c] *Demokratisches Wochenblatt* - [d] Ferdinand Lassalle (the reference is to his 'iron' law of wages). - [e] Charles Étienne Lafargue - [f] Gertrud Kugelmann - [g] Franziska Kugelmann

4

JENNY MARX (DAUGHTER)
TO LUDWIG KUGELMANN

IN HANOVER

[London,] 30 October 1869

My dear Doctor!!!

Thank you very much for your letter and the copy of the portrait of your dear mother. It is a wonderfully good one— better than the original painting. I was very glad to have it.—It gave me much pleasure to hear that you feel better—may time gradually reconcile you to the great loss you have sustained. Think—

'after life's fitful fever, she sleeps well—nothing can hurt her further'.[a]

Is there no consolation in that thought?

I have written a note to Mrs Menke. I am much obliged to you for the timely remembrancer, though to my credit be it said, that previous to the arrival of your note, I had thought of writing to 'Mariechen'—... but somehow or other—well—the way to hell, they say, is paved with good intentions. Moor also has written her a few lines. He is much better and has almost managed to get rid of the troublesome cough which so much tormented him at Hanover. He sends you his kind regards, and hopes you will excuse his [not] writing to you, as at the present moment he is very busy reading a book (which has just appeared in the Russian language, and the reading of which gives him no small amount of trouble) on the condition of the Russian peasantry,[b] which it appears is exactly the reverse of what the imaginative Carey[c] represents it to be—anything but enviable. 'Happiness doesn't grow in Russia.' This book has just appeared in the nick of time, it is very important. Moor should in his second volume[41] make known the facts contained in it. Meanwhile the French translation of the first volume is steadily progressing.[441] In a month the third chapter[676] will be ready for correction, at least so writes Paul (Lafargue) who visited the translator a few days ago.

---

[a] Shakespeare, *Macbeth*,* Act III, Scene 2 (paraphrased). - [b] Н. Флеровскій, *Положеніе рабочаго класса въ Россіи.* - [c] H. Ch. Carey, *Principles of Social Science.*

'Dans une pauvre maison, dans une chambre plus pauvre encore, où ne se trouvent que deux chaises, une table, un lit et quelques planches pour des livres,'[a]

Paul writes us, he found Mr Keller (the translator) busy at his work. He is young, intelligent, enthusiastic. Paul is delighted with him, and particularly admires his '*grand pouvoir travailleur et énergie*'[b] — and indeed who could help doing so? For the sake of pursuing his studies (he occupies himself with several sciences, but principally with the social science), this young man lives in a state of comparative misery. His father is a wealthy manufacturer, whose factory he superintended during seven years, but feeling disgusted with his '*métier de gardechiourme*'[c] Mr Keller gave up his position. Paul met two more socialists at Mr Keller's house.

'Le parti socialiste,' il nous écrit, 'se constitue à Paris et commence à tenir le haut du pavé, quoiqu'il n'ait pas de journal, il a les réunions publiques et l'agitation personnelle.'[d]

No doubt the socialist party has risen on the ruins of the Simons, Pelletans, Bancels, Gambettas. The French people have discovered that the emptiest vessels make the greatest noise — have watched those big-mouthed ranters turning tail and won't give them credit for their good intentions, their hopes, 'that they who run away, may live to fight another day'.

In London the event of the week has been a Fenian demonstration, got up for the purpose of praying the government for the release of the Irish prisoners.[452] As Tussy has returned from Ireland[677] a stauncher Irishman than ever, she did not rest until she had persuaded Moor, Mama and me to go with her to Hyde Park, the place appointed for the meeting. This Park, the largest one in London, was one mass of men, women and children, even the trees up to their highest branches had their inhabitants. The number of persons present were by the papers estimated at somewhere about 70 thousand, but as these papers are English, this figure is no doubt too low. There were processionists carrying red, green and white banners, with all sorts of devices, such as 'Keep your powder dry!', 'Disobedience to tyrants is a duty to God'. And hoisted higher than the flags were a profusion of red Jacobin caps, the bearers of which sang the *Marseillaise* — sights and sounds that must have greatly interfered

---

[a] In a poor house, in a room still poorer, where there are only two chairs, a table, a bed and a few bookshelves - [b] great working capacity and energy - [c] profession as a warder - [d] The socialist party, he writes, is constituting itself in Paris and beginning to come to the fore; although it has no press organ it holds public meetings and carries on agitation among individuals.

with the enjoyment of the portwine at the clubs.—On the following day, Monday, all the papers made a furious onslaught on those confounded 'foreigners', and cursed the day they had landed in England to demoralize sober John Bull by means of their bloodred flags, noisy choruses and other enormities....

It is tea-time—and I have promised to roast some chestnuts for Tussy, so thank your good stars or rather the chestnuts that this scrawl doesn't run on for ever.—(I am sure you have been thinking I was never going to stop.) With kindest remembrances from all at home.

Believe me dear 'Doctor'

Very faithfully yours
Jenny Marx

You seem surprised at my bestowing upon you your sonorous title. Believe me I do not grudge it to you. In 'our new society' there will be little need for priests of the body; they will go to the wall along with their brethren physicians of the soul—meanwhile I wish you joy—make the most of your dignities—while they last! I enclose Weerth's *photographie*.[a]

First published in *Movimento Operaio*, No. 2, Milan, 1955

Reproduced from the original

Published in English for the first time

5

JENNY MARX (DAUGHTER) TO LUDWIG KUGELMANN

IN HANOVER

London, 27 December 1869

My dear Doctor,

I hope you do not fancy that true to the code of certain forefathers of mine, I am indulging in a spirit of revenge. The only reason why I have so long left unanswered your very kind letter is, that I haven't been able to call one hour my own. Until two o'clock you know I am every day engaged[371]—then, as our poor Helen[b] has been very unwell, my afternoons were often

---

[a] See this volume, p. 389. - [b] Helene Demuth

spent in housework, besides which I have looked through several hundred newspapers, in order to make extracts from them to Moor of the financial swindling concerns etc.—(By the bye Overend and Gurney have just been acquitted.[227] The bourgeoisie throughout the length and breadth of the land rejoice at the liberation of these 'martyrs', whom they declare to have been more sinned against than sinning. I shouldn't be at all surprised if these thieves in broadcloth were one of these days returned to Parliament to legislate for their countrymen. The partiality of the Judge for the defendants was so glaring, that it struck even the obtuse jury, and on one occasion elicited a protest from them.)—You see I have excuses to offer for my silence. But nevertheless, I will admit, that though you were right in supposing that I do not bow down before a God of vengeance, I am just as little inclined to worship *ein sanftes Lämmerschwänzchen*.[a] To prove to you that I am not in the habit of returning 'good for evil', I have condemned you as a punishment to eat a most indigestible compound—a truly English plum-pudding, for the performance of which feat, remission for all your sins shall be granted you.

All at home send you their best wishes for the New Year, in which I most heartily join. We were *so* sorry to hear of your illness, and trust that by this time you have quite recovered from the effects of it. Moor is in pretty good health at this moment, that is to say, comparatively speaking.—A few days ago Engels paid us a visit of a few hours. He was on his way to Barmen where he intends spending the Christmas days with his mother.[513] He looked particularly well, and very happy at having effected his escape from the counting-house, in which he felt like a fish out of water. He works hard at his book on Ireland.[b] Your questions concerning that book, I am unable to answer, being altogether ignorant as to its contents. I suppose it will be something of a pendant to *The Condition of the Working-Class in England*.[c] It gave us much pleasure to see that you sympathize with us as regards the Irish question. We are all of us downright Fenians. On the day we received the news of Donovan's[d] election we all danced with joy—Tussy was quite wild.[466]

You can imagine what consternation the intelligence of the election of a Fenian produced in England. At first the Press, with the exception of *Reynolds's* and *The National Reformer*, could only

---

[a] a sweet little lamb's tail - [b] F. Engels, *The History of Ireland*. - [c] F. Engels, *The Condition of the Working-Class in England. From Personal Observation and Authentic Sources*. - [d] O'Donovan Rossa

shriek in chorus 'A felon convicted has been elected—horror of horrors!' Then having in concert rung the changes on those to them magical words, the hireling crew fell foul of each other—the Tory papers abused Gladstone, declaring this election to be the fruit of his policy—the Whig organs ranted on the subject of ingratitude and lamented the fate of a country in which messages of peace and good will were thus answered, in which treason flaunts itself in the daylight and the praises of murder are sung. The British government at once despatched thousands of soldiers to the Sister Isle. It must be admitted that as the Tories say, Gladstone's measure of Church disestablishment[678] has already borne fruit. Religious fanaticism is dying a natural death, the hostility of Catholics and Protestants is at an end, there is a split in the Orange camp[679] and Orangemen, Ribbonmen[436] and Fenians are uniting against their common enemy the British Government. Consequently the influence of the priests is vanishing, the Irish movement is no longer in their hands, in fact the election of Donovan Rossa was in direct *opposition* to the clerical party. For instance, these gentlemen being opposed to the release of the political prisoners, convoked meetings for the tinkering of some sort of land bill, which meetings were forcibly broken up by the people, who declared that they would come to no terms with the British Government, until the prisoners had been released. As the Government turned a deaf ear to amnesty meetings etc. the people elected Donovan Rossa, the Fenian, in defiance of the British Government and of the Irish professional agitators, lay and clerical, whose insincerity they had at last discovered.

Meanwhile the noblest Irish are pining in British dungeons. It is impossible to describe the sufferings of these men. Donovan Rossa had been at one time for 35 days kept in a dark cell with his hands manacled behind his back, night and day, and was not loosed even to take food—thin porridge—which was left for him on the floor of the cell. Altogether, my dear Doctor, England is at this moment a country of horrors. In the East End of London famine fever has broken out—in the workhouses the paupers are murdered wholesale. The doctors no longer satisfied with the *corpses* of the paupers are making their experiments on the *living*, and yet the time is still fresh in my memory when the English Press expressed the greatest indignation at the Practice of the vivisection of animals in France.

Last week a case happened in Wales, which makes one's hair stand on end. A Welsh farmer had spread the report that his daughter, a girl of 12 years, had lived without food for two years.

Now though this poor Welshman received money for exhibiting his child, it is possible (in Wales the belief in witches etc. still exists) that he is half a lunatic and believed his tale. But that doctors of the first London hospitals should have done so, seems incredible. Be that as it may, they formed a commission and appointed nurses from Guy's Hospital to go to Wales in order to watch this so-called fasting girl during a fortnight. Daily these same physicians issued bulletins to the public as to the girl's state. For *six* days they kept her without food, and on the seventh the miserable child died. On the night before the child's death, Doctor Davies told the father of the girl that there was no danger, and on being examined that gentleman declares, that he did not suggest food because he did not like to '*offend*' the father. How very polite and considerate to be sure!

I will try to procure the whole case for you. It certainly does not give one a high opinion of the medical profession in England. I do believe that if a person were to declare that he can walk over red-hot iron-bars *unhurt* or jump out of a window, doctors would be found to investigate the matter. We shall return to the trials by ordeal one of these days![680]

With best wishes for the new year

Believe me, very sincerely yours

Jenny Marx

First published in *Movimento Operaio*, No. 2, Milan, 1955

Reproduced from the original

Published in English for the first time

6

JENNY MARX TO ENGELS

IN MANCHESTER

[London, about 17 January 1870]

Dear Mr Engels,

Seldom can a HAMPER have arrived so *à propos* as that of yesterday. The crate had just been unpacked, and the 50 slim fellows were standing in rank and file in the kitchen when Dr Allen and his PARTNER, a young Scots doctor, arrived to operate on poor Moor, so that, immediately after the operation, Moor, and his two Aesculapii could refresh themselves with the delicious Braunenberger. The business was very bad this time. For 8 days we had applied all the remedies, compresses, *basilicum* etc., etc., that have so often been of help: but all in vain. The abscess steadily grew, the pain became unbearable, and no opening or discharge could be induced. It had to be lanced, so Moor finally decided to take the unavoidable step of calling in a doctor. Immediately after the very deep incision he felt great relief, and although he was not yet free of pain this morning, he is on the whole much much better, and will, we hope, have recovered in a few days. But now I must go into action against him with a whole register of sins. Since returning from Germany, and particularly since the Hanoverian campaign,[349] he has been unwell, coughed continually, and instead of looking after himself, began to study Russian hammer and tongs, went out seldom, ate infrequently, and only showed the CARBUNCLE under his arm when it was already very swollen and had hardened. Dear Mr Engels, how often in the past years have I wished that you had been here!! Some things would have been different. Now I hope that he will take this latest experience as a warning. Please, dear Mr Engels, don't make *any remarks* to him in your letters about this. He is very irritable at the moment, and would be very cross with me. But it has been a great relief to pour out my heart to you, since I am quite incapable of changing his lifestyle in any way. Perhaps it would be possible to speak to him seriously through Gumpert, when he comes to Manchester once again. He is the only doctor in whom he still has confidence. Dominant in our house at present is a general disdain for all medicine and all doctors; but they are still a necessary evil; you can't get along without them.

What do you say to the second New Year present with which Laura has presented us[a]? I hope that the rapid pace will soon come to an end; otherwise we could sing

1, 2, 3, 4, 5, 6...
10 LITTLE NIGGER[b] BOYS!

First published in *MEGA*, Abt. III, Bd. 4, Berlin, 1931

Printed according to the original

Published in English for the first time

---

[a] The reference is to the birth of the Lafargues' daughter (see this volume, p. 552). - [b] See p. XXXVIII of the Preface.— *Ed.*

7

JENNY MARX (DAUGHTER)
TO LUDWIG KUGELMANN

IN HANOVER

[London,] 30 January 1870

My dear Doctor,

I write these lines to tell you why Moor has not answered your letters. Since about three weeks he has had carbuncles under his arm, which were so painful that poor Moor was unable to move his arm. Twice the doctor cut them.[a] This operation brought with it almost instantaneous relief. At the present moment I am happy to say, our dear patient is almost well again, though of course he still feels very weak, the necessary effect of the great strains he has suffered. Now that it is over I think it is a good thing the illness came to a crisis as Moor had been tormented by it for months past—you will remember he was anything but well at Hanover and in that state he continued up to the present time—sometimes a little better, sometimes worse.

Your correspondence with Jacoby amused him much.[b] To judge from that venerable gentleman's rambling answer, your letter to him must have hit pretty hard.

I have also to acknowledge the receipt of your letter to myself—the contents of which surprised me not a little and have made me very anxious to hear the final decision of the Philistines of the *Künstler-Verein*.[c] Considering that this *Verein* is composed of the cream of Hanoverian society, the 'cultivation' of the Upper Classes, on the strength of which they consider themselves so much superior to the Working Classes, certainly is something to be mightily proud of! The only pity is that these blockheads have succeeded in annoying you and in robbing you of so much time.

I must ask you and dear Trautchen[d] to forgive me for not having before this informed you of the advent of a little stranger in Lafargue's family. On the second of January Paul announced to us the arrival of a girl in the rue du Cherche-Midi. She is exactly a year older than her brother,[e] the birthdays of the children being on the same day.[f] A few days ago Laura wrote us that she is much stronger.

---

a See the previous letter. - b See this volume, p. 417. - c Union of Artists - d Gertrud Kugelmann - e Charles Étienne Lafargue. There is a mistake in the original: 'older' instead of 'younger'. - f 1 January

Her letter was accompanied by a most interesting lot of French journals—the *Marseillaise, Cloche, Réforme, Rappel* and *Pays*. These journals give one a capital idea of the present state of France. The hubbub and excitement prevailing in the capital are incredible. All parties, nay all individuals are at loggerheads. Rochefort is at daggers drawn with his quondam friends and supporters Vermorel, Villemessant etc. etc. whom he openly denounces as *mouchards*,[a] and they again in their organ, the *Figaro*, return tit for tat. As for the Bancels, Gambettas, Pelletans, Favres etc., that tribe of big-mouthed spouters of sonorous phrases have altogether vanished—they are no-where. Experience has taught the people what they have to expect from the bragging '*gauche*'.[b] Not one of them dared to show his face at Victor Noir's[516] funeral or to raise his voice in the Chambers. Rochefort, supported by brave old Raspail, has annihilated them—doomed them to a living death. Whatever Liebknecht may say to the contrary,[681] Rochefort reigns supreme at Paris, and the wisdom of his conduct in preventing a collision with the military on the day of the interment is now apparent to all. Were Liebknecht to read the *Pays*, he would see that *Cassagnac* and consequently the Government do not disguise their rage at the fact—'*que le peuple ne savait pas mourir pour ses convictions,*' '*qu'ils n'ont pas élevé dans l'air le drapeau rouge*'.[c] Formerly, shrieks the ferocious clown Cassagnac:

'les révolutionnaires étaient des hommes de coeur, des hommes de principes qui se *battaient* pour des idées, et qui savaient bien que ni canons, ni fusils, ni bayonettes ne tiendraient devant la *poitrine nue* du peuple qui réclame son droit'.[d][682]

These 'naked breasts' would indeed have been a feast for the cannons and *chassepots*[230] of the Man of December,[e] the more so, stationed as they were on the outskirts of Paris, where barricades could not be erected and where consequently the 100,000 soldiers would not, as in the narrow streets of Paris, have been exposed to a hand to hand scuffle with the people.—Then the *Volksstaat* also gives an incorrect account of the strike at Creuzot.[683] It is not true that the workmen demand higher wages and a diminution of the hours of labour. They simply requested to have the management of their sick fund in their own hands and not in those of

---

[a] police agents - [b] left - [c] that the people *did not manage to die* for their convictions, that they did not raise the red banner - [d] 'the revolutionaries were brave people, people with principles, the people who *fought* for ideas and knew well that neither cannons nor rifles nor bayonets can resist the *naked breasts* of the people demanding their rights.' - [e] Napoleon III

M. Schneider, further that their fellow-workman *Assy* should not be sent away and that an under-master who had oppressed them, should be dismissed. These are the true causes of the strike. The French Government and the official press declare them to be due à *l'excitation artificielle.*[a] M. Géroult, of the *Opinion Nationale, montre les sociétés secrètes dominant, donnant des mots d'ordre et des consignes.*[b][684] These societies are of course, the International, from which Assy, the leader of the strike, is said to have received 55,000 frs. *The Times* reprints these statements and endorses them.[c] Would they were true! It is a thousand pities the International cannot keep pace in its doings with the brilliant imaginings of these worthies.

It is a significant fact that some of the soldiers sent to Creuzot at once fraternized with the miners. Four of these soldiers are to be tried for having attempted to enlist their comrades in the people's cause.

In Yorkshire a strike has also taken place, the workmen claiming the management of their own sick fund and protesting against the refusal of the Employers to allow the men to combine. As ever since the year 1824 the right of combination has been legalised in England, the masters are in fact acting in direct opposition to the laws of the country, notwithstanding which the Government supplies them with soldiers to do their bidding.

The particulars of the strike are exactly like those of Creuzot— free constitutional England and despot-ridden France—do not differ—both countries have soldiers ready at hand to shoot down the men who have the courage to assert that they think they have intelligence enough to manage their own funds—their hard earned savings.

According to an estimate made by a correspondent to one of the English papers, staying at *Creuzot,*— the workmen lose by the strike *8,000£* a day (wages) whilst the loss to the masters is about *40,000£*!!! a day.

Will you please give my best love to Trautchen and thank her for her letter. I will write to her very soon. Please also tell her that I must call upon her to hand over a certain little bracelet to 'Käuzchen',[d] for whom it was destined. As she is a sworn foe of the Communists, she will know to appreciate my respect for private

---

[a] artificial excitement - [b] shows the omnipotence of secret societies providing slogans and instructions - [c] The reference is to the statement 'The Great Strike in France', *The Times*, 24 January 1870. - [d] Franziska Kugelmann

property. But joking apart I really should not like to see the bracelet on Trautchen's arm—it is rather too 'primitive'.

With Moor's kindest regards to the *Frau Gräfin*,[a] Käuzchen *und an den Mann von der plastischen Bewegung.*[b]

I remain very sincerely yours

Jenny Marx

First published in *Movimento Operaio*, No. 2, Milan, 1955

Reproduced from the original

Published in English for the first time

8

PAUL LAFARGUE TO MARX

IN LONDON

Paris, [18 April 1870]

My dear Mr Marx,[c]

I have just returned from the labour federation conference about which Laura wrote you in her letter.[627] All the sections of the International, all the labour groups and all the corporations were convoked[644]; each group sent one or two delegates. There were at least 1,200 or 1,300 members of the International or delegates from different labour groups. The Rules which had been drawn up by a commission were adopted unanimously; except for paragraph 2 to which was added a new amendment, the gist of which is that all the sections would appoint substitute delegates who would be prepared to assume their functions should the government ever arrest the members of the Federal Council. This proves to you how far the working class has come along; your advice given in the Basle manifesto 'if you want freedom you must take it' was heeded and understood.[685] Thanks to the International, which, owing to the federal bureau of labour societies, has made enormous strides since the last elections, the working class has a sense of its power and wants to take action whatever the cost. The mutualist group[686] is shattered; it was not

---

a Gertrud Kugelmann - b and master of plastic movement (Ludwig Kugelmann). The reference is to the course of treatment advised by Kugelmann to Marx. - c Marx's answer see on pp. 489-93 of this volume.

represented at the conference; it vigorously opposed all calls for federation. What was most encouraging about the assembly was the need for centralisation felt by all members as well as the acute and precise awareness the working class had of its individuality as a class and of its antagonism towards the bourgeoisie. As champion of class struggle, you would have enjoyed attending this rally. Following the Rules vote delegates spoke about the plebiscite and of the manner in which the working class ought to conduct itself; all the speakers were in favour of abstention but considered it an opportune time to draw up a manifesto. A commission was appointed of which I am a member. It met that same evening to discuss the manifesto's groundwork, etc.[687] The document should contain the following three main points:

1) The empire is not recognised as having the right to ask questions;

2) insofar as the empire represents the bourgeoisie, the people have nothing to do with the improvements of the imperial constitution;

3) the necessity of abstaining or casting a blank ballot must be impressed upon peasants. Appointed as literary editors were Tolain, Avrial, Paul-Laurent, etc... That's what happened yesterday.

You must have seen in the *Marseillaise* the big notice of the French section[688]; fortunately, however, it has as much influence here as a spit in the sea. When the Federal Council is constituted an order will be given to the *Marseillaise* not to print anything on the International without the authorisation of the Federal Council; you must know that the *Marseillaise* is at the mercy of the International and that if the latter ever placed its notices in the *Réveil*, the *Marseillaise* would die.

I could get myself appointed by any section as a member of the Federal Council but I believe it would be better if I were the representative of the London Council; would you like to appoint me next Tuesday representative of the Council to the Paris federation? The International has some invaluable members here; Varlin in particular has a talent for organisation and an influence which cannot be overestimated. Combault, delegate of the Vaugirard section is also an invaluable member; he is a most eloquent speaker, is adept at handling matters in a lively and amusing fashion and is liked even by those he lampoons. He has the wit of a Gaudissart. Thank you for your letter. I shall heed your advice but I do not believe that it will sway Verlet, who is more of an enthusiast than a tactician.[689] As for my father, I believe you will do well to speak to him in such a manner; it will be better for you, for him and for me.

You think that the pseudonym Paul-Laurent is altogether sentimental in origin; 'sentiment' does in fact play into it to a small degree, but there is more to it than that, as the following item published in the *Libre pensée* will prove to you.

'In our last issue we said that our collaborator Paul Lafargue, not wishing to be confused with the Lafargues of the *Figaro* and *Paris-faillite* stores, felt compelled [*s'était senti forcé*] to add the name Laurent. The inveterate wit of *Figaro*, a purist of broken French, informs us that the rules of syntax do not allow the figurative use of the verb 'to feel' [*sentir*]. Do not the words '*vil me sens*' bring to mind in the Lafargue in question (Gustave) the name of a certain person (Villemessant)? At any rate the scholar Guguste, whose every lucubration is felt to reveal his character [*sentent la terroir*] should try hard to avoid appearing pedantic [*sentent le pédant*] if he does not want people to see just how ignorant he really is [*qu'on ne sente trop son ignorance*].'[690]

Since the *Libre pensée* is a purely literary newspaper it will not be possible to publish the Rules in it, but once the Federal Council reprints the Rules I shall, if I am a member of it, oversee the operation most carefully[617]; that will be more important.

Greetings to Williams (Jenny). I let Prudhomme in on the literary secret.[562] I saw Franckel who is taking great pleasure in spreading it everywhere.

Greetings to all.

Heartily,
P. Lafargue

First published in *Novaya i noveishaya istoriya*, No. 5, Moscow, 1964

Printed according to the original

Translated from the French

Published in English for the first time

9

JENNY MARX (DAUGHTER)
TO LUDWIG AND GERTRUD KUGELMANN

IN HANOVER

[London,] 8 May 1870

• Many many thanks my dear Mr and Mrs Kugelmann for the beautiful presents you have sent me. I don't know which delight me more—the engravings or the songs—my eyes and ears are equally busy. The studs have given Moor great pleasure, and indeed the flowers are most artistically worked. He is also delighted with the tapestry of Leibniz and has already given it a place in his study, where we have stuck it on the wall over the mantel-piece.[a] Unfortunately the blue paper of the tapestry has injured the beautiful engraving representing the death of Caesar, having covered it with blue colour. Altogether the engravings have been damaged by the way in which they were packed,—Kaulbach's history is partly torn. However we hope, the picture-framer will be able to patch it up again. The box only reached its destination yesterday afternoon (Saturday)[b]—so it must have been a very long time travelling.

I also have to thank you—last though not least—for your kind letters and good wishes for my birthday.[c] I was sorry to hear that you, dear 'doctor', are again unwell, and trust soon to have a better account. Moor also is far from well, having caught a very severe cold. All the other inmates of Modena Villa, four cats and dog included, are well, but in a great hubbub, in which they have been ever since last Sunday, when the news came from Paris that a plot against Bonaparte's life had been discovered. Of course you have seen from the German papers that the imbecile French government attempted at first to implicate the International in this affair, and that a great number of its members, forming the Paris and Lyons branches of the International, have been arrested.[642] The flunkeys of the English and French press of course availed themselves of this opportunity to make furious onslaughts on the International and to call upon their respective governments to suppress that odious Association as the root of all evils. For all

---

[a] See this volume, p. 512. - [b] 7 May - [c] 1 May

that, the French government has however been obliged to declare that the International has nothing to do with the plot, and that its members are solely being prosecuted for the crime of belonging to an 'illicit society'. Moor has written a declaration, unanimously adopted by the General Council, in which he repudiates any complicity of the International in the affair.[a]

According to the French government, M. Gustave Flourens is deeply implicated in the plot, and as that gentleman is in England, the French government has been secretly asking the English government to deliver him up; but Mr Gladstone, who is well aware that the doing so would cost him his premiership, (as it did Palmerston in the case of Simon Bernard[b]), declares that the ministry can do nothing in the matter without further proofs of M. Flourens' culpability. But in reality there are no proofs against M. Flourens in the hands of the French government, for granted it be proved that he sent money to Paris for the purpose of arming the people with bombs in case an insurrection should break out, that does not imply that he had anything to do with the intended assassination of the Emperor. Last Sunday (my birthday) when the news of the discovered *complot* reached us M. Flourens was at our home—so you can imagine that my birthday was anything but a tranquil or a gay one. We did not know at the time but what M. Flourens might not be at once arrested. He is the son of the celebrated naturalist of that name and has himself written a book on Ethnography[c] and delivered lectures at the Collège de France. He is a most extraordinary mixture of a *savant* and an *homme d'action.*[d]

The good result of the plot is that it has forced the man of December[e] to throw off his liberal mask and to show himself in his true colours. A system of *blanche terreur*[f] prevails at Paris. Yesterday all the opposition papers were confiscated, the people are being goaded to a state of desperation. There is no knowing what will happen to-day.

I continue to write to the *Marseillaise,* several of my letters have been quoted in *The Irishman*, the national paper of Ireland.[691] At present I am waiting for news from Ireland concerning the treatment of the political prisoners. If I do not soon receive an

---

[a] K. Marx, *Concerning the Persecution of the Members of the French Sections. Declaration of the General Council of the International Working Men's Association.* - [b] See this volume, p. 505. - [c] G. Flourens, *Histoire de l'homme. Cours d'histoire naturelle des corps organisés au Collège de France.* - [d] a scholar and a man of action - [e] Napoleon III - [f] white terror

answer I shall begin to think that the letter I have written to the wives of the prisoners has been intercepted by the British Government. Unluckily I signed my real name!
   Post-time.
   Kiss dear Fränzchen [a] for me, my good Trautchen,[b] and with ever so many thanks for your kindness
   Believe me

                                        Affectionately yours
                                                    Jenny

   Mama and Tussy send their kindest regards—I forgot to tell you that Dr Gunz called upon us three times. He sent us tickets for several operas.

First published in *Movimento Operaio,* No. 2, Milan, 1955

Reproduced from the original

Published in English for the first time

10

JENNY MARX TO ENGELS

IN MANCHESTER

                                        [London, 12 July 1870]
                                        Tuesday evening

My dear Mr Engels,

   I have just returned from a new journey of exploration, and hasten to report to you. I have now found a house, which charms all of us because of its wonderful open situation. Jenny and Tussy were with me, and both find it particularly nice. Because of its position and interior fittings it is naturally rather more expensive than Shrewsbury Villa, for which the man insists on £55. Our present house costs £60. *It is next to Primrose Hill,* so all the FRONT rooms have the finest and openest view and air. And round about, in the side streets, there are SHOPS of all sorts, so your wife will be able to buy everything herself. Now for the interior fittings. Basement, big attractive kitchen with large range. Next to this, a very spacious bathroom with large bathtub and *cheminée,*[c] BACK

---

[a] Franziska Kugelmann - [b] Gertrud Kugelmann - [c] fireplace

KITCHEN, cupboards of all kinds, COAL CELLAR, and a *dungeon lying deeper*, which although it has no flooring at present, could be a very good cool wine-cellar; a small, very small, garden, not bigger than for hanging out the washing, etc. Then *rez-de-chaussée*[a] 2 very nice rooms divided by folding doors; the back one has, instead of a window, a particularly charming GREENHOUSE or, if you like, double window, which makes the room very light and friendly. *Bel étage*,[b] in front—a very fine large room, next to it a smaller one, no folding doors. 2nd floor—3 BEDROOMS: 2 very roomy, the third rather smaller, all in full REPAIR. The two bottom rooms are just being papered. I think you could scarcely find a better house, and I am convinced your wife will like it very much. Its situation is just too cheerful and amusing. You scarcely need to leave the house to be in the open and see thousands of people.

It is naturally of the utmost importance that you and your wife see it for yourselves, and as quickly as possible, since a house situated as well as this one will certainly go quickly. But if it is not to your taste I have found another 2 nearby; but they are not situated in such a pleasant way. It would be best if your wife came with you right away and saw for herself. You know we shall be very happy to have her with us. Write straight away about it, so we know whether we should go on looking or whether you will be coming.

I would like to get these lines into the post this evening so that you might consider the matter in the course of the day.

Therefore, a hasty adieu from

Your

Jenny Marx

First published in *MEGA*, Abt. III, Bd. 4, Berlin, 1931

Printed according to the original

Published in English for the first time

---

[a] ground floor - [b] first floor

11

JENNY MARX (DAUGHTER)
TO LUDWIG KUGELMANN

IN HANOVER

[London,] 17 July 1870

My dear Doctor,

I hope you do not think that laziness or negligence has had anything to do with my silence. The fact is, that I no sooner received your letter than I wrote to Mr Pigott, the editor of *The Irishman* to enquire of him where I could obtain a photograph of O'Donovan Rossa. Mr Pigott wrote to say that he was unable to give me any information on the subject (the British Government does not allow the portraits of the Fenians to be sold) but that he had sent my letter to Mrs Rossa, as that lady could perhaps procure for me a photograph of her husband. Now I have waited from day to day for a letter from Mrs Rossa—but in vain—and as I think it will be of no use to wait any longer, I write these lines to ask you whether the enclosed print,[a] which appeared some time ago in *The Irishman* will be of any use to Mr Rissé? It certainly is a very bad likeness—but it is better than nothing.

It would be a thousand pities to give up the excellent plan of publishing Rossa's portrait. Its publication would greatly annoy John Bull—for the British Government dreads nothing so much as that its infamous treatment of the Fenian prisoners should become known on the Continent. Indeed, the Prison Enquiry is solely got up for the purpose of hushing up the unpleasant truths that were oozing out. On the eve of the Enquiry, the pretended object of which is to elucidate things, the prisoners are more *closely guarded than ever*, lest they might inform their friends of the treatment they are undergoing. A few days ago Mrs Luby, wife of one of the prisoners, visited her husband to bear to him the tidings of his mother's death, (grief for her son's sufferings hastened Mrs Luby's death) and though the unfortunate woman had not seen her husband since *three* years, she was not allowed to see him face to face without the intrusion of a jailor. Mrs Luby was led into one huge iron cage grated with heavy iron bars, Luby

---

[a] At the beginning of the letter there is a note by Kugelmann: 'Rossa's portrait is missing'.

was brought from his cell to another cage grated also with heavy iron bars, apart from that in which the wife was detained. A jailor stood close beside the prisoner watchful, ready to interfere should he utter a word relative to the Prison treatment.

But poor Luby had no need to complain—his pallid, shrunk and shrivelled form spoke but too eloquently of a tale of horrors. The fact is that Mrs Luby did not even recognize her husband— so altered, and aged does he look. The friends of the prisoners being thus carefully excluded, the evidence of the prisoners suppressed, it is not difficult to guess that the whole commission will turn out to be a regular sham from beginning to end. As the governors, jailors, warders are to have it all their own way in the coming inquiry, the end of it all will be that the venal scribes of the press will be enabled to paint in glowing colours the amenities of English prison life and to brand the statements of O'Donovan Rossa as so many lies!

For the notes required for the preface of Mr Rissé's book[692] I addressed myself to Engels who with his usual amiability and promptitude at once sent me the enclosed remarks[a] which will I think prove of interest to the German public.

As regards Carlsbad[b] I am sorry to say that thanks to that desperate gambler at Paris[c] our long projected voyage has come to nothing. To travel without a passport is of course an impossibility in the present state of affairs and to obtain one equally out of the question. Even to naturalised Englishmen the British Government refuses passports.[308] But Moor will himself write to you on the subject. Tell Trautchen[d] I will also write to her in a few days to give vent to my disappointment—and please will you also tell that lady that I think she has grown unconscionably lazy. I have not heard from her for months.

What do you think of the war? We have not yet recovered from our surprise and indignation at the turn affairs have taken. It is not easy to reconcile oneself to the thought that instead of fighting for the destruction of the Empire, the French people are sacrificing themselves for its aggrandizement, that instead of hanging Bonaparte they are prepared to enroll themselves under his banner. Who could have dreamt of such things a few months ago when the Revolution in Paris seemed a fact. This revival of chauvinism in the 19th Century is indeed a hideous farce[693]!

---

[a] F. Engels, *Notes for the Preface to a Collection of Irish Songs*. - [b] Karlovy Vary - [c] Napoleon III - [d] Gertrud Kugelmann

It is time to post this long letter—so with best love to dear Trautchen and Fränzchen.[a]

Believe me dear 'Doctor', very faithfully yours

Jenny Marx

First published in *Movimento Operaio*, No. 2, Milan, 1955

Reproduced from the original

Published in English for the first time

---

[a] Franziska Kugelmann

NOTES

1 This letter was first published in English, in a slightly abridged form, in: *Letters to Dr. Kugelmann by Karl Marx*, Co-operative Publishing Society of Foreign Workers in the U.S.S.R., Moscow-Leningrad, 1934.—3

2 Engels visited Marx in London between 1 and 5 April 1868 to attend the wedding of Laura Marx and Paul Lafargue.—3, 5, 7, 10

3 Marx is referring to the Parliamentary elections to be held in November 1868 on the basis of the second Reform Bill of 1867. The law extended suffrage to people resident in town for a period of not less than 12 months and renting houses or flats for no less than £10. In the counties, the right to vote was granted to tenants with an annual income of above £12. Suffrage was granted to a section of skilled workers. However, it was not extended to Scotland and Ireland.—3, 375

4 Marx is referring to the stand of the British trade union leaders in the 1867-68 election campaign, when George Odger, William Cremer, George Potter et al. urged the workers to come to an understanding with the Liberals and in fact refused to draw up an independent and class-conditioned election programme. In the course of the elections, trade union leaders frequently withdrew their candidatures in favour of one election coalition or another with which they were affiliated. A case in point is George Odger, who was nominated in Chelsea (London).

During the 1868 election campaign, Liberal leader Gladstone publicly promised to settle the Irish question, which since the autumn of 1867 acquired a sharper edge due to a new upsurge of the national liberation movement in Ireland against British colonial oppression. He came out with the slogans 'to pacify Ireland' and 'to reconcile England and Ireland' and he also promised a church reform. In his speech in the House of Commons on 3 April 1868, Gladstone likened the Tory policies in Ireland to the conquest of England by the Normans (see *The Times*, No. 26090, 4 April 1868). Marx warned the leaders of the British labour movement against the dangerous influence of social demagogy inherent in the Liberals' election platform on the Irish question. Trade union leaders, Lucraft in particular, actually supported bourgeois Radicals in their assessment of the Irish Fenians (see Note 86).—3

[5] The reference is to Freiligrath's letter written on 3 April 1868, in which he thanks Marx for a copy of Volume One of *Capital* sent to him in September 1867 and congratulates him on his daughter Laura's marriage. The letter contained the following opinion of *Capital*: 'This is precisely the book one would wish to study, and its success has not been quick and loud in coming, but its hidden impact will be all the more profound and durable. I know that on the Rhine, many young merchants and factory-owners are delighted by your book. In that environment, it will attain its real purpose; for the scholars, it will be, apart from this, an indispensable source.'—4, 8

[6] Marx has in mind his letter to Freiligrath of 20 July 1867 (see present edition, Vol. 42, p. 397). In his reply, dispatched the same day, Freiligrath avoided giving a direct answer to Marx's question.

Late in April 1867, a committee was set up in London to collect donations for Ferdinand Freiligrath, who had found himself without means of subsistence owing to the closing down of the London branch of the Banque Générale Suisse of which he was manager. On 25 and 26 April, the committee, which was made up of German petty-bourgeois émigrés, appealed 'to all friends of German poetry' in England and other countries for a subscription. Similar committees were set up in many German towns and in New York. Accounts of the progress on the subscription were published by the *Hermann. Deutsches Wochenblatt aus London*.—4, 373

[7] Engels is probably referring to the letter Wilhelm Liebknecht wrote to him on 29 March 1868.—5, 8

[8] In his letter to Engels of 25 February 1868 Otto Meissner requested assistance in drawing up a publisher's advertisement announcing the publication of Volume One of *Capital* so as 'to break silence through powerful advertisement'. Simultaneously, Otto Meissner sent notices containing the table of contents to about thirty newspapers.—5, 37

[9] The reason for these opinions of the *Demokratisches Wochenblatt* published by Wilhelm Liebknecht was probably the anonymous article 'Märzgedanken', printed in No. 13 on 28 March 1868. Reviewing the revolution of 1848-49 in Germany, its author (in all probability, Liebknecht himself) exaggerated the contribution of petty-bourgeois democrats to the campaign for the Imperial Constitution, specifically, of Gustav Struve, a leader of the Baden uprisings and Liebknecht's friend. For Engels' opinion of these events, see his works 'The Campaign for the German Imperial Constitution' and 'Revolution and Counter-Revolution in Germany' (see present edition, Vols. 10 and 11).—5

[10] Engels is referring to the article 'Auswanderung und Bürgerrecht', in the *Demokratisches Wochenblatt*, No. 14 of 4 April 1868, on the treaty between the North German Confederation and the USA on the citizenship of German émigrés. The draft agreement was discussed in April 1868 in the North German Reichstag.

The *North German Confederation* (Norddeutscher Bund) existed from 1867 to 1870 as a federative state under the aegis of Prussia. It was set up on the initiative of the Prussian Prime Minister Otto von Bismarck after Prussia's victory over Austria in 1866 and the disintegration of the German Confederation.—6

[11] A reference to Engels' intention to write a review of Volume One of Marx's *Capital* for *The Fortnightly Review* to which Professor Beesly was a contributor. (see Marx's letter to Engels of 8 January 1868, present edition, Vol. 42). While

working on the review, Engels wrote out excerpts from *Capital*, which later made up a synopsis (see Note 26). The review was written around 20 May-1 June 1868, but rejected by the editorial board (see present edition, Vol. 20).— 6, 30, 33, 35, 37, 38, 44, 47, 50, 52, 54, 70, 73, 74, 81, 138

12 Paul and Laura Lafargue wrote to the Marx family about their life in France. (Letters of Laura and Paul Lafargue to Karl Marx and his daughter Jenny, of 3 April 1868; to Jenny of 6 April 1868; of Laura Lafargue to her sister Jenny of 9 April 1868; and to her sister Eleanor of the same date).—7, 9

13 Marx is referring to his articles of 1856-57 for the *New York Daily Tribune* on the French joint-stock bank Crédit Mobilier—'The French Crédit Mobilier' (a series of articles) and 'Crédit Mobilier' (see present edition, Vol. 15).—7

14 A reference to the speculative machinations of the Scottish economist and financier John Law in France between 1716 and 1720; he dealt with the issue of securities and the foundation of joint-stock trading companies. The bank which he founded in 1716, and later transferred to the French Government, as well as a number of companies for trade with foreign countries, went bankrupt in 1720.—7

15 The reference is to Johann Baptist Schweitzer's review of Volume One of *Capital* anonymously printed in twelve issues of *Der Social-Demokrat* between 22 January and 6 May 1868, under the heading 'Das Werk von Carl Marx'. For Marx's opinion of this review, see his letter to Engels of 23 March 1868 (present edition, Vol. 42).—8, 11, 13, 61

16 In March and April 1868, 3,000 building workers were on strike in Geneva. They demanded that the working day be reduced to ten hours, wages be raised, and payment by the day be substituted by payment by the hour. On the initiative of the Central Committee of the International's Geneva sections, the workers in other industries rendered assistance to the strikers.
In 'The Fourth Annual Report of the General Council of the International Working Men's Association' to the Brussels Congress of 1868 written by Marx it is stated: 'In the struggle maintained by the building trades of Geneva the very existence of the International in Switzerland was put on its trial. The employers made it a preliminary condition of coming to any terms with their workmen that the latter should forsake the International. The working men indignantly refused to comply with this dictate' (present edition, Vol. 21, p. 16).
The victory of Geneva workers was made possible by the solidarity action organised by the General Council in England, France and Germany.—8, 11, 14, 94, 199, 209

17 François Graglia, member of the Committee of the Geneva Section of the International, was sent to Paris and London to arrange financial aid for the Geneva building workers who had gone on strike. He stayed in London from 6 to 9 April, attended meetings of the French Section and the General Council, and, accompanied by Hermann Jung, visited a number of workers' societies.—8

18 The bronze workers of Paris went on strike in February 1867 when, in response to their demand for fixed tariffs, their employers insisted that they dissolve their credit society, Société de crédit et de solidarité des ouvriers du bronze. Thanks to the General Council, which discussed the matter at its meetings of 5, 12, 19 and 26 March and 2 and 9 April 1867 (see *The General Council of the First International. 1866-1868. Minutes*, Moscow, 1964, pp. 101-03, 105-06, 107, 108), Paris workers received financial aid from the British trade

unions. The strike ended in a victory for the bronze workers, who managed to preserve their organisation. The employers agreed to introduce fixed rates for individual types of work.—8

19 The part of the letter intended for Laura was written by Marx in English. It was published for the first time in English, in an abridged form, in *Annali dell' Istituto Giangiacomo Feltrinelli*, Milano, 1958.—9

20 An allusion to Laura's work as Marx's secretary before her marriage.—9

21 Marx jokingly refers to Borkheim's letters written on 2 and 7 April 1868 as 'scribaille', a word that Borkheim had borrowed from Herzen's unsigned article in the French edition of the *Kolokol* (La Cloche), No. 6, 1 April 1868, prompted by an anonymous publication in St. Petersburg's *Birzheviye Vedomosty* (Stock-Exchange News), Nos. 307 and 310, 15 and 18 November 1867. Borkheim quoted Herzen in his letter of 2 April. He decided to use Liebknecht's *Demokratisches Wochenblatt* to attack Herzen and applied to Marx for certain linguistic information. Borkheim carried out his intention in the article 'Russische politische Flüchtlinge in West-Europa. III' (see *Demokratisches Wochenblatt*, Nos. 17, 20, and 25 April and 16 May 1868).—9

22 *Guillaumin & Co.*—a book-publisher in Paris dealing in literature on economics.—9

23 The part of Marx's letter of 11 April 1868 addressed to Paul Lafargue was written in German.—10

24 The events in the Charleroi coalfields occurred in the spring of 1868. In response to the mine-owners' decision to reduce production to four days a week and lower the wages by ten per cent, the workers declared a strike. On 26 March, violent clashes took place between the workers and the police. Twenty-two people were arrested and put on trial. The Belgian Section of the International launched a wide campaign to support the strikers both in Belgium and abroad. It organised protest meetings and gave wide coverage of the events in *La Tribune du Peuple*, *La Liberté* and other papers. On 12 April it issued a manifesto to the workers of Belgium and other countries (see *La Tribune du Peuple*, No. 4, 19 April 1868). The Section maintained regular contacts with the General Council. The Charleroi events were discussed at the Council meetings of 21 April, 12 May and 2 June 1868 (see *The General Council of the First International. 1866-1868. Minutes*). The Brussels Section set up a special committee to brief lawyers for the defence of the detainees. The lawyers managed to swing public opinion in favour of the defendants and on 15 August all of them were acquitted by the jury. This led to a rise in the membership of the International in Belgium.

For the *Geneva strike* of building workers see Note 16.

From 14 to 17 April 1868 a general strike took place in Bologna. The workers demanded that the income tax be cut down and distributed more fairly. A number of meetings and a demonstration were held. Troops were summoned to disperse the demonstration and numerous arrests were made.— 11, 62

25 A reference to the newspaper reports on Eichhoff's lectures on the causes of modern trade crises ('Die Ursachen der Handelsstockungen der Gegenwart'), which he delivered in Berlin in February-May 1868. In them, he quoted *Capital* and the *Manifesto of the Communist Party*, and used material that Marx had sent him. Eichhoff's lectures did a great deal to advertise Volume One of *Capital* in

Germany. The reports were printed in *Die Zukunft* and the *Norddeutsche Allgemeine Zeitung.*—11, 37

26 The 'Synopsis of Volume One of *Capital* by Karl Marx' made by Engels in the spring and summer of 1868 is extant as a manuscript covering about two thirds of the book, including the chapter 'Machinery and Large-Scale Industry' (present edition, Vol. 20, pp. 263-308, and this volume, Note 11).—11

27 A reference to Ludwig and Gertrud Kugelmann's letter to Marx of 8 April 1868, in which they expressed their joy at the prospect of Marx's visit to Germany.—12

28 Kugelmann, who corresponded with the noted German natural scientist Rudolf Virchow on certain questions of medicine, tried to get him interested in Marx's *Capital.*—12

29 The full English translation of this letter was first published in: *Letters to Dr. Kugelmann by Karl Marx*, Co-operative Publishing Society of Foreign Workers in the U.S.S.R., Moscow-Leningrad, 1934.—12, 48, 56, 67, 82, 130, 144, 173, 184, 213, 231, 278, 317, 337, 359, 433, 466, 475, 527

30 This refers to the appeal 'Internationale Arbeiterassociation. Zuruf an alle Arbeiter deutscher Sprache' for rendering material aid to the building workers of Geneva who had gone on strike, drawn up by Johann Philipp Becker on the instructions of the Central Authority of the German-language sections' group. It was published in Geneva on 11 April 1868.
On the strike of Geneva building workers, see Note 16.—14

31 Marx refers to the editorial 'Politische Uebersicht' featured in the *Demokratisches Wochenblatt*, No. 15, 11 April 1868, edited by Wilhelm Liebknecht, in which Marx's book *Herr Vogt* (see present edition, Vol. 17) was described as 'containing much that is edifying' and 'systematically silenced by the German press'.—15

32 The subjects listed by Marx were dealt with in the editorial 'Politische Uebersicht' in the *Demokratisches Wochenblatt*, No. 16, 18 April 1868.—16

33 This letter was published in English for the first time in an abridged form in: Karl Marx and Frederick Engels, *Correspondence, 1846-1895*, London, Lawrence LTD, [1934].—16, 20, 89, 152, 154, 163, 235, 306, 342, 353, 362, 369, 387, 418

34 An excerpt from this letter was first published in English in: K. Marx and F. Engels, *Letters on 'Capital'*, London, New Park Publications, 1983.—19, 99, 123, 137, 224, 478, 482

35 Engels is probably referring to the editorial 'Politische Uebersicht' in Liebknecht's *Demokratisches Wochenblatt*, No. 15, 11 April 1868, which quoted Bismarck's speech in the Reichstag commission on debts: 'Since you refuse to pass a state law on debts, not recognising the Reichstag's right independently to lodge complaints against officials at the debt collection department,—well, then there will be no law on debts, and we shall be unable to raise a loan for the Navy.'—19

36 As a result of the victory in the Austro-Prussian War of 1866, in which the Kingdom of Hanover fought on the side of Austria, Prussia annexed Hanover in September of that year and turned it into a province, to which the operation of the Prussian constitution was extended in 1867. George V, King of Hanover, fled to Austria, where he attempted to head a movement against affiliation

with Prussia. He failed and, on 1 February 1868, had to sign a treaty with Prussia under which he agreed to abdicate for a certain compensation. However, as early as 2 March 1868, the Prussian government passed a resolution on the confiscation of the ex-King of Hanover's property and lands.— 19, 221

37 A reference to the first session of the Customs Parliament held between 27 April and 23 May 1868.

The *Customs Union Parliament*—the guiding body of the Customs Union reorganised after the war of 1866 and the signing, on 8 July 1867, of a peace treaty between Prussia and the South German states, which provided for the establishment of this body. The Parliament comprised members of the North German Confederation's Reichstag and deputies from the South German states: Bavaria, Baden, Württemberg and Hesse. Bebel and Liebknecht were the two workers' deputies in it. It was to deal exclusively with issues of trade and customs policies; Bismarck's intention gradually to widen its jurisdiction by encompassing political questions was met with stubborn opposition from the South German representatives (see Note 62).— 20

38 The *German People's Party* (Deutsche Volkspartei) was set up in 1865 and encompassed the democratic elements of the petty bourgeoisie and part of the bigger bourgeoisie, chiefly from South and Central German states. As distinct from the National-Liberals, it opposed Prussia's supremacy and advocated the plan for the establishment of the so-called Great Germany incorporating both Prussia and Austria. While pursuing an anti-Prussian policy, the People's Party voiced the particularist aspirations of some German states. It was against Germany's unification as a single centralised democratic republic, advocating the idea of a federative German state.

In 1866, the German People's Party was joined by the Saxon People's Party, whose nucleus consisted of workers. This left wing of the German People's Party had, in effect, nothing in common with it except anti-Prussian sentiments and the wish jointly to solve the problems of national unification in a democratic way. Subsequently, it developed along socialist lines. The main section of the Party broke away from the petty-bourgeois democrats and took part in founding the Social-Democratic Workers' Party in August 1869.— 20, 102, 231, 242, 257, 299, 304, 308, 313, 324, 428, 478, 513

39 A reference to the female suffrage meeting held in Manchester on 14 April 1868. It was reported by *The Bee-Hive Newspaper* (No. 340, 18 April 1868).— 20

40 Paul and Laura Lafargue returned to London from Paris about 25 April 1868, and on 30 April moved into a flat rented for them on Primrose Hill (see Marx's letter to Engels of 30 April 1868, this volume, p. 25).— 20

41 After the first publication of *A Contribution to the Critique of Political Economy* appeared in 1859, Marx produced a lengthy economic manuscript throughout 1861-63, which was a second rough draft of *Capital* (the first was the manuscripts of 1857-58). In 1863, he evolved the final plan for a four-book work, the first three books theoretical and the fourth, a historical and critical one. Having finished work on the manuscripts of 1861-63, Marx began preparing them for the press in August 1863.

This work from 1863-65 resulted in the third rough draft of *Capital*, three books of a theoretical character. The notes for the fourth book, the *Theories of Surplus-Value*, were incorporated in the manuscripts of 1861-63. Later, having completed work on them, Marx went back to the first book. On Engels' advice, he decided it should appear first. Preparation for the press continued throughout 1866 and most of 1867. The first German edition of the first book appeared in September 1867 as Volume One of *Capital*. Under the plan agreed upon with Meissner, the publisher, the second and third books (devoted to the circulation of capital and the process of capitalist production as a whole) were to appear as Volume Two, while the fourth book on the history of economic theories was to be Volume Three of *Capital*.

Marx, however, had not completed the preparation of the last books of *Capital* for the press. After his death, this was done by Engels, who published Marx's manuscripts relating to the second and third books as volumes Two and Three of *Capital* (1885 and 1894). Engels also intended to prepare for the press and publish as Volume Four of *Capital* the above-mentioned manuscript of the fourth book, but did not have time to do this in his lifetime. This edition presents this book of *Capital* as part of the *Economic Manuscripts of 1861-63*, (volumes 30-34) while Volumes One, Two and Three of *Capital* are to be found in volumes 35, 36 and 37 of the present edition respectively.—21, 30, 61, 68, 119, 232, 234, 259, 408, 528, 545

42 In the first manuscript of the third book of *Capital* written by Marx in 1864-65, the entire text is divided into seven long chapters. After Marx's death, while preparing the manuscript for the press, Engels substituted this division by division into parts. In Volume Three of *Capital*, published by Engels in 1894, the chapter mentioned in the letter corresponds to Part II 'Conversion of Profit into Average Profit' (see present edition, Vol. 37).—24

43 The first German edition of Volume One of *Capital* (1867) considers the changes in the structure of capital mentioned here in the c) section of Chapter VI, 'Das allgemeine Gesetz der Kapitalistischen Accumulation'. Corresponding to this section in the second (1872) and subsequent German editions of Volume One, is Chapter XXIII of Part VII. Corresponding to this material in the English edition of 1887 edited by Engels is Chapter XXV, Part VII, 'The General Law of Capitalist Accumulation' (see present edition, Vol. 35).—24

44 Here productive capital means industrial capital, as distinct from merchant capital. Later, Marx evolved a special definition of productive capital in Part I of Volume Two of *Capital* (see present edition, Vol. 36).—24

45 Marx's reference is to the erroneous tenet of Adam Smith's theory (see A. Smith, *An Inquiry into the Nature and Causes of the Wealth of Nations*, Ld., 1776, Book I, Ch. 6) generally shared by bourgeois political economists according to which the value, and consequently the price of the commodity is reducible to neat revenue and does not include fixed capital. Marx criticised 'A. Smith's dogma' in Part III of *Capital*'s Volume Two (present edition, Vol. 36).—25

46 On 26 April 1868, Victor Schily asked Marx for his biographical data which J. J. E. Reclus needed for his review of Volume One of *Capital* for *La Cooperation* newspaper. Marx's reply to Schily has not been found.—25, 28

47 The reference is to the trial by the Central Criminal Court from 28 to 30 April 1868 of three Fenians (see Note 86), including Richard Burke, an organiser of the abortive Fenian uprising of 1867. Ernest Jones and Macdonald were the defence counsels for Burke. For a detailed report on the trial, see *The Times*, nos. 26111-26113, 29 and 30 April, and 1 May 1868.—26

[48] This letter was first published in English in an abridged form in: K. Marx and
F. Engels, *Letters on 'Capital'*, London, New Park Publications, 1983.—26, 28, 30,
32, 38, 45, 55, 84, 160, 411

[49] In his letter of 29 April 1868, Johann Baptist Schweitzer requested Marx to
define the position of the workers' party on the bill on reducing taxes for pig
iron to be discussed in the Reichstag. Enclosed with the letter were the clippings
'Jahresbericht der Handelskammer von Elberfeld und Barmen' and 'Ein
Circular der Herren Fabrikanten Funcke und Hück' (Annual Reports of the
Elberfeld and Barmen Chambers of Commerce and the Circular of Messrs
Factory Owners Funcke and Hück) (Hagen, 23 April). Marx quoted them
when drafting a reply to Schweitzer. Having received Engels' notes on this
question (see p. 29 of this volume) Marx replied to Schweitzer probably on
7 May (the letter has not been found). In his article 'An die Mitglieder des
Allgemeinen Deutschen Arbeitervereins (die Herabsetzung der Eisenzölle
betreffend)' published by *Der Social-Demokrat* on 13 May 1868, Schweitzer
referred to Marx as 'the outstanding scientific authority of our trend'. The
article also reprinted the above-mentioned documents in full. In his letter to
Marx of 13 May 1868, in which this article was enclosed, Schweitzer thanked
Marx for 'precious judgement'.— 26, 28, 30

[50] A reference to the article featured by the *Mannheimer Zeitung* reviewing
Volume One of *Capital*. It was not signed and was probably promoted by
Siebel.—28, 74

[51] In his letter to Liebknecht, which has not come down to us (see Engels' letter to
Marx of 13 March 1868, present edition, Vol. 42), as well as in his review of
Volume One of *Capital* for the *Demokratisches Wochenblatt* published on 21 and
28 March 1868, Engels advised the worker deputies to make 'themselves
thoroughly conversant with' *Capital*, which would supply them with the
necessary material for the debate on new handicraft trades Regulations in the
Reichstag (see present edition, Vol. 20, p. 336).

The draft regulations were discussed in the Reichstag in the spring of 1869
and were approved on 29 May (see Note 324).—30

[52] A reference to the spinning mill industry statistics for 1860 cited on page 186
of the first German edition of Volume One of *Capital*. Preparing the second
German edition which appeared in 1872, Marx used additional information
supplied by Engels (see Note 59), cited exact data and corrected a number of
factual mistakes which the first edition contained (see present edition,
Vol. 35).—30, 36

[53] Marx's letter to Joseph Dietzgen dated 9 May 1868, is not extant in full. The
date has been established on the basis of Dietzgen's reply written on 20 May.
Eight years later, Dietzgen had his article 'Sozialdemokratische Philosophie'
printed by *Der Volksstaat* newspaper (No. 3, 9 January 1876), in which he
quoted the excerpt given here.—31

[54] *The Royal Society* (The Royal Society of London for Improving Natural
Knowledge), the oldest British learned society founded in 1660 and endorsed
by the Royal Charter in 1662. Publishes the journals *Philosophical Transactions*
(since 1665) and *Proceedings of the Royal Society* (since 1800).—33

[55] A reference to the scandalous court trial in Austria in May 1868. Baroness Julia
Ebergenyi, mistress of Count Chorinsky, was charged with the murder of
Chorinsky's wife. The letters from Chorinsky to Ebergenyi, which featured as
evidence at the trial, gave reason to suspect Chorinsky of complicity.— 34

56 A short excerpt from this letter was published in English for the first time in: *The Letters of Karl Marx*. Selected and translated with explanatory notes and an introduction by Saul K. Padover, Prentice-Hall Inc., Englewood Cliffs, New Jersey, 1979.—35, 52, 243, 446, 511, 513, 515

57 Marx is probably referring to the incident described by Plutarch in his *Vitae parallelae*.

Decurions—members of city councils originally existing in the urban communities of Italy dependent on Rome, and later, under the empire, in all towns in the provinces; were in charge of distribution and collection of taxes, renting town lands, expenditure of public money, etc.—35

58 Marx's letters to the Philips family, his mother's relatives, written around 15 February and 5 March 1868 (see Marx's letters to Engels of 15 February and 6 March 1868, present edition, Vol. 42), have not been found.—35

59 The extant notebook II of Marx's economic manuscripts of 1861-1863 (see MEGA², II/3.1, S. 143) suggests that the information mentioned in this letter was received by Marx from Engels in August-September 1861 during his stay in Manchester. Page 87 of this notebook contains a phrase, 'Suggested by Engels...' The figures cited further completely tally with the examples on page 186 of Volume One of the first edition of *Capital* which appeared in 1867. However, this phrase is absent in the notebook Marx kept since April 1860 and until February-May 1863.—36

60 These letters from Marx to Wilhelm Eichhoff have not been found.—36

61 An allusion to the rumour that, having returned to Germany in 1867 after a long period of emigration, Wilhelm Eichhoff had abandoned politics and refused on these grounds to join the political campaign against Stieber waged by Liebknecht in the *Demokratisches Wochenblatt* between April and June 1868. However, as early as May, Liebknecht informed Borkheim that Eichhoff had promised to let him have the necessary anti-Stieber materials. The content of Liebknecht's letters was known to Marx. His associates began to distrust Eichhoff even more after he had been seen in the company of Berlin police officers, and especially after his speech at the inaugural meeting of the Democratic Workers' Society, which appeared in *Die Zukunft* newspaper in distorted form and was later reprinted by the *Demokratisches Wochenblatt*, No. 43, 24 October 1868 (see this volume, pp. 151, 153). Marx had done a great deal to clear Eichhoff's name. On Marx's request, Eichhoff wrote to him on 31 October-1 November giving full explanations which convinced Marx of his dedication to the cause of revolution (see also Marx's letter to Engels of 16 April 1869).—36, 266

62 Marx is referring to a Protest signed by representatives of South German states and four members of the Reichstag of the North German Confederation (see Note 10) on 7 May 1868. The authors opposed Bismarck's intention to expand the competence of the Customs Union Parliament (see Note 37) by stretching it to cover political issues. The text was printed by the *Demokratisches Wochenblatt*, No. 20, 16 May 1868.—38

63 Engels refers to Lasker's speech at the first session of the Customs Union Parliament held on 18 May 1868 (on the Customs Union Parliament, see Note 37).—38

64 Marx is referring to Chapter II 'Die Verwandlung von Geld in Kapital' of the first German edition of *Capital*, Volume One. In the second and subsequent

German editions, it corresponds to Part II, and in the English edition of 1887, to Part II, Chapters IV-VI (see present edition, Vol. 35).—39

[65] A reference to Chapter I 'Waare und Geld' of the first German edition of *Capital*, Volume One. Corresponding to it in the second and subsequent German editions, as well as in the English edition of 1887 edited by Engels, is Part I (see present edition, Vol. 35).—39, 68

[66] A reference to the champions of the so-called 'currency principle', a trend in bourgeois political economy advocating the quantitative theory of money. Jones Lloyd (Lord Overstone), Robert Torrens, George Arbuthnot and other representatives of this school maintained that the value and price of commodities are determined by the quantity of money in circulation, that the guarantee of stable currency is the obligatory backing of banknotes by gold and that their issue is regulated according to the import and export of precious metals, regarding violation of these 'laws' as the decisive cause of economic crises. The attempt of the British Government to rely on the 'currency principle' theory (Bank Act of 1844, etc.) failed, thus proving its scientific groundlessness and its impracticability (see critique of this theory in Marx's *A Contribution to the Critique of Political Economy*, present edition, Vol. 29).—39

[67] Marx lectured on wages in the London German Workers' Educational Society on 20 May 1868.

The *German Workers' Educational Society* in London was founded in February 1840 by Karl Schapper, Joseph Moll and other members of the League of the Just. After the Communist League had been founded, the leading role in the Society belonged to the League's local communities. In 1847 and 1849-50 Marx and Engels took an active part in the Society's work. But on 17 September 1850, Marx, Engels and a number of their followers withdrew because the Willich-Schapper sectarian and adventurist faction had increased its influence in the Society. In the late 1850s Marx and Engels resumed work in the Educational Society. At the time of the First International, the Society functioned as its German Section in London. It existed up to 1918 when it was closed down by the British government.—40, 166

[68] Marx and his daughter Eleanor stayed with Engels in Manchester from 29 May to about 15 June 1868.—42, 45, 49, 52, 58

[69] *Silesian wars*—in historical writings, the wars waged by Prussia against Austria for Silesia (which belonged to Austria). As a result of the First (1740-42) and Second (1744-45) Silesian wars, which formed part of the European war for Austrian succession, the most of Silesia was captured by Prussia. Austria's attempts to recover the territory in the Seven Years' War (1756-1763), sometimes referred to as the Third Silesian War, were futile.—42

[70] The Lausanne Congress of the International in 1867 designated Brussels as the venue of the next general congress (1868). However, since the Belgian Chamber of Deputies had renewed the Aliens Law of 1835, under which any foreigner could be expelled from the country as politically unreliable, Marx raised the issue of not meeting in Brussels at the General Council sitting of 26 May 1868 (see *The Bee-Hive Newspaper*, No. 346, 30 May 1868). The resolution on the transfer of the site of the Congress to London drawn up by Marx was read at the Council sitting of 2 June (see present edition, Vol. 21, p. 6).

The speech made in the Chamber of Deputies by the Belgian Minister of Justice Jules Bara on 16 May 1868, in which he urged the deputies to abolish the convocation of the congress in Brussels, the protest of the Brussels Section of the International evoked by this speech and printed in the *Tribune du Peuple* No. 5, 24 May 1868, and the letters of De Paepe and Vandenhouten, the leaders of the Brussels Section, prompted Marx to propose a new resolution at the General Council's sitting of 16 June, under which Brussels remained the venue for the next annual congress. The text of the resolution was included in the Minutes of the General Council meeting of 2 June 1868, and was also printed by *The Bee-Hive Newspaper*, No. 347, 6 June 1868.—43, 45

71 Engels did not carry out his intention to write a second review of *Capital* for *The Fortnightly Review*.—44, 53, 74

72 A reference to the French Section of the International in London, founded in the autumn of 1865. Besides proletarian elements (Eugène Dupont, Hermann Jung, Paul Lafargue), the branch included representatives of the petty-bourgeois émigrés (Le Lubez, Pierre Vésinier and later Félix Pyat). See also this volume, p. 62 and Note 89.—45, 62, 63, 75, 78, 83, 91, 173, 272, 481, 488, 497

73 Marx is referring to the General Council of the First International which, up to the end of 1866, was usually referred to as the Central Council.—45, 82, 102, 161, 228, 275, 341, 396, 445, 449, 475, 488, 497

74 The Brussels newspaper *La Cigale*, No. 25, 21 June 1868, carried a piece by Pierre Vésinier from London, 'Bulletin du travailleur', which featured in a distorted way the debate on changing the place of the International's congress at the 9 June General Council meeting and contained slanderous attacks on Hermann Jung and Eugène Dupont, the Council members. In this connection on 22 June the central section in Brussels unanimously decided not to accept responsibility for Pierre Vésinier's article, and to voice the protest against making public the internal affairs of the International. The protest of the Belgian Section was printed in *La Cigale*, No. 26, 28 June 1868.—45

75 Marx paraphrases a passage from Hegel's *Phänomenologie des Geistes* (see G. W. F. Hegel, *Sämtliche Werke*, in 20 Bde., Bd. 2, Stuttgart, 1927, S. 270-71).—46

76 The *Schiller Institute*, founded in Manchester in November 1859 in connection with the centenary of Friedrich Schiller's birth, was conceived as a cultural and social centre of the city's German colony. At first Engels was critical of a society notorious for its tendency towards formalism and pedantry, and he kept aloof from it. But after certain amendments had been made to its Rules, he became a member of its Directorate in 1864, and later its President, devoting much time to it and exercising a considerable influence on its activities. In 1867-68, Engels was particularly occupied with its affairs since a new building was under construction. While Engels was away from Manchester in 1868, the Directorate invited Karl Vogt, who was connected with Bonapartist circles and had been casting aspersions on the proletarian revolutionaries, to give a lecture at the society. In view of this Engels decided that his political reputation would be compromised if he remained President (see this volume, p. 100 and present edition, Vol. 21, p. 18). On 2 October the secretary Davisson approached Engels on behalf of the Directorate asking him to reconsider his decision, but Engels refused. In April 1870 he was again elected member of the Directorate, but did not take an active part in its work.—46, 64, 100, 113, 345, 526

[77] Marx is referring to his stay with the Kugelmanns in Hanover from around 17 April to 15 May 1867. He visited them after his talks with Otto Meissner in Hamburg about the publication of Volume One of *Capital*.—48, 158

[78] Engels' letters to Eleanor Marx have not been found.—49, 75

[79] A reference to the collection of material for Wilhelm Eichhoff's work on the history of the International Working Men's Association, its foundation, organisation, political and social activity and growth: *Die Internationale Arbeiterassociation. Ihre Gründung, Organisation, politisch-sociale Thätigkeit und Ausbreitung.* Wilhelm Eichhoff conceived it in the summer of 1868 when his brother Albert, a publisher, planned to put out a Workers' Calendar for 1869. Wilhelm Eichhoff proposed to write a leading item on the establishment, development and activity of the International Working Men's Association. On 6 June 1868, he informed Marx of his intention and asked him to send the necessary material and help him with the article. As early as 27 June Marx sent to Berlin a great number of documents of the Association, newspaper clippings and his own notes. In his reply of 29 June Eichhoff thanked Marx for the material and informed him that he was going to use his notes word for word and supplement and expand them as advised by Marx. Eichhoff's work grew into a pamphlet because of the abundance of material. It was written with Marx's direct assistance. Eichhoff's letters show that as his work progressed, Marx answered his numerous questions, gave advice, made suggestions, and wrote certain parts of the pamphlet. From 12 to 22 July 1868, Marx edited the pamphlet and read the proofs. On 29 July the work was completed and the edition came out in August (see present edition, Vol. 21, p. 322).—50, 80

[80] This letter was first published in English in full in: *The Letters of Karl Marx.* Selected and translated with explanatory notes and an introduction by Saul K. Padover, Prentice-Hall, Inc., Englewood Cliffs, New Jersey, 1979.—51, 111, 171, 314, 355

[81] The article has not been found.—53

[82] In his letter of 29 June 1868 Eichhoff thanked Marx for the material for his pamphlet *Die Internationale Arbeiterassociation. Ihre Gründung, Organisation, politisch-sociale Thätigkeit und Ausbreitung* (see Note 79), and told him about an unsigned review of Volume One of *Capital* published by the *Vierteljahrschrift für Volkswirthschaft und Kulturgeschichte* (see Note 83).—55

[83] A reference to the review of Volume One of *Capital* in the magazine *Vierteljahrschrift für Volkswirthschaft und Kulturgeschichte*, of which Faucher was an editor (Bd. XX, Berlin, 1868, S. 206-19). It appeared under the heading 'Das Kapital. Kritik der politischen Oekonomie von Karl Marx. Erster Band. Buch I. Der Produktionsprozess des Kapitals. Hamburg, Otto Meissner, 1867'.—55, 56, 65, 86

[84] The letter in question has not been found.—55, 78, 109, 121, 127, 151, 153, 166, 169, 189, 202, 211, 217, 222, 223, 224, 229, 249, 256, 258, 262, 266, 267

[85] A reference to the bourgeois peasant reform of 1861 in Russia which abolished serfdom and launched the development of capitalism. Under the Manifesto and the Statute on the Peasants Leaving the State of Serfdom signed by Alexander II on 19 February 1861, the peasants were granted personal freedom and the right to dispose of their property; the system of land ownership was preserved, and the peasants had to pay for the land allotments they received. Until the payment had been made, they remained 'under

temporary duty' and had to make payments in kind or do corvée for the landowner. (See Marx's opinion of the Reform, then in the state of preparation, in 'The Emancipation Question', present edition, Vol. 16, pp. 139-47).— 55

86 *Fenians*—Irish revolutionaries who took their name from the warriors of Ancient Erin. The first Fenian organisations were founded in the 1850s in the USA and later in Ireland itself. The secret Irish Revolutionary Brotherhood, as the organisation was known in the early 1860s, aimed at establishing an independent Irish republic by means of an armed uprising.

The Fenians, who represented the interests of the Irish peasantry (see Marx's letter to Engels, 30 November 1867, present edition, Vol. 42), came chiefly from the urban petty bourgeoisie and intelligentsia and adhered to conspiratorial tactics. The British Government attempted to suppress the Fenian movement by severe police reprisals (see Note 452).— 57, 224

87 This letter was first published in English in an abridged form in: K. Marx and F. Engels, *Letters to Americans. 1848-1895*, International Publishers, New York, 1953.— 58

88 The London German Workers' Educational Society (see Note 67) jointly with certain other organisations in London held annual gala evenings to mark the anniversary of the June 1848 uprising of the Paris proletariat; members of the General Council also took part in these gatherings.— 62

89 At a public meeting in Cleveland Hall, London, held on 29 June 1868, Félix Pyat read out an address, allegedly received by him from the secret society *La commune révolutionnaire de Paris* and moved a provocative resolution declaring the assassination of Napoleon III as the sacred duty of every Frenchman. The resolution was published by *The Bee-Hive*, No. 351, 4 July 1868. In response, at its meeting of 7 July, the General Council, on Marx's proposal, resolved to disavow Pyat's behaviour in a resolution to this effect (see present edition, Vol. 21, p. 7). When the General Council Resolution appeared in the press, a split took place in the French Section in London (see Note 72). Eugène Dupont, Hermann Jung, Paul Lafargue expressed their disapproval of Pyat's adventurist and provocative tactics and withdrew from it (see this volume, p. 78). Pyat's group lost contact with the International but continued to act on its behalf and repeatedly supported anti-proletarian elements opposing Marx's line in the General Council. On 10 May 1870 the General Council officially dissociated itself from this group (see present edition, Vol. 21, p. 131).— 62

90 The letter of the Brussels committee of 23 June 1868 reported on the decision of the central section in Brussels concerning Vésinier's piece in *La Cigale*, No. 25, 21 June 1868. It was read out at the General Council meeting on 7 July 1868 (see Note 74).— 62

91 A reference to the members of the second bureau of the Paris sections of the International (Combault, Varlin, Landrin, Malon, Molin, Granjon and others) who were sentenced to imprisonment. In March 1868, they had been elected to replace the 15 previously arrested members of the first bureau (on the court trial over the members of the first bureau, see Marx's letters to Engels, 8 and 11 January 1868, present edition, Vol. 42). The members of the second bureau were kept at the Paris Saint-Pelagie prison after they were brought to trial for the second time on 22 May 1868 on the pretext that no official permission had

been granted for membership of the new Paris bureau. The defendants were sentenced to three months' imprisonment and a fine.— 62

92 This letter was first published in English in an abridged form in: *The Letters of Karl Marx*. Selected and translated with explanatory notes and an introduction by Saul K. Padover, Prentice-Hall Inc., Englewood Cliffs, New Jersey, 1979.— 65

93 A reference to Kugelmann's intention to write to Faucher about the review of *Capital* (see Note 83). Marx ironically likens Faucher to Mannequin Piss (manneken-Pis), the well-known statue of a boy on the 17th-century fountain in Brussels executed by the Flemmish sculptor F. Duquesnoy.— 65, 68

94 Joseph Dietzgen's article ' "Das Kapital. Kritik der politischen Oekonomie" von Karl Marx. Hamburg, 1867' was sent by Marx to Liebknecht and published in the *Demokratisches Wochenblatt* in No. 31 (supplement) and nos. 34, 35 and 36 of 1, 22 and 29 August and 5 September 1868.— 65, 70

95 *Demagogues* in Germany were participants in the opposition movement of intellectuals. The name became current after the Karlsbad Conference of Ministers of the German States in August 1819, which adopted a special decision against the intrigues of the 'demagogues'.— 66

96 Marx gave a more detailed analysis of Schmalz's views in his economic manuscripts of 1861-63 'A Contribution to the Critique of Political Economy' (see present edition, Vol. 31).— 67

97 See the article by Karl Marx, 'My Plagiarism of F. Bastiat' (present edition, Vol. 20, p. 260).
   The article, probably written that very day, was not published in Marx's lifetime.— 67

98 Together with a letter of 9 July 1868, Kugelmann sent Marx a copy of the newspaper *Literarisches Centralblatt für Deutschland* of 4 July 1868, which contained an unsigned review of Volume One of *Capital*, analysed by Marx in the present letter. Kugelmann also sent Marx his letter to Faucher written in connection with the review in the *Vierteljahrschrift...* (see Note 83).— 67

99 Marx gave a critique of the views of the French vulgar economist Bastiat and his German followers in the afterword to the second German edition (1872) of Volume One of *Capital* and elsewhere in that volume (see present edition, Vol. 35).— 68

100 Marx's idea was that the chapter on vulgar political economy should conclude the fourth, historical-critical part of *Capital* (see present edition, Vol. 32). The material containing a critique of vulgar bourgeois political economy was first used by Marx in his manuscript of 1861-63 (see Note 41).— 68

101 In his letter of 9 July 1868, Kugelmann asked for Marx's opinion of his intention to publish Schweitzer's review of Volume One of *Capital* as a pamphlet. The review appeared in *Der Social-Demokrat* between January and May 1868 (see Note 15).— 69

102 Ernest Jones was nominated for the Parliamentary elections of 1868 by Manchester's workers, but lost.— 71, 92, 136, 162

103 K. Boruttau dedicated his book *Gedanken über Gewissens-Freiheit* (Königsberg, 1867) to 'Fräulein Ottilie Schurzel in Moskau'.— 72

104 The *General Association of German Workers*—a political organisation of German workers founded in Leipzig on 23 May 1863, at a meeting of workers' societies.

Its foundation was an important step in the advancement of an independent nation-wide working-class movement in Germany and promoted the workers' emancipation from the ideological domination of the liberal bourgeoisie. However, Lassalle, who had been elected chairman, and his followers chose to direct the Association's activities along reformist lines, restricting it to a public campaign for universal suffrage. One of the items on the programme was the establishment of production cooperatives financed by the state, which were expected to resolve social contradictions. The Lassallean leadership of the Association supported the Prussian government's policy of the unification of Germany from above, through dynastic wars.

Thanks to the experience of the working-class movement, and especially the International, and supported by Marx and Engels, the more advanced section of the Association began to drift away from the Lassallean dogmas. The Lassallean leaders, who were afraid to lose their influence among the workers, were forced to manoeuvre. The programme of the Hamburg Congress of the Association (which in its final version appeared in *Der Social-Demokrat*, No. 98, 21 August 1868) contained points that went against Lassalle's doctrine, i.e., advocated complete political freedom, positively assessed Marx's *Capital*, and urged the international cooperation of the working class. In the letter 'To the President and Executive Committee of the General Association of German Workers" (see present edition, Vol. 21), a reply to the invitation which had been extended to him, Marx gave his opinion of the programme and, as he remarked in a letter to Engels of 26 August, congratulated the members of the Association on 'having abandoned *Lassalle's programme*' (see this volume, p. 90).

The Hamburg Congress (22-26 August 1868) adopted important decisions: it approved the strike movement in principle, unanimously acknowledged that 'Marx had rendered outstanding services to the working class with his work *Capital*', and pointed to the necessity for joint action by the workers of different countries. In fact, however, the Lassallean leaders continued to oppose its affiliation with the International and adhered to their former standpoint.

At the Gotha Congress (May 1875), the General Association of German Workers merged with the German Social-Democratic Workers' Party (the Eisenachers) founded in 1869 and headed by August Bebel and Wilhelm Liebknecht. The united party assumed the name of the Socialist Workers' Party.—73, 75, 98, 105, 115, 117, 132, 134, 358, 420

105 Engels is referring to Liebknecht's letter to Marx of 17 July 1868 about the arrangement made by Liebknecht and Schweitzer in Berlin in July 1868. During the meeting, Liebknecht told Schweitzer about his and Bebel's intention to recommend the forthcoming congress of the Union of German Workers' Associations in Nuremberg (see Note 135) to adopt the programme of the International, and insisted that the Lassallean Association be affiliated with it, believing that this would remove the cause for dissent between the Lassalleans and the followers of Bebel and Liebknecht, and make unification possible.—73, 110

106 A reference to Kugelmann's letter to Engels of 26 July 1868, which stated that, according to Kertbény, Keil of Leipzig agreed to feature Marx's biography in *Die Gartenlaube* magazine. However, the biography written by Engels was not printed. In July 1869, Engels revised it for *Die Zukunft* newspaper, and it appeared in No. 185 under the heading 'Karl Marx' on 11 August 1869 (see present edition, Vol. 21).—73, 77, 81

107 In the late 1850s-early 1860s, Beta, who was contributing to the newspaper *Hermann. Deutsches Wochenblatt aus London* and was also a correspondent of *Die Gartenlaube*, which was published in Leipzig, repeatedly calumniated Marx in his articles. For Marx's opinion of Beta's activities as a newspaperman, see his letters to Engels, 19 and 26 November and 11 (or 12) December 1859, and 10 January 1861, and his letters to Ferdinand Freiligrath, 23 November 1859 and 23 February 1860 (present edition, Vols. 40 and 41).— 74

108 On 23 July 1868, on behalf of the Union of German Workers' Associations (see Note 169) Bebel sent the General Council of the International an invitation to the Nuremberg Congress (see Note 135) in which he wrote: 'Among the more important items on the agenda the principal place belongs to the *question of the programme...* We ... intend to recommend the Congress to adopt the programme of the International Working Men's Association and ... also suggest that the organisation be affiliated to the International Working Men's Association.' The invitation was enclosed into Liebknecht's letter to Marx of the same date. Liebknecht insisted that Marx go to Nuremberg as the General Council delegate, but Marx declined this offer. The General Council meeting of 25 August 1868 decided that its representative at the Nuremberg Congress would be Georg Eccarius.— 75

109 The solidarity congress of workers of all nationalities inhabiting Austro-Hungary, which was to be held in Vienna in September 1868, was banned by the government of Austria-Hungary.— 75

110 Marx probably means two legal actions brought against Schweitzer in 1868. On 14 February, speaking at a meeting in Berlin, Schweitzer said that the Royal police headquarters, by the repeated banning of meeting, had violated human rights. Schweitzer's speech was interpreted as undermining the King's state power and he was sentenced to two weeks' imprisonment which he served in September 1868.

The Elberfeld court sentenced Schweitzer to three weeks' imprisonment for the distribution of leaflets, and he served his term in Berlin prison from 8 to 29 July 1868.— 75

111 Marx's reply to Schweitzer's letter of 28 June 1868 has not been found. In his letter Schweitzer asked if Marx would be able to attend the Hamburg Congress of the General Association of German Workers (see Note 104). If Marx agreed, Schweitzer intended, before going to prison (see Note 110) to send him an invitation signed by 24 members of the Association's committee (see also this volume, pp. 89-90).— 76

112 Marx's notes refer to his biography written by Engels (see Note 106). The first one refers to the *Rheinische Zeitung für Politik, Handel und Gewerbe.* The newspaper was founded by members of the Rhenish liberal bourgeoisie which was opposed to Prussian absolutism. In May 1842, Marx began to contribute to it, and in October became one of the editors. It published a number of Engels' articles (see present edition, Vol. 2). Under Marx's editorship, the newspaper began to follow an increasingly coherent democratic trend. Its character, which was to a large extent determined by Marx's articles containing criticism of Germany's social, economic and political development (see present edition, Vol. 1) attracted the attention of the Prussian authorities. On 12 November 1842, the government imposed a rigorous censorship of it, and on 19 January passed a decision banning the newspaper as of April 1843, and introducing even stricter censorship for the remaining period. The decree was promulgated

on 21 January (see 'Erlass der drei Zensurminister betr. Unterdrückung der *Rheinischen Zeitung* zum. 1. April 1843,' Berlin, 1843, 21 January). At the end of January 1843 Marx was already thinking of resigning the editorship (see Marx's letter to Ruge, 25 January 1843, present edition, Vol. 1, p. 397), but he did not consider it possible to carry out his intention at the height of the campaign for the repeal of the ban. In March, however, he became convinced that changes in the editorial board could provide a chance of saving the newspaper, and he decided to resign officially from his post (the announcement of his resignation was published on 17 March 1843. See present edition, Vol. 1, p. 376).

But the royal rescript was not repealed. The last issue of the newspaper appeared on 31 March 1843.— 76

113 Marx is referring to the reprisals against the *Neue Rheinische Zeitung* published in Cologne in 1848-49. In April-early May 1849, Minister of the Interior Manteuffel repeatedly urged the Cologne authorities to take legal action against the newspaper's editorial board (see present edition, Vol. 9, pp. 492-93, 496-97). By the spring of 1849, 23 lawsuits had been brought against it. However, the procurator's office, which had already failed twice to get a conviction from the jury (7 and 8 February 1849. See present edition, Vol. 8, pp. 304-39) did not dare to challenge the newspaper on legal grounds. On 16 May Marx was ordered to leave Prussia within 24 hours.— 76

114 In a letter to Engels of 26 July 1868 (see Note 106) Kugelmann suggested that Marx's biography be printed under the heading 'Ein deutscher National-Ökonom'.— 77

115 The *Jacobin Club* ('Société des amis de la constitution')—a political club founded at the time of the French Revolution, in October 1789; initially represented different political trends in the anti-absolutist camp.— 79

116 A reference to Moses Hess' review of Volume One of *Capital*, which he had already begun writing in November 1867 for the French press. Marx suggested that it should contain a synopsis of the theory of value as expounded in *Capital*. In 1868, Hess tried for several months to get the review published in a number of newspapers, including *Courrier français* and *Morale indépendante*. It is not known what has happened to the review.— 79, 84

117 Marx considered the expediency of transferring the General Council to Geneva for the year 1869 in connection with the forthcoming Congress of the International in Brussels.— 79

118 Engels refers to the resolution of the Communist League's Central Authority in London of 15 September 1850 (see present edition, Vol. 10, pp. 625-29) passed as a result of the adventurist activities of the Willich-Schapper faction which transferred the powers of the Central Authority to the Cologne district authority.

The *Communist League*—the first German and international communist proletarian organisation set up under the leadership of Marx and Engels in early June 1847 in London and operating until 1852. Its programme and organisational structure were evolved with the direct participation of Marx and Engels. On the instruction of the League's Second Congress held on 29 November-8 December 1847, which unanimously approved the principles of scientific communism elaborated by Marx and Engels, the two men wrote the League's programme, *Manifesto of the Communist Party*, published in February 1848 (see present edition, Vol. 6, pp. 477-519).

During the 1848-49 revolution, the Communist League was the organisational centre and vanguard of the revolutionary movement in Germany.

After the defeat of the revolution, the Communist League was restructured in 1849-50 and continued working. The 'Address of the Central Authority to the League' written by Marx and Engels in March 1850 (see present edition, Vol. 10, pp. 277-87) summed up the results of the 1848-49 revolution and emphasised the need to set up an independent proletarian party; it also developed the idea of permanent revolution.

The decision mentioned above was adopted as a result of the dissent, which became more acute in the summer of 1850, over the tactics to be adopted in order to protect the workers from the influence of the Willich-Schapper faction, which tried to make the League adopt an adventurist policy of starting revolution in total disregard of the objective laws and the situation prevailing in Germany and other European countries. The faction's activities gave the police an excuse to stage provocative acts against the Communist League. However, the transfer of the Central Authority to Cologne had certain undesirable consequences: the Cologne district authority proved incapable of exercising leadership over the entire League; moreover, the transfer had put the Central Authority in danger of police reprisals. In fact, the police persecution and the arrests of May 1851 put an end to the work of the League in Germany. On 17 November 1852, soon after the Communist Trial in Cologne, the League dissolved itself on Marx's suggestion, but its members continued their propaganda and revolutionary work.

The Communist League had played a major historical role as a school for proletarian revolutionaries and the embryo of a proletarian party, the forerunner of the International Working Men's Association.— 80, 140, 397

119 In his letter to Marx of 7 August 1868, John Morley, editor of *The Fortnightly Review*, explained that he had rejected Engels' review of Volume One of *Capital* (see Note 11) because he had 'no room for it'.— 81, 84

120 As is apparent from Kugelmann's letter to Marx of 2 August 1868, the matter under discussion is the financial assistance to the weavers in Linden (Hanover) who were on strike. Kugelmann wrote to Marx: 'A few days ago, the workers of the local mill, about 1,000 of them, launched an entirely justified strike. They are working for about 14 hours a day and earn 3 shillings a week. This is the first strike of such scope here, and its successful conclusion is of major importance... It would be of *particular significance* for Germany if England could render support to the striking weavers. The *moral* impact of this factor would be tremendous for both sides.' This message was discussed at a meeting of the General Council held on 4 August 1868 (see *The Bee-Hive*, No. 355, 8 August 1868).— 82

121 In 1866-67 in London, Lafargue resumed and completed his medical studies interrupted by his expulsion from Paris University in 1865. He returned to Paris in the autumn of 1868 and tried to get a doctor's certificate allowing him to set up a practice in France, without taking his exams for a second time, but failed. After becoming involved in political activities and journalism, Lafargue abandoned the idea of a medical career.— 82, 155

122 *Tranquillity is the first duty of citizens*, a phrase from the address by F. W. von Schulenburg-Kehnert, acting Governor of Berlin, to the city's population on 17 October 1806, after the defeat at Jena.— 83

123 Enclosed in this letter was the text of an 'Appeal to the German Workers in London' written by Lessner on behalf of the London German Workers' Educational Society (see Note 67) in connection with the Congress of the International to be held in Brussels in September 1868, and sent to Marx for review (see present edition, Vol. 21, p. 385-86).—83

124 This letter was first published in English in an abridged form in: Karl Marx, Frederick Engels, *Selected Letters. The Personal Correspondence, 1844-1877*, Ed. by F. J. Raddatz, Little, Brown and Company, Boston, Toronto, 1981.—85, 86, 255, 303

125 These letters from Karl Marx to his relatives have not been found.—85

126 Marx was on holiday at Ramsgate approximately from 21 to 24 August 1868.—87

127 Engels refers to Bernhard Becker, whom Lassalle nominated in his will as his successor to the post of President of the General Association of German Workers. Becker called himself 'heir by Lassalle's will' on the title page of his *Enthüllungen über das tragische Lebensende Ferdinand Lassalle's.*—88, 89

128 A reference is to a number of works by Marx and Engels, including statements in *Der Social-Demokrat* and *Berliner Reform*, the pamphlets 'The Prussian Military Question and the German Workers' Party' and 'The "President of Mankind"', which expose Schweitzer's political stand and Bernhard Becker's slanderous attacks (see present edition, Vol. 20).—88

129 Engels' mother wrote on 2 September 1868 to tell him that she had arrived in Ostend the day before. Engels joined her for about 10 days there. *En route* he met Marx in London.—88,90, 92, 95, 100, 128

130 The official invitation to Marx to be guest of honour at the Hamburg Congress of the General Association of German Workers (see Note 104) was sent on behalf of the President and the Committee of the Association on 13 August 1868 and published in *Der Social-Demokrat*, No. 95, 14 August 1868. It was read out at the General Council meeting of 18 August 1868 and included in a brief report of the meeting in *The Bee-Hive Newspaper*, No. 358, 22 August 1868.—89

131 Engels' letter to Marx of 27 August 1868 has not been found.—90

132 In 1868, the members of the International in Naples maintained contacts with the International Working Men's Association through Eugène Dupont, member of the General Council, who was their delegate at the Brussels Congress.
    The Neapolitan branch of the International became finally established in 1869. It was the first section of the International Working Men's Association in Italy, and quite a large one at that; it had many workers among its members. It was under the strong influence of the Bakuninists. Early in 1871, however, it disintegrated; with the help of Cafiero, who received instructions from Engels, it was reorganised and maintained regular contacts with the General Council. Cafiero kept its members informed about Engels' letters and the Association's documents. Soon, it became the International's principal centre in Italy, but was routed by the police in August 1871.—91

133 Marx is referring to the reports of the International's Italian sections on the situation in the country. Specifically, on 18 August 1868, a letter read out at the General Council meeting stated that 'at Bologna and vicinity the right of

meeting is suppressed; the officers of the working men's societies are in prison'
(see *The Bee-Hive Newspaper*, No. 358, 22 August 1868).

On 3 November 1867 at Mentana, the French army, jointly with the Pope's
mercenary guards, defeated Garibaldi's army which had undertaken a new
campaign against Rome to liberate it from the French and annex it to the Italian
state.—91

134 Since the members of the second bureau of the International's Paris sections
(see Note 91) had been arrested, more than ten representatives to the Brussels
Congress (see Note 138) were sent mostly by the French professional unions
affiliated with the International. Among them were mechanics, tin-smiths,
cotton printers, bookbinders, house painters, marble and bronze workers.—91

135 The *Nuremberg Congress* of the Union of German Workers' Associations led by
Bebel was held on 5-7 September 1868. In all, 115 delegates from 93 sections
in Germany, Austria and Switzerland were present. Apart from Georg Eccarius,
the official representative of the General Council, several other members of the
International attended. By 69 votes against 46, the Congress resolved to join
the International Working Men's Association and adopted a programme
recognising its basic principles. It also elected a committee of 16 to carry out
this resolution. On 22 September 1868, the General Council approved the
committee membership giving it the status of the Executive Committee of the
International Working Men's Association in Germany. On 7 September liberal
bourgeois members, who found themselves in the minority and were opposed
to the Congress resolutions, announced their withdrawal from the Union. The
Nuremberg Congress also resolved to organise trade unions and heard
Liebknecht's report on armaments, in which he demanded that standing armies
be disbanded. The Congress was an important step towards the foundation of a
proletarian party in Germany.—91, 102, 115, 118, 128, 135, 166, 172, 249, 304

136 *The Times* published five reports by Eccarius on the work of the Brussels
Congress of the International. They appeared on 9, 11, 14, 15 and 17
September 1868 under the heading 'International Working Men's Congress
(From a Correspondent)'.

Eccarius' reports on the Nuremberg Congress of the Union of German
Workers' Associations (see Note 135) were not printed by *The Times*.—91, 97,
101

137 The last meeting of the General Council before the Brussels Congress was held
on Tuesday, 1 September 1868. It heard, and unanimously approved the
report of the General Council to the Brussels Congress drawn up by Marx (see
present edition, Vol. 21, p. 12).—92

138 A reference to the Third Congress of the International held in Brussels on
6-13 September 1868. It was attended by nearly 100 delegates representing
workers of Britain, France, Germany, Belgium, Switzerland, Italy and Spain.
Marx, who took part in the preparations for the Congress, was not present.
The annual report of the General Council written by Marx (see present edition,
Vol. 21, p. 12) was read out at the Congress on 7 September 1868. The
Congress adopted an important resolution on the necessity for introducing
public ownership of railways, mineral resources, collieries and mines, forests
and arable land. This resolution showed that most of the French and Belgian
Proudhonists had become supporters of collectivism and it marked the victory
of proletarian socialism over petty-bourgeois reformism in the International.
The Congress also adopted the resolutions (drawn up by Marx) on the

eight-hour working day, on the use of machinery and on the attitude towards the congress of the bourgeois-pacifist League of Peace and Freedom (see present edition, Vol. 20, p. 204), and a resolution, moved by a group of German delegates, recommending the workers of all countries to study Marx's *Capital* and promote its translation from German into other languages (see Note 150).—93, 95, 96, 115, 131, 143, 166, 202, 221, 258, 404

[139] The original letter has not been found. Friedrich Lessner first quoted it in his reminiscences *Vor 1848 und nachher* published in the *Deutsche Worte*, Wien [1898]. There, the letter was erroneously dated 10 August.

This letter appeared in English for the first time in: Lessner F., *Sixty Years in the Social Democratic Movement*, London, 1907.—93

[140] A reference to Friedrich Lessner's letter to Marx posted in Brussels on 8 September 1868, in which Lessner gave a detailed account of the work of the International Working Men's Association's Congress in Brussels.—93

[141] Marx is probably referring to the question of the strike movement entered onto the agenda of the Brussels Congress on the suggestion of the French delegate Tartaret in addition to the points proposed by the General Council earlier. The reports of the French Section in Geneva and the Belgian Section in Liége contained Proudhonist ideas on the issue; strikes were denounced as a matter of principle and only recognized as the inevitable evil. The Congress resolution, passed despite the opposition of the Proudhonists, defined strikes as a necessary and legitimate means of struggle between labour and capital.—94

[142] A reference to the Nuremberg Congress of the Union of German Workers' Associations (see Note 135) and the general congress of the Lassallean Association in Berlin (see Note 164).—94

[143] Marx means the opposition to the trade unions put up by the Belgian unions and French Proudhonists at the Geneva and Lausanne congresses of the International.

The *Geneva Congress*, the first congress of the International Working Men's Association, was held on 3-8 September 1866. It was attended by 60 delegates from the Central Council (see Note 73), various sections of the International and workers' associations in Britain, France, Germany and Switzerland. Hermann Jung was elected its chairman. The Congress approved the Rules and Administrative Regulations of the International Working Men's Association (see present edition, Vol. 20, p. 441). Marx's 'Instructions for the Delegates of the Provisional General Council. The Different Questions' were read as the official report of the Central Council (see present edition, Vol. 20, p. 185). The Congress became a scene of struggle between Marx's followers and the Proudhonists, who had a third of the votes and countered the 'Instructions' with their own programme on all items on the agenda. They were particularly opposed to trade unions and preached political indifferentism. In heated debates with the Proudhonists, Jung, Eccarius, Dupont, Carter and other supporters of the Central Council succeeded in having 6 items out of 9 of the 'Instructions' adopted in the form of Congress resolutions, including the one on trade unions.

The *Lausanne Congress* of the International was held on 2-8 September 1867. Marx took part in the preparations, but, as he was busy reading the proofs of Volume One of *Capital*, he was unable to attend. He withdrew his candidature at the General Council meeting of 13 August 1867. The Congress was attended by 64 delegates from six countries (Britain, France, Germany,

Switzerland, Belgium and Italy). Apart from the annual report of the General Council, the Congress heard reports from the local sections, which indicated the increased influence of the International on the proletarian masses and the growing strength of its organisations in different countries. Despite the efforts of the General Council's delegates, the Proudhonist-minded delegates imposed their agenda on the Congress. They sought to revise the decisions of the Geneva Congress in a Proudhonist spirit. They managed to pass a number of their resolutions, including the ones on cooperation and credit, which they regarded as the chief factors of changing a society through reform. However, they failed to achieve their main objective. The Congress confirmed the Geneva resolutions on the economic struggle and strikes. The Proudhonists likewise failed to seize the leadership of the International. The Congress re-elected the General Council in its former composition and retained London as its seat.— 95, 221, 258

144 Marx sent Sorge's credentials to Meyer (see this volume, p. 59) in response to Meyer's letter of 20 May 1868, which contained the following request: 'In the middle of next month, Sorge is planning to go to Chicago and will be able to establish all sorts of contacts. Would you be so kind as to supply us with some useful addresses?'— 96

145 As President of the Central Committee of the Social Party of New York and its environs, (between November 1867 and September 1868), the first workers' party in the USA, Friedrich Sorge was a vigorous promoter of the ideas of the International in the USA. Early in 1868, disagreements of principle began to arise, which later turned into a personal hostility between Sorge on the one hand, and Sigfrid Meyer and August Vogt on the other. Meyer and Vogt insisted on more vigorous action to draw the unions of American workers into the International, even though they were not yet ready to take that step. Sorge strove to organise a more active popularisation campaign that would gradually make them realise the need for joining the International. In the end he failed to achieve the official affiliation of the Social Party to the International, but in his activity he adhered to the International's principles and the decisions of its congresses.

Having been stripped, on Meyer's and Vogt's insistence, of the General Council's Corresponding Secretary's powers, Sorge did not belong to any organisation for over a year. Only in December 1869, he resumed his work of popularising the International's ideas among the German workers within the reorganised General Association of German Workers.— 97

146 The *National Labor Union* was founded in the USA at a congress in Baltimore in 1866, with the active participation of William Sylvis, a prominent member of the American labour movement. It made a major contribution to the growing struggle for an independent policy of workers' associations, for solidarity of white and coloured workers, for an 8-hour working day and for the rights of working women. Soon after its foundation, it established contacts with the International Working Men's Association. The Union's congress in Chicago held in August 1867 elected Richard Trevellick delegate to the Lausanne Congress of the International, but he was unable to attend. At the last sessions of the Basle Congress of the International (1869) Andrew Cameron was the National Labor Union delegate. The Union's congress in Cincinnati in August 1870 adopted a resolution on its adherence to the principles of the International and its intention to join it. The resolution was not implemented, however. In 1870 and 1871, many trade unions withdrew, and in 1872 the Union virtually ceased to exist.— 97, 184, 351

147 Marx planned to have *Capital* translated into English back in 1865, when working on the manuscript (see Marx's letter to Engels, 31 July 1865; present edition, Vol. 42). Reporter Peter Fox, a member of the British labour movement, was to help him find a publisher. However, due to the latter's death in 1869 nothing was settled. The English translation of Volume One of *Capital* edited by Engels appeared after Marx's death, in January 1887. The translation was done by Samuel Moore and Edward Aveling between mid-1883 and March 1886; Eleanor Marx-Aveling assisted in preparing the translation for the press.—97, 442.

148 At the General Council meeting of 8 October 1867 Peter Fox, James Carter and Robert Shaw accused Eccarius of misrepresenting the reports on the Lausanne Congress published in *The Times* on 6, 9, 10 and 11 September 1867. See also Marx's letters to Engels of 4 and 9 October 1867, present edition, Vol. 42.—97, 106, 148

149 Excerpts from Volume One of *Capital* were published in the USA, in *The Sun* on 26 January 1868.—97

150 At the Brussels Congress of the International (see Note 138), on 11 September 1868, a group of German delegates moved the following resolution on Marx's *Capital*: 'We, the German delegates at the International Working Men's Congress at Brussels, recommend to the working men of all countries the work of Carl Marx, *Das Kapital*, published last year, and urge upon them the desirability of endeavouring to cause that important work to be translated into those languages into which it has not yet been translated, and declare that Carl Marx has the inestimable merit of being the first political economist who has scientifically analysed capital and dissolved it into its component parts.' The resolution was unanimously approved by the Congress and published in *The Times* on 15 September 1868 as part of Eccarius's report. See also Note 136.

The article 'Der fünfte Vereinstag deutscher Arbeitervereine zu Nürnberg (5-7. September)', which appeared in the *Demokratisches Wochenblatt*, No. 37, 12 September 1868, quoted Liebknecht's speech at the Nuremberg Congress of the Union of German Workers' Associations (see Note 135), in which he lashed out against bourgeois science and the press which kept deliberately silent about Volume One of *Capital*.—99, 101

151 Marx is referring to a speech made by Moses Hess at the meeting of the Brussels Congress of the International Working Men's Association on 11 September 1868. Hess spoke out against the Proudhonist theory of 'gratuitous credit' (crédit gratuit), which was criticised by Marx in his work *The Poverty of Philosophy. Answer to the 'Philosophy of Poverty' by M. Proudhon* (see present edition, Vol. 6, pp. 105-212).—100, 102

152 The Brussels Congress resolution (adopted on 13 September 1868) on the ownership of land, mines and collieries and railways was the first concrete statement of the socialist principle underlying the International's approach to the issue of property. In connection with land ownership, the Congress emphasised that the contemporary economic development of the capitalist system determines the need for introducing public ownership of land and the mineral resources, including arable land (for the text of the resolution, see: 'Troisième congrès de l'Association Internationale des Travailleurs. Compte rendu officiel. Bruxelles, septembre 1868. Supplément au journal *Le Peuple belge*, 24 septembre 1868').—101

153 The question of Eccarius' reports published in *The Times* (see also notes 136, 155) was not discussed at the General Council meetings because of his long illness.— 101, 106

154 Lessner, who informed Marx almost daily about the course of the Brussels Congress, wrote in a letter of 11 September 1868: 'On Wednesday, the question of machinery was discussed. I took the floor, mentioned your book and quoted from it... *Daily News* had something about this. Its reporter approached me and inquired about the name of the book and the part from which I quoted. My reading out of the excerpts was welcomed by applause. Friend Eccarius, however, did not deem it worthwhile, or not to his advantage, to mention this in his report for *The Times*.'— 101

155 The text of the resolution on war proposed by a group of German delegates at the Brussels Congress was printed in full in the supplement to *Le Peuple belge*, 22 September 1868, and the *Vorbote* magazine, No. 10, October 1868. Eccarius' report in *The Times*, 17 September 1868, contained an incomplete and inaccurate exposition of the resolution.— 101

156 The Brussels Congress of the International Working Men's Association elected a special commission to investigate the accusations brought by Vésinier against certain members of the International (see notes 74 and 90). On 3 November 1868, at the sitting of the General Council, a letter from the Brussels commission was read out which said that Vésinier had failed to adduce any proof and that the commission had not been able to find the slightest grounds for these accusations. The commission members proposed expelling Vésinier from the International as a slanderer.— 102

157 A reference to an article by Johann Philipp Becker 'Was wir wollen und sollen' printed in 1866 in the first issue of the *Vorbote*. Before the Nuremberg Congress of the Union of German Workers' Associations, this article appeared, mistakenly, in the Union organ, *Deutsche Arbeiterhalle* on 27 July and 12 August 1868, as the International's programme, and was reprinted by the *Demokratisches Wochenblatt* (nos. 31-32, supplements, and 33, 1, 8 and 15 August 1868). It gave an incoherent and vague account of the aims and tasks of the International working-class movement, especially in Germany and Switzerland. However, it was not mentioned at the Nuremberg Congress, as the error had been rectified earlier. The *Demokratisches Wochenblatt*, No. 35, 29 August, published the chief points of the International's programme which the Congress adopted without any changes. Delegates Stuttman, Eichelsdörfer and Sonnemann stated that the reference to Becker's article as the International's programme was an error. In a letter to Marx of 20 September 1868, Liebknecht wrote: 'The quiproquo happened while I was *absent* on my wedding trip. I had given orders to print *your* "Address"; and Bebel, who could not find it, wrote to Becker for the "Programme" and received the unfortunate document that brought us to despair in Nuremberg. When I discovered the mistake, it was too late to mend it, especially as we could not well *disavow* old Becker. Luckily, Pfeiffer and Co. were so confused by our vigorous onslaught that they quite forgot to prove the stupidities of the pseudo-programme. Now the thing is explained, and our people know, that under the circumstances the error was excusable.'— 102

158 In the summer of 1869, the Ermen-Engels partnership agreement signed on 30 June 1864 for the term of 5 years, which had made Engels a co-owner of the firm of Ermen and Engels in Manchester, was to expire. As Engels had

expected, his talks with G. Ermen about his withdrawal from the firm became protracted. A draft agreement is extant, drawn up by Engels on 2 December 1868, which specified the terms of the withdrawal: '1) Mr. Engels retires from business on the 30th June 1869 and engages not to be interested, either directly or indirectly, as principal or assistant, in any similar or competing business either in England or on the Continent for the term of five years after that date. 2) Mr. Engels consents that Mr. G. Ermen, if he should think proper to do so, continues the firm of Ermen and Engels as long as he is a partner in the concern. 3) Mr. G. Ermen pays Mr. Engels on 30th June 1869 the sum of £1750, Seventeen Hundred and fifty Pounds St. 4) Mr. Engels to have the right of keeping £5000—in the concern at 5% Interest between 30th June 69 to 30th June 1870. Manchester December 2 d 1868' (see also Note 369).— 104, 167

[159] On 22 August 1868 Bismarck, Prime Minister of Prussia, had a fall while riding and withdrew temporarily from his duties because of his injury, while King William I, as the press reported, incessantly toured the country, taking part in military reviews, festivals and receptions.— 104

[160] In a letter of 15 September 1868, Schweitzer wrote to Marx: 'I consider you to be the head of the European working-class movement—not only through democratic election but by the will of God. You can also be assured that I will promote your intentions as best I can. Of course no prestige is great enough to prevent one, under certain circumstances, from adhering to one's own opinion. I believe, however, that conflict does not arise easily. When it appeared to me that you were not right, subsequent consideration showed me, at least until now, that I was mistaken myself. Yet I cannot find much in common with your followers—at least with some of them.

'...I intend to get you the Statutes which we want to propose to the organisation at the congress after they have been discussed by a limited number of persons, so that before the congress, has started you will have a chance to note the points which may not tally with the spirit of the [congress's] organisation, although this shouldn't occur.

'It may happen that it will be too late to send the Statutes to you; however, I shall try to make the dispatch possible.'— 105, 107, 115, 118, 127, 132,

[161] Marx is referring to the six editorials printed under the common heading 'Der allgemeine deutsche Arbeiter-Congress' in Der Social-Demokrat in September 1868, which mirrored the ideological conflict between dedicated Lassalleans and the followers of Schweitzer. Fearing that their influence among the workers might dwindle under the impact of the mounting strike movement and the International's ideas, Schweitzer's followers were forced to abandon some of the Lassallean concepts and change their attitude towards the economic struggle of the working class. Specifically, a general German workers' congress in Berlin that Schweitzer and Fritzsche had been planning (see Note 164) was to consider the issues of the strike movement and the trade unions of German workers. The address drawn up by Schweitzer and Fritzsche for the congress and published by Der Social-Demokrat, No. 101, 30 August 1868, read: 'It is urgently necessary to establish a mass and stable organisation of all workers throughout Germany for the purpose of jointly moving forward by means of strikes... We are convening a general German workers' congress to set up, and also strengthen and evolve the uniform organisational principles of general trade unions in all industries throughout Germany, as well as to discuss the general lines along which strikes can be organised.'— 105

162 The principle of setting up production associations on the basis of state credit as a means of emancipating the workers from exploitation was first proclaimed by Philippe Buchez in 1831 in the philosophical journal *L'Européen*, which he published. His plan was popularised in the 1840s by *L'Atelier* magazine, which represented the interests and ideas of French handicraftsmen and workers influenced by the doctrine of Christian socialism (see also this volume, p. 260).— 105, 133, 260

163 Marx's letter to Liebknecht has not been found. In his reply of 20 September 1868, Liebknecht wrote that '...there are a few dozen of "Vogts" in Berlin. I had to leave them there when I was expelled; and *most* copies were distributed by me to political persons,— sold *very* few. In 5 or 6 days I hope to have news'.— 106

164 A reference to the general congress of the General Association of German Workers convened by Schweitzer and Fritzsche on 26-29 September 1868 in Berlin with the permission of the Hamburg Congress of the Lassallean Association to discuss the establishment of trade unions (see Note 104). Represented at the congress were mostly workers from North German towns. The workers' societies comprising the Nuremberg organisation headed by Bebel and Liebknecht were refused permission to send their members to the congress. As a result the Berlin congress promoted the foundation of a number of unions built after the pattern of the sectarian Lassallean Association and brought them together in a single general union. Schweitzer became president, while the most prominent members of the General Association of German Workers headed the individual, and for the most part newly-established, unions. Marx sharply criticised Schweitzer for such an organisation of the congress, which brought about a split in the German trade unions (see this volume, pp. 134, 135), and for the adoption of the Statutes, which went completely against the goals and nature of the trade-union movement.— 108, 112, 118, 125, 127, 132, 133, 134, 140

165 A reference to the bourgeois revolution in Spain (1868-74) which began on 18 September 1868 with a naval mutiny in Cádiz against the reactionary monarchy of Isabella II. The masses, supported by almost all the royal troops, were actively involved in the revolution. As a result, state authority passed to the bourgeoisie and bourgeois landowners, who on 18 October formed a provisional government headed by General Francisco Serrano. The Constituent Cortes, convened in February 1869, passed a bourgeois-monarchist constitution which proclaimed Spain a hereditary monarchy and introduced a number of bourgeois freedoms (universal suffrage for men, freedom of press, assembly, associations, etc.). Against the background of fierce class clashes, a bourgeois-democratic federative republic was proclaimed in Spain in 1873. However, in 1874, big bourgeoisie and landowners engineered a restoration of the Bourbons.— 108, 113, 115, 119, 126, 131, 137

166 In a letter to Marx of 16 September 1868, Liebknecht proposed that an address to the German workers be drawn up urging unification and criticising Schweitzer and his followers as opponents of unity in the ranks of Social-Democrats.— 109, 110, 112

167 A reference to the ban imposed on 16 September 1868 by the Leipzig police on the General Association of German Workers (see Note 104) centred in Leipzig, and on its local branch in Berlin (see Engels' article 'On the Dissolution of the Lassallean Workers' Association', present edition, Vol. 21). On 10 October,

however, a group of Lassalleans headed by Schweitzer restored the association under the same name, transferring its seat to Berlin. The new Statutes of the Association published in *Der Social-Demokrat*, No. 119, 11 October 1868, stated that the Association would abide by Prussian laws and act only in a peaceful, legal way. Adapting itself to Prussian law, the Association dissolved its local branches. (For Marx's and Engels' opinion of these manoeuvres, see letters of Marx to Engels of 25, 26 and 29 September and of Engels to Marx of 21, 24 and 30 September and 2 October, as well as Marx's letter to Schweitzer of 13 October 1868.)— 109, 111, 134, 140

168 The bourgeois revolution of 1848 in the Kingdom of Naples began on 12 January 1848 with a popular uprising in Sicily against the feudal absolutist monarchy of Ferdinand II of the Bourbon dynasty. It triggered off revolutionary events in other Italian states. However, as a result of the conciliatory stand of the liberal bourgeoisie, the revolution was suppressed in May 1849.— 109

169 Engels is referring to the Union of German Workers' Associations, which was set up at the workers' educational societies' congress in Frankfurt am Main on 7 June 1863, in opposition to the Lassallean General Association of German Workers (see Note 104). Wilhelm Liebknecht and August Bebel were actively involved in its activities, heading the workers' movement for a revolutionary and democratic way of Germany's unification and against the influence of the liberal bourgeoisie, which was quite strong in the first years of the Union's existence. At the Nuremberg Congress (see Note 135), it in fact affiliated itself with the International. Later, the Union was instrumental in the formation, at the Eisenach Congress of 1869, of the Social-Democratic Workers' Party of Germany (see Note 373).— 110, 118

170 In late September 1868, Engels wrote an article 'On the Dissolution of the Lassallean Workers' Association' for the *Demokratisches Wochenblatt* published by Liebknecht (present edition, Vol. 21). In it he quoted excerpts from his pamphlet 'The Prussian Military Question and the German Workers' Party' (present edition, Vol. 20).— 111, 112, 114

171 A reference to a speech made by Bernhard Becker, President of the Lassallean General Association of German Workers, at the meeting of its Hamburg branch on 22 March 1865, in which he slandered the International Working Men's Association and Marx, Engels and Liebknecht personally. Becker's speech appeared in the supplement of *Der Social-Demokrat*, No. 39, 26 March 1865. Marx exposed Becker's lies in his essay 'The "President of Mankind"' (present edition, Vol. 20).— 112

172 Following Marx's advice, in early October 1868 Engels wrote a postscript to his article 'On the Dissolution of the Lassallean Workers' Association' (see present edition, Vol. 21), in which he exposes Becker's plagiarism in his pamphlet, mentioned in this letter.— 112

173 *Blue Books*—collected documents of the British Parliament and Foreign Office published since the seventeenth century.— 113, 128, 264, 481

174 An excerpt from this letter was published in English for the first time in: Karl Marx and Friedrich Engels, *Correspondence, 1846-1895*, London, Lawrence LTD, [1934].— 114, 127, 188, 191, 195, 262, 349, 428, 462, 471

175 A reference to the agreement reached by British trade unions at the first national congress in 1868, which was convened in connection with the campaign for completely legalising them. Ever since, congresses have been held

on a regular basis, and an executive body of the congress, the Parliamentary committee heading the campaign, was formed.

The *London Trades Council* was first elected at a conference of trade union delegates held in London in May 1860. It headed the London trade unions numbering thousands of members and was fairly influential among the British workers. The leaders of the following trade unions played a major role in the Council: the Amalgamated Society of Carpenters and Joiners (Robert Applegarth), the Shoemakers' Society (George Odger), the Operative Bricklayers' Society (Edwin Coulson and George Howell) and the Amalgamated Engineers (William Allan). All of them, except Allan, were members of the General Council of the International Working Men's Association. The General Council did its best to draw the broad mass of British workers into the International and endeavoured, on the one hand, to get the local trade union organisations affiliated to it and, on the other, to induce the London Trades Council to join the International as a British Section. After the repeated deferment of the question, which was due to the struggle between the reformer leaders of the London Council who opposed affiliation and local trade union representatives, it was finally decided at the London Trades Council meetings of 9 and 14 January 1867, to co-operate with the International Association 'for the furtherance of all questions affecting the interests of labour; at the same time continuing the London Trades Council as a distinct and independent body as before' (*The Times*, No. 25708, 15 January 1867). This decision was discussed at the General Council sitting of 15 January 1867. Afterwards, the contacts between the London Trades Council and the International were maintained through the General Council members who also sat on the Trades Council.

The *London Workingmen's Association* was founded in 1866 on the initiative of George Potter and his followers for the purpose of launching a movement for trade union representation in Parliament. From the start, Potter's platform was of a conciliatory character; he and his followers made advances to the workers and professed themselves champions of universal suffrage, but in fact were ready to compromise and accept the election reform on any terms. The work of Potter's association was in fact hampering the movement for universal suffrage, headed by the Reform League (see Note 228), whose programme and tactics had been evolved under Marx's influence. The association functioned up to the 1870s.

By the *Amalgamated Trades Unions* here is meant the United Kingdom Alliance of Organised Trades set up in June 1866 at the conference of trade union delegates in Sheffield. The Alliance, which embraced 53 trade unions with the membership of nearly 60,000, existed up to late 1870.— 114, 135

[176] A reference to Eichhoff's letter to Marx of 27 September 1868.— 116, 118

[177] Marx is referring to the speech made by the leader of the Party of Progress Schulze-Delitzsch at the meeting of members of the machine-builders' union in Berlin on 24 September 1868. The meeting elected twelve delegates to the general congress of the General Association of German Workers (see Note 164). A detailed report of the meeting and Schulze-Delitzsch's speech were published in *Der Social-Demokrat*, No. 113, 27 September 1868.— 116

[178] A reference to the conflict in the Paris Section of the International which was discussed at the General Council sittings on 24 January, 7, 21 and 28 February, and 7 and 14 March 1865. This was the first occasion when the General Council acted as arbiter in a section's internal affairs.

The Paris Section, which was founded at a meeting held on 28 September 1864 at St. Martin's Hall, where the International had been inaugurated, began its work in late December 1864. It was headed by an Administration comprising three correspondents approved in London, Proudhonist workers Henri Tolain, Fribourg and Charles Limousin. Alongside with Tolain's group, a lawyer and bourgeois republican Henri Lefort also claimed to be a founder and leader of the International Working Men's Association in France. Lefort's followers accused Tolain and other members of the Paris Administration of being in contact with the Bonapartists (Marx and Engels exposed this insinuation in the statement to *Der Social-Demokrat*, see present edition, Vol. 20, p. 36). Nevertheless, wishing to draw into the International the workers grouped around Lefort and trying to reduce his influence on them, Marx supported the Central Council resolution of 7 February 1865 on Lefort's appointment as 'Counsel for the literary defence' of the International in France. Those present at the meeting of the Paris Section, however, lodged a protest against this decision, and sent Tolain and Fribourg to London on 28 February to speak on this point at the Central Council meeting. The Council referred the problem to the Standing Committee, which discussed it on 4 and 6 March. Marx proposed a draft resolution which actually annulled the previously adopted decision on Lefort's appointment. This resolution has survived in his notebook (see present edition, Vol. 20, p. 330). When Marx drew it up, he tried to protect the French organisation of the International from attacks by bourgeois elements and to strengthen the leadership of the Paris Section by bringing in revolutionary proletarians. The draft formed the basis for the Central Council resolution on this issue which was passed on 7 March 1865 (see present edition, Vol. 20, p. 82).— 118

[179] A reference to a lecture delivered by Karl Vogt in September 1868 at the Schiller Institute in Manchester. See Engels' letter 'To the Directorate of the Schiller Institute' (present edition, Vol. 21).— 118

[180] An excerpt from this letter was published in English for the first time in: Karl Marx, Friedrich Engels, *Selected Letters. The Personal Correspondence, 1844-1877*, Ed. by F. J. Raddatz, Little, Brown and Company, Boston, Toronto, 1981.— 119, 239, 241, 264, 268, 295, 299, 372, 408, 416, 425, 436, 508, 519

[181] A reference to the French constitution of 14 January 1852 issued after the Bonapartist coup d'état, under which state authority was concentrated in the hands of the president elected for a term of 10 years at a general election (see also Marx's letter to J. B. Schweitzer of 13 October 1868, this volume, p. 135).— 120

[182] A reference to Wilhelm Eichhoff's letters to Marx of 27 September and 2 October 1868.— 120

[183] A reference to Wilhelm Liebknecht's letter to Marx of 2 October 1868.— 120

[184] A reference to a letter from Sigismund Borkheim to Marx of 3 October 1868.— 120

[185] A reference to Joseph Dietzgen's manuscript 'Das Wesen der menschlichen Kopfarbeit' (The Essence of Human Brainwork) sent to Marx for review from St. Petersburg, where Dietzgen lived from 1864 to 1869. The work was published for the first time in Hamburg in 1869.— 120, 126, 151, 152, 154, 173

186 Marx is referring to a letter written to him by Nikolai Danielson on 30 (18)
    September 1868, with a postscript by Nikolai Lyubavin dated 14 (2) October.
    Danielson wrote: 'The significance of your latest work— *Capital. Critique of
    Political Economy*—has prompted one of local publishers (N. Polyakov) to
    undertake its translation into Russian. The various attendant circumstances
    make it desirable to publish the second volume simultaneously with the first.
    Therefore, as the publisher's representative, I request you, should you consider
    it possible, to send me sheets of the second volume as soon as they have been
    published.'
        In his reply, Marx enclosed a note on his own literary and political activities,
    which was used in the preface to *Capital*'s Russian edition (see this volume,
    pp. 123-25 and Note 196).— 120, 123, 149

187 At the time, Marx planned to publish the second and third books of *Capital*
    ('The Process of Circulation of Capital' and 'The Process of Capitalist
    Production as a Whole') as Volume Two of *Capital* (see also Note 41).— 123,
    160, 412

188 The notes about Marx's literary and political work were used in the Preface to
    the Russian edition of Volume One of *Capital* which appeared in St. Peters-
    burg in the spring of 1872. (On the history of its translation into Russian, see Note
    196.)— 123

189 In the original Marx wrote '1847' instead of '1848'. The matter is that the
    basis of this 'Speech on the Question of Free Trade' was the material
    prepared by Marx for a speech he was to have delivered at the International
    Congress of Economists in Brussels in September 1847 (see present edition,
    Vol. 6, pp. 279-81 and 287-90 and also notes 116 and 246).
        The speech was published as a pamphlet in French at the end of January
    1848.— 124

190 Marx is referring to a series of articles by Engels 'The Armies of Europe'
    (present edition, Vol. 14) published in *Putnam's Monthly. A Magazine of
    Literature, Science, and Art* in August, September and December 1855 through
    Marx's mediation (see Marx's letter to Engels of 15 June 1855, present edition,
    Vol. 39). Marx helped Engels by collecting data on various European armies,
    the Spanish and the Neapolitan in particular, at the British Museum
    Library.— 124

191 In Britain, the different workers' societies functioning within the same industry
    were admitted to the International on equal terms.— 125

192 In his letter of 8 October 1868 Johann Baptist Schweitzer complained to Marx
    as the 'secretary of the International' about the policies pursued by Bebel,
    Liebknecht and their followers towards the General Association of German
    Workers which he headed. He mentioned the decision of the Hamburg
    Congress (see Note 104) to become affiliated, 'with the consent of the
    authorities', with the International Working Men's Association. Schweitzer
    demanded that Marx support him and help him check Bebel's and Liebknecht's
    attacks against him. Otherwise, Schweitzer threatened, he would begin 'open
    hostilities'.
        Enclosed with his letter were the Statutes of the general Trade Union
    Association founded at the general congress of the General Association of
    German Workers in Berlin (see Note 164).— 127

193 The decision to abolish the office of the General Council's President was moved
    on Marx's initiative by John Hales and adopted at the General Council meeting

of 24 September 1867. (See Marx's letter to Engels, 4 October 1867: present edition, Vol. 42.) The abolition of this post, which had been permanently held since 1864 by one of the British trade union leaders, George Odger, considerably weakened the position of the reformist wing of the International. Odger did not get any post when the appointment of officers in the Council took place. The International's Basle Congress (September 1869) approved the General Council's decision.— 128, 135

194 The address written by Marx on instructions from the General Council and approved by the Council on 13 October 1868, is not extant.— 128

195 After Volume One of *Capital* had been published, Kugelmann and Engels took considerable trouble to blow up the conspiracy of silence of bourgeois science and the bourgeois press against this work. Kugelmann's connections made it possible to distribute the book and popularise it in the democratic and bourgeois press. He managed to get published anonymously a number of reviews by Engels in the *Beobachter, Staats-Anzeiger für Württemberg* and other newspapers.— 130

196 A reference to the publication of the Russian translation of Volume One of *Capital*, which was undertaken by the St. Petersburg publisher N. Polyakov; on 30 (18) September 1868, Danielson wrote to Marx on his behalf (see this volume, pp. 123-25). At the end of 1869 it was decided that the translation would be made by Bakunin. However, the specimens he submitted were not accepted as satisfactory. Starting with the summer of 1870, the translation was being done by Lopatin, who used his stay in London to consult Marx. He translated chapters II, III and IV (in part) of the first German edition of Volume One. Late in 1870, with the translation still unfinished, Lopatin returned to Russia to help organise Chernyshevsky's escape from Siberia. By October 1871, the translation was finished by Danielson (he completed Chapter IV, and did chapters V and VI) and Lyubavin, a former fellow-student of Danielson, professor of chemistry at Moscow University (he translated Chapter I and the supplement). The first Russian edition of Volume One of *Capital*, which was also the first foreign edition, appeared in St. Petersburg on 8 April (27 March) 1872.— 130, 480

197 Marx is apparently referring to his Paris acquaintance with N. Sazonov, M. Bakunin and G. Tolstoy, a Russian landowner.— 130

198 A reference to the *Adresse de l'Association internationale des femmes, à l'Association internationale des travailleurs. Bienne, le 1er Sept. 1868*, signed on behalf of the Association by Marie Goegg, President of the Central Committee. The Address made it clear that the Association, which had by that time existed for about three months, was a feminist organisation which showed no interest in the issue of class struggle. It demanded that suffrage be extended to women, and advocated their equal rights to work and education. Its further history is unknown.— 131

199 An excerpt from this letter was published in English for the first time in: Karl Marx and Friedrich Engels, *Correspondence, 1846-1895*, London, Lawrence LTD [1934]; a more complete version was published in: Marx, Engels, *Selected Correspondence*, Moscow, Progress Publishers, 1975.— 132

200 Schulze-Delitzsch, a German bourgeois economist and a leader of the Party of Progress (see Note 317), advocated small savings banks and loan offices, and consumer and producer cooperatives based on the workers' own means with the aim of diverting the workers from the revolutionary struggle against

capital. Schulze-Delitzsch advocated harmony of capitalists' and workers' interests, asserting that cooperatives could help improve workers' conditions under capitalism and save small producers and artisans from ruin. Lassalle criticised Schulze-Delitzsch's cooperative plans and advanced his own idea of production associations set up by workers and sponsored by the Junker-bourgeois Prussian state.—133

201 A reference to a demand advanced by the Chartist movement in Britain which was entered into the People's Charter published on 8 May 1838 in the form of a Bill to be submitted to Parliament. It consists of six clauses: universal suffrage (for men over 21 years of age), annual elections to Parliament, secret ballot, equal constituencies, abolition of property qualifications for candidates to Parliament, and salaries for M.P.s. In 1839, 1842 and 1848 petitions for the Charter were rejected by Parliament.—133

202 Marx is referring to the new Regulations for handicraft trades, which extended the workers' right to form coalitions and stage strikes. On 29 May 1869 the Regulations were approved by the North German Reichstag (see also Note 324).—134

203 Between 14 and 22 September 1868, 13,000 miners were on strike in Essen. They demanded that deductions from wages be stopped and an eight-hour working day introduced. The strike ended in victory for the workers.—136

204 A reference to the distribution of Marx's book *The Poverty of Philosophy...* (see present edition, Vol. 6), which was written in 1847 in Brussels and published (1,500 copies) that same year by two publishers simultaneously, Vogler's in Brussels and Frank's in Paris, who in 1865 sold his business to publisher F. Vieweg. The publication was undertaken on a commission basis: Marx paid part of the expenses as the author and was to receive a certain sum from the sale of each copy. By 1868, the demand for the book grew steeply owing to the mounting campaign against the Proudhonist elements in the International, while the book became a bibliographical rarity. In view of this, Marx applied, in October 1868, to the Paris publisher, who, as is clear from the letter, had stopped the sales altogether. Nothing is known about the results of Lafargue's negotiations on this issue.—137, 217

205 Alexandre Besson and Victor Le Lubez (see Note 72) had sent a letter to Hermann Jung in October 1868 in which they protested against the decision of the Brussels Congress to expel Pierre Vésinier from the International (see Note 156). In their letter they also attacked Hermann Jung and Eugène Dupont, members of the General Council. On 19 October 1868, Jung informed Marx about the French Section's meeting at which he was going to defend the International.—139

206 A reference to the reactionary Prussian Law on Associations passed on 11 March 1850.—140

207 Engels is referring to the Democratic Labour Union (Der Demokratische Arbeiterverein) that was formed in October 1868 following a split in the Berlin Workers' Union, which rejected, by 32 votes against 28, the resolutions of the Nuremberg Congress (see Note 135). A leading role in the founding of the new Union belonged to Eichhoff, who kept in constant touch with Marx and was the Berlin correspondent of the General Council of the First International. On 3 November 1868, at a General Council meeting, Marx reported on the formation of the Democratic Labour Union. On Eichhoff's suggestion, the Union joined the Union of German Workers' Associations headed by Bebel and

Liebknecht, and adopted its programme based on the International's principles. The Democratic Labour Union also maintained close contacts with the Berlin Section of the International. Almost all of its members were also members of the International. To emphasise its proletarian character, two workers, Wilcke and Kämmerer, were elected its Presidents. The Democratic Labour Union actively opposed the Lassalleans. Wilhelm Liebknecht used to speak at its meetings. In 1869 it joined the Social-Democratic Workers' Party set up at the Eisenach Congress.— 140

[208] A reference to Chapter VI, 'Der Accumulationsprozess des Kapitals' of the first German edition of *Capital's* Volume One (1867). Corresponding to it in the second and subsequent German editions is Part VII. In the English edition of 1887 which was prepared by Engels this is Part VII ('The Accumulation of Capital') and Part VIII ('The So-Called Primitive Accumulation') (see present edition, Vol. 35).— 141

[209] In his letter to Marx of 15 October 1868 Kugelmann wrote about a review of *Capital* by Hansen, a Berlin professor of political economy, who said, among other things, that it was 'the most significant phenomenon of this century'. Hansen also offered Marx a professorship in political economy.— 142, 144

[210] A reference to a meeting held on 20 October 1868. It was organised by the French Section in London (see Note 72). It was held mainly by petty-bourgeois refugees headed by Pyat, who had lost contact with the International. They came out against the resolution on the bourgeois pacifist League of Peace and Freedom (see Note 271) passed by the Brussels Congress on 12 September 1868. It stated that the existence of a pacifist league claiming to be the leader of the international workers' movement is superfluous given the existence of the International Working Men's Association. It was suggested that the League should join the International and its members should become members of International's sections. On 20 October Marx wrote to the General Council about the forthcoming meeting. The Council referred the issue for consideration to its executive body, the Sub-Committee, granting it special powers for exposing the intentions of the meeting's organisers should this prove necessary.— 143

[211] Probably a reference to the strike of British tailors which began in March 1866. It was headed by the Executive Committee of the Journeymen Tailors' Protective Association formed at the national conference of British tailors held in Manchester on 12-17 March 1866. London entrepreneurs tried to recruit apprentices in Belgium, France and Switzerland through their agents. In this connection, the General Council published an appeal in these countries' newspapers urging the tailors to refuse to go to England on account of the strike under way there. The entrepreneurs' plans were foiled, and they were obliged to make concessions and raise the wages.— 143

[212] A reference to Kugelmann's letter to Marx of 24 October 1868.— 144

[213] This letter has come down to us as a copy written in English in Sigfrid Meyer's hand.— 147

[214] The General Council's credentials for August Vogt, which Marx enclosed with his letter to Meyer and Vogt of 28 October 1868, are published according to the copy made by Sigfrid Meyer on the copy of Marx's letter to Jessup of 28 October 1868.— 148

[215] In his letters to Marx of 31 October and 31 October-1 November 1868, Eichhoff cleared himself of the charge of being connected with the Prussian

police (see Note 61). Among the reasons that had led to this suspicion was an inaccurate report of Eichhoff's speech at the first meeting of the Berlin Democratic Labour Union (see Note 207) on 15 October 1868 published by *Die Zukunft* and later by the *Demokratisches Wochenblatt*, No. 43, 24 October 1868.—151, 152

216 A reference to the 'Adresse an die Demokraten Spaniens' (Address to the Democrats of Spain) issued in October 1868 on behalf of the Social-Democrats of Saxony in connection with the revolution in Spain (see Note 165). The Address was published in the supplement to the *Demokratisches Wochenblatt*, edited by Liebknecht, No. 44, 31 October 1868.—151

217 An allusion to the June 1848 uprising of Paris workers which ended in the defeat of the insurgents, and at the coup d'état accomplished in France on 2 December 1851, which established the military bourgeois dictatorship of Louis Napoleon. On 2 December 1852, the Empire was proclaimed, and Louis Bonaparte became Emperor Napoleon III.—152, 242

218 A reference to the 'Adresse au peuple et au Congrès des États-Unis d'Amérique' (Address to the People and Congress of the United States of America) which was read on 2 November 1868 at a meeting convened in London by petty-bourgeois democrats Felix Pyat, Victor Le Lubez, J. V. Weber, etc. The Address was printed by *La Cigale*, No. 45, 8 November 1868, and *L'Espiègle*, No. 45, 8 November 1868.—155

219 A reference to Borkheim's letter to Engels of 9 November 1868.—156

220 The 'gang system' mentioned here has been described by Marx on pages 684-87 of the first German edition of Volume One of *Capital* (1867). In the second (1872) and subsequent German editions, this information was to be found in Part VII, Chapter XXIII, 'The General Law of Capitalist Accumulation'. Corresponding to it in the English edition of 1887 prepared by Engels was Ch. XXV Section 5e ('The British Agricultural Proletariat') of Part VII ('The Accumulation of Capital').—156

221 The meeting convened in Paris on 10 October 1868 by French economists and journalists, including Horn, was devoted to the problem 'capital and interest from the point of view of labour'. A report of the meeting was published by *Le Figaro*, No. 285, 11 October 1868, under the heading 'Chronique de Paris'.—158

222 A reference to the subscription launched by the democratic and republican Paris press to raise money for a monument to Victor Baudin, deputy of the Legislative Assembly, who died on the barricades during the Bonapartist coup of 2 December 1851. Against the background of mounting anti-Bonapartist sentiments, the subscription assumed the nature of a mass political campaign. Its organisers had legal proceedings instituted against them on the charge of inciting hatred against the government. The trial took place on 13-14 November 1868. The accounts were published in pamphlet form under the heading 'Affaire de la souscription Baudin (The affair of Baudin's subscription) in Paris, in 1868. The monument was unveiled only in 1872.

The *banquet movement*—a campaign for an electoral reform in France in 1847, on the eve of the revolution. Bourgeois-democratic elements took an active part in it alongside the bourgeois liberals. Engels gave his opinion of this movement in a number of articles (see present edition, Vol. 6, pp. 364-66, 375-82, 385-87, 393-401, 409-11, 438-44).—159, 188, 191

223 The *Bank Charter Act* (An Act to Regulate the Issue of Bank-Notes, and for Giving to the Governor and Company of the Bank of England Certain Privileges for a Limited Period) was introduced by Robert Peel on 19 July 1844. It provided for the division of the Bank of England into two separate departments, each with its own cash account—the Banking Department, dealing exclusively with credit operations, and the Issue Department issuing bank-notes. The Act limited the quantity of bank-notes in circulation and guaranteed them with definite gold and silver reserves, which could not be used for the credit operations of the Banking Department. Further issues of bank-notes were allowed only in the event of a corresponding increase in the precious metal reserves. The issue of bank-notes by provincial banks was stopped. The Act was suspended several times by the government itself, in particular, during the economic crises of 1847, 1857 and 1866. Marx gave an analysis of the meaning and significance of the 1844 Act in a series of articles written in 1857-58 for the *New-York Daily Tribune*: 'The Vienna Note.—The United States and Europe.—Letters from Shumla.—Peel's Bank Act' (see present edition, Vol. 12), 'The Bank Act of 1844 and the Monetary Crises in England', 'The British Revulsion' (Vol. 15), 'The English Bank Act of 1844' (Vol. 16), etc. A detailed description of the Act was given by Marx in *Capital*, Vol. III (Chapter XXXIV) (Vol. 37).—159, 166

224 Marx is referring to the Chapter 'Spaltung von Profit in Zins und industriellen Profit. Das zinstragende Kapital' of his manuscript of Book Three of *Capital* written in 1864-65. In Volume Three of *Capital* published by Engels in 1894 it corresponds to the entire Part V 'Division of Profit into Interest and Profit of Enterprise. Interest-Bearing Capital' (see present edition, Vol. 37).—160

225 A reference to the confidential address of the Permanent Central Committee Bureau of the League of Peace and Freedom (see Note 271) of 22 September 1868. It was published as a leaflet signed by Gustav Vogt, the President of the Bureau and Editor-in-Chief of the League's press organ, *Les États-Unis d'Europe*. The address called on the League 'to become a *pure political expression* of great economic and social interests and principles which are now developed and spread so triumphantly by the great International Working Men's Association of Europe and America' (see also K. Marx, F. Engels, *The Alliance of Socialist Democracy and the International Working Men's Association*, present edition, Vol. 23.).—161

226 The decision to publish the resolutions of the Geneva and Brussels congresses was adopted by the General Council on 6 October 1868 on a suggestion by Lafargue and Dupont. The preparatory work was done by Eccarius, while Marx put the finishing touches and checked the translation into English. The first part of the pamphlet was published in *The Bee-Hive*, No. 371, 21 November and the second, in No. 374 on 12 December 1868. In February 1869 the resolutions were published in London in pamphlet form, under the heading: 'The International Working Men's Association. Resolutions of the Congress of Geneva, 1866, and Congress of Brussels, 1868'.—161, 221, 223

227 A reference to the bankruptcy of Overend, Gurney and Company, a major British bank. It financially ruined a large number of depositors. The matter was brought to court; the trial ended in December 1869 with the acquittal of the company directors.—161, 208, 305, 548

228 The *Reform League* was founded in London in the spring of 1865 on the initiative and with the direct participation of the International's General

Council as a political centre of the mass movement for the second election reform. The League's leading bodies—the Council and Executive Committee— included the General Council members, mainly trade-union leaders. The League's programme was drafted under the influence of Marx, who called upon the working-classes to pursue their policy independently of bourgeois parties. Unlike these parties, which confined their demands to household suffrage, the League advanced the demand for manhood suffrage. This revived Chartist slogan (see Note 201) evoked a sympathetic response among the working class and won the League the support of the trade unions, hitherto indifferent to politics. The League had branches in all major industrial towns and counties. However, the vacillations of the bourgeois radicals in its leadership, and the conciliation of the trade union leaders prevented the League from following the line chartered by the General Council. The British bourgeoisie succeeded in splitting the movement, and a moderate reform was carried out in 1867 which granted franchise only to the petty bourgeoisie and the upper layer of the working class (see Note 3).— 161, 245

229 In St. Stephen's Chapel, where the House of Commons sat between 1547 and 1834. Later, came to designate the House of Commons of the British Parliament.— 162

230 *Chassepot*—a needle-gun invented in 1866 by a French worker and named after him; the French army was supplied with this type of weapon in 1866-74.— 162, 553

231 Marx exposed the slanderous attacks of the French bourgeois newspaper *Le Constitutionnel* against the Paris workers, participants in the June 1848 uprising, in the *Neue Rheinische Zeitung* (see present edition, Vol. 7, pp. 154, 156, 479).— 162

232 *Rotten boroughs*—sparsely populated or depopulated small towns and villages in England which enjoyed the right to send representatives to Parliament since the Middle Ages. These representatives were in fact appointed by the landed aristocracy, who controlled the handful of 'free voters' who nominally elected them. The 'rotten boroughs' were disfranchised by the electoral reforms of 1832, 1867 and 1884.— 163

233 The *Mobile Guard* was set up by a decree of the Provisional Government on 25 February 1848 with the secret aim of fighting the insurgent people. Its armed units consisted mainly of lumpen-proletarians and were used to crush the June uprising of the Paris workers. Subsequently, it was disbanded on the insistence of the Bonapartists, who feared that in the event of a conflict between President Bonaparte and the republicans the Mobile Guard would side with the latter.

For Marx's description of the Mobile Guard, see his work *The Class Struggles in France, 1848 to 1850* (present edition, Vol. 10, pp. 62-63).— 164

234 Marx's article for *The Diplomatic Review* was written on request of Collet Dobson Collet, the publisher, on 9 November 1868 (see this volume, p. 159), and published under the heading 'How Mr. Gladstone's Bank Letter of 1866 Procured a Loan of Six Millions for Russia' (see present edition, Vol. 21). The editors of *The Diplomatic Review* prefaced it with a note which introduced Marx as the author of *Capital* and the *Revelations of the Diplomatic History of the 18th Century* (see present edition, vols. 35 and 15).— 166

235 The *National Sunday League*—a philanthropic educational organisation which campaigned to get the cultural establishments—museums, concert halls,

etc.—to stay open on Sundays, since the working population was unable to visit them on weekdays. Its honorary secretary was R. M. Morell, and a member of the council—the bourgeois radical Baxter Langley. The League's activities met with a strong opposition from the Anglican Church and the religious organisations which demanded a strict observance of Sundays.

The League's premises at 256, High Holborn, London, W.C. were the venue of the General Council meetings held between June 1868 and February 1872.— 166

236 A reference to the anonymous article 'Look before You Leap, and Beware of Traitors' (*Reynolds's Newspaper*, No. 949, 18 October 1868), which sharply criticised Jones' attitude to the Whigs and accused him of being a renegade. During the Parliamentary election campaign, Jones openly supported the Whig candidates from Carlisle saying that 'the Whigs had now come round to the Democrats, and joined hands with them'. The article in the *Reynolds's Newspaper* quoted Jones' remarks of more than ten years before (published by the *Democrat* newspaper of Carlisle) which did not tally with his later actions: 'The Whigs are the political adventurers; ... they are the men who keep their hands in the pockets of the people; they are tricky politicians. On each side of them stand two classes—one on each side of them, and the thief is in the middle. The one is the Tory; the other is the Radical; and the Whig—the thief—is in the middle.'— 166

237 This letter is the rough draft of Engels' reply to W. Holzenhauer's letter of 18 August 1868. Holzenhauer wrote that he had been employed by the firm of Ermen and Engels in Engelskirchen for 18 years, from the time of its foundation (see Note 238), and had been dismissed after a quarrel with Adolf von Griesheim.— 169

238 A reference to the German branch of the firm Ermen & Engels—at Engelskirchen (near Cologne) founded c. 1840 by Friedrich Engels Sr., which ran the German side of the enterprise with the assistance of Anthony Ermen. The firm had its offices in Barmen.

After their father's death in March 1860, Engels' brothers Hermann, Rudolf and Emil suggested that Frederick should give his share in the business over to them. One of the reasons they named was that he had been living abroad since 1849. Engels was to receive £10,000 in compensation to consolidate his legal and financial position in the firm of Ermen & Engels in Manchester. He became its co-owner in 1864 (see also Note 158).— 169

239 This letter was published in English in full for the first time in: Karl Marx, Friedrich Engels, *Selected Letters. The Personal Correspondence, 1844-1877*, Ed. by F. J. Raddatz, Little, Brown and Company, Boston, Toronto, 1981.— 169, 269

240 A reference to Schweitzer's reply of 2 December 1868 to Marx's letter of 13 October 1868 (see this volume, pp. 132-35). Schweitzer defended the draft Statutes of the Lassallean trade unions (which Marx had criticised) and the political course of the General Association of German Workers which he headed (see notes 104 and 164). Schweitzer declared that he had more reason for leadership of the German workers' movement than Liebknecht, and claimed that control should be concentrated in his hands. As he put it, a reconciliation between Liebknecht and him was possible only if Marx, whom both sides recognised as the 'spiritual Eminence' should personally intervene to support Schweitzer against Liebknecht.— 172, 175, 176

241 A reference to the letter from the Saxon miners of Lugau, Nieder-Würschnitz and Oelsnitz, dated 15 November 1868, which expressed their wish to join the International, was sent to Marx and read at the General Council meeting of 24 November 1868 (see Note 281).—172, 176

242 In his letter to the General Council of 29 November 1868, written on behalf of the Central Committee of the German-speaking sections in Geneva, Johann Philipp Becker wrote that Bebel, President of the Union of the German Workers' Associations (see Note 169), had stated in his circular letter that societies could join the International Working Men's Association without paying membership dues. Bebel's purpose in doing so was to popularise the resolution on joining the International passed by the Nuremberg Congress (see Note 135). This question was discussed at the General Council meeting on 15 December 1868, at which Marx stated that he had requested Liebknecht to remove that point from the circular letter.—172

243 A reference to the formation of a new Cabinet under Gladstone. On that occasion, *The Times* featured an editorial which contained, among other things, predictions about the appointments likely to be taken up by Lowe and Bright (see *The Times*, No. 26300, 5 December 1868).—176

244 Above the address in the original is the oval seal of the General (Central) Council with the inscription: 'International Working Men's Association, Central Council, London'.—177, 195

245 A reference to Sigfrid Meyer's letter of 24 November 1868, which was a reply to Marx's letter of 28 October 1868 (see this volume, pp. 148-49). Meyer wrote about the progress of the labour movement in the USA and the work he was doing with August Vogt to set up a German Section of the International in New York.—177

246 A reference to the cotton crisis produced by the cessation of cotton deliveries from the USA due to the blockade of the slave-owning Southern states by the Northern states' navy during the Civil War of 1861-65. The cotton famine in Britain began just before the overproduction crisis and merged with it. Since 1862, and for two or three years, three-quarters of the cotton mills in Lancashire, Cheshire, and some other counties stood totally or partially idle.—179

247 Marx quotes Kugelmann's letter of 7 December 1868 that contained Joseph Dietzgen's address for which Marx had asked (see this volume, p. 173) and some information about him. Enclosed with the letter was Dietzgen's photograph and W. A. Freund's letter.—180

248 A reference to the lecture 'On the Physical Basis of Life' delivered by Th. H. Huxley in Edinburgh on 8 November 1868. Later, on 1 February 1869, it was published in *The Fortnightly Review*, No. XXVI.—183, 242

249 See Note 247.—184

250 This letter is a rough draft of Marx's reply to the letter from the firm of Asher & Co., Foreign Booksellers & Publishers, 12 December 1868. It contained a request for a copy of Marx's pamphlet *Herr. Vogt*, which was not available in London.
The fair copy of the letter has not been found.—185

251 A reference to the letter from A. A. Serno-Solovyevich to Marx of 20 November 1868, in which he requested Marx, on behalf of the commission

preparing the workers' newspaper *L'Égalité*, to be a permanent correspondent of this printed organ of the French Section of the International Working Men's Association.— 186

252 The *Brimstone Gang* —a students' association at the University of Jena in the 1770s which was notorious for its brawls; subsequently the expression became widespread. In 1849-50, it was the jocular nickname of the group of German petty-bourgeois émigrés in Geneva. In 1859, petty-bourgeois democrat Karl Vogt made a number of slanderous statements in which he associated the activities of the Brimstone Gang with Marx and his followers. Marx refuted his allegations in his pamphlet *Herr Vogt* (see present edition, Vol. 17, pp. 28-37).— 186

253 A reference to the blockade of the Southern ports, from which cotton was shipped to England, declared by Lincoln on 19 April 1861. The blockade, which lasted till August 1865, was not very effective, however, since contraband trade developed between the Southern states and England and also between the South and the North. Liverpool played a special role in the smuggling of commodities between England and the Confederation: for the first two years of the war 31 thousand bales of pressed cotton were delivered there. (See K. Marx, 'The British Cotton Trade' and 'The Crisis in England', present edition, Vol. 19, pp. 17-20 and 53-56.)— 186

254 Marx refers to the speech made by Louis Michel on 13 November 1851 in the Legislative Assembly (see *Le Moniteur universel*, No. 318, 14 November 1851, supplement 1) concerning the Bill introduced on 6 November 1851 by the royalists Le Flô, Baze and Panat, questors of the Legislative Assembly (deputies of the Assembly in charge of economic and financial matters and security). The Bill, which gave the Chairman of the Legislative Assembly the right to summon troops, was rejected on 17 November. When the vote was taken, the Montagne supported the Bonapartists, seeing the royalists as the principal danger.— 188

255 A reference to the meeting of the deputies of the Party of Order at the French Legislative Assembly held in the Mayor's office of Paris' 10th district on 2 December 1851. It adopted a resolution on Louis Napoleon's resignation from the post of President and the transition of power to the Legislative Assembly. The deputies refused to apply to workers for support. This attempt at legalised opposition to the coup d'état was immediately suppressed by the police and the troops. Participants in the meeting were arrested.

  A detailed report of the meeting was published in: E. Ténot, *Paris en décembre 1851. Étude historique sur le coup d'état,* Paris, 1868, pp. 142-64.— 188, 191

256 A reference to the Frankfurt Parliament or the German National Assembly, which was convened after the March revolution in Germany and first met on 18 May 1848 in Frankfurt am Main. Its principal goal was to overcome the political fragmentation of the country and work out a German constitution. The liberal deputies, who were in the majority, turned the Assembly into a mere debating club. It did not dare call upon the people to rebuff the onslaught of counter-revolution and defend the constitution. When the major German states recalled their deputies, and the authorities of Frankfurt am Main banned meetings within the city limits, the left-wing elements moved to Stuttgart and tried to launch a legal campaign in defence of the imperial constitution, but were dispersed by the troops on 18 June 1849. Marx and Engels severely criticised the activities of the Frankfurt National Assembly in the *Neue Rheinische Zeitung* (see present edition, vols. 7, 8 and 9).— 189

257 This refers to the Programme and Rules of the International Alliance of Socialist Democracy (Programme et Règlement de l'Alliance Internationale de la Démocratie Socialiste), founded by Mikhail Bakunin, in Geneva in October 1868. Besides Bakunin, members of its Provisional Committee were Brosset, Duval, Guétat, Perron, Zagorsky and Johann Philipp Becker. In 1868 leaflets in French and German containing these documents were published in Geneva. On 29 November, Becker, who shortly afterwards broke with Bakunin, sent the Alliance's Programme and Rules to the General Council for approval. On 15 December, the General Council spoke against the admission of the Alliance to the International Working Men's Association, and on 22 December unanimously approved, with insignificant amendments, a circular letter 'The International Working Men's Association and the International Alliance of Socialist Democracy' (see present edition, Vol. 21, pp. 34-36) written by Marx and approved by Engels, which exposed the Alliance's wish to split the workers' movement (see this volume, p. 192). The circular letter was sent out to all the sections of the International as a confidential communication.

For the text of the Programme and Rules of the International Alliance of Socialist Democracy with Marx's remarks, see present edition, Vol. 21, pp. 207-11.— 190, 191, 201, 211, 218, 413, 424, 489

258 After the victory of the bourgeois-democratic revolution in France in February 1848, foreigners residing in Paris conceived the idea of setting up armed legions for the purpose of establishing republics in their home countries. Marx and Engels were resolutely opposed to the export of revolution as an adventurist and unsound venture which doomed the revolutionary forces to destruction. A case in point was the fate of the Belgian republican legion which was making its way home from Paris and was ambushed by Belgian government troops on 29 March 1849 immediately after crossing the French border near the village of Risquons-Tout (see also Engels' article 'The Antwerp Death Sentences', present edition, Vol. 7, pp. 404-06).— 195

259 In November 1868, the reformist trade union leaders in Britain (Applegarth, etc.) took part in the setting up of a committee for the organisation on behalf of the workers of a banquet in honour of the American Ambassador in London Reverdy Johnson. On 1 December 1868, the General Council made public the committee's letter which suggested that the Council should send its representative to the banquet. Marx, who was opposed to the workers' participation in the organisation of such a function, said that Johnson 'did not represent the working classes of America [and that] the working classes ought not to go in the wake of the upper and middle classes'. The General Council resolved to send Robert Shaw and Hermann Jung to the committee's organisational meeting to campaign against this sort of undertaking. Thanks to the steps taken by the General Council representatives, the attempt to give a reception in honour of Johnson on behalf of the workers failed.— 195

260 An excerpt from this letter was published in the Sotheby Parke Bernet and C° catalogue on 19 April 1977.— 196

261 Marx apparently sent his daughter Laura a volume of poetry by Rückert, a German Romantic poet, whose work was influenced by Goethe's Oriental poetry.— 196

262 The Corn Laws (first introduced in the fifteenth century) imposed high import duties on agricultural produce in the interests of landowners in order to maintain high prices for these products on the home market. In 1838 the

Manchester factory owners Cobden and Bright founded the Anti-Corn Law League, which demanded the lifting of the corn tariffs and urged unlimited freedom of trade with the aim of weakening the economic and political power of the landed aristocracy and reducing workers' wages. The struggle between industrial bourgeoisie and the landed aristocracy over the Corn Laws ended in 1846 with their repeal.— 196

263 Marx refers to the second section of Chapter VI in the first German edition (1867) of Volume One of *Capital* entitled 'Die s.g. ursprüngliche Accumulation'. In the second (1872) and subsequent German editions the structure of the volume underwent changes. The above-mentioned Chapter VI came to form Part VII, while the second section of it became Chapter XXIV. Corresponding to this section in the English edition of 1887 prepared by Engels are chapters XXVI-XXXII, Part VIII ('The So-Called Primitive Accumulation', see present edition, Vol. 35).— 197

264 A reference to Bakunin's letter to Marx of 22 December 1868 (see *Die Neue Zeit*, Bd. I, No. 1, Stuttgart, 1900-1901, S. 6-8).— 198, 202

265 De Paepe took a firm stand on the policy of Bakunin and his followers who intended to split and disorganise the International. In a letter of 16 January 1869, addressed to the initiating committee of the International Alliance of Socialist Democracy (see Note 257), De Paepe criticised the activities of the Bakuninists and their programme and supported the decision of the General Council on the Alliance passed on 22 December 1868 (see present edition, Vol. 21, pp. 34-36).— 198

266 Marx is referring to the economic struggle of the Swiss weavers and building workers, which began on 9 November 1868 with the strike of the ribbon-weavers and dyers in Basle and lasted until the spring of 1869. Marx described it in detail in the 'Report of the General Council to the Fourth Annual Congress of the International Working Men's Association' (see present edition, Vol. 21, pp. 68-82).— 198, 199, 203, 209

267 A reference to the meeting of the General Council Sub-Committee held on Saturday, 2 January 1869, which discussed the question of the lockouts declared by the textile manufacturers in Rouen and Basle (see notes 266, 272).— 198

268 Herzen announced his decision not to take any further part in the publication of the *Kolokol* (The Bell) in 'Lettre à N. Ogareff' in No. 14-15, 1 December 1868.— 200

269 *Seven Dials* was a poor district in London between Charing Cross and Oxford Street. The place got its name because on this crossing of seven streets once stood a pillar surmounted by seven dials, one for each street. The pillar was removed in 1773.— 201

270 The 'Provisional Rules of the Association' written by Marx (see present edition, Vol. 20), which the General Council unanimously approved on 1 November 1864, was published in English, together with the 'Inaugural Address', as a pamphlet entitled *Address and Provisional Rules of the Working Men's International Association...* in London in November 1864, and in *The Bee-Hive Newspaper*, No. 161, 12 November 1864. The translation of the 'Provisional Rules' into French made in late 1864-early 1865 contained a number of inaccuracies through the fault of the Proudhonist leaders of the Paris Section. The new and corrected French translation was made by Charles

Longuet under Marx's supervision and was included in the pamphlet *Manifeste de l'Association Internationale des Travailleurs suivi du Règlement provisoire*, which appeared in Brussels in 1866. The Geneva Congress of 1866 approved the Rules (General Rules) and amplified them with Regulations (later Administrative Regulations). These documents were published in late November 1866 in the pamphlet *Association Internationale des Travailleurs. Statuts et réglement*, Londres, 1866 (see present edition, Vol. 20, p. 441). However, the publication remained little known, as out of the 1,000 copies issued, 800 were held up at a frontier post on their way to France. A separate edition of the Rules and Regulations in English appeared in London in 1867 under the heading 'Rules of the International Working Men's Association', London, 1867.—202

271 The *League of Peace and Freedom* was a pacifist organisation set up in 1867 in Switzerland with the active participation of Victor Hugo and Giuseppe Garibaldi. In 1867-68, Bakunin took part in its work. At the outset the League, influenced by Bakunin, tried to use the workers' movement and the International Working Men's Association for its own ends. Voicing the anti-militarist sentiments of the people, the League's leaders, however, approached peace action from a pacifist stand, refused to reveal the social causes of wars and not infrequently reduced anti-militarist actions to mere declarations. The League's Inaugural Congress was scheduled for 9 September 1867 (originally 5 September) in Geneva to coincide with the conclusion of the Lausanne Congress of the International (2-8 September 1867). At the General Council meeting of 13 August (see *The Bee-Hive Newspaper*, 17 August 1867), Marx spoke against the International's official participation in the League's Inaugural Congress, since this would have signified approval of its bourgeois programme, but suggested that some members of the International should attend the Congress on their own to try and make it adopt revolutionary and democratic decisions. The Lausanne Congress ignored the decision of the General Council and, influenced by petty-bourgeois elements, resolved to be officially represented at the League's congress. Marx's tactics against the League of Peace and Freedom were fully approved by the Brussels Congress of the International (see Note 138).—202, 489

272 In December 1868, following the wage cuts in the cotton yarns and goods industry, a wave of strikes began in various regions of France, the most important being the one in Sotteville-lès-Rouen. The Rouen Section of the International arranged for the strikers to receive support from workers in other industries in Paris and Rouen. The Rouen Section applied for aid to the General Council. The question of the strikes in Rouen and Vienne was discussed on 5 January 1869 at the Council meeting. On Marx's proposal, it was unanimously decided to voice a protest against the arbitrary rule of the French manufacturers (the resolution was published in *The Bee-Hive*, No. 379, 16 January 1869). The Council requested the British workers to render aid to the locked-out workers of Rouen and took other steps to give material aid to the strikers.

A detailed account of the strike in Rouen was presented in the 'Report of the General Council to the Fourth Annual Congress of the International Working Men's Association' written by Marx (see present edition, Vol. 21, pp. 73-74).—203

273 A reference to the Polish Insurrection Cross, the symbol of the Polish people's national liberation struggle, given to Jenny Marx on her birthday. Since late

1867 Jenny wore this cross on a green ribbon, the national colour of Ireland, as a sign of mourning for the Fenians executed on 23 November 1867.—206, 214

274 On Marx's advice, Borkheim wrote eleven articles brought together in the series *Russische Briefe* (Russian letters): on the Russian railways (I-VII), on Mikhail Bakunin (VIII-X), and on the Russian press (XI). They appeared in *Die Zukunft* in January-August and November of 1869 and in February and March of 1870. In a letter to Engels of 19 January 1869, Borkheim asked him to recommend books for use in his work on the articles.—206, 436

275 This letter is written on a form with the letterhead: 'Memorandum from *Ermen & Engels* to M'.—206, 207

276 A reference to the Constitution of the Swiss Confederation adopted on 12 September 1848. It granted the population the right to take part in exercising legislative power in the forms of Volksanregung and Initiativbegehren. In place of a former Diet, the central legislative body, the Federal Assembly, consisting of a National Council and Council of States, was set up.—209

277 A reference to the fact that up to August 1869, the *Demokratisches Worchenblatt* edited by Liebknecht remained a joint press organ of the German People's Party (see Note 38) and the Union of German Workers' Associations (see Note 169).—210

278 Marx's work *The Eighteenth Brumaire of Louis Bonaparte* (see present edition, Vol. 11), in which, following the events, Marx revealed the essence of Bonapartism, drew attention of the leaders of the working-class movement in the 1860s. In 1864 Wilhelm Liebknecht tried to arrange a new publication of the work in Switzerland. Sophie von Hatzfeldt, Lassalle's friend and associate, offered assistance. Marx, however, turned it down (see Marx to Sophie von Hatzfeldt, 22 December 1864, present edition, Vol. 42).

In 1865, Marx apparently had the idea of publishing a collection of his and Engels' works in Germany. The edition was to include also *The Eighteenth Brumaire...* (see Marx to Wilhelm Liebknecht, 24 June 1865, present edition, Vol. 42). Marx and Engels planned to enlist the services of Otto Meissner, the publisher of Volume One of *Capital* (see Engels to Marx, 27 April 1867, present edition, Vol. 42). The negotiations were, however, protracted. Against the background of the exacerbating crisis of the Second Empire in France, Marx stepped up his efforts to get a second edition of the work printed. Already in late January 1869, Marx, who on 27 January had received Meissner's agreement to undertake a second edition of *The Eighteenth Brumaire...*, sent him a corrected version (see this volume, Marx to Ludwig Kugelmann, 11 May 1869, and p. 222). The second authorised German edition of this work appeared in Hamburg in late July 1869.—211

279 Marx addressed the same request concerning his work *The Eighteenth Brumaire of Louis Bonaparte* to a number of his friends, including Borkheim. It was F. Wohlauer who sent Marx a copy of the book probably together with the letter of 1 February 1869.—211

280 Marx refers to Gustav Adolf Bachmann's letter of 31 January 1869 with the request of the Lugau workers to be affiliated with the International Working Men's Association. See *Die I. Internationale in Deutschland*, Berlin, 1964, S. 295.—214, 219

281 Engels wrote the 'Report on the Miners' Guilds in the Coalfields of Saxony' (see present edition, Vol. 21) at Marx's request on the basis of material sent in by

the Saxon miners from Lugau, Nieder-Würschnitz and Oelsnitz, who informed the General Council and Marx personally of their wish to join the International (see Note 241). The report, which Engels had written in English, was read at the General Council meeting of 23 February 1869. An abridged version appeared in *The Bee-Hive*, No. 385, 27 February 1869. Other English newspapers, including *The Times*, *The Daily News* and *The Morning Advertiser*, refused to carry the report. In early March 1869 Marx himself translated it into German, and it was published in *Der Social-Demokrat*, No. 33, 17 March, *Demokratisches Wochenblatt*, No. 12 (supplement), 20 March, and *Die Zukunft*, nos. 67 and 68, 20 and 21 March 1869.—214, 219, 220, 221, 223, 226, 227, 230, 244

282 As is clear from Lafargue's letter to Marx's wife Jenny, written before 12 February 1869, the matter under discussion was Lafargue's negotiations with the French authoress Clémence Royer about the translation of Volume One of *Capital* into French. The negotiations proved unproductive. On the translation of *Capital* into French, see also notes 309 and 441.—217

283 A reference to the plan for the publication of a French daily political newspaper *La Renaissance*, to be started in 1869. Among the proposed staff members were Blanquists (Jaclard, Tridon etc.) and republicans (Ranc). A major contribution to the work was made by Lafargue, who wrote two articles, one a critique of Proudhonism, and the other a concise exposition of the *Manifesto of the Communist Party* (the manuscripts are not extant). Lafargue tried to persuade Marx to contribute to the newspaper. Due to a shortage of funds the project fell through, but the preparations had gone so far that in early 1869, a prospectus 'Pour paraître le 24 février [18]69. La Renaissance, Journal politique hebdomadaire' was brought out.—217, 220, 225, 287, 290, 308, 316

284 The Berne Congress of the League of Peace and Freedom (see Note 271) took place on 21-25 September 1868.—218

285 A reference to the preparatory materials for Borkheim's articles 'Michael Bakunin' (VIII-X) in the *Russische Briefe* series (see Note 274), brought out by *Die Zukunft* on 21 July, 13 and 15 August and 2 November 1869. Among the materials used by Borkheim was Bakunin's 'Address to the Russian, Polish and All Slavic Friends' (printed in the *Kolokol*, No. 123-124, supplement, 15 February 1862).—219, 223

286 Engels visited Marx in London from around 4 to 7 February 1869.—222

287 Marx is referring to the book: J. L. Foster, *An Essay on the Principles of Commercial Exchanges between England and Ireland*, London, 1804. The source of this research was the material collected by two Parliamentary commissions, the Secret Committee of the House of Lords and the Select Committee of the House of Commons, appointed in 1797 to investigate the affairs of the Bank of England in connection with the operation of the so-called Bank Restriction Act, promulgated on 3 May 1797. It introduced a compulsory exchange-rate of the Bank of England bank-notes and cancelled the exchange of bank-notes into gold. In 1819, the British Parliament adopted a new law which re-established the exchange of bank-notes into gold. The exchange was completely restored by 1821.

A synopsis of Foster's book made by Marx is extant. Marx made it in his notebook of excerpts entitled 'Heft II. 1869' probably right after he had received the book.—224

288 This is probably an error. W. Blake's work *Observations on the Principles Which Regulate the Course of Exchange; and on the Present Depreciated State of the Currency*, which deals with the difference between the nominal and the real rate of exchange, appeared in London in 1810. In 1802, a book by W. T. Thornton *An Inquiry into the Nature and Effects of the Paper Credit of Great Britain* was published in London. W. Blake repeatedly refers to Thornton's work in the sections on the real and nominal rate of exchange. Marx's synopses of the works by Blake and Thornton have come down to us. They are to be found in Marx's II and VI London notebooks of excerpts of 1850-53 (see MEGA², IV/7, S. 115-27 and 506-27).

Marx mentions William Petty's works dealing with the difference between the nominal and the real rate of exchange in the *Theories of Surplus-Value* (see present edition, Vol. 34).—224

289 Marx is referring to the decision of the British Government to pardon some of the Fenians who took part in the 1867 uprising. A statement to this effect was made by C. Fortescue-Parkinson, Chief Secretary for Ireland, at the House of Commons on 22 February 1869 (see *The Times*, No. 26368, 23 February 1869). Under the new decision, 49 out of 81 convicts, at that time undergoing penal servitude in Australia and Great Britain, were liable to unconditional pardon. 'The class to which he referred might be described as partly young men, hot-headed and easily led, literally the dupes and tools of others and incapable, as far as can be ascertained, of doing mischief to the public hereafter, if undirected,' wrote *The Times*.—224

290 Marx likens Gladstone's cabinet (1868-74) to the 'Cabinet of All the Talents'; this ironic name had been given to the notorious Coalition Ministry of Lord Aberdeen (1852-55). A characteristic of the 'Cabinet of All the Talents' is contained in the article by Marx and Engels, 'The Late British Government' (see present edition, Vol. 13, p. 620).—224

291 A reference to the negotiations on the payment of damages inflicted on the United States by Britain, which during the American Civil War of 1861-65 rendered assistance to the insurgent slave-owning Southern states, specifically, by equipping warships for them. Among these, the principal one was the *Alabama*, which operated against the Northerners from August 1862 to July 1864. On 23 November 1868, representatives of the USA and Great Britain signed a convention to cover all Anglo-American claims since 1853 but ignoring those of the *Alabama*. The dispute was finally settled on 14 September 1872, when the Geneva tribunal ruled that Britain should pay $15.5 mln to the United States.—225

292 Marx quotes a translation into Scots made by John Bellenden of a Scottish 16th century chronicle originally written by Hector Boece, a poet and chronicler. The translation was published in Edinburgh in 1536 under the title *The History and Chronicles of Scotland* and reprinted in 1821. The original, written in Latin, first appeared in Paris in 1527 under the title *Scotorum Historiae a prima gentis origine cum aliarum et rerum et gentium illustratione non vulgari* and reprinted, with supplements, in 1574.—226, 230

293 A reference to *La loi relatif à des mesures de sûreté générale* (Law on Public Security Measures) known as *La loi des suspects* (Suspects Law) adopted by the Corps législatif on 19 February and promulgated on 28 February 1858. It gave the Emperor and his government unlimited power to exile to different parts of France or Algeria or to banish altogether from French territory any person suspected of hostility to the Second Empire.—230

294 A reference to Liebknecht's statement of 18 February published by the *Demokratisches Wochenblatt*, No. 8, 20 February 1869. In that statement, Liebknecht proposed to appoint the General Council the arbiter in the conflict between Schweitzer and his General Association of German Workers on the one hand, and Bebel, Liebknecht and the workers' unions they headed, on the other. The note that Schweitzer had refused to recognise the General Council as arbiter appeared in *Der Social-Demokrat*, No. 24, 24 February 1869.—230, 234, 405

295 Wilhelm Hasenclever was elected to the North German Reichstag at the by-elections of 25 January 1869 not in Essen but in the Duisburg constituency. He received 6,792 votes while Dr. Hammacher, a National-Liberal, and Landrat Keßler polled 2,665 and 2,142 votes respectively (4,807 in all). As the source of the information about the outcome of the elections Engels used *Der Social-Demokrat*, 28 February 1869, which mistakenly stated that Hasenclever's superiority amounted to 992 votes.—230

296 In a letter of 14 February 1869, Kugelmann advised Marx to send an autographed copy of Volume One of *Capital* to A. Quételet, probably hoping to prompt the latter to contribute a review to the press. Kugelmann was impressed by Quételet's book *Zur Naturgeschichte der Gesellschaft...*, Hamburg, 1856, which he quoted in his letter to Marx.—232

297 A reference to A. Quételet's books *Sur l'homme et le développement de ses facultés, ou Essai de physique sociale*, Tomes I-II, Paris, 1835 (Marx used the English translation published in Edinburgh in 1842) and *Du système social et de lois, qui le régissent*, Paris, 1848. Extracts are extant which Marx copied out of these books in 1851 and probably in 1865-66.—232

298 The *Liberal Union* (l'Union Libérale), a coalition of bourgeois republicans, Orleanists and a part of the Legitimists formed as a result of their joint opposition to the Empire during the 1863-64 election campaign to the Corps législatif. Another attempt to form a liberal union at the time of the 1869 election campaign failed owing to dissent between the parties which had comprised the coalition in 1863. Moderate bourgeois republicans (Jules Favre, Jules Simon and others) advocated a union with the monarchists and supported the Orleanist Dufaure who, however, lost the elections.—232

299 A reference to the second letter of the Alliance of Socialist Democracy Central Bureau (see Note 257) of 27 February 1869, a reply to the General Council's circular letter which contained a refusal to admit the Alliance to the International Working Men's Association as an independent international organisation. The Alliance voiced its readiness to disband if the General Council approved its Programme and agreed to admit individual sections of the Alliance to the International.

Marx received the Alliance's address from Eccarius, who enclosed it with his letter of 4 March 1869.—235, 240

300 Marx discussed the draft of the reply 'The General Council of the International Working Men's Association to the Central Bureau of the International Alliance of Socialist Democracy' with Engels; it was unanimously approved by the Council at the meeting of 9 March 1869. The document was written by Marx in English and French (see present edition, Vol. 21), and confidentially communicated to the corresponding secretaries of the International's sections. The document was published for the first time in 1872, in the private circular of the General Council *Fictitious Splits in the International* (see present edition, Vol. 23).—235, 237

301 On the insistence of the General Council, Article 2 of the Alliance's Programme was changed in April 1869 to read as follows: 'It is above all working for the complete and final abolition of classes and for the political, economic and social equalisation of persons of both sexes.'—236, 491

302 The second edition of Engels' *The Peasant War in Germany* (see present edition, Vol. 10) was published in Leipzig in October 1870 as a separate pamphlet with the author's preface, which highlighted the role of the peasantry as an ally of the proletariat (see present edition, Vol. 21).—237

303 Marx's work *The Eighteenth Brumaire of Louis Bonaparte* was translated into French after Marx's death by the French socialist Edouard Fortin. The translation was published in the central organ of the Workers' Party of France *Le Socialiste* (Paris) in January-November 1891. It appeared as a separate edition that same year in Lille: *Le Dixhuit Brumaire de Louis Bonaparte* par Karl Marx.—238

304 Engels refers to Wilhelm Angerstein's letter of 9 March 1868, in which the latter requested him to contribute to a new Austrian workers' newspaper. On 11 March 1868 Marx received an offer from Angerstein to contribute to the Viennese newspapers *Der Telegraph* and *Arbeiter-Zeitung*. See Engels to Marx, 13 March, and Marx to Engels, 14 March 1868 (present edition, Vol. 42).—238

305 Following in the steps of the ribbon-weavers, the Basle dyers also went on strike on 9 November 1868 (see Note 266). The strike lasted until spring of 1869 and developed into a campaign for the existence of the International in Basle, where its next congress was to be held by decision of the Brussels Congress. In many countries, members of the International launched a mass campaign of solidarity with the striking Basle workers.

   Apart from the 'Bericht über die Arbeiterbewegung in Basel' published in *Der Vorbote* for December 1868, the events were described by Johann Philipp Becker in his pamphlet *Die Internationale Arbeiter-Association und die Arbeiter-bewegung in Basel im Winter 1868 auf 1869*, Genf, 1869.—238

306 In a letter to Marx of 8 March 1869, Otto Meissner wrote that the printing of the second German edition of *The Eighteenth Brumaire of Louis Bonaparte* had been postponed for commercial reasons (the time between the New Year and Easter being unfavourable for book-publishing, while later, Marx could have counted on proofs).—239, 241

307 A reference to three articles by Marx, 'The Defeat of June 1848', 'June 13, 1849' and 'Consequences of June 13, 1849' published in 1850 in the *Neue Rheinische Zeitung. Politisch-ökonomische Revue*, nos 1, 2 and 3, which later formed the principal part of the book *The Class Struggles in France, 1848 to 1850* (see present edition, Vol. 10, pp. 45-131).

   In 1895, Engels reprinted the articles from the *Revue* in German with his introduction (see present edition, Vol. 27).—241, 242

308 When he was about to travel to Karlsbad for a cure, Marx made an attempt to become a British subject in August 1874, as a precaution against possible reprisals by Austrian authorities. In Austria, as in a number of other European countries, members of the workers' and democratic movement could be taken to court for merely corresponding with Marx. A Special Report of the Metropolitan Police Office, Scotland Yard, is extant which was drawn up in connection with Marx's application for citizenship and in which Marx is characterised as follows: '... he is the notorious German agitator, the head of

the International Society, and an advocate of Communistic principles. This man has not been loyal to his own King and Country.'

Marx's request was not granted for reasons which had probably not been explained to him.—243, 248, 563

309 Marx attached considerable importance to the publishing of the French translation of *Capital*. Ever since 1867, negotiations with Élisée Reclus through Victor Schily had been under way in Paris. Reclus undertook to do the translation in collaboration with Moses Hess. Judging from Schily's letter to Marx of 24 January 1868, Élisée Reclus and Moses Hess intended not so much to translate *Capital* as to abridge it in order to adapt it to the needs and tastes of the French public. The negotiations, which lasted for almost three years, were unproductive. In early 1868, an offer to translate *Capital* came from Jósef Cwierczakiewicz (alias Card), a Polish émigré in Geneva. Marx turned the offer down (see present edition, Vol. 42, p. 528, 532-33). In December 1868 Lafargue entered into negotiations with the French authoress Clémence Royer over a translation of *Capital* (see Note 282).

For subsequent attempts to get *Capital* translated into French, see Note 441.—243

310 See below for a letter from Hirsch to Kugelmann of 8 February and Kugelmann's letter to Marx of 22 March 1869.—249

311 A reference to August Bebel's letter to Marx of 27 March 1869 written in connection with the dispute between Bebel and Liebknecht, on the one hand, and Schweitzer, on the other, at the congress of the General Association of German Workers held in Barmen-Elberfeld on 28-31 March 1869. Pressured by the workers, Schweitzer was obliged to meet half-way the demand of the Association's Leipzig members for an open discussion with Liebknecht, and for his and Bebel's presence at the Barmen-Elberfeld congress (see Note 318). Afraid of losing his prestige in the Association, Schweitzer intended to submit for discussion a proposal on establishing closer contacts with the International. Bebel, who had with Liebknecht arrived at Barmen-Elberfeld on the eve of the congress, warned Marx about Schweitzer's demagogic manoeuvres in the above-mentioned letter of 27 March 1869: 'We have heard so much about Schweitzer's mean tricks here that our hair is standing on end. It is now abundantly clear that Schweitzer has proposed the International's programme solely for the purpose of dealing us a strong blow and splitting up or winning over to his side the majority of the opposition. I request you therefore on my behalf, and also on that of Liebknecht and our other friends, to ignore for the time being the request to approve the corresponding decision of the congress or at least to give Schweitzer a very cautious reply.'—249, 250

312 Seeking to stem the growth of the opposition in the General Association of German Workers Schweitzer proposed to join the International Working Men's Association at the general congress in Barmen-Elberfeld (see notes 311 and 318). His proposal, which was published on 3 February by *Der Social-Demokrat*, may be summed up as follows: 'a) the Association shares the Programme and goals of the International Working Men's Association;

'b) if the Association does not join the International, this will be solely due to the Law on Associations operating in Germany;

'c) the Association considers itself under obligation to work for a repeal of this law and the realisation of a full and unlimited right to form unions and hold assemblies; and especially to popularise the principle according to which the state has no right to use its laws to prevent a free development of a peaceful workers' movement;

'd) until it becomes possible to join the International, the Association will try, as far as it can, to remain in real accord and maintain real cooperation with the International.'

Schweitzer's proposal was approved by the general congress with an amendment introduced by Bremer, the head of the International's Magdeburg Section:

'e) each member of the General Association of German Workers has a right to be a member of the International Working Men's Association.'

In actual fact, Schweitzer refused to cooperate with Liebknecht and Bebel in uniting the German working-class movement under the International. The General Association of German Workers did not join the International.— 249

313 Marx is referring to Joseph Dietzgen's letter of 20 March 1869, in which he wrote about the success of his work in setting up a section of the International Working Men's Association in Siegburg and its environs.— 249

314 Engels is referring to his 'Report on the Miners' Guilds in the Coalfields of Saxony' (see present edition, Vol. 21, and this volume, Note 281). *Die Zukunft* published it on 20 and 21 March 1869, ascribing it to Marx and providing it with an editorial comment: 'The General Council of the International Working Men's Association has resolved to publish the *following report by Karl Marx*, Secretary of the General Council for Germany, both in the English original and the German translation.'— 250

315 *The Bee-Hive*, No. 390, 3 April 1869, carried a report on the conference of cooperative societies held in Leeds at which Lloyd Jones, a figure in the British cooperative movement, made a speech on the need to set up a joint press organ of cooperatives and trade-unions, and proposed to call it the *Citizen Newspaper*. The project had not been carried out.— 251, 253

316 Between 1867 and 3 April 1869, Engels' domicile was at 25 Dover Street; he referred to 86 Mornington Street, the house he rented for Lizzy Burns and where he himself lived most of the time since August 1864, as his 'unofficial address'. From 3 April and until September 1870 when he moved to London, Engels' domicile was at 86 Mornington Street.— 251

317 A reference to the members of the German Party of Progress founded in 1861. Among its most prominent members were Waldeck, Virchow, Schulze-Delitzsch, Forckenbeck and Hoverbeck. The Party advocated German unification under Prussia, the convocation of an all-German parliament, and the establishment of a liberal ministry accountable to the Chamber of Deputies. Frightened by the possibility of a popular revolution, it did not support the basic democratic rights, i.e., universal suffrage and freedom of the press, association and assembly. In 1866, its Right wing broke away to form a National-Liberal Party which capitulated before the Bismarck Government.— 252

318 A reference to the dispute between Liebknecht, Bebel and Schweitzer at the congress of the General Association of German Workers held in Barmen-Elberfeld on 28-31 March 1869 (see Note 311). Bebel and Liebknecht accused Schweitzer of having contacts with the Bismarck Government and of attempts to prevent the formation of a united workers' party in Germany. The congress showed that Schweitzer's authority had been undermined: 14 delegates representing 4,635 of the Association's members refused to give him a vote of

confidence, while 42 delegates with 7,400 votes gave such a vote. The congress adopted a number of resolutions aimed at restricting Schweitzer's dictatorial powers and making the internal life of the Association more democratic: in addition to the President, it was to be headed by a board of twelve members and its seat was to be in Hamburg. A proposal was moved to convene a Social-Democratic congress in Germany with a view to 'founding a united organisation'. On Schweitzer's suggestion, it was resolved to establish closer contacts with the International to the extent permitted by the German law. In fact, however, the Association's leadership continued to pursue a sectarian policy and obstruct the affiliation of the Association with the International.— 253, 255, 264

319 Marx is probably referring to a General Council meeting of 1 December 1868, which discussed the question of workers' participation in the campaign to organise the reception for the American Ambassador in London, Reverdy Johnson (see Note 259).— 253

320 *Boustrapa*—nickname of Louis Bonaparte, composed of the first syllables of the names of the cities where he staged putsches: Boulogne (6 August 1840), Strasbourg (30 October 1836), and Paris (coup d'état of 2 December 1851, which culminated in the establishment of a Bonapartist dictatorship).— 253, 523

321 A printers' strike in Geneva began in March 1869 when the owners of printing presses refused to raise the workers' wages, for which the latter had been campaigning for ten years. The strike was headed by the Romance Federal Committee and the International's sections in Geneva which secured financial support for the strikers from workers in Switzerland, France, Germany and Italy.

    For a detailed account of the strike, see Marx's 'Report of the General Council to the Fourth Annual Congress of the International Working Men's Association' (present edition, Vol. 21, p. 71).— 254

322 *Die Zukunft* wrote about this statement by Schweitzer on 2 April 1869: 'It should be noted that Herr von Schweitzer had earlier stated unambiguously that if even the most insignificant minority should refuse to grant him confidence, he would immediately resign. It seems, however, that he changed his mind again after the voting.'— 255

323 On 3 April 1869, the political affairs section of *Demokratisches Wochenblatt*, No. 14, reported: 'Since now there is every reason to hope for, if not the influence, then at least the unification of the various factions of Social-Democracy, we shall henceforth refrain from attacking Herr von Schweitzer in the *Demokratisches Wochenblatt* so as not to obstruct the unification. We assume, naturally, that the other side will terminate its attacks against us.'— 255

324 When under discussion during the spring of 1869, the Bill on regulations for handicraft trades in the North German Reichstag was severely criticised by the working-class deputies. Following Engels' directions (see Note 51), on 18 March Bebel demanded that factory work be subjected to some sort of reglamentation, i.e., that a ten-hour working day be introduced, work on Sundays prohibited, factory inspection organised and freedom of association granted to trade unions (see *Die Zukunft*, No. 67, 20 March 1869). Of the numerous proposed amendments, only Bebel's suggestion that 'workers' books' be abolished was adopted. On 29 May the Bill was passed (see 'Stenographische Berichte über die Verhandlungen des Reichstages der Norddeutschen Bundes. I. Legislatur-Periode-Session 1869', I. Bd. Berlin, 1869, S. 114-19, 124 and

146-48). Reporting to the General Council on 13 April 1869 about the speeches of the worker deputies at the North German Reichstag, Marx mentioned Bebel's speech in particular (see *The General Council of the First International, 1868-1870. Minutes,* Moscow, 1974, pp. 81-82).— 255, 274

325 In a letter to Marx of 3 April 1869, Liebknecht gave an optimistic account of the outcome of the struggle against Schweitzer at the congress of the General Association of German Workers in Barmen-Elberfeld (see Note 318). According to him, Schweitzer had sustained a crushing defeat, the leadership had passed into the hands of the Hamburg board and strife was extinguished. Summing up his information, Liebknecht wrote: 'The General Association of German Workers numbers only 11,000 men who have *extremely* vague political notions and mostly support Bismarck. *Our* Union is more numerous and enlightened.'

Liebknecht also wrote about his intention to bring out Engels' work *The Peasant War in Germany* as a separate pamphlet (2,000 copies) (see present edition, Vol. 10).— 256

326 The strike of workers in the cotton yarns and goods industry in Preston (Lancashire) began in March 1869 as a response to the provocative decision of the manufacturers to cut wages by ten per cent. The General Council and the trade unions organised financial support by workers in other towns, as a result of which the strike lasted until August 1869, and ended in a compromise (wages were reduced by 5 per cent). Reports on the progress of the strike appeared regularly in *The Bee-Hive.*— 257, 278, 296

327 A reference to Moll's letter to Marx of 6 April 1869, written on the instructions of the Solingen Section of the International. Moll wrote: 'The congress of the General Association of German Workers in Barmen-Elberfeld (see notes 311 and 318) has, as you know, largely destroyed Dr. Schweitzer's personality cult by blowing away the smoke-screen surrounding that power-hungry dictator; the congress advocated joining the International Association, as far as this is permitted by the existing laws.

'Bebel and Liebknecht vigorously championed the International's principles, made accusations against Schweitzer and other delegates and took them by the throat. Schweitzer did not try to defend himself, although he had intended to do so before the congress. The *assured* speeches of many, if not all delegates have made it clear that this Association has many *viable* elements; our section, like the International Association in general, will grow stronger, since the disunited workers' organisations will join the International.'— 259

328 This letter was published in English for the first time in: *The Times. Literary Supplement,* 1.VI.1967.— 259

329 On the instructions of the Solingen Section of the International (see Note 330), Friedrich Wilhelm Moll wrote to Marx about the disagreements with Schweitzer in his letter of 6 April 1869 (see Note 327).— 260

330 The Solingen Section of the International was set up in February-March 1866. Its members were in touch with the Central Committee of the German-language sections in Geneva and applied for assistance to the General Council and to Marx and Engels personally. The most active members of the Section, including Klein and Moll, took part in the International's congresses. In the autumn of 1867, this Section initiated the establishment of a cooperative of workers engaged in the production of steel and iron goods; it played a major

part in the work of the Section (the Rules of the cooperative were drawn up by
J. Ph. Becker).—260

[331] In the summer of 1866, the Greek population of Crete rebelled against
Turkish rule demanding that the island be incorporated into Greece. Turkish
troops undertook harsh punitive measures against the rebels and the island's
civilian population. However, supported by volunteers from many countries,
the insurgents carried on their struggle.

The events in Crete provoked a fresh exacerbation of international
contradictions in the Balkans. In November 1866 the Russian tsarist authorities
suggested that the European powers should urge the Turkish Empire to hand
Crete over to Greece. However, fearing that Russia would further consolidate
its position in the region and that the national liberation movements of the
peoples under the Sultan would mount, the Western states preferred Crete to
remain under Turkish rule. Support for the Cretan insurgents was confined to
a joint statement by Russia, France, Italy and Prussia on 29 October 1867. It
advised the Turkish Government to refrain from bloodshed on the island. The
conference convened by the European states in Paris in January 1869 to settle
the Turkish-Greek conflict forced Greece to discontinue support for the
uprising, thereby hastening its defeat. In 1869, the uprising was suppressed.—
260

[332] Marx's daughters Jenny and Eleanor visited the Lafargues in Paris on 26
March 1869. Jenny returned to London on 14 April, and Eleanor's visit lasted
till 19 May 1869.—262, 269

[333] A reference to Liebknecht's letter to Marx of 12 April 1869.—262, 264

[334] Ludlow's review of *Capital* was not published. The only item about the work in
the British bourgeois press appeared in January 1868 in the conservative
weekly *The Saturday Review of Politics, Literature, Science and Art*. Despite open
hostility to the author of *Capital*, the item noted 'the plausibility of his logic,
the vigour of his rhetoric, and the charm with which he invests the driest
problems of political economy' (see present edition, Vol. 42, p. 529).—263

[335] Marx is referring to a work by J. Janin *La fin d'un monde et du neveu de Rameau*,
written in 1861; it was a sequel to Diderot's novel *Le neveu de Rameau*, as
re-interpreted by Janin.—263

[336] Engels is probably referring to an article by J. M. Ludlow 'Ferdinand Lassalle,
the German Social-Democrat' published in *The Fortnightly Review* on 1 April,
and Ludlow's letter to Marx of 12 April 1869, a reply to Marx's letter of
10 April (see this volume, pp. 259-60).—264

[337] This letter was written by Marx over Liebknecht's letter to him of 12 April
1869. Marx deciphered the names explaining to Engels the following passage
from Liebknecht's letter: 'E. I had always defended against B.'—266

[338] On 12 February 1867, at the elections to the North German Reichstag in
Barmen-Elberfeld, Sophie von Hatzfeldt, who headed a small group of
Lassalleans that had split away from the General Association of German
Workers in 1867 (see Note 104), launched a campaign against Schweitzer. His
candidature was opposed by that of Hillmann which the workers did not
support: Hillmann received only 52 votes. However, Schweitzer, who received
4,668 votes, was not elected either.—268

[339] At the meeting of the General Council held on 20 April 1869 Marx was
instructed to draw up a protest on behalf of the General Council against the

massacre of the strikers in Seraing and Frameries (Belgium) in April 1869 (see Note 343).— 270

340 An allusion to the origin of Paul Lafargue, who was born in Santiago de Cuba. His mother's father was a mulatto, and her mother was an American Indian.— 271, 446

341 Marx's source of information was probably *The Times* of 24 April 1869, which featured a report 'New York, April 13' in the *Telegraphic Despatches* column stating that 'Mr. Clay (to Liberia) and Mr. Bassett (to Hayti) are the first two coloured diplomatists appointed'.— 271

342 Marx forwarded to Engels Alphonse Vandenhouten's letter to Marie Bernar, Corresponding Secretary for Belgium, which dealt with the so-called *Brussels Liberation Section* (or the *Revolutionary Committee of the International Association*) founded by bourgeois and petty-bourgeois republicans in Brussels in April 1869. One of the section's leaders was a former police chief. Its provocative activities and calls for plunder and violence provided the Belgian police with an excuse for persecuting members of the International Association. The manifesto of this organisation, connected as it was with the French branch in London (see Note 72), was published in *La Cigale*, No. 16, 18 April 1869. It was discussed at the General Council meeting of 20 April 1869, which stated that 'there was a party at Brussels who would not conform to the policy of the Central Committee but desired to be affiliated as an independent branch. In case an application should be made to this effect the Council was asked not to comply till after the Congress.'— 272

343 A reference to the bloody reprisals of the Belgian authorities against the strikers at the Cockerill Ironworks in Seraing and miners in Frameries in April 1869. These events were discussed at the General Council meetings of 20 and 27 April and 4 May. Marx was instructed (see Note 339) to draw up an address in English and French on behalf of the Council, and read it out on 4 May 1869, at a General Council meeting. It was decided to publish and distribute it (see K. Marx, 'The Belgian Massacres', present edition, Vol. 21). On his suggestion, it was also decided to launch a mass protest campaign and secure material relief for the victims.— 275

344 The report of the General Council meeting of 4 May 1869 published in *The Bee-Hive*, No. 395, 8 May 1869, stated that the General Council had decided to translate the address 'The Belgian Massacres' into four languages to make it known throughout the world.— 275

345 A reference to the letter of Louis Borhardt's daughter Malvine to Marx written on 19 April 1869. Her father had instructed her to apply to Marx for information on one M. Gromier, who had brought Borhardt letters of recommendation from Felix Pyat and Louis Blanc.— 276

346 Marx quotes Eccarius' letter of 29 April 1869, informing Marx about the publication of his pamphlet *Eines Arbeiters Widerlegung der national-ökonomischen Lehren John Stuart Mill's*, Berlin, 1869. The work was written by Eccarius with Marx's substantial assistance and published for the first time in *The Commonwealth* newspaper in late 1866-early 1867.— 276

347 A reference to the second edition (1869) of Marx's work *The Eighteenth Brumaire of Louis Bonaparte* (see Note 278).— 276

348 A reference to a number of diplomatic documents published since the 1830s by David Urquhart, a British political figure and writer, and his works on foreign

policy. They appeared in a variety of publications edited by Urquhart, including *The Portfolio* magazine and the newspapers *The Morning Advertiser* and *The Free Press*, which in 1866 was renamed *The Diplomatic Review*, and also as separate books and pamphlets.— 278

349 Marx and his daughter Jenny left for a visit to Ludwig Kugelmann in Germany around 10 September 1869 (see this volume, p. 353), and stayed in Hanover until 7 October. On the way back, they stopped over in Hamburg (8 and 9 October), where Marx had an appointment with Otto Meissner. On 11 October, Marx returned to London.— 279, 312, 318, 337, 359, 551

350 A reference to the reprisals of the Belgian authorities against workers in Charleroi in the spring of 1868 and in Seraing and Frameries in April 1869 (see notes 24 and 343).— 279

351 Marx wrote the 'Address to the National Labour Union of the United States' (see Note 146) in connection with the threat of war between Britain and the USA which arose in the spring of 1869, and read it on 11 May at the General Council meeting. The English text was published as a separate leaflet and also in *The Bee-Hive*, No. 396, 15 May 1869; the German version appeared in the *Demokratisches Wochenblatt*, No. 21, 22 May, and *Der Vorbote*, No. 8, August 1869 (see present edition, Vol. 21).— 279, 283

352 A reference to a single system of weights and measures introduced in Germany in 1868.— 280

353 Marx and his youngest daughter Eleanor stayed with Engels in Manchester from 25 May to 14 June 1869. Eleanor's visit probably lasted until early October.— 286, 290, 291, 317, 337, 370, 466

354 This letter was published for the first time in the article of D.G.C. Allan, 'The Red Doctor amongst the Virtuosi: Karl Marx and the Society', brought out by *The Royal Society of Arts Journal*, London, 1981, Vol. CXXIX, Nos. 5296-5297, pp. 259-61, 309-10. The original is kept in the Archive of the Greater London Library (Greater London Council).— 287

355 Marx's letter was addressed to London from Manchester, where he and his daughter Eleanor were staying with Engels between 25 May and 14 June 1869.— 287

356 In May 1869, Peter Le Néve Foster, Secretary of the Society of Arts and Trades Board of Directors, sent out letters to a number of persons, including Marx, requesting their consent to be elected to the Society. Marx's letter of 28 May 1869 was a reply to this proposal. On 30 June 1869, the Society's general meeting considered 132 candidatures and took a vote, as a result of which Marx was elected a member. To be admitted, a person had to have three members, at least one being his personal acquaintance, to back his candidature. For Marx, this was Peter Lund Simmonds, a Dane residing in England, a well-known political writer and author of numerous works on botany and agriculture.

Marx's admittance to the Society of Arts and Trades signified recognition by British scientific quarters of his merits as a scholar and political writer.

The *Society of Arts and Trades*, which was founded in 1754, set itself the philanthropic and educational goal of 'promoting the arts, trades and commerce'. Its social composition was varied: its managing bodies included both members of the aristocracy, patrons of the Society, and representatives of a broad cross-section of bourgeoisie and bourgeois intellectuals; among the members were also representatives of trade unions. In the 1860s, the Society's membership was in excess of 4,000.

In 1853-54, as the mass strike movement began to grow, the Society tried to act as an intermediary between the workers and the manufacturers seeking to take the edge off the class struggle. Marx sharply criticised this position and even called the organisation the '"Society of Arts" and tricks' (see present edition, Vol. 12, p. 612).

Marx's admission to the Society gave him greater access to scientific literature to be found in the Society's library, including its extremely large collection of works by the 17th-19th century economists. Many of them he used when working on *Capital*. He was particularly interested in recent research in the field of economics and natural sciences, specifically, chemistry and agriculture, whose results were published in the Society's journal. Marx used the materials of the journal for 1859, 1860, 1866 and 1872 in Volume One of *Capital* (the first and second editions) (see present edition, Vol. 35).— 287, 297, 372

357 Written across Marx's letter were the words which meant that Marx had signed a written commitment to observe the Rules and Regulations of the Society. In the bottom right corner, by Marx's signature, his name and academic degree (Ph. D.) are written again in a more legible hand.— 287

358 A reference to Austria's defeat in the war with Prussia in 1866, which resolved the long-standing rivalry between the two states. Its outcome was the unification of Germany under Prussia.— 289

359 J. B. Schweitzer stated at the sitting of the North German Reichstag on 17 May 1869: 'When a red banner is hoisted in Paris over the Tuileries, Europe will go up in flames as it did at the time of the French bourgeoisie's revolution, which opened up the way for European revolutions.'— 289

360 Marx's letter was written on the fourth page of Eleanor Marx's letter to her sister Jenny. The letter was published in English for the first time in: *Annali dell' Istituto Giangiacomo Feltrinelli*, an I, Milano, 1958.— 290

361 Between 27 March and 19 May 1869, Eleanor Marx was staying with the Lafargues in Paris, from where she went to Manchester with her father to visit Engels (see Note 355).— 290

362 *Edda*—a collection of epic poems and songs about the lives of the Scandinavian gods and heroes. It has come down to us in a manuscript dating from the 13th century, discovered in 1643 by the Icelandic Bishop Sveinsson—the so-called *Elder Edda*, and in a treatise on the poetry of the scalds compiled in the early 13th century by Snorry Sturluson (*Younger Edda*). The Eddas mirrored the state of Scandinavian society at the time of the disintegration of the tribal system and the migration of the peoples. They include plots and characters from Nordic folklore.— 295

363 J. B. Schweitzer, President of the General Association of German Workers, and Fritz Mende, President of the Lassallean General Association of German Workers which was under the influence of Sophie von Hatzfeldt (see Note 338), published in *Der Social-Demokrat*, No. 70, 18 June 1869 an address 'Wiederherstellung der Einheit der Lassalle'schen Partei', urging the two rival organisations to unite on the basis of Lassalle's Rules drawn up in 1863. The address enjoined them, in categorical form, to hold a vote on this issue within three days and to elect a president of the united Association. Playing on the

desire for unity voiced by the workers belonging to the two organisations Schweitzer succeeded in getting the more democratic forms of leadership evolved by the general congress in Barmen-Elberfeld in the spring of 1869 (see Note 311) abolished, in reorganising the Association along the principles proclaimed by Lassalle's Rules, in accordance with which the President was invested with dictatorial powers, and in getting himself re-elected as President of the united Association. Schweitzer's activities provoked indignation among the members of the Association and hastened the withdrawal from it of its more advanced elements.

Leaders of the opposition in the General Association of German Workers, Wilhelm Bracke, Julius Bremer, Samuel Spier and Theodor Yorck, who consulted Liebknecht and Bebel on 22 June 1869, addressed the Association's members in Magdeburg, urging them to convene a congress for the unification of all Social-Democratic workers in Germany. The address was published in the *Demokratisches Wochenblatt*, No. 26, 26 June 1869, and as a separate leaflet. On 27 June 1869, the Union of German Workers' Associations officially supported the address, which was the first step in the practical preparations for the congress in Eisenach (see Note 373).—295, 300, 304

[364] In a letter to Marx of 24 June 1869, Wilhelm Eichhoff wrote about the difficulty of selling his pamphlet *Die Internationale Arbeiterassociation...* (see Note 79), and his brother's inability, for financial reasons, to undertake the reprinting of Engels' work *The Peasant War in Germany* (see present edition, Vol. 10). The second edition of *The Peasant War* appeared in 1870 (see Note 302).—297, 299

[365] In a letter to Engels of 2 July 1869, Marx's daughter Jenny gave an ironical account of a soirée at the Kensington Museum: 'What genius the English have for the inventing of melancholy pleasures! Fancy crowd of some 7,000 mutes in full evening dress, wedged in so closely as to be unable either to move about or to sit down, for the chairs, and they were few and far between, a few imperturbable dowagers had taken by storm and stuck to throughout the evening. Of the works of art (the Queen has sacked all the museums of the people, in order to carry off their treasures to this aristocratic and favourite resorts of the "belated lamented"), it was next to impossible to get a glimpse.'—297

[366] Marx is referring to a passage from Laurence Sterne's novel *The Life and Opinions of Tristram Shandy, Gentleman* (Paris, 1832, p. 20) saying that gravity 'was no better, but often worse, than what a French wit had long ago defined it,—viz. *A mysterious carriage of the body, to cover the defects of the mind.'*—297

[367] On 23 June 1869 Marx took part in a mass trade union meeting in Exeter Hall in London held in support of the Bill for expanding the rights of trade unions.—298

[368] A reference to the June 1848 uprising of the French proletariat. See Marx's and Engels' articles 'The 23rd of June', 'The 24th of June', 'The 25th of June', and 'The June Revolution' (present edition, Vol. 7, pp. 130-49, and 157-64).—298

[369] On 30 June 1869, the contract signed by Engels with his partner Gottfried Ermen (see Note 158) expired. Since that time, Engels terminated his participation in the Manchester firm Ermen & Engels and devoted himself exclusively to writing, scientific research and party work.—299, 310, 312

370 On 29 June 1869, George Henry Moore, an Irish M. P., spoke in the House of Commons disclosing the atrocities perpetrated by the British authorities against the Fenian prisoners and demanded that conditions be improved for those Fenians who had been arrested at the time of the 1867 uprising and had no charge preferred against them. Replying to Moore's speech, Henry Austin Bruce, the Home Secretary, hypocritically tried to refute the facts cited by Moore and vindicate the actions of the British Government. The other Irish M.P.s, who voiced the wish that the prisoners be treated in a more humane way, by and large justified the repressions against the Fenians. Moore's proposal was voted down. Marx defined his attitude to this issue in his articles 'The English Government and the Fenian Prisoners' and 'Record of a Speech on the Irish Question'. See also 'Articles by Jenny Marx on the Irish Question' (present edition, Vol. 21).— 300

371 Starting from January 1869, Marx's daughter Jenny gave lessons to the Monroe children. She stayed in Eastbourne with the Monroe family from 4 to 21 July 1869.— 300, 327, 547

372 In a letter to Marx of 29 June Liebknecht explained his long silence by family matters and party work. He wrote: 'The conflict with Schweitzer is very much there, and *victory will soon* be attained; 3/4 of the General Association of German Workers already support us, we are having a conference in Brunswick this coming Sunday, and a congress in August, to which you, Engels and Eccarius will be invited. You *must attend.* In case of extreme need, we'll get hold of some money. You must show yourself to the German workers. Write to me straight away so that I can show your letter in Brunswick...

'You *must immediately send us* the International's membership cards. I've been waiting for them for several months. *All German Social-Democrats are now becoming "international"*, and we shall discuss the best forms of joining at our, probably *Basle* congress, to which Bebel and I are going.

'You must *adapt the 'Communist Manifesto' for the requirements of agitation.* I never pay heed to *enemies*, but enemies and those who will become such are worthy of some attention.

'*Becker* insists that we obey *him*, but I've told him quite definitely that we are maintaining *direct* contacts with the General Council.'

In another part of the letter Liebknecht explained in detail the considerable financial difficulties involved in the publication of the *Demokratisches Wochenblatt* and asked Marx to appeal to Engels for financial assistance.— 303, 306.

373 A reference to the all-German congress of the Social-Democrats of Germany, Austria and Switzerland held in *Eisenach* on 7-9 August 1869. Taking part in it were 263 delegates representing over 150,000 workers; the congress founded an independent revolutionary party of the German proletariat which was called the Social-Democratic Workers' Party. The congress adopted a programme which incorporated, word for word, the basic provisions of the International's Rules. The draft Programme was published in the supplement to the *Demokratisches Wochenblatt*, No. 31, 31 July 1869. It showed some influence of Lassalleanism but was mostly based on Marxist principles. The congress defined the status of the Social-Democratic Workers' Party as a section of the International. Since the Prussian Law on Associations banned all societies which had contacts with other organisations, especially those abroad, the congress decided that the party members should join the International as private persons. It also discussed the organisational principles of the party. The plan proposed by J. Ph. Becker (see Note 409) did not meet with support. August

Bebel, who made a report on the Programme and the organisational issue, emphasised the need to adopt Rules which would preclude a personal dictatorship. The Rules that were approved were drawn up along democratic lines.—303, 332, 335, 345, 544

374 A reference to the clash of miners with the police and troops near Mold, Denbighshire. The workers protested against the lowering of the wages and the atrocities of the mine manager. On 28 May 1869 a crowd of unarmed miners made an attempt to set free their arrested fellow-workers but they were fired on. Five people were killed and many wounded. The court acquitted the authorities and sentenced the 'rebels' to ten years' hard labour. Home Secretary Bruce declared in the House of Commons that the troops had a right to shoot at the crowd in self-defence without obtaining permission from the authorities.

On this issue, see also: K. Marx, 'Report of the General Council to the Fourth Annual Congress of the International Working Men's Association' (present edition, Vol. 21, pp. 80-81).—305, 308

375 The *Riot Act*, which was promulgated in 1715, banned all 'riotous assemblies' of more than 12 persons; in case of its violation, the authorities were obliged to read out a special warning and use force if the assembly did not disperse within an hour.—305

376 The *Arms Act* regarded everyone carrying arms without a permit as a violator of public law and order, liable to a court trial. Under George III, in the late 18th century, an act was promulgated which also banned learning the use of arms without prior official permission.—305

377 As a result of a vigorous campaign by the British trade unions for their legalisation, in the spring of 1869 the Royal Commission submitted to Parliament a Bill on the recognition of the unions' legal rights. The Trade Union's Act was passed in 1871.—305

378 The collection *Agricultural Statistics, Ireland. Tables showing the estimated average produce of the crops for the year 1866*, Dublin, 1867, was used by Marx when preparing the second edition of *Capital's* Volume One to supplement Part VII, 'The Accumulation of Capital', Chapter XXV, 'The General Law of Capitalist Accumulation', Section 5, 'Illustration of the General Law of Capitalist Accumulation, f. Ireland'.—306

379 A reference to the Congress of the First International held in Basle on 6-11 September 1869. It was attended by 78 delegates from England, France, Germany, Switzerland, Belgium, Austria, Italy, Spain and North America. Marx was not present at the Congress but took an active part in preparing it. The General Council Minutes include his speeches dealing with individual items on the Congress's agenda: the agrarian question (6 July), the right of inheritance (20 July) and public education (10 and 17 August) (see present edition, Vol. 21).

The question of the right of inheritance was entered on the agenda, which was approved on 22 June 1869, at the suggestion of the Geneva Section headed by the Bakuninists. They proposed to annihilate the right of inheritance, believing this to be the only means of eliminating private property and social injustice.

At the General Council meeting of 3 August, Marx read out a *Report of the General Council on the Right of Inheritance*, prepared by him, which was approved and submitted to the Congress on behalf of the Council. However, at the Congress itself the question of the right of inheritance provoked a heated debate. Despite the opposition of Liebknecht and De Paepe, Bakunin managed to win some of the delegates over to his side. No resolution concerning this matter was passed.

After discussing the land question for a second time (the first discussion of land ownership took place at the Brussels Congress [see Note 138]) the majority of the Basle Congress delegates voted for abolishing private property in land and converting it over into common property; the Congress also passed resolutions on the unification of trade unions at the national and international levels.

The Basle Congress was the scene of the first clash between supporters of Marx and Engels, and the followers of Bakunin's anarchist doctrine. The latter failed to assume leadership in the International Working Men's Association. The Basle Congress confirmed that the General Council was to remain in London.

In order to consolidate the unity and organisation of the International, the General Council was granted a right to expel from the International any section that did not comply with its Rules, on condition that the Federal Council and the Congress approved.—306, 322, 325, 335, 338, 351, 355, 364, 393, 405, 413, 463

380 A reference to Liebknecht's speech at the meeting of the Berlin Democratic Labour Union of 31 May 1869, 'Ueber die politische Stellung der Sozial-Demokratie' and Bebel's article 'An Herrn Dr. Schweitzer in Berlin' published in the *Demokratisches Wochenblatt*, No. 27, 3 July 1869. The end of Liebknecht's speech was published in the *Demokratisches Wochenblatt*, No. 32, 7 August 1869 (supplement).—307

381 Marx used the alias A. Williams when staying in Paris between 6 and 12 July 1869.—309, 314, 315

382 This letter was first published in the original (English with German words and phrases) in the book: *Friedrich Engels. 1820-1970. Referate, Diskussionen, Dokumente*, Hanover, 1971.—310

383 Replies by Engels to letters from Marx's daughter Jenny of 24 June and 2 July 1869. In the letter of 2 July, Jenny gave an ironic description of an aristocratic soirée at the Kensington Museum on 1 July, to which she and Marx were invited by the educational Society of Arts (see this volume, pp. 297-98 and Note 365).—310.

384 Enclosed with the invitation to the Kensington Museum was a printed warning that said: 'The Council of the Society of Arts appeal with confidence to the members to assist in preventing the mobbing and following any Royal and distinguished persons who may attend the Conversazione of the Society on the 1st of July, and request them to assist in enabling such visitors to enjoy the privilege of walking about unmolested, and seeing the objects of art, like any private person.'—310

385 An excerpt from this letter was published in English for the first time in: Marx K., Engels F., *Selected Correspondence*, Moscow, 1975.—312

386 Engels refers to the unification of the General Association of German Workers headed by Schweitzer and the Lassallean General Association of German Workers headed by Mende and acting under the influence of Sophie von Hatzfeldt (see Note 363).—313

387 A reference to the reconstruction of Paris undertaken by G. E. Haussmann,

Prefect of the Seine Department, for the purpose of building new suburbs with broad streets and avenues. The reconstruction also aimed at preventing barricade fighting during uprisings.— 316

388 The elections to the Corps législatif in May-June 1869 spelled considerable success to the anti-Bonapartist opposition despite the repressions of Napoleon III's government. At an extraordinary session in July 1869, 116 deputies belonging to the liberal opposition and Left Centre signed a statement on the need to form a responsible ministry and expand the rights of the Corps législatif. At the sittings of 5 and 8 July, deputy François Vincent Raspail exposed the blatant violations of the freedom of vote by Bonapartist authorities and accused the church of conducting election propaganda during services, and the police, of overstepping their powers at the time of preparations for the election campaign, when a massacre took place in Paris (see *Annales du Sénat et du Corps législatif. Session extraordinaire du 28 juin au 6 septembre 1869*, Paris, 1869, pp. 204-05). In his message of 12 July Napoleon III promised to expand the Corps' rights and appoint ministers from among deputies, but shirked the issue of the ministry's responsibility, stressing the inviolability of the emperor's power. On 13 July he postponed the session of the Corps législatif for an indefinite period, and on 17 July introduced into the government a number of persons who suited the big bourgeoisie and the clericals but who did not belong to the opposition.— 316, 325

389 In a letter of 2 June 1869 Ludwig Kugelmann wrote to Marx that Meissner had assured him that the first signatures of the proofs of Marx's work *The Eighteenth Brumaire of Louis Bonaparte* (second edition) had already been sent to Marx and that the work would appear in two weeks' time.— 318

390 In a letter of 6 July 1869, Ludwig Kugelmann suggested to Marx that after the negotiations with Guido Weiß, the editor of *Die Zukunft*, a short biography of Marx written by Engels for another publication should appear in that newspaper (see also Note 106).—318, 328, 333

391 On 11 July 1869, Friedrich Wilhelm Fritzsche addressed Marx, on Liebknecht's recommendation, as a member of the General Council, to render financial support to the Leipzig cigar-makers' strike.

Wilhelm Liebknecht also approached Marx with a similar request on 7 and 12 July.

In his letter of 14 July Wilhelm Eichhoff enclosed a variety of material about the working-class movement in Germany and informed Marx that he would probably be elected delegate to the Eisenach Congress (see Note 373).—322, 327

392 On 1 July 1869, the Geneva Central Committee of the German-language sections of the International Working Men's Association passed a resolution published in *Der Vorbote* in July 1869, which censured Schweitzer's dictatorial behaviour and welcomed the proposal to convene an all-German Social-Democratic Workers' Congress (see Note 373). In this connection, on 14 July, a piece entitled 'Schwindel' appeared in *Der Social-Demokrat*, whose author was most probably Fritz Mende. He accused Johann Philipp Becker as Chairman of the Geneva Central Committee, and the International, of meddling in the affairs of the General Association of German Workers.—322, 327

393 A reference to Liebknecht's letter to Engels of 11 December 1867, in which he explained the reasons for his cooperation with the German People's Party (see Note 38).—324

394 On 13 July 1869 Ludwig Kugelmann wrote to Engels about his intention to ask Marx to prolong his stay in Hanover so that they could go to Karlsbad (now Karlovy Vary) for a cure together. While they were absent, Marx's daughter Jenny was to stay with Gertrud Kugelmann in Hanover.

On 17 July 1869, Kugelmann replied to Marx's letter of 15 July, in which he again asked Marx to go with him to Karlsbad in August.— 324, 327, 334

395 The reference is to an item published in the *Demokratisches Wochenblatt*, No. 29, 17 July 1869, which stated: 'We can assure you further that the *General Council* of the International Working Men's Association shares our opinion of Herr von Schweitzer but at present considers it inexpedient to interfere, so as to fully preserve the independence of the German workers' movement. But if Herr von Schweitzer proves stupid enough to turn up at the forthcoming congress of the International, as he has stated he will do, he will simply be ordered to leave.'— 324, 331

396 Engels is referring to the elections of the President of the united General Association of German Workers in late June 1869 (see Note 363). The official communication on the results of the elections signed by Mende and published in *Der Social-Demokrat* on 9 July stated that Schweitzer had been elected by an 'absolute majority' and 'stronger minority' vote. The latter meant that Mende voted for Schweitzer.— 324

397 In early April 1814, after the troops of the anti-French coalition invaded Paris, Talleyrand prepared a convocation of the Senate which declared Napoleon I deposed. In June 1815, after Napoleon I's armies were defeated at Waterloo, the majority of the Chamber of Representatives demanded that he abdicate.— 325

398 Excerpts from this letter were first published in English in: *The Letters of Karl Marx*, Selected and translated ... by Saul K. Padover, New Jersey, USA, 1979; *Karl Marx, Friedrich Engels, Selected Letters. The Personal Correspondence. 1844-1877.* Edited by Fritz J. Raddatz. Boston, Toronto, 1981.— 326, 329

399 Marx's letter to Wilhelm Liebknecht written around the beginning of July (earlier than 10 July), 1869, has not been found.— 326

400 A reference to an item carried by the *Demokratisches Wochenblatt*, No. 28, 10 July 1869, which stated that only '*full members* of the International Working Men's Association would be admitted to the Basle Congress'.— 326

401 Marx's letter to Liebknecht written around 17 July 1869, has not been found.— 326

402 Marx's letter to Otto Meissner, probably written on 19 July 1869, has not been found.— 327

403 As Kugelmann's letter to Marx of 17 July 1869 makes clear, the reference is to Bracke's intention to appeal to the General Council of the International for financing the propaganda campaign against Schweitzer in Germany.— 327, 331

404 A reference to Liebknecht's letter to Marx of 22 July 1869.— 328

405 Marx's reply to Liebknecht's letter of 22 July 1869 has not been found.— 328

406 Marx is referring to the sections 'Arbeitsprozess und Verwerthungsprozess' and the 'Theilung der Arbeit und Manufaktur' of the first German edition of Volume One of *Capital*. Corresponding to them in the second and subsequent German editions of this volume are Chapters V and XII (see present edition,

Vol. 35). In the English edition of 1887 prepared by Engels, this material is to be found in Part III, Chapter VII, 'The Labour-Process and the Process of Producing Surplus-Value', and Part IV, Chapter XIV, 'Division of Labour and Manufacture'.—329

407 In connection with the intention of Karl Vogt, the German natural scientist, to go on a lecture tour of Germany in 1869, Engels suggested that, with help from Kugelmann, Marx's book *Herr Vogt* should be circulated in Berlin (see present edition, Vol. 17). Wilhelm Liebknecht possessed a number of copies. (See also this volume, Engels' letter to Marx of 29 January 1869 and Marx's letter to Engels of 29 March 1869.)—330

408 Marx used the book by Nassau William Senior mentioned here while preparing the second German edition of Volume One of *Capital,* which appeared in 1872 (see present edition, Vol. 35).—331

409 Johann Philipp Becker published, on behalf of the Central Committee of the German-language sections, an address to the Eisenach Congress, which was published by *Der Vorbote,* No. 7, July 1869 (see Note 373). It contained a plan of a working-class organisation. Becker, who was under Bakunin's influence, refused to recognise the need for a proletarian political party. He regarded the trade unions as the only acceptable organisational form of workers' movement and sought to put the German Social-Democracy under the control of the Central Committee of the German-language sections. Marx, Engels and Bebel were sharply critical of this plan.—332, 335

410 A receipt written by Bernard, Corresponding Secretary for Belgium, has come down to us: 'Received from Mr. Marx the sum of 25 thaler for the victims of Seraing and Borinage (Belgium). London, 22 July 1869. Bernard, Secretary for Belgium, twenty-five thaler.' Marx wrote on the receipt: '(This money was sent to me by Bebel in the name of the Leipzig workers. K.M.)' (See: *The General Council of the First International 1868-1870. Minutes,* Progress Publishers, Moscow, 1974, pp. 443-44).—332

411 A reference to the General Council meeting of 20 July 1869, at which Marx made a speech on the right of inheritance as part of the preparations for the Basle Congress. A report of the meeting was printed by *The Bee-Hive,* No. 406, 24 July 1869, but was not accurate. Marx's speech, which has been preserved in its original form in the minutes taken by Eccarius, is reproduced in the present edition (see Vol. 21, p. 394).—334

412 A reference to the *National Reform League* set up in 1849 in London by Chartist leaders James (Bronterre) O'Brien, Reynolds, etc. The League's goal was to attain universal suffrage and introduce social reforms. In 1866, it joined the International and worked under the guidance of the General Council, having turned into a branch of the Reform League. The latter's leaders, Alfred Walton and George Milner, were members of the General Council and participants in a number of the International's congresses.
On Marx's stay in Paris, see Note 381.—334

413 *Der Vorbote,* No. 7, July 1869, carried a report of the meeting of the Nuremberg Section of the International. At the meeting, which was convened to establish closer contacts among the Bavarian workers' organisations, representatives of 13 such organisations were present. Amongst others, the meeting passed a resolution on the campaign for 'direct popular legislation'. In a commentary to the resolution, Johann Philipp Becker proposed to submit it for discussion to the Eisenach Congress (see Note 373).—336

414 A reference to the letters of August Bebel of 30 July 1869, and Wilhelm Liebknecht, late July 1869. Bebel's letter was a reply to Marx's letter (not extant) of 27 July 1869 (see this volume, p. 332). Bebel and Liebknecht supported Marx's critical attitude to Becker's plan for a workers' organisation in Germany (see Note 409) and advocated its formation on the basis of the International's principles.— 338, 339

415 A reference to the address to the German Social-Democrats 'An die deutschen Sozial-Demokraten' on the convocation of an all-German workers' congress in Eisenach with a view to founding an independent workers' party in Germany. The address appeared in the *Demokratisches Wochenblatt*, No. 29, 17 July 1869. It was signed by representatives of workers' societies of Germany, Austria and Switzerland. Among the signatures of the members of the Central Committee of the German Workers' societies in Switzerland was that of petty-bourgeois democrat Amandus Goegg. This fact gave ground for an article featured by *Der Social-Demokrat*, No. 84, 21 July 1869, which identified the views of Liebknecht and his followers with those of Goegg.— 339

416 A reference to the address of the Geneva Central Committee to the Spanish revolutionaries, 'Der Internationale Arbeiterbund von Genf an die Arbeiter Spaniens' issued on 21 October 1868. It was published as a separate leaflet in German and in French and in *Der Vorbote*, No. 12, December 1868.— 340

417 This letter was published in English for the first time in: *Friedrich Engels. 1820-1970. Referate, Diskussionen, Dokumente*, Hanover, 1971.— 341

418 Engels stayed in Ostend and Engelskirchen with relatives from around 19 August to early September 1869.— 342, 352, 357

419 Marx refers to Liebknecht's speech 'Ueber die politische Stellung der Sozial-Demokratie' made at the meeting of the Berlin Democratic Labour Union of 31 May 1869 (see Note 380). Liebknecht said that August Brass, editor of the *Norddeutsche Allgemeine Zeitung* was willing to give Marx, Engels and himself space in his newspaper to popularise the ideas of socialism and communism, but that he had turned down this proposal.— 344

420 On Marx's recommendation, Hermann Jung, member of the General Council, evidently attended the meeting of the Amalgamated Society of Carpenters and Joiners which discussed a nominee to the Basle Congress. On 17 August, Jung informed the General Council that the Society would probably send a representative to the Congress. This was the Society's General Secretary Robert Applegarth, who, however, carried only a General Council member's mandate.— 346

421 Engels, Lizzy Burns and Eleanor Marx toured Ireland from 6 to 16 September 1869.— 348, 351, 356

422 A reference to Dupont's statement at the General Council meeting of 17 August 1869, that the Paris bronze-workers had paid off their debt to the London trade unions (see Note 18).— 350

423 Marx quotes Neumayer's letter to the General Council of 14 August 1869.— 350

424 Zabicki made a report on the 1869 strike at woodworking factories and brickworks in Posen at the General Council meeting of 17 August 1869, at which Marx was present. Zabicki said that 'the building operatives of Posen

(Polish) had won their first strike; they had been assisted by the men of Berlin'.— 350

425 Hiltrop's essay mentioned by Engels, 'Ueber die Reorganisation der Knappschaftsvereine', appeared in the *Zeitschrift des königlich preussischen statistischen Bureaus*, nos. 4, 5 and 6, April, May and June, 1869. The magazine was edited by Ernst Engel. Engels examined the rules of the miners' guilds (guild funds) in the coalfields of Saxony on Marx's instruction, and in February 1869 prepared a report on this question for the General Council (see Note 281).— 352

426 On 21 August 1869, Liebknecht reprinted Marx's biography in the *Demokratisches Wochenblatt*, No. 34. It was written by Engels and first appeared in *Die Zukunft*, No. 185, 11 August (see present edition, Vol. 21). When reprinting the material, Liebknecht omitted the following phrases (printed in italics): '*Everything he* [Lassalle— Ed.] *wrote was derived from elsewhere, not without some misunderstandings either*; he had a forerunner *and an intellectual superior, whose existence he kept a secret, of course, whilst he vulgarised his writings*, and the name *of that intellectual superior* is Karl Marx.' By way of explanation, Liebknecht wrote to Marx on 17 August 1869, that he had abridged the text since it could 'offend' the Lassalleans if printed in full.— 352

427 The item published by Liebknecht in the *Demokratisches Wochenblatt*, No. 35, 28 August 1869, read: 'It has been decided in Eisenach that alongside with the general party organ (*Der Volkstaat*, for the present, the *Demokratisches Wochenblatt*), there should be a press organ for Austria— *Die Volkstimme*, and for Switzerland, *Felleisen*.'— 352

428 Engels refers to the lengthy discussion at the Eisenach Congress (see Note 373) around a name for the party, which involved, among others, the German petty-bourgeois democrat Rittinghausen. The name agreed upon was the Social-Democratic Workers' Party (Sozial-demokratische Arbeiterpartei). A report of the Eisenach Congress was published in the *Demokratisches Wochenblatt*, No. 33, and supplements to nos. 33 and 34, 14 and 21 August 1869.— 352

429 In the 1860s, in Prussia's Rhine Province, Baden and some other German lands, Catholic priests, including Ketteler, the Bishop of Mainz, launched a campaign for universal suffrage, laws protecting workers' rights, etc. In this way the Catholic clergy sought to prevent socialist ideas from taking hold of the German workers. On 6 September 1869, a congress of Catholic communities opened in Düsseldorf, which adopted a resolution 'To demand from all Christians of all estates that they take care of the working class and promote its economic and moral flourishing'.— 354

430 A reference to the second edition of Marx's work *The Eighteenth Brumaire of Louis Bonaparte*, which appeared in late July 1869. In reply to Marx's note, which is not available, Meissner wrote on 28 September 1869 that all copies of Marx's book have been sent off with the exception of the 25 he had.— 354

431 Liebknecht's letter to Marx in which he asked for Engels' work *The Peasant War in Germany* for reprinting has not come down to us. There is Liebknecht's letter to Kugelmann of 20 September 1869, in which Liebknecht writes that he intends to reprint this work. On 20 December, Liebknecht wrote to Engels for permission to reprint the work and to ask for a short introduction to it. The second edition of *The Peasant War in Germany* appeared in Leipzig in October 1870.— 354, 356

[432] On 26 September 1869, Marx's second daughter Laura Lafargue turned twenty-four.— 355

[433] Marx quotes an old German song (c. 1200).— 355

[434] In July 1865, Liebknecht was expelled from the Prussian state by the Berlin police 'for political reasons'. In 1867, he was elected deputy to the North German Reichstag from Saxony and enjoyed a deputy's immunity. However, in September 1869, he was unable to visit Marx in Hanover, as the Prussian police had a right to arrest him during a break in the Reichstag work between 22 June 1869 and 14 February 1870. Marx originally planned a meeting with Liebknecht in Brunswick, and later in Hamburg. However, the meeting never took place.— 356, 358

[435] Marx is referring to Paul Lafargue's letter of 14 September 1869, in which the latter gives an account of the General Council meeting of 14 September, the first after the Basle Congress of the International Working Men's Association.— 356, 445

[436] *Ribbonmen*—participants in an Irish peasant movement whose members were united in secret societies and wore a green ribbon as an emblem. The Ribbonmen movement, which emerged in late 18th century in Northern Ireland, was a form of popular resistance to the arbitrary rule of the English landlords and the forcible eviction of tenants from the land. The Ribbonmen attacked estates, organised attempts on the lives of hated landlords and managers. The activities of the Ribbonmen had a purely local, decentralised character; they had no common programme of action.— 357, 549

[437] Marx was conducting negotiations with Meissner in Hamburg on 8 and 9 October 1869.— 357

[438] Engels first conceived the idea of a book on the history of Ireland in the summer of 1869. He studied a vast selection of literary and historical sources: works of classical and medieval authors, annals, collections of ancient law codes, legislative acts and legal treatises, folklore, travellers' notes, numerous works on archaeology, history, economics, geography, geology, etc. Engels' bibliography, embracing over 150 titles, is selective and includes but a fraction of the sources he studied. Preparatory materials take up the bulk of 15 paginated notebooks of excerpts, as well as notes, fragments on separate sheets and newspaper clippings. Marx attached great importance to Engels' book and helped him all he could. The views of Marx and Engels on major problems of Irish history took shape in the course of joint discussions.

In May 1870, Engels began working on it.

Engels actually succeeded in finishing only the first chapter, 'Natural Conditions'. The second chapter, 'Old Ireland', is unfinished (see present edition, Vol. 21), while the two last chapters were not even begun. The Franco-Prussian War and the Paris Commune, which were soon to follow, made Engels concentrate on his work in the International and left him no time for the book.— 357, 358

[439] A report of this talk, which touched on the vital issues of the working-class movement, was published by J. H. W. Hamann, member of the delegation, cashier of the metalworkers' union, in *Der Volksstaat* on 27 November 1869. Marx spoke about the significance of trade unions as a school of socialism. He said that in trade unions, workers were getting ready to become socialists, since there they had an opportunity to watch the daily struggle between labour and capital.

He emphasised the importance of an independent printed organ for the working-class movement. 'It is a printed organ of trade unions,' said Marx, 'that can serve as a means of the workers' mutual communication; it is there that the "pros" and "contras" must be discussed. It is necessary to discuss the issue of wages in the different regions, and to collect, as far as this is possible, the opinions of workers in different trades. However, this printed organ must never become the property of a private individual. If we want it to fulfil its purpose, it must belong to a collective. It is probably unnecessary to dwell on the reasons for this attitude, they are so obvious that everyone can be expected to understand: if you wish to see your union flourish, this tenet must be accepted as one of the basic conditions.' 'The talk ended', wrote Hamann, 'with Marx stressing once more the need never to try to cling to individuals but bear in mind the cause, and draw conclusions only to promote it. "Be it Liebknecht, be it Dr. Schweitzer, or be it myself, always think about the cause, for the truth is not to be found outside it."' Unfortunately, while recording the conversation, Hamann seriously distorted some of Marx's remarks in the Lassallean spirit, specifically, on the issue of the relationship between the political party of the working class and the trade unions. (See *Internationale wissenschaftliche Korrespondenz zur Geschichte der deutschen Arbeiterbewegung*, Berlin (W), 1986, Heft 1, S. 63-71).— 358

440 On Marx's meeting with the delegation of the Brunswick Committee of the German Social-Democratic Workers' Party, see Note 447.— 358

441 A reference to the French translation of Volume One of *Capital* made by Charles Keller, member of the Paris Section of the First International. Keller began the work in October 1869, and on 16 October sent Marx the translation of Chapter II of the first volume for corrections. Keller took part in the Paris Commune and emigrated to Switzerland after its defeat. The work remained unfinished. The translation of Volume One of *Capital* into French was made by Joseph Roy and published in Paris in 1872-75 in instalments, which were later brought together in a book (on the French translation of *Capital*, see also Note 309).— 359, 378, 399, 450, 545

442 Chapter IV of Volume One of *Capital* (first German edition) corresponds to chapters IV, V and VI of the French edition. Marx feared that the chapter in its original form would not suit the French readers.— 360

443 N. Flerovsky's book *The Condition of the Working Class in Russia* (Н. Флеровскій, *Положеніе рабочаго класса въ Россіи*) was sent to Marx by Danielson on 30 September (12 October), 1869. Danielson expressed the hope that it would supply Marx with the necessary material for the subsequent parts of his classical work *Capital*. This work prompted Marx to take up Russian seriously. (For Marx's opinion of Flerovsky's book see this volume, pp. 390, 423, 424).— 360, 362, 429

444 A reference to the atheistic congress (Anticoncilio) convened in Naples on 8 December 1869 by petty-bourgeois democrats who stood close to the League of Peace and Freedom (see Note 271) as a gesture of opposition to the Catholic oecumenical council which was held in Vatican from 8 December 1869 to 20 October 1870, and adopted the dogma of the Pope's infallibility in the matters of faith. The atheistic congress was broken up by the Neapolitan authorities.— 362

445 *Pale*—the name of an English medieval colony in Ireland established as a result of the seizure by the Anglo-Norman feudal lords of the island's south-eastern part in the 12th century. The colony, whose boundaries were fortified (hence

the name), served as the base for incessant wars against the population of the free part of Ireland which ended in the 16th-17th centuries with the conquest of the entire country.— 363, 415

446 This letter was first published in English in an abridged form in: Marx K., Engels F., *Selected Correspondence*, Moscow, 1979.— 363, 365, 522

447 After the Basle Congress (see Note 379), members of the People's Party in Germany (see Note 38) and the *Felleisen* newspaper, organ of the German workers' unions in Switzerland, launched a campaign against the Congress decisions to abolish private property in land as essentially communist ones. Seeking to reconcile the People's Party and the petty-bourgeois supporters of *Felleisen* with the decisions of the Basle Congress, Goegg, its editor-in-chief, made a long statement in *Der Volksstaat*, No. 3, 9 October 1869, in which he attempted to belittle the revolutionary importance of Congress decisions. He declared that there was nothing communist about them. Marx is apparently referring to this statement as 'Goeggiana'.

At that time, Liebknecht and *Der Volksstaat*, fearing that a break with the petty-bourgeois democratic elements in the South-German states might occur, refrained from a large-scale popularisation campaign of the Basle decisions to convert the land into public property; *Der Volksstaat* repeatedly stated that these decisions were applicable only in Britain, where large landed property existed, and were unsuitable either for Germany or France, where small peasant holdings predominated. Liebknecht believed that the party approval of the Basle decisions would be premature and could have prompted the proletarian supporters of the South-German People's Party to depart from the Social-Democratic Workers' Party. This tactic met with disapproval on the part of his associates and soon Liebknecht himself became convinced that it was erroneous, and began actively to popularise Basle Congress decisions.

On 3 October 1869, at a meeting with Marx in Hanover (see Marx's letter to Engels of 30 September 1869), members of the Central Committee Bonhorst, Bracke and Spier discussed the possibility of implementing the Basle Congress decisions and the tactics of the Social-Democratic Workers' Party in Germany with respect to the peasantry. On 25 October Bonhorst wrote a letter to Marx requesting him to give as clear an account of the matter as possible in order to use it to organise a popularisation campaign among German peasants (see Note 453). This letter from Bonhorst was forwarded by Marx to Engels.— 363

448 Marx learned that Bakunin had the writings of A. A. Serno-Solovyevich, who committed suicide on 16 August 1869, from *L'Égalité*, No. 37, 1 October 1869, which carried an announcement requesting all persons in possession of manuscripts, letters and other documents of the deceased to submit them for the use of the newspaper, which was intending to publish his works and compile a bibliography.— 364, 366

449 Marx refers, specifically, to the article by Hermann Greulich 'Die Heulmaierei gegen den Basler Kongress' published in *Der Volksstaat*, No. 5, 16 October 1869.— 364

450 By 'the antiquated manner of 1789' Marx means the transfer to the peasants of the land confiscated from the feudal lords (parcelling) at the time of the French Revolution. Marx and Engels believed that this way of dealing with the agrarian problem was unsuitable for the proletarian party, leading as it did to the establishment of a petty-bourgeois peasant class and dooming the peasantry to gradual impoverishment and ruin (see K. Marx and F. Engels, 'Address of

the Central Authority to the League, March 1850', present edition, Vol. 10, pp. 284-85).—364

451 The *Land and Labour League* was founded in London in October 1869 with the participation of the General Council. Its Executive Committee included more than ten General Council members. The League's programme was drawn up by Eccarius on Marx's instruction and edited by Marx (see Vol. 21, pp. 401-06). Along with general democratic demands, like the reform of the finance and tax system and of public education, it contained demands for the nationalisation of the land and the reduction of working hours, as well as the Chartist demands for universal suffrage and home colonisation.

   Marx held that the League could play a role in revolutionising the English working class and could promote the establishment of an independent proletarian party in England. However, by the autumn of 1870, the influence of bourgeois elements had grown in the League and it gradually began to lose contact with the International.—364, 375, 377, 412

452 In the summer and autumn of 1869, a mass movement developed in Ireland for an amnesty of the Fenian prisoners (see Note 86).

   In 1867, the Fenians were preparing an armed uprising; in September of that year, the British authorities managed to arrest the leaders of the Fenian movement and put them on trial. The Fenians were persecuted, their newspapers were closed down, and the operation of the Habeas Corpus Act suspended (see Note 486). The campaign for the defence of the convicted Fenians launched in England was supported by the General Council of the First International.

   Numerous meetings presented petitions to the British Government demanding that the Irish revolutionaries be released, but Prime Minister Gladstone refused to meet these demands. On 24 October 1869, a mass demonstration in defence of the Fenians took place in London (for an account of the event, see this volume, pp. 546-47), after which the General Council resolved to address the English people in defence of the Fenians, and set up a special commission consisting of Marx, Lucraft, Jung and Eccarius. On Marx's suggestion, the issue was expanded, and in November 1869 the General Council held a broad discussion on the attitude of the British Government to the Irish prisoners. Marx spoke twice (see present edition, Vol. 21, pp. 407-12), and wrote a 'Draft Resolution of the General Council on the Policy of the British Government Towards the Irish Prisoners' (see present edition, Vol. 21, p. 83, and this volume, p. 375), which was approved by the General Council on 30 November 1869.—365, 449, 546

453 In a letter to Marx of 25 October 1869 (see Note 447), Bonhorst wrote: 'You should know better than anyone what the sore spot of the *German* peasant is. If we promise him to operate on that spot, he will be all for us. Thus, I believe, ... the mortgages may provide a wonderful opportunity. Just as raising the fertility of the soil. Insurance based on reciprocity. The ability to compete with the large estates. Schools. Everything must rest on the state principle.'—365

454 A reference to the destruction on 16 October 1869, by order of the Prussian military authorities and against court ruling, of the monument to the citizens of Celle (Hanover) who took part in the Langesalza (Thuringia) battle against the Prussians on 27 June 1866, at the time of the Austro-Prussian war, in which Hanover fought on the side of Austria. The Prussians had been defeated. War Minister Roon stated during the discussion of this issue in the Prussian Landtag: '*Prussia is a military state*, and the military authorities in Celle only

executed their inalienable supreme right' (see *Der Volksstaat*, No. 11, 6 November 1869).—366, 371

455 A reference to the issue of *The Bee-Hive* of 30 October 1869 (No. 420), which featured the editorial 'Ministers and the Fenian Prisoners'. It vindicated the policies pursued by Gladstone with regard to the Irish national liberation movement.—366

456 A strike of spinners in Bolton caused by reduction of wages by 5 per cent and the overall deterioration of the workers' conditions due to an industrial slump lasted from 29 October to 4 November 1869 and ended in defeat for the workers.—367

457 The reference is apparently to the article 'Unser Redakteur' published in *Der Pionier*, No. 42, 13 October 1869, which attacked Marx's *Capital*.—367

458 Liebknecht's inconsistent behaviour when popularising the decisions of the Basle Congress (see Note 447) was used by Schweitzer, who in a series of provocative articles in *Der Social-Demokrat* accused the Eisenachers of deceiving the workers, denouncing a socialist programme, and toeing the line of the People's Party (see Note 38). Bonhorst responded with an article 'Der famose Diktator und eine der Braunschweiger "Strohpuppen" im Lichte der Baseler Beschlüsse', in which he made it clear that the Lassallean General Association of German Workers only paid lip service to socialist principles while in fact doing nothing to implement them. Schweitzer, Bonhorst wrote, will never manage to pass himself off as a champion of the rural proletariat's interests, for he enjoys the support of the Prussian junkers. The attacks of the democratic press on the resolutions of the Basle Congress, he stated by way of conclusion, only serve to show where the dividing line lies between the Social-Democratic Party and its fellow-travellers in the People's Party. The article appeared in *Der Volksstaat*, Nos. 8 and 9, 27 and 30 October 1869.—367, 369.

459 Bonhorst was arrested in Magdeburg on 27 October 1869, on the charge of agitating against the Prussian Government, and was sentenced to four weeks' imprisonment.—367

460 On 6 November 1869, a ceremony of the opening of Blackfriars Bridge and Holborn Viaduct was held in London. Queen Victoria was present.—367

461 *Repealers*—people campaigning for a repeal of the Anglo-Irish Union of 1801 imposed upon Ireland by the British Government after the suppression of the Irish uprising of 1798. The Union, which came into force on 1 January 1801, put an end to the autonomy of Ireland and abolished the Irish Parliament. One of the consequences of its introduction was the abolition of tariffs established by the Irish Parliament at the end of the 18th century to protect the rising Irish industry, and this led to its total decline. Since the 1820s, the movement for the repeal of the Union began to gain momentum in Ireland. However, its bourgeois liberal leadership (O'Connell and others) regarded the campaign only as a means to wrest insignificant concessions for the Irish bourgeoisie from the British Government. Under the impact of the mass movement, the liberals were forced to found the Repealer Association (1840), and they attempted to make it agree to a compromise with the British ruling classes.—368, 390, 398, 473

462 Arthur O'Connor, a prominent member of the Irish national liberation movement, was a leader of the secret revolutionary organisation, the United

Irishmen, whose goal was to establish an independent Irish republic. In May and June 1798, the members of the United Irishmen staged an uprising against the British rule. O'Connor and other leaders were arrested on the eve of the uprising. The uprising was brutally suppressed (see Note 461).—368, 398

463 Marx ironically likens Freiligrath to the manufacturer Classen-Kappelmann, member of the Cologne city council, who became a notorious figure in 1865. In July 1865 he took part in the preparation of a banquet for the Party of Progress members who were deputies of the Chamber of Representatives of the Prussian Landtag in opposition to the Prussian Government. The banquet was banned and Classen-Kappelmann, who feared arrest, left for Belgium. The guests arrived to find the premises closed and assembled at the Zoo. The assembly was dispersed by the police.—371

464 Marx refers to the circular letter to the French electors drawn up by Ledru-Rollin, participant in the 1848-49 revolution, who lived in London as an émigré up to 1870. Describing it as that of a pretender, Marx alludes to the fact that in the Presidential elections in France on 10 December 1848, Ledru-Rollin nominated himself as a representative of petty-bourgeois democrats. His letter, dated 7 November 1869, was published in *Le Réveil* on 10 November under the heading 'Aux électeurs'.—371

465 The original of this letter is kept in the archives of the Greater London Library (Greater London Council).—372

466 Jeremiah O'Donovan Rossa, a leader of the Irish national liberation movement, who was under arrest at the time, was elected to the House of Commons as member for Tipperary on 25 November 1869.

An amnesty in Italy—Engels means a partial amnesty announced in Italy in November 1869 covering individual categories of political offences, specifically, service misdemeanors in the National Guard.—373, 387, 420, 548

467 This letter was first published in English in an abridged form in: *The Labour Monthly*, Vol. 14, No. 12, London, 1932; fragments of this letter were published in: Marx K., Engels F., *Correspondence. 1846-1895*, London [1934], and Marx K., Engels F., *Selected Correspondence*, Moscow, 1975.—375

468 The reference is to Marx's speeches on the policy of the British Government towards the Irish prisoners, which he made at the General Council meetings of 16 and 23 November 1869, and which were recorded by the Council's Secretary Eccarius in the Minute Book (see present edition, Vol. 21, pp. 407-12).—375

469 In a speech made on 7 October 1862 in Newcastle, Gladstone (then Finance Minister) greeted the Confederation of the Southern States in the person of its President Jefferson Davis, justifying the rebellion of the southern slaveowners against Lincoln's lawful government. The speech was published in *The Times*, No. 24372 on 9 October 1862. It was referred to at the General Council discussion mentioned above.—375

470 In a letter of 13 November 1869, Wilhelm Liebknecht requested Marx and Engels to write several scientific articles for *Der Volksstaat*. He also voiced his regret that they had failed to meet during Marx's stay in Germany (see Note 349).—376

471 Élisée Reclus, a French geographer and sociologist, member of the International Working Men's Association, was staying in London in July and August of 1869 and attended two meetings of the General Council.—377, 378

472 A fragment of this letter was first published in English in: *The Labour Monthly*, Vol. 14, No. 12, London, 1932.—377

473 The amnesty in Russia issued on 25 May (6 June) 1868 extended to political prisoners sentenced before 1 January 1866, and a section of prisoners of foreign extraction who, according to Imperial Edict, were expelled from the country for good. Under the amnesty, a number of Poles sentenced to less than twenty years' imprisonment were able to return home.—377

474 The *Guelphic conspiracy*—a reference to the events that developed after the Austro-Prussian war of 1866 in Hanover, which lost its independence and was annexed by Prussia. The former King of Hanover, George V, who strove for the restoration of the Guelph dynasty, set up the so-called Guelph Legion in France in the spring of 1867. It comprised mostly émigrés from Hanover. On 8 April 1868, the Prussian legal bodies sentenced a number of officers who had taken part in its foundation to ten years' imprisonment. However, seeking to consolidate its position in Hanover, the Prussian Government announced an amnesty of the rank-and-file members early in May that year.—377

475 See present edition, Vol. 38, pp. 423-24.—382

476 Engels is referring to the report 'Vom Rechte das mit uns geboren' read at the Berlin General Union for the Defence of Rights by Scheffer, champion of the idea of free religious communities. The purpose of such communities was to 'foster a higher degree of awareness in the people'. The report was published in *Der Volksstaat*, nos. 12 (supplement), 13 14 and 15; 10, 13, 17 and 20 November 1869.—382

477 An excerpt from this letter was published in English in: *The Labour Monthly*, Vol. 14, No. 12, London, 1932; in an abridged form, it was published in: Marx K., Engels F., *Correspondence. 1846-1895*, London [1934]. It was published in English in full for the first time in: Marx K., Engels F., *Selected Correspondence*, Moscow, 1975.—383

478 Marx is referring to the General Council meeting of 23 November 1869, which continued the discussion of the policies of the British Government with respect to the Irish political prisoners (see notes 452 and 468).—386

479 Engels is referring to an armed uprising staged in the spring of 1867 by the Irish revolutionaries, the Fenians (see notes 86 and 452). The British authorities, who had been informed that preparations for an uprising were under way, easily suppressed the isolated outbursts. Many Fenian leaders were arrested and tried.—387

480 *Chetham Library*—the oldest library in Manchester, founded in 1653. Marx worked there together with Engels in 1845 during his first stay in England.—388, 402, 518

481 *Brehon Law*, the general name of the Celtic common law code, took its name from the Brehons, judges in Celtic Ireland. The laws operated in Ireland until 1605, when they were repealed by the British Government. Their publication was started by the Brehon Law Commission set up by the British Government in 1852. The first three volumes of the *Ancient Laws of Ireland* appeared in 1865, 1869 and 1873 and made up the collection *The Senchus Mor*, or *Great Old Law Book*. The publication continued up to 1901.—388, 409, 442, 451, 509, 519

482 J. Davies, *Historical Tracts*, London, 1787. Engels sets forth the contents of two of Davies' tracts, 'A letter from Sir John Davies to Robert Earl of Salisbury,

1607', and 'A letter from Sir John Davies to Robert Earl of Salisbury concerning the State of Ireland, 1610'.—388

483 Engels is referring to the speech made by Napoleon III on 29 November 1869, at the opening of an extraordinary session of the French National Assembly (published on 30 November in the *Journal des Débats* and other French newspapers), and the speeches of Prévost-Paradol in Edinburgh during his tour of Britain in November 1869 (published in the British press and in a number of French papers, including the *Journal des Débats* on 16 and 18 November 1869).—388

484 This letter was published in English for the first time in: *Irish Opinion. The Voice of Labour*, No. 26, 25 May 1918, Dublin.—389

485 At the time of the English Revolution an uprising broke out in Ireland which resulted in the Catholic part of the island splitting with England. The uprising was suppressed in 1649-52. The 'pacification' of Ireland was executed with the utmost brutality and ended in the mass transfer of land to the new English landlords; this strengthened the landowner and bourgeois strata and paved the way for the restoration of the monarchy in 1660.—391

486 A writ of *Habeas Corpus*—the name given in English judicial procedure to a document enjoining the appropriate authorities to present an arrested person before court on the demand of the persons interested to check the legitimacy of the arrest. Having considered the reasons for the arrest, the court either frees the arrested person, sends him back to prison or releases him on bail or guarantee. The procedure, laid down by an Act of Parliament of 1679, does not apply to persons accused of high treason and can be suspended by decision of Parliament. The British authorities frequently made use of this exception in Ireland.—391, 394, 419

487 At one of the sittings of the Prussian Landtag, Minister for the Interior Count von Eulenburg made a statement justifying the violations of the law by the Prussian military authorities in Celle (see Note 454).—391

488 This is Marx's reply to Kugelmann's request to give him the address of E. Reich, to whom Kugelmann was going to send Volume One of *Capital*. Reich's book *Ueber die Entartung des Menschen, ihre Ursachen und Verhütung* (Erlangen, 1868) was given by Kugelmann to Marx during the latter's stay in Germany in September and October 1869. The Introduction to the book is marked 'Gotha, 5. Mai 1868'. —391

489 An excerpt from this letter was first published in English in: *The Labour Monthly*, Vol. 15, No. 1, London, 1933.—392, 394, 396

490 Marx refers to the reports of the General Council meetings of 16 and 23 November 1869, at which he made a speech on the policies of the British Government with regard to the Irish prisoners (see present edition, Vol. 21). The reports were written for the press by two General Council members, Eccarius ('The British Government and the Irish Political Prisoners', in: *The Reynolds's Newspaper*, nos. 1006 and 1008, 21 November and 5 December 1869) and Harris ('International Working Men's Association', in: *The National Reformer*, 28 November and 5 December 1869).

By Harris' 'currency panacea', Marx means his article 'Yours or Mine; or Short Chapters, Showing the True Basis of Property and the Causes of its Unequal Distribution' in: *The National Reformer*, 5 December 1869. *The Reynolds's*

Newspaper and *The National Reformer* were published on Saturday but were dated Sunday; that is why the Sunday 5 December issue of *The National Reformer* was sent by Marx to Engels on Saturday, 4 December.— 392, 394

491 A reference to the second issue ('the attitude of the British working class to the Irish question') in the discussion on Ireland in the General Council (see this volume, pp. 371-72). Marx had proposed to open it on 7 December 1869, but was unable to attend on account of an illness. The General Council never took up the issue again. Marx expounded his views on the position of the British working class with regard to Ireland in his letter to Engels of 10 December 1869 (see this volume, p. 398) and in the circular letter 'The General Council to the Federal Council of Romance Switzerland' (present edition, Vol. 21).— 392

492 After the defeat of the 1867 armed uprising in Ireland (see Note 479), many Fenians were arrested and tried. On 18 September 1867 in Manchester, the Fenians made an armed attack on a prison van in an attempt to liberate Kelly and Deasy, two of their leaders. Five Irishmen captured on the spot were sentenced to death, which triggered off a wave of protests in Ireland and England. Members of the General Council also voiced their protest. Seeking to work out a coordinated tactic of the proletariat in the national question and to popularise the ideas of proletarian internationalism among English workers, Marx persuaded the General Council to hold a public discussion of the Irish question to which representatives of the Irish and English press were to be invited. The discussion began on 19 November, and on 20 November, at an extraordinary meeting, the General Council adopted the petition 'The Fenian Prisoners at Manchester and the International Working Men's Association' (see present edition, Vol. 21). This is the document that Marx mentions in a letter to Engels.— 392.

493 Marx's letter to Robert Applegarth of 1 December 1869 has not been found.— 393

494 Marx is referring to Robert Applegarth's letter to him of 2 December 1869:

'Amalgamated Society
of Carpenters and Joiners, General Office.
113 Stamford Street,
Waterloo Road, S.E.
London, Dec 2d 1869

'My dear Marx,
'Your note is just to hand.
'I have not replied to the enquiries—made as to whether I voted for Common property in Land and I don't intend doing so till I hear from you.
'I send you a copy of the question put to me.
'"Was any resolution passed to which you were, or were not a party, against all private property in land?"
'The above is the question and the first words of my reply will be.
'"A resolution *was passed* declaring 'That society has a right to abolish private property in land and to convert it into common property and that there was a necessity for doing so'. And for this resolution I gave my vote most cordially."
'I then want to say in a few words why Land ought to be made common property.
'I would not have troubled you had I been asked the question only as reference to some opinion I had expressed apart from the International but as

my reply will be placed in the hands of those who would *by one means or another*
have to disgorge their ill gotten acres, if land was made common property and
as my vote was given at one of our Congresses I feel I ought to ask the advice
of those who understood the question thoroughly before I was born.
'I shall therefore wait till I hear from you.
'I am yours truly
'R. Applegarth'.—393, 395

495 Marx's letter to R. Applegarth of 3 December 1869, has not been found.—393

496 In a letter to Marx of 11 November 1869, Wilhelm Bracke noted that the
arrest of Leonard von Bonhorst had created additional difficulties for the
Committee of the Social-Democratic Workers' Party (see Note 459).
Bonhorst was Secretary of the Brunswick Party Committee.—393, 395

497 The demand for the repeal of the Union (see Note 461) had been the most
popular slogan in Ireland since the 1820s.—394

498 A reference to the letter from Klein and Moll to Engels of 3 December 1869.
They wrote about the financial difficulties encountered by the Solingen
cooperative for the production of steel and iron goods (see Note 330) and
requested Engels for assistance. Inscribed on the letter in Engels' hand is:
'Answered on 8 February 1870. Fifty thaler sent by registered mail, with the
interest to be added to the cooperative's reserve fund'.—395, 396, 420

499 On 30 November 1869, at a sitting of the Corps législatif, bourgeois
republican Jules Favre made an inquiry into illegal actions by the government,
including postponement of the Corps' assemblies and interference of the
authorities in the elections to the Corps in May and June 1869. Particularly
scandalous facts were revealed at the sitting of 7 December at which deputy
Durand's mandate was being confirmed. Minister for the Interior Forcade-
Laroquette spoke in defence of Durand. The proposal to hold an investigation
into the results of the vote on Durand's candidature was advanced by Jules
Favre. Liberal deputies who belonged to the oppositional parliamentary group
of French bourgeoisie, the so-called third party, did not support Jules Favre
and abstained from voting. Jules Favre's proposal was rejected by 135 votes to
86.—395

500 The toast to Marx and Engels as editors of the *Neue Rheinische Zeitung* was
proposed by Karl Klein in May 1864 in Cologne on the occasion of the
anniversary celebration of the General Association of German Workers in the
presence of Ferdinand Lassalle.—397

501 Marx is referring to his contributions to the *New-York Daily Tribune* (in
1851-62). See, for instance, Marx's essays 'Forced Emigration.—Kossuth and
Mazzini.—The Refugee Question.—Election Bribery in England.—Mr. Cobden'
published in the spring of 1853 in that newspaper (present edition, Vol. 11,
pp. 528-34).—398

502 Engels proposed to include the section 'Rebellion and Union. 1780-1801' into the
chapter 'English Rule' (see present edition, Vol. 21, p. 307). Marx's recommendation to Engels that he should write a separate chapter on the period from 1779 to
1800 for his book on Irish history (see Note 438) was based on his own research.
Marx prepared excerpts on Irish history from 1776 to 1801.—398

503 Marx is probably alluding to the presence of Empress Eugénie Montijo at a
session of the French Cabinet of Ministers of 9 December 1869, which pro-

voked deep indignation among the liberal and democratic opposition in Paris.—399

504 A fragment of this letter was published in English for the first time in: Marx and Engels, *On the United States,* Moscow, 1979.—401

505 Engels probably means the English edition of the book by W. Camden *Britannia or Chorographical Description of the most flourishing Kingdoms England, Scotland and Ireland and the Islands adjoining,* London, 1637. The book, originally written in Latin, was published in 1590 as one volume with another work by Camden, *Hiberniae et insularum Britanniae adiacentium descriptio,* which Engels ascribed, apparently erroneously, to Giraldus Cambrensis. In his further work on the history of Ireland (see Note 438), Engels used the publication (in Latin) *Giraldi Cambrensis Opera,* ed. J. S. Brewer, London, Longmans, 1863. *Expugnatio* was included in Vol. V of this edition, which was published in 1867 (see Note 528), and also appeared in the English translation published by Bohn in London in 1863, *The Historical Works of Giraldus Cambrensis.*—402

506 Probably an error in the text; the first edition of Robert Kane's *The Industrial Resources of Ireland* appeared in 1844, and the second—in 1845 in Dublin. Engels probably refers to the latter.—402

507 Having failed to move to the forefront in the International's leadership at the Basle Congress (see Note 379), Bakunin altered his tactics and launched an open campaign against the General Council. His followers came to form the majority in *L'Égalité* weekly published in Switzerland, and as early as 6 November 1869, No. 42 carried an editorial 'Le Bulletin du Conseil Général', accusing the General Council of violating articles 2 and 3 of the Regulations on the publication of an information bulletin dealing with the conditions of workers in various countries. On 13 November, No. 43 published another article, 'L'Organisation de l'Internationale', which proposed the establishment of a federal council for England, allegedly to make it easier for the General Council to manage the more general affairs of the International. On 27 November, No. 45 featured an article 'Les Parties Politiques à Genève et l'Internationale', which suggested abstention from politics, and on 11 December, *L'Égalité* No. 47 lashed out against the Council's position on the Irish question in the editorial entitled 'Réflexions'. *Le Progrès* newspaper, which was published in Switzerland, assumed a similarly critical stand.

The question of *L'Égalité* and *Le Progrès* was discussed at the General Council for the first time at a meeting of 14 December 1869. On 1 January 1870, an extraordinary Council meeting approved a circular letter, drawn up by Marx, 'The General Council to the Federal Council of Romance Switzerland', which was sent out to the International's sections (see present edition, Vol. 21, p. 84).—404, 411, 489, 492

508 A reference to a resolution of the Basle Congress adopted on 9 September 1869, on the procedure of settling conflicts between the International's sections. (See 'Report of the Fourth Annual Congress of the International Working Men's Association', London [1869], p. 21.) It is included in the work of Marx and Engels *Fictitious Splits in the International. Private Circular from the General Council of the International Working Men's Association* (present edition, Vol. 23).—404, 480

509 Marx is referring to the Resolution of the Geneva Congress of the International on publishing a bulletin (in: *Rules and Administrative Regulations of*

the International Working Men's Association, London [1867], Articles 2, 3, present edition, Vol. 20, p. 442. See also: K. Marx, 'The General Council to the Federal Council of Romance Switzerland', present edition, Vol. 21, p. 84).— 405

510 Marx is referring to the Central Committee of the German-language sections in Switzerland headed by J. Ph. Becker. Since November 1865, it was the organisational centre for the sections of German-language workers not only in Switzerland but in Germany, Austria and the countries where German workers were living in emigration.— 405

511 On 5 January 1870, Marx was a member of the General Council delegation to the funeral of Robert Shaw, a house-painter and member of the General Council. The obituary Marx had written on the instruction of the Council was published in the Belgian newspaper *L'Internationale,* No. 53, 16 January 1870 (see present edition, Vol. 21, p. 92).— 406

512 The report to the Belgian Federal Council written by Marx as a temporary Corresponding Secretary for Belgium is not extant. It had been forwarded to De Paepe through Hins alongside a copy of the circular letter 'The General Council to the Federal Council of Romance Switzerland' (see present edition, Vol. 21, p. 84) and Robert Shaw's obituary (see Note 511).— 406, 411, 414

513 Engels left for Barmen to visit his mother in late December 1869, and returned to Manchester on 6 January, 1870.— 407, 548

514 Apparently a reference to Ollivier's liberal ministry's assuming office in France on 2 January 1870. In Germany, this event was regarded as a step towards normalising relations between France and the North German Confederation.— 407

515 Engels refers to Fritz Mende's book *Herr J. B. von Schweitzer und die Organisation des Lassalle'schen All[gemeinen] deutschen Arbeitervereins,* Leipzig, 1869. Mende headed a small group of Lassalleans who had split off from the General Association of German Workers (see Note 104) under the influence of Sophie von Hatzfeldt and formed the Lassallean General Association of German Workers in 1867. In 1872, it virtually ceased to exist.— 408

516 On 10 January 1870, Prince Pierre Napoléon Bonaparte murdered Victor Noir, a reporter on the republican newspaper *La Marseillaise,* in his house. Noir visited Pierre Napoléon as a second of the Blanquist Pascal Grousset, also a *La Marseillaise* reporter, who had challenged the prince to a duel. The murder was committed a few days after the coming into office of Ollivier's liberal ministry, which the liberal bourgeoisie expected to introduce a number of reforms. The murder of Noir provoked an outburst of indignation in democratic quarters and bolstered the republican movement in France.— 409, 423, 553

517 Prévost-Paradol's article was published on Monday, 17 January 1870, in the *Journal des Débats.*— 409

518 A reference to the speech by John Bright, Minister of Trade in Gladstone's liberal government, made at Birmingham on 11 January. It was published by *The Times* on 12 January 1870.— 409

519 Marx read in Russian Herzen's book *Prison and Exile* (London, 1854; published under the pen-name of Iskander) which belonged to Engels and contained his

marginal notes. On page 196 Marx wrote: 'Finished 9 January 1870'. The copy is kept at the International Institute of Social History in Amsterdam.— 411

520 In a letter of 20 December 1869, Liebknecht asked Engels for permission to reprint his work *The Peasant War in Germany* (see present edition, Vol. 10, pp. 397-482) in *Der Volksstaat*, and subsequently as a separate pamphlet. He also asked for a short preface to the work.

Liebknecht's letter of 8 February 1870 shows that Engels had given his consent. The preface (see present edition, Vol. 21, p. 93) and five chapters appeared in *Der Volksstaat* between 2 April and 25 June 1870; in October 1870 the work was published as a pamphlet.— 411, 417, 425

521 *Land League*—a reference to the Land Tenure Reform Association founded in July 1869 on the initiative of John Stuart Mill. Its stated purpose was to restore the small peasantry by renting plots of land to the unemployed.— 412

522 Marx intended to expound the issues of landed property and rent in the third book of Volume Two of *Capital*, but altered the original plan in the course of his work. The manuscript of the third book of *Capital* was written in 1864-65. After Volume One of *Capital* appeared in 1867, Marx did a great deal of work collecting new material about landed property in Belgium and a number of other European and American countries. However, it did not allow him to re-write the section on land rent. Later, Engels included the part on landed property into Volume Three of *Capital*. For details, see Engels' preface to Volume Three of *Capital* (present edition, Vol. 37).— 412

523 De Paepe listed the works on landed property in Belgium in a letter to Marx of 1 February 1870.— 412

524 A reference to Hins' letter to Stepney of 21 January 1870, which was forwarded to Marx by Eccarius on 27 January 1870.— 412, 424, 431

525 Even before the Romance Federal Council had received the circular letter 'The General Council to the Federal Council of Romance Switzerland' (see Note 507), it managed to change the composition of the editorial board of *L'Égalité*. After the Bakuninists had withdrawn, the newspaper began to support the policy of the General Council. The report on the withdrawal of seven members from *L'Égalité* editorial board ('Aux sections romands') appeared in the newspaper on 8 January 1870, No. 2 and on 15 January the next issue (No. 3) carried a statement by the editors themselves. It was signed, among others, by J. Ph. Becker, who prior to April 1870 vacillated in his attitude to the Bakuninists. Soon, however, he went back on his decision to withdraw.— 412, 430

526 The private letter from Perret to Jung mentioned here was dated 4 January 1870, like the official letter. The excerpt that follows has also been preserved as a copy made by Marx's daughter Jenny. The last passage of the excerpt was copied by Marx.— 413

527 Later, in his letter to Hermann Jung of 15 April 1870 Henri Perret gave a detailed account of the incident. James Guillaume's father was secretary of the State Council in Neuchâtel, and it was he who signed Martinaud's mandate.— 413

528 In 1863, Volume III of Giraldus Cambrensis' complete works was published (*Giraldi Cambrensis Opera*, voluminis I-VII, Londini, 1861-1877). Volumes I-IV were brought out by J. S. Brewer, and volumes V-VII—by James F. Dimock.

His works *Expugnatio Hibernica* and *Topographia Hibernica* were included in Volume V, which appeared in 1867. (See also this volume, p. 402).—416

529 On 20 January 1870, at an electors' meeting in Berlin, bourgeois democrat Johann Jacoby, deputy of the Prussian Landtag, made a speech on the goals of the labour movement, in which he said, among other things: 'From the viewpoint of a future historian of culture, the emergence of the tinies workers' association will be of more value than the Battle of Sadowa'. On 23 January, having received a report of the meeting, Kugelmann wrote to Jacoby: 'Why, making references to Aristotle, de Maistre, Owen, von Gentz and John Stuart Mill do you ignore the name of *Karl Marx*, a researcher compared to whom all the above-mentioned, with the exception of Aristotle, are mere pygmies, a thinker who can by right be called *the brain of the 19th century*; whose teaching you have not only failed "to develop further" but the other way round, ... his epoch-making works, specifically, the *Manifesto of the Communist Party* and *Capital*, have provided you with *the most significant* material.' On 24 January, Jacoby wrote to Kugelmann acknowledging Marx's indisputable merits; still he tried to justify himself, saying that his popular exposition required no specific references. These letters of Kugelmann's and Jacobi's were forwarded by Marx to Engels.—417

530 The first attempt to translate Marx's book *The Eighteenth Brumaire of Louis Bonaparte* into French was made by Keller in December 1869, who interrupted his work on the French translation of *Capital* (see Note 441). Keller's work remained unfinished. On the first publication of the book in French see Note 303.—419

531 Engels is referring to the German translation of the work by P. Lilienfeld *Land and Freedom* (Лилиенфельд, *Земля и воля*), which appeared in St. Petersburg in 1868. The translation, 'Land und Freiheit', was published in: J. Eckardt, *Russlands ländische Zustände seit Aufhebung der Leibeigenschaft*, Leipzig, 1870.— 419, 426

532 A reference to the revolutionary events that took place in Elberfeld in May 1849. The city Committee of Public Safety appointed Engels supervisor of all works to build defensive works and barricades, and commander of the artillery. Local bourgeoisie, who feared that Engels' authority might become too great, demanded that the Committee issued an order for his arrest. The Solingen workers, with whom Engels had arrived in Elberfeld, and also the workers of Elberfeld were outraged by the bourgeoisie's behaviour and resolutely rose to his defence. Unwilling to be the cause of a split in the insurgents' camp, Engels left Elberfeld for Cologne on 15 May. He gave a detailed account of these events in his report 'Elberfeld' to the *Neue Rheinische Zeitung*, No. 300, 17 May 1849 (see present edition, Vol. 9, pp. 447-49), and in his work 'The Campaign for the German Imperial Constitution' (see present edition, Vol. 10, pp. 159-71).—420

533 A reference to the arrest of Rochefort on 7 February 1870, in La Villette, a workers' suburb of Paris, for his article about Victor Noir's murder (see Note 516) published by *La Marseillaise*, 12 January 1870.

White smocks was a name for French police agents. In June 1869, the Police Prefecture of Paris made an attempt to provoke a spontaneous outburst among the workers using the 'white smocks' who staged manifestations, built barricades, sang the *Marseillaise*, etc. Engels expressed his apprehensions that similar provocations would be staged after Rochefort's arrest.—422, 427

534 Excerpts from this letter were first published in English in: Marx K., Engels F., *Correspondence. 1846-1895*, London [1934]; and in: Karl Marx, Friedrich Engels, *Selected Letters. The Personal Correspondence. 1844-1877* edited by Fritz J. Raddatz, translated from the German by Ewald Osers, Boston, Toronto, 1981.—422

535 Probably a reference to the book by P. Lanfrey, *Histoire de Napoléon I*, Tomes I-IV, Paris, 1867-1870. Excerpts from Chapter VII, Volume IV, 'Le Guet-apens de Bayonne', were printed in *La Cloche*, Nos. 44-46, 1-3 February 1870.—423, 426

536 A reference to Perret's letter to Jung of 4 January 1870. It was quoted by Marx in his letter to De Paepe, 24 January 1870 (see this volume, p. 413).—424, 426

537 Marx is referring to an item that appeared in *La Marseillaise* on 2 February 1870, and was inspired by Blind. It dealt with the fact that in 1849, Blind was unlawfully arrested in France and put into prison, although as an official representative of the revolutionary Baden government he enjoyed diplomatic immunity. The item contained a demand for an amnesty for Blind as an alleged former member of the German National Assembly and a diplomatic representative of the Frankfurt Parliament. In actual fact, Karl Blind and Jacob Friedrich Schütz (Blind wrote Schurz, since that name was better known belonging as it did to a Brigadier General of the Northern States of America, subsequently the American Secretary for Home Affairs) had never been members of the National Assembly. Schütz had been sent to Paris as a chargé d'affaires of the Palatinate to establish diplomatic relations with France, buy munitions, and recruit commanding officers.
On the *German National Assembly*, see Note 256.—425

538 Engels is referring to Wilhelm Liebknecht's letter of 8 February 1870. To explain why he did not know about the publication of the second edition of Marx's *The Eighteenth Brumaire of Louis Bonaparte* (see present edition, Vol. 11, pp. 99-197), Liebknecht wrote that Otto Meissner had not informed either *Der Volksstaat* or *Die Zukunft* about this, and as he put it, 'a week ago, I did not know for sure if the book had appeared'.—426, 428

539 A reference to the article by Alfred Naquet featured by *La Marseillaise*, No. 43, on 30 January 1870: 'La Révolution et la science. De la fabrication du coton-poudre et de son application, soit comme poudre de guerre, soit comme poudre de mine'.—426

540 A reference to Bouverie's speech in the House of Commons on 10 February 1870, in connection with the proposal of the government to deprive O'Donovan Rossa of the right to attend its sessions (see Note 466). His speech was published by *The Times* on 11 February 1870, in a report on the session.—429

541 Marx is referring to a group of Russian political refugees from among the young intellectuals, followers of the noted Russian revolutionary democrats Chernyshevsky and Dobrolyubov. In the spring of 1870, they founded the Russian Section of the First International in Geneva. A substantial contribution to its organisation had been made by A. A. Serno-Solovyevich, a member of the International, who died in 1869. On 12 March 1870, the Committee of the Section sent the General Council its Programme, Rules, and a letter to Marx requesting him to be their representative at the General Council. The programme of the Russian Section defined its objectives as follows: '1. To popularise the ideas and principles of the International Association in Russia by

every possible rational means, whose special character and mode of influence stem from the very position of the country. 2. To promote the establishment of international sections among Russian workers. 3. To help establish stable, mutual contacts between the working classes of Russia and Western Europe, including assistance to each other in order to more successfully attain their common goal, emancipation.' This document, and the official reply of the General Council written by Marx, 'The General Council of the International Working Men's Association to Committee Members of the Russian Section in Geneva' (see present edition, Vol. 21) were published by the press organ of the Russian Section, *Narodnoye Dyelo* (People's Cause), No. 1, 15 April 1870.

At its meeting of 22 March 1870, the General Council admitted the Russian Section to the International, and Marx agreed to represent it at the General Council. The Section rendered Marx and Engels substantial assistance in counteracting the Bakuninists' attempts to split the International. Members of the Russian Section, including Nikolai Utin, Anton Trusov, Yekaterina Barteneva, Victor Bartenev, Yelena Dmitriyeva, and Anna Korvin-Krukovskaya, took an active part in the Swiss and international working class movement. The Section made an attempt to establish contacts with the revolutionary movement in Russia. Its work was terminated in 1872.—430, 462, 492

542 Marx apparently means the January 1870 issue of *Der Vorbote*, edited by J. Ph. Becker, which featured materials describing the activities of the International, specifically, the fourth article in the series *Der vierte Kongress der internationalen Arbeiterassoziationen in Basel*, written in the spirit of the policies pursued by the General Council.
On Bakunin's statements in *L'Égalité*, see Note 507.—431

543 A reference to the events connected with the decision of the French National Assembly to withdraw Rochefort's deputy's mandate for his appeal to rise against the Empire after the murder of Victor Noir, reporter from *La Marseillaise*, by Prince Pierre Napoléon Bonaparte (see notes 516 and 553). Flourens was an organiser of meetings and assemblies for the defence of Rochefort. One of such meetings was to be held on 7 February 1870, on the premises of *La Marseillaise* editorial offices, but Rochefort was arrested when entering the room. The initiative passed to Flourens, who immediately announced that the government had been overthrown, and declared uninterrupted revolution. Assisted by those present, he arrested the police commissary present at the meeting, led the people out into the street, and they made for Belleville. Sixty people actually got there. Flourens hoped to use the assistance of a number of junior officers to seize arms at the Prince Eugene's barracks and the Belleville Theatre, where rifles were kept. However, Flourens' plan fell through. The liaison men failed in their task and workers did not come to the assistance, and in the end only Flourens and one young man remained at the barricade, leaving it late at night. By morning, it was taken by soldiers.—431

544 Engels is referring to the *Irish Land Bill*, which was discussed in the British Parliament in the first half of 1870. Submitted by Gladstone on 15 February 1870 for the British Government on the pretext of assisting Irish tenants, it contained so many provisos and restrictions that it actually left the basis of big landownership by the English landlords in Ireland intact. It also preserved their right to raise rents and to drive tenants off the land, stipulating only that the landlords pay compensation to the tenants for land improvement, and instituting a definite judicial procedure for this. The Land Act was passed in

August 1870. The landlords sabotaged the implementation of the Act in every way and found loopholes in it. The Act greatly promoted the concentration of farms in Ireland into big estates and the ruination of small Irish tenants.—432, 437, 456

545 A reference to the separate *Peaces of Basle* of 1795 signed by the French Republic on the one hand, and Prussia and Spain on the other. The signing of these treaties isolated Britain and Austria and led to the disintegration of the first anti-French coalition which had included Britain, Austria, Spain and Prussia.—432

546 Marx touched on these issues in a number of his works. See, for instance, *A Contribution to the Critique of Political Economy*, Chapter 1 (present edition, Vol. 29); *The Economic Manuscripts of 1857-58*, § 1 'Production' (present edition, Vol. 28); also in Volume One of *Capital* (present edition, Vol. 35, Part I, Chapter One).—434

547 The theory that the Russians are descendants of the Mongols was advanced by Franciszek Duchinski in his works published in 1854-61, specifically *Les origines slaves. Pologne et Ruthénie*, Paris, 1861. H. Martin expounded this theory in his work *La Russie et l'Europe*, Paris, 1866, which was translated into German by Kinkel in 1869.—435

548 Under the treaty of 30 March 1867, Russia's territories in North America (Alaska) passed over to the USA on payment of $7,200,000 (11 million roubles by contemporary exchange rate).—435

549 A reference to Bakunin's *Confession* to Tsar Nicholas I written in 1851 during his imprisonment at the Peter and Paul Fortress. Bakunin acknowledged his errors and characterised his revolutionary activities as 'political madness'. Marx communicated to Engels some data from the article published by *Moskovskiye Vedomosty*, No. 4, 6 January 1870.—437

550 On 8 March 1870, using its right of an arbiter in conflicts between the International's sections (see Note 508), the General Council examined the Sub-Committee's report and ruled on the conflict that had emerged in Lyons between the old Lyons Section represented by Schettel and other persons who stood close to Left-wing republicans, and the group headed by the Bakuninist Albert Richard. The General Council found the accusations groundless, and approved Richard's appointment as Corresponding Secretary of the International Working Men's Association. The statement made by the General Council stressed the need to be careful and avoid personal animosities fraught with conflict, and to concentrate all the strength and all the energy for the speedy triumph of the principles of the International Working Men's Association.— 437, 480

551 In February 1870, three candidates stood for Parliament in Southwark: Beresford (Conservative Party), Odger (a workers' candidate), and Waterlow (Liberal Party). They received 4,686, 4,382 and 2,966 votes respectively.—437

552 This is a reply to Collet's letter of 26 January 1870. C. D. Collet had asked for details of the Russian railway loan. Collet sent this letter by Marx on to Urquhart with his own postscript. At its first publication in the first Russian edition of Marx's and Engels' *Works*, Urquhart was mistakenly named as the addressee. The letter first appeared in English in: *Bulletin of the Society for the Study of Labour History*, Leeds, 1967, No. 14, pp. 16-17.—438

553 The Russian Railway Loan bonds worth £12 mln were released for sale by
Lionel Nathan Rothschild in Paris on 27 January 1870. This was reported,
specifically, by *Moskovskiye Vedomosty*, No. 11, 27 (15) January 1870.—438

554 This letter was written by Marx on the back of Borkheim's letter to him of
19 February 1870. Borkheim informed Marx about his intention to translate
Flerovsky's book (Н. Флеровскій, *Положеніе рабочаго класса въ Poccиu*) into
English and requested Marx to write a preface to it.—440

555 A reference to Peter Imandt's letter to Marx of 18 February 1870, in which he
asked for Marx's advice concerning the Prussian Government's demand, lodged
through the Consul of the North German Confederation, that he pay the fees
for the course of lectures on theology he attended at Bonn University in
1844-45. Before replying to Imandt, Marx consulted Engels. (For Marx's reply
to Peter Imandt, see this volume, pp. 443-44.)—440, 443

556 On 21 February, Marx forwarded to *L'Internationale* certain material disclosing
the cruel treatment of the members of the Irish national liberation movement
by the British authorities. Marx expected that De Paepe would use this material
for an article. However, the editorial board decided to print Marx's sketch
verbatim dividing it into two instalments, which appeared on 27 February and
6 March, nos. 59 and 60 (see K. Marx, 'The English Government and the Fenian
Prisoners', present edition, Vol. 21). On the publication of this material see also
this volume, p. 453.—440

557 Engels quotes articles from Napoleon I's *Code civil* passed in 1804 and
introduced also in the West and South-West German territories conquered by
France. The Code continued to operate in the Rhine Province after its
annexation by Prussia. Article 2265 quoted by Engels reads in full: 'Those who
acquire real estate in good faith (bona fides) through honest work and on legal
grounds, are acquiring property by virtue of the expiry of the ten years' statute
of limitations if the owner is residing on the territory under the jurisdiction of
the court of appeal in which the property is located, and twenty years
limitations, if he is residing outside this territory.'—441

558 Engels refers to Favre's speech made on 21 February 1870 at a session of the
Corps législatif and featured by the *Journal des Débats* on 22 February
1870.—442

559 The reference is to the death of the Lafargues' daughter born on 1 January
1870. She died at the end of February.—444

560 See Note 556.—444

561 A. Talandier's article 'L'Irlande et le catholicisme', spearheaded against the
Irish national liberation movement appeared in *La Marseillaise*, No. 58,
16 February 1870; a synopsis of the article featured by *The Daily News*
appeared in *La Marseillaise*, No. 60, 18 February 1870. A. Talandier's obituary
Nécrologie. Alexandre Hertzen, originally carried by the Paris newspaper
Democratie, was reprinted by the Brussels' *L'Internationale*, No. 56, 6 February
1870.—445

562 A reference to the series of eight articles on the Irish question written by
Marx's daughter Jenny and published in *La Marseillaise* between 1 March and
24 April 1870, under the pen-name of J. Williams (see present edition, Vol. 21,
pp. 414-41). The third article was written by Jenny in collaboration with her
father. In subject-matter they have a connection with Marx's essay 'The English

Government and the Fenian Prisoners' (see Note 556) — 445, 449, 458, 466, 488, 501, 557

563 On 15 February 1870, the House of Representatives of US Congress passed a resolution obliging the President to submit to it the information on the cases of American citizens kept in British prisons on the charge of involvement with the Fenians.— 445

564 The soirée at the place of the French petty-bourgeois socialist Moilin at which the plans for social reform were discussed, was described by Lafargue in his letter to Marx of January 1870.— 449

565 *Fenians*—see Note 86.
Head Centre, head of the secret Fenian organisation within the structure of the Fenian brotherhood.— 449

566 The column 'Irishman in Paris' (*The Irishman*, No. 36, 5 March 1870) featured a report from Paris, which praised highly Jenny Marx's first article on the Irish question published by *La Marseillaise*. Jenny's article was published under the pen-name J. Williams; Marx also used this alias in some of his letters for considerations of secrecy, but his initial was A. That is why Engels writes that he 'could not explain the Christian name'.— 451

567 A reference to the second edition of Engels' work *The Peasant War in Germany* (see Note 520).— 452

568 A letter about his mother's sickness, who was taken ill on Wednesday, 2 March, was posted by Hermann Engels on 5 March, and received by Frederick Engels on 8 March 1870 (see this volume, pp. 452-53). Hermann asked Frederick to come over and wrote that he had sent a telegram. Enclosed with the letter was a copy of Hermann's letter to Emil Blank which contained the details.— 452

569 In his article, Marx made use of the material on the death of Michael Terbert provided by *The Irishman*, No. 34, 19 February 1870 (see Note 556).— 453

570 Huxley's first public lecture 'The Forefathers and Forerunners of the English People' was delivered in Manchester on 9 January 1870. A detailed account of the lecture, headed 'Professor Huxley on Political Ethnology', was published in the *Manchester Examiner & Times* on 12 January 1870.— 454

571 An express issue of *La Marseillaise* (No. 79, 9 March 1870) carried letters of prominent members in the republican and the national liberation movements in France, Spain and other countries who in their time had been kept or were still in prison. Among others, the newspaper featured letters from Rochefort, Raul Rigo, O'Donovan Rossa, and a posthumous letter from Victor Noir. The headline opening O'Donovan Rossa's letter read: 'Letter of the Citizen O'Donovan Rossa, Fenian deputy to the British Parliament, condemned to the galleys and held at the Newgate Prison'.— 454

572 Engels informs Marx about Friedrich Moll's letter of 28 February 1870 and of Klein's letter of the same date. Their authors thanked Engels for the 50 thaler he had sent to the Solingen production cooperative (see this volume, pp. 415-17). This is what Klein told Engels about the incident with Schapper: during Schapper's and Engels' stay in Sollingen in 1849, Schapper said to Engels: 'Brother Engels, why do you argue with these dogs wearing kid gloves, take out your sword and cut off their heads'. Further on, Klein told the story of how Engels, as a young man, once paid his workers' wages 'on the basis of the communist principle'.— 456

573 A reference to the series of articles on the Irish question written by Jenny Marx (see Note 562). In this letter, Engels refers to the publication of the second article in *La Marseillaise* on 9 March 1870, which reproduced O'Donovan Rossa's letter about the harsh treatment of political prisoners in English prisons (O'Donovan Rossa was arrested in 1865). On 10 March, this letter was reprinted by *The Times* (on the publication of O'Donovan Rossa's letter, see also this volume, pp. 454-55).—457

574 *The Daily News* of 16 March 1870 carried an anonymous article officially initiated by the Home Office headed by Bruce. It made an attempt to deny the facts cited in O'Donovan Rossa's letter, but recognised that Rossa 'has been put in irons'.—457

575 Engels quotes the evidence given by a prisoner published in: *Things not Generally Known, Concerning England's Treatment of Political Prisoners*, Dublin, 1869.—457

576 *Shamrock*—the national emblem of Ireland, usually represented as a clover leaf, which symbolises the Holy Trinity in the Christian Church. The Irish pin the emblem on their hats on 17 March, the birthday of St. Patrick, who is traditionally considered Ireland's patron saint.—458

577 This letter was written on a form stamped: 'General Council of the International Working Men's Association, 256, High Holborn, London, W.C.'; the letter carries an oval stamp 'International Working Men's Central Council London'.—458, 504, 511

578 Marx's letter to R. Pigott of 19 March 1870 has not been found.—458

579 A. Talandier's article '*La Marseillaise* et la presse anglaise' appeared in *La Marseillaise*, No. 85, 15 March, and dated 14 March 1870; it contained a review of the articles carried by *The Times* on 10 March and *The Daily Telegraph* and *The Daily News* on 11 March 1870.—459

580 Marx refers to the General Council meeting of 15 March 1870. He had not attended the Council meetings since 11 January because of illness.—459

581 A programme of the Paris society of proletarians-positivists was read at the General Council meeting of 15 March 1870. It stressed that the society members 'aim at social regeneration without God or King and hope to bring it about by the propagation of the positivist doctrine'. When discussing their admittance to the International, Marx stated that 'their rules were too exclusive and contrary to the General Rules of the Association'. Marx and Mottershead spoke out 'against admitting them as positivists'. On Milner's suggestion, a decision was reached to instruct Dupont as Corresponding Secretary for France to try and make the proletarians-positivists aware of the discrepancies in their programme.

    Comtism (positivism), a trend in bourgeois philosophy and sociology founded by Auguste Comte which opposes both speculative idealism and materialism; it recognises the practical results achieved by science but rejects its philosophical materialist conclusions from the position of agnosticism. Comtism reduces all scientific cognition, including that in history and sociology (the latter term has been coined by Comte) to empirical knowledge. Social development is considered from a biological angle. According to Comte, capitalism is the highest stage of social development, and attempts at its revolutionary change are supposed to be futile. Comte believed that the road to social harmony lies through 'new religion', a cult of an abstract higher being.— 460

582 Engels' letter to Marx posted on 21 March 1870 has not been found.— 460

583 After three of Jenny Marx's articles on the treatment of the Irish political prisoners in English prisons were published in *La Marseillaise* (see present edition, Vol. 21), the Irish M. P. George Henry Moore demanded, on 17 March 1870, that the Government launch a 'full and free' public inquiry into the matter. Under pressure from public opinion, Gladstone was forced, when replying to Moore, to agree to such an inquiry, but made a significant stipulation as to the character of the commission, stating that he 'shall be responsible for the manner in which the inquiry is conducted'. Thus Gladstone secured the right to appoint not a Parliamentary but a Royal commission which would not be accountable to Parliament. Moore's inquiry and Gladstone's reply were published in *The Times* on 18 March; on 19 March, in the column 'Treatment of Political Prisoners' and under the heading 'Probable Inquiry', *The Irishman* featured the item (mentioned by Engels) which, contrary to what Gladstone had stated, said that a Parliamentary commission was to be appointed.— 461

584 In 1844, to please the Austrian Government, J. R. G. Graham, the British Home Secretary (1841-1846), ordered the postal department to submit letters of the Italian revolutionary refugees to the police for inspection.— 462

585 Marx is referring to two of Becker's letters: the one to Jung of 12 March, in which Becker explains his behaviour in the conflict between the General Council and *L'Égalité* (see notes 507 and 525), and to Marx of 13 March 1870.— 463

586 *La Marseillaise*, Nos. 72 and 73, 2 and 3 March, carried the obituary of Herzen written by Bakunin in a letter form in which Bakunin called Herzen his friend and fellow-countryman and said that his death 'was a tremendous loss to his friends, to the cause of Russian emancipation and ... to that of all mankind'. He wrote that he had been closely connected with Herzen for 30 years and that Herzen, Ogarev and himself had always had a common goal. The obituary was reprinted in full in Nos. 10, 11 and 12 of *Le Progrès* on 5, 12 and 19 March 1870.— 463, 492

587 A reference to the money sent to Herzen in 1858 by the Russian landowner P. A. Bakhmetev for propaganda purposes (the so-called Bakhmetev Fund). Marx learned about this from J. Ph. Becker's letter of 13 March 1870. In 1869, under pressure from Bakunin and Ogarev, Herzen agreed to divide the fund into two parts, one of which Ogarev sent to Nechayev. After Herzen's death in 1870, Nechayev received the other part from Ogarev.— 463, 492

588 A reference to the evidence for the defence in the murder case of the journalist Victor Noir by Prince Pierre Napoléon Bonaparte (see Note 516). At the trial, which took place in March 1870, it was alleged that Noir slapped Pierre Bonaparte on the face.— 463

589 When publishing this letter in the book *Der Braunschweiger Ausschuss der socialdemokratischen Arbeiter-Partei in Lötzen und vor dem Gericht*, Brunswick, 1872, Bracke pointed out that the letter was written on a form stamped: 'General Council of the International Working Men's Association, 256, High Holborn, London, W.C.'.— 464

590 Acting on the decisions of the Eisenach Congress (see Note 373), the Committee of the Social-Democratic Workers' Party of Germany urged Party members to join the International Working Men's Association as private persons, since to establish the organisational links between the two bodies, it was necessary to circumvent the Law on Associations operating in Prussia. In a Committee letter of 17 March 1870, Wilhelm Bracke noted that Johann Georg Eccarius had long been commissioned with obtaining 3,000 International membership cards which could have been distributed in the Party. On receiving the letter, Marx immediately forwarded the requested membership cards to Leonhard von Bonhorst as the Committee Secretary.— 464

591 A reference to Bonhorst's letter to Marx of 21 February 1870 and Bonhorst's letter to Borkheim of 17 March 1870, which Borkheim forwarded to Marx on 21 March. Bonhorst also wrote to Engels about the financial predicament of the Social-Democratic Party of Germany (a letter of 17 March 1870).— 464

592 This letter is reproduced from a copy made in an unidentified handwriting. It begins with the written stamp of the General Council: 'General Council of the International Working Men's Association, 256, High Holborn, London, W.C.'.— 464

593 The *Coercion Bill* was introduced in the House of Commons by Gladstone on 17 March 1870, and passed by it. Aimed against the national liberation movement, the Bill provided for the suspension of constitutional guarantees in Ireland and the introduction of extraordinary powers for the English authorities in the struggle against the Irish revolutionaries.

Mentioning Clanricarde, Marx refers to his speech of 21 March 1870, during the discussion of the Bill in the House of Lords. Clanricarde accused Gladstone's government of leniency towards Ireland and demanded a harsher policy to restore 'social order' there.— 466

594 This phrase is a reply to Kugelmann, who had requested Marx in a letter of 21 March 1870, to let him know whether Jenny Marx had Goethe's *Works*; Kugelmann wanted to give her a birthday present.— 466

595 Marx is apparently referring to a story about a boy which he had told on a visit to the Kugelmanns. The boy used to complain: 'O that I should be learning French instead of Latin!' (see *Mohr und General. Erinnerungen an Marx und Engels*, Berlin, 1982, pp. 278-79). Gertrud Kugelmann used this phrase in a letter to the Marx family of 21 March 1870.— 467

596 *Omladina* (i.e., the Association of Serb Youth), a political organisation of Serb liberal bourgeoisie which existed in 1866-72 in the town of Novi Sad which used to belong to Austria-Hungary. Its stated goal was promotion of culture and education, but it really campaigned for political unification of all Serb territories. The democratic wing headed by S. Marković opposed the liberal trend prevailing in the Omladina, which tended to ignore the class aspect of this issue. The organisation was disbanded because of internal strife.

Burschenschaften—German student organisations which at the time of the liberation war against Napoleonic France championed Germany's unification. Alongside with progressive ideas, the Burschenschaften advocated nationalism.— 468

597 This letter was first published in English in an abridged form in: *The Labour Monthly*, Vol. 15, No. 1, London, 1933.— 470

598 Due to a serious illness, in the winter of 1869-70 Marx was able to attend only three General Council meetings (14 December, 4 January and 15 March). On 29 March, on Lucraft's suggestion, the General Council passed a resolution 'expressing the sympathy of the Council with Cit. Marx on account of his continued illness'. The resolution was communicated to Marx by Eccarius on 4 April 1870.—471

599 A reference to Friedrich Lessner's letter to Marx of 6 April 1870, which dealt with the motion, introduced by Hales at the General Council meeting, to appoint a finance commission.—471

600 Marx mentions the letter of 26 March 1870 addressed by Sigfrid Meyer to Eccarius as General Secretary of the International, but forwarded by the author to Marx with permission to dispose of it as he saw fit.—471

601 In the address 'L'Union des Travailleurs allemands de New-York aux ouvriers de Paris' published by La Marseillaise, No. 103, 2 April 1870, F. Carl and F. Jubitz welcomed the revolutionary actions of the Paris workers. They described them as front-rank fighters for freedom and equality on the road to social revolution.—472

602 Between 22 February and 28 May 1870, the North German Reichstag held a debate on the criminal code. On 1 March, the Reichstag voted for the abolition of capital punishment; on 15 March, the liberals suggested that for political prisoners, hard labour should be replaced by imprisonment, but whenever a political crime had been committed for dishonest reasons, penal servitude should be retained. This motion, which gave the government an opportunity to put political prisoners in convict prisons, was passed by the Reichstag. The debate on the criminal code ended on 25 May 1870, with capital punishment restored on the insistence of the government on 23 May.—477

603 In a letter to Engels of 5 April 1870, Liebknecht wrote about his plan to go to Berlin and try and found a cheap daily newspaper there. In the same letter, he spoke highly of Engels' preface to the second edition of The Peasant War in Germany (present edition, Vol. 21), and wrote that the views expounded by Engels coincided with his own. He also intended to publish his report on the land question in Germany in connection with the decisions of the Basle Congress to abolish private property on land (see notes 447 and 458).—477

604 A reference to Sigismund Borkheim's letter to Marx of 8 April 1870, in which he quoted Liebknecht who complained in a letter to Borkheim that Marx disliked him.—478, 482

605 Pfänder was elected member of the General Council on 1 November 1864, and remained one until 1867. On 18 January 1870, Pfänder was again elected to the General Council, but did not take an active part in its work until 12 April 1870.—478

606 After L'Égalité editorial board had been reorganised (see notes 507 and 525), the Bakuninists, attempting to retain their lost positions, secured a formal majority of votes at a regular congress of the Romance Federation held in La Chaux-de-Fonds on 4-6 April 1870. The congress discussed the attitude of the working class towards the political struggle. In contrast to the Geneva sections, the Bakuninists advocated abstention from political struggle referring to the French text of the Rules (see Marx's work 'The General Council to the Federal Council of Romance Switzerland', present edition, Vol. 21, pp. 89-90). On Bakunin's insistence, the congress began its proceedings with the admission of

the newly-formed sections to the Federation. A sharp controversy arose over the admission of the section named 'Alliance of Socialist Democracy—Central Section' founded by Bakunin in Geneva in June 1869 which, in fact, exercised leadership in the secret International Alliance of Socialist Democracy, and the Chaux-de-Fonds pro-Bakunin section. Utin, one of the leaders of the Russian Section in Geneva, exposed Bakunin's schismatic activities. A split occurred; the Geneva delegates and other General Council supporters continued their work independently. An announcement about the Chaux-de-Fonds split mentioned by Marx was published in *L'Égalité*, No. 15, 9 April 1870.

The Bakuninists had assumed the name of the Romance Congress, elected a new Federal Committee and transferred its seat to La Chaux-de-Fonds. Thus two Federal Committees appeared in Romance Switzerland, in Geneva and in La Chaux-de-Fonds. The Bakuninists started publication of a newspaper *La Solidarité*, under the editorship of James Guillaume, first in Neuchâtel (11 April 1870-12 May 1871), and then in Geneva. In fact it was the continuation of *Le Progrès*. In early April 1870, representatives of the Romance Federal Committee and supporters of the Alliance sent the General Council detailed reports on the congress in La Chaux-de-Fonds and requested that it pass a decision concerning the split. On 12 April, the Council instructed Jung to collect additional material, and, having received exhaustive information in April and May, on 28 June 1870 it passed a resolution proposed by Marx which confirmed the powers of the old Federal Committee. The Bakuninist Federal Committee was instructed to assume another title (see present edition, Vol. 21, p. 136).— 480, 493

607 A reference to the famine that struck Ireland in 1845-47. It was caused by the potato crop failure and the large-scale exports of other foodstuffs from the country. According to the data of 1851, between 1841 and 1851, the famine and eviction of small tenants from land ('the clearing of estates') resulted in the death of over a million people and emigration of another million.— 480

608 Marx is referring to the section on Ireland in Chapter VI of the first German edition of *Capital* in 1867 (pp. 688-99), which in the first English edition (1887) corresponded to Part VII, 'The Accumulation of Capital', Chapter XXV, 'The General Law of Capitalist Accumulation', Section 5. 'Illustrations of the General Law of Capitalist Accumulation. f. Ireland' (see present edition, Vol. 35).— 481

609 *Freeholders*—a group of small landowners in England. They paid the landlord an insignificant fixed rent and had the right to dispose freely of their plots. They enjoyed low property qualifications of 40 shillings (£2) (annual income). In 1829, this figure was raised five times over, and 40-shilling freeholders lost the right to vote. In the 1830s-40s, more and more freeholders were rapidly ruined, their lands passing into the hands of landlords who leased them to big farmers, capitalist tenants.— 481, 484

610 A reference to the congress of German natural scientists, researchers and medical men held in Hanover on 18-23 September 1865. At one of the sessions, Schulze made an attempt to disprove Darwin's theory.— 482

611 Under the Poor Law that had existed in England since the 16th century, each parish levied a tax for the benefit of the poor; parishioners unable to provide for themselves and their families received aid through poor relief funds. In 1834, a new Poor Law was passed in England that recognised only one form of help, placing the poor into workhouses under a prison-like regime which the people nicknamed 'poor men's Bastilles'.— 484

612 Engels is referring to preparations for the so-called plebiscite which Napoleon III hoped to use to consolidate his somewhat shaky position. On 20 April 1870, the government made public a new constitution which was a compromise between the authoritarian and the parliamentary systems. It was followed by a decree on 23 April, which proposed that the French people use the plebiscite to approve or reject the following: 'The People approves the liberal reforms effected in the Constitution since 1860 by the Emperor, with the cooperation of the great bodies of the State, and ratifies the *Senatus-Consultus* of the 20th April 1870.' The issue was worded in such a way that a positive answer to it would sound like an approval of the overall political structure of the Second Empire. As a result of a plebiscite held on 8 May 1870, about 3.5 million citizens in fact opposed the Empire (1,894,681 abstained, and 1,577,939 voted against). A large share of the votes against the Empire belonged to the French army; in Paris alone, 46,000 servicemen gave a negative answer.— 484, 508, 513, 514

613 Engels uses the term *'gouvernement direct par le peuple'* meaning the so-called direct popular legislation, referendums on the various issues of the internal affairs and policies of the Swiss cantons (see Note 276). Thus, on 6 February 1870, the canton of Ticino held a referendum on the changes in the cantonal constitution (administrative division, representation in the cantonal council, etc). On 20 February, the canton of Zurich held referendums on the tax bill, etc.— 485

614 The excerpt from this letter from the words 'I am now forced...' to the end was published in: *The Letters of Karl Marx. Selected and translated with explanatory notes and an introduction by Saul K. Padover*, New Jersey, USA, 1979. According to the editors, Marx wrote it to Paul and Laura Lafargue.— 485

615 *Paul-Laurent*—the pen-name of Paul Lafargue, made up of his own name and that of his wife Laura.— 485, 489

616 On Marx's suggestion, on 12 April 1870, the General Council granted the credentials of the International's correspondent in France to Henri Verlet.— 485

617 The first French edition of the International's Rules, 'Congrès ouvrier. Association Internationale des Travailleurs. Règlement Provisoire', was published by the French Section of the International set up in Paris in 1864 by the workers Tolain, Fribourg and others, who had Proudhonist sympathies. The translation, which appeared in early January 1865, contained a number of distortions and errors. (See present edition, Vol. 21, pp. 89-90.)

In November 1866, after the Geneva Congress, which approved the Provisional Rules, Marx and Lafargue published a verified translation of the Rules of the International Working Men's Association and the Administrative Regulations, but that edition was not widely distributed in France, since it was almost entirely confiscated by the French police.

On 18 April, replying to a proposal by Marx, Lafargue wrote that it was impossible to publish the Rules in *La Libre pensée*, since the newspaper was registered as a purely literary publication (see this volume, p. 557). However, Lafargue managed to get the verified translation of the Rules published, and it appeared in Paris after 20 April 1870. The translation had been checked by Lafargue. Against a background of mounting police reprisals in France, it became necessary to expedite the publication of the Rules and Lafargue had no chance to send the manuscript to Marx for review. In June 1870, Lafargue's translation was published for the second time in: *Procès de l'Association Internationale des travailleurs. Première et deuxième commission du Bureau de Paris,* Deuxième édition, Paris, juin 1870.—486, 557

618 Marx is referring to H. Verlet's article 'Force et matière' published in *La Libre pensée,* No. 13, 16 April 1870. The author spoke highly of Büchner's book *Kraft und Stoff.*—486

619 Marx sent Engels Perret's letter to Jung of 15 April 1870, in which Perret described in detail the split that occurred at the Chaux-de-Fonds Congress (see Note 606) and the Bakuninists' intrigues in the Swiss sections of the International.—488

620 On 7 April 1870, the Federal Committee newly established by the Bakuninists (at the Chaux-de-Fonds Congress; see Note 606), which had its headquarters at Chaux-de-Fonds, directed a letter to the General Council requesting it to settle the conflict between itself and the Romance Federal Council. The letter, which was signed by the Federal Committee Secretary F. Robert, also informed the General Council about the establishment of a new *La Solidarité* newspaper by the Bakuninists.—488

621 Laura and Paul Lafargue's letters of 18 April (see this volume, pp. 556-57) and after 20 April 1870, informed Marx about the foundation, in Paris, of the Federal Council of the International Working Men's Association (see Note 644). Lafargue believed that for expediency's sake, he should not become a member of the newly established Council but should be a representative of the London General Council at the Paris Federation. He asked Marx to discuss granting him these powers at the next meeting. This was done by the General Council on 17 May 1870.—489

622 Replying to Marx's letter before 4 May 1870, Laura Lafargue stated that Marx's warning about Paul Robin's splitting activities had been communicated to Leo Frankel.—489

623 A reference to the resolutions proposed by Bakunin at the congress of the League of Peace and Freedom held in Berne in 1868 in connection with the discussion of the League's draft programme. Bakunin spoke several times in defence of his proposals. His speeches, as well as his and his followers' announcement about their withdrawal from the League, were published in Herzen's *Kolokol,* No. 14-15, 1 December 1868.—489

624 The demand to abolish the right of inheritance was put forward by Saint-Simon's followers (Enfantin, Bazard, Rodrigues, Buchez, etc.) who, in the late 1820s, set out to popularise and develop Saint-Simon's doctrine. In 1830, a book was published in Paris which, based as it was on Bazard's lectures, expressed the views of Saint-Simon's followers on the right of inheritance: *Doctrine de Saint-Simon Exposition.* Première année. 1829, Paris, 1830, pp. 143-69.—490

625 A reference to the General Council entering the question of the right of inheritance on the Basle Congress agenda (see Note 379). A major preliminary discussion on the issue was held at the General Council in the summer of 1869. On 3 August the Council approved Marx's 'Report of the General Council on the Right of Inheritance' (see present edition, Vol. 21). Marx's report was read at the Congress by Eccarius on 11 September 1869.—492

626 A reference to *Kolokol,* the Russian revolutionary democratic newspaper edited by Alexander Herzen and Nikolai Ogarev. It was published in Russian in

1857-67, and in French with Russian supplements in 1868-70, in London up to 1865 and later in Geneva. After Herzen's death in 1870, an attempt to keep up the newspaper was made by Sergei Nechayev, who was in close contact with Bakunin. This is probably what Marx means. Six issues appeared in April-May 1870.—492, 508, 516

627 Marx refers to Laura Lafargue's letter of 18 April 1870. Calling her Laurent, Marx hints at Paul-Laurent, the pen-name of Paul Lafargue (see Note 615; see also this volume, p. 557).—493, 555

628 Engels is referring to a speech at the Chaux-de-Fonds Congress (see Note 606) by François Dupleix, who accused Bakunin's followers of atheism and alleged that the workers were unwilling to have the question of their faith discussed.—495

629 On 16 and 20 April 1870, Liebknecht published in *Der Volksstaat*, nos. 31 and 32, Bakunin's article 'Briefe über die revolutionäre Bewegung in Russland. I.'—496, 499, 519

630 Marx is referring to the lectures on ethnology read by Flourens at the Collège de France in the early 1860s and published in 1863 as a book: G. Flourens, *Histoire de l'homme. Cours d'histoire naturelle des corps organisés au Collège de France*, Paris, 1863.—497

631 On 12 April 1870, the General Council instructed Marx and Dupont to draw up a protest, on behalf of the International, concerning the harsh verdict brought in against the participants in the March strike at Eugène Schneider's metal works in Creuzot. However, the large-scale police reprisals against members of the International which began in France in late April forced the General Council to revise its plans and replace the protest with a leaflet, written by Marx, 'Concerning the Persecution of the Members of the French Sections. Declaration of the General Council of the International Working Men's Association' (see present edition, Vol. 21, p. 127).—497

632 On 3 May 1870, Bracke and Bonhorst requested Engels' permission to publish his letter to Bracke of 28 April in *Der Volksstaat*, organ of the Social-Democratic Workers' Party, saying that it was of general interest and importance to Party members. Engels was to write to them before 10 May if he did not agree. On 14 May, an excerpt from Engels' letter was published in *Der Volksstaat*. The editors of the present edition do not possess the original letter.—498

633 On 17 March 1870, Leonhard von Bonhorst, Secretary of the Committee of the Social-Democratic Workers' Party of Germany, sent Engels a cashier's report for 1869, in which he wrote about the poor state of the Party's finances.—498

634 On 17 March 1870, Bonhorst as Secretary of the Social-Democratic Workers' Party Committee wrote to Marx and Engels that the workers forming the basis of the party were too passive. He also stated, 'since our party is, amongst other things, the youngest of those that have entered the social and political arena, it is probably also lacking in strength.'—499

635 Engels' letter to Borkheim, written later than 28 April 1870, has not been found.—499, 507

636 The Commission for the Publication of the Ancient Laws and Institutes of Ireland was set up by the British Government in 1852 (see Note 481).—501, 519, 520

637 A reference to the first Russian edition of the *Manifesto of the Communist Party* by Marx and Engels, which appeared in Geneva in 1869 in Bakunin's

translation. The book was printed at the *Kolokol* printshop. The inadequacies of Bakunin's translation, which in places somewhat distorted the meaning of this major programme document of the proletarian party, were corrected in Plekhanov's translation, which was published in Geneva in 1882.— 502

638 A reference to Wilhelm Liebknecht's letter to Engels of 27 April 1870.— 503

639 Marx and his daughter Eleanor went on a visit to Engels in Manchester on 23 May and stayed there until about 23 June 1870.— 504, 520, 529

640 On 3 May 1870, the French Section in London (see Note 72) gave a banquet for Flourens, who had fled from France under threat of arrest. An account of the banquet was forwarded to France, Germany and some other countries by Reuter and Havas-Bullier agencies and published, specifically, in the *Journal des Débats* on 5 May. It stated that the banquet was chaired by 'M. Le Lubez, président de la Société Internationale', when Le Lubez had in fact been expelled from the International for slander back in 1866. On 10 May 1870, the General Council approved Marx's 'Draft Resolution of the General Council on the "French Federal Section in London"', in which it resolutely dissociated itself from the provocative activities of the French Section (see present edition, Vol. 21).— 504

641 *Société du dix Décembre* (Society of December 10), a Bonapartist organisation established in 1849 and consisting, for the most part, of déclassé elements. A detailed account of the Society can be found in Marx's work *The Eighteenth Brumaire of Louis Bonaparte* (see present edition, Vol. 11, pp. 149-51, 186, 193-96).— 504, 523

642 In view of the preparations for the plebiscite to be held in France (see Note 612), commencing in late April 1870, arrests of socialists began throughout the country. They were charged with belonging to the International Working Men's Association, as well as with 'complicity' in the plot against Napoleon III (the so-called Blois trial), which was in fact staged by the Prefect of the Paris Police Pietri. On 5 May 1870, the *Journal officiel* made public the verdict of guilty passed by the Procurator General Grandperret, who charged a number of persons, including Flourens, with complicity in the fictitious plot. On the same day, *La Gaulois* alleged that Flourens, who was at that time in England, had been persecuted by the British police and thus forced to go into hiding.— 505, 522, 558

643 After an attempt on the life of Napoleon III made by the Italian revolutionary Orsini, in February 1858, Palmerston introduced in the House of Commons the *Conspiracy to Murder Bill*, under which émigrés and natives were to be severely punished for participation in political plots. The Bill was introduced under the pretext of threats by the French Government, which accused England of granting asylum to political refugees. Under pressure from a mass protest movement, the Bill was voted down by the House of Commons and Palmerston was obliged to resign.— 505

644 The *Paris Federation* of the International Working Men's Association was founded on 18 April 1870, at a general meeting of the International's sections in Paris under the chairmanship of Louis Eugène Varlin. The meeting, which attracted 1,200-1,300 participants, adopted the Rules of the Federation (see this volume, pp. 555-56). However, the police reprisals and arrests of the International's members which began in France late in April 1870 in connection with preparations for the plebiscite (see Note 612) disrupted the activities of the Federation.— 506, 555

[645] Marx refers to the programme article of *Kolokol*'s new editorial board 'To the Russian Public from the Editors' published in No. 1, 2 April 1870.— 507

[646] A reference to Sigismund Borkheim's letter to Marx of 3 May 1870, in which he thanked Marx for sending him Charles Lever's novel *Harry Lorrequer*.— 506

[647] On 2 April 1870, *Der Volksstaat*, edited by Liebknecht, began the publication of Engels' work *The Peasant War in Germany*. A serious blunder was made by the editorial board when printing Chapter II: on 4 May, the newspaper featured the end of this chapter, while the preceding page had been left out and appeared only on 7 May with the editorial board's note: 'The excerpt contained in today's issue was to have appeared *before* the part published in the last issue. This vexing error was caused by the absence of our type-setter who is responsible for imposing the issue (this type-setter is away on an agitation tour).'

Engels is referring to Liebknecht's footnote on Hegel that appeared in *Der Volksstaat* on 30 April 1870.— 509, 513

[648] Marx gives Engels an account of Liebknecht's letter of 7 May 1870, in which Liebknecht invited Engels, through Marx, to the Stuttgart Congress of the German Social-Democratic Workers' Party scheduled for 4-7 June 1870.— 511, 513, 519

[649] This letter, written after 7 May 1870, has not been found.— 511, 519

[650] A reference to a suggestion by Bebel and Liebknecht that the annual congress of the International Working Men's Association should be held in 1870 in Germany, either in Mainz or Mannheim. Liebknecht wrote to Marx about this on 7 May 1870. On 9 May, the Brunswick Committee of the Social-Democratic Workers' Party sent the General Council an official proposal to hold the congress in Germany.— 511, 515

[651] A reference to the following books: R. O'Flaherty, *Ogygia: seu, Rerum Hibernicarum Chronologia*. In tres partes. Londini, 1685; *Rerum Hibernicarum Scriptores Veteres*, Tomes I-IV, Buckingham, 1814-1826, ed. Ch. O'Conor; J. Ware, *Inquiries concerning Ireland and its Antiquities*, Dublin, 1705; J. Ware, *Two Books of the Writers of Ireland*, Dublin, 1704.— 516, 517

[652] The *Annales Ultoriences* were compiled by various chroniclers between the 15th and 17th centuries and described events beginning from the mid-fifth century; they were published by Ch. O'Conor in the fourth volume of his collection *Rerum Hibernicarum Scriptores Veteres* (Ancient Annalists of Ireland).

Annales IV Magistrorum were compiled in 1632-36 in the Donegal Monastery by four monks. The first part of the *Annales* was published in the third volume of Ch. O'Conor's collection; in full, they were put out by J. O'Donovan, together with an English translation, in 1856; *Annala Rioghachta Eireann. Annals of the Kingdom of Ireland, by the Four Masters, from the earliest Period to the Year 1616*.— 517

[653] Engels' letter to Liebknecht, written around 15 May 1870, is not extant.— 519

[654] In the first publication of this letter in: MEGA, Abt. III, Bd. 4, Berlin, 1931, and in: Marx and Engels, *Works*, First Russian Edition, Vol. XXIV, Moscow, 1931, this letter was erroneously dated 16 March 1870.— 519

[655] Marx forwards to Engels Liebknecht's letter of 11 May 1870, in which the latter explained the errors, including the footnote on Hegel, made when publishing Engels' work *The Peasant War in Germany* (see Note 647) in *Der Volksstaat*.

Liebknecht promised to put in a statement to the effect that the notes had been supplied by the editorial board and not Engels. He considered it unnecessary to publish Engels' official statement (see this volume, pp. 508-09).— 519

656 On 16 March 1870, *Der Volksstaat*, No. 22, carried Borkheim's article 'Ein Brief Netschajeffs' (in German, with a Russian translation made by Borkheim himself). The article was signed 'Der Autor der *Russischen Briefe* in der Berliner *Zukunft*'. *Russischen Briefe* was the name of Borkheim's articles about Russia featured by *Die Zukunft* in 1869-70 (see Note 274). On 14 May the editorial board of *Der Volksstaat* published the opening passages of Nechayev's reply, which is what Marx is writing about to Engels.— 519, 521

657 Engels visited Marx in London on his way to Germany late in December 1869.— 521

658 Marx sent Engels an anonymous article 'Das Treiben der deutschen Kommunisten' from the American newspaper *Der Pionier* of 27 April 1870. The editor-in-chief of the newspaper, which was published in New York by German petty-bourgeois democratic émigrés, was Karl Heinzen. The author of the article, who was obviously concerned about the successes of the newly-founded Social-Democratic Workers' Party of Germany and its newspaper *Der Volksstaat*, made libellous statements about Marx, Engels, Liebknecht and Eccarius, contrasting communists and the 'German revolutionary democracy'. Specifically, with reference to Lassalle, the article stated that in 1849 he had made all the necessary preparations for an uprising in Cologne but that Marx, who had promised to do the same in Düsseldorf and certain other localities, had failed to do so thus letting Lassalle down.

In this letter, Marx refers to Heinzen as Heineke, a character in the German song of the same name, which is a folk parody of the so-called grobian literature of the 16th century. Marx thus nicknamed Heinzen for the first time in 1847 in his work *Moralising Criticism and Critical Morality*, in which he likened Heinzen's journalism to specimens of this brand of literature (see present edition, Vol. 6, pp. 312-40).— 522, 524

659 A reference to Jenny Marx's letter to Manchester of 30 May 1870.— 524

660 The address of Engels' house, in which he spent his last years in Manchester and where Marx and his daughter Eleanor stayed in May-June 1870, was 86 Mornington St.— 525

661 This is Marx's reply to Le Lubez' letter of 11 June, in which he asked whether Marx was the author of the item 'Aus England' carried by *Der Volksstaat* on 11 May 1870. It exposed the provocative activities of the so-called French Section in London and especially its action on behalf of the International at the banquet for Flourens given in London on 3 May 1870 (see Note 640).— 526

662 A reference to Kugelmann's letter to Marx of 13 June 1870, in which he inquired what sort of flat to rent for Marx in Karlsbad (now Karlovy Vary).— 527

663 A reference to Otto Meissner's letter to Marx of 25 June 1870, in which he informed Marx that he was planning to make the final payment for the first edition of Volume One of *Capital* in August 1870.— 527, 529

664 This phrase can be found in the preface to the second edition of *Encyclopädie der philosophischen Wissenschaften im Grundrisse. Zum Gebrauch seiner Vorlesungen von Georg Wilhelm Hegel*, 2 Ausg. Heidelberg, Osswald, 1827, S. XVI: 'Lessing said in his time that Spinoza is treated as a dead dog.' Hegel referred to the talk between Lessing and Jacobi that took place on 7 June 1780, in the course

of which Lessing said: 'The people are still referring to Spinoza as a dead dog.'
See: F. H. Jacobi, *Werke*, Bd. IV, Abt. I, Leipzig, 1819, S. 68.—528

665 In early July 1870, Lafargue wrote in a letter to Marx that he would be visited
by a young Russian revolutionary, one Hermann Lopatin, to whom he had given
Marx's address and a letter of introduction. Marx and Lopatin met on 2 July
1870. Describing his meeting with Marx, Lopatin wrote: '...I was afraid to run
out of subjects for discussion with this luminary, and then I was secretly
puzzled—what language except that of signs could I use to communicate with
him? All my fears proved groundless on both of my visits (of which the last
lasted for ten hours), the conversation did not stop for a minute.' Lopatin
visited Marx for a second time on 3 July same year.—530

666 This excerpt from Marx's letter was quoted by Lopatin in a letter to Lavrov of
6 July 1870. First, Lopatin gave a short exposition of Marx's letter: 'Today, I
received from him (Marx) a new issue of the *Narodnoye Dyelo* (People's Cause)
and a very nice note with the latest news about the court trial of our Paris
comrades (the reference is to the third trial of the International's members in
France; see Note 667— *Ed.*). He concluded by asking if I should like him to
find me a clerk's job at some London office.'—535

667 A reference is to the third trial of the members of the Paris Federation of the
International arrested by the French police on the eve of the plebiscite (see
notes 612 and 642). The trial was held between 22 June and 5 July 1870. The
prosecution failed to bring in the charge of conspiracy; the defendants were
charged not with complicity in the fictitious plot, but with being members of
the International.—537

668 Marx enclosed with this letter the text of the 'Confidential Communication to All
Sections' and the 'Programme for the Mainz Congress of the International',
which was to open in Mainz on 5 September 1870. Both documents were written
in French. They are to be found in Vol. 21 of the present edition.
On the top of the first page is the International's round seal with the
inscription: 'International Working Men's Association. Central Council London'.—537

669 Engels' 'Confession' is a joking reply to the questionnaire compiled by Marx's
eldest daughter Jenny. It is published in this volume from the handwritten text
preserved in her album. This was a favourite parlour game in England and
Germany at the time (see Marx's 'Confession', Vol. 42 of the present
edition).—541

670 *Reineke de Vos* (Reynard the Fox)—a popular character of the medieval epic
poems about animals, a satire of feudal society. The first literary version
appeared in 1498 in Lübeck under the title of *Reynke de Vos*. Goethe's *Reineke
Fuchs* is the most popular embodiment of the epic.—541

671 Ruge's letter to Steinthal of 25 January 1869 was forwarded to Marx on
4 February by W. Strohn with whom Steinthal was friendly. Marx let Engels,
Borkheim and Kugelmann read it. He sent it to the latter on 11 February (see
this volume, p. 213).—542

672 Around 10 September, 1869, Marx and his daughter Jenny left for Belgium
and Germany. They visited Bruges, Liège, Aachen, Cologne, Siegburg (where
they called on Dietzgen), Bonn, Mainz (where they spent a day with the
German socialist Paul Stumpf) and Wiesbaden. Marx and Jenny arrived in
Hanover around 18 September 1869 (see this volume, p. 353 and Note 349).—
543

673 Eccarius' report on the first meetings of the Basle Congress (see Note 379) published in *The Times* of 15 September 1869, quoted in full the speech made by the American delegate Andrew Cameron.—543

674 A reference to Lessner's letters to Marx which gave a detailed account of the Basle Congress. Lessner sent five letters in all (6, 7, 8, 9 and 11 September 1869). Of Liebknecht's letters dealing with the Congress, the one of 7 September is extant.—544

675 In a report made at the Basle Congress meeting of 7 September 1869, Liebknecht touched on the question of his disagreement with Schweitzer and criticised Lassalle's views.—544

676 A reference to Chapter III 'Die Production des absoluten Mehrwerts' of the first German edition of Volume One of *Capital*. Corresponding to it in the second and subsequent German editions of this volume and in the first (1887) English edition is the entire Section Three (see present edition, Vol. 35).—545

677 Eleanor Marx toured Ireland with Engels and his wife Lizzy Burns from 6 to 23 September 1869.—546

678 A reference to the *Act of Disestablishment of the Church* passed by Gladstone in Ireland in 1869.—549

679 The *Orangemen*—members of the Orange Society (Order), a Protestant terrorist organisation founded in 1795 and employed by the authorities, Protestant landlords and the clergy against the Irish national liberation movement. The name was derived from William III, Prince of Orange, who suppressed the 1689-91 Irish uprising for the restoration of the Stuart monarchy. The Order had a particularly powerful influence in Ulster, Northern Ireland, with its predominantly Protestant population.—549

680 *Ordeal* or *Dei iudicum*, an ordeal by red-hot iron, boiling water, etc., used in the Middle Ages to ascertain the guilt or innocence of the accused.—550

681 Rochefort's position, who sought to avert unnecessary bloodshed on the day of Noir's funeral, was criticised in the 'Politische Uebersicht' column, *Der Volksstaat*, No. 7, 22 January 1870. Rochefort was described as 'a vacillating man, lacking principles', 'a frondeur', not a revolutionary.—553

682 Jenny Marx quotes the editorial written by P. Granier de Cassagnac for *Le Pays*, 15 January 1870.—553

683 A reference to the strike by over 10,000 workers at Schneider's engineering and metal works in Creuzot in the second half of January 1870. The strike began in protest against the dismissal of the members of the delegation which was to negotiate with the management about transferring the pensions fund to the workers. After government troops had been sent to Creuzot, the strike took on a political character. The Bonapartist government managed to suppress it by making mass arrests. One leader of the strike was Adolphe Alphonse Assi, a mechanic. The progress of the strike was described by *Der Volksstaat*, No. 8, 26 January 1870 in the 'Politische Uebersicht' column.—553

684 Jenny Marx quotes A. Guéroult's article 'Les Grèves' published in *L'Opinion Nationale* newspaper on 28 January 1870.—554

685 A reference to Marx's 'Report of the General Council to the Fourth Annual Congress of the International Working Men's Association' read at the Basle Congress meeting on 7 September 1869. Lafargue paraphrases the following

passage: 'But the workmen on the Continent ... begin ... to understand that the surest way to get one's natural rights is to exercise them at one's personal risk' (present edition, Vol. 21, p. 77).—555

⁶⁸⁶ *Mutuellistes*—in the 1860s, the name given to the right wing of the Proudhonists who were members of the French sections of the International.—555

⁶⁸⁷ A reference to the document in which the Paris Federation of the International's sections defined its tactics with respect to the plebiscite scheduled for 8 May 1870 (see Note 612). The leadership of the International's sections in France recommended that the voters should abstain or cast their ballots blank.

Manifeste antiplébiscitaire des Sections parisiennes fédérées de l'Internationale et de la Chambre fédérale des Sociétés ouvrières à tous les travailleurs français was published in *La Marseillaise*, No. 125, 24 April 1870 and issued in Paris as a leaflet at the same time.—556

⁶⁸⁸ A reference to the address of the so-called London French Section on the question of the plebiscite, 'Adresse aux citoyens français', which appeared in *La Marseillaise*, No. 116, 15 April 1870. In connection with this and other documents of this organisation, which illegally used the name of the International, on 10 May the General Council approved Marx's statement which stressed that the Section had 'ceased ... to have any connection whatever with the General Council in London or any Branch of that Association on the continent' (see present edition, Vol. 21, p. 131).—556

⁶⁸⁹ Lafargue is replying to Marx's advice to avoid any distinctive names except territorial designations when setting up new sections of the International (see this volume, p. 485). Later, the London Conference of the International held on 17-23 September 1871, granted this recommendation, which was spearheaded against sectarianism, the status of a clause in the Rules (see present edition, Vol. 22, pp. 423-24).—556

⁶⁹⁰ The note quoted by Lafargue appeared in *La Libre pensée*, No. 13, 16 April 1870. It puns on the pen-name of Villemessant, well known reactionary journalist, and the French expression 'vil me sens' (I am feeling low). 'Paris-faillite' (Bankrupt Paris) is a dig at the gutter police sheet *Paris-Journal.*—557

⁶⁹¹ *The Irishman*, No. 40, 2 April 1870 published excerpts from Jenny Marx's second article on the Irish question. The sixth article, 'Agrarian Outrages in Ireland', was published in full in *The Irishman*, No. 45, 7 May 1870.

On Jenny Marx's articles on the Irish question, see Note 562.—559

⁶⁹² A reference to a collection of Irish songs *Erins-Harfe. Irländische Volksmelodien nach Thomas Moore*, with the lyrics, *Irish Melodies*, written by Thomas Moore. The collection was prepared and published in Hanover in 1870 by the singer Joseph Rissé, whom Marx and Jenny met in 1867 during a visit to the Kugelmanns. Engels' note mentioned in this letter probably was not used in the preface.—563

⁶⁹³ The letter was written two days before the Franco-Prussian war, which began on 19 July 1870. Jenny, who was misled by the Bonapartist press, was unable to give a sound assessment of the French public's mood on the eve of the war. The chauvinistic demonstrations were organised in Paris and the provinces by the government, which made use of police agents and déclassé elements. Paul Lafargue wrote to Marx in July 1870 that in Paris, 'the police were obliged to feign enthusiasm so as to make it credible'.—563

NAME INDEX

ised the trade union of mechanics; member of the Federal Council of the Paris sections of the First International.—556

Aycard, M.—Paris banker.—7

B

Badinguet—see *Napoleon III*

Bakunin (Bakounine, Bakunine), Mikhail Alexandrovich (1814-1876)—Russian revolutionary, journalist; participant in the 1848-49 revolution in Germany; later an ideologist of Narodism and anarchism; opposed Marxism in the First International.—121, 142, 153, 154, 190, 193, 198, 200, 202, 208, 218, 222, 223, 235, 237, 240, 327, 332, 335, 362-63, 364, 404, 405, 411, 413, 414, 424, 428, 430, 431, 436, 441, 462, 468, 479, 480, 488, 489-94, 499, 502, 506, 508, 511, 516, 518, 523, 530, 531

Bakunina, Antonina Xaveriyevna (née *Kvyatkovskaya*) (c. 1840-1887) — Mikhail Bakunin's wife.—193

Balzac, Honoré de (1799-1850)—French realist writer.—85, 189

Bancel, Jean Baptiste François Désiré (1822-1871)—French lawyer and politician; bourgeois radical; deputy to the Legislative Assembly (1849-51); exiled from France after the coup d'état of 2 December 1851; member of the Corps législatif from 1869.—546, 553

Bangya, János (1817-1868)—Hungarian journalist and officer, participant in the 1848-49 revolution in Hungary; after its defeat, Kossuth's emissary abroad and at the same time secret police agent; later served in the Turkish army under the name of Mehemed Bey, acting as a Turkish agent in the Caucasus (1855-58).—58

Bara, Jules (1835-1900)—Belgian statesman, Liberal, Minister of Justice (1865-70, 1878-84).—43

Baring, Thomas (1799-1873)—financier, head of a banking house in London, Conservative M.P.—438

Barrot, Camille Hyacinthe Odilon (1791-1873)—French lawyer and politician; leader of the liberal dynastic opposition until February 1848; headed the monarchist coalition ministry (December 1848-October 1849); withdrew from political activities after the dismissal of the ministry in November 1849.—216

Barry, Charles Robert (b. 1834)—Irish lawyer; Public Prosecutor in Dublin (1859-65); M.P.; Solicitor-General (1869-70) and Attorney-General (1870-71) for Ireland.—162

Bartels, Marie (d. 1869)—Engels' niece, daughter of his sister Marie and Karl Emil Blank.—212

Bartels, Robert—Marie Bartels' husband.—212

Bartenev, Viktor Ivanovich (pseudonyms *Alexeyev, Netov*) (1838-1918)—Russian army officer; emigrated to Switzerland in 1867; member of the initiating group of the Alliance of Socialist Democracy; in 1869 broke with the Bakuninists; member of the Russian Section Committee of the International in Geneva; vigorously opposed the Bakuninist splitting activities.—193

Bassot—trustee of A. Frank's (Paris publisher) inheritance.—138, 150

Bastiat, Frédéric (1801-1850)—French economist and politician; preached harmony of class interests in bourgeois society.—65, 66, 68

Baudin, Jean Baptiste Alphonse Victor (1801-1851)—French politician, physician; Republican; deputy to the Legislative Assembly; was killed on the barricades in the faubourg of Saint-Antoine on 3 December 1851.—159, 188, 191

Bauer, Bruno (1809-1882)—German philosopher; Young Hegelian; author

Bernard, Marie—Belgian house-painter; member of the General Council of the International (September 1868-1869); Corresponding Secretary for Belgium (September 1868-November 1869).—272, 275

Bernard, Simon François (Bernard le Clubiste) (1817-1862)—French politician, republican; refugee in England in the 1850s; in 1858 was accused by the French government of complicity in Orsini's attempt on Napoleon III's life, acquitted by the British court.— 505, 559

Bervi, Vasily Vasilyevich (pseudonym *Flerovsky, N.*) (1829-1918)—Russian economist and sociologist, democrat; Narodnik utopian socialist; author of *The Condition of the Working Class in Russia.*—362, 390, 423, 426, 429-31, 433, 440, 441, 450, 462, 480, 487, 508, 531, 545

Besson, Alexandre—French worker, mechanic; refugee in London; member of the General Council of the International (1866-68); Corresponding Secretary for Belgium; a leader of the French Section in London; joined Félix Pyat's group.—139

Beta (pen name of *Bettziech*), *Johann Heinrich* (1813-1876)—German journalist, democrat; refugee in London, follower of Gottfried Kinkel.—74

Bethell, Richard, 1st Lord Westbury (1800-1873)—British lawyer and liberal statesman; Attorney-General (1856-59 and 1860-61) and Lord Chancellor (1861-65).—219, 506

Beust, Friedrich von (1817-1899)—Prussian army officer, took part in the 1849 Baden-Palatinate uprising; emigrated to Switzerland; member of the Zurich local section of the International; professor of pedagogics.—366

Beust, Friedrich Ferdinand, Count von (1809-1886)—Saxon and Austrian statesman; opposed the unification of Germany under the supremacy of Prussia and supported the independence of small German states; held several ministerial posts in the Government of Saxony (1849-66); Foreign Minister (1866-71) and Chancellor of Austria-Hungary (1867-71).—58, 64, 261, 366

Birley—M.P. from Manchester, elected in the autumn of 1868; Conservative.—163

Biscamp (Biskamp), Elard—German democratic journalist; took part in the 1848-49 revolution in Germany; emigrated after the defeat of the revolution, member of the editorial board of *Das Volk*, organ of the German refugees in London published with Marx's collaboration.—121, 126, 444

Bismarck (or *Bismarck-Schönhausen*), *Otto, Prince von* (1815-1898)—Prussian and German statesman, diplomat; Ambassador to St. Petersburg (1859-62) and Paris (1862); Prime Minister of Prussia (1862-71 and 1873-90); Chancellor of the North German Confederation (1867-71) and of the German Empire (1871-90).—6, 19, 104, 141, 151, 209, 276, 289, 307, 330, 343, 407, 436, 470

Blake, William—English economist of the first half of the 19th century; author of works on money circulation.—224

Blanc, Jean Joseph Louis (1811-1882)—French socialist, historian; member of the Provisional Government and President of the Luxembourg Commission in 1848; pursued a policy of conciliation with the bourgeoisie; a leader of petty-bourgeois emigrants in London from August 1848; deputy to the National Assembly of 1871; opposed the Paris Commune.—373, 377, 497

Blank, Karl Emil (1817-1893)—German merchant, closely connected with socialist circles in the 1840s-50s; married Frederick Engels' sister Marie.—212, 322

of the Augsburg *Allgemeine Zeitung.—* 238

Cluseret, Gustave Paul (1823-1900)— French politician, general; joined Garibaldi's volunteers in Italy (1860); took part in the American Civil War (1861-65) on the side of the Northerners; member of the International; was close to the Bakuninists; in the spring of 1870 acted as the General Council's correspondent in the USA; member of the Paris Commune; emigrated to Belgium after its suppression.—472

Cobbett, William (c. 1762-1835)— English politician and radical writer; from 1802 published *Cobbett's Weekly Political Register.—* 368, 429

Coenen, Philippe—prominent figure in the Belgian working-class movement, shoemaker; secretary of the Antwerp newspaper *Werker*; delegate to the Brussels Congress (1868), London Conference (1871) and the Hague Congress (1872) of the International; subsequently a founder of the Belgian Workers' Party (1885).—464

Collet, Collet Dobson—English radical journalist and public figure; editor and publisher of the Urquhartist *Free Press* (1859-65) and *Diplomatic Review* (from 1866).—159, 165, 168, 264, 296, 346, 438, 468

Combault, Amédée, Benjamin Alexandre (c. 1837-d. after 1884)—prominent figure in the French working-class movement, jeweller; member of the General Council of the International (1866-67), founder of a Paris section of the International in 1870; prosecuted during the third trial of the First International in France; member of the Paris Commune; subsequently emigrated to London.— 556

Comte, Isidore Auguste François Marie (1798-1857)—French philosopher and sociologist, founder of positivism.—242

Congreve, Richard (1818-1899)— English positivist philosopher; journalist; follower of Comte.—261, 293

Coningsby, Robert—prominent figure in the British democratic movement, journalist.—195

Conneau, Henri (1803-1877)—French doctor, personal physician and favourite of Napoleon III.—495

Coppel, Carl—banker in Hanover.—3

Costello, Augustin—Fenian, American army officer; came to Ireland in 1867 to take part in the uprising; was arrested and sentenced to twelve years of penal servitude; released on 25 February 1869.—224

Cremer, Sir William Randall (1838-1908)—active participant in the British trade union and pacifist movement; member of the London Trades Council, carpenter; participant in the inaugural meeting of the International held at St. Martin's Hall (28 September 1864); member of the General Council of the International and its General Secretary (1864-66); delegate to the London Conference (1865) and Geneva Congress (1866) of the International; member of the Executive Committee of the Reform League; opposed revolutionary tactics; subsequently Liberal M.P.; Nobel peace prize winner (1903); was knighted in 1907.—178

Crompton, Henry (1836-1904)—English lawyer and radical politician; positivist; took part in the trade union movement; E. S. Beesly's brother-in-law.—271

Cromwell, Oliver (1599-1658)—leader of the English Revolution; Lord Protector of England, Scotland and Ireland from 1653.—217, 363, 376, 391, 398, 416

Curran, John Philpot (1750-1817)—Irish politician and judge, radical; member of the Irish Parliament; defended leaders of the United Irishmen rev-

olutionary society at state trials.—
398, 401

Currer Bell—see *Brontë, Charlotte*

D

Dakyns—English geologist; member of
the International from 1869; was on
friendly terms with Marx and Engels.—242, 291-93, 423, 426, 454,
459, 525

Daniels, Roland (1819-1855)—German
physician; member of the Communist
League and of its Cologne Central
Authority from 1850; one of the
accused in the Cologne communist
trial (1852); friend of Marx and
Engels.—35

Danielson, Nikolai Frantsevich (pseudonym *Nikolai—on*) (1844-1918)—
Russian economist and writer; an
ideologist of Narodism in the 1880s-
90s; translated into Russian volumes
I (together with Hermann Lopatin
and N. N. Lubavin), II and III of
Marx's *Capital*; corresponded with
Marx and Engels for several years.—
120, 123, 211

Darwin, Charles Robert (1809-1882)—
English naturalist; founded the
theory of natural selection.—141,
162, 206, 217, 423, 482, 527

Davenport, Samuel Th.—treasurer of the
Society of Arts and Trades.—372

Davies—doctor at a London hospital.—
550

Davies, Edward (1756-1831)—English
clergyman, author of works on the
ancient Celts.—515

Davies, Sir John (1569-1626)—English
statesman, lawyer, Attorney-General
for Ireland (1609-19), author of several works on the history of Ireland,
supporter of the English colonisation
of Ireland.—388, 398, 401, 483, 501

Davis, Thomas Osborne (1814-1845)—
Irish democrat, historian and poet; a
Young Ireland leader.—398

Davisson, A. N.—Secretary of the
Schiller Institute in Manchester.—
118

Defoe, Daniel (c. 1660-1731)—English
journalist and novelist.—344

Delescluze, Louis Charles (1809-1871)—
French revolutionary, journalist; participant in the revolutions of 1830
and 1848, founder, editor and publisher of *Le Reveil* (1868-71), member
of the Paris Commune of 1871.—
195, 232

Demuth, Helene (*Lenchen*) (1820-
1890)—housemaid and devoted
friend of the Marx family.—270,
271, 399, 458, 526, 547

De Paepe, César (1841-1890)—Belgian
socialist, compositor, subsequently
physician; a founder of the Belgian
Section of the International (1865);
member of the Belgian Federal
Council; delegate to the London
Conference (1865), the Lausanne
(1867), Brussels (1868) and Basle
(1869) congresses and to the London
Conference (1871) of the International; following the Hague Congress
(1872) supported the Bakuninists for
some time; a founder of the Belgian
Workers' Party (1885).—9, 43, 198,
243-44, 405, 411-15, 424, 440, 453

Diderot, Denis (1713-1784)—French
philosopher of the Enlightenment,
atheist, leader of the Encyclopaed-
ists.—263, 265

Dietzgen, Joseph (1828-1888)—prominent figure in the German and
international working-class movement, leather-worker; philosopher
who independently arrived at dialectical materialism; champion of Marxism; member of the International;
delegate to the Hague Congress
(1872) of the International; emigrated to the USA in 1884.—31, 54,
65, 70, 120, 121, 126, 149, 152, 154,
173, 249, 353, 357

Dixon—managing director of a Liverpool bank.—113

Germany; opposed Luther many times.—249

Edwards, Edward Watkin—an official assignee in the · Court of Bankruptcy.—208

Eichhoff, Albert—book-seller and publisher, Wilhelm Karl Eichhoff's brother.—211, 237, 238, 261, 264, 266, 277, 282, 322, 356

Eichhoff, Wilhelm Karl (1833-1895)— German socialist; in 1859 exposed Stieber as a police spy in the press and was brought to trial for this; refugee in London (1861-66); member of the International from 1868; one of its first historians; member of the German Social-Democratic Workers' Party from 1869.—11, 36, 37, 50, 55, 78, 80, 100, 116, 118, 120, 140, 151, 152, 153, 162, 223, 230, 239, 273-74, 277, 282, 297-99, 531

Einhorn—see Horn, Eduard (Ignácz)

Eliot, George (pen name of Mary Ann Evans) (1819-1880)—English woman novelist.—292, 423

Elpidin, Mikhail Konstantinovich (1835-1908)—took part in the Russian students' revolutionary movement in the early 1860s; emigrated to Geneva in 1865, founded a Russian printing plant where the newspaper Narodnoye Dyelo (People's Cause) was published; member of the initiating group of the Alliance of Socialist Democracy.—193

Emma—see Engels, Emma

Engel, Ernst (1821-1896)—German statistician; director of the Royal Prussian Statistical Bureau in Berlin (1860-82).—253, 352

Engels, Elizabeth Franzisca Mauritia (née van Haar) (1797-1873)—Frederick Engels' mother.—34, 88, 90, 93, 194, 195, 281, 300, 302, 317-20, 336, 348, 452, 453, 548

Engels, Emma (née Croon) (1834-1916)—wife of Frederick Engels'

brother Hermann Engels.—195, 282, 322

Engels, Friedrich (1796-1860)—Frederick Engels' father.—456

Engels, Hermann (1822-1905)— Frederick Engels' brother.—194, 280, 318, 319, 320, 322

Engels, Rudolf (1831-1903)—Frederick Engels' brother.—195, 322, 352, 452-53

Ensor, George (1769-1843)—Irish journalist; opposed Anglo-Irish Union; in his works exposed the colonial policy of the British ruling classes; criticised Malthusianism.—368, 375

Ermen, Anton Gottfried (1807-1886)—a partner in the Manchester firm of Ermen & Engels.—36, 140, 280, 301, 302

Ermen, Gottfried Peter Jakob (1811-1899)—a partner in the Manchester firm of Ermen & Engels.—33, 92, 104, 167, 170, 182, 187, 194, 206, 210, 280-82, 299, 301-02, 320, 321, 329, 336, 346, 395, 402, 435

Ermen, Heinrich (Henry) Eduard (1833-1913)—a partner in the firm of Ermen Brothers; nephew of Gottfried Ermen; manager of Bridgewater Mill at Pendlebury.—32-33

Ermen, Johanna Emilié Julie (née Sartorius)—Anton Ermen's wife.—302

Ermen, Peter (Pitt) Albertus Ermen (1800-1889)—a partner in the Manchester firm of Ermen & Engels.—281, 321

Eugénie Marie Ignace Augustine de Montijo de Guzmán, comtesse de Teba (1826-1920)—Empress of France, Napoleon III's wife.—399

Eulenburg, Friedrich Albrecht, Count von (1815-1881)—Prussian statesman and diplomat; Minister of the Interior (1862-78).—391, 395

Ewald, Georg Heinrich August (1803-1875)—German orientalist; Bible scholar.—408

F

Failly, Pierre Louis Charles Achille de (1810-1892)—French general.—36

Falloux, Frédéric Alfred Pierre, comte de (1811-1886)—French politician and writer, Legitimist and clerical; in 1848 initiated the closure of the national workshops and organised the suppression of the June uprising of the Paris workers; deputy to the Constituent and Legislative Assemblies during the Second Republic; Minister of Education (1849).—232

Faucher, Julius (Jules) (1820-1878)—German economist and journalist, Young Hegelian; advocate of Free Trade; refugee in England from 1850 till 1861; returned to Germany in 1861; member of the Prussian Chamber of Deputies; member of the Party of Progress; National Liberal from 1866.—55, 56, 62, 65, 68, 86, 142

Favre, Jules Gabriel Claude (1809-1880)—French lawyer and politician; a leader of the bourgeois republican opposition from the late 1850s; deputy to the Corps législatif (1860s); Foreign Minister (1870-71); together with Thiers headed the struggle against the Paris Commune; inspired the struggle against the International.—232, 442, 553

Fechner, Gustav Theodor (1801-1887)—German physicist and philosopher.—528

Fehrenbach—photographer in London.—231, 278

Feuerbach, Ludwig Andreas (1804-1872)—German philosopher.—152, 154, 354

Firdousi (Firdausi or Firdusi) (pen name of Abul Kasim Mansur) (c. 940-1020 or 1030)—Persian and Tadjik poet.—336

Flavigny de, Marie, comtesse d'Agoult—see Stern, Daniel

Flerovsky, N.—see Bervi, Vasily Vasilyevich

Flocon, Ferdinand (1800-1866)—French politician and journalist, democrat; an editor of the newspaper La Reforme; in 1848 member of the Provisional Government.—76

Flourens, Gustave (1838-1871)—French revolutionary and naturalist, follower of Blanqui; advocate of Marxism; member of the Paris Commune; was brutally killed by the Versaillese in April 1871.—419, 423, 431, 442, 481, 488, 493, 497, 504-06, 559

Flourens, Pierre Jean Marie (1794-1867)—French physiologist and physician; member of the Paris Academy of Sciences from 1828 and its secretary from 1833; Peer of France (1846-48); Gustave Flourens' father.—423, 559

Forcade-Laroquette, Jean Louis Victor Adolphe de (1820-1874)—French statesman, Bonapartist; Minister of Finance (1860-61), Minister of the Interior (1868-69).—395

Foster, John Leslie (c. 1780-1842)—Irish lawyer, Tory.—113, 215, 219-21

Foster, Peter Le Neve (1809-1879)—Secretary of the Board of the Society of Arts and Trades.—287

Fouché, Joseph, duc d'Otrante (1759-1820)—prominent figure in the French Revolution and the Napoleonic Empire; Minister of Police (1799-1810); notorious for his unscrupulousness.—225

Fourier, François Marie Charles (1772-1837)—French utopian socialist.—512

Fourlong, J.—487

Fowler—judge in Manchester.—265

Fox—Peter Fox's mother.—285

Fox, Peter (André, Peter Fox) (d. 1869)—journalist; prominent figure in the British democratic and working-class movement; Positivist; a leader of the British National League for the Independence of Poland; participant in the inaugural meeting

his teaching.— 183, 242, 261, 293, 454, 482

I

Imandt, Peter (b. 1824)—German teacher; took part in the 1848-49 revolution; member of the Communist League; emigrated to London in 1852; supported Marx and Engels.— 440, 443

Isabella II (1830-1904)—Queen of Spain (1833-68); overthrown by the 1868-74 revolution; fled to France on 30 September 1868.— 108, 114, 115, 119, 137

Ivanov, Ivan Ivanovich (d. 1869)—student of the Agricultural Academy in Moscow; took part in the student movement of the 1860s and the Nechayev organisation; murdered by Nechayev.— 530

J

Jaclard, Charles Victor (1843-1900)—French journalist, Blanquist; member of the International; active in the Paris Commune; following the suppression of the Paris Commune, emigrated to Switzerland and then to Russia; after the 1880 amnesty returned to France and continued to take part in the socialist movement.— 9, 480

Jacoby, Johann (1805-1877)—German radical journalist and politician; a Left-wing leader in the Prussian National Assembly (1848); member of the Prussian Chamber of Deputies (1862); founder of *Die Zukunft* (1867); joined Social-Democrats in the 1870s.— 371, 417, 418, 435, 552

Jäger, Gustav (1832-1916)—German zoologist; follower of Charles Darwin; author of several works on natural sciences.— 162

Jaeger.— 266

Jakub Beg, Mohammed (1820-1877)—ruler of Kashgar (1865-77).— 373

James I (1394-1437)—King of Scotland from 1424.— 226

James I (1566-1625)—King of Great Britain and Ireland (1603-25).— 388

Janin, Jules Gabriel (1804-1874)—French writer, critic and journalist.— 263

Jenny (Jennychen)—see *Marx, Jenny*

Jessup, William J.—American worker, carpenter; active participant in the American labour movement; Vice-President (1866) and Corresponding Secretary (1867) of the National Labour Union of the United States for the State of New York, a leader of the Workers' Union of New York; General Council's correspondent in the USA.— 58, 96, 147, 149

Johannard, Jules (1843-1888)—active in the French working-class movement, lithographer; member of the General Council of the International (1868-69 and 1871-72) and Corresponding Secretary for Italy (1868-69); in 1870 founded a section of the International in St. Denis; member of the Paris Commune; Blanquist; after the defeat of the Commune emigrated to London; delegate to the Hague Congress (1872).— 78, 485

Johnson, Reverdy (1796-1876)—American lawyer and statesman; Attorney-General (1849-50); member of the Democratic Party (conservative wing); Minister to Great Britain (1868-69).— 195

Johnston, James Finlay Weir (1796-1855)—English agricultural chemist.— 384

Jones—librarian in the British Museum Library.— 518

Jones, Ernest Charles (1819-1869)—prominent figure in the English labour movement; proletarian poet and journalist, leader of the Left-wing Chartists; friend of Marx and Engels; took part in the work of the International in the 1860s.— 26, 71,

Hague (1872) congresses of the International; member of the British Federal Council; friend and associate of Marx and Engels.—83, 93, 98, 101, 102, 120, 122, 127, 161, 166, 203, 252, 284, 290, 465, 471, 478, 544

Lever, Charles James (1806-1872)—Irish novelist.—507, 509

Levy, Joseph Moses (1812-1888)—English journalist, a founder and publisher of *The Daily Telegraph.*—101, 454

Lichfield, Thomas George Anson, Earl of (b. 1825)—British Liberal politician.—393

Liebig, Justus, Baron von (1803-1873)—German chemist.—51

Liebknecht, Wilhelm (1826-1900)—prominent figure in the German and international working-class movement, participant in the 1848-49 revolution, member of the Communist League and of the International, delegate to the Basle Congress of the International (1869), deputy to the Reichstag from 1867, a founder and leader of the German Social-Democratic Party, friend and associate of Marx and Engels.—5-6, 8, 11, 15, 19, 20, 30, 38, 40, 48, 58, 73, 75, 102, 105, 106, 108-13, 114-18, 120, 121, 126-27, 131, 135, 136, 141-42, 147, 148, 151, 153, 161, 172, 175, 177, 189, 208, 209, 210, 220-23, 227-31, 234, 236, 239, 242, 248-50, 253, 255-57, 260, 262, 265-67, 274, 276, 282-84, 295-97, 299, 303, 304, 306, 307, 313, 322-28, 330-32, 338, 339, 343, 344, 353, 354, 355, 356, 364, 367, 369, 371, 376, 378, 382, 405, 411, 417-19, 426, 428, 431, 442, 445, 452, 477, 478, 482, 485, 496, 500, 503, 508-11, 513, 519-20, 544, 553

Lifford—see *Hewitt, James, 1st Viscount Lifford*

Lilienfeld-Toal, Pavel Fedorovich (1829-1903)—Russian sociologist, a Baltic country squire and high-ranking Tsarist official.—55, 154, 419, 426, 430, 434

Livy (Titus Livius) (59 B.C.-A.D. 17)—Roman historian.—85

Lizzie—see *Burns, Lydia (Lizzy)*

Lloyd—see *Jones, Lloyd*

Lochner, Georg (born c. 1824)—prominent figure in the German and international working-class movement, carpenter, member of the Communist League, the German Workers' Educational Society in London and of the General Council of the International (November 1864 to 1872), delegate to the London conferences of 1865 and 1871; friend and associate of Marx and Engels.—184

Longfellow, Henry Wadsworth (1807-1882)—American poet, translator and literary critic.—275

Lopatin, Hermann Alexandrovich (1845-1918)—Russian revolutionary, Narodnik, member of the General Council of the International (1870), translated into Russian Volume I of Marx's *Capital,* friend of Marx and Engels.—530-31, 533, 535

Louis XIV (1638-1715)—King of France (1643-1715).—429, 434, 512

Louis Napoleon—see *Napoleon III*

Louis Philippe I (1773-1850)—Duke of Orleans, King of the French (1830-48).—105, 159, 260, 264, 316, 389

Lowe, Robert, 1st Viscount Sherbrooke (1811-1892)—British statesman and journalist, contributor to *The Times,* Whig and later Liberal, M.P., Chancellor of the Exchequer (1868-73), Home Secretary (1873-74).—176

Luby—Thomas Clarke Luby's wife.—562

Luby, Thomas Clarke (1821-1901)—Irish revolutionary, Fenian, journalist, contributor to *The Irish People;* sentenced to twenty years of penal servitude in 1865, was released in 1871 and emigrated to the USA where he worked as a journalist.— 399, 563

Lucraft, Benjamin (1809-1897)—a reformist leader of the British trade unions; furniture-maker, participant in the inaugural meeting of the International held at St. Martin's Hall (28 September 1864), member of the General Council of the International (1864-71), delegate to the Brussels (1868) and Basle (1869) congresses, member of the Executive Committee of the Reform League, opposed the Paris Commune, refused to sign the General Council's address *The Civil War in France* (1871) and left the International.— 245, 248, 376, 386

Ludlow, John Malcolm Forbes (1821-1911)—participant in the British co-operative movement, lawyer and journalist, Christian socialist.— 259, 260, 261, 262-64

Ludwig III (1806-1877)—Grand Duke of Hesse-Darmstadt (1848-77).— 16, 141, 209

Lupus—see *Wolff, Wilhelm*

Luther, Martin (1483-1546)—German theologian and writer, prominent figure of the Reformation; founder of Protestantism (Lutheranism) in Germany.— 249, 271, 434

M

Macleod, Henry Dunning (1821-1902)—Scottish economist, engaged mainly in credit problems.— 38

Maddison—Marx's doctor.— 417

Maguires, the—ancient Irish aristocratic family.— 484

Malthus, Thomas Robert (1766-1834)—English clergyman and economist, author of a theory of population.— 270, 381

Manteuffel, Otto Theodor, Baron von (1805-1882)—Prussian statesman, Minister of the Interior (November 1848 to November 1850), Prime Minister (1850-58).— 124

Marie, Alexandre Thomas (1795-1870)—French lawyer and politician, moderate republican, Minister of Public Works in the Provisional Government (1848); later Minister of Justice in Cavaignac's government.— 232

Marryat, Frederick (1792-1848)—British naval officer and writer.— 507

Martin, Bon Louis Henri (1810-1883)—French historian and politician, republican, joined the International in 1865.— 435

Martinaud—former French abbot, then compositor, anarchist, member of the Paris Section of the International, delegate to the Basle Congress (1869).— 413

Marx, Eleanor (Tussy) (1855-1898)—Karl Marx's youngest daughter, took part in the British and international working-class movement.— 6, 7, 12, 14, 37, 40, 44, 45, 47-54, 60, 63, 64, 67, 71, 74, 75, 79, 82, 87, 91, 122, 159, 167, 187, 189, 200, 205, 211, 243, 246-48, 253, 256, 261, 270, 273, 275, 278, 284, 286, 290, 294, 295, 298-99, 308, 311, 317, 324, 336, 338, 339, 341, 342, 345, 347-51, 354, 357, 359, 368, 370, 382, 389, 393, 399, 410, 419, 423, 425, 433, 447, 458, 521-22, 525, 534, 546, 548, 560

Marx, Henriette (née *Pressburg*) (1787-1863)—Karl Marx's mother.— 25

Marx, Jenny (née *von Westphalen*) (1814-1881)—Karl Marx's wife.— 30, 40, 53, 56, 64, 73-75, 79, 87, 95, 122, 171, 187, 200, 205, 211, 261, 269, 272-76, 278, 284, 286, 309, 315, 326, 327, 342, 355, 359, 399, 410, 419, 458, 465, 488, 519, 525, 528, 560

Marx, Jenny (1844-1883)—Karl Marx's eldest daughter, journalist, took part in the international working-class movement.— 15, 19, 30, 45, 47-51,

53, 57, 60, 63-67, 74, 82, 87, 122, 171, 172, 187, 205, 207, 211, 213, 214, 232, 243, 246-48, 253, 261, 273, 275, 284, 286, 290, 291-94, 297, 300, 308, 310, 312, 318, 324, 325, 327, 329, 330, 334, 339, 341, 351, 354, 355, 357, 359, 361, 389, 399, 400, 410, 419, 423, 426, 429, 444, 447, 451, 455, 458-61, 466, 471, 473, 476, 487, 488, 500, 501, 503, 522, 523, 525, 532, 533, 537, 543, 545, 547, 552, 557, 558, 560, 561, 564

Marx, Laura—see *Lafargue, Laura*

Massol, Marie Alexandre (1805-1875)— French journalist, utopian socialist; Proudhon's friend; editor-in-chief of *La Morale indépendante* (1865-70).— 79

Mayer.—155

Mayer, Karl (1819-1889)—German petty-bourgeois democrat, deputy to the Frankfurt National Assembly (1848-49), editor of the Stuttgart newspaper *Der Beobachter* in the 1860s.— 325, 343, 364

Mazzini, Giuseppe (1805-1872)—Italian revolutionary, democrat, a leader of the Italian national liberation movement; headed the Provisional Government of the Roman Republic (1849); an organiser of the Central Committee of European Democracy in London (1850); when the International was founded in 1864 tried to bring it under his influence.— 240

Meissner, Otto Karl (1819-1902)—publisher in Hamburg, printed Marx's *Capital* and other works by Marx and Engels.— 5, 9, 37, 55, 74, 78, 99, 100, 102, 104, 106, 211, 214, 217, 222, 223, 234, 237-39, 241, 243, 249, 257, 276, 277, 279, 285, 297, 300, 305, 308, 318, 327, 333, 339, 354, 357, 358, 417, 428, 446, 452, 511, 527, 528, 529, 533

Mende, Fritz (d. 1879)—member of the General Association of German Workers; President of the Lassallean General Association of German

Workers founded by Hatzfeldt (1869-72), deputy to the North German Reichstag (1869).— 276, 322, 408

Mendelssohn, Moses (1729-1786)—German deist philosopher.— 528

Menke—Theodor Heinrich Menke's wife.— 545

Menke, Theodor Heinrich—German statistician, Ludwig Kugelmann's friend, member of the International.— 397, 407, 427, 456, 465

Merriman, J. J.—member of the General Council of the International (November 1864 to 1867).— 139

Meyen (Mayen), Eduard (1812-1870)— German journalist, Young Hegelian, after the 1848-49 revolution emigrated to England, later National Liberal.— 479

Meyer, Carl Joseph (1796-1856)—German industrialist, journalist and publisher, founded the Bibliographical Institute which put out several editions of the Encyclopaedic Dictionary named after him (1826).— 144

Meyer, Gustav—manufacturer in Bielefeld, Ludwig Kugelmann's acquaintance.— 13

Meyer, Hermann (1821-1875)—leading figure in the German and American working-class movement; merchant; took part in the 1848-49 revolution in Germany, emigrated to the USA in 1852; an organiser of the International's sections in St. Louis; Joseph Weydemeyer's friend.— 97, 354

Meyer, Sigfrid (c. 1840-1872)—prominent figure in the German and American working-class movement; engineer, member of the General Association of German Workers; opposed Lassalleanism, member of the International; emigrated to the USA in 1866, member of the New York Communist Club and an organiser of the International's sections in the USA; follower of Marx and Engels.— 58-59, 96-98, 148-49, 177, 184, 354, 471-76

Michaelis, Otto (1826-1890)—German economist and journalist; member of the Prussian Chamber of Deputies from 1861; a publisher of the journal *Vierteljahrschrift für Volkswirthschaft und Kulturgeschichte*; National Liberal (from 1867); deputy to the North German Reichstag.—59

Michel, Louis Chrysostome (1798-1853)— French lawyer and politician, petty-bourgeois republican; counsel for the defence at several trials against republicans during the July monarchy, deputy to the Legislative Assembly (1849-51), belonged to the Montagne Party.—188

Mill, John Stuart (1806-1873)—English economist and positivist philosopher.—166, 263, 293

Milner, George—prominent figure in the British working-class movement, Irish by birth, follower of James O'Brien; member of the National Reform League, of the Land and Labour League, and of the General Council of the International (1868-72); delegate to the London Conference (1871), member of the British Federal Council (autumn of 1872 to 1873), fought the reformist wing in the Council.—376, 386

Milton, John (1608-1674)—English poet.—348

Miquel, Johannes (1828-1901)—German lawyer, politician and financier; member of the Communist League up to 1852; a leader of the National Liberals (Right wing) from 1867, member of the Prussian Chamber of Deputies; deputy to the North German Reichstag and later German Reichstag.—142, 255, 376

Mitchel, John (1815-1875)—Irish revolutionary democrat, Left-wing leader of the Young Ireland group; deported to a penal colony for taking part in the preparation of an uprising in 1848; escaped in 1853 and emigrated to the USA; fought on the side of the Southerners during the US Civil War (1861-65), author of *The History of Ireland.*—445

Moelmud, Dufnwal (second half of the 5th cent.-first half of the 6th cent.)— semi-legendary legislator of ancient Britain.—515

Moilin, Jules Antoine (Tony) (1832-1871)—French physician and journalist, petty-bourgeois socialist; took part in the Paris Commune (1871), shot by the Versaillese.—225, 230, 242, 244, 449

Moll, Friedrich Wilhelm (c. 1835-1871)—Solingen worker, member of the General Association of German Workers, emigrated to the USA (1864), a founder of the General Association of German Workers in New York, member of the International after his return to Germany, delegate to the Geneva Congress (1866).—420-21, 456, 465

Moll, Joseph (1813-1849)—German watch-maker, a leader of the League of the Just, member of the Central Authority of the Communist League, took part in the Baden-Palatinate uprising of 1849, was killed in the battle of the Murg.—456, 465

Mollin, Gabriel—French gilder, member of the International, delegate to the Basle Congress (1869).—459

Monroe—physician, Scottish by birth; Marx's daughter Jenny gave lessons to his children.—171, 300, 357, 423, 429

Monroe—wife of Dr Monroe.—171, 300, 327, 330, 357

Mont(h)eil, Amans Alexis (1769-1850)— French historian.—423, 429

Montijo—see *Eugénie Marie Ignace Augustine de Montijo de Guzmán, comtesse de Teba*

Moore, George Henry (1811-1870) — Irish politician and leader of the tenant-right movement, M.P. (1847-

(1863-65), was arrested and sentenced to life imprisonment in 1865, amnestied in 1870, emigrated to the USA where he headed the Fenian organisation; retired from political life in the 1880s.—162, 373, 386, 389, 391, 429, 445, 451, 454, 455, 457, 458, 476, 518, 530, 532, 548-49, 562, 563

O'Donovan Rossa, Mary J.—Jeremiah O'Donovan Rossa's wife; organised collection of funds for the families of the Irish political prisoners in 1865-66; author of an appeal to Irish women published in the *Workman's Advocate* on 6 January 1866 by the General Council's decision.—458

Offenbach, Jacques (1819-1880) — French composer.—507

O'Flaherty, Roderic (1629-1718)—Irish historian.—516

Ogarev, Nikolai Platonovich (1813-1877)—Russian revolutionary, journalist, poet, friend and associate of Alexander Herzen.—516, 518

Ollivier, Émile (1825-1913)—French politician and statesman, bourgeois republican, deputy to the Corps législatif (from 1857); was close to the Bonapartists in the late 1860s; head of government (January-August 1870) and Minister of Justice and Cult.—409, 411, 422, 451

O'Neills, the—ancient Irish aristocratic family.—483

Oppenheim, Heinrich Bernhard (1819-1880)—German democratic politician, economist and journalist; an editor of the Berlin newspaper *Die Reform* (1848); refugee (1849-50), subsequently National Liberal.—85

Orsini, Cesare—Italian refugee; member of the General Council of the International (1866-67); spread the International's ideas in the USA; Felice Orsini's brother.—57

Orsini, Felice (1819-1858)—Italian democrat, republican, a prominent figure in the struggle for Italy's national liberation and unification, executed for his attempt on the life of Napoleon III.—57, 505

O'Shea, William Henry (1840-1905)—Irish public figure, defended the imprisoned Fenians in 1869.—375

Overend—a director of an English banking firm, Overend, Gurney and Company.—305, 548

Owen, Sir Richard (1804-1892)—English zoologist and paleontologist, was the first to describe archaeopteryx, a primitive reptile-like bird.—162, 509

P

Palmerston, Henry John Temple, 3rd Viscount (1784-1865)—British statesman, Tory, from 1830 Whig; Foreign Secretary (1830-34, 1835-41, 1846-51), Home Secretary (1852-55) and Prime Minister (1855-58, 1859-65).—64, 161, 243, 261, 278, 390, 505, 506, 559

Parker, Sarah—Frederick Engels' housekeeper.—156, 204

Parsons, William, 3rd Earl of Rosse (1800-1867)—British astronomer, published a pamphlet on relationship between landowners and tenants in Ireland (1867).—374

Peel, Sir Robert (1788-1850)—British statesman; moderate Tory; Prime Minister (1834-35, 1841-46); repealed the Corn Laws in 1846.—113, 159, 166

Pelletan, Pierre Clément Eugène (1813-1884)—French journalist and politician, bourgeois republican, deputy to the Corps législatif; member of the Government of National Defence (1870-71).—232, 546, 553

Pelletier, Claude (1816-1881)—French democrat, deputy to the Constituent and Legislative Assemblies (1848-51); exiled from France after the coup d'état of 2 December 1851; emigrated to the USA; the International's

questions, was close to Narodniks, published the first Russian edition of Volume I of Marx's *Capital* (1872).— 130, 429

Pollock, George D.—British army doctor; member of the commission, which in 1867 submitted to Parliament a report on treatment of political prisoners in English convict prisons.—224, 457, 459

Potter, George (1832-1893)—a reformist leader of the British trade unions, carpenter, member of the London Trades Council and a leader of the Amalgamated Union of Building Workers; founder, editor and publisher of *The Bee-Hive Newspaper.*—3, 114, 375, 377, 395

Prendergast, John Patrick (1808-1893)— Irish historian, Liberal, author of works on the history of Ireland.— 374, 388, 401, 403, 409, 415

Prévost-Paradol, Lucien Anatole (1829-1870)—French journalist and liberal politician.—388, 409

Probert, William (1790-1870)—British clergyman, specialist on ancient Welsh laws and customs.—515

Proudhon, Pierre Joseph (1809-1865)— French writer, economist and sociologist; a founder of anarchism.—101, 130, 225, 260, 383, 429

Prudhomme (b. 1843)—member of the International, its correspondent in Bordeaux (France).—557

Pyat, Félix (1810-1889)—French journalist, playwright and politician, democrat; took part in the 1848 revolution; emigrated to Switzerland in 1849 and later to Belgium and England; opposed independent working-class movement; conducted a slander campaign against Marx and the First International; member of the Paris Commune (1871).—43, 63, 64, 75, 78, 91, 143, 155, 159, 174, 272

Q

Queen Annabella—see *Annabella Drummond of Stobhall*

Quételet, Lambert Adolphe Jacques (1796-1874)—Belgian scientist, statistician, mathematician and astronomer.—232

Quo-Quo—see *Marx, Eleanor*

R

Racowiţa, Janko von (d. 1865)—Romanian nobleman; mortally wounded Lassalle in a duel (1864).—88

Ramsay, Sir Andrew Crombie (1814-1891)—British geologist, professor in London, conducted geological explorations in England and Wales (from 1862).—291

Ranc, Arthur (1831-1908)—French politician and journalist, moderate republican.—361, 486

Randall, G. W.—participant in the American working-class movement, secretary of the workers' society in Boston (USA), member of the International.—98

Rasch, Gustav (1825-1878)—German democrat, journalist and lawyer; took part in the 1848 revolution in Berlin, after the defeat of the revolution, refugee in Switzerland and France.—4

Raspail, François Vincent (1794-1878)— French naturalist and writer; socialist, sympathised with the revolutionary proletariat; took part in the revolutions of 1830 and 1848; after the revolution of 1848 was imprisoned, then lived in exile in Belgium; returned to France in 1863; deputy to the Constituent Assembly (1869).—316, 317, 369, 553

Real, W.—78

Reclus, Jean Jacques Élisée (1830-1905)—French geographer, sociologist and politician, theorist of anarchism; member of the International, editor of *La Cooperation* (1866-68), participant in the Paris Commune (1871).—9, 28, 79, 377, 378

Reich, Eduard (1836-1919)—German physician, author of works on public hygiene and sanitation.—391

Rémy, Theodor—Swiss teacher, Secretary of the Central Committee of the German-speaking sections in Geneva; follower of Bakunin; member of the Geneva Section of the International named Alliance of Socialist Democracy and of the initiating group of the Alliance of Socialist Democracy.—332

Reuter, Paul Julius, Baron von (1816-1899)—German-born founder of the British news agency.—505

Ricardo, David (1772-1823)—English economist.—69, 224, 263, 378-81, 383, 385

Richard, Albert (1846-1918)—French journalist, a founder of the Lyons Section of the International, follower of Bakunin, member of the secret Alliance of Socialist Democracy; took part in the Lyons uprising in September 1870.—414, 437, 492

Richelieu, Armand Jean du Plessis, duc de (1585-1642)—French statesman; Cardinal; Chief Minister to Louis XIII.—344

Ris, F.—194

Rissé, Joseph (b. 1843)—singer in Hanover, composed and published a collection of Irish folk songs (1870).—532, 562, 563

Rittinghausen, Moritz (1814-1890)—German democratic journalist, contributed to the *Neue Rheinische Zeitung* (1848-49); member of the Cologne Democratic Society, of the International, later (till 1884) of the German Social-Democratic Party.—352

Robert III (c. 1340-1406)—King of Scotland (1390-1406).—226

Robert, Fritz (1845-1899)—Swiss teacher, Bakuninist, delegate to the Brussels (1868) and Basle (1869)

congresses of the International, editor of *La Solidarité.*—488

Robespierre, Maximilien François Marie Isidore de (1758-1794)—Jacobin leader in the French Revolution, head of the revolutionary government (1793-94).—259, 260

Robin, Paul (1837-1912)—French teacher, Bakuninist, a leader of the Alliance of Socialist Democracy (from 1869), member of the General Council (1870-71), delegate to the Basle Congress (1869) and the London Conference (1871) of the International.—413, 489, 492, 506

Rochefort, Henri, marquis de Rochefort-Luçay (c. 1831-1913)—French journalist and politician, Left-wing republican; publisher of the journal *La Lanterne* (1868-69) and the newspaper *La Marseillaise* (1869-70); after the revolution of 4 September 1870, a member of the Government of National Defence; monarchist from the end of the 1880s.—199, 422, 427, 445, 451, 553

Roesgen, Charles—employee of the Manchester firm of Ermen & Engels.—80, 84, 119, 238, 302, 325, 333, 349, 469, 533

Roesgen von Floss, Philipp von—Dutch journalist, member of the working-class movement, mechanical engineer.—463, 464, 468, 469

Rogeard, Auguste Louis (1820-1896)—French democratic journalist, a founder and editor of *La Rive gauche* (1864); in 1865, persecuted for an anti-Bonapartist pamphlet, emigrated to Belgium and then to Germany; a leader of the Paris Commune (1871).—507

Roon, Albrecht Theodor Emil, Count von (1803-1879)—Prussian statesman and military leader; field marshal-general from 1873, War Minister (1859-73) and Naval Minister (1861-71); carried out reorganisation of the Prussian army.—376

Serno-Solovyevich, Alexander Alexandrovich (1838-1869)—Russian revolutionary of the early 1860s, refugee from 1862, member of the Geneva Section of the International (from 1867).—172, 177, 186, 189, 202, 363, 376

Serraillier, Auguste (b. 1840)—a prominent figure in the French and international working-class movement, shoemaker, member of the General Council of the International (1869-72); Corresponding Secretary for Belgium (1870) and France (1871-72); member of the Paris Commune (1871), delegate to the London Conference (1871) and the Hague Congress of the International (1872); supporter of Marx.—430, 529, 533, 535

Seume, Johann Gottfried (1763-1810)—German writer and poet.—7, 9

Seward, William Henry (1801-1872)—American politician and statesman; a leader of the Right wing of the Republican Party, US State Secretary (1861-69).—195

Shakespeare, William (1564-1616)—English playwright and poet.—216, 466, 507, 541, 545

Shaw, Robert (d. 1869)—a leader of the British working-class movement, house-painter, attended the inaugural meeting of the International held at St. Martin's Hall (28 September 1864), member of the General Council of the International (1864-69), Treasurer of the Council (1867-68), Corresponding Secretary for America (1867-69), delegate to the London Conference (1865) and the Brussels Congress (1868) of the International.—96, 406

Shee—partner of a German publisher in Brussels, Carl Georg Vogler, and owner of a bookshop.—138

Siebel, Carl (1836-1868)—German poet, helped to propagate works by Marx and Engels, including Volume I

of Capital; a distant relative of Engels.—5, 8, 28, 34, 35, 74

Simon, Jules François Simon Suisse (1814-1896)—French statesman and idealist philosopher, moderate republican, deputy to the Constituent Assembly (1848-49), member of the Corps législatif.—232, 546

Slack—London correspondent of The New-York Daily Tribune.—544

Slade, Sir Adolphus (1804-1877)—English naval officer, later admiral, served in Turkey (1849-66).—139

Smith, Adam (1723-1790)—Scottish economist.—25, 39, 45, 46, 67

Smith, Goldwin (1823-1910)—British historian, economist and journalist, Liberal, supported England's colonial policy in Ireland, moved to the USA (1868) and then to Canada (1871).—374, 388

Sonnemann, Leopold (1831-1909)—German politician and journalist, a founder of the National Association (1859); in the 1860s took the stand of South German Federalists; supported working-class movement.—102, 479

Sorge, Friedrich Adolf (1828-1906)—prominent figure in the international and American working-class and socialist movement, took part in the 1848-49 revolution in Germany, emigrated to the USA (1852), organised the International's sections there, delegate to the Hague Congress (1872), General Secretary of the General Council in New York (1872-74), active propagandist of Marxism, friend and associate of Marx and Engels.—58, 59, 97, 149, 471-72

Spencer, Herbert (1820-1903)—British positivist philosopher and sociologist.—38

Speyer, Carl (b. 1845)—carpenter, Secretary of the German Workers' Educational Society in London in the 1860s, member of the International and its General Council (from 1870) in London and then in the USA.—166

Spier, Samuel (1838-1903)—German Social-Democrat, teacher; member of the General Association of German Workers (from 1867) and the Social-Democratic Workers' Party (from 1869), member of the Brunswick Section of the International, delegate to the Basle Congress (1869).—358

Spinoza (Baruch or Benedictus) de (1632-1677)—Dutch philosopher.— 528

Spurgeon, Charles Haddon (1834-1892)—well-known English Baptist preacher.—541

Steinthal—clergyman in Manchester, Unitarian, an acquaintance of Engels.—118

Steinthal—owner of the Manchester trading firm where Georg Weerth worked from 1852 to 1856.—118, 542-43

Steinthal—wife of the above.—543

Stepney, Cowell William Frederick (1820-1872)—active participant in the British working-class movement, member of the Reform League, member of the General Council of the International (1866-72), and its Treasurer (1868-70), delegate to the Brussels (1868) and Basle (1869) congresses and to the London Conference (1871) of the International; member of the British Federal Council.—95, 160, 213, 217, 220, 412, 424, 430, 472-73

Stern, Daniel (real name Flavigny de, Marie, comtesse d'Agoult) (1805-1876)—French authoress and journalist.—217

Sterne, Laurence (1713-1768)—English writer.—297

Steuart, Sir James, afterwards Denham (1712-1780)—British economist, one of the last Mercantilists.—39

Stewart, David, Duke of Rothesay (c. 1378-1402)—son of King Robert III

of Scotland, Lieutenant of Scotland (1399-1402).—226

Stieber, Wilhelm (1818-1882)—Prussian police officer, chief of the Prussian political police (1850-60), organised the prosecution in the Cologne Communist trial (1852) and acted as main witness, chief of military police during the Austro-Prussian (1866) and Franco-Prussian (1870-71) wars.—36, 221, 266, 268, 276, 307, 461, 525

Stirling, James Hutchinson (1820-1909)—Scottish philosopher, propagated Hegel's philosophy in England.—39, 481

Strohn, Eugen (d. 1868)—Wilhelm Strohn's brother.—190, 191

Strohn, Wilhelm—member of the Communist League, a friend of Marx and Engels, refugee in Bradford.—109, 112, 142, 147, 213, 256, 403, 454

Strousberg, Bethel Henry (1823-1884)—big German railway contractor and industrialist.—352

Struve, Gustav von (1805-1870)—German democratic journalist, a key figure in the Baden uprisings in April and September 1848 and the Baden-Palatinate uprising in 1849; a leader of the German petty-bourgeois refugees in England, took part in the US Civil War (1861-65) on the side of the Northerners.—4, 110, 175

Stumpf, Paul (c. 1826-1913)—participant in the German working-class movement, mechanic; member of the German Workers' Society in Brussels (1847), of the Communist League; took part in the 1848-49 revolution in Germany, member of the International, delegate to the Lausanne Congress of the International (1867), member of the Social-Democratic Workers' Party in Germany.—354

Sulla (Lucius Cornelius Sulla) (138-78 B.C.)—Roman general and statesman, Consul (88 B.C.), dictator (82-79 B.C.).—35

cal explorations in Yorkshire (1865-69).— 292

Ware, Sir James (1594-1666)— Irish historian and statesman, Auditor-General of Ireland (1632-49, 1660-66); author of works on the history of Ireland.— 516, 517

Waterlow, Sydney Hudley (1822-1906)— British Liberal politician.— 437

Watts, John (1818-1887)— English journalist, utopian socialist, follower of Robert Owen; later Liberal.— 182, 275

Weber, Josef Valentin (1814-1895)— German watch-maker, took part in the revolutionary movement in Baden (1848); in 1849 emigrated to Switzerland and then to London; member of the German Workers' Educational Society in London.— 151, 155, 159, 174

Weber, Wilhelm— German watch-maker; Lassallean; refugee in New York (after 1864); President of the General Association of German Workers in New York (1866); Josef Valentin Weber's son.— 522

Weerth, Georg (1822-1856)— German proletarian poet and journalist, member of the Communist League, an editor of the Neue Rheinische Zeitung (1848-49); friend of Marx and Engels.— 35, 118, 389, 502, 547

Wehner, J. G.— German refugee in Manchester, Treasurer of the Schiller Institute in the 1860s; an acquaintance of Engels.— 221

Weiß, Guido (1822-1899)— German democratic journalist; took part in the 1848-49 revolution; belonged to the Party of Progress (Left wing) in the 1860s; editor of the Berliner Reform (1863-66) and Die Zukunft (1867-71).— 333, 369, 428, 479

Welcker, Karl Theodor (1790-1869)— German lawyer, liberal writer.— 511

Werner, Ernst— bookbinder in Leipzig, participant in the German working-class movement.— 350

Werner, Johann Peter— German lawyer, deputy to the Frankfurt National Assembly (1848), belonged to the Left Centre.— 253

West, Charles (1816-1898)— English physician, specialised in pediatrics.— 353, 355

Westbury— see Bethell, Richard, 1st Lord Westbury

Weston, John— prominent figure in the British working-class movement; carpenter, subsequently manufacturer; Owenite; attended the inaugural meeting of the International held at St. Martin's Hall (28 September 1864), member of the General Council of the International (1864-72); delegate to the London Conference (1865); member of the British Federal Council and of the Executive Committee of the Reform League, a leader of the Land and Labour League.— 245, 376, 386

Weydemeyer, Joseph (1818-1866)— prominent figure in the German and American working-class movement; member of the Communist League; took part in the 1848-49 revolution in Germany; editor of the Neue Deutsche Zeitung (1849-50); emigrated to the USA after the defeat of the revolution, took part in the US Civil War (1861-65) on the side of the Northerners; helped to propagate ideas and documents of the International in the USA; friend and associate of Marx and Engels.— 35, 97, 142, 502

Whaley, J. C.— prominent figure in the American working-class movement, President of the National Labour Union (1867).— 58

Wigand, Otto (1795-1870)— German publisher and bookseller, owner of a firm in Leipzig which printed works by radical writers.— 276, 297

William I (1797-1888)— Prince of Prussia, Prince Regent (1858-61), King of Prussia (1861-88) and Emperor of Germany (1871-88).— 19, 104

Williams, J.— see *Marx Jenny*

Willich, August (1810-1878) — Prussian officer, resigned from the army on account of his political views; member of the Communist League, participant in the Baden-Palatinate uprising of 1849; a leader of the separatist group that split away from the Communist League in 1850; emigrated to the USA in 1853, took part in the US Civil War (1861-65) on the side of the Northerners.— 495

Wilhelm, Wilhelmchen— see *Liebknecht Wilhelm*

Winterbottom.— 150

Wolff, Wilhelm (Lupus) (1809-1864) — German teacher, proletarian revolutionary; member of the Central Authority of the Communist League; an editor of the *Neue Rheinische Zeitung*; took an active part in the 1848-49 revolution in Germany; emigrated to Switzerland in the summer of 1849 and later to England; friend and associate of Marx and Engels.— 34, 35, 77, 210, 211, 312, 502

Y

Yor(c)k, Theodor (1830-1875)—prominent figure in the German working-class movement, carpenter, Lassallean; in 1869 left the General Association of German Workers and helped to organise the Social-Democratic Workers' Party, its Secretary in 1871-74.— 242, 250

Young, Arthur (1741-1820) — English economist and writer on agriculture, supporter of the quantity theory of money.— 361, 362, 388

Z

Zabicki, Antoni (c. 1810-1871) — a leader of the Polish national liberation movement; compositor; left Poland after 1831; participant in the Hungarian revolution of 1848-49; from 1851 a refugee in England; from 1863 published *Głos Wolny*— newspaper of the Polish democratic refugees; Secretary of the Polish National Committee; member of the General Council of the International (1866-71); Corresponding Secretary for Poland (1866-71).— 347, 350

Zhukovski, Nikolai Ivanovich (1833-1895) — Russian anarchist, a refugee in Switzerland from 1862; member of the committee of the League of Peace and Freedom; a leader of the secret Bakuninist Alliance of Socialist Democracy.— 193

Zitschke— one of Marx's creditors in London.— 285

Zweiffel— Prussian official, Chief Public Prosecutor at Cologne; deputy to the Prussian National Assembly (Right wing) in 1848.— 124

INDEX OF LITERARY AND MYTHOLOGICAL NAMES

Caliban— character in Shakespeare's *The Tempest*; half-man, half-monster.— 10

Clare Vair de Vair— title character in Alfred Tennyson's poem; a heartless and arrogant aristocrat.— 275

Crispinus— character in Juvenal's Satire 4.— 228

Eve (Bib.).— 379, 382

Excelsior— title character in Longfellow's poem.— 275

Falstaff, Sir John— character in Shakespeare's tragedy *King Henry IV* and his comedy *The Merry Wives of Windsor*; a fat, sly braggart and jester.— 216, 507

INDEX OF QUOTED
AND MENTIONED LITERATURE

WORKS BY KARL MARX AND FREDERICK ENGELS

Marx, Karl

Address to the National Labour Union of the United States. London, 1869 (present edition, Vol. 21).—279, 283
— In: *The Bee-Hive,* No. 396, May 15, 1869 (in the column 'The International Working Men's Association').—279, 283

The Belgian Massacres. To the Workmen of Europe and the United States. London, May 4, 1869 (present edition, Vol. 21).—275, 279, 283
— Les Massacres en Belgique. Manifeste du Conseil Général de Londres. A tous les membres de l'Association Internationale des Travailleurs. In: *L'Internationale,* No. 18, 15 mai 1869.—275, 279
— Die Belgischen Metzeleien. An die Arbeiter von Europa und der Vereinigten Staaten! In: *Demokratisches Wochenblatt,* Nr. 21, 22. Mai 1869.—275

Capital. A Critique of Political Economy. Vol. I, Book I: The Process of Production of Capital (present edition, Vol. 35)
— Das Kapital. Kritik der politischen Oekonomie. Erster Band. Buch I: Der Produktionsprocess des Kapitals. Hamburg, 1867.—5, 9, 10, 13, 24, 30, 36, 38, 39, 56, 58, 65, 68, 70, 72, 78, 81, 84, 97, 98, 99, 101, 102, 103, 106, 121, 123, 125, 126, 130, 136, 138, 141, 149, 152, 156, 166, 180, 184, 196, 210, 213, 214, 238, 243, 258-59, 261, 263, 277, 300, 328, 329, 352, 354, 360, 367, 368, 378, 385, 398, 399, 441, 480, 525, 527, 528, 529, 542-43, 546

Das Kapital. Kritik der politischen Oekonomie. Von Karl Marx. 2-te verbes. Aufl. Bd. I. Hamburg, Meissner, 1872.—31, 32, 33, 34, 68, 329

Capital. A Critique of Political Economy. Vol. II, Book II: The Process of Circulation of Capital (present edition, Vol. 36)
— Das Kapital. Kritik der politischen Oekonomie. Von Karl Marx. Bd. II, Buch II: Der Cirkulationsprocess des Kapitals. Herausgegeben von F. Engels. Hamburg, 1885.—21, 22, 30, 119, 123, 232, 234, 259, 409, 528, 546

—The Effects of Machinery in the Hands of the Capitalist Class. In: *The International Working Men's Association. Resolutions of the Congress of Geneva, 1866, and the Congress of Brussels, 1868.* London, [1869].—98, 221
—[Eccarius, J. G.] From a Correspondent. Brussels, Sept. 9. In: *The Times,* No. 26229, September 14, 1868.—96, 98
—(From our Special Correspondent.) Brussels, Sept. 10. In: *The Daily News,* September 12, 1868.—97, 98

[*Economic Manuscripts of 1857-58*] (present edition, Vols 28-29)
—[Grundrisse der Kritik der politischen Ökonomie (Rohentwurf) 1857-58].—434

The Eighteenth Brumaire of Louis Bonaparte (present edition, Vol. 11).—333, 399
—Der 18te Brumaire des Louis Napoleon. In: *Die Revolution.* Erstes Heft. New-York, 1852.—108, 113, 124, 211, 222, 223, 238, 325

—Der Achtzehnte Brumaire des Louis Bonaparte. Zweite Ausgabe. Hamburg, 1869.—211, 216-17, 238, 239, 241, 243, 276, 279, 285, 297, 318, 325, 330, 333, 338, 339, 349, 352, 354, 417-18, 426, 428, 446, 511

The English Government and the Fenian Prisoners (present edition, Vol. 21)
—Le Gouvernement anglais et les prisonniers fénians. In: *L'Internationale,* Nos. 59, 60; 27 février, 6 mars 1870.—440, 444, 449, 451, 453, 455, 475

The Fenian Prisoners at Manchester and the International Working Men's Association (present edition, Vol. 21)
—A. M. G. Hardy, secrétaire d'Etat de Sa Majesté. In: *Le Courrier français,* No. 163, 24 novembre 1867.—392

Forced Emigration.—Kossuth and Mazzini.—The Refugee Question.—Election Bribery in England.—Mr. Cobden (present edition, Vol. 11). In: *New-York Daily Tribune,* No. 3722, March 22, 1853.—398

The Fourth Annual Report of the General Council of the International Working Men's Association (present edition, Vol. 21)
—International Working Men's Congress. In: *The Times,* No. 26225, September 9, 1868.—93, 95, 96, 101

The French Crédit Mobilier (present edition, Vol. 15)
—In: *New-York Daily Tribune,* Nos. 4735, 4737 and 4751; June 21, 24 and July 11, 1856; No. 5128, September 26, 1857.—7

The General Council of the International Working Men's Association to the Central Bureau of the International Alliance of Socialist Democracy (present edition, Vol. 21)
—Le Conseil Général de l'Association Internationale des Travailleurs au Bureau Central de l'Alliance Internationale de la Démocratie Socialiste.—236-37, 240, 491

The General Council of the International Working Men's Association to Committee Members of the Russian Section in Geneva (present edition, Vol. 21)
—Главный Совѣтъ Международнаго Товарищества Рабочихъ. Членамъ Комитета Русской секціи в Женевѣ. In: *Народное Дѣло,* № 1, 15 апреля 1870.—462-63

The General Council to the Federal Council of Romance Switzerland (present edition, Vol. 21)
— Le Conseil Général au Conseil Fédéral de la Suisse Romande.—404-05, 406, 412-15, 424, 430, 436, 444, 449, 451, 473-75, 492

Herr Vogt (present edition, Vol. 17)
— Herr Vogt. London, 1860.—15, 106, 124, 142, 184-85, 189, 208-10, 231, 248, 250, 282, 434

How Mr. Gladstone's Bank Letter of 1866 Procured a Loan of Six Millions for Russia (present edition, Vol. 21). In: *The Diplomatic Review,* 2 December 1868.—166

Inaugural Address of the Working Men's International Association Established September 28, 1864, at a Public Meeting Held at St. Martin's Hall, Long Acre, London (present edition, Vol. 20)
— Address. In: *Address and Provisional Rules of the Working Men's International Association, Established September 28, 1864, at a Public Meeting Held at St. Martin's Hall, Long Acre, London.* [London,] 1864.—124

The International Working Men's Association and the International Alliance of Socialist Democracy (present edition, Vol. 21)
— L'Association Internationale des Travailleurs et l'Alliance Internationale de la Démocratie Socialiste.—190, 198, 201, 202, 219, 491

Lord Palmerston (present edition, Vol. 12). In: *The People's Paper,* Nos. 77, 78, 79, 80, 81, 84, 85 and 86; October 22, 29; November 5, 12, 19; December 10, 17, 24, 1853
— *I. Palmerston; II. Palmerston and Russia; III. A Chapter of Modern History; IV. England and Russia.* In: *New-York Daily Tribune,* Nos. 3902, 3916, 3930 and 3973, October 19, November 4, 21, 1853; January 11, 1854
— *Palmerston.* In: *Die Reform,* Nr. 72, 73, 74, 77, 78; 2., 3., 4., 8., 9. November 1853
— *Palmerston and Russia,* 1 ed. London, E. Tucker [1853] (*Political Fly-Sheets,* No. I); 2 ed. London, 1854
— *Palmerston. What Has He Done? (Palmerston and the Treaty of Unkiar Skelessi),* London, E. Tucker [1854] (*Political Fly-Sheets,* No. II).—124, 278, 390

My Plagiarism of F. Bastiat (present edition, Vol. 20)
— Mein Plagiat an F. Bastiat.—66

On the Jewish Question (present edition, Vol. 3)
— Zur Judenfrage. In: *Deutsch-Französische Jahrbücher.* 1-ste und 2-te Lieferung. Paris, 1844.—123

On Proudhon (present edition, Vol. 20)
— Ueber P. J. Proudhon. In: *Der Social-Demokrat,* Nr. 16, 17, 18; 1., 3., 5. Februar 1865.—135

The Poverty of Philosophy. Answer to the 'Philosophy of Poverty' by M. Proudhon (present edition, Vol. 6)
—Misère de la philosophie. Réponse à la philosophie de la misère de M. Proudhon. Paris, Bruxelles, 1847.—124, 130, 138, 141, 150, 217, 225, 260, 383-84

Preface to the First German Edition of Volume I of 'Capital' (present edition, Vol. 35)
—Vorwort. London, 25. Juli 1867. In: Marx, K. *Das Kapital. Kritik der politischen Oekonomie.* Erster Band. Buch I: Der Produktionsprocess des Kapitals. Hamburg, 1867.—259-60

Preface to the Second Edition of 'The Eighteenth Brumaire of Louis Bonaparte' (present edition, Vol. 21)
—Vorwort. In: Marx, K. Der Achtzehnte Brumaire des Louis Bonaparte. Zweite Ausgabe. Hamburg, 1869.—297, 318, 330

Programme for the Mainz Congress of the International (present edition, Vol. 21)
—Programme. In: The Fifth Annual Congress of the International Working Men's Association. London, 1870.—537

Provisional Rules of the Association (present edition, Vol. 20)
—In: Address and Provisional Rules of the Working Men's International Association, Established September 28, 1864, at a Public Meeting Held at St. Martin's Hall, Long Acre, London. [London,] 1864.—125
—In: Congrès ouvrier. Association Internationale des Travailleurs. Règlement provisoire. Paris, [1864].—486

[Record of Marx's Speech on *The Bee-Hive.* From the Minutes of the General Council Meeting of April 26, 1870] (present edition, Vol. 21).—497

[Record of Marx's Speech on the Policy of the British Government with Respect to the Irish Prisoners. From the Minutes of the General Council Meeting of November 16, 1869] (present edition, Vol. 21).—375-76, 390
—The British Government and the Irish Political Prisoners. In: *Reynolds's Newspaper,* No. 1006, November 21, 1869.—386, 392
—International Working Men's Association, 256, High Holborn. In: *National Reformer,* November 28, 1869.—392, 394

[Record of Marx's Speeches on the Policy of the British Government with Respect to the Irish Prisoners. From the Minutes of the General Council Meeting of November 23 and 30, 1869] (present edition, Vol. 21)
—The British Government and the Irish Political Prisoners. In: *Reynolds's Newspaper,* No. 1007, November 28, 1869.—390
—International Working Men's Association, 256, High Holborn. In: *National Reformer,* December 5, 1869.—390

[Record of Marx's Speech on the Right to Inheritance. From the Minutes of the General Council Meeting of July 20, 1869] (present edition, Vol. 21). In: *The Bee-Hive,* No. 406, July 24, 1869, in the column 'The International Working Men's Association'.—334

Report of the General Council on the Right of Inheritance (present edition, Vol. 21). In: Report of the Fourth Annual Congress of the International Working Men's Association, held at Basle, in Switzerland. From the 6th to the 11th September, 1869. London, [1869].—414, 492

[Resolution of the General Council on *The Bee-Hive*] (present edition, Vol. 21)
—Beschluß des Generalraths der Internationalen Arbeiterassoziation bezuglich des 'Bee-Hive'. In: *Der Volksstaat*, Nr. 38, 11. Mai 1870.—400, 497, 503

[Resolution of the General Council on Félix Pyat's Provocative Behaviour] (present edition, Vol. 21)
—Communication du Conseil général de Londres de l'Association Internationale. In: *La Liberté*, No. 55, 12 juillet 1868.—60
—Communiqué. In: *La Cigale*, No. 29, 19 juillet 1868.—60, 174

[Resolution on Changing the Place of the International's Congress in 1868] (present edition, Vol. 21). In: *The Bee-Hive Newspaper*, No. 347, June 6, 1868 (in the column 'The International Working Men's Association').—43, 44

Revelations Concerning the Communist Trial in Cologne (present edition, Vol. 11)
—Enthüllungen über den Kommunisten-Prozeß zu Köln. Basel, 1853.—124, 229
—[Boston, 1853].—124

Speech on the Question of Free Trade. Delivered to the Democratic Association of Brussels at Its Public Meeting of January 9, 1848 (present edition, Vol. 6)
—Discours sur la question du libre échange, prononcé à l'Association Démocratique de Bruxelles, dans la séance publique du 9 janvier 1848 [Bruxelles, 1848].—124

Statement to the German Workers' Educational Society in London (present edition, Vol. 21)
—Herrn C. Speyer, Sekretär des Deutschen Arbeiterbildungsvereins.—166

To the President and Executive Committee of the General Association of German Workers (present edition, Vol. 21)
—An den Präsidenten und Vorstand des Allg[emeinen] deutsch[en] Arbeiter-Vereins. In: *Der Social-Demokrat*, Nr. 100, 28. August 1868.—89

Engels, Frederick

The Condition of the Working-Class in England. From Personal Observation and Authentic Sources (present edition, Vol. 4)
—Die Lage der arbeitenden Klasse in England. Nach eigner Anschauung und authentischen Quellen. Leipzig, 1845.—6, 213, 424, 548

Democratic Pan-Slavism (present edition, Vol. 8)
—Der demokratische Panslavismus. In: *Neue Rheinische Zeitung*, Nr. 222, 223; 15., 16. Februar 1849.—121, 153-55

The History of Ireland (present edition, Vol. 21).—357, 358, 399, 402, 500, 524, 548

Karl Marx (present edition, Vol. 21).—74, 76, 77, 81
—Karl Marx. In: *Die Zukunft*, Nr. 185, 2. August 1869; *Demokratisches Wochenblatt*, Nr. 34, 21. August 1869, Beilage.—144, 318, 325, 328, 333

[A Letter to W. Bracke, 28 April 1870] (this volume). In: *Der Volksstaat*, Nr. 39, 14. Mai 1870.—520, 521

Notes for the Preface to a Collection of Irish Songs (present edition, Vol. 21).—532, 533, 563

On the Dissolution of the Lassallean Workers' Association (present edition, Vol. 21)
—Zur Auflösung des Lassalleanischen Arbeiter-Vereins. In: *Demokratisches Wochenblatt*, Nr. 40, 3. Oktober 1868.—110, 112, 115, 117
On the Dissolution of the Lassallean Workers' Association (*Postscript*) (present edition, Vol. 21)
—Zur Auflösung des Lassalleanischen Arbeitervereins. In: *Demokratisches Wochenblatt*, Nr. 41, 10. Oktober 1868.—112

The Peasant War in Germany (present edition, Vol. 10)
—Der deutsche Bauernkrieg. In: *Neue Rheinische Zeitung. Politisch-ökonomische Revue*, Nr. 5-6, 1850.—228, 229, 234, 237
—In: *Der Volksstaat*, Nr. 27-43, 45-51; 2.-30. April; 4.-28. Mai; 4.-25. Juni 1870.—425, 445, 508, 509, 513
—Der deutsche Bauernkrieg. Leipzig, 1870.—237, 239, 241, 256, 257, 262, 265, 267, 273, 278, 282, 283, 307, 354, 356, 419
Preface to the Second Edition of 'The Peasant War in Germany' (present edition, Vol. 21)
—Der deutsche Bauernkrieg. Vorbemerkung. In: *Der Volksstaat*, Nr. 27, 28; 2., 6. April 1870.—425, 428, 478
—Vorbemerkung. In: *Der deutsche Bauernkrieg*. Leipzig, 1870.—419

The Prussian Military Question and the German Workers' Party (present edition, Vol. 20)
—Die preussische Militärfrage und die deutsche Arbeiterpartei. Hamburg, 1865.—89, 111, 112, 234, 237

Report on the Miners' Guilds in the Coalfields of Saxony (present edition, Vol. 21). In: *The Bee-Hive*, No. 385, February 27, 1869 (in the column 'The International Working Men's Association').—214-15, 219, 220, 221, 222, 223, 226, 227
—Bericht über die Knappschaftsvereine der Bergarbeiter in den Kohlenwerken Sachsens. In: *Der Social-Demokrat*, Nr. 33, 17. März 1869; *Demokratisches Wochenblatt*, Nr. 12, 20. März 1869 (Beiblatt); *Die Zukunft*, Nr. 67, 68; 20., 21. März 1869.—220, 221, 244, 250

Review of Volume One of 'Capital' for the 'Beobachter' (present edition, Vol. 20)
—Karl Marx. Das Kapital. Kritik der politischen Oekonomie. Erster Band. Hamburg, Meißner, 1867. In: *Der Beobachter*, Nr. 303, 27. Dezember 1867.—58

Review of Volume One of 'Capital' for 'The Fortnightly Review' (present edition, Vol. 20)
—Karl Marx on Capital.—5, 7, 30, 35, 37-40, 44, 45, 50, 52-54, 70, 73, 74, 81, 84, 138, 140-41, 217

Review of Volume One of 'Capital' for the 'Staats-Anzeiger für Württemberg' (present edition, Vol. 20)
—Karl Marx. Das Kapital. Kritik der politischen Oekonomie. Erster Band. Hamburg, Meissner, 1867. In: *Staats-Anzeiger für Württemberg*, Nr. 306, 27. Dezember 1867.—60

Review of Volume One of 'Capital' for the 'Zukunft' (present edition, Vol. 20)
—Karl Marx, das Kapital. Erster Band. Hamburg, Meissner, 1867, 784 Seiten. 8° In: *Die Zukunft*, Nr. 254, 30. Oktober 1867, Beilage.—60

Synopsis of Volume One of 'Capital' by Karl Marx (present edition, Vol. 20)
—Das Kapital von K. Marx. I. Band. I. Buch. Produktionsprozess des Kapitals.—11-12

To the Directorate of the Schiller Institute (present edition, Vol. 21)
—An das Direktorium der Schiller-Anstalt.—100

Marx, Karl and Engels, Frederick

The First Trial of the 'Neue Rheinische Zeitung'. The Trial of the Rhenish District Committee of Democrats (present edition, Vol. 8)
—Preßprozeß der Neuen Rheinische Zeitung. Der Prozeß gegen den rheinischen Ausschuss der Demokraten. In: Zwei politische Prozesse verhandelt vor den Februar Assisen in Köln. Köln, 1849.—124

The Holy Family, or Critique of Critical Criticism. Against Bruno Bauer and Company (present edition, Vol. 4)
—Die heilige Familie, oder Kritik der kritischen Kritik. Gegen Bruno Bauer und Consorten. Frankfurt am Main, 1845.—123

Manifesto of the Communist Party (present edition, Vol. 6)
—Manifest der Kommunistischen Partei. London, 1848.—124, 262, 267, 300, 303, 304
—Манифестъ Коммунистической партіи. [Geneva, 1869].—502

WORKS BY DIFFERENT AUTHORS

Affaire de la souscription Baudin. Troisième édition. Paris, 1868.—188, 191

Aycard, N. *Histoire du Crédit mobilier. 1852-1867*. [Paris,] 1867.—7

Бакунинъ, М. *Исповедь*. In: *Московскія вѣдомости*, № 4, 6 января 1870.—437, 441
— *Редакторамъ «Колокола»*. In: *Колоколъ*, № 2, 9 апреля 1870.—516
— *Русскимъ, польскимъ и всѣмъ славянскимъ друзьямъ*. In: *Колоколъ*, №№ 122-123, 15 февраля 1862 (supplement).—221, 222

Bakounine, [M.] *Discours de Bakounine au deuxième congrès de la paix, à Berne.* In: *Kolokol (La Cloche),* No. 14-15, 1 décembre 1868.—200, 489
—*Hertzen.* In: *La Marseillaise,* Nos. 72, 73; 2, 3 mars 1870; *Le Progrès,* Nos. 10, 11, 12; 5, 12, 19 mars 1870.—463, 592, 593

Bakunin, M. *Aufruf an die Slaven. Von einem russischen Patrioten Michael Bakunin. Mitglied des Slavenkongresses in Prag.* Koethen, 1848.—154
—*Briefe über die revolutionäre Bewegung in Russland. I.* In: *Der Volksstaat,* Nr. 31, 32; 16., 20. April 1870.—496, 499, 519

Balzac, Honoré de. *Le curé de village.*—189
—*L'Illustre Gaudissart.*—85

Bara, J. [Speech in the Chamber of Deputies on May 16, 1868.] In: *La Voix de l'avenir,* No. 23, 7 juin 1868; *La Liberté,* No. 47, 17 mai 1868.—43

Bastiat, F. *Harmonies économiques.* Paris, 1850.—65

Batrachomyomachia.—174

Bebel, A. [Speech in the North German Diet on March 18, 1869.] In: *Die Zukunft,* Nr. 67, 20. März 1869.—255
—*An Herrn Dr. Schweitzer in Berlin.* In: *Demokratisches Wochenblatt,* Nr. 27, 3. Juli 1869.—307

Becker, B. *Enthüllungen über das tragische Lebensende Ferdinand Lassalle's.* Schleiz, 1868.—87, 89, 92, 112, 250, 252, 285
—*Rede des Vereins-Präsidenten, Bernhard Becker, gehalten in der Versammlung der Hamburger Mitglieder des Allgemeinen deutschen Arbeiter-Vereins am 22. März 1865.* In: *Der Social-Demokrat,* Nr. 39, 26. März 1865, Beilage.—112

Becker, J. Ph. *Die Internationale Arbeiter-Association und die Arbeiterbewegung in Basel im Winter 1868 auf 1869.* Genf, 1869.—238
—*Mahnruf. An unsere Bundesgenossen und die Arbeiter und Arbeitervereine aller Länder.* Signed by the members of the Central Committee of the group of the German-language sections. In: *Der Vorbote,* Nr. 10, Oktober 1869.—392
—*Rundschreiben des Zentralkomite's der Sektionsgruppe deutscher Sprache an die Sektionen und mitgenössischen Gesellschaften.* Signed by the members of the Central Committee. In: *Der Vorbote,* Nr. 11, November 1868.—392
—(anon.) *Was wir wollen und sollen.* In: *Der Vorbote,* Nr. 1, Januar 1866.—102
—*Programm der Internationalen Arbeiter-Association.* In: *Demokratisches Wochenblatt,* Nr. 31-33, 1., 8., 15. August 1868, Beilagen.—102

Beesly, E. S. *Catiline as a Party Leader.* In: *The Fortnightly Review,* Vol. I, 15. Mai-1. August 1865.—217
—*The Social Future of the Working Class.* In: *The Fortnightly Review,* Vol. V, No. XXVII, March 1, 1869.—230

Bible
The New Testament
Luke.—148
Matthew.—307
2 Samuel.—408

[Biscamp, E.] *London, 25 Sept.* In: *Allgemeine Zeitung,* Nr. 273, 29. September 1868 (in the column 'Grossbritannien' (marked Δ).—121

Blake, W. *Observations on the Principles Which Regulate the Course of Exchange; and on the Present Depreciated State of the Currency.* London, 1810.—224

Blanc, J. J. [Correspondence on the Brussels Congress of the International Working Men's Association.] In: *L'Opinion nationale*, 10 septembre 1868.—107

Boethius, H. *The History and Chronicles of Scotland.* Edinburgh, 1536.—225-27, 230

Boisguillebert, [P.] *Dissertation sur la nature des richesses, de l'argent et des tributs où l'on découvre la fausse idée qui règne dans le monde à l'égard de ces trois articles.* In: *Economistes financiers du XVIII-e siècle.* Paris, 1843.—429

Bonhorst. *Der famose Diktator und eine der Braunschweiger 'Strohpuppen' im Lichte der Baseler Beschlüsse.* In: *Der Volksstaat,* Nr. 8, 9; 27., 30. Oktober 1869.—367

[Borkheim, S.] *Russische Briefe.* I-VII. *Russische Eisenbannen.* In: *Die Zukunft,* Nr. 23, 36, 49, 68, 82, 158; Januar-Juni 1869
— VIII-X. Michael Bakunin. In: *Die Zukunft,* Nr. 167, 187, 189; 21. Juli, 13., 15. August, 2. November 1869.
— XI. *Ein russischer penny-a-liner.* In: *Die Zukunft,* Nr. 44, 45, 47 (Beilage), 58; 22., 23., 25. Februar, 10. März 1870.—206, 436
— *Russische politische Flüchtlinge in West-Europa.* In: *Demokratisches Wochenblatt,* Nr. 5, 6, 17, 20; 1., 8. Februar; 25. April; 16. Mai 1868 (the first two articles are signed with the initials S. B.).—142

Boruttau, C. *Gedanken über Gewissens-Freiheit.* Königsberg, 1867.—71, 72

Bright, J. [Speech at the meeting in Birmingham on January 11, 1870.] In: *The Times,* January 12, 1870.—409

Buchez, Ph. J. B. et Roux, P. C. *Histoire parlementaire de la révolution française, ou Journal des assemblées nationales, depuis 1789 jusqu'en 1815.* Tomes 1-40. Paris, 1834-1838.—260

Büchner, L. *Kraft und Stoff.* 10. vermehrte und verbesserte Auflage. Leipzig, 1869. First edition was issued in Frankfurt am Main in 1855.—486
— *Sechs Vorlesungen über die Darwin'sche Theorie von der Verwandlung der Arten und die erste Entstehung der Organismenwelt, sowie über die Anwendung der Umwandlungstheorie auf den Menschen, das Verhältniß dieser Theorie zur Lehre vom Fortschritt und den Zusammenhang derselben mit der materialistischen Philosophie der Vergangenheit und Gegenwart.* Zweite Auflage. Leipzig, 1868.— 131, 159, 162, 167, 168, 173, 206, 210

Butt, I. *The Irish People and the Irish Land: a Letter to Lord Lifford.* Dublin, 1867.—361, 374

Cabanis, P.-J.[-G.] *Considérations générales sur l'étude de l'homme, et sur les rapports de son organisation physique avec ses facultés intellectuelles et morales.* In: *Mémoires de l'institut national des sciences et arts, pour l'an IV de la République. Sciences morales et politiques.* T. 1., Paris, An VI [1797-1798].—159, 173

Camdenus, G. *Britannia, sive florentissimorum regnorum Anglioe, Scotoe, Hibernioe, et insularum adiacentium ex intima antiquitate.* Chorographica descriptio. Francofurdi, 1590. First published in Latin in 1586.—402
— *Britannia or Chorographical Description of the most Flourishing Kingdoms England, Scotland and Ireland and the Islands Adjoining.* London, 1637.—402

Cannon, J. *History of Grant's Campaign for the Capture of Richmond (1864-1865).* London, 1869.—402

Carey, H. Ch. *The Harmony of Interests, Agricultural, Manufacturing, and Commercial.* Second edition. New-York, 1856. The first edition came out in 1851.—59

— Principles of Social Science. In three volumes. Philadelphia, 1868-1869.—369-70, 374, 398-407, 545

Carl, F., Jubitz, F. *L'Union des travailleurs allemands de New-York aux ouvriers de Paris.* In: *La Marseillaise,* No. 103, 2 avril 1870.—472

Castille, H. *Les Massacres de juin 1848. D'après des documents historiques.* Paris, 1869.—232, 242, 244, 246

[Charras, J.-B.-A.] *Monsieur Napoléon Bonaparte (Jérôme).* Troisième édition. Fribourg en Suisse, 1861.—138

Clement, K. J. *Schleswig, das urheimische Land des nicht dänischen Volks der Angeln und Frisen und Englands Mutterland, wie es war und ward.* Hamburg, 1862.—459

Cluseret, G. P. *Aux travailleurs américains.* In: *La Marseillaise,* No. 103, 2 avril 1870.—472

Cobbett, W. *To the Boroughmongers. On Castlereagh's Cutting his Throat, and on Their Own Probable Fate.* In: *Cobbett's Weekly Register,* Vol. 43, No. 8, August 24, 1822.—429

Congreve, R. *Mr. Huxley on M. Comte.* In: *The Fortnightly Review,* Vol. V, No. XXVIII, April 1, 1869.—261

Curran, J. Ph. *The Speeches of the Right Honourable John Philpot Curran,* first edition, London, 1843.—398
— The Speeches of the Right Honourable John Philpot Curran, second edition, Dublin, 1855.—401

Cyclopaedia Americana—see *The New American Cyclopaedia*

Dante, A. *La Divina commedia.*—201

Darwin, Ch. *De l'origine des espèces ou des lois du progrès chez les êtres organisés. Traduit en français avec l'autorisation de l'auteur par Mlle Clémence-Aug. Royer.* Avec une préface et des notes du traducteur. Paris, 1862.—217
— On the Origin of Species by Means of Natural Selection, or the Preservation of Favoured Races in the Struggle for Life. London, 1859.—206
— The Variation of Animals and Plants under Domestication. In two volumes. London, 1868.—141

Davies, E. *Celtic Researches, on the Origin, Traditions and Language, of the Ancient Britons; with Some Introductory Sketches, on Primitive Society.* London, 1804.—515

Davies, J. *Historical Tracts.* London, 1787.—388-89, 398, 400, 483, 501

[Defoe, D.] *Memoirs of a Cavalier or a Military Journal of the Wars in Germany and the Wars in England from the Year 1632, to the Year 1648.* London, [1720].—344

Diderot, [D] *Le Neveu de Rameau précédé d'une étude de Goethe sur Diderot suivi de l'analyse de 'La fin d'un monde et du neveu de Rameau' de M. Jules Janin par N. David.* Quatrième édition. Paris, 1865.—263, 265

Dietzgen, J. *Das Kapital. Kritik der politischen Oekonomie von Karl Marx.* Hamburg, 1867. In: *Demokratisches Wochenblatt,* Nr. 31 (Beilage) Nr. 34, 35, 36; 1., 22., 29. August, 5. September 1868.—65, 70
—(anon.) *Das Wesen der menschlichen Kopfarbeit.* Dargestellt von einem Handarbeiter. Eine abermalige Kritik der reinen und praktischen Vernunft. Hamburg, 1869.—120, 121, 126, 150, 152-54, 173, 249

Duchiński, F. *Les origines slaves. Pologne et Ruthénie.* Paris, 1861.—435

Dühring, E. *Marx, Das Kapital, Kritik der politischen Oekonomie,* I. Band, Hamburg, 1867. In: *Ergänzungsblätter zur Kenntniß der Gegenwart.* Bd. 3, 3. Auflage. Hildburghausen, 1867.—59

Dupont, E. [Speech at the final sitting of the Brussels Congress of the International Working Men's Association on September 13, 1868.] In: *The Daily News,* September 15, 1868.—101

Eccarius, J. G. *Eines Arbeiters Widerlegung der national-ökonomischen Lehren John Stuart Mill's.* Berlin, 1869.—276
—(anon.) *The British Government and the Irish Political Prisoners.* In: *Reynolds's Newspaper,* Nos. 1006, 1008, November 21 and December 5, 1869.—386, 392, 437
—(anon.) *The International Working Men's Congress.* (From a Correspondent.) In: *The Times,* Nos. 26225, 26227, 26229, 26230, 26232; September 9, 11, 14, 15 and 17, 1868.—93, 97-98, 99, 101, 102, 109, 543
—(anon.) *The International Working Men's Congress.* (From a Correspondent.) In: *The Times,* No. 26543, September 15, 1869.—99, 543-44
—*Die Schneiderei in London oder der Kampf des grossen und des kleinen Capitals.* In: *Neue Rheinische Zeitung, Politisch-ökonomische Revue,* Heft 5-6, Mai-Oktober 1850; *Demokratisches Wochenblatt,* Nr. 2-5, 7; 9., 16., 23., 30. Januar und 13. Februar 1869, Beilagen.—228

Edda—295

Edwards, E. W. [Speech as a witness at the Overend, Gurney and Co. trial on January 23, 1869.] In: *The Times,* No. 26343, January 25, 1869.—208

Eichhoff, W. *Die Internationale Arbeiterassociation. Ihre Gründung, Organisation, politisch-sociale Thätigkeit und Ausbreitung.* Berlin, 1868.—50, 78, 80, 100
—[Speech at the sitting of the Democratic Workers' Association in Berlin on October 15, 1868.] In: *Demokratisches Wochenblatt,* Nr. 43, 24. Oktober 1868.—151

Eliot, G. *Felix Holt, the Radical.*—292, 423, 459

Ensor, G. *An Inquiry Concerning the Population of Nations: containing a Refutation of Mr. Malthus's Essay on Population.* London, 1818.—368, 375

Erins-Harfe. Irländische Volksmelodien nach Thomas Moore; Deutsch herausgegeben und arrangirt von Joseph Rissé. Hannover, [1870].—563

Favre, J. [Speech in the Corps législatif on February 21, 1870.] In: *Journal des Débats,* 22 février 1870.—442

Der Feldzug der preussischen Main-Armee im Sommer 1866. Bielefeld und Leipzig, 1867.—64, 283

Der Feldzug von 1866 in Deutschland. Redigirt von der kriegsgeschichtlichen Abtheilung des Grossen Generalstabes. Berlin, 1867.—283

Ferdinand Flocon to Marx in Brussels. March 1, 1848 (present edition, Vol. 6).—76, 124

Firdusi. *Heldensagen.* In deutscher Nachbildung nebst einer Einleitung über das Iranische Epos von Adolf Friedrich von Schack. 2. verm. Aufl. der 'Heldensagen' und der 'Epischen Dichtungen'. Berlin, 1865.—336

Флеровскій, Н. *Положеніе рабочаго класса въ Россіи. Наблюденія и изслѣдованія.* С.-Петербургъ, 1869.—360, 362, 363, 390, 423-24, 426, 429-31, 433, 440, 441, 450, 462, 480, 487, 508, 529

Flourens, G. *Histoire de l'homme. Cours d'histoire naturelle des corps organisés au Collège de France.* Paris, 1863.—559

Fonvielle, A. de. *Une Dénonciation.* In: *La Marseillaise,* No. 139, 8 mai 1870.—511

Fonvielle, U. de. *L'amnistie, cette concession tardive...* In: *La Marseillaise,* No. 46, 2 février 1870.—425

Foster, J. L. *An Essay on the Principle of Commercial Exchanges, and More Particularly of the Exchange Between Great Britain and Ireland: with an inquiry into the practical effects of the bank restrictions.* London, 1804.—113, 215, 222-24

Fourlong, J. *The Irish Roman Catholic Bishops on the Land Question.* In: *Manchester Examiner and Times,* March 30, 1870.—487

Frankel, L. *Ein belauschtes Zwiegespräch. VIII.* In: *Volkswille,* Nr. 10, 2. April 1870.—479, 483

Freiligrath, F. *An Joseph Weydemeyer,* I-II. In: *Die Revolution,* Nr. II, 1852.—142
— *Banditenbegräbnis.*—323
— *Piratenromanze.*—323

Gambetta, L. *Plaidoirie de M. Gambetta, avocat de M. Delescluze. Audience du 14 novembre 1868.* In: *Affaire de la souscription Baudin.* Troisième édition. Paris, 1868.—188

Ganilh, Ch. *Des systèmes d'économie politique, de la valeur comparative de leurs doctrines, et de celle qui parait la plus favorable aux progrès de la richesse.* Seconde édition. Tomes I-II. Paris, 1821. The first edition came out in Paris in 1809.—67

[Garnier, G.] *Abrégé élémentaire des principes de l'économie politique.* Paris, 1796.—67

Gaumont, Ch. *La Grève à Genève.* In: *Le Peuple,* 29-30 mars 1869.—253

The Genealogies, Tribes, and Customs of Hy-Fiachrach, Commonly Called O'Dowda's Country. With a translation and notes... by John O'Donovan. Dublin, 1844.—518

Giraldus Cambrensis. *Opera.* Vol. I-VII. London, 1861-1877.—416
— *Topographia hibernica et expugnatio hibernica.* In: *Giraldi Cambrensis Opera,* Vol. V. London, 1867.—402, 416, 442

Gladstone, W. E. *Ecce homo.* London, 1868.—445
— *A Letter to the Right Rev. William Skinner, d.d., Bishop of Aberdeen, and Primus, on the Functions of Laymen in the Church.* London, 1852.—445
— *A Manual of Prayers from the Liturgy.* London, 1845.—445
— *Propagation of the Gospel.*—445
—[Speech in the House of Commons on February 15, 1870.] In: *The Times,* February 16, 1870 (in the column 'Land Tenure (Ireland)'); *The Manchester Daily Examiner and Times,* February 17, 1870.—432, 437
—[Speech in the House of Commons on March 3, 1870.] In: *The Times,* March 4, 1870.—445, 454

Gobineau, J. A. *Essai sur l'inégalité des races humaines.* Tomes I-IV. Paris, 1853-1855.—446

Goegg, A. *Erklärung.* In: *Der Volksstaat,* Nr. 3, 9. Oktober 1869.—363

Goethe, J. W. von. *Egmont.*—331
— *Faust.*—292
— *Götz von Berlichingen.*—331
— *Hermann und Dorothea.*—295
— *Reineke Fuchs.*—541

[Granier de] Cassagnac, P. [The Leader]. In: *Le Pays*, 15 janvier 1870.—419, 553

Greulich, H. *Die Heulmaierei gegen den Basler Kongress.* In: *Der Volksstaat*, Nr. 5, 16. Oktober 1869.—364

Guéroult, A. *Les grèves.* In: *L'Opinion national*, 28 janvier 1870.—554

Haeckel, E. *Generelle Morphologie der Organismen.* Allgemeine Grundzüge der organischen Formen-Wissenschaft, mechanisch begründet durch die von Charles Darwin reformirte Descendenz-Theorie. 2 Bde. Berlin, 1866.—162
— *Monographie der Moneren.* In: *Jenaische Zeitschrift für Medicin und Naturwissenschaft.* Bd. IV. Leipzig, 1868.—162

H[arris], G. E. *International Working Men's Association.* In: *The National Reformer*, November 28 and December 5, 1869.—392, 394, 397-98, 401
— *Yours or Mine; or short chapters, showing the true basis of property and the causes of its unequal distribution.* In: *The National Reformer*, December 5, 1869.—392

Hegel, G. W. F. *Phänomenologie des Geistes.* In: G. W. F. Hegel, *Werke*, Band II, 2. Auflage. Berlin, 1841.—46, 263

Heine, H. *Atta Troll. Ein Sommernachtstraum.*—371
— Disputation (Romanzero).—249
— Lutetia.—489

Held, A. *Die ländlichen Darlehenskassenvereine in der Rheinprovinz und ihre Beziehungen zur Arbeiterfrage.* Jena, 1869.—527

Herzen, A. *Lettre à N. Ogareff.* In: *Kolokol* (*La Cloche*), Nos. 14-15, 1 décembre 1868.—200

[Герцен, А. И.] *Тюрьма и ссылка. Изъ записокъ Искандера.* Лондонъ, 1854.—411, 424, 426

Heß, M. [Speech at the Brussels Congress of the International Working Men's Association on September 11, 1868.] In: *The Times*, No. 26230, September 15, 1868.—99, 102
— (anon.) 'Die Woche, welche...'. In: *Der Volksstaat*, Nr. 15, 19. Februar 1870 (in the column 'Aus Frankreich').—422

Hewitt, J. *Ireland, and the Irish Church.* London, 1842.—374
— *Thoughts on the Present State of Ireland.* London, 1849.—374
— *A Plea for Irish Landlords.* Dublin, 1867.—374

Hiltrop. *Ueber die Reorganisation der Knappschaftsvereine.* In: *Zeitschrift des Königlich preussischen statistischen Bureaux*, Nr. 4-6, April, Mai, Juni 1869.—352

Hobbes, Th. *Leviathan, or the Matter, Form and Power of a Commonwealth Ecclesiastical and Civil.* London, 1651.—217

Horace (Quintus Horatius Flaccus). *De Arte Poetica.*—216
— *Epistolae.*—115, 136,
— *Satirarum.*—171, 435, 437

Horn, I. E. *Frankreichs Finanzlage*. Pest, Wien, Leipzig, 1868.—7, 11
— *La Liberté des banques*. Paris, [1866]. (The title erroneously had: 'J.-E.'). The German edition came out in Stuttgart and Leipzig in 1867.—158

Hugo, V. *Napoléon le Petit*. Londres, 1852.—255

Humbert, A. *Le Plébiscite de boquillon*. Paris, [1870].—507, 509

Huxley, T. H. *The Forefathers and Forerunners of the English People*. In: *The Manchester Examiner and Times*, January 12, 1870 (in the article 'Professor Huxley on Political Ethnology').—454
— *On the Physical Basis of Life*. In: *The Fortnightly Review*, Vol. V, No. XXVI, February 1, 1869.—183, 242, 482
— *The Scientific Aspects of Positivism*. In: *The Fortnightly Review*, Vol. V, No. XXX, June 1, 1869.—293

Jacoby, J. [Speech at the sitting of electors in Berlin on January 20, 1870.] In: *Die Zukunft*, Nr. 18, 22. Januar 1869.—417, 418

Jäger, G. *Zoologische Briefe*. I. Lieferung. Wien, 1864.—162

[Jerusalem.] *La Dictature universelle*. In: *L'International*, 3 août 1869.—342

Johnston, J. F. W. *Notes on North America Agricultural, Economical and Social*. In two volumes. Edinburgh and London, 1851.—384

Juárez, B. P. *Mexico, 9 mars 1868*. In: *Le Courrier français*, 21 avril 1868.—16, 18

Jubitz, F., Carl, F. *L'Union des travailleurs allemands de New-York aux ouvriers de Paris*. In: *La Marseillaise*, 2 avril 1870.—472

Juvenal (Decimus Junius Juvenalis). *Satirarum*.—228

Kane, R. *The Industrial Resources of Ireland*. 2nd ed. Dublin, 1845. The first edition came out in 1844.—402

Kirchmann, J. H. V. *Aesthetik auf realistischer Grundlage*. Bd. 1-2. Berlin, 1868.—258
— *Ueber die Unsterblichkeit. Ein philosophischer Versuch*. Berlin, 1865.—258

Klemm, G. *Die Werkzeuge und Waffen, ihre Entstehung und Ausbildung*. Sondershausen, 1858.—328-29

Kock, Paul de. *L'amant de la lune*.—159

Kolb, G. F. *Handbuch der vergleichenden Statistik der Völkerzustands-und Staatenkunde. Für allgemeinen praktischen Gebrauch*. 5. umgearb. Aufl. Leipzig, 1868.—485

Lafargue, Paul-Laurent. *Le Roman d'une Conspiration par A. Ranc*. In: *La Libre pensée*, No. 13, 16 avril 1870.—486

Lanfrey, P. *Le Guet-apens de Bayonne. Histoire de Napoléon I*. Tome IV. In: *La Cloche*, Nos. 44-46; 1-3 février 1870.—423, 426

Lange, F. A. *Die Arbeiterfrage. Ihre Bedeutung für Gegenwart und Zukunft*. 2. umgearbeitete und vermehrte Auflage. Winterthur, 1870. The first edition came out in 1865.—525, 527
— *Geschichte des Materialismus und Kritik seiner Bedeutung in der Gegenwart*. Bd. I-II. Iserlohn, 1866.—158, 173

La Rochefoucauld, F. de. *Réflexions ou sentences, et maximes morales.* Paris, 1789. The first edition came out in 1665.—297-98

Lassalle, F. *Herr Bastiat-Schultze von Delitzsch, der ökonomische Julian, oder: Capital und Arbeit.* Berlin, 1864.—461

— *Offenes Antwortschreiben an das Central-Comité zur Berufung eines Allgemeinen Deutschen Arbeitercongresses zu Leipzig vom 1. März.* Zurich, 1863.—90

Lavergne, L. de. *The Rural Economy of England, Scotland and Ireland. Translated from the French.* Edinburgh and London, 1855.—374

Ledru-Rollin, [A. A.] *Aux électeurs.* In: *Le Réveil,* No. 168, 10 novembre 1869; *Journal des Débats,* 11 novembre 1869.—371

Lever, Ch. *Harry Lorequer.*—453, 509

Leßner, F. [Speech at the sitting of the Brussels Congress of the International Working Men's Association on using machinery under capitalism of September 9, 1868.] In: *The Times,* No. 26229, September 14, 1868; *The Daily News,* September 11, 1868.—97-99

Liebknecht, W. *Erklärung.* In: *Demokratisches Wochenblatt,* Nr. 8, 20. Februar 1869.—230, 405

— *Ueber die politische Stellung der Social-Demokratie, insbesondere mit Bezug auf den Norddeutschen 'Reichstag'.* In: *Demokratisches Wochenblatt,* Nr. 27, Nr. 32 (Beilage), 3. Juli, 7. August 1869.—307, 343

Л[илиенфельд,] *Земля и воля.* С.-Петербургъ, 1868.—55, 154, 430, 434

— *Land und Freiheit.* In: Russlands ländliche Zustände seit Aufhebung der Leibeigenschaft. Drei russische Urteile. Übersetzt und commentiert von Julius Echhart. Leipzig, 1870.—419, 426, 430

Livius, Titus. *Rerum Romanorum ab Urbe condita libri.*—85

Longfellow, H. W. *Excelsior.*—278

Ludlow, J. M. *Ferdinand Lassalle, the German Social-Democrat.* In: *The Fortnightly Review.* Vol. V, No. XXVIII, April 1, 1869.—255, 259, 261, 262, 264

Marryat, F. *Peter Simple.*—507

Marseillaise (French revolutionary song).—546

Martin, H. *La Russie et l'Europe.* Paris, 1866.—435

— *Russland und Europa.* Deutsche vom Verfasser durchgesehene und vermehrte Ausgabe. Uebersetzt und eingeleitet von G. Kinkel. Hannover, 1869.—435

Marx, J. [Articles on the Irish Question] (present edition, Vol. 21). In: *La Marseillaise,* Nos. 71, 79, 89, 91, 99, 113, 118, 125; 1, 9, 19, 21, 29 mars; 12, 17, 24 avril 1870 (signed: J. Williams) (see K. Marx, F. Engels, *Collected Works,* Vol. 21).—445, 449, 451, 454, 455, 458, 459, 462, 473, 476, 488, 500, 501, 503, 559

— In: *The Echo,* No. 391, March 11, 1870.—454

— In: *The Irishman,* Nos. 40, 45, April 2, May 7, 1870.—559

Mende, F. *An die Mitglieder des Allgem. deutschen Arbeiter-Vereins.* Am 5. Juli 1869. In: *Der Social-Demokrat,* Nr. 79, 9. Juli 1869.—324

— *Herr J. B. von Schweitzer und die Organisation des Lassalle'schen Allg. deutschen Arbeitervereins.* Leipzig, 1869.—408

Mende, F., Schweitzer, J. *Wiederherstellung der Einheit der Lassalle'schen Partei*. In: *Der Social-Demokrat*, Nr. 70, 18. Juni 1869.—295

Mill, J. S. *Thornton on Labour and its Claims*. Part II. In: *The Fortnightly Review*, Vol. V, No. XXX, June 1, 1869.—293

Milton, J. *Paradise Lost*. A Poem, in Twelve Books. Book II.—348

Miquel, J. [Speech in the Reichstag on March 18, 1869.] In: *Die Zukunft*, Nr. 67, 20. März 1869.—255

Moilin, T. *La liquidation sociale*. Paris, 1869.—242, 244

Monteil, A. A. *Histoire des français des divers états aux cinq derniers siècles*. Volumes I-X. Paris, 1828-1844.—423, 429

Moore, Thomas. *Irish Melodies*. Paris, 1821.—341

Müllner, A. *Die Schuld*.—231

Napoléon III. [Speech at the opening of the Extraordinary Session of the French National Assembly on November 29, 1869.] In: *Journal des Débats*, 30 novembre 1869.—389

Naquet, A. *La révolution et la science. De la fabrication du coton-poudre et de son application, soit comme poudre de guerre, soit comme poudre de mine*. In: *La Marseillaise*, No. 43, 30 janvier 1870.—426

The New American Cyclopaedia. A popular dictionary of general knowledge. Edited by George Repley and Charles A. Dana. In 16 volumes. New York, 1858-1863.—124

Nechayev, [S. G.] [To the editors of *Der Volksstaat*.] In: *Der Volksstaat*, Nr. 39, 14. Mai 1870 (in the column 'Netschajeff an den *Volksstaat*').—519, 521

O'Donovan, J. *A Grammar of the Irish Language*. Dublin, 1845.—513

O'Donovan Rossa. *Letter from the Member for Tipperary*. In: *The Irishman*, No. 32, February 5, 1870.—445, 454, 458, 476
—In: *La Marseillaise*, No. 79, 9 mars 1870.—445, 454, 455, 458, 476
—In: *The Echo*, No. 391, March 11, 1870.—454

O'Flaherty, R. *Ogygiá: seu, rerum hibernicarum chronologia*. In tres partes. Londini, 1685.—516, 517

Ovid. *Remedia amoris*.—29

Parsons, W. *A Few Words on the Relation of Landlord and Tenant in Ireland, and in Other Parts of the United Kingdom*. London, 1867.—373

Petrie, G. *The Ecclesiastical Architecture of Ireland, Anterior to the Anglo-Norman Invasion*. In: *The Transactions of the Royal Irish Academy*, Vol. XX. Dublin, 1845.—409

Petty, W. *The Political Anatomy of Ireland*. London, 1691.—402
— *Political Survey of Ireland*. London, 1719.—402

Prendergast, J. P. *The Cromwellian Settlement in Ireland*. London, 1865.—374, 388, 401, 403-04, 409, 415

Schorlemmer, C. *Researches on the Hydrocarbons of the Series C_nH_{2n+2}.* In: *Proceedings of the Royal Society,* No. 94, 1867 and No. 102, 1868.—33, 57

Schweitzer, J. B. *An die Mitglieder des Allgemeinen deutsch. Arbeiter-Vereins.* In: *Der Social-Demokrat,* No. 80, 10. Juli 1868.—73
— *An die Mitglieder des Allg. deutsch. Arb.-Vereins.* In: *Der Social-Demokrat,* Nr. 110, 20. September 1868.—109, 114
—[Speech in the North German Diet on March 17, 1869.] In: *Die Zukunft,* Nr. 66, 19. März 1869.—256
—(anon.) *Das Werk von Carl Marx I-XII.* In: *Der Social-Demokrat,* Nr. 10, 11, 12, 14, 15, 24, 25, 30, 39, 49, 50, 54; 22., 24., 26., 31. Januar; 2., 23., 26. Februar; 8., 29. März; 24., 29. April; 6. Mai 1868.—8, 11, 13, 61-62, 72

Senior, N. W. *Journals, Conversations and Essays Relating to Ireland.* In two volumes. 2nd ed. London, 1868.—331, 357

[Serno-Solowiewitsch, A.] *A propos de la grève. Réponse à M. Goegg.* Genève, 1868 (signed A. Ebéniste).—172, 186

Seume, J. G. *Der Wilde.*—7, 9

Shakespeare, W. *Julius Caesar.*—244
— *King Henry IV.*—216, 507
— *Macbeth.*—546

Silva de romances viejos. Publicada por Jacobo Grimm. Vienna, 1831.—156

Slade, A. *Turkey and the Crimean War: a narrative of historical events.* London, 1867.—139

Smith, A. *An Inquiry into the Nature and Causes of the Wealth of Nations.* Book I, Ch. 6. London, 1776.—23
— *An Inquiry into the Nature and Causes of the Wealth of Nations.* In three volumes. Edinburgh, 1814.—39, 45-46

Smith, G. *Irish History and Irish Character.* Oxford and London, 1861.—374, 388

St. Clair, S. G. B. and Brophy, Ch. A. *A Residence in Bulgaria: or Notes on the Resources and Administration of Turkey.* London, 1869.—345

Stern, D. *Histoire de la révolution de 1848.* Deuxième édition. Tomes I-II. Paris, 1862. The first edition came out in 1851.—217

Sterne, L. *The Life and Opinions of Tristram Shandy, Gentleman.* Paris, 1832.—297

Steuart, J. *An Inquiry into the Principles of Political Oeconomy.* In two volumes. London, 1767.—39

Stirling, J. H. *As Regards Protoplasm in Relation to Prof. Huxley's Essay on the Physical Basis of Life.* London, 1869.—481-82
— *The Secret of Hegel: Being the Hegelian System in Origin, Principle, Form, and Matter.* In two volumes. London, 1865.—39, 481

Struve, G. und Rasch, G. *Zwölf Streiter der Revolution.* Berlin, 1867.—5

Swift, J. *The Works.* Volumes 1-14. London, 1760.—512, 513

Sybel, H. *Oestreich und Deutschland im Revolutionskrieg. Ergänzungsheft zur Geschichte der Revolutionszeit 1789 bis 1795.* Düsseldorf, 1868.—432-33
— *Polens Untergang und der Revolutionskrieg.* In: *Historische Zeitschrift,* Bd. 23. München, 1870.—433, 442

Talandier, A. *Alexandre Hertzen.* In: *L'Internationale*, No. 56, 6 février 1870 (in the column 'Nécrologie').—445
— *L'Irlande et le catholicisme.* In: *La Marseillaise*, No. 58, 16 février 1870.—445, 459, 476
— *La Marseillaise et la presse anglaise.* In: *La Marseillaise*, No. 85, 15 mars 1870.—459

Tennyson, Alfred Lord. *Lady Clara Vere de Vere.*—275

Ténot, E. *Paris en décembre 1851. Étude historique sur le coup d'état.* Quatrième édition. Paris, 1868.—157, 168, 178, 188, 191, 205, 232, 244
— *La Province en décembre 1851. Etude historique sur le coup d'état.* Neuvième édition. Paris, 1868.—178, 188, 191, 195, 232, 244

Terence (Publius Terentius Afer). *Andria.*—174

Tholuck, F. A. *Blüthensammlung aus der morgenländischen Mystik.* Berlin, 1825.—196

Thornton, W. Th. *A New Theory of Supply and Demand.* In: *The Fortnightly Review*, Vol. VI, No. XXXIV, October 1, 1866.—158
— *On Labour; its wrongful claims and rightful dues; its actual present and possible future.* London, 1869.—264, 293

Tone, Th. W. *Memoirs of Theobald Wolfe Tone.* Written by himself. In two volumes. London, 1837. The first edition came out in Washington in 1826 under the title 'Life of Theobald Wolfe Tone', 2 Vols.—374

Tooke, Th. *An Inquiry into the Currency Principle; the Connection of the Currency with Prices, and the Expediency of a Separation of Issue from Banking.* 2nd ed. London, 1844.—39

Trench, W. S. *Realities of Irish Life.* London, New-York, [1868].—356-57, 456

The Tribes and Customs of Hy-Many, Commonly Called O'Kelly's Country. With a translation and notes ... by John O'Donovan. Dublin, 1843.—518

Tridon, G. *La Commune révolutionnaire de Paris.* In: *La Cigale*, No. 29, 19 juillet 1868.—175
— *Gironde et Girondins. La Gironde en 1869 et en 1793.* [Paris,] 1869.—233, 308

Turgot. *Réflexions sur la formation et la distribution des richesses.* In: *Oeuvres de Turgot.* Nouvelle édition par E. Daire. Tome premier. Paris, 1844.—39

Ulrichs, K. H. *'Argonauticus'. Zastrow und die Urninge des pietistischen, ultramontanen und freidenkenden Lagers.* Leipzig, 1869.—295, 403

Urquhart, D. *Au grand Vizir. 16 Août 1867.* In: *The Diplomatic Review*, 7 April 1869 ('*Insurrection en Candie. M. Urquhart à Fuad Pasha*').—260

Vallancey, Ch. *A Grammar of the Iberno-Celtic, or Irish Language.* 2nd ed. Dublin, 1782. Engels used the first edition of 1773.—518

Vambéry, H. *Eine neue Wendung in der central-asiatischen Frage.* In: *Allgemeine Zeitung*, Nr. 308, 4. November 1869; *The Times*, November 8, 1869.—375

Vauban, S. *Projet d'une dime royale.* In: *Economistes financiers du XVIII-e siècle.* Paris, 1843.—429

Venedey, J. *Irland.* Theile I-II. Leipzig, 1844.—467

Verlet, H. *Force et matière.* In: *La Libre pensée*, No. 13, 16 avril 1870.—485

Vermorel, A. *Les Hommes de 1848.* Troisième édition. Paris, 1869.—216, 233, 244

V[ésinier], P. *Bulletin du travailleur.* In: *La Cigale*, No. 25, 21 juin 1868.—45

Virchow, R. *Die Cellularpathologie in ihre Begründung auf physiologische und pathologische Gewebelehre.* Berlin, 1858.—13

Vogt, C. *Mémoire sur les microcéphales ou hommes-singes.* Genève, 1867. In: *Mémoires de l'institut national genevois.* Tome onzième, 1866. Genève, 1867.—210

Vogt, G. *Monsieur, le bureau du Comité central permanent de la Ligue...* Bern, le 22 sept. 1868.—161

Wachsmuth, W. *Europäische Sittengeschichte vom Ursprunge volksthümlicher Gestaltungen bis auf unsere Zeit.* Zweiter Theil. Leipzig, 1833. This five-part work was published from 1831 to 1839.—515, 516

Wagener, H. [Speech in the North German Diet on March 17, 1869.] In: *Die Zukunft*, Nr. 66, 19. März 1869.—255

Wagner, A. *Die Abschaffung des privaten Grundeigenthums.* Leipzig, 1870.—527

Wakefield, E. *An Account of Ireland, Statistical and Political.* In two volumes. London, 1812.—361, 362, 367, 374, 388, 442, 477, 483

—(anon.) *England and America. A Comparison of the Social and Political State of Both Nations.* In two volumes. London, 1833.—384

Ware, J. *Inquiries Concerning Ireland, and Its Antiquities.* Dublin, 1705. The first two editions came out in Latin in London in 1654 and 1658.—516, 517

— *Two Books of the Writers of Ireland.* Dublin, 1704. In: Ware, J. *Inquiries Concerning Ireland, and Its Antiquities.* Dublin, 1705.—516, 517

Watts, J. *The Facts of the Cotton Famine.* London, Manchester, 1866.—181

— *Trade Societies and Strikes*: their good and evil influence on the members of trades unions, and on society at large. Machinery. Co-operative societies. Manchester, 1865.—278

Young, A. *A tour in Ireland; with general observations on the present state of that kingdom: made the year 1776, 1777, and 1778 and brought down to the end of 1779.* Volumes I-II. London, 1780.—361, 360, 388

DOCUMENTS OF THE INTERNATIONAL WORKING MEN'S AS-
SOCIATION[a]

The Geneva Congress of the International Working Men's Association (1866)

The International Working Men's Association. Resolutions of the Congress of Geneva, 1866, and the Congress of Brussels, 1868. London, [1869].—161, 221, 222

[Resolution of the Geneva Congress on Publishing the Bulletin.] In: *Rules of the International Working Men's Association. Administrative Regulations.* London, [1867,] articles 2, 3.—405

[a] Documents written by Marx and Engels see in the section 'Works by Karl Marx and Frederick Engels'.

The Lausanne Congress of the International Working Men's Association (1867)

Procès-verbaux du congrès de l'Association Internationale des travailleurs réuni à Lausanne du 2 au 8 septembre 1867. Chaux-de-Fonds, 1867.—223

[Resolution of the Lausanne Congress on the obligation of sections to make contributions.] In: *Procès-verbaux du...,* p. 37.—258

The Brussels Congress of the International Working Men's Association (1868)

Troisième Congrès de l'Association Internationale des travailleurs. Compte rendu officiel. Bruxelles, septembre 1868. Supplément au journal *Le Peuple belge,* 1868.—221

[Resolution on war proposed by the German delegates at the Brussels Congress.] In: *Troisième Congrès de...* Supplément au journal *Le Peuple belge,* 22 septembre 1868.—In: *The Times,* No. 26232, September 17, 1868.—94, 101-02 —In: *Der Vorbote,* Nr. 10, Oktober 1868.—94

[Resolution of the Brussels Congress on land property.] In: *Troisième Congrès de...* Supplément au journal *Le Peuple belge,* 24 septembre 1868.—101

[Resolution on Marx's *Capital* proposed by the German delegates at the Brussels Congress.] In: *The Times,* No. 26230, September 15, 1868.—99, 101

[Resolution of the Brussels Congress on the League of Peace and Freedom.] In: *Troisième Congrès de...* Supplément au journal *Le Peuple belge,* 18 septembre 1868.—202

[Resolution of the Brussels Congress on the obligation of sections to make contributions.] In: *Troisième Congrès de....* Supplément au journal *Le Peuple belge,* 24 septembre 1868.—258

[Resolution of the Brussels Congress on the consequences of using machinery.] In: *Troisième Congrès de...* Supplément au journal *Le Peuple belge,* 14 septembre 1868.—98, 221

The Basle Congress of the International Working Men's Association (1869)

Report of the Fourth Annual Congress of the International Working Men's Association, held at Basle, in Switzerland. From the 6th to the 11th September 1869. London, [1869].—375, 378, 405, 414, 430, 472, 473, 555

[Resolution of the Basle Congress on land property.] In: *Report of the Fourth Annual Congress...,* p. 26.—364, 365, 369, 393

[Resolution of the Basle Congress on settling the conflicts between the Association's sections.] In: *Report of the Fourth Annual Congress...,* p. 21.—314, 480

À Monsieur Bara, ministre de la justice. Signed by the members of the Board and Federal Council of the Brussels section. In: *La Tribune du peuple,* No. 5, 24 mai 1868.—43

Aux sections romandes. Signed on behalf of the Federal Council of Romance Switzerland by Guétaz, Chairman, and A. Perret, General Secretary. In: *L'Égalité,* No. 2, 8 janvier 1870.—430

Avis de la Redaction. Signed by Ch. Perron, A. Robin, Guilmeaux, J. Dutoit, A. Lindegger, Ph. Becker, Pinier. In: *L'Égalité*, No. 3, 15 janvier 1870.—430

[Becker, J. Ph.] *Internationale Arbeiterassociation. Zuruf an alle Arbeiter deutscher Sprache.*—14

Der Internationale Arbeiterbund von Genf an die Arbeiter Spaniens, Genf, 21. Oktober 1868. Signed by the members of the Central Committee of the International Working Men's Association in Geneva and members of the German-language sections' group. (Leaflet). In: *Der Vorbote*, Nr. 12, Dezember 1868.
—L'Association Internationale des Travailleurs de Genève aux ouvriers d'Espagne. Genève, le 21 octobre 1868. Signed by the members of the Central Committee of the International Working Men's Association in Geneva. (Leaflet.)—340

[Leßner, F.] *Appeal to the German Workers in London* (present edition, Vol. 21)
—Aufruf an die deutschen Arbeiter Londons. Signed: Im Namen des Deutschen Arbeiterbildungsvereins, deutscher Zweig der Internationalen Arbeiter-Assoziation: Der Vorstand. In: *Hermann. Deutsches Wochenblatt aus London*, Nr. 502, 15. August 1868.—83

Mahnruf. An unsere Bundesgenossen und die Arbeiter und Arbeitervereine aller Länder. Genf, den 21. Oktober 1869. Signed on the instructions of the Central Committee by the German-language sections' group: Becker, Jährig, Kannenberg. In: *Der Vorbote*, Nr. 10, Oktober 1869.—396

Manifeste antiplébiscitaire des Sections parisiennes fédérées de l'Internationale et de la Chambre fédérale des Sociétés ouvrières à tous les travailleurs français. In: *La Marseillaise*, No. 125, 24 avril 1870.—556

[Protest of the Brussels section of the International Working Men's Association in connection with P. Vésinier's publications in the press on June 25, 1868. Signed: B. Delesalle, secrétaire.] In: *La Cigale*, No. 26, 28 juin 1868 (published in the column 'Correspondance').—60

Первая Русская секцiя. Программа. In: *Народное Дѣло*, № 1, 15 апрѣля 1870.—430

Règlements. In: *Association Internationale des Travailleurs. Statuts et règlements.* Londres, 1866.—125, 135, 236, 557

Rules of the International Working Men's Association. Founded September 28th 1864. London, [1867].—75, 102, 134, 191, 202, 235, 332, 461, 464, 486

Rundschreiben des Zentralkomite's der Sektionsgruppe deutscher Sprache an die Sektionen und mitgenössischen Gesellschaften. Genf, den 12. November 1868. In: *Der Vorbote*, Nr. 11, November 1868.—396

Statuts pour la Fédération des Sections Romandes adoptés par le Congrès Romand, tenu à Genève... les 2, 3 et 4 janvier 1869.—495

DOCUMENTS

Accounts Relating to Trade and Navigation for the Year Ended December 31, 1861. In: *The Economist,* Vol. XX, No. 966, March 1, 1862 (Supplement).—189

An Actuary. Life Assurance Companies: their Financial Condition. Discussed, with Reference to Impending Legislation, in a Letter Adressed to the Right Hon. W. E. Gladstone, M. P., First Lord of the Treasury. London, 1869.—228, 230

Adresse an die Demokraten Spaniens. In: *Demokratisches Wochenblatt,* Nr. 44, 31. Oktober 1868, Beilage.—151

Adresse au peuple et au Congrès des Etats-Unis d'Amérique. Signed by F. Pyat, Weber and others. In: *La Cigale,* No. 45, 8 novembre 1868; *L'Espiègle,* No. 45, 8 novembre 1868.—155

Adresse aux citoyens français. Londres, le 11 avril 1870 (signed: J. Barbernt). In: *La Marseillaise,* No. 116, 15 avril 1870 (in the column: Association internationale des travailleurs, branche française).—556

Adresse de l'Association internationale des femmes, à l'Association internationale des travailleurs. Bienne, le 1 er Sept. 1868.—131

Agricultural statistics, Ireland. General abstracts showing the acreage under the several crops, and the number of live stock, in each county and province for the year 1867. Dublin, 1867.—140

Agricultural statistics, Ireland. Tables showing the estimated average produce of the crops for the year 1866. Dublin, 1867.—306

Allgemeiner deutscher Arbeiter-Congreß. In: *Der Social-Demokrat,* Nr. 114, 115, 116, 117; 30. September, 2., 4., 7. Oktober 1868 (with supplements to these Nos).—306

The Ancient Laws of Cambria: containing the institutional triads of Dyvnwal Moelmud, the laws of Howel the Good, triadical commentaries, code of education, and the hunting laws of Wales. Translated from the Welsh by W. Probert. London, 1823.—515-16

Ancient Laws and Institutes of Wales; comprising laws supposed to be enacted by Howell the Good, the anomalous laws. Volumes I-II. 1841.—534

Ancient Laws of Ireland. Senchus Mor. Volumes I-II. Dublin, London, 1865, 1869.—382, 409, 422, 423, 442, 451-52, 501, 509, 519

An die deutschen Sozial-Demokraten. Signed by the former members of the General Association of German Workers, Lassallean General Association of German Workers, German section of the International Working Men's Association in Geneva, Central Committee of the German Workers' unions in Switzerland, Union of German Workers' Associations and others. In: *Demokratisches Wochenblatt,* Nr. 29, 17. Juli 1869.—339

An Herrn Karl Marx in London. Berlin, 6. Juli 1868. Signed by the President and members of the Board of the General Association of German Workers. In: *Der Social-Demokrat,* Nr. 95, 14. August 1868.—89

Annala Rioghachta Eireann. Annals of the Kingdom of Ireland, by the Four Masters, from the earliest period to the year 1616. Edited with translation by John O'Donovan. Second edition. Volumes I-VII. Dublin, 1856.—517

Annales du sénat et du Corps législatif. Paris, 1869.—227

Annales IV Magistrorum. Ex ipso O'Clerji Autographo in Bibliotheca Stowense. Nunc primum editit. C. O'Conor. In: *Rerum Hibernicarum Scriptores.* T. 3. Buckinghamiae, 1826.—517

Annales ultonienses, ab anno D.CCCC XXXI, ad annum D.MC XXXI, ex Codice Bodleiano: itemque indicem generalem. Nunc, primum editit. O'Conor. In: *Rerum Hibernicarum Scriptores.* T. 4. Buckinghamiae, 1826.—517

Annual Statement of the Trade and Navigation of the United Kingdom with Foreign Countries and British Possessions in the Year 1861. Presented to Both Houses of Parliament by Command of Her Majesty. London, 1862.—188

An die Vorstands-Mitglieder des Allgemeinen deutschen Arbeiter-Vereins. Signed by W. Real. In: *Der Social-Demokrat*, Nr. 90, 2. August 1868.—78

Ein Circular der Herren Fabrikanten Funcke und Hück in Hagen.—26, 28

Correspondence, 1839-1841, relative to the affairs of the East, and the conflict between Egypt and Turkey. 4 Parts.—264

Erlaß der drei Zenzurminister betr. Unterdrückung der Rheinischen Zeitung zum 1. April 1843. Berlin, 1843, Januar 21.—76

Die Generalversammlung des Allg. deutsch. Arbeiter-Vereins. In: *Der Social-Demokrat*, Nr. 100, 101, 102; 28., 30. August, 2. September 1868.—106

Gewerbeordnung für den Norddeutschen Bund. 1869.—28, 255, 274

The Irish Land Bill. 1870.—434, 437, 456

Jahresbericht der Handelskammer von Elberfeld und Barmen.—26, 28

[Knox, A. and Pollock, G. D.] *Report of the Commissioners on the Treatment of the Treason-Felony Convicts in the English Convict Prisons.* London, 1867.—224, 457, 459

Leabhar na g-Ceart, or the Book of rights... With translation and notes, by John O'Donovan. Dublin, 1847.—518

Monsieur, le bureau du Comité central permanent de la Ligue..., Bern, le 22 sept. 1868. [Confidential Address of the Bureau of the Permanent Central Committee of the League of Peace and Freedom].—161

Mustersatzung für die einzelnen Arbeiterschaften. In: *Der Social-Demokrat*, Nr. 118, 9. Oktober 1868, Beilage.—129

Österreichs Kämpfe im Jahre 1866. Nach Feldacten bearbeitet durch das k. k. Generalstabs-Bureau für Kriegsgeschichte. Bände I-V. Wien, 1867-1868.—283

Pour paraître le 24 février [18]69. *La Renaissance, Journal politique hebdomadaire.*—218, 220, 225

Programm der Generalversammlung des Allgemeinen deutschen Arbeiter-Vereins, stattfindend in Hamburg, vom 22. bis 25. August 1868. In: *Die Zukunft*, Nr. 266, 10. Juli 1868; *Der Social-Demokrat*, Nr. 98, 21. August 1868.—75, 90

Programme et Règlement de l'Alliance internationale de la démocratie socialiste. Genève, [1868].—189-92, 202, 218, 235-37, 240, 241, 489-91

Protest [of the South German federalists and seven members of the North German Diet of May 7, 1868]. In: *Demokratisches Wochenblatt*, Nr. 20, 16. Mai 1868.—38

Public Health. Seventh Report. With Appendix. 1864. London, 1865.—196

Public Health, Eighth Report. With Appendix. 1865. London, 1866.—196

Reports from the Poor Law Inspectors. Agricultural Holdings in Ireland. Returns 1870.—480

Reports from the Poor Law Inspectors. Landlord and Tenant Right in Ireland 1870.—480

Reports from Poor Law Inspectors on the Wages of Agricultural Labourers in Ireland. Dublin, 1870.—480, 481

Report from the Select Committee on the Bank Acts; together with the Proceedings of the Committee, Minutes of Evidence, Appendix and Index. Ordered, by the House of Commons, to be Printed, 1 July 1858.—113

Report of Commission on Bombay Bank, 1869.—306

Report of Committee of H.o. Commons of July, 1843 on results of the allotment system etc.—306

Rerum Hibernicarum Scriptores [veteres]. Tomes I-IV. Buckinghamiae, 1814-1826. Editit C. O'Conor.—516, 517

[Resolution of the Hamburg general congress of the General Association of German Workers on Volume One of Marx's *Capital.*] In: *Der Social-Demokrat,* Nr. 101, 30. August 1868, Beilage.—98

[Resolution of the Hamburg general congress of the General Association of German Workers on the attitude to working-class movement in different countries.] In: *Der Social-Demokrat,* Nr. 102, 2. September 1868.—117

[Resolution of the Nuremberg Congress of the Union of German Workers' Associations on their joining the International Working Men's Association and adopting its programme.] In: *Demokratisches Wochenblatt,* Nr. 37, 12. September 1868.—114, 118

Satzung für den Arbeiterschaftsverband. In: *Der Social-Demokrat,* Nr. 118, 9. Oktober 1868, Beilage.—129, 134, 140

Statistical Abstract for the U. Kingdom, No. 16. London, 1868.—306

Statut. Geschäfts-Reglement. In: *Der Social-Demokrat,* Nr. 119, 11. Oktober 1868.—140

Things not Generally Known, Concerning England's Treatment of Political Prisoners. Dublin, 1869.—457, 459

ANONYMOUS ARTICLES AND REPORTS PUBLISHED IN PERIODIC EDITIONS

Allgemeine Zeitung, Nr. 55, 24. Februar 1869, Beilage: ◆◆ *Genf, 21. Febr.* (in the column 'Neueste Posten').—238
— Nr. 63, 4. März 1869: ◆◆ *Genf, 28. Febr.* (in the column 'Schweiz').—238

The Bee-Hive, No. 364, October 3, 1868: *The International Working Men's Association.*—148-49
— No. 420, October 30, 1869: *Ministers and the Fenian Prisoners.*—366

—No. 422, November 13, 1869: [Report on the marriage ceremony of Duke of Abercorn's daughters].—374

Börsenhalle. Hamb. Abend-Zeitung, 14. Februar 1868: [Review of Volume One of Marx's *Capital*].—61

La Cigale, No. 16, 18 avril 1869: *Association Internationale des Travailleurs. Formation d'une nouvelle section à Bruxelles.*—272, 273

The Daily News, September 8-12, 1868: *The Congress of the International Association of Workmen. From Our Special Correspondent. Brussels, sept. 6, 7, 8, 9, 10.*—93, 99
—September 11, 1868: *The International Working Men's Congress. From Our Special Correspondent. Brussels, sept. 9.*—97, 98
—No. 7445, March 11, 1870.—459
—March 16, 1870: [On O'Donovan Rossa's letter].—458

The Daily Telegraph, No. 4598, March 11, 1870.—459

Demokratisches Wochenblatt, Nr. 14, 4. April 1868: *Auswanderung und Bürgerrecht.*—5
—Nr. 15, 11. April 1868: *Politische Uebersicht.*—15, 19
—Nr. 16, 18. April 1868: *Politische Uebersicht.*—15
—Nr. 34, 36, 47, 48; 22. August, 5. September, 21., 28. November 1868; Nr. 10, 6. März 1869: *Die demokratischen Ziele und die deutschen Arbeiter.*—239
—Nr. 37, 12. September 1868: *Der fünfte Vereinstag deutscher Arbeitervereine zu Nürnberg (5.-7. September).*—99
—Nr. 40, 3. Oktober 1868: *Politische Uebersicht.*—141
—Nr. 41, 10. Oktober 1868: *Der Staat und die soziale Frage.*—136, 149, 175
—Nr. 42, 17. Oktober 1868, Beilage: *Ein Hannoveraner...*—141
—Nr. 14, 3. April 1869: *Politische Uebersicht.*—255
—Nr. 28, 10. Juli 1869: '*Vom Londoner Generalrath...*'.—326
—Nr. 29, 17. Juli 1869: *An die deutschen Sozial-Demokraten.*—339
—Nr. 29, 17. Juli 1869: *Man schreibt uns...*—325, 326, 331
—Nr. 29, 17. Juli, Beilage: *Was Bürger drüben können und hüben könnten.*—325
—Nr. 33 und Nr. 33, 34, Beilagen; 14., 21. August 1869: *Protokoll des Kongresses am 8. und 9. August.*—353
—Nr. 35, 28. August 1869: '*In Eisenach ist angeordnet worden...*'.—353

The Diplomatic Review, April 7, 1869: *The 'Eastern Question' Closed. Summary from the Blue-Books.*—260
—*Le Ministre Grec à Londres à son Gouvernement.* 29 décembre 1868 [extrait].—260

The Economist, Vol. XXIV, No. 1181, April 14, 1866: *A Phase of the Cotton Trade during the Civil War.*—179, 182, 186
—Vol. XXIV, No. 1210, November 3, 1866: *The 'Law' of Demand and Supply.*—158

L'Égalité, No. 37, 1 octobre 1869.—364
—No. 39, 16 octobre 1869: *Nouvelles de l'étranger. France.* Lyon, le 1er octobre 1869, Paris, le 21 vendémiaire, an 78 (12 octobre 1869).—364
—No. 47, 11 decembre 1869: *Réflexions.*—404, 424
—No. 15, 9 avril 1870: *Nouvelles du congrès.*—479

L'Emancipation belge, No. 254, 10 septembre 1868: leader.—107

L'Espiègle, No. 27, 5 juillet 1868: [Adresse aux Parisiens par le Comité central d'action de Paris du 24 juin 1868] (in the column 'Documents historiques').—62

The Evening Star, September 15, 1868: *The International Congress of Workmen.*—101

Le Figaro, No. 285, 11 octobre 1868: *Chronique de Paris.*—158

Gazette médicale de Paris, 11 janvier 1868: *Traitement arsénial de la phthisie pulmonaire.*—3

Hermann. Deutsches Wochenblatt aus London, 4. Juli 1868: [Report on the reception for Freiligrath in Cologne].—57

L'International, 22 avril 1869: Berlin (In the column 'Dernières nouvelles').—277

The Irishman, December 4, 1869; *Great Excitement* (From the Belfast papers).—399
—No. 34, February 19, 1870: *Inquest at Spike Island-Condemnation of the Prison Treatment.*—453
—No. 36, March 5, 1870: *Schrove-Tuesday-Procession of the Boeufs-Gras—The Carnival Dying out—Conscripts 'Under the Influence'—The 'Marseillaise' Coming Round to Reason—A London Irishman's Letter to the Reds-Ollivier Holding his Ground* (in the column 'Irishman in Paris').—451
—No. 37, March 12: *'The Marseillaise, Paris "irreconcilable" organ...'* (in the column 'Current Notes').—455
—No. 38, March 19, 1870: *Probable Inquiry* (in the column 'Treatment of Political Prisoners').—460
—No. 40, April 2, 1870: *Rochefort's 'Marseillaise' and the Fenian Prisoners.*—559

Journal de Bruxelles, Nos. 252, 254-260; 8, 10-16 septembre 1868: [Reports on the Brussels Congress of the International Working Mens' Association].—107

Kölnische Zeitung, Nr. 284, 12. Oktober 1868: *Essen, 8. Okt.; Gladbach, 10. Okt.* (in the column 'Vermischte Nachrichten').—136
—Nr. 122, 3. Mai 1870: *Die Tiefsee-Untersuchungen.*—509

Колоколъ, № 1, 2 апреля 1870: *Къ русской публикъ отъ редакціи.*—506

La Libre pensée, No. 13, 16 avril 1870: '*Dans notre dernier numero...'.*—556-57

Literarisches Centralblatt für Deutschland, Nr. 28, 4. Juli 1868: *Marx, Karl. Das Kapital. Kritik der politischen Oekonomie (in 3 Bdn.). Erster Bd. Buch I. Der Produktionsprozess des Kapitals. Hamburg. 1867. O. Meissner* (signed 'h').—65, 68

Lloyd's Weekly London Newspaper, March 21, 1869: *International Labour Laws.*—249

Manchester Daily Examiner and Times, March 17, 1870; leader.—457

La Marseillaise, No. 60, 18 février 1870: *Le Daily-News donne à la presse libérale française...*—445
—No. 79, 9 mars 1870: *Lettre d'O'Donovan Rossa.*—454

The Morning Advertiser, September 16, 1868: *London, Wednesday. September 16.*—101

The Morning Herald, November 18, 1868; leader.—165

Московскія въдомости, № 207, 23 сентября 1869: *Бомбардированіе корейской крепости винтовой лодкой «Соболь».*—371
—№ 4, 6 января 1870: *Москва, 5 января.*—436, 440, 441

The Observer, November 28, 1869.—391

Der Pionier, Nr. 42, 13. Oktober 1869: *Unser Redakteur.*—367
—Nr. 17, 27. April 1870: *Das Treiben der deutschen Kommunisten.*—528, 529

Reynolds's Newspaper, No. 949, October 18, 1868: *Look before You Leap, and Beware of Traitors.*—166

Der Social-Demokrat, Nr. 100-102; 28., 30. August, 2. September 1868: *Die Generalversammlung des Allg. deutsch. Arbeiter-Vereins.*—105
—Nr. 104, 6. September 1868: *Der Allgemeine deutsche Arbeiter-Congreß. II*—105
—Nr. 112, 113; 25., 27. September 1868.—116, 120
—Nr. 112, 25. September 1868: *Zum Allgemeinen deutschen Arbeiter-Congreß. Berlin, 24. September.*—117
—Nr. 114-117 (mit Beilagen zu diesen Nummern), 30. September, 2., 4., 7. Oktober, 1868: *Allgemeiner deutscher Arbeiter-Congreß.*—140
—Nr. 118, 9. Oktober, 1868, Beilage.—127
—Nr. 24, 24. Februar 1869: [Report on Schweitzer's refusal to admit the General Council as an Arbiter in the conflict between Schweitzer and the General Association of German Workers, on the one hand, and Liebknecht and Bebel with their workers' unions, on the other].—405
—Nr. 21, 22, 24, 25, 30, 31, 32; 17., 19., 24., 26. Februar, 10., 12., 14. März 1869: *Zur Agitation in Sachsen.*—241
—Nr. 81, 14. Juli 1869: *Schwindel* (presumably written by Fritz Mende).—322, 327
—Nr. 84, 21. Juli 1869: *Berlin, 20. Juli* (in the column 'Politischer Theil').—329
—Nr. 93, 94, 95; 10., 13., 15. August 1869: *Der Congreß zu Eisenach.*—349
—Nr. 117, 6 Oktober 1869: [Announcement of the second edition of Marx's *The Eighteenth Brumaire of Louis Bonaparte*] (in the column 'Literarisches').—428
—Nr. 123, 124, 126; 20., 22., 27. Oktober 1869: *Der Baseler Beschluß wegen des Grundeigenthums.*—367, 369
—Nr. 132, 10. November 1869: *Aus Leipzig geht uns folgendes Telegramm zu...* (signed: Petzoldt).—382
—Nr. 133, 12. November 1869: (*Wir constatieren*)... (in the column 'Vermischtes').—382

The Standard, September 16, 1868: leader.—101
—May 5 and 6, 1870: [Articles on the First International].—504

The Times, No. 26096, April 11, 1868: *Switzerland, Geneva, April 10.*—8
—No. 26225, September 9, 1868: leader.—93, 96-97
—No. 26396, March 27, 1869: *The Demonstration in Trafalgar-Square.*—248
—November 22, 23 and 25, 1869: [Articles marked 'From Our Own Correspondent' in the column 'Ireland'], (leaders).—387
—December 1, 1869: *From Our Correspondent. Dublin, November 30* (in the column 'Ireland').—399
—January 24, 1870: *The Great Strike in France.*—554
—No. 26694, March 10, 1870: *The Fenian Convict O'Donovan Rossa.*—458
—March 16, 1870: *The Fenian Convict O'Donovan Rossa.*—458

Vierteljahrschrift für Volkswirthschaft und Kulturgeschichte, Bd. XX, 5. Jg. Berlin, 1868: *Das Kapital. Kritik der politischen Oekonomie von Karl Marx. Erster Band. Buch I.*

Der Produktionsprozess des Kapitals. Hamburg, Otto Meissner. 1867 (in the column 'Bücherschau').—54, 56, 59, 65, 68

Der Volksstaat, Nr. 11, 6. November 1869: *Politische Uebersicht.*—366
—Nr. 7, 22. Januar 1870: *Politische Uebersicht.*—553
—Nr. 8, 26. Januar 1870: *Politische Uebersicht.*—553
—Nr. 17, 26. Februar 1870: *Hamburg.*—445
—Nr. 27, 2. April 1870: *Anfrage.*—485
—Nr. 35, 30. April 1870: [Editorial Comment on F. Engels' *The Peasant War in Germany*].—508, 511, 519
—Nr. 38, 11. Mai 1870: *Die Pariser Polizei hat ihrem Kaiser...* (in the column 'Aus England'.)—526

Der Vorbote, Nr. 11, November 1868: *Zur Geschichte der Internationalen Arbeiterassociation.*—199, 200
—Nr. 12, Dezember 1868: *Bericht über die Arbeiterbewegung in Basel.*—199, 200, 203
—Nr. 12, Dezember 1868: *Der Internationale Arbeiterbund von Genf an die Arbeiter Spaniens.* (The address was also published as a leaflet in German and French).—340
—Nr. 1, Januar 1869.—208
—Nr. 1, Januar 1869: [Report on the money raised for the striking Basle workers].—209
—Nr. 7, Juli 1869: [Report from Basle] (in the column 'Zur Geschichte der Internationalen Arbeiterassociation').—335
—Nr. 7, Juli 1869: [Report from Nuremberg] (in the column 'Zur Geschichte der Internationalen Arbeiterassociation').—336
—Nr. 7, Juli 1869: *Denkschrift. Das Zentralkomité der Sektionsgruppe deutscher Sprache.* Genf, den 20. Juli 1869.—332, 335
—Nr. 1, Januar 1870.—431
—Nr. 4, April 1870: *Zur Geschichte der Internationalen Arbeiterassociation.*—502

Die Zukunft, Nr. 174, 15. Mai 1868 (Morgen-Blatt): [Report on W. Eichhoff's final lecture 'Die Ursachen der Handelsstockungen der Gegenwart' at the Alt-Köln district organisation (Berlin)].—37
—Nr. 292, 298; 25., 29. Juli 1868: *Oekonomische Briefe.*—78
—Nr. 32, 35, 37, 40, 47; 7., 11., 13., 17., 25. Februar 1869: *Die Gewerksgenossenschaften.*—230, 239
—Nr. 60, 12. März 1869: 'Bei der in engerer Wahl vollzogenen Ersatzwahl...' (in the column 'Berlin, 11. März').—250
—Nr. 61, 13. März 1869: 'In Bezug auf das Vereins und Versammlungs-Gesetz ist vom Obertribunal folgender Rechtsgrundsatz angenommen worden...' (in the column 'Berlin, 12. März').—258
—Nr. 71, 72; 25., 26. März 1869: *V. Kirchmann's Aesthetik* (anonymous review on J. H. v. Kirchmann's *Aesthetik auf realistischer Grundlage*. 2 Bde, Berlin, 1868).—258
—Nr. 76, 2. April 1869: *Barmen, 30. März. (Priv.-Mitth.).*—264
—Nr. 79, 6. April 1869: *Barmen, 31. März. (Die Generalversammlung des allgemeinen deutschen Arbeitervereins).*—264
—Nr. 80, 7. April 1869: *Barmen, 31. März. (Priv.-Mitth.) Generalversammlung des allgemeinen deutschen Arbeitervereins.—Fortsetzung.)*—264
—Nr. 86, 14. April 1869: *Barmen, 5. April. (Privat-Mitth.) Generalversammlung des allgemeinen deutschen Arbeitervereins. Schluß).*—264

INDEX OF PERIODICALS

Neue Rheinische Zeitung. Politisch-ökonomische Revue—a theoretical journal of the Communist League; it was founded by Marx and Engels in December 1849 and published till November 1850.—228, 237, 241, 242, 267

Neues Wiener Tagblatt—an Austrian liberal paper published in Vienna from 1867 to 1945.—15

New-York Daily Tribune—a newspaper founded by Horace Greeley in 1841 and published until 1924; organ of the Left-wing American Whigs until the mid-1850s and later of the Republican Party; in the 1840s and 1850s it voiced progressive views and opposed slavery. Marx and Engels contributed to it from August 1851 to March 1862.—7, 124, 398, 544

El Obrero—a Spanish weekly newspaper published in Palma (Majorca) from 1870 to 1871. It was banned by the government in January 1871 but continued to appear under the name *La Revolucion social.*—497, 498

The Observer—an English conservative weekly published in London since 1791.—391, 508

L'Opinion nationale—a daily published in Paris from 1859 to 1874.—107, 511-12, 554

The Pall Mall Gazette—a conservative daily which appeared in London from 1865 to 1921.—543

Paris-faillite—see *Paris-Journal*

Paris-Journal—a reactionary daily published in Paris from 1868 to 1874; was connected with the police.—557

Le Pays, Journal de l'Empire—a daily founded in Paris in 1849; during the Second Empire (1852-70) was a semi-official newspaper of Napoleon III's government.—419, 455, 553

The People's Paper—a Chartist weekly published by Ernst Jones in London from 1852 to 1858. Marx and Engels contributed to it from October 1852 to December 1856 and helped with its editing.—157

Père Duchêsne—see *Le vrai Père Duchêsne*

Le Peuple—a Bonapartist daily published in Paris from October 1868 to September 1870; from February 1869 it appeared under the title *Le Peuple français.*—254

Le Peuple. Journal de la République démocratique et sociale—a socio-reformist newspaper published in Paris from 1848 to 1850; from April 1848 it appeared under the title *Le Représentant de Peuple*; from September 1848 to 13 June 1849, under the title *Le Peuple*; from 1 October 1849 to 14 May 1850 under the title *La Voix du peuple,* and from 15 June to 13 October 1850, under the title *Le Peuple de 1850.* Its editor was Proudhon.—217

Der Pionier—a weekly published in New York (1854-58), then in Boston (1859-79); organ of the German petty-bourgeois democratic refugees; its editor-in-chief was K. Heinzen.—285, 367

Political Register—see *Cobbett's Weekly Political Register*

Post—see *Londoner Deutsche Post*

Le Progrès—a Bakuninist newspaper which opposed the General Council of the International; it was published in French in Le Locle under the editorship of James Guillaume from December 1868 to April 1870.—404, 413, 479-80, 492

SUBJECT INDEX